AMNESTY
INTERNATIONAL
REPORT
1995

This report
covers the period
January to December
1994

Amnesty International is a worldwide voluntary movement that works to prevent some of the gravest violations by governments of people's fundamental human rights. The main focus of its campaigning is to:

- *free all prisoners of conscience.* These are people detained anywhere for their beliefs or because of their ethnic origin, sex, colour or language – who have not used or advocated violence;

- *ensure fair and prompt trials for political prisoners;*

- *abolish the death penalty, torture and other cruel treatment of prisoners;*

- *end extrajudicial executions and "disappearances".*

Amnesty International also opposes abuses by opposition groups: hostage-taking, torture and killings of prisoners and other deliberate and arbitrary killings.

Amnesty International, recognizing that human rights are indivisible and interdependent, works to promote all the human rights enshrined in the Universal Declaration of Human Rights and other international standards, through human rights education programs and campaigning for ratification of human rights treaties.

Amnesty International is impartial. It is independent of any government, political persuasion or religious creed. It does not support or oppose any government or political system, nor does it support or oppose the views of the victims whose rights it seeks to protect. It is concerned solely with the protection of the human rights involved in each case, regardless of the ideology of the government or opposition forces, or the beliefs of the individual.

Amnesty International does not grade countries according to their record on human rights; instead of attempting comparisons it concentrates on trying to end the specific violations of human rights in each case.

Amnesty International has more than 1,100,000 members, subscribers and regular donors in over 170 countries and territories. There are 4,329 local Amnesty International groups registered with the International Secretariat and several thousand school, university, professional and other groups in 89 countries in Africa, the Americas, Asia, Europe and the Middle East. To ensure impartiality, each group works on cases and campaigns in countries other than its own, selected for geographical and political diversity. Research into human rights violations and individual victims is conducted by the International Secretariat of Amnesty International. No section, group or member is expected to provide information on their own country, and no section, group or member has any responsibility for action taken or statements issued by the international organization concerning their own country.

Amnesty International has formal relations with the United Nations (UN) Economic and Social Council (ECOSOC); the United Nations Educational, Scientific and Cultural Organization (UNESCO); the Council of Europe; the Organization of American States; the Organization of African Unity; and the Inter-Parliamentary Union.

Amnesty International is financed by subscriptions and donations from its worldwide membership. No funds are sought or accepted from governments. To safeguard the independence of the organization, all contributions are strictly controlled by guidelines laid down by the International Council.

AMNESTY INTERNATIONAL REPORT

1995

Amnesty International Publications
1 Easton Street, London WC1X 8DJ
United Kingdom

First published 1995
by Amnesty International Publications
1 Easton Street, London WC1X 8DJ, United Kingdom

© Copyright Amnesty International Publications 1995

ISBN: 0 86210 245 6
AI Index: POL 10/01/95
Original language: English

Typesetting and page make-up by:
Accent on type, 30/31 Great Sutton Street, London EC1V 0DX, United Kingdom

Printed by: The Bath Press, Lower Bristol Road, Bath, United Kingdom

Cover design: John Finn, Artworkers

Cover photograph: Woman in Cambodia, © Leah Melnick/Format
Back cover photograph: Woman in Bosnia and Herzegovina, © Katz Pictures/John Reardon

This report documents Amnesty International's work and its concerns throughout the world during 1994. The absence of an entry in this report on a particular country does not imply that no human rights violations of concern to Amnesty International have taken place there during the year. Nor is the length of a country entry any basis for a comparison of the extent and depth of Amnesty International's concerns in a country. Regional maps have been included in this report to indicate the location of countries and territories cited in the text and for that purpose only. It is not possible on the small scale used to show precise political boundaries. The maps should not be taken as indicating any view on the status of disputed territory. Amnesty International takes no position on territorial questions. Disputed boundaries and cease-fire lines are shown, where possible, by broken lines. Areas whose disputed status is a matter of unresolved concern before the relevant bodies of the United Nations have been indicated by striping only on the maps of the country which has *de facto* control of the area.

CONTENTS

APPENDICES

INTRODUCTION

Human rights are women's right

In a world racked by violence, women face rape, mutilation and death at the hands of armed men. Yet all too often these women remain invisible. Their tales are not heard. Their plight is hidden by the sheer scale of the tragedies.

This report exposes a range of specific human rights violations suffered by women, men and children around the world. It shows who was responsible and documents the activities of Amnesty International's worldwide membership in combating the violations and promoting greater respect for all human rights.

In 1994 women suffered every known abuse and violation of fundamental human rights. Torturers, executioners, jailers and killers did not discriminate on grounds of sex, unless it was to subject women to abuses to which they are particularly vulnerable.

Their suffering continued despite an historic declaration by the international community the previous year. In the Declaration of the 1993 World Conference on Human Rights,

Yeni Damayanti outside the Central Jakarta District Court in March 1994. She and 20 other students were arrested in December 1993 for demonstrating against human rights violations in Indonesia under the government of President Suharto and sentenced to up to 14 months' imprisonment for "insulting" the President.

2

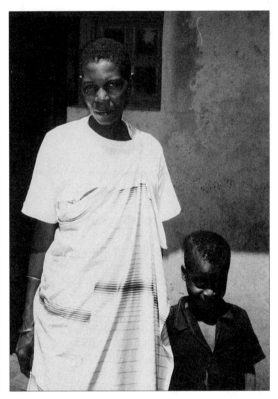

"The Tutsi took 11 Hutu, including my son Richard Ntahomvukiye, and other men I knew. The soldiers then commanded the Tutsi to kill them, which they did with machetes and clubs while the soldiers stood by to encourage them... The dogs had eaten the bodies in two days."

Sylvie Ntungiyabani and her family fled from their home in Ngozi province, Burundi, after witnessing the killing of three Tutsi. On 29 October 1994, hours after they arrived at a camp for displaced Hutu in Gashikanwa, her husband Paul Bavakure was taken by soldiers and stabbed to death. Then they killed her son. No one was brought to justice for the killings.

governments acknowledged that women's rights are human rights. They promised to guarantee women their social and economic rights – their rights to peace, development and equality. They also promised to uphold women's civil and political rights – their rights not to be killed, tortured, sexually abused, arbitrarily imprisoned or made to "disappear". On both counts, they have failed abysmally to match their words with deeds.

This report, which covers 151 countries, shows the extent to which women, as well as men, continue to be victims of indiscriminate state repression. Women like Aung San Suu Kyi, the 1991 Nobel Peace Prize winner, who has been under house arrest in Myanmar for over five years because she dared to oppose the government. Or Agathe Uwilingiyimana, the Rwandese Prime Minister, who was one of the first victims of the carnage that tore through her country in 1994. Or Angélica Mendoza de Ascarza, a 70-year-old woman who has been persistently persecuted and was falsely accused of "terrorism" for working on behalf of the "disappeared" in Peru.

Armed opposition groups, many of which have adopted the methods of terror used by the state, do not spare women either. Thiagarajah Selvanithy, for example, has been a prisoner of a Sri Lankan armed opposition group, the Liberation Tigers of Tamil Eelam, since 1991. Women in Peru have been shot or hacked to death by Shining Path. Women in Algeria have been killed and threatened by armed Islamist groups for not wearing the Islamic veil or for being related to members of the security forces.

The climate of violence which is perpetuated or condoned by governments makes a mockery of the Declaration on the Elimination of Violence against Women, adopted by the UN General Assembly in December 1993. The more violence there is in general, the more likely it is that women will be subjected to horrific abuses. The particular tragedies of Rwanda, Bosnia-Herzegovina, Liberia and other war-torn areas are a powerful reminder of how those who seek to win power by force of arms are often willing to eliminate anyone who stands in their way – whether they be armed men, civilians or even whole communities. Women, who because of their families are often less mobile than men, are frequently obliterated in the trail of devastation. Women who are defenceless are easy targets for acts of vengeance.

Moreover, they are also subjected to specific abuses because they are women. Women such as the expectant mother in Rwanda who was slashed to death by a doctor when she was in the final stages of labour because she was a Tutsi and he was a Hutu. Or the Muslim woman who was beaten and raped by masked Serbian soldiers in front of her daughter and parents in Bosnia-Herzegovina.

These conflicts suggest that the deliberate violation of the human rights of women has increasingly become a central

© Brenda Prince/FORMAT

Barzani women in Qushtapa, Iraq, hold photographs of their husbands who were among 8,000 Kurds of the Barzani clan who "disappeared" after arrest in August 1983. The Iraqi authorities have never acknowledged the arrests.

4

Ayşe Nur Zarakolu, a member of the Human Rights Association in Istanbul, Turkey, was sentenced to five months' imprisonment for publishing a book by Ismail Beşikçi about the Kurdish minority. She was released at the end of August, but faces further prosecutions for publishing other books by the same author.

component of military strategy. Rape is not an accident of war, or an incidental part of armed conflict. Its widespread use in times of conflict reflects the special terror it holds for women, the special contempt it displays for its victims. It also reflects the inequalities and discrimination women face in their everyday lives in peacetime.

Around the world women are being raped by the very people who are supposed to protect them. In the southern Mexican state of Chiapas, for instance, three sisters aged 16, 18 and 20 were raped by soldiers at a road-block. In Haiti, the 14-year-old sister of a government opponent was raped by members of an armed civilian militia who were looking for her brother.

Millions of other women are the victims of mass terror and hardship. Over 80 per cent of the world's 20 million refugees are women and children. Many of them suffer not only the poverty, humiliation and disorientation of displacement, but also cruelty and abuse during their flight in search of safety. Women like the Ethiopian mother who was raped by border guards when she was five months pregnant as she tried to flee to a neighbouring country. Or the Haitian woman seeking political asylum in the USA who was reportedly raped by an immigration guard at a Florida detention centre. Or the hundreds of Somali women refugees who have been raped in the refugee camps in the North Eastern Province of Kenya.

Discrimination against women is a deadly disease. More women and girls die every day from various forms of gender-based discrimination and violence than from any other type of human rights abuse. Every year, according to the UN Children's Fund (UNICEF), more than a million infant girls die because they are born female. Every year, because of discrimination, countless women are battered to death by their husbands, burned alive for bringing "disgrace" on the family, killed for non-payment of dowries, bought and sold in unacknowledged slave markets for domestic or sexual purposes, or have their genitals mutilated in the name of tradition. In some countries, women are subjected to forced virginity tests or humiliating strip searches. In others they are cruelly punished for violating dress codes, committing adultery, engaging in lesbian relationships, or even because they are victims of rape.

Some of these abuses fall outside Amnesty International's mandate for research and direct action and are therefore not covered in this report. Amnesty International does, nevertheless, work to promote all the human rights enshrined in the Universal Declaration of Human Rights and other international standards, through human rights education programs and campaigning for ratification of human rights treaties. We believe that if women are treated as second-class citizens, they are more likely to be abused by soldiers during conflicts, more likely to be persecuted for standing up for their rights, and more likely to be silenced if they protest against violations.

Increasingly women have fought the anonymity which hides their suffering and their struggles. The Declaration on the Elimination of Violence against Women welcomed "the role that

Vasiliya Inayatova, an engineer, poet and member of the *Birlik* opposition organization in Uzbekistan. She was arrested on 12 May, on her way to a human rights conference in Kazakhstan, and taken to the police headquarters in Tashkent where she was interrogated for some five hours and charged with "insulting a police officer". After seven days under "administrative arrest" she was released.

6

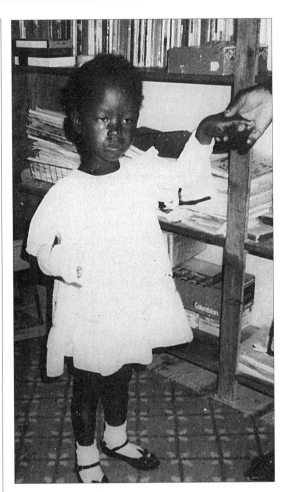

© Roussiere

Jocelyne Jeanty, aged four, was beaten by a patrol of soldiers and *attachés* when they attacked the town of Raboteau, Gonaïves, Artibonite department, Haiti. The bandages on her arm conceal the wounds she sustained. The military carried out a spate of attacks on inhabitants in the Gonaïves area in late 1993 and in the first months of 1994.

women's movements have played in drawing increasing attention to the nature, severity and magnitude of the problem of violence against women". Yet in numerous countries it is precisely such women who are threatened, imprisoned, tortured, made to "disappear" and killed by agents of governments who have pledged to uphold the Declaration.

Many such women can be found in the pages of this report. Eren Keskin, a lawyer in Turkey, has been subjected to death threats, apparently because she defended alleged members of a Kurdish armed opposition group, and was prosecuted for her statements about human rights in Turkey. Scores of Tibetan nuns have been tortured and imprisoned by the Chinese authorities for supporting independence for Tibet. The office of the Salvadorian Women's Movement was ransacked and the guard killed during an apparent campaign of intimidation against the opposition involving the security forces in El Salvador. Members of the Progressive Organisation of Women in India were beaten on the breasts and between the legs by police because they staged a silent protest for women's rights. A mother who led a campaign to find a group of 11 "disappeared" children in Brazil was gunned down in broad daylight in the street.

Women such as these have contributed to the vibrant movement of women's and human rights organizations that has emerged around the world in the past two decades. Some work for their "disappeared" relatives; some are community activists, fighting for basic rights such as freedom from want; some are lawyers seeking justice for the unrepresented; some campaign against torture, some against domestic violence, some for equal treatment at work or for land rights.

This wave of courage, creativity and commitment has too often met a wall of government indifference or state repression of the cruellest kind. Few governments recognize the work of women's human rights organizations as a legitimate exercise of fundamental civil and political rights. At the same time, many governments have done almost nothing to ensure that women enjoy the full range of rights to which they are entitled. The international community pays lip-service to equality – "Equality by the Year 2000" is the UN's slogan for the present decade. But will this slogan ever become reality?

The answer may become clear shortly after this report is published, when the world's governments meet at the Fourth UN World Conference on Women, being held in Beijing, China's capital, in September 1995. The early signs were not encouraging. In the run-up to the conference women's human rights were under attack by governments and individuals who argue that the extent to which civil and political rights are enjoyed must be subordinate to regional or cultural traditions.

As this report makes clear, all human rights, including women's human rights, are indivisible and universal. A woman

Elfinesh Kano, a professional Oromo singer, was detained on 31 December 1993 following a demonstration in Addis Ababa, Ethiopia. She was released without charge in May 1994 after paying a bond. She was reported to be seriously ill as a result of being beaten and denied medical treatment while detained.

who is assassinated, tortured or arbitrarily imprisoned has no chance of exercising any of her economic, social or cultural rights, including the rights to equality, development and peace. All human rights are interdependent. They also apply to all people in all circumstances. No government has the right to hide human rights crimes behind a smokescreen of "tradition", "culture" or economic imperatives. The murder of an Indonesian woman trade unionist by state officials cannot be justified on the grounds of the country's economic development. The Sudanese Government is wrong to allow women to be degraded and subjected to cruel floggings for the "cultural crime" of not covering their hair.

The Fourth UN Conference on Women offers both a focal point for campaigning on women's human rights and an opportunity to press governments attending the conference to guarantee that real action to promote and protect women's human rights is placed at the heart of the international agenda.

But the work must continue after the delegates have gone home. History shows that upholding women's human rights cannot be left to governments. Any protection that has been won, has been won by grassroots campaigning. If the international human rights movement is serious about promoting women's human rights, it must work in partnership with women's organizations.

Women are fighting back all over the world. They are demanding justice, opposing discrimination, demonstrating for equal rights. The human rights movement must make governments listen to these women's voices. We must demand that they take action to protect and promote women's human rights. Join us in our campaign to make the new millennium an era in which all women, men and children can enjoy the full range of their human rights.

The search for truth and justice

"It is almost two years and the search for my son continues. Every morning I get up at four o'clock to search for Harjit, before starting work... If it were not for Amnesty International and other international pressure, my family and I would probably not have survived elimination or the police would have broken us down enough to give up our search for Harjit. Tears of gratitude reach my eyes when I think Harjit would not have been alive today if it were not for your support and hard work."
A letter from the father of Harjit Singh, India

"The campaign has worried the government ... who have found themselves obliged to respond... Thanks to international pressure, the accused is being held and has been placed at the disposition of a civilian court. I had already lost hope. The threats and attacks had nearly finished me off. That all changed with your campaign."
A letter from the father of Luis Landa Diaz, Venezuela

"I wish I could thank everyone who sends me a card or a letter, because your work gives me great hope and courage... I don't know what I would have done without the letters that I receive from the members of Amnesty – you really give me great strength and hope that one day I will be able to see my son thanks to your efforts."
A letter from the mother of George Salsa, Kuwait

Two fathers and a mother. Three parents of three sons who "disappeared" or were killed by the security forces of their governments. These three tragic stories were among 24 cases featured in Amnesty International's 1994 Campaign against "Disappearances" and Political Killings. The moving responses of these parents reflect eloquently the tremendous impact this campaign had on those closest to the victims of "disappearance" or political killing.

On every continent the names and faces of these three young men and 21 other men and women were rescued from the obscurity into which they had been consigned by members of state security forces, paramilitary organizations or police squads responsible for their "disappearance" or death. The perpetrators of these violations were relying on the passage of time and the shortness of human memory to cover their crimes. They could not have expected that their victims' names and faces would be plastered on walls, published in newspapers, broadcast on television and radio, and raised high on placards in cities and towns around the world.

The immense creativity and commitment generated by Amnesty International's worldwide membership during this campaign deprived these perpetrators of their ultimate victory. Harjit Singh, Luis Landa, George Salsa and others like them will never be forgotten.

The search for these "lives behind the lies" and for their abductors or killers goes on. Even when we cannot physically save the life of an individual, Amnesty International's campaign demonstrated clearly that we can at least recover that person's identity through pursuing the truth and justice. The campaign dramatically illustrated the point made by the Guatemalan human rights lawyer, Frank LaRue, that "the right to identity does not end with death. Death is the end of life, but not of identity."

That enduring right to identity has been asserted imaginatively by Amnesty International's members around the globe in a host of compelling public events and actions. In Belgium, a huge barge floated up and down the waterways of the country bearing 840 pairs of shoes symbolizing the "disappeared". The Danish Section brought a herd of cows to Copenhagen's town hall to commemorate an incident where 43 men of a single Colombian village were made to "disappear" by armed men as an act of revenge for the theft of 43 cattle from a local landowner. In Yemen, dozens of school children participated in 10 days of events to launch the campaign. In West Africa, Ivorian musician and Amnesty International member Waby Spider toured the region on behalf of the campaign and recorded a special song about "disappearances". An Egyptian group helped to prepare two documentaries on "disappearances" and political killings, and designed a series of cards illustrating the campaign.

The Brazilian Section enlisted the support of prominent men and women from a number of professions as "Ambassadors of Hope" to represent victims of "disappearance" and political killing in media and public events around the country. The Hong Kong Section staged an open-air mime performance presenting the theme of the campaign. Slovenian members of Amnesty International published black-bordered funeral announcements in national newspapers, marking the deaths of several victims of political killings.

A Polish children's art centre held an international graphic art competition on "disappearances", attracting outstanding works of art by young people in more than a dozen countries. Several other European Amnesty International sections hosted the children's theatre group FIND – an organization of families of the "disappeared" from the Philippines. Their remarkable dramatization of the impact on families of the "disappearance" of fathers and brothers moved audiences wherever they performed.

For nine months, Amnesty International members regularly filled streets, market places and lecture theatres on "Days of

Presence" held on behalf of individual victims of "disappearance" and political killing featured in the campaign. Through press conferences, embassy vigils and concerts, the "Days of Presence" made the names and faces of the 24 "Lives behind the Lies" familiar to the public in places as far apart as Guyana and the Czech Republic, New Zealand and Mexico, Canada and Taiwan. Leaflets telling the stories of these cases were produced and distributed by Amnesty International members in Nigeria and Finland, Hungary and the United States of America, Croatia and Brazil. Exhibitions of photos, posters and works of art on "disappearances" and political killings attracted attention in Zambia and Mongolia, Pakistan and Ireland, Lithuania and Malaysia. Some 5,000 letters streamed out of Nepal to government authorities in targeted countries. Amnesty International members and supporters staged a demonstration in the town centre of Tel Aviv, Israel. The shaming symbol of a black wreath was left at an embassy door in London, the United Kingdom. There was also a special worldwide week of action focusing on the appalling human rights tragedies of Burundi and Rwanda.

The conviction that such work against these particular violations must be placed at the heart of the organization's research

© Per Daugaard

Amnesty International members in Denmark brought 43 cattle to Copenhagen's town hall to demonstrate against the "disappearance" of 43 men from Pueblo Bello, Colombia. The men had been abducted in reprisal for the theft of 43 cattle from a local paramilitary leader.

Monique Mujawamaliya, a human rights activist from Rwanda, with other Amnesty International members in the Netherlands during the 1994 campaign against political killings and "disappearances". Michel Karambizi, shown on the poster, his wife and their 10-year-old daughter were among some 1,000 people, most of them Tutsi, who were massacred by government soldiers in October 1990.

and campaigning agenda in the 1990s was a catalyst for inspiring membership activity beyond the framework of the theme campaign. Amnesty International's campaigning on the specific human rights situations in Colombia and Indonesia prompted equally committed and creative action on "disappearances" and political killings in these countries from sections and groups in all regions of the world. A meeting of the African Urgent Action Coordinators held in Ghana considered how recent advances in information technology could increase the effectiveness of African sections in their campaigns against "disappearances", political killings and other human rights violations – with particular regard to their ability to respond rapidly to situations of crisis.

The energy and vitality of the movement, so vividly displayed in Amnesty International's theme campaign in 1994, put the perpetrators of "disappearance" and political killings on notice – and provided a beacon of hope for the families of victims who persist in their search for truth and justice.

Strength through diversity

What links a former prisoner of conscience who is now a member of parliament in South Africa, a schoolgirl on the Caribbean island of Curaçao, and a masseuse from the remote mining town of Gremyachinsk in the northern Urals? The answer is their commitment to protecting human rights throughout the world. It is people like them, from all walks of life, who are the backbone of Amnesty International. It is people like them who devote time and energy to raising awareness about human rights and organizing campaigns against abuses.

This diversity reflects the fundamental aims of Amnesty International – to defend specific human rights of all people, irrespective of their nationality, religion or race. Only by building a movement that is rooted in all cultures in every continent, with women and men of all ages actively involved, can the organization's ideals be realized.

Today, there are over a million Amnesty International members, donors and subscribers in over 150 countries and territories. Many are organized in the 4,329 local groups that meet regularly in every region of the world. In 55 countries, the groups have established Amnesty International sections to coordinate their efforts at a national level.

Every year the movement becomes larger and more diverse, with long-established sections working alongside fledgeling groups such as those in Eastern and Central Europe and southern Africa. In addition, special networks of people such as lawyers, medical workers, trade unionists, journalists and students are organized to use their expertise and influence to promote human rights. Amnesty International's diversity is also reflected at the organization's headquarters in London, the International Secretariat, whose staff of over 300 people is drawn from more than 50 countries.

A further indication of the internationalism of the organization is the number of languages into which Amnesty International's publications are translated. The organization works in four core languages (Arabic, English, French and Spanish) and translates as many publications as possible into other languages. The Hong Kong office, for example, translates the monthly *Amnesty International Newsletter* into eight languages: Bangla, Chinese, Hindi, Korean, Nepali, Tamil, Thai and Urdu. The Israeli Section produces a newsletter and translations in Hebrew. In the newly democratized South Africa, Amnesty International publications have been translated into Afrikaans, Xhosa and Zulu and distributed throughout the country.

This drive towards greater multi-lingualism is one of many

14

© Associated Press/Pavel Rahman

Taslima Nasrin, a Bangladeshi writer and campaigner for women's rights, was forced to flee into exile after being charged with blasphemy and threatened with death by Islamist groups. She wrote to Amnesty International:

"Please accept my sincere gratitude for what you have done for me... Indeed, your support along with that of a few others may have been a critical factor in my being able to leave my country in safety."

policy initiatives launched by Amnesty International members in recent years. The members determine policies and overall strategies through local democratic structures, special international meetings on key issues, and the biennial International Council Meeting (ICM) – Amnesty International's supreme policy-making body.

Another important initiative of recent years has been mobilizing the youth of the world to take up Amnesty International's message and carry it forward into the next generation. Young people bring to the movement fresh ideas and inspiring levels of energy and bravery. They are not inhibited by the weight of past tradition, so feel free to experiment with effective new approaches to human rights work.

These qualities have been demonstrated in Slovenia where the first-ever group in Eastern and Central Europe was set up in 1988 by a 16-year-old high-school student. Since then the Slovenian members, whose average age is just over 20, have made remarkable progress through imaginative campaigning and skilful use of the media. By early 1994 they had a national office coordinating the work of six groups and in December they won section status, becoming the first section in the region. In 1995 they will host Amnesty International's ICM.

Other sections are also encouraging youth interest. The Tunisian Section, for instance, recently translated into Arabic an illustrated guide to the Universal Declaration of Human Rights. In Botswana, secondary-school students in Maru held an "Amnesty week" in which they staged a symbolic imprisonment of students and staff. They also organized a 24-hour letter-writing marathon in which 1,550 letters were sent asking for justice for

AMNESTY INTERNATIONAL REPORT 1995

people featured in the Worldwide Appeals section of the *Amnesty International Newsletter.*

Amnesty International is now planning an International Youth Program to develop this work. It will gear resources specifically towards the youth membership and create an organizational structure which can maximize the contribution they make.

Fundraising to support human rights work is another ongoing challenge to Amnesty International's members, particularly in the developing world. Working in very different social and economic conditions, the members' ingenuity and imagination are vital components of successful initiatives. Around the world, a wide variety of activities – ranging from intimate coffee mornings to huge concerts – are organized to suit local needs.

One of several long-term fundraising efforts was initiated in 1994 by the Venezuelan Section. The first stage of the project was designed to promote awareness of Amnesty International through an intensive media and public relations campaign. Interviews were given on radio and television and advertisements were placed in newspapers and magazines. Billboards with the words "We Defend Life – Amnesty International" were put up in the major cities.

During 1995 the Venezuelan Section hope to benefit from this increased awareness of Amnesty International in the form of returns on their direct mail campaign. The money raised will be

Amnesty International members in Warsaw, Poland, publicize the organization's 1994 campaign against political killings and "disappearances".

16

used partly for preparatory work for future fundraising initiatives and partly for funding the Section's vital human rights work. The Venezuelan Section was also involved in an exchange of fundraising personnel with the British Section, just one example of inter-section cooperation that took place in 1994.

Other places with fundraising successes included Bratislava, where the group raised money on Human Rights Day by selling mock world passports. The Hong Kong Section organized a fundraising walk called "The Search for the 'Disappeared'" and the Bahamas group raised funds by organizing a diving expedition.

The ingenuity of the membership is also crucial to the success of Amnesty International's campaigning efforts, given the many and varied cultures in which members are working. In 1994, for example, the Japanese Section asked all 45-year-olds in their country to join Amnesty International to commemorate the 45th anniversary of the signing of the Universal Declaration of Human Rights. It urged them to sign petitions and write letters for the campaign against "disappearances" and political killings. Equally inventive was the "Ambassadors of Hope" scheme launched by the Brazilian Section (see page 10).

In 1994 Amnesty International members also responded to the many human rights emergencies around the world. Most sections worked hard to bring to the world's attention the plight of people in Burundi and Rwanda, whether by lobbying their own government or member of parliament, or by attracting media coverage. The African sections in particular worked tirelessly for

Amnesty International children's group in Bangladesh.

Children's drawings (*above*) and a street display of posters (*left*): just two of the initiatives organized by the Mexican Section during Amnesty International Week which in 1994 focused on human rights violations against children.

effective action to be taken. The Ghanaian Section, for example, concentrated on lobbying their government. This included distributing to government officials Amnesty International's 15-point program for implementing human rights in international peace-keeping operations (see **Appendix VIII**). In Côte d'Ivoire, a poster campaign with the message "Today it's Rwanda! And tomorrow?" was initiated.

Tens of thousands of participants in the Urgent Action Network responded to the immediate risk of torture, execution or other serious abuses. They wrote letters, used the telephone or sent faxes to intervene at a moment's notice on behalf of hundreds of individuals whose cases were featured in "Urgent Action Appeals" issued throughout 1994.

These actions are based on information carefully researched and analysed by the staff of the International Secretariat. The information is sent out in "Urgent Action Appeals", as well as in the monthly *Amnesty International Newsletter*, reports and other campaigning materials. Once a year it is summarized in this annual report.

During the year Amnesty International continued to train its members to use the information and initiate campaigns with even greater effect. Part of this project is to provide first-class information and coaching to the people who are responsible for training in each country. In 1994 a "training of trainers" workshop took place in Africa for the first time. Held in Ghana, it

18

lasted five days and involved participants from Gambia, Ghana, Nigeria, Sierra Leone, South Africa and Zambia. The workshop led to the setting up of training programs, covering issues such as fundraising, in these countries.

Such workshops are designed for the specific needs of those taking part. For example, in Eastern and Central Europe members identified their main difficulty in attracting new members and funds as the general public's lack of awareness of Amnesty International. The regional workshop held in Bulgaria in June 1994 and attended by representatives of 13 countries was therefore geared towards tackling this problem.

A diverse, well-trained and committed membership in a wide variety of countries provides a firm base from which to spread the message of Amnesty International even more widely. That message is simple. Everyone, everywhere has the right to enjoy their fundamental human rights. Amnesty International members will continue to develop and improve their work to make sure the message is heard even more clearly around the globe.

Building the future

In August 1994 a group of professionals from international and local human rights institutions involved in human rights education met at Amnesty International's headquarters in London. They discussed three issues: preventative human rights work, the challenges facing the international community in the field of human rights education, and the role of Amnesty International in this work.

The meeting was just a small part of Amnesty International's increased efforts to develop a strategy for promoting human rights and preventing violations worldwide. It concluded, among other things, that Amnesty International should be more systematic about drawing together the experiences of its sections and groups in human rights education. To this end, a four-year Human Rights Education Strategy was formulated to improve co-ordination between sections and groups throughout the world and to enhance their efforts to prevent human rights violations.

Human rights awareness

Most Amnesty International sections run human rights awareness campaigns. These aim to spread information about human rights, create a climate of opinion which promotes greater respect for human rights, and encourage action in defence of those rights.

A group of children aged 11 and 12 in Chusovoy, Ural Region, Russia, play a game on the theme of human rights as part of an extra-curricular course.

In early 1994, for example, the Japanese Section organized a competition to promote the UN Convention on the Rights of the Child. Participants of all ages were asked to translate the Convention from English into Japanese and to explain what the Convention means to them. In July a panel of well-known personalities judged the 630 entries and a book with the 10 winning entries is to be published. Media coverage of the event raised awareness of the Convention.

In Macao, Amnesty International members organized seminars in English and Cantonese, as well as poetry readings. They also organized human rights courses and produced human rights education materials.

Many other initiatives continued during 1994. In the Caribbean region, Amnesty International sections and groups join together every year to send postcards with a human rights message. In 1994 school children in Bermuda sent messages of solidarity to human rights activists in Guatemala. The Bermuda Section organized its third annual local jazz festival, and in Argentina and Mexico concerts were staged to bring the human rights message to young people.

Amnesty International groups also promoted human rights in countries which have recently experienced the devastation of war. In Croatia, Amnesty International members organized 10 days of public action on human rights during September. The event focused on a poster exhibition on Amnesty International's

Children in Taiwan sign appeals organized by local Amnesty International members for the release of prisoners of conscience around the world.

work, with lectures, concerts and other public events organized each day to promote human rights.

The dissemination of the African Charter on Human and Peoples' Rights throughout Africa continued to be one of Amnesty International's major human rights awareness efforts. Despite some weaknesses in its text, the Charter seeks to apply many fundamental and universal human rights standards in the African context. In the three years since Amnesty International's project started in 1991, an additional eight states have ratified the Charter (Ethiopia and Swaziland, along with recent Organization of African Unity members Eritrea and South Africa, are now the only African countries not to have done so).

At the beginning of the project, Amnesty International produced an illustrated Guide to the Charter written in plain language. With the help of local non-governmental organizations, it has subsequently produced both the African Charter and the Guide in Afrikaans, Arabic, English, French, Portuguese, Spanish, Swahili, Xhosa and Zulu, and the Charter also in Hausa and Kirundi. During 1994 a special effort was made to translate the Charter and Guide into languages spoken in South Africa to coincide with the ending of *apartheid*.

Amnesty International groups and sections in Africa have also organized many events to increase knowledge and understanding of the Charter. For example, members in Côte d'Ivoire with the support of local musicians and singers produced and continue to distribute a cassette of songs explaining the Charter in several languages spoken in Africa. In Sierra Leone, Amnesty International members with the support of local communities have had passages of the Charter read in churches and mosques.

Since 1991 Amnesty International groups in Africa and elsewhere have organized special events on 21 October to commemorate the promulgation and coming into force of the African Charter. Drawing competitions for children, debates on the radio, music concerts, conferences and other public events have been staged to highlight the document. Amnesty International is now trying to make governments aware of the obligations they have to the African Commission on Human and Peoples' Rights.

As in past years, hundreds if not thousands of Amnesty International groups around the world organized stalls, miniconcerts, public meetings, seminars and outdoor events on 10 December to commemorate and celebrate Human Rights Day. These occasions aim to focus public attention on the importance of promoting and protecting the rights of all people, regardless of creed, race or sex. These events have received very positive responses from the public.

Human rights education

A growing number of Amnesty International sections are developing new and challenging human rights education programs to help individuals understand human rights as well as the underlying attitudes which lead to respect for them. They also promote knowledge of the instruments which codify and protect human rights, and train people in the skills necessary for human rights work.

Many local projects in developing regions have received support from Amnesty International's "Teaching for Freedom" project based in Norway. In 1994 Amnesty International members in Ecuador, Guyana, Hong Kong and the West Bank and Gaza Strip started new programs under this scheme.

In several countries human rights education work expanded in 1994. One developing area has been the training of security forces. While Amnesty International seeks to contribute to this process, governments remain responsible for ensuring that their security forces abide by international standards and that they are properly trained.

In Brazil, Amnesty International's human rights training in police academies continued to expand during 1994. Work with the Brazilian police was initiated in 1984 and developed rapidly; in 1988 a law was passed unanimously by the state parliament of Rio Grande do Sul introducing human rights education into the training of the state police. The Brazilian Amnesty International Section has subsequently been involved in setting the syllabus. In 1989 a similar law was passed in Bahia state and in 1990 agreement was reached with the authorities of São Paulo to work with civil and military police there.

By the end of 1994 the Brazilian Section was involved in human rights education work with: the municipal guards in seven cities; the military police in Bahia (in collaboration with UNICEF); the military police and civil police in São Paulo (in collaboration with the local university); the military police in Rio Grande do Sul (in collaboration with the local university); and the civil police in Rio Grande do Sul, where they have worked with half of the civil police personnel.

In 1994 Amnesty International also concentrated on human rights training in civil society. In the West Bank and Gaza Strip, Amnesty International groups, in collaboration with other local institutions, organized two human rights training workshops for human rights activists and educators who were developing human rights education programs. The workshops were assisted by a trainer from the Philippines.

Another major human rights initiative took place in Lilongwe, Malawi, at the beginning of August – a symposium entitled "Malawi: Human Rights – The Way Forward". The symposium was initiated by Amnesty International and the Public Affairs Committee, a body representing all religious communities in Malawi. It was attended by representatives from Malawi's human rights non-governmental organizations and religious organizations as well as by members of the security services. Delegates discussed the problems encountered by human rights organizations and looked at practical ways of building a human rights movement in the country. During the workshop that followed the two-day symposium, a human rights training program was planned for 1995.

In Guyana, the Amnesty International Section held a curricula development seminar, "Educating for Citizenship", in April in conjunction with another local non-governmental organization and the Ministry of Education. Its aim was to enable educators to view school curricula from a global perspective, taking into account the rights of children, and to improve the integration of human rights issues. The seminar was attended by educators and teachers from different regions of Guyana, and from Barbados, Grenada, Jamaica and Trinidad and Tobago.

In 1994 Amnesty International produced a Human Rights Education Pack for Eastern and Central Europe (including the countries of the former Soviet Union). The pack is aimed at educators working with young people in primary and secondary education, and suggests how human rights issues can be incorporated into school curricula. It also contains practical exercises for the classroom. At the end of the year sub-regional workshops were planned to test the pack and to show people how to use it.

In Western Europe, French-speaking groups from France, Italy and Switzerland met in Lausanne, Switzerland, in early October to discuss the need to develop human rights education work in the region. The Greek, Irish and Portuguese sections of Amnesty International continued to develop programs in their respective

© Cees de Rover

UN civilian police in Mozambique receive Amnesty International's cards listing 10 basic rules for safeguarding human rights during a course organized by the UN Centre for Human Rights. Over 8,000 cards were printed and distributed to both the UN civilian police and to the Mozambican Police.

countries, as did the Austrian, Belgian, British, Dutch, French and German sections, which also supported the efforts of other Amnesty International sections and other organizations in Africa, Eastern and Central Europe, and the Middle East.

Amnesty International is committed to developing awareness and understanding of international human rights standards as well as to promoting knowledge of the relevant national, regional and international mechanisms for the protection of human rights. The ultimate goal is to encourage ordinary citizens and government leaders, groups and institutions, to adopt beliefs, behaviours and policies that will safeguard all human rights everywhere in the world.

Protecting refugees

There were over 23 million refugees worldwide by the end of 1994, according to the Office of the UN High Commissioner for Refugees (UNHCR). Some had fled outside their own region, but the vast majority had sought safety in countries neighbouring their own. Many were denied their fundamental human rights and their rights as asylum-seekers.

Serious human rights violations are among the complex root causes of refugee movements. The millions of men, women and children who have been forced to abandon their homes need protection, and states have a duty under international law to provide it. The principle of *non-refoulement*, as set out in the 1951 Convention relating to the Status of Refugees and reflected in other human rights instruments, prohibits states from forcibly returning refugees to countries where they would risk serious human rights violations. This principle is widely recognized as a norm of customary international law, binding on all states, yet it is often violated.

Around the world

The largest and most sudden refugee crisis in 1994 was in Central Africa. Within weeks of mass killings in Rwanda by the former government forces and militia, over 300,000 people had fled the country. Among them were refugees from Burundi who a few months earlier had sought safety in Rwanda from intercommunal violence and political killings in Burundi (see *Amnesty International Report 1994*). Most of those who fled went to Tanzania, others to Zaire, Uganda and Burundi. Hundreds of them were killed or "disappeared" in Burundi in June and July (see **Burundi** entry).

Over a million more Rwandans fled in July 1994 shortly after a new government took control in Rwanda. The majority were Hutu – the predominant ethnic group in the former Rwandese Government and security forces. Most went to Zaire, where at one stage hundreds were dying daily from disease in the camps (see **Rwanda** and **Zaire** entries). Thousands of the refugees subsequently returned to Rwanda. But many others feared to return because of reports of abuses in Rwanda by the new government's security forces and supporters, and because of intimidation, death threats and killings in the camps by leaders, militia and soldiers linked to the ousted government.

Amnesty International called on the Rwandese authorities to take urgent steps to end the cycle of human rights violations and to investigate fully all alleged abuses. It also urged the UN to establish an adequate and effective human rights monitoring presence in Rwanda. Such measures would provide the refugees with some assurance about their future safety if they were to return.

In May, after two years of summarily returning all Haitians intercepted at sea (see *Amnesty International Report 1994*), the US Government announced that Haitian asylum-seekers would be allowed to present asylum claims on board US ships or in other countries in the region. In another change in policy some weeks later, such asylum-seekers were offered so-called "safe haven" protection at the US naval base at Guantánamo Bay, Cuba, but were no longer able to apply for asylum in the USA. While the end of the policy of forcible return of all intercepted Haitians was a positive development, these arrangements meant that asylum-seekers fleeing Haiti had no opportunity for a proper hearing of their claims, which they would have had if allowed to seek asylum in the normal way. Amnesty International was concerned about this restriction on the rights of these asylum-seekers, as well as the similar restriction on Cubans intercepted at sea and taken to Guantánamo, a substantial number of whom, the organization believed, could be at risk of human rights violations if returned home (see **Cuba** entry). An Amnesty International delegation visiting Guantánamo some weeks later, immediately after the US military intervention in Haiti in September, was concerned that Haitians were opting to return home, and apparently being encouraged to do so, without being given access to reliable independent information about the still unstable situation in Haiti.

In Iraq, the government's continuing crack-down on the Shi'a Muslim population in the south, including military attacks on the population, meant that many Iraqi Shi'a Muslims fled across the border into Iran to join thousands who had fled there in previous years (see **Iraq** entry). Over 20,000 Iraqis in Saudi Arabia who feared returning to Iraq following the 1991 Gulf War remained in a purpose-built camp. A report issued by Amnesty International in May described how some of them had reportedly suffered gross human rights violations, such as arbitrary arrest, torture and ill-treatment, and some had reportedly been extrajudicially executed. Since 1991 hundreds had been forcibly returned to Iraq, despite the risk they faced there.

Many thousands of asylum-seekers from Iraq and Iran, as well as other countries, have fled to Turkey in recent years, but Turkey has limited its formal obligations under the 1951 Convention to refugees coming from Europe. As a result, there is inadequate protection in Turkey for refugees from countries outside Europe. Even those recognized as refugees by the UNHCR are not entitled to remain – their only option is to obtain resettlement in other countries. But resettlement is offered only at the discretion of other governments – it is not guaranteed. In March Amnesty International reported that the situation for non-European refugees and asylum-seekers was reaching crisis point: some had been forcibly returned to the countries they had fled and others faced harassment by the Turkish police.

In Thailand, there are no proper procedures by which asylum-

More than half a million people were massacred in Rwanda following the death of President Habyarimana in April. By August well over a million people had fled the country. *(Left)* A Rwandan refugee arrives at Benako refugee camp in Tanzania. Refugees arriving at the camp walked for up to a week to reach safety. *(Below)* Katale refugee camp in Zaire, which lacked even the most basic facilities. Conditions in many of the refugee camps to which Rwandans fled were atrocious. In Goma, also in Zaire, up to 80,000 people died within weeks in a cholera epidemic.

© Howard J. Davies

seekers can obtain legal recognition of their special situation. Many of them, particularly those from Myanmar who are now the largest single group of asylum-seekers in Thailand, suffered from a general crack-down on "illegal immigration". Many faced lengthy detention in conditions falling far below basic international standards, and some were deported to areas of Myanmar where they would be at risk of human rights violations (see **Thailand** entry).

Governments' response to refugees

The 1993 World Conference on Human Rights reaffirmed the right to seek and enjoy asylum from persecution in other countries and recognized the need for a comprehensive approach to the protection of refugees. Such an approach should include effective action to tackle the situations causing refugees to flee, as well as to provide them with effective protection. Amnesty International called on the UN Commission on Human Rights in February to take urgent and strong measures to ensure that governments put a stop to the human rights violations which cause refugees to flee.

However, many governments seem more concerned with reducing the number of asylum-seekers who reach their borders than with stopping the human rights disasters which make people flee. Moreover, it is often the countries with the greatest resources, to which comparatively few asylum-seekers flee,

Haitian asylum-seekers at the US base at Guantánamo Bay, Cuba. Both Haitian and Cuban boat people were offered so-called "safe haven" protection at the base without the opportunity to apply for asylum in the USA.

AMNESTY INTERNATIONAL REPORT 1995

Afghan refugees from Kabul City recently arrived at Nasir Bagh Camp, Peshawar, Pakistan. Many academics and professionals – particularly educated women – were among a recent wave of Afghan refugees fleeing to Peshawar.

which have the most restrictive attitudes towards refugees.

The visa requirements imposed by European countries on nationals of Bosnia-Herzegovina after the war started there and people started to flee (see *Amnesty International Report 1994*) are just one example of measures taken by European governments to limit the protection they offer refugees. In recent years many European governments have taken steps to restrict the number of asylum-seekers whose cases are given full examination by categorizing some types of claim as inadmissible or otherwise not deserving substantive examination. In addition, a growing number of asylum-seekers are returned to third countries – usually countries they have previously travelled through where, it is held, they should submit their claims. Such arrangements have for some years been developing among the European Union (EU) member states, and more recently these states have adopted policies for sending asylum-seekers back to third countries outside the EU.

Many asylum-seekers who come to Western Europe have travelled through countries in Eastern and Central Europe, to which they might be returned on this basis. Some such countries, however, do not have a sufficiently developed infrastructure to provide effective protection to large numbers of refugees and asylum-seekers. In addition, Hungary limits its formal obligations under the 1951 Convention to asylum-seekers coming from European countries.

An elderly Tibetan woman in a refugee camp near Pokhara, Nepal, where she has lived since the 1950s. The UN High Commissioner for Refugees estimated that the number of refugees around the world in 1994 was over 23 million. Many of the countries where large numbers of people sought protection were among the world's poorest.

Amnesty International believes that policies for transferring asylum-seekers to third countries must ensure that arrangements are made for the proper examination of their claims. Otherwise, asylum-seekers may be returned successively from one country to another, ending up in a country where they risk persecution.

Access to full and fair procedures

Even where asylum-seekers manage to get access to asylum procedures, in some countries these procedures fall short of what is required by international standards. Governments have often been reluctant to remedy such deficiencies, arguing that a relatively good asylum procedure can be a "pull factor" attracting people who want to migrate for economic or other reasons not related to persecution. But the international principle of *non-refoulement* prohibits states from returning asylum-seekers against their will to a country where they fear human rights violations unless it is established that they would not be at risk. This can only be done by a complete examination of the merits of the case in a full and fair procedure.

Amnesty International has identified a number of basic principles, based on international standards, which form an essential minimum for a fair and satisfactory asylum procedure, and calls on all states to ensure that their asylum procedures comply with them. The most fundamental of these are that the asylum-seeker is granted access to the procedures, has a fair hearing, has an effective right of appeal, and is allowed to await the decision on that appeal before being expelled. Amnesty International also urges that these essential principles be used as a basis to develop an international agreement on minimum procedural standards for dealing with asylum requests.

In June Amnesty International's European sections reported on deficiencies in asylum procedures in several European states. They called on EU member states to establish common basic standards for fair and satisfactory asylum procedures in Europe complying with the requirements of international standards, and to codify these in an international agreement.

Amnesty International raised its concerns again with EU member states in November, when specific proposals were under discussion for a common policy on minimum standards for asylum procedures. The organization feared that the proposed common policy would undermine existing safeguards in the procedures in some member states, by allowing a further erosion of the standard of protection to the lowest common level.

Many Amnesty International sections raised concerns about changes in national legislation which would not provide asylum-seekers with adequate protection. For example, in the Netherlands, legislation introducing the notion of "safe" countries of origin was adopted in December, and legislation introducing provisions for returning asylum-seekers to third countries was going through parliament at the end of the year. In Ireland, legislation under discussion for regulating the asylum procedure made insufficient provision for legal assistance and advice to asylum-seekers.

A comprehensive system for determining refugee status on an individual basis can place a major administrative load on governments, particularly when large numbers of asylum-seekers arrive within a short time. But this cannot absolve governments of their obligations under international law towards refugees who arrive at their borders. International standards underline that the fundamental principle of *non-refoulement* – including non-rejection at the border – must be scrupulously observed at all times, and that asylum-seekers should always be admitted to the state where they seek refuge and given all necessary provision to enable them to obtain durable protection. Amnesty International was concerned that in some countries asylum-seekers who had had no proper examination of their claim were forcibly expelled or threatened with forcible expulsion to countries where they might be at risk, or to other countries where they might not be afforded proper protection (see **Thailand**, **Ukraine** and **Russia** entries). In Estonia, asylum-seekers were held in detention throughout the year without any opportunity to find effective and durable protection; their situation remained unresolved at the end of the year (see **Estonia** entry).

Detention

International standards state that the detention of asylum-seekers should normally be avoided and used only where necessary for certain specified reasons. All detained asylum-seekers should be given a prompt individual hearing before a court or similar body to determine whether the detention is lawful and in accordance with international standards. Under international standards unauthorized entry is not regarded as a legitimate reason for detaining asylum-seekers, since asylum-seekers may have no choice but to try to enter a country without prior authorization. Despite this, there are signs that governments are increasingly detaining asylum-seekers, often in breach of international standards.

In Belgium, asylum-seekers arriving at the airport without valid papers are routinely detained pending a decision on whether their application is admissible. In Germany, asylum-seekers arriving at major international airports without valid papers, or who come from countries considered by the authorities to be "safe" countries of origin, are detained while their asylum application is examined.

In Austria, asylum-seekers who have come through a "safe" third country – which includes all neighbouring countries – are considered illegal entrants. Once they contact the authorities to make an asylum claim they are in most cases detained while the asylum and the expulsion procedures are handled concurrently. While detained, their access to lawyers is very limited and often the proceedings happen so fast that they cannot obtain a lawyer

© Migrant Media

A demonstration at Campsfield House Detention Centre, Oxfordshire, the United Kingdom, by asylum-seekers protesting about their detention. Hundreds of asylum-seekers were detained in the UK pending the outcome of their asylum claims.

before the asylum claim and permission to remain in the country have been refused, leading to an expulsion.

In Australia, those arriving without a visa who claim asylum at the border are automatically detained. They can be held throughout the entire asylum procedure until they are granted refugee status, or, if their asylum claim is refused, until they are expelled. Those who appeal against refusal of asylum are liable to be detained throughout all stages of the procedure, which can take several months or longer. Amnesty International has repeatedly called on the government to make its policy on detention of asylum-seekers comply with international standards, but new legislation which came into effect in 1994 provides for the continuation of the policy (see **Australia** entry).

In the United Kingdom, hundreds of asylum-seekers were detained in 1994 pending determination of their asylum claim. Detainees can be held indefinitely, are not properly informed of the reasons for their detention, and have no effective opportunity to challenge those reasons before a court or independent review body. Many are held in ordinary prisons. A study by Amnesty International's British Section of 50 individual cases demonstrated that this lack of accountability, and the absence of proper judicial control, results in arbitrary decision-making and unnecessary detentions. It also indicated that the average length of such detention had increased significantly – to over five months – since new asylum procedures came into force in mid-1993.

In Switzerland, detention of asylum-seekers has not been a regular practice to date, but new legislation adopted in 1994 provides for asylum-seekers to be detained during the appeal stage of the asylum procedure.

There were also some encouraging developments during the year. Monica Castillo, who had been expelled from Sweden with the intention of returning her to Peru despite the risks she would have faced there (see *Amnesty International Report 1994*), was granted refugee status in the Netherlands. In addition, some courts ruled against the restrictive policies of governments. In Belgium, a court ordered the government to improve access for lawyers to asylum-seekers held in detention. In Germany, some courts challenged the return of asylum-seekers to third countries under new legislation introduced in 1993 (see *Amnesty International Report 1994*), and at the end of the year some of these cases were before the Constitutional Court. At the political level, in April the Parliamentary Assembly of the Council of Europe called for the European Convention on Human Rights and Fundamental Freedoms to be amended to include a right of asylum, and identified certain minimum guarantees, including some of those specified by Amnesty International, which should be included in all asylum procedures.

Working with international organizations

The killing of more than half a million civilians in Rwanda in 1994 and the continuing atrocities in countries such as Afghanistan, Algeria, Angola, Bosnia-Herzegovina, Burundi, Colombia and Turkey threw into stark relief the inability of the UN and other intergovernmental organizations to prevent or stop gross human rights violations. Repeated declarations of high ideals look increasingly hollow in the face of unchecked extra-judicial executions, torture and "disappearances".

There is no shortage of knowledge about impending human rights crises around the world. Amnesty International and other non-governmental organizations, independent UN experts and journalists all publicly document escalating human rights violations. Embassy officials keep their own governments informed about the latest developments in all corners of the world. The problem is the failure of governments and intergovernmental organizations to listen to these warnings and act quickly.

In April 1993 the UN's own Special Rapporteur on extrajudicial, summary or arbitrary executions visited Rwanda, one year before the mass killings began. In a report dated 11 August 1993 he recommended that structures be set up to protect civilians from massacres in which "it has been shown time and time again that government officials were involved". Later he warned:

> "[l]essons should be drawn from the past and the cycle of violence which has drenched both Burundi and Rwanda in blood must be broken. To this end, the impunity of the perpetrators of the massacres must be definitively brought to an end and preventive measures to avoid the recurrence of such tragedies must be designed".

Yet governments failed to heed this warning.

This chapter looks at some of the events in 1994 which reveal the lack of political will, resources and coordination that have sometimes paralysed international action against gross human rights violations. Events show the reluctance of governments to heed the warning signs and take early preventive action, and their failure to react swiftly in the face of massive violations, for example by tackling the impunity enjoyed by the perpetrators.

Nevertheless, there were some encouraging signs in 1994. These included moves to address impunity by developing further the system of international justice, the adoption of a new

AMNESTY INTERNATIONAL REPORT 1995

human rights treaty prohibiting "disappearances", and the start of the term of office of the new High Commissioner for Human Rights, who launched field initiatives to monitor and protect human rights.

Peace-keeping and human rights

While the UN's peace-keeping operations have mushroomed dramatically over recent years, the UN has not really come to terms with its new role. Human rights work in peace-keeping operations has been carried out haphazardly and much of the thinking and many of the existing organizational structures remain mired in the practices of the past, rather than meeting the challenges of today.

Most peace-keeping operations and their human rights components have been worked out in New York at UN headquarters, with a marked lack of involvement, consultation or cooperation with the UN's own human rights bodies and experts or its Centre for Human Rights based in Geneva – and with hardly any reference to other UN programs such as the Vienna-based Crime Prevention and Criminal Justice Branch. As a result the UN is sometimes ill-equipped to deal with the human rights aspects of conflicts such as that in Somalia, often lacking the expertise and resources necessary to make an effective impact.

Amnesty International believes that the UN must now consistently build essential measures for human rights promotion and protection into its peace-keeping activities, right from the first planning stages. In 1994 Amnesty International published a report, *Peace-keeping and human rights*, together with a 15-point program of recommendations for peace-keeping activities (see **Appendix VIII**). There needs to be a coherent approach to these operations which insists on a central role for the protection and promotion of human rights – even after the peace-keeping troops have left.

In 1994 Amnesty International produced training documents for the UN civilian police (UNCIVPOL) monitors in Mozambique. These materials, together with bilingual pocket-sized cards to remind them of basic human rights principles for law enforcement, were distributed to the UNCIVPOLs and the Mozambican police. During the year the UN itself produced a handbook of criminal justice standards for UNCIVPOLs.

Amnesty International also worked for greater human rights awareness and expertise to be built into a number of UN operations including those in Angola, Liberia and Somalia. Amnesty International advocates deploying civilian human rights advisers in these operations in order to help prevent human rights violations, assist military observers to compile reports on violations of humanitarian law, and to train local human rights organizations in methods of investigation and reporting.

When the Security Council decided in May to cut the size of its peace-keeping force in Rwanda from just over 2,000 to 270,

Amnesty International called for the immediate return to Rwanda of the operation's civilian police monitors and unarmed military observers and an increase in their number. They had a vital role to play in helping to act as a dissuasive presence and in reporting systematically on the abuses, yet their deployment still took months, even after the Security Council authorized a 1,500-strong force.

The year saw an increased use of multinational military operations authorized by the Security Council but carried out outside UN command and control. These included the US-led force in Haiti, the French-led force in Rwanda and the Russian-led force in Georgia. In these situations Amnesty International has sought to ensure independent monitoring of the conduct of such forces. It has urged them not only to respect international human rights standards, but also to report any human rights violations they witness. When it became clear that the USA was seeking authority for a military intervention in Haiti, Amnesty International called for an international human rights monitoring operation to monitor the conduct of the international troops as well as the activities of the Haitian military and paramilitary forces.

> " ... the United Nations has not been able to act effectively to bring to an end massive human rights violations. Faced with the barbaric conduct which fills the news media today, the United Nations cannot stand idle or indifferent."
>
> UN Secretary-General Boutros Boutros-Ghali, writing in 1992, the year he took up office

There are signs that the UN recognizes the potential threat to human rights of operations which are not under UN command and control and are conducted without proper supervision. By December the UN Secretary-General was warning that states acting with such authority "can claim international legitimacy and approval for a range of actions which may in fact not have been envisaged by the Security Council" and that therefore such "peace enforcement operations ... must be closely monitored by the Council if international acceptance of those actions and their consequences is to be assured".

Amnesty International has sought to reinforce the principle that peace-keeping personnel should never be silent witnesses to human rights violations and abuses. All incidents should be documented and taken up with the domestic authorities. Where institutions to ensure accountability exist, such as the Truth Commission in El Salvador or the International Criminal Tribunals for Rwanda and the Former Yugoslavia, such information should be passed on to these bodies so that perpetrators can be brought to justice.

In December 1994 the UN General Assembly adopted the UN Convention on the Safety of United Nations and Associated Personnel. This Convention was drafted in response to the increasing attacks on UN personnel and the gaps in international law for bringing to justice the perpetrators of such attacks. Amnesty International successfully urged that this Convention should also include provisions outlining the duties of UN personnel to respect human rights.

Integrating human rights – the High Commissioner for Human Rights

New opportunities have been opened up with the appointment of the first High Commissioner for Human Rights, José Ayala Lasso from Ecuador. The High Commissioner began work on 5 April 1994, just two days before the genocide began in Rwanda. In early May Amnesty International launched an initiative to persuade members of the UN Commission on Human Rights to convene a special session of the Commission to address the crisis in Rwanda. The High Commissioner made similar appeals which were decisive to the success of this initiative. The special session, convened on 24 and 25 May, resulted in increased attention to the crisis in Rwanda and the appointment of a Special Rapporteur, René Degni-Ségui from Côte d'Ivoire, who was immediately sent to Rwanda.

On 2 August the High Commissioner launched an appeal for US$2.1 million to fund 20 human rights monitors to carry out deterrent, confidence-building, preventive and investigatory functions in Rwanda. When sufficient funds failed to materialize rapidly, Amnesty International deplored the failure of many wealthy countries to contribute quickly, or at all. In August, following a mission to the country, Amnesty International called for many more human rights monitors to be deployed in every one of Rwanda's 70 districts to help protect people and to build a climate of confidence. The organization welcomed the initiative launched by the High Commissioner in September to send 147 human rights monitors to the country, but regretted the months of delay caused by lack of funds, personnel and logistical back-up. By the end of the year the operation was still not up to full strength.

One of the High Commissioner's key functions is to coordinate all the human rights work of disparate institutions scattered throughout the UN system such as the Centre for Human Rights in Geneva; the New York-based UN Development Programme, departments of Peace-Keeping, Humanitarian Affairs, and Political Affairs, and the Division for the Advancement of Women; the Vienna-based Crime Prevention and Criminal Justice Branch; and the UN Educational, Scientific and Cultural Organization (UNESCO) in Paris. He can play a central role in ensuring that human rights concerns are integrated into almost every corner of UN decision-making at an early stage, including preparations for peace-keeping operations, as well as when the UN facilitates political settlements of armed conflicts. The High Commissioner can also press governments and the UN system to heed early warning signs of deteriorating human rights situations.

38

The High Commissioner is able to use both confidential dialogue and public statements to persuade, and if necessary shame, governments into cooperating with the UN system and reforming their law and practice to prevent human rights violations. Amnesty International hopes he will fulfil the promise he made, as quoted in a Swiss newspaper in 1994, that he would not hesitate to raise his voice if necessary, and with the utmost frankness.

In 1994 the High Commissioner visited 19 countries in four continents and committed himself to listening to the views of local non-governmental organizations as a regular part of these visits. Non-governmental organizations play a vital role in informing the High Commissioner about the human rights situations in countries. Amnesty International regularly submits to him a wide range of information about the human rights situation in individual countries and on particular themes. The organization has made recommendations to the High Commissioner about his working methods and the role it believes he should play in ensuring countries cooperate with UN human rights bodies and mechanisms, and in coordinating and increasing the profile of human rights throughout the UN system and in the world generally.

International justice

For more than 30 years Amnesty International has consistently argued that perpetrators of human rights violations must be brought to justice if the cycle of crime and impunity throughout the world is to be broken. Impunity breeds contempt for the law and encourages even more brazen human rights violations by officials who act as if they are above the law.

While the world's focus has been on Rwanda, nothing has been done to bring to justice those responsible for more than 50,000 killings in neighbouring Burundi following a coup attempt in October 1993. In Haiti, thousands of women and men, including human rights monitors, trade unionists, journalists, members and leaders of popular grassroots and religious groups, as well as children, were victims of widespread and systematic abuses in the years after the 1991 military coup. Amnesty International believes that letting killers and torturers off the hook undermines long-term solutions to the human rights crises because it sends a message that they can continue their abuses.

Many of the human rights violations and abuses committed in places such as Angola, Bosnia-Herzegovina, Burundi, Haiti and Rwanda are so heinous and so shock the conscience of humankind that they are considered crimes for which individuals can be held personally responsible under international law. The past two years have seen glimmers of hope that public outrage at massive violations of human rights is pushing governments to fulfil their promise to create a better system of international justice.

In 1994 the International Criminal Tribunal for the Former

Yugoslavia created by the UN Security Council – the first such war crimes tribunal since the Nuremberg and Tokyo tribunals after the Second World War – became operational. However, it has been bedevilled by logistical, financial and practical problems. It was only in August that South African judge Richard Goldstone took up office as Prosecutor after deadlock in the Security Council delayed an appointment to this post for months. A team of only 21 investigators has been faced with the daunting task of collecting enough first-hand evidence, much of it difficult to reach in the war zones of the former Yugoslavia, to bring to justice perpetrators of gross human rights violations and abuses. By the end of the year the tribunal had issued one indictment against a Serb who was believed to be still in Bosnia-Herzegovina, and had requested the transfer of a case pending before a German court involving charges of genocide, "ethnic cleansing", torture, including rape, and murder of civilians and prisoners of war.

In another historic move, the Security Council decided on 8 November to set up an *ad hoc* international tribunal to try people responsible for genocide, crimes against humanity and violations of the humanitarian law governing internal armed conflict, committed in Rwanda between 1 January and 31 December 1994. The tribunal's jurisdiction also covers such crimes committed by Rwandans in neighbouring states.

Like the statute of the former Yugoslavia tribunal

> "In the aftermath of the Second World War... it was generally anticipated by the international community that a new era had begun. An era in which the human rights of all citizens in all countries of the world would be universally respected. It was not to be... There was no mechanism devised by the international community for establishing the guilt of the perpetrators and punishing them."
>
> Prosecutor Richard Goldstone, opening the first hearing of the International Criminal Tribunal for the Former Yugoslavia, November 1994

on which it is modelled, the statute of the Rwanda tribunal lays the foundation for a just, fair and effective process. It reaffirms that carrying out a crime on the orders of a superior is not a defence. Anyone who planned, instigated or ordered crimes, even if a senior official, cannot escape prosecution. The tribunal has the power to take over trials in national courts which might be a sham or unfair. It must observe a number of important guarantees for fair trial and has a duty to protect victims and witnesses from possible reprisals. Amnesty International also welcomes the exclusion of the death penalty from the statutes of the two tribunals.

All of the powers of the tribunals will be of little use unless states and the UN ensure they have sufficient money, staff and political support. Amnesty International has urged states to contribute to the special UN voluntary funds set up for the tribunals, to ensure the UN General Assembly grants adequate funding and

40

swiftly to pass laws to enable their national authorities to co-operate with the tribunals.

Amnesty International advocated the establishment of both *ad hoc* tribunals. But these fulfil relatively short-term needs in only two areas of the world. The need for a *permanent* international criminal court to try grave violations of international human rights and humanitarian law wherever they occur remains over-whelming and urgent. Almost half a century ago the UN General Assembly asked experts in the International Law Commission (ILC) to draft a statute for a permanent criminal court. The Cold War, however, stifled progress until out-rage over the atrocities in the former Yugoslavia stimulated renewed interest in the proposal.

> " ...massacre, rape, ethnic cleansing, the wanton killing of civilians, affect each and every one of us, whatever our nationality and wherever we live. They affect each and every one of us because they imperil the great principles of civilisation enshrined in international legal standards on human rights."
> Antonio Cassese, President of the International Criminal Tribunal for the Former Yugoslavia, addressing the UN General Assembly, November 1994

In 1994 the ILC presented a final draft statute to the 49th session of the UN General Assembly. Despite overwhelming agreement on the need for a perma-nent court, some states have continued to delay the adoption of the proposal. After long and difficult negotiations, the General Assembly could agree only on setting up an *ad hoc* committee to look further at the draft statute and report back in 1995. In a report, *Establishing a just, fair and effective international criminal court*, Amnesty International set out its detailed critique of the ILC draft statute with recommendations to ensure the proposed court meets all fundamental international standards. Amnesty International is calling on states to adopt the necessary treaty no later than 24 October 1996, the end of the 50th anniversary year of the UN.

Evading scrutiny: the UN Commission on Human Rights

Time and again governments with abysmal human rights records have won the support of enough other governments, acting in their perceived self-interests, to block action in the UN, particu-larly by the Commission on Human Rights. Through such con-certed obstruction governments evade accountability, and the UN system for human rights protection is undermined.

Once again Amnesty International put before members of the 1994 Commission on Human Rights overwhelming evidence of severe and systematic human rights violations in countries such as Algeria, China (including Tibet), Indonesia and East Timor, Peru and Turkey. Yet the Commission blatantly disregarded the need to act on these countries.

Even though the UN's own Committee against Torture con-cluded in a unique public statement issued as a last resort in

November 1993 that "...the existence of systematic torture in Turkey cannot be denied", the Commission on Human Rights in 1994 refused to take action on Turkey. The Turkish Government has escaped criticism by the Commission because of a skilful mix of political initiatives, public relations gestures and the support in the international arena of powerful allies for whom the strategic significance of this country is far more important than its human rights record.

In contrast to a strong resolution the year before, in 1994 the Commission expressed only muted concern about continuing human rights violations in East Timor. Serious human rights violations, however, are part of Indonesia's official response to political opposition and also the means of removing perceived obstacles to economic policies throughout the Indonesian archipelago, including Aceh, Irian Jaya, Java and the capital Jakarta. Amnesty International argues strongly that the Commission has a duty to address the human rights situation throughout Indonesia and East Timor.

Sometimes procedural ploys are used by governments to evade scrutiny. Amnesty International deplored the way the Chinese Government was able to use a procedural motion at the 1994 Commission, for the fourth time, to block any Commission resolution on human rights violations in China, including Tibet. In other cases, such as Kashmir, the reality of grave human rights violations was again obscured by the acute politicization of the debate, so that states felt unable to act without seeming to take sides in a political dispute.

Most governments have been largely uninterested in countries such as Burundi where they have few strategic interests, even though some 50,000 people died in Burundi following a coup attempt in October 1993 and political killings continued almost daily in 1994. The UN Commission on Human Rights in 1994 declined to appoint a Special Rapporteur on Burundi. The High Commissioner for Human Rights did implement a program of advisory services, but this was based on an assessment of the situation prepared six months before mass killings devastated the country. During 1994 Amnesty International urged the UN to establish a civilian human rights operation to work with the Organization of African Unity's observation mission in Burundi and to help prevent a recurrence of the appalling cycle of violence. After months of delay, a small presence from the Centre for Human Rights had been established by the end of the year.

The regional experience: Africa and Europe

Regional intergovernmental organizations in Europe and Africa are facing a crisis of credibility as they struggle to carve out new roles and find sufficient resources to tackle gross human rights violations and abuses both within and outside armed conflict.

The Conference on Security and Co-operation in Europe (CSCE), which changed its name as of 1 January 1995 to the Organisation for Security and Co-operation in Europe, encompasses 53 states from Vancouver to Vladivostok. The CSCE sees itself as the main body for preventing conflicts erupting into war and for resolving crises in Europe. A major human rights challenge for the CSCE is whether it is able to place the protection of human rights at the heart of the search for peace and security and also deal with serious human rights violations occurring outside armed conflicts. The end of an armed conflict does not necessarily mean the end of human rights violations and violent conflict often erupts after many years in which human rights grievances have been ignored.

In 1994 Amnesty International urged the CSCE to systematize the ill-defined role human rights protection has played in its long-term diplomatic missions which are stationed in countries across the region, including Bosnia-Herzegovina, Estonia, Georgia, Latvia, Moldova and Tadzhikistan. After a two-month Review Conference the CSCE heads of state met in Budapest in December and agreed that "respect for human rights ... is an essential component of security and co-operation in the ... region". If so, human rights protection should be an essential part of the work of these CSCE diplomatic missions on the ground. At the very least the missions should report regularly on the human rights situation, include human rights advisers and never become silent witnesses to atrocities. Amnesty International argued that human rights guarantees and mechanisms for their implementation should always play a central role in any peace negotiations brokered by the CSCE and in the despatch of any CSCE peace-keeping force.

The past three years have seen a growing tide of concern, expressed publicly by experts and parliamentarians in the UN, CSCE and Council of Europe and by the Council of the European Union, about escalating human rights violations in Turkey. However, the Committee of Ministers, the highest decision-making organ in the Council of Europe, remained unwilling to tackle patterns of gross or systematic human rights violations such as those in Turkey. This makes it even more important for the CSCE to act. Amnesty International has repeatedly urged that as a first step, a CSCE expert mission under the so-called Moscow mechanism should go to Turkey to investigate torture and attacks on freedom of expression, and make clear recommendations which would require the main CSCE bodies to decide on follow-up action.

In Africa, a conflict prevention and resolution mechanism, set up by the Organization of African Unity (OAU) in 1993, aims to prevent conflicts and to help establish a fair and just society. Recent conflicts in Africa have been characterized by gross violations of human rights and humanitarian law. Yet despite several significant initiatives, such as an important but under-resourced monitoring operation in Burundi, the mechanism has no express human rights component.

In addition to the mass killings in Rwanda and Burundi, 1994 saw continuing gross human rights violations and abuses in armed conflicts throughout the region, including in Algeria, Angola, Liberia, Somalia and Sudan. Despite the scale of the suffering, the OAU failed to take a leading role in ensuring that measures for the protection and promotion of human rights were an essential part of the search for national reconciliation, peace and justice.

During 1994 Amnesty International reiterated its call for the OAU to implement a six-point program to promote and protect human rights, which Amnesty International first proposed in 1993. Amnesty International welcomed the appointment in April 1994 by the African Commission on Human and Peoples' Rights of a Special Rapporteur on extrajudicial executions. He was requested urgently to address the situation in Rwanda but, disappointingly, was not given the resources to do so.

International action to protect women

Any woman who is extrajudicially executed, tortured, made to "disappear" or arbitrarily detained cannot exercise her rights to equality, development and peace. This is the message which Amnesty International is taking to the Fourth UN World Conference on Women, to be held in Beijing in September 1995. It is a message that emerges clearly from the catalogue of gross violations suffered by women and girls throughout the world (see **Introduction**).

The five regional preparatory meetings held in 1994 in Argentina, Austria, Jordan, Indonesia and Senegal produced final documents which in varying degrees reflect women's rights as human rights. However, Amnesty International has consistently pointed out that the 1994 draft Platform for Action – to be adopted at the Conference – barely mentions human rights and fails to refer to governments' responsibilities to prevent and stop human rights violations suffered by women and girls. In its paper, *Equality by the year 2000?*, Amnesty International has set out 10 recommendations for the Platform for Action, which include fully acknowledging the universality and indivisibility of women's civil, cultural, economic, political and social rights and ensuring that all governments ratify – and implement – human rights treaties.

The human rights of women and girls have suffered in the UN from neglect and because responsibility has been split between two UN bodies, now located in different continents. Amnesty International welcomed the appointment in 1994 by the UN Commission on Human Rights of a Special Rapporteur on violence against women, Radhika Coomaraswamy from Sri Lanka. Her work should enrich the world's understanding of the causes of continuing, entrenched violations against women and ensure that no part of the UN system can ignore this issue. However, it was disappointing that the Commission on Human Rights failed to decide on practical measures to integrate women's human rights into the UN system or on measures to make a reality the commitments made in 1993 at the UN World Conference on Human Rights. Amnesty International hopes that a new awareness by the New York-based Commission on the Status of Women of the vital need to coordinate with other bodies will move this body towards closer cooperation with the Geneva-based Commission on Human Rights.

Historic treaty on 'disappearances'

In 1988 the Inter-American Court of Human Rights deplored the fact that the phenomenon of "disappearances" had "occurred with exceptional intensity in Latin America". Six years later the Americas have become the first region to adopt a binding treaty aimed at the prevention and eradication of "disappearances" and the punishment of perpetrators.

On 9 June 1994 the 24th regular session of the General Assembly of the Organization of American States (OAS) unanimously adopted the Inter-American Convention on the Forced Disappearance of Persons (see **Appendix IX** for full text). The Convention was eight years in the making but it was not until the year leading up to the 1994 OAS General Assembly that serious flaws in the draft were removed, resulting in a final text which contains a number of important developments or reaffirmations of international standards on the prohibition of "disappearances".

The Convention refers to "disappearances" as "an affront to the conscience of the Hemisphere and a grave and abominable offence against the inherent dignity of the human being". One aim of the Convention is the eradication of "disappearances" and States Parties commit themselves "not to practice, permit or tolerate [enforced] disappearance, even in states of emergency". Most importantly, the Convention meets a long-standing demand by the human rights movement and relatives of the "disappeared" by "reaffirming that the systematic practice of the forced disappearance of persons constitutes a crime against humanity". The defence of obedience to orders from superiors is expressly excluded and perpetrators may not be tried in military courts. The Convention creates an urgent, although confidential, procedure under which the Inter-American Commission on Human Rights can act on allegations of "disappearance" even before a case has been declared admissible.

Amnesty International and other international and regional non-governmental organizations contributed during the drafting process and actively urged the OAS to adopt the Convention. The Convention will enter into force after it has been ratified by two states. Unfortunately, although it had been signed by 12 states, by the end of the year none had yet ratified or acceded to the Convention. Amnesty International has urged all members of the OAS to become States Parties as a matter of priority.

Under-funding of human rights at the UN

Under-funding is a chronic problem for the UN human rights program, making it almost impossible to do the intensive work needed to make any impact in countries where violations are gross or systematic. Each year the UN Secretary-General and the relevant bodies of the UN General Assembly fail to provide adequate resources to meet the needs of the Centre for Human Rights as outlined by its Director. By withholding funds, member states effectively ensure that the UN human rights program will be unable to function properly: vital country visits by UN experts are postponed or suffer from lack of adequate back-up, human rights field operations muddle through without even basic supplies such as vehicles, and, no sooner does the UN raise expectations of a human rights field operation, than they are dashed when the Centre finds itself unable to deliver.

Despite small increases in 1993 and 1994, less than two per cent of the total UN budget is spent on the Centre for Human Rights. Yet the workload of the Centre continues to expand, as new experts are appointed by the UN Commission on Human Rights, more countries ratify human rights treaties, and demands increase for the Centre to operate field offices in several continents. In 1993 the UN Secretary-General proposed a woefully inadequate budget of just over US$1 million to implement the Vienna Declaration and Programme of Action, far short of the almost US$40 million bid originally submitted by the Centre for Human Rights.

It is perhaps not surprising that the call from within the UN to consider human rights priorities is often lost in the overwhelming weight of other interests. Amnesty International believes that states, who every year pledge their commitment to the UN's human rights program and the importance of respect for human rights, should take a hard look at the impact of under-funding and radically reassess their attitude to staffing the human rights program. If states are serious about addressing human rights problems they will have to approve extra staff and other resources for the program.

COUNTRY
ENTRIES

AFGHANISTAN

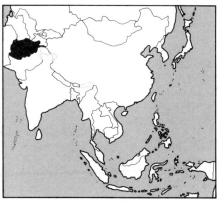

Thousands of civilians were killed and thousands more were wounded in artillery attacks deliberately aimed at residential areas by all factions in the civil war. Hundreds of men, women and children were deliberately and arbitrarily killed by members of the main armed groups during raids on civilian homes. Torture, including rape of women and children, was reportedly widespread. People were unlawfully imprisoned in private detention centres because of their political opinions, religion or ethnic origin, or as hostages. Journalists covering the war were detained or imprisoned by the warring factions. Hundreds of people "disappeared". Warlords acted as Islamic judges and ordered punishments including executions.

As in previous years, no effective central authority was established. Leaders of the main warring factions, Borhannudin Rabbani of the *Jamiat-e-Islami* (Society of Islam) and Gulbuddin Hekmatyar of *Hezb-e-Islami* (Party of Islam), remained President and Prime Minister respectively. An alliance of Mujahideen groups led by *Jamiat-e-Islami* retained control over most of the capital, Kabul, and an opposition alliance led by *Hezb-e-Islami* controlled other parts. Autonomous commanders allied to one or other of the rival alliances controlled the rest of the country. Some set up quasi-governmental structures and conducted their own foreign affairs.

Continuing armed conflict and political instability made it difficult to verify reports of human rights abuses within the country, but newly arriving Afghans interviewed in the border areas in Pakistan

testified to an unfolding human rights catastrophe. Hundreds of thousands of Afghans were displaced or fled to the neighbouring countries. In February food convoys organized by international aid agencies had their access into Kabul blocked by the allied forces of Prime Minister Gulbuddin Hekmatyar and General Abdul Rashid Dostum. Despite repeated warnings by the aid agencies that mass starvation of the Kabul population was imminent, six UN-organized trucks of relief supplies were not permitted to reach the city for several weeks. Following international appeals, three of the trucks were allowed to move on to Kabul on 6 March. However, on 7 March, in the northern Kabul suburb of Khair Khana where thousands of displaced Kabul inhabitants had fled to escape fierce fighting, people awaiting emergency food distribution were attacked with cluster bombs, reportedly by the forces of Gulbuddin Hekmatyar. At least six people were reportedly killed and 30 injured. The blockade remained in force until December when UN food convoys arrived in Kabul.

The UN Commission on Human Rights Special Rapporteur on the situation of human rights in Afghanistan, whose mandate was renewed for a further year in March, visited the country several times and submitted his interim report to the UN General Assembly in November, stating that the most basic elements of humanitarian law applicable to civilians were not being observed in Afghanistan.

Fighting over control of territory resulted in the killing of thousands of civilians caught in cross-fire or subjected to indiscriminate artillery attacks. The vast majority of the victims were unarmed civilians killed in the streets of Kabul, in their houses or in dwellings in the city where they had sought shelter after their homes had been destroyed. Other civilians were deliberately killed in their homes by members of the warring factions on suspicion of supporting rival armed groups. The fighting and attacks on civilians, originally confined to Kabul and the northern town of Mazar-e-Sharif, spread during 1994 to the provinces of Kunduz, Herat, Kandahar, Baghlan, Badghis and Nangarhar.

On 1 January the allied forces of General Abdul Rashid Dostum and Prime Minister Gulbuddin Hekmatyar launched

50

an attack on President Rabbani's forces at Kabul's Presidential Palace and the Ministry of Defence. Rival groups took up positions in residential areas on both sides of the River Kabul. Within a few weeks, hundreds of people, the majority of whom were unarmed civilians, had been killed in indiscriminate artillery attacks aimed at residential areas.

Attacks on Kabul continued throughout the year, reportedly killing dozens of people almost daily. In August, three hospitals in Kabul were reportedly attacked with rockets which killed over 30 patients and destroyed a store holding medical supplies provided by international aid organizations.

Armed clashes broke out in September between two Shi'a factions – *Hezb-e-Wahdat*, allied to Gulbuddin Hekmatyar, and *Harakat-e-Islami*, allied to Borhannudin Rabbani. Hundreds of people were killed and thousands were injured during the clashes. Scores of them were believed to have been killed deliberately and arbitrarily.

Factional fighting and attacks against Kabul led to thousands more civilian casualties in the last third of the year. According to one estimate, up to 800 people were killed and over 17,000 wounded between 12 September and 12 October alone. Several hundred of them were unarmed men, women and children killed in their houses by armed faction members who suspected them of supporting their political rivals. In a round of artillery and mortar fire on 21 October around Kabul University, the Deh Mazang area and the so-called Television Mountain, at least 45 people were killed and 150 wounded. Eye-witnesses reported that one of the bombs hit a school housing displaced people, killing 10. Another round of rocket attacks on Kabul on 23 October reportedly left at least 15 people dead and 43 injured; and in a barrage of rockets on Kabul on 24 October, at least 35 people were killed and 98 wounded. By the end of the year over 3,000 people had reportedly been killed in Kabul.

Members of armed political groups routinely entered civilian houses in Kabul and other parts of the country, killing male members of the family who resisted their entry and confiscating household property. For example, in March a man was killed in Kabul's Chel Sotoon district by armed faction members who entered his house, allegedly because he had allowed his 15-year-old daughter to go to school. She was repeatedly raped by the killers.

Unarmed civilians suspected of belonging to rival groups were reportedly tortured and ill-treated. Hundreds of women, young girls and boys were reportedly subjected to brutal torture and rape by members of the armed factions. Beatings were widespread. All armed groups reportedly held captives for long periods in private jails and tortured them. Former detainees said they had been beaten with rifle butts, tied to dead bodies for several days and forced to eat what they were told was human flesh. Some detainees reportedly received electric shocks, were subjected to suffocation, or had their testicles crushed by pliers. Scores of detainees reportedly died under torture. Prisoners who could not buy their release were at risk of being killed deliberately and arbitrarily.

In Kabul, secret detention centres known as *riasats* were reportedly used as torture centres. In at least three cities – Mazar-e-Sharif, Jalalabad and Herat – prisoners were reportedly kept in official jails and it was believed that former prison buildings in other cities were also used to hold prisoners.

The vast majority of those held were believed to be detained because of their ethnic origin or their association with rival political or religious factions. Among the hundreds of detainees were scores who had been arrested in previous years. Some prisoners were reportedly released during the year in exchange for money or for prisoners held by rival political groups. Prisoners held in previous years in private jails run by armed political groups in border areas in Pakistan were believed to have been transferred to detention centres inside Afghanistan.

Over a dozen journalists were captured and ill-treated at the hands of various Mujahideen groups. They were then warned not to report on armed groups' involvement in weapons transfers or drug-trafficking; many had to leave the country. In January an Afghan journalist was reportedly arrested and beaten repeatedly with a rifle butt by members of an armed political group. They accused her of spying and told her she would only be released if she had sex with six armed guards. She was released, reportedly after payment of a large sum of money. A New Zealand journalist, Shane Teehan, illegally detained since early January in Kunduz because of his journalistic activities, was released on 2 March when the city was captured by a rival Mujahideen group. In March a representative of the UN Children's Fund UNICEF, Sami Saqeb, was abducted in northern Kabul and his whereabouts remained unknown. Mir Wais Jalil, an Afghan journalist with the BBC World Service, was killed after being abducted in an area reportedly controlled by *Hezb-e-Islami*. He was apparently returning home after he had interviewed Gulbuddin Hekmatyar. There had been no moves to bring his killers to justice by the end of 1994.

Hundreds of people were believed to have "disappeared" in all parts of Afghanistan during the year after being abducted by armed guards belonging to the various armed political groups. Najmuddin Musleh, an Uzbek employed as a personal assistant of President Rabbani, was arrested and detained on 31 December 1993 in Kabul. He had been sent to negotiate with General Dostum. Members of the alliance between Gulbuddin Hekmatyar and General Dostum were reported to have publicly admitted detaining him, but his family was unable to establish his whereabouts or to contact him.

By mid-March at least 200,000 people had reportedly fled Kabul for the eastern town of Jalalabad, and some 300,000 people had reportedly been displaced within the city. Tens of thousands managed to cross Pakistan's officially closed border by paying bribes. Afghan refugees in Pakistan with professional or academic backgrounds reported receiving frequent death threats from Afghan armed groups in Pakistan.

The majority of refugees from Tadzhikistan were believed to have returned home voluntarily, with an estimated 6,000 Tadzhiks remaining in Afghanistan (see *Amnesty International Report 1994*).

Armed political groups acted with total impunity. The judicial system was virtually non-existent in most parts of the country and armed warlords acted as Islamic judges and ordered prisoners to be executed, stoned to death or whipped, with no legal safeguards. In a few areas, Islamic courts were reported to have dispensed summary justice, including public floggings and executions.

In March Amnesty International called attention to the continuing human rights abuses in the context of the country's civil war. In a report released in April, *Afghanistan: Incommunicado detention and "disappearances"*, Amnesty International expressed concern about the safety of scores of Afghans, and urged all the Mujahideen groups to observe minimum international humanitarian standards and to respect the right to life and security of the person. In August Amnesty International called for an impartial investigation into the killing of Mir Wais Jalil, reiterating the fact that since there was no civil structure in Afghanistan, only the international community could take action to ensure that there was an impartial investigation to bring those responsible to justice.

In December Amnesty International issued a statement, based on interviews with Afghans in refugee camps in Pakistan, raising its concern about reports of mass murder, arbitrary detention and torture – including widespread rape of women and children – being carried out by all armed political groups in Afghanistan. It called on the international community to take action to bring the human rights catastrophe in the country to an end.

ALBANIA

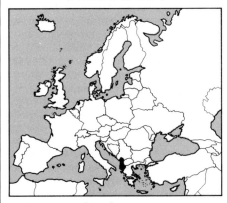

At least 12 political prisoners were convicted during the year in unfair trials; some were prisoners of conscience. Other prisoners of conscience were detained for short periods. There were frequent reports that police had beaten or otherwise

52

ill-treated people during arrest or in custody. At least five people died after being severely beaten in police custody. Seven men were sentenced to death for murder; two were executed.

In July former President Ramiz Alia and nine other former leading communist party officials were sentenced to between three and nine years' imprisonment for misappropriation of state property and abuse of office.

In November a new constitution was rejected in a referendum.

There were several trials of political prisoners during the year which failed to meet international standards of fair trial. Some of those convicted were prisoners of conscience.

In January Martin Leka and Aleksandër Frangaj, journalist and editor respectively of the newspaper *Koha Jone*, were arrested on charges of "slander" and revealing state secrets, together with two military officers. *Koha Jone* had published and commented on an order of the Minister of Defence forbidding off-duty officers to carry personal weapons outside barracks. At their trial in February Martin Leka was sentenced to 18 months' imprisonment and Romeo Liçi, an army officer, was sentenced to four years' imprisonment. Aleksandër Frangaj was acquitted and he and the second army officer were released. An appeal by the prosecution was heard in March. Martin Leka's sentence was confirmed. Aleksandër Frangaj, who was out of the country at the time, was sentenced to five months' imprisonment. In early May Martin Leka and Aleksandër Frangaj received a presidential pardon and Martin Leka was released. At the end of the month he and Aleksandër Frangaj were acquitted by the Court of Cassation, which also reduced Romeo Liçi's sentence to two years' imprisonment. In November Romeo Liçi was released under an amnesty.

In March the district court of Tirana sentenced Fatos Nano, leader of the Socialist Party and former prime minister, to 12 years' imprisonment on charges of embezzlement of state property and falsification of official documents in connection with shipments of Italian emergency aid to Albania in 1991. Three co-defendants, accused of abuse of office, were also convicted. They received prison sentences of three years, one year and three years suspended for one year respectively. The

Court of Appeal upheld these sentences in May. The defendants all rejected the charges. Fatos Nano refused to cooperate with the court, stating that he considered the trial to be fabricated with the aim of discrediting the Socialist Party. His lawyer pointed to numerous violations of his client's right to defence: the failure to inform Fatos Nano of the charges against him until September 1993, two months after his arrest; arbitrary restrictions on the time allowed for consultation with his lawyer prior to the trial; lack of access to the full investigation file and the elimination from this file of material relevant to the defence. Evidence produced in court did not convincingly substantiate the charges against the accused. In November his prison sentence was reduced to eight years under an amnesty.

In August Kurt Kola, President of the Association of Former Political Prisoners, was placed under house arrest. He was charged with obstructing the execution of a court decision after the Association refused to comply with a court order (based on legislation dealing with industrial strikes) to end a hunger-strike by some 2,500 former political prisoners demanding economic compensation for their detention under communist rule prior to 1991. He was released in November and charges against him were withdrawn.

In September, five leading members of *Omonia*, an organization representing the Greek minority, were sentenced by a court in Tirana to between six and eight years' imprisonment on charges of treason and espionage for Greece. Only one of the defendants, Theodhor Bezhani, had a lawyer throughout investigation proceedings; the defendants were denied full access to the court file; the court refused requests by the defendants to call additional witnesses and it admitted as evidence statements by witnesses who did not appear in court, even when, as in one case, the witness had subsequently repudiated his statement. The defendants and a number of witnesses alleged that statements had been obtained from them by ill-treatment and threats. There was little evidence to substantiate the charges of espionage and treason (including arming members of the Greek minority) brought against them. Three of the defendants, Kosta Qirjako, Theodhor Bezhani and Irakli Sirmo, were also convicted of possessing unlicensed weapons (two bullets, a pistol and a hunting rifle, respectively). On appeal all five defendants had their sentences reduced to between five and seven years' imprisonment. These sentences were further reduced by a third under an amnesty in November. In December Irakli Sirmo was pardoned and released.

There were reports of some 100 incidents during the year in which police beat people, including political opponents of the government, during or following arrest. For example, in March police in Tirana arrested and beat Ilir Lulja, a supporter of the Socialist Party. He and members of his family were repeatedly detained and released without charge by police during the year. In November he was again arrested by police who beat and injured him allegedly on the pretext that he was reading the Socialist Party newspaper. In August former political prisoners on hunger-strike in Tirana were evicted from their headquarters and beaten by police in the streets as they dispersed. Police also reportedly arrested and beat a number of their fellow hunger-strikers and supporters in other towns, including Pogradec, Shkodër, Durrës and Fier. Also in August, three members of the Greek minority in Himara were arrested and beaten at state security police headquarters in Tirana after they were found in possession of leaflets printed in Greece calling for the release of the arrested *Omonia* leaders. In October, three homosexual activists, members of Albania's first and only homosexual organization, founded in March, were arrested and beaten by police in Tirana. One of them suffered multiple fractures to a leg. In November Socialist Party supporters in many regions complained that they had been briefly detained, and sometimes beaten, by police in connection with the referendum on a new constitution which they opposed.

At least five people died apparently as a result of ill-treatment in custody. No police officer responsible for these deaths appeared to have been brought to trial by the end of the year. Among the victims was Irfan Nanaj who was beaten at a police station in Saranda after being arrested during a brawl in a bar in January; he was admitted to hospital in a coma and died 10 days later. One police officer was subsequently arrested on charges of having caused his death and a warrant was issued for the arrest of another officer. In September police in Korça were called to the home of Dhimitraq Petro who had quarrelled with his wife. They arrested and beat him; he died of an intra-cranial haemorrhage several days later.

At least three people died after being shot by police in suspicious circumstances. In February a police officer in Vlora entered a café in pursuit of someone. When a waiter, Fitim Bitri, approached to find out what was happening, the police officer fatally wounded him. The police officer was later arrested. In June five police officers were sentenced to between one and 17 years' imprisonment for the murder of David Leka in August 1993 (see *Amnesty International Report 1994*). On appeal their sentences were reduced to between one and 11 years in prison. A press report in September said that the police officer responsible for the death of Romeo Gaçe, who was shot in May 1993, had received "at least a symbolic punishment" (see *Amnesty International Report 1994*).

Seven men were sentenced to death for murder and two were executed.

Amnesty International called on the government of President Berisha to release prisoners of conscience and to institute impartial and independent investigations into incidents in which police were alleged to have killed or beaten people. The organization also called for death sentences to be commuted. In September Amnesty International wrote to the authorities expressing the hope that the Court of Appeal reviewing the conviction of the five members of *Omonia* would take into account breaches of the defendants' right to a fair and open trial and the weakness of the evidence produced in support of charges of espionage and treason.

Amnesty International expressed its concern that provisions of a draft criminal code due to go before parliament drastically increased the number of offences punishable by the death penalty and called for the abolition of this punishment. It called for the elimination of provisions allowing for up to three years' imprisonment for adult men found guilty of consensual homosexual acts in private. The organization also expressed concern about articles which it feared could be used to restrict the rights to freedom of expression, assembly and association.

54

ALGERIA

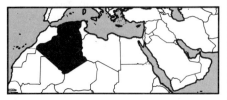

Hundreds of civilians were extrajudicially executed by the security forces or deliberately and arbitrarily killed by armed opposition groups. Thousands of suspected supporters of Islamist groups detained in 1994 or previous years were tried on terrorism charges; most were sentenced to prison terms by special courts whose procedures fall far short of international fair trial standards. Among them were possible prisoners of conscience. Torture of detainees, often held in illegally prolonged incommunicado detention, was widespread; scores of detainees are reported to have died as a result. At least 300 people arrested since 1992 remained in administrative detention without charge or trial. Over 600 people were sentenced to death but no executions were reported.

President Liamine Zeroual was appointed in February to replace the five-member *Haut Comité d'Etat*, High Council of State, and multi-party elections which had been cancelled in 1992 were not rescheduled (see *Amnesty International Report 1993*). The state of emergency, which had been extended indefinitely in 1993 in breach of the Constitution, remained in force. A curfew imposed on 10 provinces in 1992 and 1993 remained in place.

Armed clashes between the security forces and armed Islamist groups continued during the year, resulting in thousands of deaths and injuries. In September the government stated that at least 10,000 people had been killed since the state of emergency was imposed in 1992, but other sources estimate the number killed to be more than 30,000.

The civilian population was frequently caught between the security forces and armed Islamist groups. Teachers who, under threat by armed Islamist groups, advised female students to wear the *hidjab* (Islamic veil) were arrested and impris-oned for encouraging civil disobedience. Men eligible for conscription to the army faced imprisonment if they refused to enlist, and were threatened with death by armed Islamist groups if they enlisted. Relatives of suspected members of armed Islamist groups were taken hostage and ill-treated by the security forces as a means of putting pressure on those sought for arrest; relatives of members of the government and security forces were threatened and killed by armed Islamist groups.

Violent attacks by both sides on individuals escalated in 1994, resulting in thousands of deaths. The authorities claimed that all those killed by the security forces had died in armed clashes. However, security forces were reported to have extrajudicially executed hundreds of civilians. Most were alleged supporters of armed Islamist groups or people suspected of helping such groups. The victims included unarmed people often killed at night during curfew hours in or near their homes, sometimes in front of their families. Others were reportedly arrested and killed in custody. Scores of extrajudicial executions appeared to have been carried out in retaliation for attacks by armed opposition groups on security forces, or as an alternative to arrest.

On 19 March the body of Kouider Melal was found in the street outside his home in El Ataf, Ouedfoda, alongside the bodies of three other men from the same district who had also been under arrest. Kouider Melal had been arrested by security forces at his workplace two weeks earlier. All four bodies reportedly had bullet wounds to the head.

On 3 June Fouad Bouchelaghem, a professor of physics at Blida University, was arrested from his home at night. Despite repeated requests to the authorities for information, his family were unable to obtain any information on his whereabouts for over three months. He was reportedly seen on 20 July being taken away from the Chateauneuf detention centre in the capital, Algiers. On 8 September his family learned that his body had been brought to the morgue in Bologhine on 21 July and buried some weeks later.

Other killings by the security forces were reported in Cherarba, a suburb of Algiers, in April, May, July and August following attacks by armed groups on the security forces. On one occasion, on 16

August at least 20 people were killed by the security forces, reportedly after an armed group had ambushed two army vehicles earlier that day. Witnesses said the victims were killed outside their homes when security forces went from house to house questioning people about the ambush. One of them, 18-year-old high-school student Fatah Mizreb, was said to have been shot dead when he opened the door of his house.

Several killings were committed during curfew hours, apparently by the security forces or by paramilitary groups acting with their consent: gendarmes or police nearby made no attempt to intervene. No public inquiries were opened into any deaths caused by law enforcement officials.

Hundreds of civilians were killed by armed Islamist groups, particularly the *Groupe islamique armé* (GIA), Armed Islamic Group, and the *Armée islamique du salut* (AIS), Islamic Salvation Army. The victims included journalists, academics, civil servants, teachers, magistrates and political activists who supported the cancellation of the 1992 elections or opposed the political agenda of the Islamist groups. Scores of foreigners were also killed. In September 1993 the GIA had warned all foreigners to leave Algeria or face death. Spokesmen for the *Front Islamique du salut* (FIS), Islamic Salvation Front, which had gained a majority in first-round elections in December 1991 before being banned in March 1992 (see *Amnesty International Reports 1993* and *1994*), denied responsibility for killings carried out by armed Islamist groups, but failed to condemn such killings and sometimes justified them.

In April two cousins who had just completed their military service were abducted from their home by members of an armed Islamist group. They were found dead the next day: their bodies had been mutilated with an axe. Their family later received a letter signed by the GIA threatening to kill them if they did not stop criticizing the GIA.

The husband of Leila Aslaoui, Mohamed Redha Aslaoui, was stabbed to death on 17 October, shortly after his wife had resigned as government spokesperson and Minister for National Solidarity in protest at the release from prison of two senior FIS leaders.

Journalists continued to be killed and threatened with death by armed Islamist groups, and at least 15 were killed during the year. They included Mohamed Salah Benachour, a journalist working for the *Algerian Press Service* (APS), who was shot dead on 27 October. He was the third APS journalist killed since July.

Women were also killed or threatened with death by armed Islamist groups. The victims included a 17-year-old student who was killed in February, reportedly for not wearing the *hidjab*, and the wife of a retired gendarme who was stabbed to death in June, along with her two children.

An anti-Islamist organization, the *Organisation des Jeunes Algériens Libres* (OJAL), Organization of Young Free Algerians, also issued death threats. In March, for example, they threatened to kill 20 veiled women and 20 bearded Islamist men for every woman killed for not wearing the veil. Shortly after, on 29 March, two veiled high-school students were shot dead at a bus stop in the suburbs of Algiers.

The OJAL had also claimed responsibility for the abduction in November 1993 of Mohamed Bouslimani, the President of an Islamic charity and a founding member of the Islamist party *Hamas*. His body was found buried, with the throat slit, in January. His abduction had also been claimed by the GIA.

Often it was not clear who was responsible for attacks on specific individuals. In June, for example, the President of the Algerian League for Human Rights (LADH), Youcef Fethallah, was shot dead by unknown gunmen as he went to his office in Algiers. The LADH had repeatedly condemned killings and other abuses by both the security forces and armed opposition groups.

Thousands of militants and suspected supporters of Islamist opposition groups arrested since 1992 were tried on terrorism charges by three special courts in Algiers, Oran and Constantine. The special courts were set up under the anti-terrorist decree of September 1992 (see *Amnesty International Reports 1993* and *1994*). These trials violated fundamental requirements of international law. Detainees were routinely tortured during *garde à vue* (incommunicado) detention, which was frequently prolonged beyond the maximum

56

12-day period permitted by the 1992 anti-terrorist decree. Confessions extracted from detainees under torture were accepted as evidence by judges, and the courts consistently failed to investigate torture allegations, even when detainees appeared in court with obvious marks of torture. Defence lawyers were given insufficient time to prepare their case, were often not allowed to call defence witnesses, and were denied access to part of their clients' files. Defendants were denied the full right of appeal available in ordinary courts (see *Amnesty International Report 1994*).

Over 300 people detained during mass arrests in 1992 remained administratively detained without charge in a desert camp in Ain M'Guel, in the south of the country. Lieutenant Lembarek Boumaarif, arrested in June 1992 accused of killing President Mohamed Boudiaf, and Yassine Simozrag, arrested in July 1993, who was allegedly tortured during prolonged *garde à vue* detention, had not been brought to trial by the end of the year (see *Amnesty International Report 1994*).

In September Abbassi Madani and Ali Belhadji, two FIS leaders sentenced to 12 years' imprisonment in 1992, were released from prison and placed under house arrest. Five other FIS leaders sentenced in the same trial were released: two in February and three in September.

The dramatic increase in torture which began in 1992 continued. Methods of torture most commonly cited were: the "*chiffon*" (cloth), whereby the detainee is tied to a bench and a cloth soaked with chemicals or dirty water is forced into the mouth; burning using a blowtorch (*chalumeau*); electric shocks to the ears, genitals and other sensitive parts of the body; tying a thread around the penis and progressively tightening the thread; sexual abuse using bottles and sticks; beatings; and death threats and mock executions. Drilling holes in the back, feet or legs was also reportedly used as a method of torture. The authorities failed to investigate a single torture allegation, to Amnesty International's knowledge.

Noureddine Lamdjadani, a doctor, alleged he was repeatedly tortured for two months. He was arrested on 17 May and remained in *garde à vue* detention until 17 July. He stated that he was blindfolded, subjected to the "*chiffon*" torture, and

beaten for three days in the central police station in Algiers. He was then transferred, blindfold and in the boot of a car, to the detention centre of Chateauneuf, where he alleged he was again repeatedly tortured by the same methods and threatened with death. He remained in detention awaiting trial at the end of the year.

At least 600 people were sentenced to death, most of them *in absentia*, by special courts in trials which violated international standards for fair trial. However, the moratorium on executions announced in December 1993 remained in force throughout 1994.

At least eight Tunisian asylum-seekers, all recognized as refugees by the UN High Commissioner for Refugees, were forcibly returned to their country despite fears that they would be at risk of serious human rights violations.

Amnesty International urged the authorities to investigate allegations of extrajudicial executions and to take the necessary steps to stop them being committed by the security forces. It urged the authorities to end the use of prolonged incommunicado detention and torture. The organization called for those tried by the special courts on terrorist charges to be given fair trials, and for the authorities to review the procedures of the special courts. Amnesty International also called for the commutation of all death sentences.

Amnesty International repeatedly called on the armed Islamist groups to put an end to killings of civilians and to other abuses such as abductions of civilians. It also called on the FIS leaders to condemn killings and other abuses against civilians and to call on the armed Islamist groups to end human rights abuses.

In October Amnesty International published a report, *Algeria: Repression and violence must end*.

In an oral statement to the UN Commission on Human Rights in February, Amnesty International included reference to its concerns in Algeria.

ANGOLA

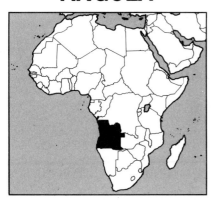

Critics of the government were briefly detained and may have been prisoners of conscience: there were attempts on the lives of others. Hundreds of unarmed civilians were reported to have been deliberately killed by both the government army and forces of the *União Nacional para a Independência Total de Angola* (UNITA), National Union for the Total Independence of Angola.

In November, amidst news of continued fighting and deliberate killings of defenceless civilians, officials deputizing for President José Eduardo dos Santos and UNITA leader Jonas Savimbi signed a new peace agreement, known as the Lusaka Protocol. This supplemented and modified the 1991 peace agreement which collapsed after UNITA disputed the results of the September 1992 elections (see *Amnesty International Report 1994*). Under the terms of the Lusaka Protocol, the UN was to monitor government troops and supervise the confinement to assembly areas of UNITA troops. UNITA's weapons and those in civilian hands were to be collected and stored under UN supervision. The formation of a joint army, which was incomplete when war broke out in late 1992, was to be completed and any soldiers not incorporated into the army were to be demobilized. The Lusaka Protocol provided for UNITA members to be incorporated into the police and for the police to be properly trained and to abide by internationally recognized human rights standards. UNITA was to participate in all levels of government. The peace agreement was to be implemented by a Joint Council composed of government and UNITA rep-

resentatives and chaired by the UN with representatives of the governments of Portugal, Russia and the USA as observers. The strength of the UN Angola Verification Mission (UNAVEM II) was to be increased to some 7,000 military and police observers and other staff. Finally, the UN would supervise the second round of presidential elections between President dos Santos and Jonas Savimbi – this had not taken place when war resumed in late 1992.

In November the government passed an amnesty law to give effect to the Lusaka Protocol's provision that all civilian and military prisoners detained as a result of the conflict were to be released under the supervision of the International Committee of the Red Cross. No details of any releases had been published by the end of the year.

During the year Angolans continued to die in their thousands in besieged towns and in devastated rural areas, either in the fighting or from hunger or disease. Both sides deliberately killed prisoners; bombed or shelled predominantly civilian areas; and prevented the delivery of food aid to areas controlled by the other side. Three million of Angola's 10 million people were in need of emergency relief. The government forcibly conscripted youths under 18, the minimum age in Angola for compulsory military service. UNITA also forced civilians to serve as soldiers and porters.

Government forces in Cabinda, an Angolan enclave separated from the rest of Angola by Zaire's corridor to the sea, faced attacks by both UNITA and the two armed factions of the *Frente de Libertação do Enclave de Cabinda* (FLEC), Cabinda Enclave Liberation Front.

Four journalists were briefly detained and appeared to be prisoners of conscience. Leopoldo Baio and Ricardo de Melo were arrested in May and held for several hours while they were questioned about articles they had written about government corruption. In Cabinda, also in May, João Mavinga was detained for about a day and questioned about his report that FLEC had set up a radio station. Mariano Costa was detained for a day after returning from Lisbon, Portugal, in September and was reportedly asked to reveal his sources for a story on UNITA.

A human rights worker was prosecuted in circumstances which suggested that he

58

was being punished on account of his human rights activities. Lourenço Adão Agostinho, Secretary General of the *Associação Angolana dos Direitos Humanos* (AADH), Angolan Human Rights Association, had been detained in 1989 on charges of embezzlement but did not stand trial. In May 1994 he was rearrested when six plainclothes police stopped him in the street at gunpoint. He claimed that his defence counsel was unable to consult the trial dossier until shortly before the trial started in late May. Lourenço Adão Agostinho was acquitted of charges of theft and falsification of documents but convicted of "abuse of confidence" in connection with missing money and sentenced to two and a half years' imprisonment.

It was impossible to establish how many political prisoners were arrested in 1994 or how many arrested in previous years were still held. UNITA claimed that some of the hundreds of suspected UNITA supporters arrested between November 1992 and January 1993 (see *Amnesty International Report 1994*) were still held without charge or trial. The government occasionally reported that it had captured UNITA soldiers. Other sources indicated that captured UNITA soldiers were often shot.

There were attempts on the life of some government opponents, some of which may have been attempted extrajudicial executions. The government failed to establish who was responsible. Mfulumpinga Lando Victor, leader of the *Partido Democrático para o Progresso – Aliança Nacional Angolana*, Democratic Progress Party – Angolan National Alliance, had just entered his apartment in central Luanda in April when his car and apartment were sprayed with machine-gun bullets. In July an explosion wrecked the apartment of Nelson Bonavena, leader of the *Frente para a Democracia*, Front for Democracy, who was not at home at the time.

There were many reports of government soldiers carrying out extrajudicial executions after taking control of villages and towns which had been held by UNITA. Usually few details were available and it was impossible to find witnesses who could corroborate the accounts. In January, four people, including a six-year-old boy, Francisco Lele, were reportedly shot dead in their homes in Luavo village, Cabinda, by soldiers conducting a house-to-house search for UNITA or FLEC soldiers. UNITA said in June that government troops had extrajudicially executed about 300 people after they occupied Quilengues, in Huila province, in August 1993. It named about 20 of those killed, including a doctor, two Portuguese businessmen, and two members of the local Roman Catholic church. It appeared that some extrajudicial executions had occurred but it was not possible to establish how many. UNITA said that some of the victims were forced under torture to name people hostile to the government.

Eduardo Domingos, an economics professor and a well-known UNITA supporter, was killed in Lubango in October, allegedly by government forces. He had been detained for a month in January 1993 because of his membership of UNITA.

A parliamentary Commission of Inquiry reported in January on its investigations into the killings of members of the Bakongo ethnic group in Luanda a year earlier, in January 1993 (see *Amnesty International Report 1994*). The commission found that 12 people had been killed in an isolated incident but that those responsible – police and members of the Civil Defence (militia) – had been motivated not by the ethnic origin of the victims but by a desire to revenge themselves against Zairians who had assisted UNITA troops in expelling government forces from the town of Soyo in northwestern Angola. Some 20 people had been detained in connection with the killings but they were released without charge a few weeks after they were arrested. The findings were disputed by the leaders of some political parties and members of the Bakongo ethnic group who claimed that many people had been killed.

By the end of the year there was no news of prisoners whom UNITA had detained in 1994 or in previous years (see *Amnesty International Report 1994*). Those detained in 1994 included four Roman Catholic missionaries, the Congolese husband of a US aid worker, and two other people captured in August after UNITA soldiers attacked a convoy of vehicles travelling between Luanda and Porto Amboim. In July UNITA threatened to execute two South Africans whose plane UNITA forces had shot down and whom they regarded as mercenaries. The two men were employees of a South African company which said it had a contract with the Angolan Government to provide guards and military instructors. UNITA representatives later said they had not been killed.

There were many accounts of defenceless civilians, particularly government officials or supporters, being deliberately and arbitrarily killed by UNITA. Witnesses from N'Dalatando, which the government reoccupied in May, reported having seen UNITA soldiers shooting civilians or hacking them to death with machetes. Journalists who visited Huambo shortly after government forces recaptured the city in early November found the bodies of dozens of prisoners held by UNITA who had apparently been deliberately killed a few days earlier. Some were found in the precincts of a prison and of houses which local people said had been used as prisons: other bodies had been deposited in wells.

Another armed political organization, *FLEC-Renovada* (Renewed FLEC), captured government soldiers in Cabinda and threatened to shoot 10 of them. It later appeared that these threats were not carried out. In November *FLEC-Renovada* captured three Polish employees of a logging company, apparently to draw attention to its complaints that the government did not use profits from extractive industries to benefit Cabinda. The three hostages were released in December.

Amnesty International was concerned about the arrest of possible prisoners of conscience and continued to appeal for an end to all unlawful killings. In response to Amnesty International's inquiries, the Minister of Justice told the organization that Lourenço Adão Agostinho had received a fair trial. The organization received no response to its inquiries about people who had been extrajudicially executed or had "disappeared" after war resumed in 1992. Nor did it receive any reply from UNITA to its inquiries about people who were reported to have "disappeared" or been killed in UNITA custody.

ARGENTINA

There were reports of torture and ill-treatment resulting in at least two deaths. There was little progress in investigations into past "disappearances". Several people were killed by the police in circumstances suggesting that they had been extrajudicially executed.

A new Constitution was approved in August, allowing presidents to stand for re-election. It granted constitutional status to a number of international and regional human rights treaties and created the office of Ombudsman for the defence and protection of human rights. An article was incorporated which gave formal recognition to the rights of indigenous peoples. In December parliament passed a law awarding compensation to the relatives of those who had "disappeared" between 1976 and 1983 during the so-called "dirty war".

In July a car-bomb razed a building in Buenos Aires housing two Jewish cultural organizations, killing 96 people. No one had been charged with the bombing by the end of 1994, and no political group had admitted responsibility.

There were violent demonstrations by public employees in the province of Jujuy in April, in the province of El Chaco in October, and in the province of Tucumán in December. The demonstrations were called to demand the payment of unpaid wages and wage increases. There were also riots, hunger-strikes and other protests against prison conditions in the Federal Capital and several provinces, including Buenos Aires, Córdoba, Jujuy, Mendoza and Salta.

In October, for the first time ever, a serving navy officer, Captain Antonio

60

Pernías, publicly admitted that the navy had engaged in torture of prisoners during the "dirty war" of 1976 to 1983. Captain Pernías acknowledged that the navy had used torture as "a tool" in the fight against subversion. Another navy officer, Captain Juan Carlos Rolón, stated that the so-called "task groups" that were engaged in the clandestine operations of the "dirty war", including torture and extrajudicial executions, were an intrinsic part of the navy's operations. The officers made the admission before a Senate committee which subsequently withheld agreement for their promotion. Criticizing the Senate's decision, President Carlos Menem said that it was better to forget the past. President Menem further stated that it was thanks to the armed forces "that we fought and triumphed in that dirty war which took our community to the brink of collapse".

In September Guillermo Maqueda, a student convicted as a result of a miscarriage of justice (see *Amnesty International Report 1990*), was released early: he had served five years of a 10-year prison sentence.

There were reports of torture and ill-treatment in several provinces, resulting in at least two deaths. In February Diego Rodríguez Laguens, a forestry expert, was reportedly detained by the Jujuy provincial police and allegedly beaten to death in San Pedro police station. The police denied that Diego Rodríguez Laguens had been detained and claimed that he was killed in a road accident. Following a judicial inquiry, three police officers were indicted with unlawful detention and murder. At the end of the year they were awaiting trial. A witness who saw the torture was severely beaten by unidentified assailants and the lawyer acting for the victim's family reportedly received death threats.

In April the body of an 18-year-old military conscript, Omar Octavio Carrasco, who had been declared missing and a deserter, was found within the grounds of 161 Army Battalion in Zapala, Neuquén province. The body reportedly had severe injuries on the chest and shoulder and had one eye missing. Omar Octavio Carrasco apparently died inside the barracks after being kicked unconscious by low-ranking officials. A military officer, a soldier and a former soldier were in custody awaiting trial charged with his murder,

and two officers were charged with being involved in a cover-up. In August, following a national outcry caused by the crime, a presidential decree abolished compulsory military service and granted an amnesty to past draft avoiders.

A number of police officers were convicted of torture and sentenced to prison terms. In March two police officers were sentenced to life imprisonment for the killing under torture in 1993 of Ramón Buchón, a builder, in San Nicolás, Buenos Aires province. In October a police officer was sentenced to life imprisonment and seven other officers to prison terms ranging from three to eight years for torturing to death Oscar Mario Sargiotti in Córdoba province in December 1990. The convicted officers appealed against the sentences.

There was no progress in investigations into "disappearances". Miguel Brú, a student, was alleged to have "disappeared" in August 1993 after filing a complaint against members of La Plata 9th Police Station for illegally searching his house (see *Amnesty International Report 1994*). However, two police officers were charged with illegally searching Miguel Brú's home in April 1993. No progress was reported in the investigations into the "disappearances" of Pablo Cristian Guardatti in May 1992 and three others in 1990 (see *Amnesty International Report 1993*).

Human rights campaigners accused the government of failing to act to obtain information on thousands of people who "disappeared" after being abducted by the military and security forces during the "dirty war". In August General Cristiano Nicolaides, former commander-in-chief of the army, stated in court that during the years of military rule the army kept files on "disappeared" children and that the army had kept written records about the functioning of the clandestine detention centres. He also stated that all aspects of the fight against subversion were closely regulated.

In September Dr Elena Mendoza, a lawyer working on "disappearances" with the human rights organization Grandmothers of Plaza de Mayo, reportedly received death threats. In November a judge in a civil damage suit ordered two former commanders-in-chief of the navy to pay a total of US$1 million each in compensation to the relatives of four members of a family who "disappeared" during the "dirty war".

There were several reports of police killings in circumstances which suggested they were extrajudicial executions. In January Norberto Corbo, Héctor Bielsa, Gustavo Mendoza and Edgardo Cicuttín were killed by the police in Wilde, Buenos Aires province. The four men were travelling in two separate cars which were intercepted by members of the Lanus Investigations Brigade, who alleged they were searching for criminal suspects. The police fired more than 200 bullets at the cars, killing three occupants of one car and one of the other. The police alleged that they were returning fire. However, the only survivor of the shooting denied that there was any exchange of fire and no arms were found in his car. Ten police officers were initially charged with homicide and placed in preventive detention, but were later released.

In September Roberto Fabián Coronel, an inmate of Mendoza Provincial Penitentiary, was killed in suspicious circumstances. Initially the authorities claimed that Roberto Fabián Coronel had been beaten to death by other inmates. However, further investigations established that he had been shot dead, allegedly by a prison guard. A judicial investigation was opened.

In July, three police officers were condemned to 11 years' imprisonment for the extrajudicial execution, in May 1987, of three youths in Ingeniero Budge, Buenos Aires province. The officers were released pending an appeal and at least one of them remained on active duty.

In January Amnesty International published a report, *Argentina: Journalism, a Dangerous Profession*, which described physical attacks on journalists, death threats and other forms of intimidation. Amnesty International repeatedly appealed to the government to investigate thoroughly and impartially reports of torture and ill-treatment by police and prison officers and to take steps to prevent such abuses. Amnesty International condemned the bombing in Buenos Aires in which 96 people were killed.

ARMENIA

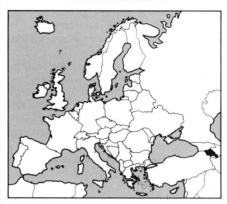

Seventeen members of the Hare Krishna religious sect alleged that they were ill-treated in detention. Six Azerbaijani prisoners were allegedly killed in custody. At least four people were sentenced to death, but there were no judicial executions.

Parliamentary discussion of a new draft constitution continued (see *Amnesty International Report 1994*), but it had not been adopted by the end of the year. President Ter-Petrosyan again met his Azerbaijani counterpart in talks aimed at resolving the Karabakh conflict (see **Azerbaijan** entry).

The continuing Karabakh conflict made it difficult to investigate allegations that Azerbaijani civilians taken hostage in connection with the fighting were held in Armenia, in private hands but with the complicity of the authorities. The whereabouts of Yolchu Gyoyushov and Ramazan Mamedov (see *Amnesty International Report 1994*), said to have been seized from neighbouring Georgia and held pending an exchange for Armenian hostages in Azerbaijan, remained unknown at the end of the year.

Seventeen devotees of the Hare Krishna sect alleged that they were beaten in police custody on 31 August in the capital, Yerevan. They had been detained at their temple after an altercation with four men who the devotees claimed had been among a group who had entered the premises two days earlier and had assaulted several sect members. The devotees also alleged that the police refused to respond to their request for protection during the earlier attack, or to investigate the incident.

62

There were conflicting reports about the circumstances in which eight Azerbaijani prisoners died on 29 January in Ministry of Defence custody in Yerevan. Six died of gunshot wounds to the head, and in three cases the muzzle of the gun was in contact with the head at the time the shot was fired. An independent forensic expert dismissed an early claim that these men were shot while trying to escape, saying that the pattern of their injuries suggested "execution-type shootings". However, the expert did not absolutely exclude the possibility of mass suicide, a later explanation given by the Armenian Military Procurator who said seven of the men shot themselves with one pistol in several minutes after an escape bid failed. The seventh victim died of a gunshot wound to the chest, and the eighth of throat wounds typical of suicide. A commission of inquiry was established, but no results were known to have been published by the end of the year.

Two other Azerbaijani prisoners, Bakhtiar Khanali ogly Shabiev and Garay Muzafar ogly Nagiev, were sentenced to death in Yerevan in April. They were convicted of murdering three ethnic Armenians in the Kelbajar district of Azerbaijan and of attempting to poison a reservoir in Armenia. According to official statistics, at least two other people were sentenced to death during the first half of 1994. In all, 13 death sentences had been passed since 1990, but no executions had taken place since 1991.

Amnesty International continued to express concern about allegations that hostages from the Karabakh conflict were held in Armenia. The authorities responded that their investigations failed to substantiate any of the reports raised with them. Amnesty International urged comprehensive and impartial investigations into reports of ill-treatment in custody and allegations that at least six Azerbaijani prisoners had been killed in custody. Amnesty International also called for all pending death sentences to be commuted. A response from the authorities in August confirmed that no executions had taken place during President Ter-Petrosyan's term of office, and that this policy would not change for the remainder of his tenure.

AUSTRALIA

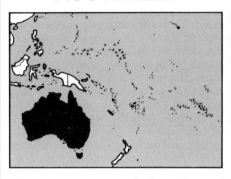

There was a continuing high incidence of deaths of Aboriginal prisoners in custody. Government policy on the detention of asylum-seekers failed to meet international standards.

In April the UN Human Rights Committee ruled that Tasmania's criminal law on homosexuality breached the International Covenant on Civil and Political Rights (ICCPR), in particular the right to privacy. However, the Tasmanian authorities maintained that the law would not be changed as it "reflects the opinion of the Tasmanian general public". The Australian Federal Government called for talks with the Tasmanian State Government about the ruling. In October the lower house of the Australian Federal parliament passed a law aimed at overruling the Tasmanian law prohibiting sex between consenting adult homosexuals in private.

In November 1993, the New South Wales State Government removed from the Summary Offences Act the penalty of imprisonment for using offensive language although it retained the possibility of imposing a fine. In its 1993 report entitled *Australia: A criminal justice system weighted against Aboriginal people*, Amnesty International had specifically called for a review of this Act which appeared to discriminate against Aboriginal people. Although they form only one per cent of the New South Wales population, Aboriginal people still accounted for more than 15 per cent of those sentenced to imprisonment, and about 25 per cent of juveniles in institutions under control orders.

Despite detailed recommendations made by the Royal Commission into Aboriginal Deaths in Custody (RCIADC) (see *Amnesty International Report 1993*), at least nine Aboriginal prisoners died in custody during 1994. In February the Australian Institute of Criminology reported that the rate of Aboriginal deaths in custody had continued at the same level as during the 10-year period 1980 to 1990 investigated by the RCIADC.

Official investigations into the deaths of Aboriginal prisoners Barry Raymond Turbane and Daniel Yock after alleged ill-treatment by the police (see *Amnesty International Report 1994*) found early in the year that no person could be prosecuted or blamed for their deaths. A report by the Queensland Criminal Justice Commission, contested by Daniel Yock's family, said his arrest was lawful and not racially motivated.

In the state of Victoria at least eight people were shot dead by police, who may have used excessive force. Four different investigations into the shootings were carried out by the state government and the police. A Task Force was appointed to monitor the implementation of the recommendations contained in the investigation reports. There were 22 fatal police shootings in Victoria between 1988 and 1995, five of which involved people with histories of mental illness.

Under the Migration Reform Act of 1992, asylum-seekers who arrived at the border without prior authorization to enter the country continued to be automatically detained. In November and December 1994, there was a dramatic increase in the number of asylum-seekers arriving by boat, mostly from southern China, bringing the annual total to 952. The majority of asylum-seekers were detained for the entire duration of the prolonged asylum procedure, which often took months.

Amnesty International called on the government to ensure that asylum-seekers were afforded rights which would enable them, on their own initiative, to challenge their detention in the courts, in accordance with international standards.

Amnesty International was concerned about the continuing high incidence of deaths in custody of Aboriginal prisoners and about the victims of police shootings in the state of Victoria. Amnesty International called for adequate investigations and for those responsible for abuses to be brought to justice.

AUSTRIA

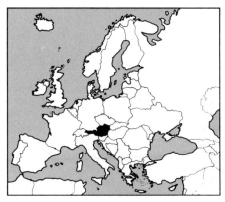

Allegations were received of ill-treatment of detainees by police officers.

In February the Austrian Parliament passed an amendment to the Law on Alternative Military Service, increasing the length of alternative service from 10 to 11 months. The length of military service was left unchanged at eight months. The new legislation also imposed new restrictions on the time limits within which conscientious objectors are able to submit applications for alternative service.

A number of reports were received of ill-treatment in police custody. For example, in May, Naser Palushi, an ethnic Albanian from Kosovo province, Yugoslavia, alleged that he was kicked, jabbed behind the ears with a pen and hit in the face by officers of East Vienna Police Detention Centre. At the time Naser Palushi was on hunger-strike in protest against his detention following the rejection of his application for asylum.

In April four officers of Vienna Provincial Court prison were acquitted of charges of ill-treating Turkish national Ahmet S. in March 1993 (see *Amnesty International Report 1994*). In delivering its ruling the court commented that although the prisoner's allegations were credible, it had not been possible to establish the identity of the officer responsible.

In July two police officers were fined by Salzburg Regional Court for ill-treating Rudolf Reumann while he was held at a Salzburg police station in August 1992 (see *Amnesty International Report 1994*).

Also in July the European Commission of Human Rights concluded that Ronald Ribitsch's rights under Article 3 of the

64

European Convention for the Protection of Human Rights and Fundamental Freedoms had been violated. The Commission was satisfied beyond reasonable doubt that Ronald Ribitsch was subjected to physical violence amounting to inhuman and degrading treatment when he was held in police custody for three days in 1988.

In January and March Amnesty International expressed concern to the authorities about the new time limits introduced for submitting applications for alternative military service. The organization pointed out that the new legislation took no account of the fact that a person's conscientiously held beliefs may change over time.

In August Amnesty International asked the authorities for information about the steps taken to investigate the alleged ill-treatment of Naser Palushi.

The organization received no substantive replies to its letters.

In June Amnesty International published a report, *Austria: The alleged ill-treatment of foreigners – a summary of concerns.*

AZERBAIJAN

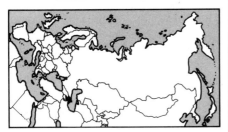

Scores of people were reportedly held hostage because of their ethnic origin by both sides to the conflict over the disputed Karabakh region. Over 100 suspected opponents of the government were arrested after a failed coup attempt in October: some alleged they were ill-treated in detention. The death penalty was abolished for women. At least 10 death sentences came to light, and one was commuted. No executions were reported. One death sentence was passed and subsequently commuted in the self-proclaimed Nagorno-Karabakh Republic (NKR).

The political situation remained unstable. At the beginning of October members of a special police unit briefly occupied the Procurator-General's office in the capital, Baku, and forces loyal to the Prime Minister were said to have tried to seize key buildings in the city of Ganja. President Heidar Aliyev declared a state of emergency, and the Prime Minister fled after being dismissed and charged with treason. Over 100 people were subsequently arrested.

A July cease-fire in the disputed region of Karabakh (see *Amnesty International Report 1994*) was generally observed for the rest of the year, and in December the Conference on Security and Co-operation in Europe agreed in principle to send a peace-keeping force to the area.

In October the death penalty was abolished for women.

Both the NKR and the Azerbaijani authorities alleged that the other side held large numbers of people hostage because of their ethnic origin. For example, Armen Amirbekyan, an ethnic Armenian, was detained on a train at the beginning of the year while in transit through Azerbaijan. He was taken first to the Security Ministry prison in Baku, then to a special holding camp for Armenian detainees in Gobustan. Officially, ethnic Armenians held under such circumstances were detained only as a security precaution, to allow an identity check, and released if shown to be *bona fide* travellers. However, Armen Amirbekyan's relatives allegedly received a telegram from Security Ministry officials offering to exchange him for two Azerbaijani prisoners. He was still in Gobustan camp in December.

Dozens of hostages were released in negotiated exchanges during the year. Among them was 13-year-old Sevda Nukhiyeva, an ethnic Azeri, who had been detained by ethnic Armenian forces in July 1993 along with 18 other members of her extended family. They had gathered for a wedding in the village of Gorazly in Fizuli district, and were taken to Khankendi (known to the Armenians as Stepanakert) in the NKR. Sevda and five female relatives were released in September, and all family members were free by the end of the year.

In April the trial by military tribunal began of seven former government officials arrested after a successful mutiny by a military unit in Ganja in June 1993 (see *Amnesty International Report 1994*).

Three defendants – Ikhtiyar Shirinov, Gabil Mamedov and Sulkheddin Akperov – had been in custody since then until the trial opened. The charges included exceeding authority and using armed force against the Azerbaijani people. Sulkheddin Akperov was taken back into custody in September, allegedly as a punishment for delaying the trial when he changed his lawyer, but escaped the following month. Other defendants reported problems in calling witnesses they felt were pertinent. The trial continued at the end of the year.

Throughout the year opposition figures alleged that many of their number were imprisoned solely for their peaceful opposition to the government, although official sources stated that they were held in connection with criminal offences, often involving loss of life.

Reports of ill-treatment in pre-trial detention continued, but restricted access made verification difficult. Many of the over 100 known or suspected supporters of the former prime minister arrested in October were said to be kept in very cramped conditions in investigation prisons in Ganja and Baku. They allegedly had to take it in turns to sleep while others in the cell stood. It was also alleged that many were denied parcels, and that food and medical provision in the prisons were inadequate.

At least 10 death sentences came to light, although in the absence of official statistics the real total, which may have been higher, was not known. Unofficial sources reported that 60 to 70 men were awaiting execution on death row at the end of the year, in grossly overcrowded conditions.

No executions were reported, and at least one death sentence was commuted. Private Yemin Salimov had been sentenced to death by a military tribunal in early 1993 for battlefield desertion, but he was pardoned by presidential decree in January.

One death sentence was passed in the NKR in May. Captain Yury Belicheko, a Ukrainian citizen, was accused of being a mercenary for Azerbaijan and carrying out a number of bombing raids over the NKR which resulted in loss of life and material damage. He was sentenced without right of appeal by a military tribunal, but he was later pardoned and his sentence commuted by the NKR parliament.

In July the UN Human Rights Committee examined Azerbaijan's first periodic report regarding implementation of the International Covenant on Civil and Political Rights. It was concerned that allegations of hostage-taking and torture had not been properly addressed. The Committee was also disturbed at the number of death sentences pronounced, and recommended that the use of the death penalty be reduced and provision made for the right to appeal against death sentences.

Throughout the year Amnesty International urged all parties involved in the conflict over Karabakh to release anyone held hostage, or held solely on grounds of their ethnic origin.

Amnesty International sought further information on allegations that opposition figures were imprisoned solely for their political beliefs, and urged that all political prisoners receive a fair trial in line with international standards.

Amnesty International welcomed the abolition of the death penalty for women, but continued to urge the authorities to commute all pending death sentences and to take steps towards abolition of the death penalty.

BAHAMAS

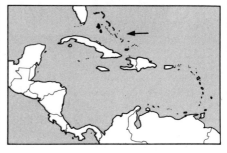

Two death sentences were imposed. No executions were carried out and there were 36 prisoners under sentence of death at the end of the year. A final decision on the challenge to the constitutionality of the death penalty was still pending.

Prime Minister Hubert Ingraham stated that executions would be resumed as soon as outstanding appeals had been heard. There had been no hangings since April 1984 and 36 prisoners were under sentence of death. Fourteen of them had spent over five years on death row and

66 should have had their sentences commuted according to a November 1993 ruling by the Judicial Committee of the Privy Council (JCPC) in London, the final court of appeal for the Bahamas. The JCPC ruled that execution after more than five years on death row constitutes "inhuman or degrading punishment or other treatment", and that such prisoners should have their sentences commuted. However, the government had taken no steps to commute the relevant sentences by the end of 1994.

The appeal of Anthony Neely and Jeremiah Poitier to the JCPC, challenging the constitutionality of the death penalty, was still awaiting a full hearing. They had argued that, as the method of execution was not specified in the Constitution or any specific law, execution would be unconstitutional.

In March Amnesty International urged the government to implement the November 1993 JCPC decision and also called for the commutation of all death sentences.

BAHRAIN

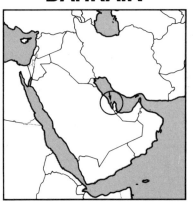

At least 30 political prisoners, including possible prisoners of conscience, continued serving long prison sentences imposed after unfair trials in previous years. Several of them were reportedly tortured. Hundreds of people were arrested during the year in connection with their religious or political activities. Some were released days after their arrest, but others remained in incommunicado detention without charge or trial for up to three months before being released. Dozens of Bahraini nationals were forcibly exiled, although restrictions preventing the return of 64 others were lifted.

At least 30 political prisoners, including possible prisoners of conscience, remained in prison at the end of the year. They were all serving long prison sentences imposed in previous years after unfair trials. Some were held in connection with membership of banned opposition groups; others in connection with an alleged coup attempt in 1981 (see *Amnesty International Report 1994*). A number of them were transferred to other prisons where they were held incommunicado for several weeks and reportedly tortured. For example, in April a number of political prisoners, including Mohammad Jamil 'Abd al-Amir al-Jamri, 'Abd al-Jalil Khalil Ibrahim, al-Sayyid Ja'far al-'Alawi, 'Ali Ahmed Jassim al-Dayri and Nabil Baqir, were reportedly transferred from Jaw Prison No.1 to al-Qal'a Prison following the discovery of a radio during a cell inspection. They were allegedly placed in solitary confinement and tortured to extract information regarding the source of the radio. Some of them were transferred to hospital for urgent medical treatment before being returned to al-Qal'a Prison.

In January dozens of people were arrested at al-Mu'min Mosque in Manama during a commemoration by members of the Shi'a community of the death of Grand Ayatollah Golpayegani, the Iranian *marja' al-taqlid* (source of emulation) of Shi'a communities worldwide. Some were released a few days later, but 18 people, including Tawfiq al-Mahrous, 'Abd al-Ridha al-Shuweikh, 'Ali 'Omran and Mohammad Hassan, remained in incommunicado detention without charge or trial until March when they were all released. In December hundreds of people were arrested in connection with a petition initiated by 14 well-known figures calling on the Amir of Bahrain, al-Sheikh 'Isa Bin Salman Al Khalifa, to reinstate the parliament which was dissolved in 1975. Among them were al-Sheikh 'Ali Salman, who led prayers at al-Khawaja Mosque in Manama, and Ibrahim Hassan; both were arrested on 5 December in their homes in Bilad al-Qadim, southwest of Manama. At the end of the year they remained held as possible prisoners of conscience in al-Qal'a Prison and both were reportedly tortured.

The arrest of al-Sheikh 'Ali Salman sparked off widespread demonstrations calling for his release. At least four people, Hani 'Abbas Khamis, Hani Ahmed al-

Wasti, Haj Mirza 'Ali 'Abd al-Ridha and Ya'qoub al-Ma'touq, were reportedly shot dead by members of the security forces.

An amnesty for political prisoners was declared in March by the Amir. The number and identities of those who benefited were not known.

Dozens of Bahraini nationals were denied entry when they tried to enter Bahrain after they had lived abroad for some time. Ahmed Hussein Akbar 'Abbas and his family returned to Bahrain in January. They were detained at the airport for 12 days before being expelled to Lebanon. Before the expulsion, they were reportedly threatened that if they returned again to Bahrain they would be put on a boat bound for Iran. Ahmed Hussein Akbar 'Abbas had been expelled three times previously when trying to return to Bahrain – once in 1982 and twice in 1993 (see *Amnesty International Report 1994*). 'Abd al-Hadi 'Abdullah al-Khawaja, resident in Denmark, returned to Bahrain in February, after he was informed of his father's death in Bahrain. He was held at the airport and interrogated, and reportedly ill-treated before being expelled to Lebanon.

The practice of forcible exile extended to political prisoners who had served their prison terms. Nabil Baqir (see above) and Ahmed Hussein Mirza were forcibly exiled to Iran in June. They had been imprisoned on political grounds since 1987, and had reportedly served their respective seven-year prison sentences. Sixty-four political exiles were amnestied by the Amir in March, although their identities were not made public.

Amnesty International wrote to the Minister of the Interior in January urging the immediate and unconditional release of those arrested at al-Mu'min Mosque if they were detained as prisoners of conscience. The organization welcomed the Amir's decision to permit some Bahraini exiles to return but continued to call for the practice of forcible exile to be ended. In December the organization wrote to the Minister of the Interior twice calling for independent investigations into the circumstances of the killing of the four demonstrators (see above) and for all those held to be granted access to a lawyer of their own choosing, family and medical attention if necessary. At the end of the year no response had been received from the authorities.

BANGLADESH

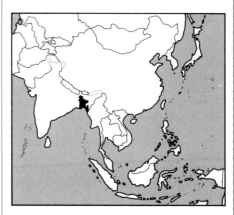

Dozens of prisoners of conscience were held under the Special Powers Act (SPA) or on criminal charges for exercising their right to freedom of expression. Political prisoners tried under anti-terrorist legislation may not have received a fair trial. Torture in police stations and jails continued, allegedly resulting in at least 40 deaths. At least six people were sentenced to death. No executions were reported.

From late February opposition parties boycotted parliament and demanded fresh elections under a neutral caretaker government. Prime Minister Khaleda Zia rejected this demand as "unconstitutional and undemocratic". Frequent demonstrations by opposition parties and Islamist groups involved a high level of political violence. In December all opposition members resigned from parliament.

In the Chittagong Hill Tracts, several rounds of talks between government and tribal representatives failed to bring a political solution. A cease-fire was periodically extended and sometimes broken. Following an agreement between India and Bangladesh, repatriation of some of the 56,000 tribal refugees from India began in February when over 1,800 people returned. Around 3,300 more refugees returned in July and August, even though land and homes had been restored to only a few of the returning refugees. A demand by tribal representatives for international supervision of their repatriation and rehabilitation was not conceded. A commission set up to investigate the possible extrajudicial execution of 12 to 20 tribal people in Naniarchar in November 1993 (see *Amnesty International Report 1994*) had not published its report by the end of 1994.

In April the Home Minister said that all political cases brought under the previous government would be dropped and that 109 cases had already been withdrawn. These cases related to political opponents of the previous government who had frequently been arrested on false criminal charges. The Suppression of Terrorist Activities Act of 1992 lapsed on 5 November and an ordinance provided for completion of prosecutions already begun under the Act. A law reform commission, announced in April, had not been established by the end of the year.

Feminist writer Taslima Nasrin received death threats from Islamic clerics after she was quoted as saying that the Koran should be revised. The clerics offered cash rewards for anyone killing her. Islamist groups engaged in violent protests demanding the death of all "apostates", including several journalists, and ransacked the offices of the newspapers *Janakantha* and *Banglar Bani*. Journalists were injured and newspapers burned. Non-governmental organizations which provide training, healthcare and legal aid particularly to women were attacked by Islamist groups on the grounds that such services alienate women from their Islamic lifestyle. The Islamist groups demanded that the country's small Ahmadiyya religious minority be declared non-Muslim and that a blasphemy law carrying the death penalty as the maximum punishment be introduced. Violent clashes ensued between secular and Islamist groups during which several people died.

In June the government brought charges against Taslima Nasrin under Section 295A of the Bangladesh Penal Code for having "maliciously and deliberately outraged the religious sentiments of the people". She went into hiding after a warrant for her arrest was issued and left the country in August after she had been granted bail. Also in June, similar charges were brought against four editors of *Janakantha* in connection with an article which described how village clerics misinterpreted Koranic verses and misled illiterate villagers. Three of the journalists were arrested, but were released on bail after about three weeks. The trial of all four began in late 1994.

The SPA, which allows detention without charge or trial for an indefinite period, continued to be used to detain dozens of people, including prisoners of conscience. The High Court declared about 80 per cent of SPA detention orders issued during the year to have been unlawful. Abul Hasnat, a barrister and member of the Jatiya Party, was detained under the SPA in November 1993. After the High Court ruled the detention order unlawful, he was released on 8 January but immediately rearrested. He was detained for a further 120 days under the SPA.

By September, 663 people were officially reported to have been arrested under the Curbing of Terrorist Activities Act since the beginning of the year. They included members of political parties, trade unionists and student activists. Scores faced trials which may have fallen short of international fair trial standards; the Act permits the trial of people *in absentia*, limits defendants' rights to present a full defence, rules out bail during pretrial detention, and provides punishments of five years' imprisonment to the death penalty for offences including harassment of women and obstructing traffic.

The vagueness of the Suppression of Terrorist Activities Act led to it being used to harass political opponents. Three student activists of the Bangladesh Chhatra League, affiliated to the Awami League, were arrested under the Act in March, and 13 others in June in Rangpur; all were accused of shoplifting. Local residents believed that the students had been charged for political reasons. One of them, 19-year-old Ashrafuddin Alam, died on 11 July in Rangpur jail in suspicious circumstances.

Torture, consisting mostly of beatings by police, continued to be reported. During demonstrations police often indiscriminately beat peaceful protesters. In July police injured some 15 journalists in Chittagong who were covering a rally.

Over 40 people died in police and judicial custody allegedly as a result of torture. Five men died in the mental ward of Sylhet prison in February. Their bodies reportedly bore marks of injuries and at least two appeared to have been strangled. Prison staff said one of the men had died in a scuffle and the others had died of natural causes. A similar official explanation was given when three prisoners died in Comilla jail in April within days of each other. A human rights group in Bangladesh which investigated the deaths said they had been the result of torture. On 20 August Abdul Khaleque died in Tejgaon police station in Dhaka on the day of arrest. His father filed a complaint that he was beaten to death; an investigation was set up but its findings had not been made public by the end of 1994.

The government took no effective measures to stop unlawful trials and arbitrary punishments imposed by village mediation councils or *salish* which have no legal authority to hear criminal cases. On 11 May Sapnahar, a 13-year-old girl who had become pregnant after being raped in 1993, was tried by *salish* in Dhamsa village, Brahmanbaria district. The alleged rapist was acquitted for want of four adult Muslim male witnesses, which are required under Islamic law to prove rape. Sapnahar's pregnancy was considered sufficient evidence to "convict" her of unlawful sexual intercourse. She was "sentenced" to be publicly flogged 40 days after delivery, but a women's rights group intervened and gave her shelter. An investigation was reportedly ordered by the Inspector General of Police but had not begun by the end of the year. Six other cases of "conviction" of women by *salish* had been reported by October.

Police apparently condoned killings of political activists by failing to intervene during clashes between rival political groups. In July at least six people were killed when members of the *Jamaat-e Islami*, Islamic Society, and the All Party Students Unity clashed in Chittagong during demonstrations and police failed to protect peaceful participants.

Perpetrators of human rights violations and abuses were rarely brought to justice; only two instances were reported. A police constable, charged with the attempted rape of a seven-year-old girl in February 1992, was sentenced in March to nine years' imprisonment by a court in Sirajganj. In February, nine participants of the *salish* which had sentenced a couple to death by stoning in January 1993 were sentenced to seven years' imprisonment in Moulvibazar; all nine filed an appeal.

At least six people were sentenced to death, all of them for murder. No execu-

tions were reported. A government bill to extend the death penalty for the offences of trafficking in women and children was pending in parliament.

Amnesty International urged the government to release all prisoners of conscience immediately and unconditionally, including journalists held solely for exercising their freedom of expression. It repeatedly appealed to the government to ensure the safety of writers, journalists and people associated with non-governmental organizations who were threatened by Islamist groups. In February Amnesty International issued a report, *Bangladesh: Further reports of extrajudicial executions by security forces in 1993*. It described three incidents in 1993 in which between 30 and 40 unarmed civilians had been extrajudicially executed by members of the security forces. In August Amnesty International appealed to parliamentarians not to support a re-enactment of the Suppression of Terrorist Activities Act, due to lapse in November. In October Amnesty International issued a report, *Bangladesh: Fundamental rights of women violated with virtual impunity*, and urged the government to safeguard effectively women's rights which had been frequently abused by Islamist groups. No substantive response was received from the government during the year.

BARBADOS

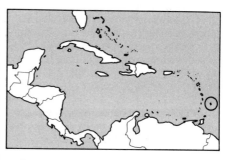

A decision was handed down on the case of Ryan Jordan who died in police custody in 1992. At least two death sentences were imposed; there were no executions and 21 people remained on death row at the end of the year.

Prime Minister Erskine Sandiford of the Democratic Labour Party lost a vote of confidence in June. A general election in

70

September was won by the Barbados Labour Party (BLP) led by Owen Arthur, who became Prime Minister. In its election manifesto the BLP had committed itself to the use of the death penalty and the reintroduction of corporal punishment.

The decision of the inquest in the case of Ryan Jordan, a 17-year-old who died in April 1992 allegedly as a result of injuries sustained while being interrogated by police, was delivered in September (see *Amnesty International Reports 1993* and *1994*). The coroner noted that the death had been caused by bruising of the left lung and heart, and kidney failure under the influence of drugs. He found no evidence of cruel or unusual punishment and concluded that the fundamental human rights of Ryan Jordan had not been violated. However, he returned an open verdict.

At least two people were sentenced to death; there were no executions. The government had still taken no steps at the end of the year to implement the November 1993 decision of the Judicial Committee of the Privy Council (JCPC) in London, the final court of appeal for Barbados. The JCPC had ruled that execution after more than five years on death row constitutes "inhuman or degrading punishment or other treatment", and that prisoners held on death row for more than five years should have their sentences commuted to life imprisonment. By the end of 1994 at least six prisoners had spent over five years on death row and should have had their sentences commuted.

Amnesty International wrote to the Attorney General in March calling for steps to be taken to commute the relevant death sentences under the JCPC ruling and also urged him to commute all death sentences.

BELARUS

At least one person on death row was awaiting the outcome of a petition for clemency.

Elections to the newly created post of President were won in July by Alyaksandr Lukashenka. Parliament rejected a draft law on a civilian alternative to compulsory military service in February, and did not include provisions for conscientious objectors in the new constitution adopted in March. The Constitution also retained the death penalty as "an exceptional measure of punishment for particularly serious crimes". A draft new criminal code which would decriminalize consenting homosexual acts between adult males and limit the scope of the death penalty (see *Amnesty International Report 1994*) had still not been adopted by parliament by the end of the year.

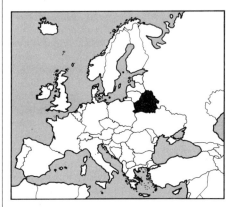

Statistics on the application of the death penalty in 1993 were released at the beginning of the year. They revealed that 21 people on death row had submitted petitions for clemency and that 16 people had been executed in 1993. One death sentence had been commuted. All death sentences and executions were for premeditated, aggravated murder. No such statistics were known to have been published for 1994. At least one man, Sergey Kutyavin, had his appeal against his death sentence rejected by the Supreme Court in March. At the end of the year he was on death row awaiting the outcome of a petition for clemency. He had been sentenced to death for murder in July 1993.

Amnesty International continued to urge the authorities to introduce a civilian alternative to military service, of non-punitive length, for conscientious objectors. The organization also urged the President to grant clemency to Sergey Kutyavin and to commute all other pending death sentences.

BELIZE

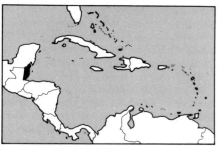

Six people were sentenced to death and seven people remained on death row. On appeal, four death sentences were commuted and one case was dismissed. No executions were carried out.

Lorna James was sentenced to death in February for murder, but on appeal to the Belize Court of Appeal, the verdict was overturned and a retrial ordered. At her retrial she was found guilty of manslaughter and sentenced to five years' imprisonment. Marco Tulio Ibañez, a Guatemalan citizen, was sentenced to death for murder on 3 March, but the case against him was dismissed by the Court of Appeal on 8 March. Another Guatemalan citizen, Roberto Yotxol, who was sentenced to death for murder on 6 July, had his sentence reduced by the Court of Appeal to 25 years' imprisonment for the lesser charge of manslaughter. At the end of the year three men who were sentenced to death during 1994 in separate cases – Pascual Bull, Hernan Mejia and Wilfredo Orellano – were awaiting the outcome of their appeals which took place in November and December.

In late November Governor General Sir Colville Young signed three death warrants for the execution on 9 December of Lindsberth Logan, Alfred Codrington and Salvadorian citizen Nicolás Antonio Guevara. All three, who had been sentenced to death for murder, had their appeals to the Court of Appeal and the Advisory Council dismissed. They were granted stays of execution by the Governor General following a decision on 7 December to allow leave to appeal to the Judicial Committee of the Privy Council (JCPC) in London, which is the final court of appeal for Belize.

Ellis Taibo remained on death row awaiting the outcome of an appeal hearing before the JCPC. He had been sentenced to death in August 1992 for rape and murder (see *Amnesty International Reports 1993* and *1994*).

Dean Edwardo Vasquez and Catalino O'Neil won their appeals to the JCPC, which on 29 June announced that the verdicts in both cases should be reduced from murder to manslaughter (see *Amnesty International Report 1994*). The JCPC concluded that having regard to the provisions of the Belize Criminal Code and the Constitution, the judge's direction of the jury was not sound in that he had wrongly directed the jury that the "onus was upon the accused to prove extreme provocation on the balance of probabilities". The cases were returned to the Court of Appeal in Belize for sentencing.

In December Amnesty International appealed to the Governor General and the Prime Minister, the Right Honourable Manuel Esquivel, on behalf of those under sentence of death, expressing concern about the possible resumption of executions in Belize after an interval of nine years. Amnesty International called for the abolition of the death penalty.

BENIN

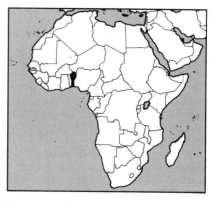

Three possible prisoners of conscience and five political prisoners, all arrested in 1992, continued to be held without trial throughout the year. There were reports that detainees had been ill-treated.

A campaign against a local tax, organized by the *Parti communiste du Bénin* (PCB), Communist Party of Benin, continued until January when the authorities agreed to abolish the tax. Several PCB members were arrested during the campaign of civil disobedience. In January an

72

apparently peaceful PCB meeting held near Aguégué, northeast of Cotonou, was broken up by security forces. In the violence which ensued, four PCB members were seriously injured and gendarmes were attacked. The four PCB members were among nine people arrested and charged with assaulting members of the security forces. There was no official investigation to establish why the security forces used violence to break up the meeting. The nine were held for six weeks before being provisionally released and later convicted and fined.

Three possible prisoners of conscience continued to be held in pre-trial detention throughout the year. All members of a farmers' union, *Migbe Aya* (We Reject Poverty), they had been arrested in December 1992 and were apparently awaiting trial on murder charges despite the fact that none had been present at the scene of the murder. They appeared to have been arrested solely because they had advised the victim of an attempted armed robbery in which gendarmes were implicated to lodge a complaint (see *Amnesty International Report 1994*). The three remained in the prison of Athiémé, in southern Benin, where conditions are particularly harsh. No investigation was held into reports that they had initially been held in chains. They had no access to a lawyer; the authorities claimed they had refused a lawyer but other sources indicated that the detainees had been coerced into not appointing a lawyer.

Prisoner of conscience Edgar Kaho, a journalist, was released in March, after serving 10 months of his one-year prison sentence (see *Amnesty International Report 1994*).

Five people were still awaiting trial throughout the year in the prison of Kandi, in the north of the country. They had been arrested in March 1992 after participating in a demonstration against police corruption during which a police officer was injured (see *Amnesty International Report 1993*).

Eleven army and police officers detained for more than two years in connection with an attempted coup in May 1992 (see *Amnesty International Report 1994*) were brought to trial in September. Three were acquitted and eight received sentences of between three and 10 years' imprisonment with hard labour. Among

them was Gomina Seydou Fousseini, a security official under former President Kérékou's government, who received a 10-year prison sentence. Sixteen others, including Captain Pascal Tawès, deputy commander of the Presidential Guard under President Kérékou, were sentenced *in absentia* to life imprisonment with hard labour.

Three PCB members from So-Ava, a town near Cotonou, who had reportedly been tortured in custody in 1993, were convicted. The men, all farmers, had been arrested during a PCB meeting in September 1993. During pre-trial detention they were reportedly severely beaten, their hands and feet were chained and their relatives beaten when they arrived to bring food. Despite a request from their lawyer, there was no investigation into these allegations of torture, nor did the court give any consideration to their complaints. In January they were each sentenced to a term of imprisonment for refusing to pay the local tax.

Amnesty International expressed concern to the government of President Nicéphore Soglo about the continuing detention without trial of the three members of *Migbe Aya*. In January government officials gave assurances that the three were to be promptly tried, but in September the Minister of Justice told a visiting Amnesty International representative that the judicial inquiry into the case had not yet been completed. Amnesty International was also concerned at reports that detainees were subjected to beatings or other cruel, inhuman or degrading treatment and that the courts failed to investigate reports of torture when these were brought to their attention. It urged the authorities to initiate independent inquiries into all allegations of torture.

BHUTAN

A prisoner of conscience spent his fifth year in prison. More than 50 political prisoners, including possible prisoners of conscience, remained in detention without charge or trial. Prison conditions reportedly improved. "Village volunteer groups" were reportedly responsible for possible extrajudicial executions in the south. More than 1,000 Nepali-speaking southern Bhutanese were forced to leave the country and some of their houses were deliberately demolished.

The governments of Bhutan and Nepal met three times to discuss the fate of more than 85,000 people living in refugee camps in eastern Nepal, the great majority of whom are Nepali-speaking people from southern Bhutan. In April agreement was reached on the procedures for classifying these people into the four categories agreed upon in 1993, with a view to some returning to Bhutan (see *Amnesty International Report 1994*). However, this work had not started by the end of the year. In October delegates of the UN Working Group on Arbitrary Detention visited Bhutan.

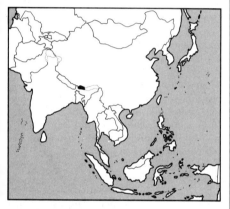

Continuing attacks on civilians in southern Bhutan, including armed robbery, rape and sometimes killings, were often attributed by the government to "anti-nationals" returning to Bhutan from the refugee camps in Nepal. There were also reports that armed members of the Bodo tribal community in Assam, India, were responsible for abuses in southern Bhutan.

Tek Nath Rizal, a prisoner of conscience, spent his fifth year in prison despite having been pardoned by Bhutan's head of state, King Jigme Singye Wangchuk, in late 1993 (see *Amnesty International Report 1994*).

More than 50 Nepali-speaking southern Bhutanese remained held without charge or trial. They included possible prisoners of conscience, many of whom had been held for more than three years. A further 50 had reportedly been charged and were awaiting trial. During 1994 the King granted an amnesty to 59 political prisoners, including Deo Datta Sharma (see *Amnesty*

International Report 1994).

In May, seven Nepali-speaking southern Bhutanese charged under the National Security Act with treason and involvement in various "anti-national" activities were sentenced to between 10 years' and life imprisonment. The trial of 17 people from Sarbhang, Geylegphug District, who faced similar charges, started in July but had not concluded by the end of the year. Details of the proceedings in both cases were not known.

A general improvement in detention conditions and the treatment of prisoners was reported. The International Committee of the Red Cross extended its visits to places of detention to include southern Bhutan.

"Village volunteer groups" were reportedly responsible for possible extrajudicial executions in the south. In February members of one such group in Sarbhang, Geylegphug District, reportedly attacked seven Nepali-speaking robbers with knives. They killed three of them, apparently without attempting to arrest them. No disciplinary action was taken.

Approximately 1,100 Nepali-speaking people from southern Bhutan arrived in the refugee camps in eastern Nepal. Many of them were believed to have been forcibly exiled from Bhutan. Bhutanese local government officials had taken various measures to make them leave, including forcing them to sign "voluntary migration forms" and destroying their homes (see *Amnesty International Report 1994*). In one case, the *dungpa* (local administrator) had told Nirmal Gurung that 32 families from his village in Samchi District had petitioned the government to "remove" him and his family. Nirmal Gurung was made to fill out a "voluntary migration form" and told to leave the country. The villagers then drew up a petition stating that they had not asked for the family to be removed; their alleged request had been concocted by the authorities. In June Nirmal Gurung's family was nevertheless told to leave and informed that their "voluntary migration form" could not be withdrawn. Nirmal Gurung was refused permission to appeal to the King. Three soldiers and the village headman then destroyed his home. Other villagers assisted under threat of eviction themselves. Nirmal Gurung and his relatives subsequently left for the refugee camps in Nepal.

74

In August Amnesty International published a report, *Bhutan: Forcible Exile*, highlighting its concern that people forced into exile may be denied their right to return to their own country. Amnesty International continued to appeal for the immediate and unconditional release of Tek Nath Rizal and for all political prisoners to be promptly and fairly tried or released. Its request for the transcript and judgment of the trial of Tek Nath Rizal to be made public was refused by the government on the grounds that High Court rules "prohibit publication of 'restricted documents'". Amnesty International also requested information about the estimated 4,000 "village volunteer groups" operating in southern Bhutan, and urged the government to ensure that all such groups observe basic human rights standards.

BOLIVIA

A Spanish citizen died allegedly as a result of a beating by military personnel. A farmer died in suspicious circumstances after being arrested by an anti-narcotics police patrol. There were reports of torture and ill-treatment of coca-growers detained during an operation to counter drug-trafficking.

Throughout the year there were widespread strikes and other protests against social and economic conditions and government reforms to the political, electoral and educational systems. In August coca-growers from Cochabamba and other departments marched to the capital, La Paz, to protest against the enforced eradication of their crops by anti-narcotic security agents and ill-treatment of local union members. In July the government launched an anti-narcotics operation in the El Chapare region of the department of Cochabamba. Between 200 and 300 people were detained for up to 10 days during the first phase of the operation.

As a result of constitutional reform, the government announced in August the creation of the office of State Ombudsman. An article was also incorporated into the Constitution which gave formal recognition to the rights of indigenous peoples.

Former president General Luís García Meza, sentenced *in absentia* to 30 years in jail for human rights violations and other crimes committed during the period of his military rule, was arrested in São Paulo, Brazil, in March. However, extradition proceedings, approved in October by Brazil's Supreme Court, were suspended in November because of procedural irregularities. In April, two co-defendants of the former president in the seven-year Responsibilities Trial who had also been sentenced to 30 years' imprisonment (see *Amnesty International Report 1994*) were also detained: Tito Montaño Belzu, a former senior member of the armed forces, and Juan Carlos García Guzmán, who had been sentenced *in absentia* and was detained in Argentina.

Two people were killed by security forces in circumstances suggesting that they may have been unlawfully killed. On 10 February a Spanish citizen, Manuel Ramón Puchol Pastor, died in the village of San Matías, department of Santa Cruz, allegedly as a result of a severe beating by members of the *Monte Florida 14* infantry regiment. In September the trial began of seven members of the regiment who were charged with the killing. The trial was still in progress at the end of 1994.

On 18 August Felipe Pérez Ortiz, a peasant farmer living in the El Chapare region, died in suspicious circumstances at the hands of security agents. The Subsecretary for Human Rights of the Ministry of Justice and representatives of the Chamber of Deputies' Human Rights Commission, among others, visited the area as part of a commission of inquiry into the death. They reported that Felipe Pérez had been shot at close range after being arrested. Eight of the nine security agents implicated in the killing were suspended from duty and detained pending further investigations. The ninth, reported to be the agent who fired the fatal shot, escaped.

Reports of ill-treatment of detainees by police continued. Sandalio Verdúguez Salazar alleged that on 28 July he was abducted by approximately 20 members of the Mobile Rural Patrol Unit (UMOPAR), taken to an empty house and severely beaten. No investigation into the allegations was known to have been initiated. In July an inter-institutional commission of inquiry visited El Chapare to investigate allegations of arbitrary detentions and beatings of detainees held in the context of anti-narcotics operations.

Two television journalists were the victims of politically motivated attacks. On 29 October a letter-bomb addressed to Carlos Mesa in La Paz was intercepted; accompanying it was a letter from a group calling itself the Dignity Command, an armed political group apparently linked to former president General Luís García Meza. On 30 October, in the city of Santa Cruz, three men fired on the home of Luís Soruco Barba, injuring a neighbour. Both journalists were granted police protection and investigations into the incidents were opened.

Amnesty International wrote to the government in March urging a full and independent investigation into the death of Manuel Ramón Puchol Pastor. In a letter to President Gonzalo Sánchez de Lozada in September, Amnesty International asked to be informed about the terms of reference of the investigation into the killing of Felipe Pérez Ortiz. The organization also called for assurances that all allegations of human rights violations would receive prompt and thorough investigation. Amnesty International welcomed the incorporation of the office of State Ombudsman into the reformed Constitution as a further step towards safeguarding human rights in Bolivia and asked to be kept informed of its legal status and terms of reference.

BOSNIA AND HERZEGOVINA

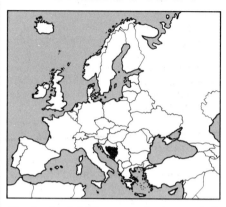

Hundreds of deliberate and arbitrary killings were reported, mostly committed by Bosnian Serb forces. Hundreds of prisoners of conscience were held by various parties to the conflict. Many detainees were reportedly tortured or ill-treated or made to perform forced labour in dangerous conditions. There were reports of rape and "disappearances". Muslims, Croats and Roma were expelled from the areas in which they lived by Bosnian Serb forces. Death sentences were ordered by Bosnian Serb courts.

At the start of the year four different armed forces were fighting in various areas of Bosnia-Herzegovina. In central Bosnia and around government-held pockets in the east and west, there was continuing conflict between the largely Muslim *Armija Bosne i Hercegovine* (ABH), Army of Bosnia and Herzegovina, and the *Vojska "Republike Srpske"* (VRS), Army of the "Serbian Republic". In central Bosnia the ABH and some Muslim paramilitaries were also fighting the Bosnian Croat force, the *Hrvatsko Vijeće Obrane* (HVO), Croatian Defence Council, which was supported by elements of the Croatian Army. In the Bihać pocket in the west, fighting continued between rebel Muslim forces, loyal to a local leader, Fikret Abdić, and the ABH. In the second half of the year the VRS and the rebel Muslim forces in the Bihać area received support from Croatian Serb forces, and in the southwest units of the Croatian Army fought against the VRS.

The siege of Sarajevo by the VRS continued throughout the year. However, in

76

February, following an international outcry over massacres of civilians in mortar attacks, a cease-fire was agreed between the VRS and ABH and the town and surrounding area were partially demilitarized.

In March an agreement was signed in Washington, the USA, by Alija Izetbegović, the Bosnian President, the Croatian President and representatives of the Bosnian Croats. An effective cease-fire between the ABH and HVO was immediately implemented. The Washington agreement provided for the establishment of a Muslim- (or Bosniac-) Croat Federation on the territories their forces controlled. The Federal Constitution contained some important human rights guarantees and mechanisms. However, little progress was made towards implementing them. Mostar was placed under European Union (EU) administration while the Western European Union provided policing.

The Croat-Muslim cease-fire brought an end to the large-scale human rights abuses which had accompanied their conflict. However, fierce fighting between the VRS on one side and ABH and HVO on the other continued in other areas.

Continuing international attempts to reach a peace agreement involving all sides, brokered by the UN, the EU and the so-called "Contact Group", failed. The government of the Federal Republic of Yugoslavia (FRY) publicly withdrew its support for the Bosnian Serb forces after Radovan Karadžić and other Bosnian Serb representatives rejected a modified peace plan in July. At the end of the year partial agreement had been reached between the various parties on a new cease-fire and the reopening of negotiations for a political settlement.

The UN Protection Force in the former Yugoslavia (UNPROFOR) continued to protect humanitarian aid. However, criticism mounted because of its ineffectiveness in its other role of protecting the UN-designated "safe areas", in particular the areas around Goražde, Sarajevo and Bihać. North Atlantic Treaty Organization (NATO) aircraft carried out a small number of air attacks in support of the "safe areas". UN personnel were harassed, detained and used as "human shields", mainly by the VRS.

All sides accused the others of breaches of international humanitarian law. Mon-itoring and verification of abuses by international observers were frequently difficult and witnesses were often reluctant to speak for fear of reprisals.

In November the International Criminal Tribunal for the former Yugoslavia issued its first indictment. A Bosnian Serb camp commander was accused of grave breaches of the Fourth Geneva Convention of 1949, relating to the protection of civilians in time of war. He was believed to be in Bosnian Serb-controlled territory and was not in custody. The tribunal also requested that the German Government hand over another Bosnian Serb soldier, detained on suspicion of committing similar acts.

VRS forces deliberately targeted civilians with artillery, mortar bombs and sniper fire. For example, in February nine people were killed when the VRS fired three mortar bombs on a queue for humanitarian aid in Sarajevo. The VRS was also believed to have been responsible for a bomb which fell on a Sarajevo market the following day killing 68 people and wounding 200. The hospital and other non-military targets were also reportedly attacked by the VRS during their advance on Goražde in April. Despite the February cease-fire and a sniping ban, VRS sniper attacks on civilians continued in Sarajevo. For example, in one incident one person was killed and 19 injured when a tram was hit by sniper fire in October. The HVO and ABH also targeted civilians, although much less frequently.

Civilians were deliberately and arbitrarily killed in towns outside the war zones. Most of the victims were Muslims, Croats and Roma living in towns under VRS control. Up to 20 people were killed in Prijedor between 29 March and 1 April. The *de facto* Bosnian Serb authorities later announced that suspects had been arrested in connection with the killings. Muslims, Croats and foreign nationals were killed in the Mostar area, despite the Croat-Muslim cease-fire. The killings were apparently carried out by members of the HVO and Croatian paramilitaries and were reportedly not investigated fully by the Bosnian Croat authorities. Among the victims was an Iranian journalist, Saeed Hussein Navaba, who was allegedly killed by HVO soldiers or paramilitaries near Mostar in September.

All sides held numerous detainees.

Many were civilians who had not used or advocated violence and had been detained solely on account of their nationality or political or other beliefs. Places of detention were often not made known. The International Committee of the Red Cross (ICRC) was not always informed of or given access to detainees. Regular exchanges of prisoners took place between the various parties. However, others were detained throughout the year. Approximately 3,000 detainees, both civilians and prisoners of war held in the context of the Croat-Muslim conflict at the start of the year, had been released by July. However, more people were detained during the year in other circumstances. Some arbitrary detentions were carried out in order to intimidate remaining minorities into leaving their homes; others for the purpose of extorting money or for use in prisoner exchanges. Some individuals who were prosecuted may have been prisoners of conscience.

For example, a group of seven medical staff, predominantly Serbs, were detained by the Bosnian Government authorities in Sarajevo in January, reportedly for attempting to cross into Bosnian Serb-controlled territory. In April the *de facto* Bosnian Serb authorities detained 11 French aid workers, alleging that they had attempted to smuggle arms into Sarajevo, although there appeared to be no real foundation to the charges. A Bosnian Serb official proposed that they be exchanged for the seven Serbian medical staff held by the Bosnian Government. The aid workers were released in May after the payment of a large sum of money. The Serbian medical staff were released in a prisoner exchange in June.

In July it was reported that about 100 men and 50 women, mainly Muslims, including disabled and injured people, were detained in Velika Kladuša by forces loyal to the rebel Muslim leader, Fikret Abdić. They were held in conditions which may have amounted to cruel, inhuman or degrading treatment. About 300 civilians were detained by the ABH in the area.

Up to 600 Muslim civilian men were held by the VRS in the Bijeljina area. They were taken into detention between July and September and many had not been released by the end of the year. Some were rounded up in Bijeljina and Janja; others had paid money to leave these towns for

government-controlled areas but were nevertheless detained before crossing the front line. Relatives were not always informed of their detention and some men "disappeared". Some of the detainees were beaten or otherwise ill-treated in detention. Some detainees held by the VRS, ABH or Muslim rebels were required to perform forced labour, sometimes in dangerous situations such as digging trenches on front lines. Six Muslim men were allegedly killed during shelling while digging trenches for the VRS near Teočak in May.

The Bosnian Government authorities detained men, including possible conscientious objectors, for deserting or avoiding military service. Many of those prosecuted were Serbs. Draft resisters and deserters were also prosecuted by the Bosnian Serb and Bosnian Croat authorities. Early in the year the authorities in Croatia and the FRY, in collaboration with the HVO and VRS respectively, mobilized men born in Bosnia-Herzegovina for service in the respective armies. As a result potential asylum-seekers were deported from the FRY and possible conscientious objectors were detained in Croatia (see **Croatia** and **Federal Republic of Yugoslavia** entries).

All sides held trials or initiated investigations for crimes connected with the war, including grave breaches of humanitarian law. The defendants were almost exclusively accused of crimes against individuals of the national group holding the trial. The investigations and trials may not have been carried out in conditions which allowed for a fair trial.

Throughout the year there were widespread human rights abuses against Muslims, Croats and Roma remaining in Bosnian Serb-controlled areas. These included bombing or shooting at houses and attacking people in their homes and subjecting them to beatings, rape and knife attacks. The perpetrators were frequently dressed in military uniforms. Victims who sought help from civilian or military police were offered little or no protection. These abuses together with arbitrary detentions of civilians and deliberate and arbitrary killings and other pressures formed clear patterns of intimidation aimed at compelling people to leave the area. There were also abuses on a lesser scale against Muslims in Bosnian Croat-controlled areas and vice versa, as well as against Serbs in those areas.

78

Around 6,000 Muslims were forcibly expelled from Bosnian Serb-controlled Bijeljina and Janja between July and September. Some were forcibly expelled in the middle of the night; others were effectively compelled to pay to leave as a result of systematic persecution, including the arbitrary detention of men of military age, threats and acts of violence. Some were forced to pass dangerously close to minefields or cross the front line while fighting was taking place.

Information came to light of a death sentence passed in 1993 by a court in a government-controlled area. Djemal Zahirović was sentenced to death in September 1993 for participating in the torture and ill-treatment of prisoners in the Bosnian Serb-controlled camp in Batković in 1992. None of the three known death sentences imposed in 1993 was carried out (see *Amnesty International Report 1994*). A Bosnian Serb military court in Banja Luka imposed a "death sentence" on a Bosnian Serb soldier, Vojislav Dimitrijević, after convicting him of multiple murder. Another Bosnian Serb soldier was allegedly shot for desertion in November.

Throughout the year Amnesty International publicized its concerns and appealed to governmental and *de facto* authorities inside Bosnia-Herzegovina and to the authorities in Croatia and the FRY to prevent human rights abuses, to investigate all reports of abuses and to ensure that suspected perpetrators were brought to justice.

In January the organization published a report, *Central and southwest Bosnia-Herzegovina: civilian population trapped in a cycle of violence*, detailing abuses which had occurred in the context of the Croat-Muslim conflict between April and December 1993. In February it appealed on behalf of Dr Dejan Kafka and other medical professionals detained by the government authorities in Sarajevo. It called on the *de facto* Bosnian Serb authorities to investigate and prevent the recurrence of the deliberate targeting of civilians in Sarajevo. In March Amnesty International appealed for the release of possible Serbian conscientious objectors detained in Sarajevo. In April it called on the Bosnian Serb authorities to prevent deliberate targeting of civilians in Goražde. In May it appealed for the release of 11 French aid workers held as hostages by the VRS.

In June Amnesty International issued a report, *Bosnia-Herzegovina: "You have no place here" – Abuses in Bosnian Serb areas*, documenting abuses in Banja Luka and other towns in western Bosnia. The same month the organization appealed on behalf of two Tunisian humanitarian aid workers who had been detained by Bosnian Serb forces. It also appealed to the Bosnian Government to prevent the harassment of Serbs in government-controlled areas. In July it called on the Bosnian Serb authorities to release civilians detained around Bijeljina and to prevent other human rights abuses in the area. It also appealed for the release of civilian detainees held in Velika Kladuša by rebel Muslim forces.

In September Amnesty International called on the Bosnian Serb authorities to make public the reasons for the detention in Banja Luka of five prominent Muslims who had reportedly been accused of working against the authorities. In November it appealed to the Bosnian Serb authorities to prevent human rights abuses by VRS units attacking Bihać. In December Amnesty International published a report, *Bosnia-Herzegovina: Living for the day – Forcible expulsions in Bijeljina and Janja*.

BRAZIL

Hundreds of people were extrajudicially executed by police and death squads. Torture and ill-treatment of detainees were reported from police stations and prisons. Journalists, human rights activists, church workers and state prosecutors investigating human rights violations by members of the police received death threats.

Elections were held in October for a new President, state governors and members of parliament at federal and state level. Fernando Henrique Cardoso of the Brazilian Social Democratic Party was elected President and was due to take office on 1 January 1995.

In November, following a wave of killings by police and by drug gangs in Rio de Janeiro, the federal government appointed an Army General to assume joint command of the civil and military police of the state to oversee the fight against arms and drug-trafficking.

Hundreds of people, including adolescents and children, were killed by death squads in cities including Rio de Janeiro, Recife, Belo Horizonte and Salvador. The involvement of civil and military police in death squad activities in many states was openly acknowledged by the authorities but little progress was made in investigations and prosecutions.

On 18 June the dead bodies of two girls and a boy aged between 12 and 15 were found semi-naked in front of Santa Cecilia Church in the Bras de Pina neighbourhood of Rio de Janeiro. The bodies had been arranged to form a cross on the tarmac. All had shotgun wounds to the head, chest and limbs; the boy had his hands tied behind his back. These were typical of death squad-style executions which were reported to have claimed 1,200 lives in Rio de Janeiro from September 1993 to June 1994. Ninety per cent of these cases remained unsolved.

In October Rio de Janeiro police shot dead 13 people in the Nova Brasília shanty town. The killings were apparently in revenge for an armed attack by a drug gang on a police station in which one policeman lost a leg. The police claimed that the 13 lost their lives in a gun battle, but members of the community alleged that some had been dragged out of their homes and extrajudicially executed.

On 9 December Wagner dos Santos was shot and seriously wounded in Rio de Janeiro. He was a key witness who had identified three military police standing trial for the Rio de Janeiro Candelária massacre in which seven street children and a youth were shot dead outside Candelária church in July 1993. On regaining consciousness Wagner dos Santos claimed that he had been abducted, handcuffed, beaten and then shot and left for dead by a group of policemen in plain clothes, who blamed him for identifying some of their colleagues. Amnesty International had repeatedly urged the Brazilian authorities to protect him and several child witnesses to the Candelária killings, but learned during the year that up to 40 of them remained sleeping on the streets.

Rural workers and trade union leaders were also extrajudicially executed with impunity. A member of an alleged death squad operating within a military police unit in Sergipe state testified that military police took part in several operations to kill cattle thieves and others in Sergipe and Bahia states, on the orders of high-ranking state police and judicial officials. In November authorities in Pará state announced an investigation into military police participation in hired killings of rural workers in the south of the state, after claims by a landowner that he had paid police to commit such crimes.

In July Ivaldo Severino da Silva, a rural trade union representative, was shot dead in Ipojuca, Pernambuco state. Six previous attempts had been made on his life. A local judge had previously refused to detain three employees of the Trapiche sugar mill in connection with an attempt on the trade unionist's life in October 1993. According to trade union sources, 16 people had been killed at the Trapiche sugar mill since 1986, the majority in connection with their trade union activities.

José Amaral Cirilo went into hiding in September; he had been tortured and nearly killed by police in Marechal Deodoro, Alagoas state, in 1993. He sought protection in a police station in the state capital, Maceió, in May 1993 after seeking compensation through the labour courts from the Sumauma sugar mill in Marechal Deodoro. Two civil policemen from Marechal Deodoro collected him from Maceió and took him away in handcuffs. He was then held at the police station in Marechal Deodoro and beaten on the hands with a wooden club. After signing papers produced by the manager of the sugar mill, he was handcuffed and taken in a car without licence plates to a waste ground. He was forced to lie down and shot twice in the face. Police removed his handcuffs when they thought he was dead. He ran away and was pursued by a police sergeant who shot at him, wounding him three times in the leg and twice in the side. After reaching safety, he reported the case to the authorities. During the subsequent investigation, evidence of a clandestine cemetery was found at the waste ground. The state authorities confined him to the state mental hospital for 14 months "for his own safety". Police officers were charged with his attempted murder but had not been brought to trial by the end of 1994.

In May a former military policeman was sentenced to 50 years' imprisonment for killing two rural trade unionists, brothers José and Paulo Canuto, and wounding Orlando Canuto in Xinguara in April 1991 (see *Amnesty International Report 1992*). This was the first trial and conviction in connection with hundreds of murders of rural workers and trade unionists in the south of Pará state which had taken place over three decades. In November the convicted policeman escaped from the central prison in Belém. Another police sergeant charged with the same crimes had escaped from police custody in 1992. In May the mayor of Coqueiro Seco, Alagoas state, was acquitted of planning the murder of town councillor Renildo dos Santos in 1993 (see *Amnesty International Report 1994*). Four military policemen and one civilian were at liberty awaiting trial for Renildo dos Santos' murder.

Torture and ill-treatment of detainees were reported from police stations and prisons. In January a rural worker, José Bernadino Algatano, died in hospital after being beaten by military police in Dionísio, Minas Gerais state. According to witnesses he was handcuffed, thrown to the ground and beaten and kicked in the abdomen, back and genitals. His brother was detained when he tried to intervene and taken to the local police station. There, he reported seeing José Bernadino Algatano being beaten, being suspended from an iron bar (a torture known as parrot's perch) and being semi-asphyxiated with a wet cloth. The autopsy report revealed severe injuries to the intestines consistent with blows to the abdomen. A military police inquiry had not been concluded by the end of 1994.

In September a judge ordered the Minors' Police Station in Belo Horizonte, Minas Gerais state, to be closed following evidence of systematic torture and sexual abuse there. Members of the Juvenile Welfare and Prosecution Service visiting the police station in August had taken testimonies from detainees who alleged that they had been beaten and given electric shocks. The prosecutors inspected a small room in the basement where torture sessions were held and found a strip of rubber attached to a wooden stave with which the juveniles had been beaten. Charges of torture were brought against two police chiefs and two detectives. The crime of torture is still not included in the Brazilian penal code, but charges of torture can be brought under the 1990 Children's Statute.

There were reports that prison guards repeatedly beat prisoners in the House of Detention prison in São Paulo. In March José Roberto dos Santos, a prisoner suffering from AIDS, was injured on his limbs, chest and back after being beaten with iron bars. In June, after inspecting wounded prisoners, the São Paulo State Public Defender's Office initiated criminal proceedings against 15 guards for injuring 40 prisoners in Block 4 of the prison. There were further reports of beatings following a number of escape attempts.

Journalists, human rights activists, church workers and state prosecutors investigating human rights violations by members of the police received death threats and some were killed. On 13 June Reinaldo Guedes Miranda, a lawyer, and Hermógenes Da Silva Almeida Filho, a poet, who were both human rights advisers to the opposition Workers Party, were shot dead in their car. They had been closely following the investigation into the 1993 Vigário Geral massacre (see *Amnesty International Report 1994*) on behalf of the local council's human rights commission. The two had reported receiving threatening notes, apparently relating to their activities on behalf of black people and homosexuals. A police informant was detained and charged with the killings. Colleagues of the two men disputed the authorities' claim that the killings were not political.

Cesar Gama, José Antônio Moura Bomfim and Marcos Cadoso, all newspaper journalists in Aracajú, Sergipe state, received repeated death threats after publishing allegations that a military police death squad was operating with the collusion of high-ranking state authorities.

In September the existence of a "hit-list" of some 40 people in the town of

Xinguara, Pará state, was reported. Six of those named on the list were already dead and two had been attacked. According to evidence given by gunmen already charged with related incidents, those named on the list had been singled out because of their links with peasant farmers involved in local land conflicts. One of the gunmen alleged that he had been contracted to kill Father Ricardo Rezende (see *Amnesty International Report 1993*). Brother Henri des Rosiers, Father Benedito Rodrigues Costa and a local councillor, Elpídio Pereira da Silva, were also named on the list.

During the year Stella Kuhlman, military state prosecutor in São Paulo, made public a series of telephone threats she had been receiving for the previous 18 months in relation to her work prosecuting military police charged with homicide and extortion – in particular from the military police battalion known locally as ROTA. Threats recorded on her private telephone included: "If you continue branding my friends, your children will die, then your mother and you will die last". Stella Kuhlman was one of the prosecutors in the trial of 120 military police charged with the House of Detention prison massacre (see *Amnesty International Reports 1993* and *1994*). Tania Sales Moreira, Rio de Janeiro state public prosecutor, continued to receive death threats because of her work prosecuting members of death squads (see *Amnesty International Report 1992*).

In September Amnesty International published a report, *Beyond Despair: An Agenda for Human Rights in Brazil*. The report analysed the increasing scale of human rights violations in urban areas over the previous four years which it attributed to the virtual impunity enjoyed by police committing human rights crimes. It also pointed to encouraging initiatives by some state prosecutors. It proposed major institutional reforms of Brazil's police and judiciary and specific measures for the effective protection of victims and witnesses of human rights violations. An Amnesty International delegation visited Brazil in September to present the report to the Minister of Justice, the Attorney General and to presidential candidates and to gain their commitment to an emergency program to improve human rights protection in Brazil.

Throughout the year Amnesty International raised individual cases with the Brazilian authorities, seeking investigations and protection for witnesses of human rights crimes in order to hold the security forces to account and so end the cycle of impunity and violence.

BULGARIA

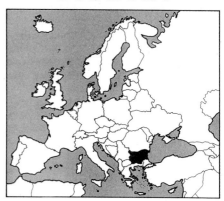

There were reports of torture and ill-treatment by the police. Many of the victims were Roma, two of whom died in detention in suspicious circumstances. Two death sentences were passed, but there were no executions.

In May Bulgaria ratified the European Convention for the Prevention of Torture and Inhuman or Degrading Treatment or Punishment.

In February the National Assembly debated a proposal to lift the moratorium on executions introduced in June 1990. When no decision was taken, 49 deputies petitioned the Constitutional Court. The court ruled in July that the decision to retain or abolish the death penalty is within the competence of the National Assembly and urged the deputies to take a decision as soon as possible.

In July the National Assembly adopted the Judiciary Act which introduced new criteria for the appointment of members of the Supreme Judicial Council, of Supreme Court judges and of the chief prosecutor. The law also made possible the removal of such officials who were appointed after elections in October 1991. In September, however, the Constitutional Court ruled that members of the Supreme Judicial Council could not be removed until the expiry of their term in 1996 and that the new criteria for appointments could not be applied retroactively.

In September Parliament adopted a law on national defence which provides for a civilian alternative to military service. However, no statutory rules for the alternative service had been enacted by the end of the year. Around 7,000 men, including some conscientious objectors, had reportedly failed to appear before army selection boards by the end of August.

Trials of suspected perpetrators of past human rights abuses continued. In September Nadia Dunkin, a witness in the trial of three former officials of the Lovech labour camp (see *Amnesty International Reports 1993* and *1994*), was killed. She had reportedly received death threats after speaking publicly about killings and torture of detainees.

Ethnic Macedonians, members of *Obedinena Makedonska Organizatsiya "Ilinden"*, the United Macedonian Organization "Ilinden", were subjected to arbitrary arrests and detained briefly in police stations. In April Stoyan Machkarov, Lyubomir Vasilev and Aleksandar Iliev were detained in Blagoevgrad while putting up posters announcing an assembly at Rozhen Monastery (see *Amnesty International Report 1994*). They were reportedly beaten by police officers who attempted to make them confess that they were being paid for their political activity. In September two men were detained in Sandanski for handing out leaflets.

Reports of apparently racially motivated torture and ill-treatment of Roma by police officers indicated that such abuses were widespread. The authorities also failed to protect Roma from racist violence. In February, in Dolno Belotintsi, racist attacks by violent crowds of local people lasted several days after a man was killed by a Rom. The crowds burned down one Roma home and broke into others smashing windows and destroying furniture and other household goods. The victims complained and reportedly failed to receive protection from the regional police department. In March and April a group of around 60 "skinheads" attacked Roma homes in Pleven. When they set fire to the home of Zaharinka Koleva they reportedly shouted: "We will burn you alive". According to witnesses, the police did not intervene to stop the attack and in some cases beat the Roma with truncheons.

None of the perpetrators was arrested although the identity of many was well known to local people.

In August police carried out a raid on the Roma community in Pazardjik. Armed officers reportedly broke into Roma homes without presenting warrants and indiscriminately beat the occupants. Police had carried out a similar raid on this community in 1992 (see *Amnesty International Report 1993*). No results of an official investigation into the first incident had been published by the end of the year and none of the victims of ill-treatment had won any redress through the courts. Kiril Yosifov Yordanov, the only victim who persisted in his complaint about ill-treatment, was allegedly beaten and intimidated by police officers on 17 October.

In two cases, alleged torture of Roma in detention resulted in death. Lyubcho Sofiev Terziev died in the police station in Kazanluk, two days after his arrest in August. In September Slavcho Lyubenov Tsonchev died in Pleven police station.

Two people were sentenced to death for murder during the year. However, no executions had taken place in Bulgaria since 1989.

In February Amnesty International wrote to the deputies of the National Assembly urging them not to lift the moratorium on executions. In March and April the organization expressed concern to the authorities about the reported failure of the police to protect Roma from racially motivated attacks in Dolno Belotintsi and in Pleven. In April and September Amnesty International expressed its concern about the detention and ill-treatment of ethnic Macedonians.

Amnesty International repeatedly urged the authorities to investigate reports of beating and other ill-treatment of Roma. In September the organization published a report, *Bulgaria: Turning a blind eye to racism*, and urged the government of Prime Minister Lyben Berov to establish an independent commission to conduct a full and impartial inquiry into all allegations of ill-treatment of Roma. In October Amnesty International expressed concern about the alleged torture resulting in death of Slavcho Lyubenov Tsonchev. No reply from the authorities had been received by the end of the year in response to any of Amnesty International's concerns.

BURUNDI

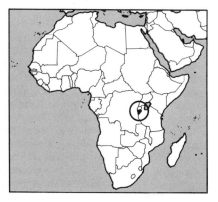

Thousands of people were killed in politically motivated massacres committed by the security forces and civilian gangs. Many of the victims were killed solely because of their ethnic origin. The authorities did little or nothing to investigate the killings or bring those responsible to account. Several hundred people were arbitrarily detained, many of whom alleged that they were tortured, and dozens of people "disappeared".

In January the National Assembly appointed Cyprien Ntaryamira to replace the country's first democratically elected President, who had been killed by soldiers in an unsuccessful coup attempt in October 1993 (see *Amnesty International Report 1994*). Both were members of the *Front pour la démocratie au Burundi* (FRODEBU), Front for Democracy in Burundi, which won the elections in June 1993.

On 6 April President Ntaryamira was killed along with President Juvénal Habyarimana of Rwanda when their plane was brought down by a missile in Rwanda. The FRODEBU interim President of the National Assembly, Sylvestre Ntibantunganya, became interim President and power-sharing negotiations began between FRODEBU and opposition political parties. An agreement reached in September included the election of President Ntibantunganya to a four-year term by the National Assembly and the appointment of 45 per cent of government ministers from opposition political parties.

Tension between Tutsi, who dominated the government until July 1993 and continued to control the armed forces, and Hutu remained high. Politically motivated killings – both massacres and sporadic political assassinations, mostly of prominent Hutu – were reported virtually daily across the country. By mid-1994 the two communities were for the most part living in mutually hostile areas, both in towns and in the countryside, although they had formerly lived alongside each other.

There was an almost complete breakdown of law and order resulting from the government's failure to control the armed forces or to prevent Hutu and Tutsi extremists from arming themselves. Responsibility for individual killings was difficult to ascertain. There were numerous claims that members of the security forces assisted groups of armed Tutsi and that leading members of FRODEBU supported armed Hutu, but the government took no action to establish the facts or to bring those encouraging political violence to justice.

Opposition leader Mathias Hitimana of the *Parti pour la réconciliation du peuple* (PRP), Party for the People's Reconciliation, was held for 10 days in August in connection with violent demonstrations which had resulted in about 15 deaths.

On rare occasions when perpetrators were arrested, they were released without charge within hours or days. In April the interim President, in collaboration with the armed forces, launched a "disarmament campaign" calling on citizens to surrender their arms. The armed forces apparently regarded this as a licence to use unrestrained lethal force and killed hundreds of people, including unarmed civilians. The army used helicopters and grenades against unarmed civilians, destroying parts of the capital, Bujumbura, and villages in several provinces. Thousands of people were displaced.

A commission of inquiry announced by the government in December 1993 to investigate human rights abuses and other crimes related to the October 1993 coup attempt – after which some 50,000 people were killed – failed to get under way (see *Amnesty International Report 1994*). However, both the army's own Procuracy and the ordinary Procuracy carried out investigations. The army's inquiry resulted in the detention of 18 soldiers suspected of complicity in former President Melchior Ndadaye's murder. None had been brought to trial by the end of the year. Criminal investigations by the ordinary

84

Procuracy started in April and were conducted by teams of magistrates at provincial level. Several hundred people, virtually all of them Hutu, were arrested as a result and were still held untried at the end of the year (see below). The official investigations were condemned as biased by many Hutu political leaders. In November President Ntibantunganya called for an international commission of inquiry into the October 1993 killings as required by the September power-sharing agreement, but no steps were taken to set it up.

In mid-March 1994 the UN Secretary-General sent a fact-finding mission to investigate the 1993 coup attempt and subsequent massacres, but its findings, which were submitted to the Burundi Government in December, were not made public. The UN Secretary-General's representative mediated in talks between FRODEBU and opposition political parties. In March the UN Commission on Human Rights condemned and demanded an end to human rights abuses in Burundi. However, the Commission did not recommend any specific measures by the UN to help end the abuses. In May the UN Centre for Human Rights set up a human rights education program for judicial and law enforcement officials. In October the UN General Assembly authorized the deployment of human rights monitors, but none was sent.

An Organization of African Unity (OAU) monitoring mission was deployed, but it did not report publicly on its activities.

Army operations resulting in extrajudicial executions were reported from March onwards, initially in the northern suburbs of Bujumbura and later in other parts of the country. On 6 March soldiers massacred more than 200 unarmed Hutu – women, men and children – during a night raid on the Kamenge zone of Bujumbura. The army denied responsibility but witnesses pointed to the use of bayonets and the swiftness of the killings as evidence of military involvement. An army officer's identity card was reportedly found at the site. Army commanders had ignored calls made by the government the previous day for the security forces to leave the area and stop attacks on civilians.

On 21 March the security forces again entered Kamenge, and its neighbouring suburbs of Cibitoke and Kinama, to disarm Hutu gangs. Soldiers sealed off the area and there were widespread reports that several hundred unarmed victims, including children, were extrajudicially executed by the army.

In September the security forces again rounded up several hundred civilians in Kamenge for "screening" to identify those suspected of involvement in armed opposition. The bodies of 13 of those rounded up, including Alexis Bandyatuyaga, a journalist, and Dr Innocent Sindayihebura were later found near Bujumbura airport. Witnesses said the bodies had been dumped by soldiers driving gendarmerie vehicles. The bodies showed signs of torture: several had had their skulls crushed.

The security forces carried out further killings outside Bujumbura. For example, on 4 October, 20 civilians were reportedly rounded up in Cibitoke province and herded into houses which were set ablaze. This followed a rebel attack in which nine soldiers were wounded. In Muramvya province, Kivoga commune, at least 17 civilians, including children, were reportedly executed by soldiers on 26 October.

Tutsi civilians killed more than 50 Hutu in Bujumbura between 31 January and 5 February. Members of the armed forces were deployed but failed to stop the violence. Further killings by armed Tutsi followed throughout the year. For example, Tutsi students at a school in Matana commune, Bururi province, attacked a group of Hutu farmers on 7 May, killing at least four. Soldiers reportedly stood by and watched. Similar incidents were reported between April and October from other provinces, including Ngozi, Muramvya and Kayanza.

There were also killings of Tutsi by Hutu civilian gangs. At least 30 Tutsi villagers were reportedly killed one night in March in Tangara district, Ngozi province. The authorities reported several days later that more than 30 Hutu had been arrested in connection with the killings, although it was unclear whether any were formally charged.

In another attack in October, Hutu gangs reportedly killed several hundred Tutsi in Tangara district. These killings were followed by several mutual reprisals, culminating in the destruction of Tangara trading centre by Tutsi.

Further killings occurred in December

when an armed political group attacked the security forces in the northwest province of Cibitoke. Responsibility was claimed by the *Forces pour la défense de la démocratie* (FDD), Forces for the Defence of Democracy, the armed wing of the *Conseil national pour la défense de la démocratie* (CNDD), National Council for the Defence of Democracy, led by a former minister in the FRODEBU government, Leonard Nyangoma. Government forces reportedly carried out reprisal killings of unarmed Hutu civilians, forcing thousands to flee to neighbouring Zaire. FDD attacks and government force reprisals were also reported in southern Burundi.

Several hundred people, most of them Hutu, suspected on the basis of little or no evidence of supporting Hutu armed groups, were detained in the capital by the gendarmerie and were routinely held incommunicado, without being referred to the Procuracy, and tortured or beaten. Most were detained at the headquarters of the *Brigade spéciale de recherche* (BSR), the gendarmerie's Special Investigation Brigade in Bujumbura, before being transferred to Bujumbura's Mpimba central prison. Among those still held at the end of the year were Emile Bucumi and Sadiki Likango.

About 300 people, most of them Hutu, accused of responsibility for massacres of Tutsi civilians in late 1993, were arrested early in the year. They included Jocker Bandemibara who was held at the BSR, where he was severely ill-treated, and then transferred to Mpimba prison. Another group of Hutu composed of about 20 civil servants were detained in Gitega prison during May and reportedly tortured. Virtually no Tutsi, either soldiers or civilians, were detained on account of the killings of Hutu which also occurred in late 1993.

Dozens of people arrested by the security forces reportedly "disappeared". Nine people were reported to have "disappeared" after being arrested by the security forces on 29 April. Most were Hutu residents of Kamenge, including Denis Niragira and Pierre-Claver Ningarukye: one, Ngoyi, was a Zairian national. Five people "disappeared" in September after they were arrested in Bujumbura. The body of one of them, Jean-Baptiste Tugirisoni, was found a few days later.

Hundreds of thousands of refugees who had fled to Rwanda in October 1993 returned to Burundi because of the violence in Rwanda from April onwards. There was also a massive influx of refugees from Rwanda. There were reports of violence between groups of refugees, which the Burundi security forces failed to prevent. There were also reports that Burundi soldiers carried out or condoned killings of Rwandese Hutu refugees.

More than 100 Rwandese asylum-seekers, particularly men and boys, were killed on 11 June after arriving at Kiri, in the northeastern province of Kirundo. According to witnesses, the victims were forced by armed men in military uniforms to get into trucks which took them a short distance away, where they were killed by Tutsi civilians with machetes and axes. Several other incidents were reported in July in which dozens of Rwandese nationals were killed in Burundi.

Thirty-one Rwandese who had crossed into Burundi "disappeared" in Kayanza province on 13 July. They were reportedly taken away by Burundi soldiers and never seen again.

Throughout the year Amnesty International repeatedly appealed to the government of Burundi, political leaders and the security forces to stop perpetrating or condoning human rights violations and instead to condemn them. In a report published in May, *Burundi: Time for international action to end a cycle of mass murder*, Amnesty International called for an independent commission of inquiry into human rights violations and urged the international community to help Burundi implement measures to end the killings and prevent their recurrence. Amnesty International also expressed concern about arbitrary arrests and torture of detainees, and called on the authorities to make public the whereabouts of people who had "disappeared" and bring to justice any officials responsible for unlawful secret detentions.

Amnesty International urged the Special Session of the UN Commission on Human Rights convened in May to consider the mass killings in Rwanda to also consider the situation in Burundi, but it did not do so. When a clandestine radio station began broadcasting inflammatory messages in July, Amnesty International called on the international community to take action to prevent a repetition of the

86

human rights crisis which had occurred in Rwanda.

In July and August Amnesty International delegates visited Burundi. They found that the criminal justice system had all but collapsed and that hundreds of people were being killed in political violence each month. The delegates called for further international action immediately, including strengthening the OAU monitoring mission and deploying international observers to ensure effective and impartial investigations into human rights abuses.

Amnesty International referred to Burundi in two statements to the UN Commission on Human Rights in February and in its statement before the Special Session of the Commission in May.

CAMBODIA

One prisoner of conscience was detained in July. Nine Thai nationals were detained for three months before being charged and tried. Evidence emerged of illegal detention, torture, ill-treatment and extrajudicial execution at an illegal detention centre run by the Royal Cambodian Armed Forces (RCAF). At least 30 people were victims of suspected extrajudicial executions. Ethnic Vietnamese Cambodians were deliberately and arbitrarily killed by both the RCAF and forces of the *Partie* of Democratic Kampuchea (PDK or Khmer Rouge). The PDK committed grave human rights abuses throughout the year, including deliberate and arbitrary killings.

Civil war between the RCAF and forces of the PDK continued throughout the year, with heavy fighting during the dry season. The coalition government, led by First Prime Minister Prince Krompreah Norodom Ranariddh, the leader of the National United Front for an Independent, Neutral, Peaceful and Co-operative Cambodia (FUNCINPEC), and Second Prime Minister Hun Sen, leader of the Cambodian People's Party (CPP), made little progress in drafting new legislation. Proceedings in the National Assembly were delayed for several months while two CPP members, who had won seats in the 1993 election but then organized an attempt at secession, tried to retake their seats (see *Amnesty International Report 1994*). In July the two men, Prince Norodom Chakropong and General Sin Song, led a coup attempt in the capital, Phnom Penh. When the coup failed, Prince Norodom Chakropong left the country, after the intervention of his father, the head of state, King Norodom Sihanouk. Sin Song was placed under house arrest, but later escaped to Thailand. Following the coup attempt, the government put increasing pressure on journalists and human rights groups not to criticize members of the government or to refer to the attempted coup.

Several laws debated in the National Assembly raised serious human rights concerns. In June, following the breakdown of peace negotiations, the government closed down the office of the PDK in Phnom Penh and in July the National Assembly passed a bill to outlaw the PDK. This law was broadly phrased and there were fears that it could be applied arbitrarily to imprison any government opponent. In August an immigration law was passed which allows the authorities to confiscate travel and identity documents from "illegal immigrants". The law does not meet minimum human rights standards on freedom of movement, and there were concerns that it could be applied arbitrarily to forcibly exile Cambodia's ethnic Vietnamese minority. A draft Press Law approved by the Council of Ministers falls far short of minimum international human rights standards.

The UN Special Representative of the Secretary-General for Human Rights in Cambodia submitted an extensive report to the UN Commission for Human Rights in February, detailing human rights violations on Cambodia. In March the Commission adopted a resolution requesting that the Special Representative report to the

Commission in 1995, and that the Centre for Human Rights continue its work in Cambodia. The Special Representative made four visits to Cambodia in 1994, and the UN High Commissioner for Human Rights visited Cambodia in July. In December the UN General Assembly adopted a resolution expressing "grave concern about the serious violations of human rights as detailed by the Special Representative" including abuses by the PDK.

Nguon Non, editor of the Khmer language newspaper *Morning News*, was arrested in July in connection with articles about the failed coup attempt. He was a prisoner of conscience. Nguon Non had already been arrested and charged in March, in connection with articles criticizing the Governor of Phnom Penh, but was later released. He was charged under the 1992 State of Cambodia Press Law, passed by the former communist government, which allows the authorities to shut down newspapers and imprison publishers. His trial was halted in July by the judge following a telephone call to the court from an unknown party, and Nguon Non was taken back to prison. Following interventions by the UN Special Representative of the Secretary-General for Human Rights in Cambodia and the UN High Commissioner for Human Rights, he was released on unconditional bail in August. His trial had not resumed by the end of the year.

Nine political prisoners were detained in July for alleged involvement in the attempted coup. The men, all Thai nationals, were arrested at Phnom Penh airport as they tried to leave the country. Initially held under arrest at a hotel, they were transferred in August to T3 prison in Phnom Penh, where they were detained in poor conditions and denied full access to their diplomatic representatives. In October, following international concern about their cases, all nine men, and two Cambodian nationals, were charged with illegally transporting weapons and participating in a plot to overthrow the government. Following a hasty trial, the nine were all found guilty, given suspended sentences and allowed to return home.

Evidence emerged in 1994 of the existence of an illegal detention centre at Cheu Kmau, a remote location in Battambang province, operated by the RCAF. At least 35 people had been illegally detained at Cheu Kmau between August and December

1993. All had been killed. During 1994 at least 19 people were illegally detained at Cheu Kmau, one of whom was severely injured in an explosion while being forced to clear landmines. A 17-year-old girl held near Cheu Kmau was repeatedly raped by soldiers in 1994. In spite of detailed investigations by the UN Centre for Human Rights Field Office in Cambodia, and requests for government action from the UN Special Representative of the Secretary-General for Human Rights in Cambodia and others, no action was taken to bring the soldiers responsible to justice. A Special Commission established by the two prime ministers to investigate the case attempted to discredit the findings of UN investigators and concluded that no one was illegally detained at Cheu Kmau. In September a five-year-old girl was shot in the leg during an attack on the family of one of the staff members of the UN Field Office. UN staff believed the attack was politically motivated and linked to the Cheu Kmau investigations. No one was brought to justice for the attack.

A prison officer, who had been arrested by the UN Transitional Authority in Cambodia (UNTAC) in 1993 for allegedly killing prisoners and then handed over to the Cambodian Government, was released without charge by the authorities (see *Amnesty International Report 1994*). Officials investigating the case concluded that "there was no evidence against him", despite eye-witness reports that he had shot dead seven prisoners. He returned to a high-ranking job in the police force in Prey Veng province. A second prison officer arrested by UNTAC in 1993 and handed over to the Cambodian authorities was found guilty of torturing prisoners, fined and sentenced to one year's imprisonment.

At least 30 unarmed people were deliberately killed during the year, some of them victims of extrajudicial executions. Some extrajudicial executions took place in the context of armed conflict between the RCAF and the PDK. For example, in May a PDK prisoner of war captured by RCAF troops in Battambang was decapitated by soldiers and his head was displayed on the wall of the regional military headquarters. Reports of at least three other such killings could not be confirmed.

Civilians were also the victims of extrajudicial executions. Hun Sokea, a villager,

88

was killed in February following a land dispute near Phnom Penh which had been violently broken up by the security forces. Hun Sokea was walking along a road near the disputed area when the military police ordered him to stop. When he did not obey, four or five military police officers beat him with rifle butts and shot him in the face as he lay on the ground. The military authorities claimed that Hun Sokea was a rebel who had attempted to "seize their guns". No one was brought to justice for the killing.

In April, four RCAF soldiers entered a village in Kratie province and demanded food from the villagers. When none was produced, the soldiers started shooting at the villagers, killing three, including a seven-year-old boy, and wounding three others. Local human rights monitors reported the attack and in June three of the four soldiers who took part in the attack were tried and sentenced to between 10 and 13 years' imprisonment. The fourth soldier escaped arrest and had not been apprehended by the end of the year.

Government critics were also killed. Newspaper editor Nuon Chan was shot dead in the street in Phnom Penh in September shortly after receiving verbal warnings from several government ministers, including the First Prime Minister, about the content of his newspaper, *Voice of Khmer Youth*. The government condemned the killing, but warned that "a number of local newspapers … have frequently published … articles groundlessly accusing the [government's] leaders, personnel and officials of being involved in this or that issue". Two local human rights organizations which condemned the killing and called for a full investigation were warned by the government that they could be shut down or taken to court. In another attack that was apparently politically motivated, journalist Chan Dara was shot dead in Kompong Cham province in December.

Local police were implicated in killings which appeared to be politically motivated. In April, four FUNCINPEC police officers were disembowelled and killed in Kompong Speu province. Available evidence suggested that provincial police officials linked to the CPP ordered these killings. No one was held to account for the killings.

Attacks on members of the ethnic Viet-

namese minority, the most vulnerable group in the country, continued to be reported. In a typical attack in April, 13 ethnic Vietnamese civilians, nine of them children, were killed in an attack on the village of Piem So, Kandal province. Five armed men entered the village and threw grenades at a group of children playing in the street. They then attacked a woman and shot dead the village headman. Seven people arrested in connection with the attack were later released in spite of clear evidence against them, and no further investigations were conducted. In August, four ethnic Vietnamese people and two Khmers were killed in an attack on a village in Kandal province. Despite evidence pointing to the involvement of RCAF soldiers, no one was brought to justice for the killings.

The PDK was responsible for grave human rights abuses throughout the year, including arbitrary killings and hostage-taking. The fate and whereabouts of some of those held by the PDK remained unknown. Amnesty International learned that in December 1993 a convoy of unarmed soldiers from the former Khmer People's National Liberation Armed Forces (KPNLAF) was ambushed by PDK soldiers. At least three people were killed and a further 17, including several KPNLAF officers, were captured. Their fate and whereabouts remained unknown.

In July PDK soldiers attacked a train in Kampot province, killing at least nine people and capturing more than 100 others, including three ethnic Vietnamese civilians and three foreign tourists. Most were released soon afterwards, but up to 16 people were held in illegal detention for three months. PDK radio broadcasts indicated that they would hold the Western tourists for as long as certain Western governments continued to assist the RCAF. In November the bodies of the three Western hostages were discovered. The second in command of the unit which had carried out the attack on the train defected to the RCAF with most of his troops. No attempt was made by the government to bring him or any of his soldiers to justice.

PDK forces launched arbitrary attacks on villages throughout the year in which an unknown number of civilians were killed and injured. In October PDK soldiers in Battambang province killed more than 40 civilians who were cutting bamboo. The civilians were forced to walk for two days before being shot dead. PDK forces also captured village officials in Siem Reap province and held them for "re-education". Hundreds of civilians were forced to work as porters and labourers for the PDK during the last three months of 1994.

In January Amnesty International published a report, *Kingdom of Cambodia: Human rights and the new Constitution*, detailing the organization's concern that the new Constitution excludes certain sections of the population, notably the ethnic Vietnamese, from full human rights guarantees under the law. The organization also expressed concern about the human rights implications of the draft immigration law. In May Amnesty International called upon both sides fighting the civil war to respect at least minimum international standards for the treatment of prisoners.

During the year Amnesty International called for a full investigation into reported extrajudicial executions at Cheu Kmau in Battambang province and elsewhere. It also appealed for the release of Nguon Non and for the fair and prompt trial of nine Thai nationals detained in connection with the attempted coup. The government did not respond to most of the organization's appeals. An Amnesty International delegation visited Cambodia in November to discuss the organization's concerns with government ministers.

CAMEROON

Dozens of critics and opponents of the government were detained without charge or trial; most were prisoners of conscience. Torture, including severe beatings, by police and gendarmes continued to be routine and prison conditions remained harsh. More than 50 civilians were extrajudicially executed by government forces in the far north of the country.

Opposition to the government of President Paul Biya continued as salaries and living standards dropped sharply; the government responded to strikes by public service employees, including teachers, with arrests and dismissals. In November President Biya announced that public debate on constitutional reform, previously abandoned, would resume. A constitutional committee was established in December to discuss amendments to the Constitution proposed by the government. Members of opposition political parties, critical of the committee's terms of reference, refused to participate. Earlier in the year the English-speaking community had advocated a federal system of government.

Conflict, including outbreaks of fighting, continued between the Kotoko and Shua Arab communities in the far north and dozens of people died in clashes in late December 1993 and early January 1994. Government forces deployed to curb violence between the two communities and also to prevent attacks by armed robbers were themselves responsible for human rights abuses. Hundreds of civilians sought refuge in Chad and Nigeria. A long-standing border dispute with neighbouring Nigeria over the Bakassi peninsula in the southwest intensified early in the year, prompting sporadic fighting between Cameroonian and Nigerian armed forces.

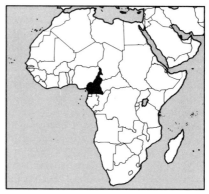

Dozens of critics and opponents of the government, who included members of opposition political parties, trade unionists and journalists, were detained, usually without charge or trial. Most were prisoners of conscience. The security forces regularly kept suspected government opponents in custody for longer than the 72 hours allowed by law before they were released or referred to a judicial authority.

Among members of opposition political parties arrested was Janvier Deny, a taxi-driver and treasurer of the local section of the *Union des forces démocratiques du Cameroun* (UFDC), Union of Cameroon Democratic Forces, who was arrested by

90 police on 12 January in Ebolowa, Southern Province. He denied any knowledge of a report found in his taxi of a meeting organized by teachers, at that time on strike; his arrest appeared to be an attempt to intimidate opposition political parties before local government elections scheduled to take place in the following months but subsequently postponed. He was held without charge or trial under successive administrative detention orders until his release on 19 February.

Members of the opposition *Union nationale pour la démocratie et le progrès* (UNDP), National Union for Democracy and Progress, were detained following an incident in Maroua, Far-North Province, on 30 July during which one person was killed and several wounded. There were clashes when government minister Hamadou Mustapha, also a UNDP member, was attacked with stones following his arrival in Maroua allegedly by some UNDP members who criticized him for remaining in President Biya's government. Some people were apparently arrested during the clashes but most were arrested at their homes later that day or in the following days. They included Hamadou Adji, president of the local section of the UNDP. Twenty-eight people were charged with complicity in joint acts of looting, assault occasioning death, obstruction of the public highway and causing slight bodily harm. In November a court ordered the provisional release of 14 of them, but the prosecuting authorities appealed against this and all remained held at the end of the year. Most of the detainees appeared to have been detained solely because they opposed participation of UNDP members in the government.

Dozens of supporters of the Social Democratic Front (SDF) were arrested following calls in October by the SDF for demonstrations to mark the anniversary of the 1992 presidential election, in which SDF leader John Fru Ndi was narrowly defeated, and in protest against deteriorating living standards. In the capital, Yaoundé, 12 SDF supporters, including a woman, were arrested on 15 October and held in police custody without charge for three days. About 100 others were reported to have been arrested and beaten by police on 18 October in Fundong, North-West Province; about 30 were subsequently transferred to a police station in Bamenda where they received further beatings. They were released uncharged on 27 October.

In November, six leaders of opposition political parties which had recently formed a new coalition – the Allied Front for Change – were arrested by police during a peaceful demonstration in Yaoundé. They were released after questioning.

The government attempted to suppress trade union protest against salary cuts by arrests and large-scale dismissals. A strike by teachers had begun in November 1993; in January, 11 teachers, including a woman, all members of the *Syndicat national autonome de l'Enseignement secondaire* (SNAES), National Autonomous Union of Secondary Education, were detained without charge by police for six days. Further arrests of trade unionists occurred in March during a strike by other public service employees. Cyprian Lionel Fofuh-Fru, president of the Cameroon Public Servants Union (CAPSU), was arrested on 1 March in Bamenda because of his peaceful trade union activities and held until the following day. Che John Njiyang, a treasury employee, was also arrested on 1 March after protesting to police about Cyprian Fofuh-Fru's detention; his wife Mary Lum Njiyang was arrested later the same day and both were held until 4 March.

Despite a government announcement in September that press restrictions would be eased, harassment of journalists and confiscation of newspapers continued. Several independent newspapers had been suspended earlier in the year. On 7 March copies of *Le Messager* carrying an article about the border dispute with Nigeria were confiscated; its editor, Pius Njawe, was questioned by police the following day. Ndzana Seme, director of the weekly *Le Nouvel Indépendant*, was detained for three days in January; he was again arrested on 14 October in Yaoundé for publishing articles questioning the activities of President Biya and Jean Fochivé, Secretary of State for Internal Security. He was released on 23 December after being convicted of defamation of the head of state and sentenced to one year's imprisonment, suspended for three years, and a fine. He had been beaten in police custody before being transferred to prison.

Torture, including severe beatings, of both political detainees and of criminal suspects by the police and gendarmerie remained routine. Some victims died as a result of their injuries. The frequency of beatings of detainees, including on the soles of their feet, was acknowledged publicly at a training seminar for law enforcement officials, including police, gendarmes and prison officers, organized in July by the Comité national des droits de l'homme et des libertés, National Commission for Human Rights and Freedoms, which had been inaugurated by President Biya in 1992.

Students arrested on 12 January following disturbances at the University of Yaoundé were reportedly beaten by police and then taken to the "Americanos", a detention centre outside Yaoundé which had become notorious for ill-treatment. They were reportedly tortured for several hours before being released.

Che John Njiyang and Mary Lum Njiyang, arrested in March (see above), were beaten and held in a small, crowded cell with male criminal suspects who were stripped to their underclothes. When Simon Nkwenti, Secretary General of CAPSU, went to the police station to inquire about them, he too was arrested and beaten unconscious; he was released the following day.

In April Desiré Nkeu was arrested by soldiers in Edéa, Littoral Province, accused of burglary. He died the same day at a military barracks after he had been severely beaten.

When a lawyer from the Public Prosecutor's office visited a police station in Yaoundé in October to inspect detainees he was himself held for five hours, stripped and beaten. Six police officers were subsequently arrested. However, the authorities were not known to have investigated other reports of torture and ill-treatment by the police and gendarmerie.

Prison conditions remained harsh and there were reports of cruel, inhuman or degrading forms of punishment for even minor infringements of regulations by prisoners. For example, in the Central Prison in Douala, prisoners were reportedly held naked in punishment cells without natural light or sanitary facilities. Others were reportedly punished by beatings or being chained and suspended upside-down. Large numbers of prisoners died because of lack of proper diet and medical care. For example, as many as 150

prisoners died in the Central Prison in Maroua during the year.

Soldiers deployed to restore order in areas affected by the conflict between the Kotoko and Shua were responsible for the arrest, torture and unlawful killing of Shua. In January several Shua, including traditional chiefs, were arrested after nine members of the security forces were killed in an ambush in the area of Logone Birni near the border with Chad in the Department of Logone and Shari. The Shua were arrested even though the government claimed that Chadian dissidents were responsible for the killings. Some of those arrested appeared to have been detained after being denounced to the security forces by rival Kotoko. One of those arrested, Malloum Eli, was reported to have died after torture at a military barracks. Other Shua were arrested on 21 January at Afadé, transferred to Kousséri and then to Waza. They included Haroun Djidda and Allakhou Mahmat who were reported to have died after being beaten and tortured with cigarette lighters and burning plastic bags, and Issa Mahmat who was believed to have been shot dead on 23 January.

On 17 February government forces extrajudicially executed more than 50 Shua villagers at Karena on the shores of Lake Chad, apparently in revenge for the killing of a soldier. The day before, the village chief and a soldier had been killed in an incident involving armed bandits. During a funeral ceremony for the village chief, soldiers surrounded the village, fired indiscriminately at villagers and set fire to their homes. Nine women and 35 children, including babies, were among those killed. Many of the victims were burned to death. More than 90 others were wounded. Despite the gravity of the incident, there was no official inquiry and none of those responsible was known to have been suspended from duty, investigated or brought to trial.

Two Chadian lorry-drivers were shot dead in July by a gendarme who had demanded money from them near Mora, Far-North Province. In a public letter to the Cameroonian authorities, the Chadian Government condemned the harassment and ill-treatment of Chadian nationals by security forces in Cameroon.

Nigerian nationals resident in the disputed territory of the Bakassi peninsula reported harassment, beatings and killings

92

by Cameroonian gendarmes.

Although courts were reported to have continued passing death sentences, no details of sentences imposed during the year were received. There were no executions.

In a report published in January, *Cameroon: 1993 – Political arrests and torture continue*, Amnesty International described the continuing pattern of human rights violations in Cameroon and urged action by the government to end detention without trial, torture and extrajudicial executions. In February Amnesty International called for the unconditional release of Janvier Deny. Amnesty International also condemned the torture and killing of Shua Arabs, in particular the massacre at Karena, and called for those responsible to be brought to justice. A reply from the Chief of Staff of the Armed Forces stated that soldiers had been convicted and sentenced to death for unlawful killings; however, this appeared to refer to killings of Shua in Kousséri in 1992 (see *Amnesty International Report 1994*). In March the UN Human Rights Committee deplored the many cases of illegal detention, torture, death sentences and extrajudicial execution in Cameroon. In July the UN Human Rights Committee upheld a complaint submitted by writer and former prisoner of conscience Albert Mukong that he had been arbitrarily detained from 1988 until 1989 and again in 1990 and subjected to cruel, inhuman and degrading treatment.

CANADA

Several members of the Canadian peace-keeping forces stationed in Somalia in 1993 were court-martialled in connection with the death under torture of a Somali

teenager. **Canada was found to be in breach of its obligations under international human rights law for its extradition in 1991 of a capital murder defendant to the USA where he faced the death penalty.**

Eight soldiers from the Canadian Airborne Regiment were charged in connection with the death in March 1993 of Shidane Abukar Arone in Belet Huem, Somalia, where they were stationed as part of the UN peace-keeping forces. Shidane Abukar Arone, aged 16, was blindfolded, beaten and tortured to death after he had been caught trying to enter the regiment's compound. One of the soldiers was sentenced to five years' imprisonment for manslaughter at a court martial in March; another was sentenced to 90 days' imprisonment and demotion for negligence; and a third received a reprimand. Others were acquitted or had the charges against them dropped and one case was pending at the end of the year. Appeals by the authorities against the acquittals or seeking stiffer penalties were pending at the end of the year, as were appeals by some of those convicted.

In November the government ordered a public, civilian inquiry into the conduct of the Canadian peace-keeping forces during their 1993 mission in Somalia. It said the inquiry – expected to take place after completion of criminal proceedings – would also investigate allegations that officers had ordered the destruction of evidence of human rights abuses against Somalis.

Amnesty International had called on the Canadian authorities in May 1993 to hold an independent public inquiry into the case of Shidane Abukar Arone and two shootings of Somalis and to bring those responsible to justice (see *Amnesty International Report 1994*, **Somalia** entry).

On 26 January the UN Human Rights Committee found that Canada had violated its obligations under the International Covenant on Civil and Political Rights (ICCPR) when in 1991 it extradited Charles Ng to California, USA, where he faced a capital murder charge, without seeking assurances that he would not be executed if convicted. At the time of his extradition, California's sole method of execution was the gas chamber, which the Committee said constituted cruel and unusual punishment prohibited under the ICCPR. The Committee expressed concern that Charles Ng was extradited while it was reviewing his case, and asked Canada to do whatever it could to prevent his execution if he was convicted. Amnesty International had appealed to the Canadian Government not to extradite Charles Ng without seeking assurances that he would not be executed (see *Amnesty International Report 1992*).

In January 1994 Amnesty International learned from the Quebec Ministry of Justice that four of the six complaints investigated by the *Commissaire à la déontologie policière*, a police ethics commissioner, in relation to ill-treatment of Mohawk Indians by members of the Quebec police during a land dispute at Oka in 1990, had been dismissed because of lack of evidence (see *Amnesty International Reports 1991* and *1992*). The Ministry stated that the complainants had been informed of the findings, but had not pursued their complaints further.

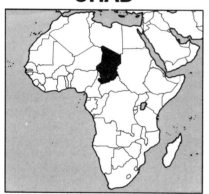

CHAD

More than 200 unarmed civilians were extrajudicially executed by government forces in areas where armed political groups were active. Several hundred civilians suspected of supporting armed government opponents were detained and some were still held without trial at the end of the year. Government opponents and human rights activists were detained briefly; some received death threats. Torture was reported. Over 20 people reportedly "disappeared". Two people remained under sentence of death and four people were sentenced to death, three *in absentia*. No executions were reported. An armed political group was responsible for the deliberate and arbitrary killing of scores of defenceless civilians.

In March a committee set up in December 1993 by the Higher Transitional Council submitted a draft new constitution, an electoral code and a charter for political parties to a commission composed of representatives of political parties and independent organizations. The texts had not been approved by the government or adopted by the Higher Transitional Council by the end of the year. Legislative and presidential elections which were announced for April 1994 were not held. In December President Idriss Déby announced that legislative elections would be held in April 1995.

A National Human Rights Committee was established in October 1994. The government decree setting up the committee stated that it was to advise the government on human rights and to bring laws into line with the Charter for Human Rights adopted by the National Conference in April 1993.

The August session of the UN Sub-Commission on Prevention of Discrimination and Protection of Minorities strongly condemned massive and persistent human rights violations committed by the security forces, including the Republican Guard, and asked the authorities to put into effect measures to promote human rights.

In May, after the International Court of Justice ruled that the Aouzou strip belonged to Chad, Libyan troops withdrew from the territory along Chad's northern border which they had occupied since 1973.

After several years of armed conflict in the south of the country, in September a peace accord was signed in the neighbouring Central African Republic between the Chadian Government and the armed political group, the *Comité de Sursaut National pour la Paix et la Démocratie* (CSNPD), Committee of National Revival for Peace and Democracy. The *Forces Armées pour la République Fédérale* (FARF), Armed Forces for a Federal Republic, a group which split from the CSNPD, did not take part in the peace negotiations.

In December President Idriss Déby decreed an amnesty for all detainees and political exiles with the exception of his predecessor, Hissein Habré.

In areas where armed political groups were active, notably in Logone Occidental and Oriental provinces in the south and around the town of Abéché in the north-east, such groups attacked and killed both soldiers and civilians. More than 250 de-fenceless local people were killed in reprisals by the armed forces. Some vic-tims were shot dead in the presence of witnesses; others were seized by the se-curity forces, then tortured and killed. Despite the findings of local human rights organizations that the security forces had extrajudicially executed civilians, the gov-ernment failed to take action against the killers.

At least 200 unarmed civilians were ex-trajudicially executed in January by gov-ernment forces including the Republican Guard, an army unit directly responsible to President Idriss Déby. The killings fol-lowed an attack on the military barracks in Abéché by members of an armed group known as the *Front National du Tchad* (FNT), Chad National Front, led by Dr Al Harris. The FNT had signed a peace treaty with the government in June 1992, but its provisions were apparently never imple-mented. There were reports of widespread looting and rape by government soldiers and by the Republican Guard. Soldiers reportedly rampaged through areas of Abéché, killing unarmed civilians sus-pected of supporting the FNT. The authorit-ies announced that 30 people had died in the attack, mostly FNT combatants. How-ever, an investigation carried out in Febru-ary by members of several Chadian human rights organizations concluded that at least 200 unarmed civilians had been extrajudicially executed by government forces within a few days of the FNT attack. Two children of Abou Annour, the village chief of Kabartou, were among the vic-tims.

In June a number of civilians in the sub-prefecture of Bousso were killed by government forces after an altercation be-tween the army and the CSNPD. Several people accused of colluding with the rebels were arrested and later released.

Further extrajudicial executions were reported in the south between 12 and 14 August, after fighting in Logone Occiden-tal province between the army and the FARF. In reprisal for the deaths of five sol-diers killed in action on 12 August, the army burned down several villages in the district of Kaga, assembled the inhabi-tants, then killed more than 25 of them. One pregnant woman and several children were among the victims. In the village of Kaga the head of a district and a village chief were tied up and beaten by soldiers.

Early in the year reports emerged of the extrajudicial execution in 1993 of Adoum Acyl, former commander in chief of the army, a day before the killing of Abbas Koty to whom he was reportedly closely allied (see *Amnesty International Report 1994*). Members of the Republican Guard tried to shoot him but their guns report-edly jammed; they then ran him over with a vehicle.

Government soldiers arrested several hundred local people apparently sus-pected of colluding or sympathizing with the FNT combatants after the attack on Abéché in January. Many were released within days, including Mahamat Yachoub, a 72-year-old imam. Other civilians were reportedly released in early February after President Idriss Déby visited Abéché.

Peaceful opponents of the government and human rights activists were detained for short periods. They appeared to be prisoners of conscience. For example, Ngarlejy Yorangar le Mohiban, a journalist and director of a satirical publication, was arrested on 3 March and held for four days. He was accused of spreading false information about President Déby. Simon Béassingar, former prefect of Kanem, was arrested and held for 16 days in the police station in Sarh before being released. He was accused of inciting the inhabitants of Moundou to protest against a visit of Pres-ident Déby to Logone Occidental. Two members of the Chadian League of Human Rights – Enoch Djondang and Abou Laoukara – received death threats from suspected government agents.

There were numerous other arrests of people accused of opposing the govern-ment, none of whom was referred to the courts. It was impossible to establish if the accusations against them were genuine or fabricated. For example, Zakaria Garba, a member of the Prime Minister's political party, was detained in July by the Intelli-gence Service and accused of planning a coup. He was released without charge after 18 days.

In July Dr Abdelazziz Kadouck, a gyn-aecologist at N'Djaména hospital, and Mahamat Koty, brother of Abbas Koty, were arrested by the National Intelligence Service and the Republican Guard on the grounds that they were members of an opposition group. They were held incommunicado in two different secret detention centres and tortured. In October both were held at the headquarters of the Intelligence Service and later Dr Abdelazziz Kadouck was transferred to N'Djaména hospital for medical treatment. In December they were released as a result of the amnesty.

In October several members of an opposition party were arrested when President Déby visited the town of Mao, Kanem. Some were beaten at the time of the arrest. They were released without charge after eight days.

Eight civilians detained in 1993 and accused of planning to overthrow the government remained in detention until they were released as a result of the amnesty at the end of the year. They appeared to have been held purely on account of their contact with Abbas Koty. Those released included Bichara Digui and El Hadj Ahmat Gueou.

Torture of detainees was reported in areas of counter-insurgency operations and also in the capital, N'Djaména. Young children and old people were among those reportedly tortured by security forces in Abéché following the FNT attack in January. The victims included eight-year-old Abdoulaye Hissein. An elderly woman, Atcha Issaka, died as a result of ill-treatment by soldiers. Izedine Ibrahim and Anour Ousmane, two farmers, were reported to have been hit on the face and to have each lost an eye. In the nearby village of Hayam-Matar, women were reported to have been raped by soldiers.

At least 19 people who were abducted from their houses in Abéché by soldiers in January were unaccounted for by the end of the year; they had apparently "disappeared". One alleged supporter of Abbas Koty arrested in October 1993, Koché Issaka, was also reported to have "disappeared" from custody in 1994.

Two members of the security forces convicted of murder in 1992 remained under sentence of death (see *Amnesty International Report 1994*). In November the criminal court sitting at Abéché passed four death sentences. Three of the accused were tried *in absentia*. The four were accused of belonging to an armed group which killed several people in a market place in Gniguilim in August 1993. There was no right of appeal to a higher court,

and one of the accused, Yachoub Issaka, faced imminent public execution at the end of the year.

Armed opposition groups, particularly the CSNPD, were responsible for deliberate and arbitrary killings of civilians. At the end of June the CSNPD shot and killed scores of unarmed civilians and burned several villages in the region of Ba-Illi in southern Chad. The victims included the village chief, some shepherds, a young schoolchild at the Koranic school and a nine-year-old girl.

In April Amnesty International submitted information about its concerns in Chad for UN review under a procedure established by the Economic and Social Council Resolutions 728F/1503, for confidential consideration of communications about human rights violations.

Amnesty International continued to appeal to the authorities to take steps to halt extrajudicial executions, including investigating reports and bringing those responsible to justice. No response was received.

CHILE

Two journalists and a human rights lawyer were prosecuted by military courts. Cases of torture by the security forces were reported. Military courts continued to close investigations into past human rights violations, but at least 18 officers were convicted for such crimes by the civilian courts. At least eight people died in circumstances suggesting they might have been victims of extrajudicial executions.

President Eduardo Frei Ruiz-Tagle, who was elected in December 1993, took office in March 1994 and replaced Patricio

96

Aylwin. Tension between the government and the military over past human rights violations resurfaced in April, when General Rodolfo Stange, Director General of the *carabineros*, refused a government request that he should resign after a civilian court recommended that he be prosecuted for obstructing an investigation into the murder of three members of the Communist Party in 1985 (see below).

The *Corporación Nacional de Reparación y Reconciliación*, National Corporation for Reparation and Reconciliation, continued to be informed of people who "disappeared" or were killed under the former military government which ruled Chile from 1973 to 1990. The Corporation's mandate was further extended until the end of 1995 (see *Amnesty International Report 1993*). By the end of 1994 the total number of people who had been killed or "disappeared" under the military government was officially acknowledged to be more than 3,000. Seventy-three bodies exhumed from clandestine graves in a Santiago cemetery were identified during the year. Most had apparently been extrajudicially executed. Among them were officials of the late President Salvador Allende's government who had been arrested by the security forces immediately after the September 1973 military coup (see *Amnesty International Report 1993*). None of those responsible for the killings was brought to justice.

·A proposal to extend the scope of the death penalty introduced in 1992 had not been considered in Congress by the end of the year (see *Amnesty International Report 1994*).

The government signed the Inter-American Convention on the Forced Disappearance of Persons in June, but had not ratified it by the end of the year.

In mid-January Juan Andrés Lagos and Francisco Herreros, director and editor respectively of *El Siglo* magazine, were briefly rearrested. They faced trial by a military court for publicly accusing the police of corruption in 1992 (see *Amnesty International Report 1994*). They were released on bail and had not been tried by the end of the year. In April Héctor Salazar Ardiles, a human rights lawyer, was charged by a military court with inciting sedition because he had criticized *carabineros* for their role in the 1985 killing of three members of the Communist

Party (see below). The case was closed in October by the Military Appeals Court but was reopened in December.

In October a military court recommended that navy captain Humberto Palmara Iribarne should be imprisoned for up to three years, for publishing a book dealing with the military's role in human rights violations. His appeal was under review at the end of the year.

All but one of the 10 remaining prisoners convicted under the former military government of politically motivated offences were released (see *Amnesty International Report 1994*). Some were sent into exile. Six other people with outstanding arrest warrants from that time were arrested after they presented themselves to the authorities. Three, including Sergio Buschmann, had returned from abroad. They were still awaiting a decision on their petition for release at the end of the year.

At least 120 people were serving prison sentences for politically motivated offences committed since the end of the military government. In February, 42 of them were transferred to a high security prison in Santiago. Many were tortured and ill-treated during the transfer. For example, Ariel Sáenz was seriously injured by prison guards who reportedly kicked and beat him with sabres and batons while he was lying on the floor with six other political prisoners. Ariel Sáenz, whose injuries were confirmed by a doctor, was released on bail in September. He had been arrested in November 1993 and tortured by members of *investigaciones*, the civilian police.

At least 11 other cases of torture by the security forces were reported. On 12 March Patricio Fuentes Zamorano, aged 16, was arrested without warrant at his home in Santiago by *carabineros*. He was forced into a vehicle and taken to a nearby detention centre, where he was allegedly beaten to confess to a crime he did not commit. Later that day he was taken back home and beaten again in front of relatives. His 13-year-old sister Silvia Fuentes Zamorano was also beaten. Patricio Fuentes Zamorano was released without charge a few days later.

Hugo Fernández Eguiluz, aged 73, was arrested without warrant in Santiago by *carabineros* on 7 April. He was taken to a police station, where he was reportedly beaten and semi-asphyxiated with a plastic bag. After his release without charge later that day he required medical treatment for his injuries.

On 29 April Valeria Baquedano Parra was arrested without warrant by *carabineros* in Santiago together with her three daughters and her grand-daughter. They were taken to a police station, where Valeria Baquedano Parra was beaten and sexually molested in front of her relatives, allegedly because her husband had lodged complaints against some of the officers from that police station. She was released days later without charge.

Few of those responsible for these and other cases of torture and ill-treatment were suspended or prosecuted. However, eight members of the police were under investigation at the end of the year in connection with the arbitrary arrest and torture of Tania María Cordeiro Vaz who was arrested in March 1993 and released without charge in March 1994 (see *Amnesty International Report 1994*).

In November the UN Committee against Torture addressed the case of Chile. While acknowledging that there had been improvements, the Committee recommended effective measures to end the practice of torture by some branches of the security forces, especially the *carabineros*, and the adoption of legal reforms to limit the scope of military jurisdiction in cases of human rights violations.

At least 18 people, many of them officials, were sentenced by civilian courts for human rights violations committed under the military government, despite the fact that military courts continued to claim jurisdiction over human rights cases, and to close cases covered by the 1978 Amnesty Law (see *Amnesty International Report 1993*). In April the Supreme Court ordered the reopening of the case of Carmelo Soria, a Spanish-Chilean UN official tortured and murdered by government officials in Santiago in 1976. The case had been closed under the 1978 Amnesty Law by a military court in December 1993. In October a court of appeal sentenced two former police officers and a civilian for the 1974 abduction and "disappearance" of two Mapuche Indians near Temuco. The court ruled that the 1978 Amnesty Law was not applicable. The law has been applied to officials responsible for human rights violations committed before 1978,

but the court ruled that the crime of "disappearance" continues until the whereabouts of the victim are established.

In March a civilian judge sentenced 16 people, including police officers on active duty, for the 1985 abduction and killing of three members of the Communist Party (see *Amnesty International Reports 1986* and *1993*). His investigation was hampered by six high-ranking police officers including General Rodolfo Stange. The six were prosecuted by a military court, on the recommendation of a civilian judge, but the charges were dropped in June.

At least eight people died in circumstances suggesting they might have been extrajudicially executed by members of the security forces. Religious community workers Ricardo Meneses Traipe and Jaime Guarda Rocco were shot at close range and killed by two reportedly drunken *carabineros* in the streets of Santiago on 22 October. The officers were suspended and were awaiting trial at the end of the year. Three *carabineros* were indicted in January for the killing of José Araya Ortiz in September 1992, but the case was transferred to military courts in November.

Amnesty International continued to call for full investigations into human rights violations and for those responsible to be brought to justice. The organization also continued to call for the abolition of the death penalty.

CHINA

Hundreds of political dissidents and members of ethnic and religious groups were arbitrarily detained. Scores of them, including prisoners of conscience, were held without charge or trial or sentenced to terms of imprisonment after unfair trials. Thousands of prisoners of conscience and political prisoners arrested in previous years remained in prison. Torture and ill-treatment of prisoners were widely reported. At least 2,496 death sentences and 1,791 executions were recorded.

The authorities stated early in the year that "political stability" was essential to continued economic development, and during 1994 the repression of people perceived as threatening the established political order intensified. There was a

98

renewed crack-down on prominent dissenters and further repressive legislation was adopted. Two new laws came into force in January which banned certain religious activities. In July the government banned specific activities "endangering state security", increasing restrictions on freedom of expression and association.

Scores of political dissidents were arbitrarily detained throughout the year. Most of them, including prisoners of conscience, were held for months without charge and were still in prison at the end of the year.

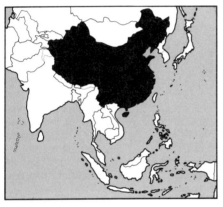

A crack-down on prominent dissidents and human rights activists started in Beijing and Shanghai in March 1994. Some of those detained in Beijing were apparently arrested for attempting to form an independent labour rights group, the League for the Protection of the Rights of the Working People (LPRWP), which was refused legal registration in March. Yuan Hongbing, a law professor at Beijing University, and Wang Jiaqi, a law graduate, were secretly detained on 2 March in Beijing. They had sponsored the LPRWP and had initiated a petition in January seeking justice in a case of alleged police brutality. Wang Jiaqi later escaped and fled the country. Zhou Guoqiang, a lawyer and a sponsor of the LPRWP, was detained on 3 March. Others associated with the LPRWP were detained between April and June. Yuan Hongbing, Zhou Guoqiang and other LPRWP sponsors remained held without charge at the end of the year.

Wei Jingsheng, a prominent dissident and former long-term prisoner of conscience, was detained on 1 April, apparently for making public comments about human rights issues, and remained held without charge at an undisclosed location at the end of the year. His assistant, Tong Yi, a professor of Chinese literature, was detained on 4 April and sentenced in December, without charge or trial, to two and a half years of "re-education through labour" for "disturbing public order". She was believed to have been detained because of her association with Wei Jingsheng.

Several human rights activists were detained in Shanghai. In March Zhu Fuming was reportedly arrested for his links with the Shanghai-based Association for Human Rights, which was formed in 1993 but refused legal registration. His whereabouts were unknown to his family. At least five other members of the association were detained in April and May and held without charge, including Li Guotao, the association's chairman, Yang Zhou, a founding member, Dai Xuezhong and Yang Qingheng. Bao Ge, another dissident associated with the Shanghai human rights group, was detained in June after sending an open letter to the government asking for a national human rights organization to be set up. Li Guotao, Yang Zhou, Bao Ge and Yang Qingheng were later sentenced without trial to three years' "re-education through labour". The fate of the others remained unknown.

Scores of members of religious groups were detained because of their peaceful religious activities. From late 1993 at least 30 Protestant and Catholic leaders were detained or placed under restriction in various regions of China. Father Zhu Tai, for instance, was reportedly detained in November 1993 while celebrating Roman Catholic mass in Zhangjiakou city, Hebei province. He was said to have been assigned to one year's "re-education through labour". Three members of a banned Protestant group known as the Shouters – Lin Zilong, aged 79, He Xiaxing and Han Kangrui – were reportedly arrested in Fujian province in December 1993. They remained in detention "under investigation for religious reasons". Pan Yiyuan, a Protestant house-church leader from Zhangzhou city in Fujian province, was arrested in February for his peaceful religious activities. He was believed to be still held without trial at Zhangzhou Detention Centre at the end of the year.

Repression of dissent continued in the Tibet Autonomous Region (TAR) as new security measures were taken to prevent nationalist demonstrations. On 10 May the authorities in Lhasa, capital of the TAR, declared a one-month period of heightened security measures before a series of anniversaries, including Tibetan religious festivals, in late May. By October at least 50 Tibetans, mostly monks and nuns, were reported to have been arrested, and many others beaten by armed police, following a series of peaceful pro-independence demonstrations in the TAR.

Demonstrators were arrested on 27 May in Lhasa during a peaceful protest by up to 200 Tibetan shopkeepers against official tax assessments. According to eye-witness accounts, 17 shopkeepers were kicked and beaten with rifle butts by armed police. They were reportedly released after officials at Gutsa Detention Centre refused to admit them because they were bleeding from head wounds. On the same night a number of suspected political activists, regarded as possible instigators of further protests, were rounded up from their homes.

Tibetan monks and nuns, who make up the majority of political prisoners in the TAR, were reported to have received heavy sentences for their pro-independence activities. In July, five Tibetan monks were sentenced to between 12 and 15 years' imprisonment for "counter-revolutionary sabotage". They had allegedly broken the name-plate on a government building and pasted up pro-independence slogans in eastern Tibet in March. The sentences were announced by a court in Pakshoe county, Chamdo Prefecture, at a show trial attended by several thousand local inhabitants, and broadcast on Tibetan television.

It was also reported during the year that 14 nuns imprisoned in Drapchi Prison, Lhasa, had their sentences increased in October 1993 by up to nine years for composing and recording pro-independence songs in prison. One of them, Phuntsog Nyidron, had her sentence extended to 17 years' imprisonment. The nuns had reportedly been arrested between 1989 and 1992 for taking part in pro-independence demonstrations.

The police continued to use "shelter and investigation", a form of administrative detention, to arbitrarily detain dissidents without charge, in violation of Chinese law. Professor Xiao Biguang, another co-founder of the Beijing-based

LPRWP, was arrested at his home on 12 April. He was reported to be administratively detained under a "shelter and investigation" order issued by the Beijing Public Security Bureau and was denied visits from his family.

Another form of administrative detention, "re-education through labour", was increasingly used to sentence dissidents without charge or trial to up to three years' detention. Such sentences were imposed on human rights activists, members of unapproved religious groups and other people branded as "troublemakers". The many cases reported included that of Yan Zhengxue, a painter from Beijing and deputy from a local People's Congress in Zhejiang province, who was assigned in April to two years' "re-education through labour" in a forced labour camp in Heilongjiang province, northern China. He was sentenced, without a trial, for allegedly stealing a bicycle – an unfounded accusation that followed his efforts to bring to justice three police officers who had assaulted him in 1993. In another case, Zhang Lin, a pro-democracy activist arrested in Beijing in May, was sentenced in August in his home province of Anhui to three years' "re-education through labour", reportedly because his marriage licence was "not in order" and he had too many contacts with foreign reporters.

Thousands of political prisoners detained or convicted after unfair trials in previous years remained held. In October the authorities acknowledged holding over 2,800 prisoners convicted of "counter-revolutionary" offences, a euphemism for political crimes. However, the figure is far below the real number of political prisoners: it excludes those held for political reasons but convicted of other offences, those held under various forms of administrative detention without charge or trial, and those detained for long periods pending trial. Among cases previously unknown which came to light during 1994 were those of several hundred political prisoners held at the Qinghe penal farm, near Tianjin, and at Beijing Prison No. 2, who had been convicted of political or criminal offences for their activities during the 1989 pro-democracy protests.

Those believed to be still held since the early 1980s included dissidents imprisoned for their involvement in the "democracy wall" movement of the late 1970s

100

(see previous *Amnesty International Reports*) and people convicted of "counter-revolutionary" offences for a variety of peaceful political or religious activities.

Some prisoners of conscience were released during 1994. Two Tibetan human rights monitors, Gendun Rinchen and Lobsang Yonten, who were arrested in May 1993 (see *Amnesty International Report 1994*), were released in January. In April and May, Wang Juntao and Chen Ziming, branded as "black hands" of the 1989 pro-democracy protests, were released on bail for medical treatment after serving over four years of their 13-year sentences. Others released included people jailed for their involvement in peaceful religious activities.

Political trials continued to fall far short of international fair trial standards. Extreme limitations were placed on the right to defence. Confessions, often extracted under torture, were accepted as evidence. Defendants had no right to call witnesses and had insufficient time and facilities to prepare their defence. Verdicts and sentences were routinely decided by the authorities before trial.

In April Ulaanshuvu, a former lecturer at Inner Mongolia University, was sentenced to five years' imprisonment for "counter-revolutionary propaganda and incitement", nearly three years after his arrest. His trial before the Hohhot Intermediate People's Court lasted less than 30 minutes and the charge against him had reportedly been changed. He was reportedly ill-treated in prison.

In another case, Gao Yu, a prominent freelance journalist held since October 1993, was sentenced to six years' imprisonment after a secret trial in November in which she had no legal representation. She was charged with "disclosing state secrets" in articles she had written for Hong Kong publications. During two previous hearings of her case, the court reportedly decided that there was insufficient evidence for conviction, but instead of acquitting her it returned the case to the procuracy for "further investigation".

A major political trial of 15 prisoners of conscience began in Beijing in July. The 15 had been detained for more than two years on charges of "counter-revolution" for forming or joining three underground dissident groups, writing and printing political leaflets and planning to distribute them before the 1992 anniversary of the 1989 massacre in Beijing. Their trial had been postponed several times since 1993, reportedly because of lack of evidence. In December, nine were sentenced to terms of imprisonment ranging from three to 20 years, five were "exempted" from criminal punishment, and one was placed under "supervision" for two years. Relatives of the defendants were reportedly not permitted to attend the court hearing.

Torture and ill-treatment of detainees and prisoners held in prisons, detention centres or labour camps were widely reported. Methods most often cited were beatings, electric shocks, use of shackles, sleep deprivation and exposure to extremes of cold or heat. Prison conditions were frequently harsh and many prisoners suffered from serious illnesses as a result. Medical care and food were often inadequate, and punishments frequently threatened the physical and psychological well-being of prisoners. Political prisoners in Hanyang Prison in Hubei province, for example, claimed that they had been beaten and held in conditions that amounted to cruel, inhuman and degrading treatment.

Phuntsog Yangkyi, a Tibetan nun and prisoner of conscience, reportedly died in a police hospital in Lhasa in June, allegedly as a result of ill-treatment. She was one of several nuns beaten at Drapchi Prison in February after singing nationalist songs. No independent investigation was conducted into her case or those of other prisoners alleged to have been tortured or ill-treated in detention.

The dramatic increase in the use of the death penalty which began in 1990 continued (see *Amnesty International Reports 1991* to *1994*). At least 2,496 death sentences and 1,791 executions were recorded by Amnesty International, but the true figures were believed to be far higher.

Amnesty International continued to urge the authorities to release all prisoners of conscience, ensure fair and prompt trials for other political prisoners, investigate torture allegations and safeguard prisoners from ill-treatment. It also urged the authorities to commute all death sentences. The government did not respond.

In oral statements to the UN Commission on Human Rights in February, Amnesty International included reference to its concerns in China.

Amnesty International published several reports on China including: in January, *China: Dissidents Detained Since 1992 – Political Trials and Administrative Sentences*; in March, *China: Protestants and Catholics Detained Since 1993*; in April, *China: Death Penalty Figures Recorded for 1993*; in June, *China: Human Rights Violations Five Years after Tiananmen*; and in November, *China: The Imprisonment and Harassment of Jesus Family Members in Shandong Province*.

COLOMBIA

Over 1,000 people were extrajudicially executed by the armed forces or paramilitary groups operating with their support or acquiescence. Human rights activists were subjected to attempts on their lives and death threats. At least 140 people "disappeared" after being seized by the security forces or paramilitary groups. Torture and ill-treatment of detainees were increasingly widespread. Armed forces personnel continued to evade accountability for thousands of extrajudicial executions in recent years. Armed opposition groups committed grave human rights abuses including deliberate and arbitrary killings and the taking and holding of hostages.

Liberal Party candidate Ernesto Samper Pizano was elected President and assumed office in August. In September he announced a program of action to improve respect for human rights, including measures to tackle impunity, to eradicate paramilitary organizations and to assist internal refugees.

Negotiations initiated in 1993 between the government and the *Corriente de Renovación Socialista* (CRS), Socialist Renewal Current, culminated in a peace agreement in April. Some 350 members of the CRS, a dissident wing of the armed opposition group *Ejército de Liberación Nacional* (ELN), National Liberation Army, were demobilized under the agreement. Following similar agreements in May and June, 650 members of three Medellín-based urban militia groups, the *Milicias Populares*, and 130 guerrillas from the *Frente Francisco Garnica*, a dissident faction of the *Ejército Popular de Liberación* (EPL), Popular Liberation Army, were also demobilized. Other guerrilla-backed militia groups continued to operate clandestinely. The majority faction of the ELN; the *Fuerzas Armadas Revolucionarias de Colombia* (FARC), Revolutionary Armed Forces of Colombia; and the EPL, maintained their campaigns of armed opposition throughout the year. Civilians, including children, continued to be injured by landmines laid by armed opposition groups, principally the ELN, in the Magdalena Medio region of central Colombia.

In November President Samper announced his government's willingness to negotiate with armed opposition groups. The government's peace program included extensive reference to human rights and international humanitarian law.

In June Congress approved a draft law against "disappearances". The law included important provisions to prevent those responsible for human rights violations benefiting from impunity, including the prohibition of amnesties or pardons. It also specified that a "disappearance" cannot be considered an "act of service" – thereby ensuring that investigations and trials would fall within the remit of the civilian rather than the military justice system – and that the concept of "due obedience" could not be invoked as a defence. The then President, César Gaviria, rejected the draft law on the grounds that these and other provisions were "unconstitutional" and "inconvenient", and the law returned to Congress for review. In September the government of President Samper withdrew two of the three objections, but continued to object to the provision bringing "disappearances" within the remit of the civilian courts. In October the Senate voted to accept the three objections raised by President Gaviria. The bill was

102

passed to the House of Representatives but had not been debated by the end of the year.

In September the Inter-American Commission on Human Rights (IACHR) of the Organization of American States together with the Colombian Government and victims' representatives agreed to create a special commission to investigate the "disappearance" and murder of more than 60 people in Trujillo, Valle del Cauca department, in 1990 (see *Amnesty International Report 1991*). The special commission's conclusions and recommendations were to be studied by the IACHR in February 1995.

In December Congress voted to ratify the Second Protocol Additional to the Geneva Conventions which regulate internal conflicts.

Intense counter-insurgency activities continued in many areas of the country. Peasant farmers, community leaders, members of left-wing political organizations and trade unionists continued to be the main targets. Children were again among the casualties.

More than 1,000 people were extrajudicially executed by the armed forces or paramilitary groups. For example, eight-year-old Gustavo Marroquin Iglesias was shot dead in March by soldiers from the army's infantry battalion "Jaime Rooke" in the community of Laureles near Ibagué, Tolima department. Some killings of civilians appeared to be in reprisal for guerrilla attacks against military targets. In January, nine civilians from Puerto Lleras, Saravena municipality, Arauca department, were shot dead by army personnel shortly after guerrilla forces had attacked the army base in Saravena killing three soldiers. The remaining inhabitants of Puerto Lleras were then detained for 24 hours and ill-treated by the military. In August the Procurator General's Public Ministry opened formal disciplinary proceedings against nine soldiers, including a lieutenant-colonel, two majors and a captain, from the General Gabriel Reveiz Pizarro Battalion in connection with the military operation which led to the killings.

An increasing number of attacks were reported against community leaders in the departments of Cesar and North Santander. David Reyes Castro was shot dead in June in Pailitas, Cesar department, by two gunmen who were later seen entering

the army's Operational Command Base No. 7. In September Jairo Barahona was taken from his home by men who identified themselves as members of the security forces' elite Anti-Extortion and Kidnapping Unit. His body was found later that day with four bullet wounds and signs of torture.

Further evidence of the armed forces' responsibility for systematic human rights violations emerged in January when two naval sub-officials reported the illegal activities of a naval intelligence unit in the town of Barrancabermeja, Santander department, to the Attorney General. According to the sub-officials, the intelligence unit – which operated under the direct command of the head of Naval Intelligence – had murdered scores of trade unionists, teachers, journalists, human rights workers and others in the city of Barrancabermeja and in the surrounding Magdalena Medio region between 1991 and 1993. Three members of the Regional Human Rights Committee (CREDHOS) – Blanca Cecilia Valero de Durán, Julio César Berrio and Ligia Patricia Cortes – were among the victims (see *Amnesty International Report 1993*). A judge ordered the arrest of the two sub-officials and took no action against the military officers implicated by their testimonies. In August the criminal investigation was transferred to the military justice system which claimed jurisdiction. Also in August the Special Investigations Unit of the Procurator General's office recommended formal disciplinary proceedings against the National Director of Naval Intelligence for having failed to control the activities of the unit.

There was a marked resurgence in serious human rights violations attributed to paramilitary organizations after a guerrilla offensive in July which included widespread attacks against civil and military targets and the killing of a leading counter-insurgency army officer, General Carlos Gil Colorado, in Meta department. At the time of his death General Gil Colorado was under investigation by the Procurator General's office for links with illegal paramilitary organizations.

In August, two days after the inauguration of President Samper, Senator Manuel Cepeda Vargas was shot dead near his home in Bogotá, the capital. Senator Cepeda was a leading member of the

Colombian Communist Party and the *Unión Patriótica* (UP), Patriotic Union party. Responsibility for the killing of Senator Cepeda was claimed by a previously unknown paramilitary organization, *Muerte a Comunistas y Guerrilleros*, Death to Communists and Guerrillas. This group also issued death threats against other opposition activists, lawyers, trade unionists and a Roman Catholic bishop. Another paramilitary organization, *Colombia Sin Guerrilla* (COLSINGUE), Colombia Without Guerrillas, claimed responsibility for a series of attacks against trade unionists. In September, five heavily armed men forced their way into the office of the *Federación Unitaria de Trabajadores de Antioquia* (FUTRAN), United Workers' Federation of Antioquia, and opened fire killing Hugo Zapata, the union's disputes secretary, and seriously injuring Carlos Posada, the union's human rights secretary. Although judicial investigations were opened, no action was taken to implement outstanding arrest warrants and judicial sentences against paramilitary leaders found responsible for serious human rights violations in previous years.

The killing of so-called "disposables" by "death squads" with links to the security forces continued in many cities and towns. Victims included petty criminals, drug addicts, prostitutes, homosexuals and "street children". In February, three homeless youths, 16-year-old Javier González, 14-year-old Jairo Murcia and a 12-year-old boy known as "Asprilla", were shot through the head as they were sleeping in front of a warehouse in the Timiza district of Bogotá. According to reports, hundreds of youths were killed in the cities of Cali and Medellín. Many of the victims had participated in local government initiatives to disarm and rehabilitate members of juvenile street gangs or militia groups. In addition to police-backed "death squads", responsibility for the killings was attributed to rival gangs and drug-trafficking organizations.

At least 140 people "disappeared" after being seized by the security forces or paramilitary groups. In November, a group of 30 heavily armed men broke into the Judicial Prison in Aguachica, Cesar department. The gunmen, some of whom were dressed in army uniforms, shot dead political prisoner Hermés Molina in his cell and forced seven others to accompany them. The bodies of four prisoners were later found on the outskirts of Aguachica with gunshot wounds. The whereabouts of three prisoners – César Cruz, Alfredo Tarazona and Eledis Rosado – remained unknown. The eight prisoners, whose names appeared on a list carried by the gunmen, were facing charges in connection with guerrilla activities.

In the vast majority of cases armed forces personnel believed to be responsible for extrajudicial executions and "disappearances" continued to evade accountability. Military tribunals investigating human rights violations by army personnel have persistently failed to bring those responsible to justice. An apparent exception to this practice was reported in June when a war tribunal sentenced an army captain and 17 soldiers to prison terms of between six and 20 years for the murder of five men in Entrerrios, Antioquia department, in December 1992. Although initially reported as "guerrillas killed in combat", the military tribunal established that the five victims were peasant farmers who had been detained and then killed by the soldiers attached to the army's Pedro Nel Ospina Battalion.

Reports of torture of detainees by both the military and police increased. In August the then Procurator General, Dr Carlos Arrieta, said that there had been a 23 per cent increase in reports of torture between January 1993 and April 1994. A report produced by three Colombian non-governmental human rights organizations stated that in the town of Barrancabermeja, Santander department, of the 183 people detained between January 1993 and June 1994 by government security agencies, 170 had been physically or psychologically tortured. The majority of cases of torture were reported to have occurred in the army's Nueva Granada Battalion in Barrancabermeja. No information was available about criminal investigations into allegations of torture, although in some cases disciplinary sanctions were imposed. In November the People's Defender called for the immediate suspension of a police lieutenant and five police agents believed to be responsible for the illegal detention and torture of three men in Bucaramanga, Santander department. The three men had been arrested in October and tortured, including by beatings and near-asphyxiation with plastic bags.

104

Despite statements by both outgoing and incoming governments recognizing the legitimacy of their work, human rights workers' lives continued to be at risk. In March human rights lawyer Luis Narváez García survived an attempt on his life when five men armed with sub-machine guns burst into his home in Sincelejo, Sucre department. The caretaker of his property, Johny Rafael Márquez, was shot dead in the attack.

Yanette Bautista and Gloria Herney Galindez, president and secretary-general of the *Asociación de Familiares de Detenidos-Desaparecidos* (ASFADDES), Association of Relatives of the "Disappeared", received anonymous death threats in September. The threats occurred after ASFADDES had led a campaign for the new government to retract former President Gaviria's objections to the draft law against "disappearances". Nancy Fiallo Araque, a human rights educationalist working in Bucaramanga, Santander department, received repeated anonymous death threats throughout the year. All three women presented official complaints to judicial authorities but little effort was apparently made to identify and bring to justice those responsible.

Armed opposition groups continued to commit grave human rights abuses including scores of deliberate and arbitrary killings. In January, 35 people were killed and 12 injured when guerrillas of the FARC's "5th Front" opened fire on a group of supporters of *Esperanza, Paz y Libertad*, Hope, Peace and Freedom – a political movement formed by demobilized EPL guerrillas – in La Chinita neighbourhood of Apartadó in the Urabá region of Antioquia department. The victims, who had been participating in a street party following a political meeting, included three children. Responsibility for the killing of Manuel Humberto Cárdenas, the mayor of Fusagasugá, Cundinamarca department, in July, was also attributed to the FARC. In May ELN guerrillas abducted a group of municipal council officials from Aguachica, Cesar department. The body of council president, Oswaldo Pájaro García, was found two days later, shot dead. The whereabouts of another of the kidnap victims remained unknown. Eleven policemen and two high-school students were killed in October when FARC and ELN guerrillas attacked a police convoy in the

municipality of Puracé, Cauca department, with rockets and grenades. According to reports, several policemen injured in the initial attack were then shot dead. The two dead students were aboard a school bus travelling behind the police vehicles. In October the ELN claimed responsibility for killing a former senator, Felix Salcedo Gauldion, in Cúcuta, North Santander department. Guerrilla groups kidnapped over 400 people, the majority of whom were held hostage until ransom demands were met.

In March Amnesty International published a report, *Colombia: Political Violence – Myth and Reality,* which documented the continuing pattern of gross human rights violations under the government of President César Gaviria. Amnesty International called on his government to end human rights violations and impunity and to dismantle paramilitary forces. It also called on opposition groups to end deliberate and arbitrary killings and hostage-taking. No formal response was received from the government.

In November an Amnesty International delegation, led by the Secretary General, visited Colombia to discuss the organization's concerns with senior government officials, including President Samper, and human rights defenders.

In an oral statement to the UN Commission on Human Rights in February, Amnesty International included reference to its concerns in Colombia.

CONGO

Government security forces and allied armed civilian militias were responsible for arbitrary detention, torture and extra-judicial executions. The authorities took no steps to investigate human rights violations. Armed opposition groups also abducted and deliberately killed unarmed civilians.

Political violence, which had erupted in 1993 (see *Amnesty International Report 1994*), continued during the first months of the year. Dozens of unarmed civilians were killed in fighting between government troops loyal to President Pascal Lissouba and armed political groups, which effectively controlled parts of the capital, Brazzaville. The main armed groups and militias opposed to the government were loyal to Bernard Kolelas, leader of the *Mouvement congolais pour la démocratie et le développement intégral* (MCDDI), Congolese Movement for Democracy and Integrated Development. A cease-fire was signed in late January under the auspices of the *Comité parlementaire inter-régional du Pool et des pays du Niari pour la paix*, Inter-regional Parliamentary Peace Committee of Pool and Niari regions, on which the major political parties were represented. President Lissouba ordered the recruitment in January of 2,000 new members of the army, national police and gendarmerie and created special units. In February one such unit, the *Force d'interposition*, Intervention Force, was deployed in Brazzaville to disarm civilians and to allow people who had been displaced by fighting to return home.

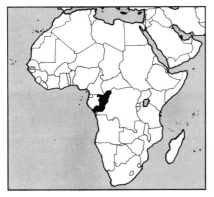

An international commission of judges from the Organization of African Unity, the European Union, Gabon and France, which was investigating alleged irregularities in elections in May 1993 (see *Amnesty International Report 1994*), reported in February. It annulled the results in nine constituencies, but this did not affect control of the National Assembly by the *Union panafricaine pour la démocratie sociale* (UPADS), Pan-African Union for Social Democracy. Parliamentarians from both the government and the opposition appealed to their supporters to accept the results. Two opposition leaders, Bernard Kolelas and Jean-Pierre Thystère-Tchicaya, were elected as mayors of Brazzaville and the town of Pointe-Noire, respectively. The elections had been delayed for two years.

Government troops and allied militia were responsible for arbitrary detention, torture and extrajudicial executions.

The level of violence made it difficult for human rights organizations to carry out independent investigations and to confirm who was responsible for individual killings of defenceless civilians, many of whom appeared to have been targeted on account of their ethnic origin. Victims reportedly included both unarmed civilians and captured opposition combatants. Marcel Mpoudi, a taxi-driver, was arrested by members of the security forces in February after being stopped at a road-block. He was taken to a detention centre where he was reportedly beaten to death. His body was allegedly buried in the grounds of the detention centre. His arrest appeared to be based solely on his ethnic origin: he came from a part of the country where support for opposition parties was strong. In June armed militia allegedly allied to the *Mouvance présidentielle,* a coalition of parties loyal to President Lissouba, arbitrarily detained the drivers and conductors of two buses owned by opposition supporters. The captives were released after the police intervened.

There were reports that scores of people, mostly young men, were tortured by members of the security forces in Brazzaville's central police station early in the year.

The authorities took no steps to investigate human rights violations committed by government and security officials, effectively allowing their forces to commit abuses with impunity. In particular, there was no official inquiry into reports of extrajudicial executions by government forces in both 1993 and 1994 (see *Amnesty International Report 1994*).

Armed militia organized by the MCDDI and other opposition political parties also committed abuses, including deliberate and arbitrary killings. In some cases prisoners appeared to be held as hostages. At the beginning of the year there were reports of abductions and of the killing of defenceless civilians who were perceived as government supporters. For example, four railway workers, including Jean Pierre Batoukounou, Fidèle Ngoma and Prosper Nkama were killed in February, apparently in retaliation for killings by government troops.

Abuses committed by armed political groups included the abduction of two political supporters of President Lissouba.

106 They were held in June for several days and reportedly ill-treated.

Amnesty International called on the authorities to take steps to prevent extrajudicial executions by the security forces. Amnesty International urged the authorities to investigate all reports of extrajudicial executions and to bring those responsible to justice. Amnesty International also condemned abuses committed by armed opposition groups including hostage-taking and deliberate and arbitrary killings.

COSTA RICA

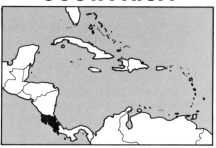

Several reports were received of the excessive use of police force.

A new president, José María Figueres Olsen, came to power in May.

At the end of 1994, the First Superior Penal Court finally heard the case of Livia Cordero Gené who had been arrested in 1990 with 14 others, and accused of "illicit association" and detonating explosives in connection with various incidents between 1986 and 1988. She was cleared of all charges, as were seven others against whom charges had remained pending. The others initially detained with her had been released over time, but Livia Cordero remained in preventive detention until freed on bail in July 1992. She maintained she had been arrested for criticizing Costa Rica's then president for allowing Costa Rican territory to be used by opponents of the Nicaraguan Government and that she had been held in preventive detention for an inordinate length of time, as pre-trial inquiries should not exceed 180 days.

In May about 36 people, including a number of members of the civil guard, were reportedly wounded when the guards clashed with banana workers, many of them Nicaraguan nationals, who were peacefully demonstrating at a foreign-owned banana estate in northeastern Costa Rica. According to reports, the guards attacked the demonstrators indiscriminately. A number of demonstrators, including minors, were briefly detained. Initially, officials maintained that the guards had not "participated" in the "activities" in which the workers were injured. However, in a July submission to the UN's Special Rapporteur on extrajudicial, summary or arbitrary executions, the Minister of Public Security acknowledged that the civil guard had been involved in the incident but maintained that the violence had been initiated by the demonstrators. In response to inquiries regarding the incident, officials, including Vice-President Rodrigo Oreamuno who met Amnesty International's Secretary General in November, failed to provide any information as to any investigations into the incident.

In April the UN Human Rights Committee found that Costa Rica had failed to provide adequate information concerning the rights of detainees held in lengthy pre-trial detention.

CÔTE D'IVOIRE

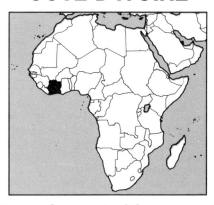

Dozens of opponents of the government were held who appeared to be prisoners of conscience. Among them were one student and three journalists who received prison terms and were imprisoned; dozens of other students were detained for short periods and at least five were held without trial for four months. Three people were sentenced to death but there were no executions.

There was political unrest throughout the year. Dozens of students and several journalists were imprisoned in an apparent attempt to stifle opposition to the government of President Henri Konan Bédié in the run-up to presidential and legislative elections scheduled to take place in 1995. In particular, the authorities targeted the *Fédération estudiantine et scolaire de Côte d'Ivoire* (FESCI), the Ivorian Federation of Students and School Pupils, which organized protests calling for improvements in conditions for students. Some FESCI leaders were arrested; others went into hiding to avoid arrest. The government claimed that FESCI had been banned in 1991, but the student organization maintained that the banning decree did not have legal force, and pointed out that it had been allowed to participate in public debate with the government over the previous two years.

In March the police arrested several FESCI members at the University of Bouaké (290 kilometres north of the capital, Abidjan) after a peaceful demonstration became violent when the security forces intervened. Eugène Gonthy, a FESCI activist, was charged with inciting violence and sentenced to one year's imprisonment although the prosecution produced no evidence of his involvement in any acts of violence. His sentence was doubled on appeal, but he was provisionally released in August. At least five other students charged with inciting violence remained in detention without trial for four months; they were probably prisoners of conscience.

The imprisonment of Eugène Gonthy provoked protests at the University of Cocody in Abidjan. In May at least 25 FESCI members, including Guirao Blé, FESCI Deputy Secretary General, were held incommunicado for two weeks after a peaceful meeting was broken up by the security forces. All the students were released on 31 May after apologizing on television; they had been threatened with continued detention if they did not apologize publicly.

Six journalists – two of whom were tried twice on separate charges – were convicted, although in three cases the sentences were not enforced. The imprisoned journalists were prisoners of conscience. In February Hamed Bakayoko, director of the weekly newspaper *Le Patriote*, was charged with insulting the head of state. An unsigned article in his newspaper had praised the former Prime Minister, Alassane Ouattara, who had challenged President Bédié's accession to power following the death of President Houphouët-Boigny. Hamed Bakayoko was sentenced to one year's imprisonment but was provisionally released in July, apparently after apologizing to President Bédié.

In March Aboudramane Sangaré, the Deputy Secretary General of the main opposition party, the *Front populaire ivoirien* (FPI), Ivorian Popular Front, and the director of the newspaper *La Voie*, was sentenced to one year's imprisonment together with four *La Voie* journalists. They had published an article claiming that President Bédié had asked the French Government for 10 billion CFA Francs to pay for President Houphouët-Boigny's funeral. The five men were not at any stage imprisoned, but the threat of imprisonment was apparently used in an attempt to exert pressure on the main opposition newspaper.

The following month, Aboudramane Sangaré and another of the journalists convicted in March, Souleymane T. Senn, were again brought to court. They were sentenced to three years' imprisonment following the publication in *La Voie* of an article by Souleymane T. Senn which, without advocating the use of violence, called on government opponents to adopt more aggressive tactics in the run-up to the 1995 elections. In this case, the sentences were enforced and the two men were imprisoned. They were released in December under a general presidential amnesty.

In August a Ghanaian refugee, Anuere Atta-Willie, was arrested and held without charge for seven weeks, apparently for having written a letter protesting about the harassment suffered by Ghanaian residents in Côte d'Ivoire. At least 23 Ghanaians were killed in anti-Ghanaian violence in Abidjan following crowd violence which occurred at a football match in Ghana in November 1993. Anuere Atta-Willie was probably a prisoner of conscience and was released after the intervention of the *Ligue ivoirienne des droits de l'homme*, Ivorian Human Rights League.

In October a Cameroonian student, Jean-Claude Um Mahop, was detained for three weeks at the *Direction de la sécurité du territoire* (DST), National Security Head-

108

quarters, because he was carrying documents concerning a Cameroonian student organization. He appeared to be a prisoner of conscience and was released without charge.

In July, three men convicted of murder were sentenced to death. No executions were carried out.

In July Amnesty International published a report, *Côte d'Ivoire: Freedom of expression and association threatened*, in which it appealed for the release of FESCI member Eugène Gonthy and the three imprisoned journalists whom it considered to be prisoners of conscience. The organization also stressed that three other journalists sentenced to terms of imprisonment in March would be prisoners of conscience if they were required to serve their sentences. No response was received from the government but all the prisoners of conscience named in the report were released before the end of the year.

CROATIA

A small number of men imprisoned for refusing mobilization into the armed forces may have been prisoners of conscience. Trials of defendants accused of politically motivated offences may not have been fair. A number of people were reportedly ill-treated by civilian or military police. There were reports of human rights abuses in rebel Serb-controlled areas.

Approximately one third of Croatian territory remained under the control of rebel Serbs in the territories known as the *Krajinas*. These areas remained UN Protected Areas (UNPAs) and little progress was made towards implementing the UN

peace plan of January 1992 which foresaw their reintegration. There were around 200,000 internally displaced people in government-controlled areas as a result of the 1991 war and a further 180,000 refugees from Bosnia-Herzegovina. Around 100,000 people in the UNPAs were refugees or displaced persons. The Croatian authorities exerted pressure on refugees from certain areas of Bosnia to return.

The mandate of the UN peace-keeping force, UNPROFOR (UN Protection Force), was extended twice during the year. As in previous years the government threatened to veto the extensions, expressing dissatisfaction with progress towards implementing the peace plan and arguing that UNPROFOR should be given greater powers to enforce the plan.

In January the government signed an agreement on the establishment of contacts with the Federal Republic of Yugoslavia. In March the government signed a cease-fire agreement with the *de facto* authorities in the *Krajinas*, although some armed clashes still occurred on the front lines.

In March the Croatian President, Franjo Tudjman, signed an agreement on forming a Bosniac-Croat federation in Bosnia-Herzegovina (see **Bosnia and Herzegovina** entry).

As a result of new research among relatives of missing persons, the Croatian Government revised the figure of those "disappeared" or missing on the Croatian side during the 1991 war down to 2,764. In addition, several hundred people were reported missing from the Serbian side.

The Croatian Army was in Bosnia-Herzegovina at the start of the year, fighting against the mainly Muslim Bosnian Government Army. Later in the year it again reportedly took part in the conflict in Bosnia-Herzegovina, fighting Bosnian Serb forces.

The Serbian army in the *Krajinas* supported Bosnian Serb forces in attacking the Bihać pocket in Bosnia-Herzegovina in November (see **Bosnia and Herzegovina** entry). There were reports of demonstrations against mobilizations into Serb forces in the *Krajinas* at the time.

Some possible prisoners of conscience were held. In late December 1993 and January 1994 the Croatian Army called up several thousand men in Croatia on behalf of the Bosnian Croat military forces to serve in Bosnia-Herzegovina. The men were Croats or Serbs who had been born in Bosnia-Herzegovina, but most had Croatian citizenship. Some who refused mobilization or deserted, including possible conscientious objectors, were reportedly imprisoned in Croatia for up to 30 days in January.

There were reports of political trials which did not meet international standards of fair trial. In March the trial began of nine men who were accused of blowing up the offices of the party *Dalmatinska Akcija* (DA), Dalmatian Action, in Split in September 1993. Some were members of the DA. The trial was adjourned several times and no verdict had been reached by the end of the year. There were allegations that several of the accused and at least one witness were forced to make incriminatory statements as a result of having been beaten by police during interrogation. Croatian courts continued to hold trials of people (mainly Serbs) accused of participating in fighting against Croatia during the war in 1991. Most defendants were tried *in absentia* and the proceedings may have fallen short of fair trial standards.

A number of people were reportedly ill-treated by police. In February a Croatian citizen of Bosnian Muslim origin was reportedly severely beaten after being arrested by police in Slavonski Brod.

There were allegations that civilian or military police failed to intervene when soldiers or civilians beat protesters during evictions of tenants from former Yugoslav National Army (JNA) apartments. Police also reportedly beat protesters or those being evicted. For example, in Split in February civilian and military police reportedly stood by while paramilitaries and their sympathizers beat Tonči Majić, an activist in a local human rights organization who had gone to an apartment where the paramilitaries were trying to evict a woman illegally. In Zagreb in September, 11 people were arrested while peacefully protesting against the eviction of another woman from a former JNA apartment. Police reportedly beat several of those arrested.

Human rights abuses were reported from the territory controlled by rebel Serbs. The *de facto* Serbian authorities failed to investigate attacks by uniformed men on civilians in the *Krajinas*. However, 30 people were arrested in Ilok in March

for attacks on both Serbs and on some of the small numbers of Croats or other non-Serbs who remained in the area. There were also reports of politically motivated abductions. In February Veljko Džakula, a former "Deputy Prime Minister" of the *de facto* authorities in the *Krajinas*, was abducted in Belgrade by police from Serbia or the *Krajinas*. He was in dispute with the *de facto* authorities over policy towards negotiations with the Croatian Government. After being held incommunicado at an unknown location in the *Krajinas* for several days, during which he was allegedly tortured, he was transferred to a prison and then released. Foreign journalists were detained in the *Krajinas* on several occasions and at least one foreign journalist was allegedly ill-treated.

In February Amnesty International appealed to the Croatian authorities to ensure that a Croatian citizen of Bosnian Muslim origin was given medical attention and called for an independent and impartial inquiry into allegations of his ill-treatment. In reply the authorities denied that ill-treatment had taken place. The organization also urged the Yugoslav authorities to investigate the "disappearance" of Veljko Džakula.

In June Amnesty International called upon the Croatian authorities to investigate the reported "disappearance" of Rasim Kahrimanović, a Muslim, in Dubrovnik in July 1993. In response they denied involvement in his reported "disappearance", but acknowledged that he had been reported as a missing person. In September Amnesty International called for an independent and impartial investigation into the reported beating of several people in the course of an eviction from a former JNA apartment in Zagreb. The authorities denied that ill-treatment had taken place.

CUBA

Some 600 prisoners of conscience were believed to be serving sentences of imprisonment. Human rights and political activists continued to face frequent short-term detention and harassment. Detention and trial procedures for political prisoners fell far short of international standards. There were frequent reports of ill-treatment in prisons and police stations. The

authorities were suspected of bearing at least partial responsibility for the death by drowning of some 40 people trying to flee Cuba by boat. One man was executed and several others were facing possible death sentences.

The government, which continued to face serious economic problems, including a US trade embargo condemned by the UN General Assembly in October 1994, carried on with its program of economic reform but resisted international pressure to initiate political reform. Independent human rights monitoring remained severely limited. Members of unofficial political, human rights and trade union groups continued to face imprisonment, short-term detention and frequent harassment. The UN High Commissioner for Human Rights visited Cuba for three days in November at the invitation of the Cuban Government but the government continued to refuse to cooperate with the UN Special Rapporteur on Cuba.

In May reports were received that a special committee of the National Assembly of Popular Power was reviewing legal procedures and individual rights but no further news was heard. In November the Assembly was said to be considering updating migration laws.

Cuban exile groups continued to threaten armed attacks inside Cuba. On 15 October the authorities captured seven armed men, said to belong to the Miami-based *Partido de Unidad Nacional Democrático* (PUND), Party of National Democratic Unity, who had landed on the coast near Caibarien and shot dead a fisherman.

Large numbers of people fled Cuba by sea in the hope of reaching the USA. President Fidel Castro accused the US Government of inciting Cubans to take to the seas and, following a series of attempted hijackings of vessels resulting in the deaths of three Cuban officials, he ordered the Cuban Coast Guard to stop preventing people from leaving the country by sea. Between 19 August and mid-September, 32,000 Cubans were picked up at sea by the US Coast Guard and taken to the US naval base at Guantánamo Bay, Cuba. During a visit to the Guantánamo base in September (see USA entry), an Amnesty International delegation found that a substantial number of the Cubans held there were former political prisoners and activ-

ists of unofficial political, human rights and trade union groups. Some said they had been told by the authorities to leave Cuba, under threat of renewed imprisonment, or even physically put on boats or rafts. Others were facing trial on political charges such as "enemy propaganda" or "disrespect".

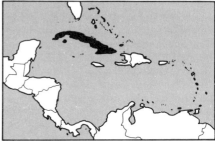

On 5 August in Havana, violent clashes took place between the Cuban security forces and crowds hoping to hijack boats. Members of the Rapid Response Brigades (see *Amnesty International Reports 1992 to 1994*), armed with sticks and metal tubes, were also called in to confront the crowds. The authorities acknowledged that some 300 people were arrested and charged in connection with the disturbances: in September it was reported that 162 of them were imprisoned in Camagüey Provincial Prison (known as "Kilo 7") charged with public order offences. Some 40 activists belonging to unofficial political and human rights groups were also arrested on 5 August and the following days, apparently as a precautionary measure, even though they had not participated in the disturbances. All were released without charge within 15 days. They and other activists subsequently reported being repeatedly subjected to short-term detention, during which they were threatened with renewed imprisonment if they did not give up their activities or leave the country.

At least 600 prisoners of conscience were believed to be awaiting trial or serving prison sentences, the majority on charges such as "enemy propaganda" and "disrespect". Prisoner of conscience Francisco Chaviano González was arrested at his Havana home on 7 May, moments after being handed a compromising document by a stranger in an apparent set-up. He was held under investigation on a charge of revealing state security secrets and had not been brought to trial by the end of

AMNESTY INTERNATIONAL REPORT 1995

1994. Francisco Chaviano is President of the unofficial National Council for Civil Rights in Cuba, which had been documenting cases of people who had died at sea while trying to flee the country.

Prisoner of conscience Marta María Vega Cabrera was arrested on 3 June in Nueva Gerona, Isla de la Juventud, following a search of her home during which she and other family members were reportedly ill-treated. After being held for several weeks by the Department of State Security, she was transferred to the Western Women's Re-education Centre in Havana charged with "enemy propaganda" in connection with her activities in the unofficial *Partido Cívico Democrático* (PCD), Civic Democratic Party. She was said to have been beaten by prison guards and prisoners in July and subsequently sent to a punishment cell after she complained about the beating of another prisoner.

A large number of people, including some prisoners of conscience, were believed to be imprisoned for up to four years under a section of the Penal Code entitled "The Dangerous State and Security Measures" which contains few fundamental judicial guarantees (see *Amnesty International Report 1994*). Some reports estimated that as many as 800 people were arrested under this legislation in Havana alone during the first eight months of the year.

Despite indications that the authorities were encouraging people to take to the seas during August, at other times of the year many of those who did so were arrested. Some were reportedly released without charge or given a non-custodial sentence if it was their first offence. Those imprisoned in previous years solely for trying to leave the country illegally continued serving prison sentences. They included Rolando Cambra Javert, arrested in 1992 and sentenced to three years' imprisonment.

Writer Norberto Fuentes (see *Amnesty International Report 1994*) was granted permission to leave the country in August following the intervention of Colombian writer Gabriel García Márquez, a close friend of President Castro.

Several prisoners of conscience were released during the year. They included four prisoners of conscience released early through the mediation of a senior Spanish politician, but only on condition they left Cuba for Spain. They were: Aurea Feria Cao (see *Amnesty International Report 1991*), María Elena Aparicio (see *Amnesty International Report 1993*), Luis Alberto Pita Santos (see *Amnesty International Reports 1992* to *1994*) and Pablo Reyes Martínez, sentenced to eight years for "enemy propaganda" in 1992. Joel Dueñas Martínez, who was released conditionally after serving 27 months of a four-year sentence for "enemy propaganda", remained in Cuba.

Detention and trial procedures again fell far short of international standards. Detainees accused of offences against state security were held under investigation for several weeks or months without access to lawyers.

Prisoner of conscience Rodolfo González González (see *Amnesty International Report 1993*), a spokesman for the unofficial *Comité Cubano Pro Derechos Humanos* (CCPDH), Cuban Committee for Human Rights, who had been arrested in December 1992, was sentenced to seven years' imprisonment in March after a show trial in Havana. He was convicted of spreading "enemy propaganda" on the grounds that he had given false information to USA-based radio stations. Unusually, foreign journalists and local human rights monitors were allowed to attend the hearing and Rodolfo González was permitted to speak at length despite criticizing the government. He was told in September that, as a result of appeals by the Spanish Government, he would be released if he agreed to go to Spain. He refused to do so and remained in prison. Other prisoners of conscience also reportedly refused to accede to pressure to accept early release in exchange for exile.

Prisoner of conscience Domiciano Torres Roca, who had been arrested in August 1993 (see *Amnesty International Report 1994*), was brought to trial in July and sentenced to three years' imprisonment, also for spreading "enemy propaganda". Domiciano Torres, Vice-President of the PCD, admitted that he had made an anti-government poster bearing the words "Down with Fidel".

Reports were received that detainees were sometimes beaten, both at the time of arrest and in prisons, and frequently sent to punishment cells for complaining about their treatment. Gloria Bravo Melgares, President of the unofficial *Movimiento 8*

112

de Septiembre, 8 September Movement, who was detained for 11 days in August and later reportedly pressurized by the authorities to flee the country on a raft, was said to have suffered severe bruising and scars after being beaten by five female officers while detained in a police station. Another activist arrested at the time of the 5 August disturbances reported hearing other detainees in a Havana police station being beaten to force them to shout pro-government slogans.

Conditions in many police stations and prisons were described as insanitary and medical attention was said to be inadequate or non-existent. Many prisoners suffered serious weight loss because of the poor diet. Although some prisoners were alleged to have been deprived of food or medical treatment as a form of punishment, the general economic conditions prevailing in the country were undoubtedly a contributory factor. Conditions at El Pitirre Prison (also known as Unit 1580) were frequently cited as being particularly poor.

On 13 July some 40 people died when a tugboat, "13 de Marzo", in which they were attempting to flee Cuba, sank. Some of the 31 survivors alleged that they had been pursued and deliberately rammed by three other tugboats causing their boat to capsize. The authorities, announcing that the incident would be investigated, claimed the boat was unseaworthy and blamed the deaths on the organizers of the escape attempt, two of whom were later charged with piracy and theft. The authorities denied there had been official involvement but survivors believed that the pursuing boats were acting under official orders. The results of the investigation were not made public.

Several government opponents were attacked by civilians, some of them armed, in circumstances suggesting official involvement. The victims included Francisco Chaviano González (see above), attacked in his home in March by four armed men; René del Pozo Pozo of the unofficial Cuban Commission for Human Rights and National Reconciliation, attacked in the street in August by a man who beat him with brass knuckles; and Lázaro Corp Yeras, President of the unofficial National Commission of Independent Trade Unions, who, together with his young son Ray, was beaten in the street in

August by three men with sticks.

One execution was known to have been carried out. The official Cuban newspaper, *Granma*, reported in August that Félix Oviedo Aguilera, who had been convicted of murder and armed robbery in November 1993, had been executed. No further news was received of six men believed to be awaiting execution in 1993. As far as was known, no death sentences were passed in 1994. However, the prosecution was said to be seeking the death penalty in three separate cases of alleged murder, involving at least eight defendants.

In March the Minister of Foreign Affairs turned down a request from Amnesty International to carry out a research visit to Cuba. The organization had not been able to visit Cuba since 1990.

Amnesty International appealed to the authorities to release all prisoners of conscience unconditionally, including those imprisoned solely for trying to leave the country, and to allow political and human rights groups to carry out their legitimate activities in peace. It urged the authorities to cease putting pressure on political prisoners and government opponents to leave Cuba, to repeal the "Dangerous State and Security Measures" legislation, and to disband the Rapid Response Brigades. It also called on the authorities to carry out an impartial investigation into the 13 July tugboat sinking, to investigate allegations of ill-treatment, and to commute the death sentence on Félix Oviedo Aguilera. Amnesty International received little substantive response to its communications.

CYPRUS

At least 21 prisoners of conscience, all Jehovah's Witnesses, were imprisoned for refusing on conscientious grounds to perform military service. One conscientious objector remained in prison in northern Cyprus.

The alternative "unarmed military service" provided for conscientious objectors is punitive in length (42 or 36 months instead of 26 months) and is suspended during periods of emergency or general mobilization.

At least 21 conscientious objectors were sentenced to up to one year's imprisonment, some for the third or fourth time, for refusing to perform military service or reservist exercises. Among them was Omiros Andreou Constantinou, a Jehovah's Witness, who was sentenced in April to six months' imprisonment for refusing to perform military service. This was his fourth term of imprisonment for the same offence. He was released a few days before completing the fourth month of his sentence.

Salih Askeroğul, a conscientious objector imprisoned in 1993 by the Turkish Cypriot authorities in northern Cyprus, remained in prison at the end of the year (see *Amnesty International Report 1994*). Amnesty International continued to appeal to the authorities in northern Cyprus for the release of Salih Askeroğul. No answer was received.

Throughout the year Amnesty International called on the Cypriot authorities to release imprisoned conscientious objectors to military service and to introduce an alternative civilian service of non-punitive length, with no restrictions on the right of conscientious objectors to apply for such service.

In May Amnesty International was informed again by the Ministry of Defence that the authorities did not consider the length of the alternative service to be punitive and that members of the armed forces who developed conscientious objections during periods of emergency or general mobilization would not be permitted to transfer to alternative civilian service.

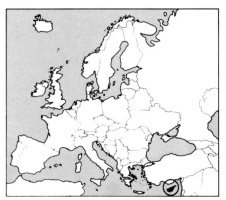

In June Amnesty International published a report, *Cyprus: A Summary of Amnesty International's Human Rights Concerns*. It covered a period of four years and described the imprisonment of conscientious objectors to military service,

documented cases of alleged ill-treatment and torture of detainees and the apparent absence of thorough investigations into these allegations, and called on the government to abolish the provision for the use of the death penalty in wartime. The report was sent to President Glafcos Clerides. No comments on the contents of the report had been received by the end of the year.

DENMARK

There were significant developments concerning alleged police misconduct in previous years.

In February Denmark ratified the Second Optional Protocol to the International Covenant on Civil and Political Rights, aiming at the abolition of the death penalty.

In June the government suspended the use of the "fixed leg-lock" as a method of restraint. This restraint method involves laying detainees face down, handcuffing them behind their backs, bending their legs, wedging one foot against the opposite knee and wedging the other foot up under the handcuffs. In December the suspension of the use of the fixed leg-lock was made permanent; assessment of other methods of restraint was under way.

In-court investigations led by prosecutors into individual cases of alleged ill-treatment in previous years, including the cases of 11 people who alleged that they had been ill-treated during a police operation in Christiania, a community in Copenhagen, had not been concluded by the end of the year (see *Amnesty International Report 1994*). Some of those detained in Christiania alleged that they had

114

been restrained in the fixed leg-lock.

The civil action on behalf of Benjamin Schou, who suffered permanent brain damage after being arrested by police in 1992, was still pending at the end of the year (see *Amnesty International Report 1994*). In the light of evidence that he had been restrained in the fixed leg-lock, the case was resubmitted for further opinion to the Danish Medical-Legal Council.

The civil action for compensation brought by Babading Fatty, a Gambian national who was ill-treated in 1990 in a Copenhagen prison, remained unresolved (see *Amnesty International Reports 1992 to 1994*).

Twenty-six people were tried in connection with a violent demonstration in the Nørrebro district of Copenhagen on 18 to 19 May 1993. Eight of the accused were sentenced to up to three months' imprisonment, one was fined and the rest were acquitted of charges relating to the incident. The convictions and all but one of the acquittals were appealed. During the demonstration, several police officers had been injured and at least 11 people, most of whom were reportedly bystanders, had been wounded by shots fired in disputed circumstances by police in riot gear and plain clothes (see *Amnesty International Report 1994*).

In August the Director of Public Prosecutions (DPP) published a report of the investigation into the events, which was in large part based on investigations by police. The report described how, outnumbered and without tear-gas, police were ordered to advance on stone-throwing demonstrators owing to imprecise and misinterpreted radio communications. The report concluded among other things that: faced with violent bombardments of stone-throwing demonstrators and diminution of their numbers owing to injuries, believing that retreat of the police chain would place injured officers in further jeopardy, and having run out of tear-gas, there were no grounds to criticize the police judgment that it was necessary to draw their weapons, fire "warning shots" and, in some instances, aimed shots. The report was critical of demonstrators' violent actions and some actions of individual officers. It recommended some changes in police procedures, regulations and equipment. However, the precise circumstances in which police fired each of the 113 shots

and in which at least 11 people were injured had not been made public at the end of the year.

The DPP started a supplementary investigation after an independent analysis of a video recording indicated that evidence that an order to shoot at demonstrators' legs might have been given had been overlooked. Charges against one police officer in connection with alleged ill-treatment during the arrest of a demonstrator and criminal investigations against three other officers, who allegedly fired shots which injured six people, were pending at the end of the year.

In October a governmental commission on the handling of complaints against the police published its report recommending that regional Public Prosecutors take over this task.

In April Amnesty International welcomed the initiative of the government and Greenland Home Rule Administration in setting up the Greenlandic Legal Commission to review and make recommendations for revision of Greenland's legal and criminal justice systems. The organization urged consideration of additional measures to ease the deterioration of the physical and psychological health of Greenlandic prisoners serving sentences in Denmark after conviction for serious crimes in Greenland (see *Amnesty International Report 1994*).

In May Amnesty International delegates met the Minister of Justice to discuss the organization's concern about reports of police ill-treatment, including the use of the fixed leg-lock.

In June Amnesty International published a report, *Denmark: Police Ill-treatment*. It highlighted cases of alleged police ill-treatment including at violent demonstrations and during a special 15-month police operation in 1992 to 1993 against hashish dealing in Christiania. It also expressed concern over the authorities' failure to address adequately complaints of ill-treatment. Amnesty International recommended an immediate end to the use of the fixed leg-lock; the establishment of an independent commission of inquiry to examine the use of force and restraint by police; establishment of an independent and impartial body to investigate and act on complaints against the police; and the review and revision of police training and equipment. The organization called on the government to initiate independent impartial investigations into allegations of ill-treatment by police, and where appropriate to pay victims compensation for the injuries and ill-treatment suffered, and to institute criminal or disciplinary procedures against alleged perpetrators. Following the publication of the report, the government announced the suspension of the use of the fixed leg-lock and the initiation of a review of restraint methods used by and taught to police.

Amnesty International welcomed the government's suspension of the use of the fixed leg-lock which the organization considers to be cruel, inhuman or degrading treatment or punishment. It also welcomed the announcement of thorough reviews of restraint techniques used by police. The organization continued to urge the government to adopt its broader recommendations.

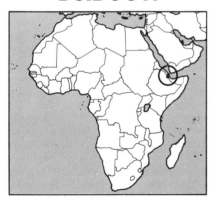

DJIBOUTI

Many government critics were detained for short periods as prisoners of conscience. A relief worker was sentenced to imprisonment; he was possibly a prisoner of conscience. Scores of suspected rebel supporters in the war zones were arrested and detained without charge or trial. In areas affected by armed conflict, there were reports of torture by government troops, including rape of women, and extrajudicial executions of unarmed civilians. At least one peaceful demonstrator was shot dead.

During the first half of the year the government of President Hassan Gouled Aptidon faced continuing armed opposition from the *Front pour la restauration de*

l'unité et de la démocratie (FRUD), Front for the Restoration of Unity and Democracy, particularly in the north. Peace talks starting in June led to suspension of fighting and a peace agreement in December.

Hundreds of peaceful demonstrators were detained in June in Arhiba, a poor area in the capital, Djibouti, when they protested against the destruction of temporary shelters erected there by people displaced by the civil war. They appeared to be prisoners of conscience. They were all released without charge after being held for some days.

Baragoita Said, a journalist, and two others were arrested in October for possession of an opposition publication criticizing government leaders. All three were prisoners of conscience. They were provisionally released in December without charge.

In late September Jean-Michel Pouchelle, a French health worker and president of SOS-Africa, a humanitarian organization, was arrested in the north where he was apparently planning a relief project for victims of the armed conflict. He was convicted of illegally entering the north and breaking a previous expulsion order. He may have been a prisoner of conscience, imprisoned on account of his humanitarian activities. He went on hunger-strike in protest at his six-month prison sentence. In December his sentence was increased by the Appeal Court to eight months; he was deported to France to serve the rest of it.

In January the Appeal Court reduced by two months a three-month prison sentence and fine imposed in October 1993 on Mohamed Houmed Soulleh, president of the *Association pour la défense des droits de l'homme et des libertés* (ADDHL), Association for the Defence of Human Rights and Liberties, for allegedly defaming the Minister of Defence (see *Amnesty International Report 1994*). He had already served most of the prison term when he was provisionally released in November 1993.

In the first half of 1994, scores of suspected FRUD supporters were detained for weeks or months without charge by the army in the war zones in the north.

Two government opponents, Awalle Guelle Assowe and Mohamed Hassan Farah, were detained when they returned

116

from exile in January. They were charged with involvement in a bomb attack on a restaurant in 1990 in which a child was killed (see *Amnesty International Report 1991*). After a few days of provisional release in November they were redetained and were still in custody without trial at the end of the year.

There were several reports in early 1994 of torture, including rape, by government soldiers of people arrested in the war zones in the north.

Government troops were also alleged to have extrajudicially executed scores of unarmed civilians. For instance, at least seven people, including Ali Balla Yousouf, a village chief, were executed in Day district in the northern Tadjourah region in January, apparently in reprisal for army casualties inflicted by FRUD rebels. A commission of inquiry was established into the incident but had not publicly reported its findings by the end of the year. In March at least 36 civilians – men, women and children – were killed by soldiers in Mabla and Oueima regions after renewed fighting in the area.

In June, during the peaceful protests in Arhiba (see above), three peaceful demonstrators were reportedly killed when troops fired indiscriminately into the crowd. The government acknowledged only one death. About 20 other people were wounded. The use of lethal force seemed to have been excessive and unlawful.

Amnesty International appealed for the release of all prisoners of conscience. It called for other suspected government opponents including alleged FRUD supporters who had been arrested to be charged with a recognizably criminal offence and given a fair trial, or released. Amnesty International also called for an impartial inquiry into reports of torture and extrajudicial executions by the security forces. It appealed for measures to stop and prevent human rights abuses in the armed conflict.

In November Amnesty International asked the government to inquire into Jean-Michel Pouchelle's conviction and hunger-strike. The government denied he was a prisoner of conscience and said his legal rights were fully respected and that he had received all appropriate medical treatment.

DOMINICAN REPUBLIC

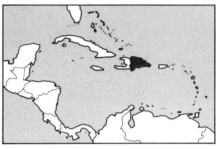

One prisoner of conscience continued to be held despite judicial orders for his release. One person "disappeared". At least eight Haitians were reportedly killed by troops near the border in unclear circumstances.

In August President Joaquín Balaguer Ricardo began a seventh term in office. His re-election, which was widely regarded as fraudulent, led to protest strikes which resulted in scores of people being detained. According to reports, at least 25 protesters were held for over 30 days. They were subsequently released, apparently without charge.

In the context of the international embargo imposed on Haiti by the UN Security Council (see **Haiti** entry) Dominican troops were placed on the border, ostensibly to prevent trade between the two countries.

By the end of the year the human rights centre announced by President Balaguer in 1993 had not apparently been established (see *Amnesty International Report 1994*).

Two independent human rights activists were reported to have been threatened by a high-ranking official at the National Penitentiary of La Victoria, during a visit to the prison. They had previously complained to the authorities about conditions in the prison, including the deaths in custody of two men.

Luis Lizardo Cabrera, a political activist detained in 1989, remained in prison, despite three judicial decisions ordering his release (see *Amnesty International Reports 1990* to *1994*). He was a prisoner of conscience.

One person "disappeared". Narciso González, a university lecturer, journalist and political activist, was detained on 26 May, after he had publicly criticized President Balaguer's re-election. According to witnesses, he was detained by soldiers in the streets of Santo Domingo, the capital. The authorities neither acknowledged his detention nor confirmed where he was held. However, his wife was reportedly later told by a military officer that Narciso González had been seen "badly injured" at the National Police headquarters on 27 May, and had apparently been transferred to a military hospital.

At least eight Haitians were reportedly killed by soldiers from the Dominican Republic in a militarized area along the border with Haiti. The victims were reported to have been suspected of involvement in gasoline smuggling, in contravention of the international trade embargo against Haiti. By the end of the year no official investigation into these killings was known to have been conducted.

Amoesty International urged the authorities to release Luis Lizardo Cabrera immediately and unconditionally, and called for an immediate, thorough and independent investigation into Narciso González' "disappearance". In June the Chief of the National Police told Amnesty International that a police investigation had found that Narciso González had not been in police custody. However, no independent investigation was apparently conducted. In September the organization appealed to President Balaguer to initiate an investigation into the reported killings of Haitians near the border.

ECUADOR

Detainees were reportedly tortured and ill-treated by members of the security forces. Judicial proceedings in one "disappearance" case resulted in the conviction of seven police officers. Numerous human rights cases documented in previous years remained unresolved.

In March the authorities announced that the Judicial Police, a new body, had come into operation in the capital, Quito, and in the city of Guayaquil, and that it would be gradually extended to the rest of the country (see *Amnesty International Reports 1992* to *1994*). However, in July the president of the Supreme Court of

Justice was reported to have declared that the Judicial Police was not yet operational and was only enshrined in the Code of Criminal Procedure. By the end of the year there was evidence that the Judicial Police had begun work in Quito.

In June President Sixto Durán Ballén promulgated an agrarian law which apparently adversely affected indigenous communal land rights. The law resulted in widespread protests by indigenous people, including the occupation of public buildings and the blocking of the Pan-American Highway. During the early days of the protest several people were reported to have been killed in clashes between indigenous people and merchants or paramilitary groups organized by landlords. The President subsequently declared a state of emergency and the army was mobilized to quell the protests.

In September President Durán Ballén issued a decree making the armed forces responsible for planning and conducting anti-crime operations together with the National Police.

Torture and ill-treatment by members of the security forces continued to be reported. Thirty people, all but one of them Colombian nationals, were reportedly tortured and threatened with death, following their detention by the army in late December 1993. The victims had been detained in connection with an ambush of an Ecuadorian border patrol by Colombian guerrillas, on the river Putumayo, in which 11 police and soldiers were killed. Nineteen detainees were released within 48 hours, and 11 were reportedly held incommunicado by the military for between six and 10 days. The 11 were reportedly blindfolded, kicked, suspended, sprayed

118

with gas, doused with a strong disinfectant, given electric shocks and subjected to mock executions. Carmen Bolaños Mora, the only female detainee, was reportedly raped until she lost consciousness. All 11, prior to their transfer into police custody, were reported to have admitted under torture to having participated in the ambush. At the end of August four of the 11 detainees were released by a judge who ruled there was no case against them. Human rights lawyers representing the seven remaining detainees protested their innocence.

On 12 April Oscar Soto and Colombian refugee John Kennedy García Petevi were detained by the police in Quito and accused of criminal offences. According to reports, Oscar Soto was severely beaten during interrogation. Human rights defenders who visited him on 24 April in the Provisional Detention Centre to which he was transferred reported that his torso was extensively bruised. An X-ray taken in mid-May showed he had a fractured rib. John Kennedy García was reportedly forced to sign a self-incriminating statement and to accuse an independent human rights defender, as well as a representative of the UN High Commissioner for Refugees in Ecuador, of aiding and abetting Colombian refugees in carrying out crimes.

On 22 June, during military operations designed to quell the protests against the new agrarian law, numerous indigenous people were reported to have been beaten by members of the army after taking refuge in a convent in Guamote, province of Chimborazo. They were reportedly forced into the convent yard by soldiers, beaten and then taken out to the edge of a gully. Some of them were seriously injured when, in circumstances which were unclear, they flung themselves into the gully.

A police investigation into the 1993 death of Luis Olmedo Aguilera López, who died days after he was allegedly beaten by the police (see *Amnesty International Report 1994*), concluded that he had died of natural causes. However, no independent investigation appeared to have been initiated into the allegations.

In November the Supreme Court of Justice sentenced seven national police force officials – including two generals and a retired director of the National Police – to prison terms ranging between two

and 16 years for the abduction, torture and murder of the brothers Carlos and Pedro Restrepo, who "disappeared" in 1988 (see *Amnesty International Reports 1992* to *1994*). Lawyers representing the seven announced appeals against the convictions and sentences. The Supreme Court of Justice ordered three other officials to be tried for having hindered investigations into the case.

The authorities failed to clarify numerous cases of human rights violations documented in past years. In February the state prosecutor named several army, navy and police officers as responsible for the arbitrary detention and torture of Serapio Ordoñez and Consuelo Benavides, and for the killing of the latter, in 1985. Two defence ministers under the government of former president León Febres Cordero were accused of being implicated in the cover-up of the case. Pre-trial proceedings had not reached a conclusion by the end of the year (see previous *Amnesty International Reports*).

No progress appeared to have been made in investigations into the cases of eight people who were killed by the security forces in 1993 (see *Amnesty International Report 1994*).

Amnesty International urged the government to set up an impartial and thorough judicial investigation into the alleged torture of the 30 people detained along the river Putumayo, and of Oscar Soto and John Kennedy García Petevi. The authorities responded only to the first case, saying that only 11 "subversives" had been detained and that "at no time had they been put under pressure, tortured or had their human rights violated." In June the organization appealed to the authorities to ensure that the security forces seeking to quell indigenous protests against the agrarian law fully respect international human rights standards and that allegations of human rights violations be promptly investigated. The authorities informed Amnesty International that talks with indigenous and other organizations had brought the protest to a peaceful end, but made no reference to allegations that numerous indigenous protesters were beaten in Guamote.

EGYPT

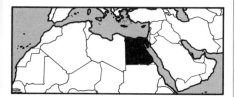

Dozens of lawyers and a number of journalists were arrested and detained as prisoners of conscience. Thousands of suspected members or sympathizers of banned Islamist groups were detained under state of emergency legislation. Some were held without charge or trial; others, almost all civilians, received grossly unfair trials before military courts. Torture of political detainees was systematic; at least one person reportedly died as a result. The security forces killed at least eight people in circumstances suggesting they may have been extrajudicially executed. At least 39 people were sentenced to death and at least 31, including 17 sentenced in previous years, were executed. Armed opposition groups committed grave human rights abuses, including deliberate and arbitrary killings of civilians.

The state of emergency, which was introduced in 1981 (see previous *Amnesty International Reports*), was extended in April for a further three years. Thousands of suspected members or sympathizers of banned Islamist militant groups were held in administrative detention without charge or trial during the year under emergency regulations.

Violent clashes, particularly in Upper Egypt and, to some extent, in Cairo, the capital, continued between armed opposition groups and the security forces. Bomb and firearm attacks were carried out by banned Islamist groups, particularly *al-Gama'a al-Islamiya* (Islamic Group) and *Gihad* (Holy Struggle). The majority of those targeted were police and state security officers, including the Deputy Head of the State Security Investigations Department (SSI) who was killed in April. Civilians killed included at least six Egyptian Copts and four foreign tourists.

Dozens of lawyers were arrested and held as prisoners of conscience. On 17 and 18 May, 36 lawyers were arrested

after the security forces violently dispersed lawyers protesting over the death in custody of 'Abd al-Harith Mohammad Madani (see below). Among those detained were three members of the Bar Association's council: Mukhtar Nouh, Galal Sa'ad and Khaled Badawi. The 36 were interrogated by the Qasr al-Nil Procuracy before being transferred to prison under 15-day detention orders. On 5 June, nine were released but 27 had their detention orders renewed. On 14 June, five other lawyers were detained, reportedly after attending a court hearing on behalf of the 27 lawyers still held. Two of the five, Gamal 'Abd al-'Aziz 'Id and al-Sayyid Fathi al-Sayyid al-Naggar, worked for the Egyptian Organization for Human Rights. By 5 July all had been released except Muntasar al-Zayyat. The court ordered his release but he remained held in Istiqbal Tora Prison. In August the State Security Prosecutor ordered his detention for a further 45 days, reportedly on charges relating to involvement in an illegal organization, spreading false information and contacts with terrorists. These charges were reportedly based on Muntasar al-Zayyat's telephone conversations with members of local and international human rights organizations, journalists, and clients who had fled the country, which had been monitored over the previous 12 months. In October he was given another 45-day detention order; he was released on 5 December.

A number of journalists were detained as prisoners of conscience during an intensified campaign of harassment against journalists working for opposition newspapers. 'Abd al-Sattar Abu Hussain, a journalist with *al-Sha'ab* (the People), the newspaper of the opposition Labour Party, which is close to the Muslim Brothers, a formally banned but tolerated Islamist movement, was arrested on 5 April. He was held in a military prison for three days and reportedly interrogated by the State Security Procuracy. On 30 April, after a grossly unfair trial before a military court, he was sentenced to one year's imprisonment for publishing, in June 1993, information about the armed forces. The offending article was apparently based on information already published in foreign newspapers circulating freely in Egypt. 'Abd al-Sattar Abu Hussain was released in early August, reportedly because of an intervention by the Minister of Defence. In

120

December 'Adel Hussein, a journalist and the Secretary General of the Labour Party, was arrested, apparently for possession of leaflets issued by al-Gama'a al-Islamiya. He was interrogated by the State Security Procuracy and given a 15-day detention order. At the end of the year he remained held.

Members of the Muslim Brothers were also held as possible prisoners of conscience. In August and September at least 90 members of this movement were detained. Most were arrested apparently for criticizing Egypt's hosting of the UN Conference on Population and Development in Cairo in September. It was not known if they were still detained at the end of the year.

The Ministry of the Interior continued to serve new detention orders, often repeatedly, on detainees who had obtained court orders for their release. Hundreds of detainees had consequently been held for more than a year without charge or trial. For instance, Hassan al-Gharbawi Shehata, a lawyer (see Amnesty International Report 1994), remained in administrative detention, despite many court orders for his release and despite being acquitted at his trial in 1990. At lea__ ___ people tried and acquitted by military courts in 1993 were still held under repeated administrative detention orders. Most of them were held incommunicado in the High Security Prison in Tora, following the Ministry of the Interior's ban on visits by families and lawyers introduced in December 1993. Among them was 'Abd al-Mun'im Gamal al-Din 'Abd al-Mun'im, a freelance journalist arrested in February 1993, who was acquitted by a military court in October 1993 (see Amnesty International Report 1994). He remained held in the High Security Prison at the end of the year.

Dozens of civilians charged with membership of banned Islamist militant groups had their cases referred to military courts by order of President Hosni Mubarak. The procedures of these courts fell far short of international fair trial standards. The judges – military officers – were not independent. Defendants were denied adequate time to prepare their defence and had no right of appeal to a higher court. Before trial, defendants were routinely held in prolonged incommunicado detention and many were reportedly tortured to extract confessions.

On 3 May, five civilians were executed after they were sentenced to death on 17 March by a military court. They were among 15 alleged members of Gihad accused of plotting to kill the Prime Minister, Dr 'Atef Sidqi. On 16 July the Supreme Military Court in Cairo sentenced five civilians to death in the case of 17 alleged members of Gihad who were charged with, among other things, attempting to assassinate the Minister of the Interior on 18 August 1993. The five were executed on 22 August. By the end of the year military courts had sentenced 21 people to death, including five in absentia, and 14 were executed. All death sentences passed by military courts are subject only to ratification by the President and review by the Military Appeals' Bureau, a non-judicial body. All death sentences were upheld by the Bureau.

Torture of political prisoners continued to be systematic, particularly in police stations, the SSI headquarters in Cairo and SSI branches elsewhere in the country. Most commonly cited torture methods included beatings, electric shocks, suspension by the wrists or ankles, burning with cigarettes and psychological torture. Hundreds of complaints of torture were lodged with the Public Prosecutor's Office but received little or no response. No investigations were made public despite the establishment in November 1993 of a special unit within the Public Prosecutor's Office to investigate reports of torture.

At least one person died in police custody apparently as a result of torture. 'Abd al-Harith Mohammad Madani, a lawyer, was arrested on 26 April and taken to the Giza branch of the SSI. He was reportedly tortured and as a result of the injuries sustained was taken to Qasr al-'Aini hospital in Cairo early the next morning. He was reported to have died later that day, although his family apparently did not learn of his death until 6 May when they were ordered to collect his body from the morgue. The body was released in a sealed coffin under police guard. He was a member of the Bar Association and the Egyptian Organization for Human Rights, and had defended many Islamist political prisoners.

The Minister of the Interior reportedly stated that 'Abd al-Harith Mohammad Madani had died following an asthma attack. However, a preliminary medical forensic report by the Public Prosecutor's Office allegedly recorded 17 injuries on various parts of the body. The final forensic report had not been made public by the end of the year. In June the authorities announced they would set up an investigation into 'Abd al-Harith Mohammad Madani's death, but no further details were made available.

At least eight people were killed by the security forces in circumstances suggesting they may have been extrajudicially executed. On 1 February, seven alleged members of al-Gama'a al-Islamiya were reportedly shot dead by SSI officers in the Cairo district of al-Zawiya al-Hamra. Eyewitnesses saw SSI officers dragging a man who then led the officers to a flat containing the seven men. Witnesses said they heard a short burst of gunfire. This contradicted the police version, which stated that the seven people had opened fire at the officers and that the shooting lasted over three hours. At the end of the year no investigation into the incident was known to have taken place.

On 25 April Amin Shafiq Hamam, a student at Asyut University and an alleged member of a banned Islamist group, was reportedly arrested in his room on the university campus by SSI officers and taken by car to a nearby village where he was killed. It appeared that no investigation into his death had been initiated.

The dramatic increase in the use of the death penalty continued. At least 39 people were sentenced to death: 21 of them, including five in absentia, for acts of violence including murder, at least 16 for murder, and two for drug-trafficking. At least 31 people were executed: of these, 14 had been sentenced by military courts in 1994 and had no right of appeal. Seventeen others had been convicted of murder and drug-trafficking in previous years. Among them was 'Abd al-Shafi Ahmad Ibrahim, who was executed in February after being sentenced to death by a state security court on 30 December 1993 for killing the writer Farag Foda (see Amnesty International Report 1994).

Armed opposition groups committed gross human rights abuses, including deliberate and arbitrary killings of civilians. In February gunmen, who were allegedly members of Gihad, shot dead Sayyid Ahmad Yahya, the owner of a car showroom, as well as one of his employees, a customer and a guard. The killings took place in Shibin al-Qanatir, a small town north of Cairo. Sayyid Ahmad Yahya was a key prosecution witness in a case against 15 alleged members of Gihad charged with plotting to kill the Prime Minister.

In March, six Copts, including two priests, were shot dead in two separate incidents in southern Egypt by armed gunmen alleged to be members of al-Gama'a al-Islamiya. The group was also reported to have been responsible for attacks on buses and boats carrying tourists which claimed the lives of four foreign nationals.

Amnesty International appealed repeatedly to President Hosni Mubarak to commute all death sentences. It called for the immediate and unconditional release of all prisoners of conscience held during the year. The organization urged an end to trials of civilians before military courts and called for all political prisoners to be given fair trials. Amnesty International also criticized the long-term detention without charge or trial of political detainees. It called for the immediate implementation of safeguards to stop torture and ill-treatment of detainees, and for urgent, thorough and impartial investigations into all allegations of torture and extrajudicial executions.

In April an Amnesty International delegation visited Egypt and met government officials to discuss human rights issues. The officials denied that there were systematic human rights violations in Egypt, saying that incidents may have occurred but these did not represent government policy. The delegation was refused a meeting with leading officials from the SSI.

In September Amnesty International published a report, Egypt: Human rights defenders under threat. In an 18-page response to the report, the authorities stated that lawyers and journalists had been held for either transgressing the law or because they were connected with banned Islamist militant groups. They also referred to the attacks by armed opposition groups – 70 policemen were killed in 1993 – and stated that the fight against "terrorism" was conducted with respect for the law. They maintained that military trials were fair. The response failed to address specific cases raised by Amnesty International or to indicate that measures would be taken to prevent or investigate human rights violations.

122

In April Amnesty International submitted information about its concerns regarding torture in Egypt to the UN Committee against Torture, pursuant to Article 20 of the Convention against Torture.

Amnesty International strongly condemned the deliberate and arbitrary killings of civilians by armed opposition groups and called on them to abide by international humanitarian standards and put an end to such killings.

EL SALVADOR

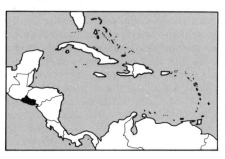

Members of the former armed opposition, including election candidates, were killed in circumstances suggesting that they had been extrajudicially executed. Despite human rights reforms introduced by the peace accords, these killings were committed with impunity. People identified with the opposition were subjected to death threats and attacks. There was concern about ill-treatment of detainees by the new police force and about harsh prison conditions.

Elections in March and April 1994 returned the ruling *Alianza Republicana Nacionalista* (ARENA), Nationalist Republican Alliance, to power. President Armando Calderón Sol, who defeated the opposition coalition candidate, Rubén Zamora, in a second round in April, took office in June. The presidential, legislative and municipal elections were to have completed the implementation of the peace accords, signed in 1992 by the government and the *Frente Farabundo Martí para la Liberación Nacional* (FMLN), Farabundo Martí National Liberation Front. However, certain key measures had still not been implemented by the end of 1994.

The new *Policía Nacional Civil* (PNC), National Civilian Police, continued to take on police and army personnel allegedly responsible for human rights violations in the past. The transfer to the PNC of members of the former *Comisión Investigadora de Hechos Delictivos*, Criminal Investigation Commission, and of the Anti-Narcotics Unit, both notorious for committing or covering up abuses in the past, was linked to continued abuses by the new police force, such as ill-treatment and excessive use of force.

The process of judicial reform was boosted by the election of a new Supreme Court of Justice in July. The role of the judiciary in human rights violations committed during the armed conflict had been particularly criticized in the 1993 report of the Truth Commission (see *Amnesty International Report 1994*). The Commission had recommended the removal of Supreme Court judges and the evaluation of all judicial personnel; this evaluation was continuing at the end of 1994.

In April the outgoing Legislative Assembly adopted a number of constitutional reforms incorporating some of the recommendations of the Truth Commission. However, key recommendations went unheeded, including further judicial reforms, reparation for victims of past human rights violations and accession to international human rights instruments.

In April the UN Human Rights Committee examined El Salvador's second periodic report on its implementation of the International Covenant on Civil and Political Rights. In its conclusions it expressed concern that the work of the Truth Commission and the future protection of human rights had been undermined by the 1993 amnesty law (see *Amnesty International Report 1994*).

Observers from the UN Observer Mission in El Salvador (ONUSAL) continued to monitor compliance with the peace accords.

The *Grupo Conjunto para la Investigación de Grupos Armados Ilegales con Motivación Política*, Joint Group for the Investigation of Politically Motivated Illegal Armed Groups, set up in December 1993 under UN auspices to investigate political violence since the end of the war, published its report in July 1994. The report concluded that organized groups carrying out political violence continued to operate, although their relation to state structures was more obscure and indirect than that of the so-called "death squads" of the past. Apparent links between political violence and organized crime made it difficult to ascertain motives in specific cases. Nevertheless, the Joint Group found evidence to suggest that many of the killings, attacks and threats reported since 1992 were politically motivated, and pointed to the absence of an official investigation in almost all cases. The Joint Group called for measures including the strengthening of El Salvador's judicial system, and the setting up of a special unit within the PNC to follow up cases of political violence. President Calderón Sol, who also received from the Joint Group a confidential appendix naming suspected perpetrators, promised to investigate all charges backed up by substantive evidence. However, the report was vehemently criticized as inconclusive and confusing by the Defence Minister, echoing the military's reaction to the Truth Commission's report in 1993. Little progress appeared to have been made by the end of the year to follow up the Joint Group's findings.

There were several killings which appeared to be politically motivated extrajudicial executions. Among the victims were members of the FMLN involved in the elections or in peace accord reforms. Most of the cases were not investigated and the pattern of killings suggested official involvement. On 27 March Heriberto Galicia Sánchez was shot dead by unidentified individuals near his home in San Miguel. Seven days earlier he had stood unsuccessfully as candidate for the Legislative Assembly for the *Movimiento Nacional Revolucionario* (MNR), the National Revolutionary Movement, which had an electoral alliance with the FMLN. Heriberto Galicia was a leading member of the MNR and of the Sugar Workers' Union, SINAZU-CAR. MNR members alleged that the murder was politically motivated and that Heriberto Galicia had previously received anonymous death threats by telephone.

FMLN member José Isaías Calzada Mejía, chair of an election monitoring committee in Jicalapa, department of La Libertad, was killed on the day of the second round of presidential elections. His body, with several bullet wounds, was found dumped near the road to San Salvador. According to witnesses, he had received death threats earlier in April during a quarrel with members of ARENA and the centrist

Partido Demócrata Cristiano (PDC), Christian Democratic Party, when he accused them of electoral irregularities. José Isaías Calzada Mejía had previously been attacked, allegedly by armed local ARENA members. He and other FMLN activists in the area had also previously received other death threats. David Merino Ramírez, FMLN coordinator of the land transfer program in Usulután, was shot dead by unidentified gunmen in a restaurant outside San Salvador on 11 November. Two FMLN leaders from San Vicente, one of whom was also involved in land transfers, were injured in the attack.

To Amnesty International's knowledge, no one was brought to justice for any of the above killings. Nor was there any apparent progress in similar cases reported since the end of the armed conflict. In July 1994 the PNC arrested two men accused of the 1993 murder of FMLN leader Francisco Velis (see *Amnesty International Report 1994*). But even in this high-profile case, proceedings appeared to have stalled by the end of the year.

The failure of the authorities to carry out effective investigations into political killings and other human rights violations was repeatedly criticized by ONUSAL. In its report of July 1994, ONUSAL's human rights division reported on the progress of judicial investigations into 75 cases of violations of the right to life since 1992. In not one case had those responsible been brought to justice. In a quarter of the cases no judicial proceedings whatsoever had been initiated.

New cases surfaced of previously unreported extrajudicial executions and "disappearances" by government forces during the armed conflict. However, the 1993 amnesty law continued to deny relatives of such victims the right to an investigation, to reparation and to justice.

Numerous opposition political figures and others identified with the opposition received death threats or were attacked. On 19 May unidentified people shot at the vehicle of Marta Valladares (formerly Commander Nidia Díaz), who had recently been elected to the Legislative Assembly as an FMLN deputy and President of the Assembly's Justice and Human Rights Commission. Her bodyguard, Elmer Cruz Pineda, who had suffered a similar attack in February, was injured. According to ONUSAL, the PNC's Criminal Investigation

124

Division appeared to have deliberately avoided pursuing significant leads in the case.

In May the offices of the women's organization *Movimiento Salvadoreño de Mujeres* (MSM), Salvadorian Women's Movement, were ransacked by unidentified assailants who destroyed documents but did not steal any valuables. The following day, Alexánder Rodas Abarca, a reserve PNC member and security guard for an FMLN faction, was shot dead as he guarded the faction's offices, which were shared with a human rights organization. Although police investigations were initiated into the incidents, no progress was reported.

Death threats continued to be issued in the name of "death squads" which had claimed responsibility for vast numbers of extrajudicial executions during the period of armed conflict, indicating the persistence of these clandestine structures. The targets of such groups included officials and church figures prominent as human rights advocates. In June individuals identifying themselves as members of the *Comando Domingo Monterrosa* (named after a military official killed in the 1980s), issued death threats against the Archbishop of San Salvador, Monsignor Arturo Rivera y Damas, and his auxiliary Monsignor Gregorio Rosa Chávez. Both had denounced the persistence of "death squads". The same month, the *Comando Domingo Monterrosa* telephoned the Salvadorian news media with death threats against a list of people including the Human Rights Procurator and the Attorney General.

Cases of torture and ill-treatment by new and existing police units were reported. On 10 May Avilio Ricardo Martínez was allegedly tortured in detention by PNC members in San Miguel who tried to force him to confess to a robbery. PNC members and soldiers carrying out law enforcement functions were also reported to have used excessive force in several incidents which resulted in suspects being killed. Jesús Molina Ramírez was shot three times while attempting to avoid arrest by members of the Fourth Military detachment for allegedly stealing a bicycle. ONUSAL reported that military officials had tried to cover up the case by coercing witnesses.

There was a series of riots in prisons around the country protesting against overcrowding and inhuman prison conditions. During the riots, it was alleged in some cases that prison guards had either been responsible for the death of inmates or had failed to protect them from other inmates.

An Amnesty International delegation visited El Salvador in June to follow up cases of apparent extrajudicial execution and death threats and to assess the progress of human rights related reforms. It held talks with government and non-governmental representatives, as well as ONUSAL. Before the elections, Amnesty International sought guarantees for the safety of all participants. It urged the authorities to investigate cases of possible extrajudicial execution and death threats, and called for the remit of the Joint Group to permit a thorough investigation into human rights violations and the bringing to justice of those responsible. Amnesty International urged the incoming government to ensure full compliance with the peace accords' provisions for the protection of human rights and to fulfil its obligation to tackle the impunity enjoyed by those committing human rights violations.

EQUATORIAL GUINEA

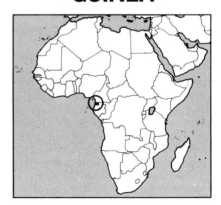

Five prisoners of conscience serving sentences imposed after an unfair trial in October 1993 were released under an amnesty in June, as were nine untried detainees who appeared to be prisoners of conscience. Hundreds of suspected government opponents were detained without charge or trial for short periods. Most appeared to be prisoners of conscience.

Many were reported to have been tortured or ill-treated. Seventeen political prisoners were convicted at two unfair trials. At least two people were extrajudicially executed by security forces. One person was reportedly sentenced to death and executed the next day.

At the opening in April of the new parliament elected in November 1993 (see *Amnesty International Report 1994*), President Teodoro Obiang Nguema promised greater respect for human rights. He announced that municipal elections would be held and promised that laws passed in 1992 and 1993, including the electoral law, would be revised. In June, at a conference of aid donors, the government agreed to compile an electoral register with the participation of opposition parties before taking a population census. However, in September the government started to compile a population census which opposition parties boycotted, on the grounds that the government might conduct local elections on the basis of a census which they had been unable to monitor.

In late November and early December the opposition Convergence for Social Democracy (CPDS) held its first congress in Bata, capital of the mainland region of Río Muni. It was the first congress to be held in Equatorial Guinea by an opposition party.

At the beginning of the year five prisoners of conscience were serving varying prison terms for conspiracy, incitement to rebellion and slander imposed in an unfair trial in October 1993 (see *Amnesty International Report 1994*). They and nine untried detainees who appeared to be prisoners of conscience were released under an amnesty in June to mark President Obiang Nguema's birthday. However, one of them, former sergeant Jacinto Nculu Abaga, was rearrested in October for reading an old Spanish military magazine: he was told that as he was no longer a soldier he should not read military publications. He remained in prison without charge or trial at the end of the year.

During the year at least 300 political activists and suspected government opponents were arbitrarily arrested in small groups or individually, especially in Río Muni. Most were released uncharged after a few days or weeks. Many had to pay what officials called "fines", but which had no legal basis, in order to be released.

Those who could not or refused to pay were detained for longer periods at the whim of provincial government officials.

About 100 people were briefly detained in several towns in Río Muni in January and February. Some were apparently arrested because they had not voted in the November 1993 elections, others because they were members of political parties which held political meetings. Others were arrested for criticizing government officials. Norberto "Tito" Mba Nze, a member of the CPDS, was arrested and tortured in February in Akonibe, in the southeast of Río Muni, for criticizing the behaviour of the government representative in the area. He was released over a week later. The government denied that Norberto "Tito" Mba Nze had been tortured or even arrested.

In March, 15 Equatorial Guineans who had been working in Gabon returned to Equatorial Guinea and were arrested in Acalayong, in southwest Río Muni. Five others evaded arrest but one, former police sergeant Antonio Ndong, was later captured and deliberately killed. The 15 were accused of attempting to attack the local military barracks as part of a plot to overthrow the government. They were taken to Bata prison where they were severely tortured. Two other people – a woman and a man – were also arrested and accused of sheltering those who had evaded arrest. They too were imprisoned in Bata.

Small groups of people were arrested on Bioko Island between March and May for allegedly belonging to the Movement for the Self-determination of Bioko Island (MAIB), a non-violent political party which had not obtained legal recognition. They included Weja Chicampo who was arrested in May in Rebola, 20 kilometres from the capital, Malabo. Members of his family and friends were also briefly detained. A week after his arrest Weja Chicampo was interrogated by security officials for several hours on two consecutive days. The interrogation was filmed and an edited version was later shown on television. Two others accused of belonging to the MAIB were interrogated with Weja Chicampo but they were not detained. Weja Chicampo was one of nine detainees released uncharged under the June amnesty.

In July Deogracias Nguema, the president of the League for the Defence of

Human Rights in Equatorial Guinea, was arrested in Malabo while he was collecting testimonies from victims of human rights violations. He was released uncharged three weeks later.

Tension mounted in September after the authorities started to compile the population census. Between September and October scores of people who opposed the census, including human rights and political activists, were arrested in Río Muni and ill-treated. Three human rights activists – Indalecio Abuy, Indalecio Eko and Tomás Nzo – were arrested in October outside Niefang in central Río Muni where they had gone to investigate reports of human rights violations. They were released uncharged a week later. Three political activists were arrested in the border town of Acalayong when they returned from a meeting organized by the European Union in Gabon in October. They were taken to the main police station in Bata where they were severely beaten. The three – Plácido Micó, a leading member of the CPDS who was a prisoner of conscience in 1992 (see *Amnesty International Report 1993*), Victorino Bolekia Banay, vice-president of the People's Democratic Alliance, and José Mecheba Ikaka, president of the National Democratic Union – were released uncharged several days later.

Three members of the CPDS were arrested in November just before their party's congress. Marcos Manuel Ndong, the CPDS representative in Spain, was arrested a few hours after his arrival in Bata. He was held without charge for several days and then expelled to Spain although he is an Equatorial Guinean citizen. This expulsion appeared to be illegal. Two other delegates were arrested in Akonibe and detained for several days.

There were two political trials. In July the 17 people who had been arrested in Acalayong in March were tried in Bata by a military court. Five defendants did not appear in court but no reason for this was given. The military trial procedures were unfair and there was no right of appeal. The court ignored the defendants' claims that they had been tortured. One defendant was acquitted and 16 were convicted of attempting to undermine the security of the state. Juan Mongomo Evolo and Rosendo Endong Nguema each received 30-year prison sentences, 12 defendants were each sentenced to 25 years' impris-

onment, and two, including María Teresa Akumu, received 12-year sentences.

There was a further political trial in November. Although the three defendants faced ordinary criminal charges of murder and were tried before a civilian court, it appeared that they had been falsely charged for political reasons. Two brothers and a sister-in-law of the president of the Progress Party were charged with killing their nephew and tried in Niefang. Three other brothers were arrested but released before the trial. A forensic doctor and the district judge in charge of investigating the death had reportedly certified it as suicide. Before their trial the defendants were shown on television, and statements they had made under torture were broadcast. The court apparently admitted these statements as evidence. Santiago Moto was convicted of homicide and sentenced to 10 years' imprisonment. The other two defendants were acquitted.

Many of those detained during the year were tortured. Two brothers were arrested in Bata in July for listening to a cassette recording of a song dedicated to Pedro Motú Mamiaga who died in police custody in August 1993 (see *Amnesty International Report 1994*). They were each beaten 250 times on the soles of the feet. Then they were made to run in front of a row of officers who beat them on the back with sticks. Santiago Moto and his brothers were also tortured in detention: their arms and legs were tied behind their backs and they were suspended from a pole and beaten with batons on their backs and the soles of their feet.

There were several reports of killings by the security forces, at least two of which appeared to have been extrajudicial executions. In March Antonio Ndong was reportedly killed by two soldiers. He was among the group of 20 who had crossed the border from Gabon in March (see above). According to reports, he surrendered to soldiers who found him hiding. Instead of arresting him, one soldier shot him in the forehead and the other shot him through the ear after he fell to the ground. In a separate case, in late September, Aguado Ndong Nguema was reportedly shot dead by a soldier in Mosok, in central Río Muni, because he refused to give his personal details to population census officials. The government denied that Aguado Ndong Nguema had been killed.

Juan Mongomo, a former army officer, was reportedly sentenced to death by a military court in December. Amnesty International had no details of the charges against him. He had no right of appeal and was reportedly executed the day after the sentence was passed.

Amnesty International delegates visited Equatorial Guinea in July to gather information about human rights violations and to discuss the human rights situation with officials. Throughout the year the organization appealed for the release of prisoners of conscience. It repeatedly called for the introduction of effective safeguards against torture and ill-treatment and urged the government to set up inquiries into all reports of torture and extrajudicial executions. In February Amnesty International published a report, *Equatorial Guinea: A missed opportunity to restore respect for human rights*, which described the human rights violations at the time of the elections held in 1993.

ERITREA

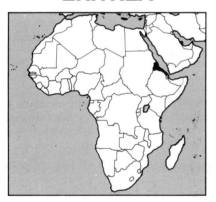

Several suspected government opponents were detained without charge or trial. Over 130 people detained on account of their involvement with the previous Ethiopian Government in Eritrea were released, but scores of others remained in detention without charge or trial. The whereabouts of over a dozen people who "disappeared" in 1991 and 1992 remained unknown. Two dissident soldiers were killed by government troops in July; it was not clear whether they had been extrajudicially executed.

The country entered its second year of independence from Ethiopia under the government of President Issayas Afewerki, **127** chair of the People's Front for Democracy and Justice (formerly the Eritrean People's Liberation Front, EPLF), the only permitted political party. A commission was appointed to draft a constitution and started work.

Information about detentions of government opponents was difficult to obtain and confirm. Several people were reportedly arrested in western Eritrea in January for alleged involvement with an armed Eritrean opposition group, Islamic Jihad, based in neighbouring Sudan, but no further details were available.

Abdusalam Mohamed Habib and three other members of the Jaberti ethnic group were arrested during a visit from Saudi Arabia in January and remained in detention without charge or trial at the end of the year. The authorities gave no explanation for their detentions.

An amnesty was declared in May for 132 prisoners detained without charge or trial since 1991 on account of alleged involvement in human rights crimes or "spying" for the former Ethiopian Government. No details were given about those released or about scores of others remaining in detention.

There was no news from the government or other sources about several detainees who had "disappeared" in the previous three years. They included Idris Saad Mahmoud and three other members of an Eritrean group working with the former Ethiopian Government who were reportedly abducted from Addis Ababa in May 1991: Ali Higo Mohamed, a former mayor of Massawa, who was abducted from Addis Ababa in July 1991; and Wolde-Mariam Bahibi and Tekle-Berhan Gebre-Tsadik of the Eritrean Liberation Front-Revolutionary Council (ELF-RC), who were abducted from Sudan in April 1992.

In July government troops reportedly shot dead two dissident soldiers at Mai Habar military camp, 30 kilometres south of the capital, Asmara. It was unclear whether or not the government troops used lethal force lawfully when they fired at the soldiers, who were reportedly demonstrating against the military authorities.

Amnesty International appealed to the government to disclose details of all political detainees, to clarify their legal status and not to detain them indefinitely without charge or trial. It called for the release

128

of the four Jaberti members whom it believed to be prisoners of conscience. It urged the authorities to account for all "disappeared" prisoners, and to establish an impartial investigation into the Mai Habar incident. No reply was received.

ESTONIA

A 17-year-old female prisoner who had been put in a punishment cell for a month hanged herself. Three prisoners were under sentence of death. Up to 100 asylum-seekers were held in detention.

In September Amnesty International learned of the death in Harku prison of 17-year-old Riina Vallikivi. She had reportedly been placed in a punishment cell in July for one month, despite the fact that she had allegedly attempted suicide on previous occasions and had been diagnosed by prison medical staff as "mentally unbalanced". On 19 August she was found hanged in her cell. Article 67 of the UN Rules for the Protection of Juveniles Deprived of Their Liberty prohibits all disciplinary measures constituting cruel, inhuman or degrading treatment, "including closed or solitary confinement or any other punishment that may compromise the physical or mental health of the juvenile concerned".

Amnesty International learned in March that Sergei Krylov had been sentenced to death the previous year for the crime of aggravated murder. Sergei Krylov and two other men convicted in 1993 (see *Amnesty International Report 1994*) were believed to be still under sentence of death at the end of the year.

Up to 100 asylum-seekers, including children, were detained throughout the

year. Their situation remained unresolved at the end of 1994.

In September Amnesty International called upon the Estonian authorities to conduct a full inquiry into the death of Riina Vallikivi. The organization urged that such an inquiry should examine, among other things, the order to place her in a punishment cell and her medical supervision during imprisonment. In November the authorities informed Amnesty International that before being placed in a "closed cell" – a punishment allowed by Estonian legislation – Riina Vallikivi had been examined by the medical chief of Harku prison who found her to be "'mentally unbalanced' but within normal limits". An inquiry into her death was currently being conducted by the prosecuting authorities. In December Amnesty International repeated its concerns and asked for further clarification of the authorities' response.

Throughout the year Amnesty International appealed for commutation of the three pending death sentences.

In June and September Amnesty International expressed concern to the Estonian authorities that asylum-seekers had not had their need for protection properly considered or been treated fully in accordance with the relevant international standards for the protection of asylum-seekers, including standards providing that asylum-seekers should not normally be detained. In a letter to Amnesty International in October the authorities acknowledged the concerns raised and the need to take steps to address them.

ETHIOPIA

Several thousand suspected government opponents were detained during 1994. Many, including several journalists and opposition party activists tried and imprisoned for political offences, were prisoners of conscience. Over 5,000 alleged opponents of the Transitional Government detained without charge since 1992 were released. Trials on charges of genocide and crimes against humanity began in December against officials of the previous government. There were widespread allegations of torture. Scores of "disappearances" and extrajudicial executions

of government opponents were reported. Two people were sentenced to death but there were no executions.

The Transitional Government headed by President Meles Zenawi, leader of the Ethiopian People's Revolutionary Democratic Front (EPRDF), extended its two-and-a-half-year term pending future general elections. A Constituent Assembly was elected to establish a new Constitution, which it ratified in December. Fighting continued in Oromo-populated areas between government forces and the Oromo Liberation Front (OLF), and violent incidents occurred in other regions.

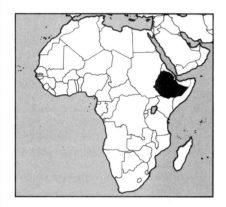

In March Ethiopia acceded to the UN Convention against Torture and Other Cruel, Inhuman or Degrading Treatment or Punishment, and in April to the Protocols additional to the Geneva Conventions of 1949.

Over 70 journalists of the independent press were arrested on account of articles criticizing the government. Many were repeatedly denied bail but eventually released provisionally: in May the Minister of Justice announced that 43 court cases were pending against journalists. Kefale Mammo, chairman of the Ethiopian Free Press Journalists Association (EFJA), was held for 19 days in April, apparently for contacting international human rights and media organizations. Several journalists were convicted under the Press Law (1992) and received prison terms, suspended prison terms or heavy fines. Tefera Asmare, editor of *Ethiopis* magazine, was sentenced to two years' imprisonment in March for criticizing the government. He was a prisoner of conscience, as was Goshu Moges, editor of *Tobia* magazine, who was sentenced to six months' impris-

onment in October and released on bail pending appeal in December for publishing a letter from an imprisoned prominent government opponent, Professor Asrat Woldeyes, which said he did not expect a fair trial (see below). Tesfaye Tadesse, a lawyer and human rights activist, was arrested in July, apparently in connection with an article in a magazine to which he was legal adviser. He was held for four months without charge.

Hundreds of opposition party members were detained on account of their peaceful political activities.

Throughout the year there were widespread arrests in eastern Ethiopia of members of the Ogaden National Liberation Front (ONLF), an ethnic Somali party. Many of those held seemed to be prisoners of conscience who were not involved in armed opposition by ONLF militias. Hajio Dama, chair of the Ogadenian Women's Democratic Alliance, was one of many people arrested in January on account of the ONLF's call for an independence referendum for the region. She was released in February with serious medical problems resulting from ill-treatment. In May government troops detained the regional assembly President, Hassan Jirreh Kalinle, and other elected members. The authorities alleged they were arrested for embezzlement of public funds. Hassan Jirreh Kalinle was released provisionally in July. Many ONLF supporters were still detained incommunicado by the army at the end of the year, including Ibado Abdullahi, a woman poet, and Haji Abdinur Sheikh Mumin, Imam of Degabur mosque.

In April, 26 members of the Eritrean Liberation Front-Revolutionary Council (ELF-RC), a political organization opposed to the government of Eritrea, were arrested in Addis Ababa and Mekelle, apparently at the request of the Eritrean Government. They were still held without charge at the end of the year pending resettlement in another country.

Scores of members of the All-Amhara People's Organization (AAPO) were detained during 1994. AAPO's chairman, Asrat Woldeyes, a professor of surgery, was imprisoned in June after being convicted with Sileshi Mulatu, an AAPO official, and three others, of conspiring to form an armed group. They had been arrested in mid-1993 and only Asrat Woldeyes had been granted bail. All five, who

130

denied calling for anti-government violence at a private AAPO meeting in October 1992, were sentenced to two years' imprisonment after an unfair trial. They were prisoners of conscience.

On 20 September up to 1,500 people, including elderly women, children, former ambassadors and AAPO supporters, were arrested at the Central High Court in Addis Ababa during a demonstration against a new trial of Asrat Woldeyes and two former AAPO officials. The protest was peaceful, but ended in scuffles after a police attack. About 1,000 people were soon released without charge; however, after a month of unlawful detention, 500 were charged with holding an illegal demonstration and public provocation. They were released on bail but no date had been set for their trials by the end of the year. Asrat Woldeyes was imprisoned for a further six months in October for contempt of court on account of a letter he wrote refusing to attend court on the grounds that he did not expect a fair trial, and for an additional three years in December on another charge.

Hundreds of members of southern opposition parties were detained in the second half of 1994. They included Lemma Sidamo, vice-chairman of the Sidama Liberation Movement (SLM), who was arrested in Addis Ababa in September but provisionally released after two months, and Merid Abebe, chairman of the Omo People's Democratic Union, who was arrested in Addis Ababa in October. Some were charged with political offences but the majority were detained without charge, and none was tried.

There were widespread arrests of suspected OLF supporters in conflict zones as well as in Addis Ababa and other towns with large Oromo populations. Most were detained illegally and incommunicado without being brought to court and charged, and many seemed to be prisoners of conscience. In September, 40 people were detained in the town of Ambo, after attending the funeral of Derara Kefana, an Oromo businessman shot dead by soldiers near his home. Over a dozen of them were still held without charge or trial at the end of 1994.

Some 5,000 suspected OLF members detained in 1992 and 1993 were released in early 1994. The government said that the others remaining in detention would be brought to court, charged and tried, and that Hurso and Dedessa special military camps for "OLF detainees" would be closed. At the end of 1994 around 300, who had been moved to Ziwai prison, were still awaiting trial.

Several hundred long-term political prisoners remained in detention throughout 1994, most of them without charge. They included many alleged OLF members, four members of the Ethiopian People's Revolutionary Party (EPRP) abducted from Sudan in 1992, and members of the SLM and ONLF (see *Amnesty International Report 1994*). The trial of Colonel Daniel Tessema and five others charged in 1993 with plotting a coup did not start during the year.

On 25 October the Chief Special Prosecutor filed capital charges of genocide and crimes against humanity against 45 of the 1,315 former officials of President Mengistu Haile-Mariam's government, security forces and ruling party who had been detained since 1991 (see *Amnesty International Report 1994*). Twenty-two others, including the former president in exile in Zimbabwe, were charged *in absentia*. Other former officials were arrested during 1994, including two who were forcibly repatriated from Djibouti in May. The trials, which opened before the Central High Court on 13 December, were adjourned to allow defence lawyers to prepare their case.

Seven exiles detained after returning to Ethiopia for a peace conference in December 1993 (see *Amnesty International Report 1994*) were freed in January. Charges of armed rebellion were withdrawn but Aberra Yemane-Ab was kept in detention for alleged crimes in the 1970s. Dozens of non-violent Oromo demonstrators arrested at the trial of the two returning OLF leaders were imprisoned for a month for contempt of court. One of the demonstrators, Elfinesh Kano, a folk-singer, was kept in detention while the authorities investigated whether her songs were seditious. A prisoner of conscience, she was released after another four months' imprisonment without charge.

Scores of suspected government opponents from different political groups "disappeared". They were believed to be held secretly by the security service. Some "reappeared" months after their relatives had given up searching for them. Those still "disappeared" at the end of the year included Nayk Kassaye, editor of *Beza* magazine, who "disappeared" in Addis Ababa in May; Mustafa Idris, a telecommunications worker, who also "disappeared" in Addis Ababa in May, and his sister Fatuma Idris, who "disappeared" in Harar in July after complaining about her brother's "disappearance"; and many alleged OLF and ONLF supporters. Several people who "disappeared" in previous years were feared to have been extrajudicially executed, including Hagos Atsbeha, held by the Tigray People's Liberation Front (TPLF) since 1988 whom the authorities claimed had committed suicide in prison; four EPRP military leaders captured in 1991; and Yoseph Ayele Bati, an OLF supporter abducted in 1992 (see *Amnesty International Report 1994*).

Torture of suspected government opponents, particularly OLF suspects, was frequently reported. Torture survivors reported having their arms tied tightly behind their backs with plastic ties; beatings with sticks and guns; whippings with electric cable; mock executions and death threats; and rape. Torture took place in secret security prisons and army camps, particularly in areas near anti-government fighting.

Oromo demonstrators arrested in Addis Ababa in December 1993 and those arrested at Asrat Woldeyes' trial in September were beaten by soldiers. They were detained incommunicado in Sendafa Police College near Addis Ababa, had their hair roughly shaved without soap or water, were made to do rigorous physical exercises, and were given little food or medical treatment.

Government soldiers were reported to have killed unarmed civilian opponents on several occasions. In February troops fired on an ONLF demonstration in Wardheer which was becoming violent, reportedly killing 60 people. Other ONLF supporters were also reported to have been extrajudicially executed by soldiers, including Mohamed Omer Tubar, a regional commissioner, in February and Mirad Leli Sigale, former mayor of Gode, in May, whom the authorities claimed was killed while escaping from detention. Among many OLF suspects killed by soldiers during 1994 was Bekele Argaw, a former army colonel, shot dead at his home in Ambo in September.

There was still no reaction from the Council of Representatives (the interim parliament) to a report submitted by a commission of inquiry into the police killing of a student demonstrator in January 1993 (see *Amnesty International Report 1994*).

Two people were sentenced to death for homicide but there were no executions.

Amnesty International appealed for the release of prisoners of conscience. It welcomed the start of trials of former officials charged with gross human rights violations but urged the authorities to rule out death sentences. It stressed that all political detainees should be charged and tried as soon as possible in accordance with international standards, or released. It called for impartial investigations into the emerging pattern of "disappearances" and torture, and into reports of extrajudicial executions of government opponents.

Amnesty International representatives visited Ethiopia in May. In November Amnesty International submitted to the government a 45-page memorandum on political imprisonment, "disappearances", torture and political killings of government opponents. It recommended a series of measures to stop these serious human rights violations.

FRANCE

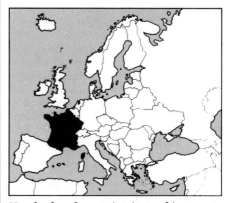

Hundreds of conscientious objectors to the national service laws were considered prisoners of conscience. There were reports of shootings, killings and ill-treatment by law enforcement officers, sometimes accompanied by racist insults. Investigations into such cases were subject to long delays.

132

In March widespread public protests followed the announcement by Prime Minister Edouard Balladur of a reduction in the guaranteed minimum wage for young professionals, the *contrat d'insertion professionelle* (CIP). Numerous demonstrators alleged that they were ill-treated by law enforcement officers.

Many domestic human rights groups were concerned by a major increase in police identity checks during the year. Police had been given sweeping new powers in 1993 to demand proof of identity even in cases where there was no evidence of suspicious behaviour. Allegations of ill-treatment during identity checks were received throughout 1994. In July a draft bill on security was presented to parliament. The control of immigration and of illegal workers was listed as one of six national priorities for the police.

There was still no right to claim conscientious objector status during military service and the alternative civilian service available to recognized objectors remained twice the length of ordinary military service. Conscientious objectors refusing to conform to the national service laws continued to receive prison sentences. The vast majority were Jehovah's Witnesses; some 500 were unofficially estimated to be imprisoned during the year for refusing to perform military service. They had not applied for conscientious objector status because they also rejected, on religious grounds, the option of civilian service.

Shootings and killings by law enforcement officers continued throughout the year. In January, two gendarmes near Rouen shot dead Ibrahim Sy, an 18-year-old youth who was a passenger in a stolen car which they were trying to stop. All three youths in the car were unarmed. In June an off-duty policeman in Paris killed two young men, Joël Nebor and Frédéric Adom, during an attempted robbery in a shop. The men, who were not carrying firearms, had thrown a chair at the officer, who was in plain clothes. He then fired nine shots at close range without attempting to subdue the men and also wounded the shop proprietor's companion.

Judicial inquiries into many other cases of shootings and killings were still unfinished at the end of the year. These included the cases of Rachid Ardjouni and Makomé M'bowole (see *Amnesty International Report 1994*). In other cases, courts imposed nominal sentences. In January the court in Chambéry gave a suspended sentence of one year's imprisonment to a police officer for manslaughter. Eighteen-year-old Eric Simonté had been shot through the head and fatally wounded by an officer who was putting handcuffs on him (see *Amnesty International Report 1994*). The prosecutor considered this "serious misconduct" and an "inadmissible error in the technique of challenging a person".

There were numerous reports of physical, including sexual, ill-treatment by law enforcement officers. Many people who had participated in or observed the anti-CIP demonstrations alleged that they had been beaten and injured by officers. Didier Laroche, who took part in a large and mostly peaceful march in Bordeaux in March, was ill-treated by officers from an "intervention squad". He claimed that they punched and kicked him and beat him with a truncheon. He was put in a van and further ill-treated on the way to the police station, where a doctor examined him and requested hospital treatment. A certificate was issued by the hospital recording a broken nose and various injuries to his eyes, face, chest, knees and thighs. His judicial complaint of ill-treatment was still under investigation at the end of the year.

At the end of 1994 judicial investigations into many complaints by people allegedly ill-treated when they were arrested after riots in Paris in April 1993 remained unfinished (see *Amnesty International Report 1994*). However, two police officers were indicted on charges of unlawful use of violence against Philippe Lescaffette, a civil servant. He had claimed that police officers armed with clubs charged him, threw him to the ground and beat him. He spent four hours in a cell without medical attention and later received 24 stitches for facial injuries.

There were numerous complaints of ill-treatment associated with identity checks, some of them relating to previous years. In June 1993 police were called to a Paris restaurant because a group of diners, including Tameem Taqi, the son of a former United Arab Emirates diplomat and a French national, had disputed a bill. Their identity papers were examined and the disagreement settled. Tameem Taqi claimed that the same officers stopped him outside, handcuffed him, and pushed him to the floor of their van. He was kicked, punched and beaten with truncheons in front of witnesses. Another diner from the same group was also detained. The police transferred both men to hospital where the officers subjected them to further ill-treatment and racial insults. A medical certificate recorded multiple contusions to Tameem Taqi's face and body consistent with his claims. His nose and mouth were particularly damaged. A prosecutor extended his custody order despite his visible physical injuries. Tameem Taqi lodged a complaint against the officers for torture and using racist insults, and against the prosecutor for illegal arrest. The judge in charge of the investigation into the two complaints indicted four police officers and remanded a sergeant in custody for assault and battery. However, her investigation was still unfinished at the end of the year.

In February Pierre Kongo, a gynaecologist from the Central African Republic, was stopped by two railway officers at the Gare du Nord railway station in Paris. He said that the police officers who arrived subsequently asked him for his identity papers and he showed his passport. The officers pushed him down the stairs, handcuffed him behind his back and knocked him to the ground. He claimed that the officers punched him while he was lying on the ground. The next morning he was treated in hospital for his injuries. A medical certificate was issued recording, among other injuries, a serious fracture to his right eye-socket. The railway and police officers gave differing and contradictory explanations for his injuries. These included statements that Pierre Kongo had injured himself by accidentally falling down; by falling over a bench trying to strike one of the officers with an arm, as he was not handcuffed; by trying to head-butt an officer because he was handcuffed; and by falling over a bench with an officer while he was resisting a body search. Pierre Kongo was released without charge. An internal police inquiry was opened and Pierre Kongo served a summons against one of the officers alleging intentional assault and battery.

Two cases illustrated the delays characteristic of the investigation and hearing of complaints of ill-treatment. In July 1993 Moufida Ksoury, a French citizen of Tunisian origin, was returning to France from Italy. At the border two Italian police officers stripped and raped her. They then took her to the French border post which was manned by two officers of the border police. A French police corporal sexually assaulted her in the toilets. He acknowledged that he had had oral sex with her but claimed that she had provoked him. In July 1994 the two Italian officers were sentenced to five years and eight months' imprisonment, but the French judicial investigation was still unfinished at the end of the year.

Two police inspectors and an investigating officer were charged with acts of violence and racist abuse against Lucien Djossouvi in September 1989 in Paris (see *Amnesty International Reports 1990* to *1994*). In September 1994 the hearing in the case was postponed for the second time until January 1995. The investigation had taken nearly four and a half years.

Ill-treatment was also alleged in prisons. In March there was a serious disturbance in Varces prison near Grenoble. News of this was largely suppressed for three weeks. Riot police were called in to support prison staff in clearing exercise yards of prisoners who were reportedly peacefully protesting. Prisoners claimed that the operation was carried out with excessive brutality. They stated that officers, wearing hoods to conceal their identity, beat them with truncheons. Unmuzzled dogs allegedly attacked prisoners who had returned to their cells. Approximately 15 prisoners were reportedly treated for their injuries in the infirmary and others were transferred to other prisons. Lawyers repeatedly demanded an inquiry into the incidents. An administrative inquiry under a gendarmerie officer was opened in March but the authorities refused a full judicial inquiry.

Amnesty International continued to express concern that, because of its punitive length, civilian service did not provide an acceptable alternative to military service. Amnesty International was also concerned that there was still no provision for conscientious objection developed after joining the armed forces. It reiterated its belief that conscientious objectors to military service should be able to seek conscientious objector status at any time.

Amnesty International sought information from the authorities about the

134 progress of investigations into incidents of shootings, killings and ill-treatment. In August 1993 the organization had written to the Ministers of the Interior and Justice regarding its concerns. In view of the failure of the government to reply to this letter and the organization's concern over the persistence of such incidents, Amnesty International published in October a report, *France: Shootings, killings and alleged ill-treatment by law enforcement officers.* This analysed 29 selected cases which occurred between January 1993 and June 1994. Seven detailed recommendations were made to the Ministers of the Interior, Defence and Justice who are responsible respectively for the police, gendarmerie and justice. Particular emphasis was placed on improvements in training for law enforcement officers and specific reforms to the judicial system. No answer had been received by the end of the year.

An Amnesty International delegate was sent to the twice-postponed trial of police officers accused of the ill-treatment and racist abuse of Lucien Djossouvi.

GABON

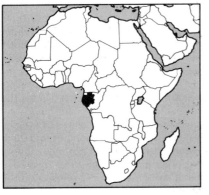

Scores of political prisoners, many of whom appeared to be prisoners of conscience, were held without trial. In a single incident, 67 prisoners were suffocated to death. Several people were shot in what may have been unlawful killings.

The opposition claimed that presidential elections in December 1993, which returned President Omar Bongo to power, were fraudulent and refused to accept the results. In early October, following international mediation, the government and opposition political parties signed an agreement to end 10 months of tension and frequent violent protests over the disputed elections.

For several months at the start of 1994 there were civil disturbances, particularly in the capital, Libreville. A state of alert, imposed from 20 December 1993 to 13 February 1994, was reintroduced between 21 February and mid-March after disturbances during the first day of a general strike organized by the *Confédération gabonaise des syndicats libres*, Gabonese Confederation of Free Trade Unions. The state of alert provided for emergency laws, including the detention without charge or trial of people considered to be a threat to public order, a night curfew and a ban on demonstrations.

At least 40 people, many of whom appeared to be prisoners of conscience, were arrested between 20 and 24 February, when members of the Presidential Guard ransacked a radio station which supported the main opposition party, the *Rassemblement national des Bûcherons* (RNB), National Rally of Lumberjacks. The authorities accused the radio station of encouraging social unrest and inciting violence. By the end of the year, most of these people were allegedly still in detention. Those arrested included journalist Vécka-Brice Nang, who was reportedly beaten while in custody. He was released provisionally in May after being charged with "inciting hatred and violence". It was unclear if he had been tried by the end of the year.

At least 14 students were arrested in June, after violent disturbances at Omar Bongo University when students went on strike to demand an increase in their allowances. Amnesty International could not confirm whether any of them had been charged, tried or released by the end of the year but several appeared to have been held in prolonged detention without access to legal counsel.

Sixty-seven prisoners held without trial died on 3 February in the Gros-Bouquet Gendarmerie detention centre in Libreville. They apparently suffocated to death after being held with over 200 other detainees in one cell. The victims were reportedly all accused of being illegal immigrants. Despite the scale of the tragedy, no action was reported against those responsible for the prisoners' conditions.

Two people, Ferdinand Nguema and Antoine Mba Ndong, both employees of RNB leader Paul Mba Abessole, died while in custody, reportedly after torture. They were arrested on 23 February when the Presidential Guard were searching Paul Mba Abessole's home. No official inquiry was announced to establish the cause of their deaths.

Seven civilians were killed in unclear circumstances during disturbances in Libreville between 20 and 24 February at the time of the general strike. In several cases the security forces apparently used disproportionate force against protesters, possibly committing unlawful killings.

Amnesty International called for independent investigations into deaths in custody and other killings by the security forces, which appeared to be violations of human rights. The UN Special Rapporteur on extrajudicial, summary or arbitrary executions raised similar concerns about the death of 67 detainees to the authorities. The authorities responded officially, but failed to reveal the precise cause of the deaths or the exact circumstances in which they had occurred, suggesting that no independent investigation had been held to collect the facts and to hold those responsible accountable.

There was no direct response from the authorities to Amnesty International on any of the concerns raised by the organization.

GAMBIA

Three journalists were detained briefly as prisoners of conscience and either convicted or deported. Following a coup in July, more than 40 former officials were arbitrarily arrested and detained without trial.

A bloodless military coup in July ended the rule of President Dawda Jawara, Gambia's only leader since independence in 1965. He was first granted temporary asylum in Senegal, and later went to the United Kingdom. The Armed Forces Provisional Ruling Council (AFPRC), led by Lieutenant (later Captain) Yahya Jammeh, which assumed power, claimed corruption had become widespread and pledged to eradicate it. It suspended the Constitution and passed several decrees which

allowed for administrative detention without charge in ways which facilitate arbitrary detention. The decrees removed the right of detainees to be informed of the reasons for their arrest and to appear promptly before a court. All political activities were banned from July 1994 and anyone who had been politically active before then could be restricted in their movements, if this was held to be in the national interest. Any member of the armed forces could be detained without trial for up to six months in the interests of national security, and their case would be reviewed in their absence by a Detention Review Tribunal which would report directly to the AFPRC. A number of commissions of inquiry were set up to investigate alleged corruption and the authorities were given far-reaching powers to obtain evidence.

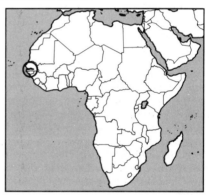

In October Lieutenant Jammeh announced that the AFPRC would remain in power until the end of 1998, when it would hold elections. However, after much criticism, internationally and within the country, on 14 December he named a National Consultative Committee which was to present its recommendations by early 1995 for a new timetable for the return to civilian rule. In November the government survived a coup attempt which resulted in a number of arrests and the deaths of at least four soldiers and possibly many more. It was impossible to establish the circumstances of these deaths or the identities of those who died. However, reports suggested that some may have been extrajudicially executed after hostilities ended.

Three prisoners of conscience were held briefly. On 19 August Halifa Sallah and Sidia Jatta were arrested after their

136

newspaper, *Foroyaa* (Freedom), the official organ of the People's Democratic Organization for Independence and Socialism (PDOIS), was banned. They were released on bail on 23 August and charged under Decree 4 which banned political activities. During their trial they argued that the newspaper was produced in the public interest, not to further the ends of their political party. In October they were sentenced to three years' imprisonment which was suspended on condition that they did not engage in any political activity during the transitional period.

In October a newspaper owner was detained and, on the grounds that he was a Liberian citizen, eventually expelled from Gambia. Kenneth Best, owner of the *Daily Observer* newspaper, was told his company had violated tax and immigration laws. However, the real reason for the authorities' actions appeared to be to curb the newspaper's criticism of the government. Other journalists working on independent newspapers were also briefly held or threatened with arrest.

Eleven former government ministers were arrested shortly after the coup in July and held in administrative detention; one other was arrested later. They were transferred to house arrest, but redetained for short periods on at least two further occasions. In mid-November they were released on condition that they did not leave the country or engage in political activities.

At least 30 members of the security forces were arrested in July and held under Decree 3 which allowed the authorities to detain members of the armed forces for up to six months without charge. It was not clear whether the detention orders were reviewed by the Vice-Chairman of the AFPRC as stipulated in the decree, but the Detention Review Tribunal began to review cases after three months. The tribunal's members were appointed by the AFPRC and its role was limited to submitting recommendations to the AFPRC which could either revoke or extend the detention order. The decree explicitly prevented a detainee from attending or being represented before the tribunal. Sixteen of the detainees were reportedly released during November, either on humanitarian grounds or after their cases had been reviewed by the Detention Review Tribunal, but at least 14 remained in detention at the end of the year. They were held incommunicado for several months, until the International Committee of the Red Cross was granted access to them in December. The secrecy surrounding their detention led to rumours that Kebba Ceesay, Director of the National Security Service, had died in custody. However, it was eventually confirmed that he was alive and receiving medical treatment.

At least 13 people, believed to be members of the security forces, were reportedly detained following the coup attempt in November and were still held at the end of the year.

Amnesty International expressed concern to the AFPRC about the numerous cases of arbitrary detention and about the inadequate Detention Review Tribunal procedures. The organization also raised its concerns about the expulsion of Kenneth Best and the conviction of Halifa Sallah and Sidia Jatta as these measures restricted freedom of expression and association.

GEORGIA

A group of 19 political prisoners was tried; the proceedings appeared to fall short of international standards for fair trials. One political prisoner was reportedly beaten. One other detainee was reported to have died following ill-treatment. At least eight people were executed after parliament lifted a moratorium on executions. At least 11 people were sentenced to death, and at least 13 death sentences were commuted. In the disputed region of Abkhazia one person was reportedly detained on ethnic grounds; the fate of a number of others

who "disappeared" in previous years remained unclear. At least six people were believed to be on death row at the end of the year in Abkhazia.

After several weeks of confusion early in the year, the death of former president Zviad Gamsakhurdia, an opposition figure, was confirmed. A state of emergency was lifted from most of the country in February. Head of State Eduard Shevardnadze survived parliamentary moves for a vote of no confidence in September.

The situation in the disputed region of Abkhazia (see *Amnesty International Report 1994*) became more stable through the year. The Georgian and Abkhaz sides agreed a cease-fire and disengagement of forces in May, and Russian troops were deployed in the area as peace-keepers the following month. Under an earlier agreement, a few of the estimated 250,000 people displaced by the fighting began to return to Abkhazia in October.

In May Georgia acceded to the International Covenant on Economic, Social and Cultural Rights as well as to the International Covenant on Civil and Political Rights together with its (First) Optional Protocol. The country acceded to the UN Convention against Torture in October.

Nineteen men, many of them supporters of former president Zviad Gamsakhurdia, were on trial on charges ranging from illegal arms possession to murder and terrorism. The trial appeared to fall short of international standards. Many of the men reported that they were not informed of the charges against them at the time of their arrest in 1992 and that access to a lawyer of their own choice had been periodically denied. The trial judge was reported to have denied defendants access to materials on the case, and in at least one instance to have denied a defence lawyer access to such materials. No confessions were excluded, despite allegations that they had been obtained under duress in pre-trial detention. Forms of torture described by defendants from that time included hanging upside-down, scalding with boiling water and systematic beatings resulting in fractured bones.

Most allegations of ill-treatment dated from before the trial opened in October 1993, although one defendant, Viktor Domukhovsky, reported that he had been beaten on 13 August by special police officers who entered his cell demanding notes

he had made of the trial. Many of the defendants suffered illness as a result of their conditions of detention; they were held in overcrowded, pest-ridden and insanitary cells. Medical attention was reportedly arbitrary and inadequate.

One man died after reportedly being beaten by the police. In July Roin Kochishvili from the village of Kurta, Tskhinvali district, was said to have died after being beaten by police officers who had detained him and several friends on suspicion of driving a stolen car.

In March parliament lifted a two-year moratorium on executions, and eight men had been executed by August. They included Suliko Chikhladze, who had been sentenced to death for murder in February. He and five others of the eight executed had been tried by the Supreme Court, and had no possibility of appeal. At least 11 death sentences were passed in the first half of the year. Thirteen death sentences were commuted in August.

At least one person was reported to have been detained on ethnic grounds in the disputed region of Abkhazia. Madlena Japaridze, aged 67, an ethnic Georgian, was said to have been visited on 8 July by an Abkhazian soldier who accused her of associating with other Georgians. The next day he and four other soldiers reportedly returned and took her away. Another family had moved into her apartment by that evening. Her whereabouts were still unclear at the end of the year.

The fate of others said to have "disappeared" in previous years during the conflict over Abkhazia also remained unresolved. They included at least seven non-Georgians said to have been detained on ethnic grounds in Sukhumi by Georgian forces in late 1992, and dozens of Georgians reportedly detained by Abkhazian forces after they recaptured Sukhumi in September 1993.

In January the Abkhazian procurator reported that there were five or six people on death row in the disputed area, all convicted of murder, and that there was no specific body at that time to review petitions for clemency.

Amnesty International sought further information on people reportedly detained solely on ethnic grounds in the Abkhazian conflict, and urged both sides to account for the whereabouts of those said to have "disappeared".

138

Amnesty International urged the authorities to ensure that Viktor Domukhovsky and his co-defendants received a fair trial in line with international standards. The organization also urged a comprehensive, prompt and impartial investigation into all allegations of ill-treatment, with the results made public and any perpetrators identified brought to justice.

Amnesty International expressed regret at the resumption of executions and urged that all pending death sentences be commuted. The organization also urged that immediate steps be taken to ensure that all those sentenced to death had the right to appeal to a court of higher jurisdiction, and to seek pardon or commutation of the sentence.

GERMANY

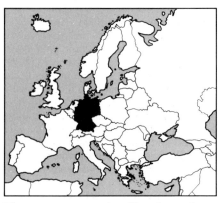

There were numerous allegations of torture or ill-treatment of detainees by police officers throughout the year. Two people died in police custody in disputed circumstances.

The majority of the victims of alleged torture or ill-treatment were foreign nationals, including asylum-seekers, or members of ethnic minorities. A high proportion of cases involved officers of the Berlin police force.

In April Bülent Demir, a 17-year-old German Turk, alleged that Berlin police officers had punched him in the kidneys and face and kicked him in the head after they had caught him spraying the wall of a house with paint. Medical certificates showed that he had suffered bruises, abrasions, two broken teeth and a broken finger which required surgery. He was later charged with resisting state authority.

In May journalist Oliver Neß alleged that he was assaulted by police officers while reporting on a demonstration in central Hamburg. According to both the journalist and a friend who witnessed the assault, two officers pinned Oliver Neß to the ground while a third removed his right shoe and deliberately and violently rotated his foot at the ankle, tearing the ligaments. Officers also allegedly punched him in the face and hit him repeatedly in the kidneys, pelvis and chest with their batons.

In August there were reports that police officers in the federal states of Berlin and Brandenburg had, over a period of more than a year, subjected Vietnamese detainees to torture or cruel, inhuman or degrading treatment. In a typical case Nguyen T., an asylum-seeker, alleged that he was punched and repeatedly kicked when plainclothes police officers stopped him and his wife in the street in the east Berlin district of Pankow in June. The residents of nearby flats were reportedly so alarmed by his screams that one of them called the police. Nguyen T. alleged that his ill-treatment continued in the police car which took him to a nearby police station, and at the station itself. His injuries included multiple bruising to his body and a hairline fracture of the bone under his left eye.

Decisions were reached by prosecuting and judicial authorities on a number of cases of alleged ill-treatment by police in previous years (see *Amnesty International Report 1994*). In February the Bremen prosecuting authorities rejected an appeal from Mehmet S. against an earlier decision not to bring charges against police officers accused of ill-treating him. Mehmet S., a Turkish Kurd, had alleged that in March 1992, when he was 14 years old, police officers had broken his arm while arresting him. In its decision to reject the appeal, the Bremen Public Procurator's Office stated that medical experts had been unable to clarify exactly how the injury to Mehmet S. had occurred.

In March the prosecuting authorities in Rostock brought charges of "arson by negligence" against two senior police officers in connection with racist attacks on an asylum hostel in Rostock-Lichtenhagen in August 1992. Over 100 Vietnamese workers housed next to the hostel had been left unprotected after the police withdrew their forces for over an hour. During their absence rioters set fire to the building, forcing the Vietnamese residents to escape on to the roof.

In September a Berlin court imposed substantial fines on three Berlin police officers found guilty of ill-treating Habib J. in December 1992. The Iranian student had alleged that after he was assaulted by a bus driver, police officers had thrown him roughly into a police van and had racially abused him and hit him in the face at the police station. The three officers appealed against their conviction.

In September a Hamburg court ruled that there was insufficient evidence to open trial proceedings against three officers charged in June with causing serious bodily harm to Frank Fennel. He had been badly beaten by members of a special police unit in July 1991. A court later awarded him compensation for his injuries, which included concussion, multiple bruising and abrasions, and a bruised kidney. Frank Fennel appealed against the court's decision.

In October the Brandenburg Higher Regional Court of Appeal ruled that three officers charged with failing to intervene in a racist attack on Amadeu Antonio Kiowa could not be tried owing to lack of evidence. Amadeu Antonio Kiowa, an Angolan immigrant worker, had been kicked and beaten unconscious by a gang of right-wing extremists in November 1990. He later died of his injuries.

Two detainees died in police custody in disputed circumstances. In June Halim Dener, a 16-year-old Turkish Kurd, was shot in the back by a Hanover police officer after being caught putting up posters for an outlawed political party. Contradictory reports were received about the shooting. Some suggested that the officer's gun had gone off accidentally after he had stumbled. Others alleged that the officer had deliberately aimed his gun at Halim Dener. Following a criminal investigation the officer concerned was charged in December with causing the death of Halim Dener through negligence.

In August Kola Bankole died at Frankfurt am Main airport following an attempt by the Federal Border Police to deport him to Nigeria. A doctor accompanying the rejected asylum-seeker had reportedly injected him with a sedative when he physically resisted the attempts to deport him. Kola Bankole died 25 minutes later. A criminal investigation was opened into the actions of the doctor.

In January the Schwerin Public Procurator's Office closed its investigation into the death of Wolfgang Grams, concluding that the suspected Red Army Faction member had not been deliberately killed by a member of an anti-terrorist unit, but had committed suicide (see *Amnesty International Report 1994*).

Amnesty International expressed its concern to the German authorities about allegations of torture and ill-treatment and about the death in custody of Halim Dener. The organization was informed that criminal investigations had been opened into all the cases it had raised. In September Amnesty International called for a full investigation into the death of Kola Bankole and the role of medical personnel in cases of forcible deportation. No reply to its letter had been received by the end of the year.

In January Amnesty International published a report entitled *Federal Republic of Germany: Police ill-treatment of detainees in Hamburg* in which it criticized the Hamburg authorities for failing to prosecute or discipline police officers responsible for ill-treating detainees in their custody.

GHANA

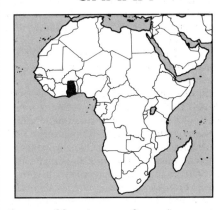

Ten possible prisoners of conscience were detained, one of whom alleged that he had been severely beaten by police. Prisoners under sentence of death had their sentences commuted to life imprisonment. The Commission on Human Rights

140 appointed in 1993 decided not to investigate allegations of extrajudicial executions dating from the early 1980s.

In February the government imposed a state of emergency in some northern districts when inter-ethnic conflict resulted in the killing of at least 1,000 people, and possibly many more. Members of the Konkomba community were in dispute with other ethnic groups over their rights to a chieftaincy and land ownership. About 150,000 people fled their homes, some into neighbouring Togo. In June the government negotiated a cease-fire between the various groups and in August the state of emergency was lifted.

Six possible prisoners of conscience were arrested and charged with plotting to overthrow the government of President J.J. Rawlings. Karim Salifu Adam, a former army sergeant and member of the National Patriotic Party (NPP), was arrested in May. He was detained without charge for nearly two months, apparently illegally, before being brought before a court and charged in connection with an alleged coup plot. The prosecution alleged that he had recruited young men for military training in Burkina Faso with the aim of overthrowing the government. He denied the charges in court and said that they had been fabricated by the Bureau of National Investigations (BNI), the security police, because he had refused to implicate opposition leaders in a fictitious coup plot. He alleged that BNI officers had beaten him severely. His trial was repeatedly adjourned, apparently because investigations had not been completed, and had not proceeded by the end of the year.

Five Ghanaians who had recently returned to Ghana from the United Kingdom were arrested on 2 September on suspicion of plotting a coup attempt: Sylvester Addae-Dwimoh, a teacher; Alex Kwame Ofei, of dual Ghanaian/British nationality; Kwame Ofori-Appiah; Emmanuel Kofi Osei; and John Kwadwo Owusu-Boakye, a student nurse. They were detained without charge until 23 September, when they were brought before a circuit court in Accra and charged with treason, a capital offence. The prosecution said that they came to Ghana in August 1994, recruited soldiers and obtained arms and ammunition, and that others involved had escaped arrest. The court denied them bail and repeatedly remanded them in custody. By the end of the year they had not been informed of the details of the charges against them, had not been asked to plead to the charges and had not been formally charged before the High Court. The five appeared to have been detained illegally for three weeks – beyond the 48 hours allowed by law – before being brought before the court and charged. They also appeared to have been held illegally in military custody at Gondar Barracks, Burma Camp, Accra, before being transferred to the custody of the security police. Following complaints to the court from their lawyers that access and private interviews with their clients were being denied by the security police, the court ordered their transfer to prison. According to unofficial reports, the defendants, all members of the same church, were conducting prayers together in a guest house at the time of their arrest. It appeared that the motive for their arrest might have been political and that they might have been prisoners of conscience.

In December police arrested Dr Charles Wereko-Brobby, an opposition journalist, and three others, and seized telecommunications equipment. They were charged with operating a private radio station without a licence and released on bail; their trial had not taken place by the end of the year. It appeared that they might have been prisoners of conscience.

In January prisoners who had been under sentence of death for more than 10 years had their sentences reduced to life imprisonment; those who had been sentenced to death for economic sabotage had their sentences reduced to 15 years' imprisonment. The numbers and identities of those who benefited were not announced. However, at least one prisoner known to have been sentenced to death in 1987 for economic sabotage was believed to have had his sentence reduced. Amnesty International estimated that as many as five prisoners under sentence of death for more than 10 years may have benefited. No death sentences were known to have been passed or executions carried out during the year.

In late 1994 the Commission on Human Rights and Administrative Justice, set up in July 1993 to monitor the observance of human rights in Ghana, said that it would not investigate allegations of extrajudicial executions committed in the early 1980s after Flight-Lieutenant Rawlings seized power for the second time. It had received requests to investigate the killings, particularly from the opposition Popular Party for Democracy and Development (PPDD). The Commission said that the PPDD was not allowed to bring such a request on behalf of those killed, that the volume of work from similar outdated complaints could swamp the Commission and that investigation after such a long time would be difficult.

Amnesty International investigated the detention of possible prisoners of conscience.

GREECE

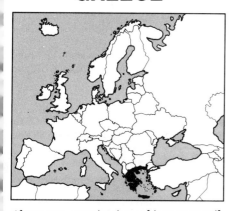

About 400 conscientious objectors to military service were held; all were prisoners of conscience. Legal proceedings continued in the cases of 14 people prosecuted for peacefully exercising their right to freedom of expression. There were further reports of ill-treatment by police.

Continuing political tensions between Greece and its neighbours – Albania, the Former Yugoslav Republic of Macedonia and Turkey – were reflected in domestic policies. In August and September Greece expelled at least 70,000 Albanian nationals following the trial of five ethnic Greeks in Tirana, Albania (see **Albania** entry). Members of the Macedonian and Turkish minorities in Greece were tried for peacefully exercising their right to freedom of expression.

There is no alternative civilian service for conscientious objectors to military service. About 400 Jehovah's Witnesses who refused to perform military service on reli-

gious grounds continued to serve sentences of up to four years and eight months' imprisonment. All were prisoners of conscience. However, conscientious objectors were given the possibility of halving their sentences by working in agricultural prisons. As an indirect consequence of a new law aimed at reducing prison overcrowding, about 90 conscientious objectors were released in mid-1994 from the agricultural prisons of Kassandra and Kassavetia. However, 76 of the men released as a result of the law received new call-ups for military service due to start in April 1995. Arrest warrants were issued against three conscientious objectors who were not Jehovah's Witnesses, but these had not been enforced by the end of the year. Some 80 other conscientious objectors who were not Jehovah's Witnesses publicly declared their opposition to military service but were not imprisoned.

Legal proceedings continued in the cases of 14 people who had been prosecuted as a result of their criticism of government policies on ethnic minorities and foreign affairs (see *Amnesty International Report 1994*). In January the Court of Appeal dropped the charges against four members of the *Antipolemiki Antiethnikisti Syspirosi,* Anti-War Anti-Nationalist Movement, as well as those against Christos Sideropoulos and Anastasios Boulis on the grounds that the statute of limitations had expired. However, Christos Sideropoulos faced further charges (see below). The appeal hearings of Michail Papadakis and of six members of the *Organosi gia tin Anasingrotisi tou Kommounistikou Kommatos Elladas* (OAKKE), Organization for the Reconstruction of the Communist Party of Greece, had not been heard by the end of the year.

In April criminal charges against Sadik Ahmet, a former member of parliament, were dropped (see *Amnesty International Report 1991*). The charges had been brought following an article published in the newspaper *Güven* in November 1989 in which he alleged that the ethnic minority which he described as "Turkish" were subjected to discrimination and repression. Proceedings against him had been suspended between April 1990 and September 1993 because of parliamentary immunity.

In September the trial of Christos

142

Sideropoulos was postponed until September 1995. He had been charged in November 1993 with "spreading false information which may cause disruption of the international relations of Greece" because of a statement he had made at a press conference in Copenhagen, Denmark, during the meeting on minority rights of the Conference on Security and Co-operation in Europe (CSCE) in June 1990. He had declared that he belonged to the Macedonian ethnic minority living in Greece and that his cultural rights were being violated.

Allegations of ill-treatment by police were received throughout the year. For example, in February Charalambos Kabiotis was arrested by police officers from the Attica Security Force for suspected possession of a small quantity of drugs. He alleged that the police officers handcuffed and beat him in the street before taking him to a bar owned by his girlfriend where they continued to beat him, particularly on the head and chest, in front of witnesses until he almost lost consciousness. His girlfriend also alleged that she was insulted, punched and beaten by the police officers.

There were allegations of ill-treatment of Albanian nationals in the course of mass expulsions during August and September. Ilia Makta, an Albanian from Fier who came to Greece in about 1990 and was working legally in Kalamata, alleged that a few days before his expulsion in September he was called to Kalamata police station where the Chief of Police tore up his authorization papers. He was then put in a cell and allegedly beaten by police officers before being expelled.

In April Amnesty International submitted information about its concerns regarding torture and ill-treatment in Greece to the UN Committee against Torture, pursuant to Article 20 of the UN Convention against Torture and Other Cruel, Inhuman or Degrading Treatment or Punishment. Its report, *Greece: Torture and Ill-treatment, Summary of Amnesty International's principal concerns,* documented cases of ill-treatment in police custody, allegations of brutality by the riot police, and ill-treatment of conscientious objectors and Albanian nationals. It also reported the failure of the Greek authorities to investigate past allegations. The Committee expressed its concern that the practice of

severe ill-treatment seemed "to be an on-going problem occurring in some police stations" and recommended that the legislation designed to prevent the ill-treatment of detainees be fully implemented.

In November the government authorized the publication of the report of the European Committee for the Prevention of Torture and Inhuman or Degrading Treatment or Punishment. The report, based on visits to prisons and police establishments in March 1993, documented cases of ill-treatment and torture, including the alleged use of electric shocks, corroborating information published by Amnesty International in 1992 (see *Amnesty International Report 1993*), and made specific recommendations for safeguards to protect detainees and improve conditions of detention. The government's preliminary reply stated that it had implemented or would implement some of the recommendations.

In June Amnesty International published a report, *Greece: Christos Sideropoulos, Ethnic Minority on Trial.* The organization called for the charges against Christos Sideropoulos to be dropped.

GUATEMALA

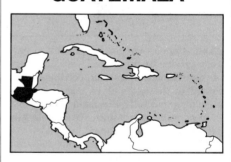

The number of extrajudicial executions increased significantly over the previous year. Victims included human rights workers, indigenous activists, suspected government opponents, returning refugees, students, academics, trade unionists and journalists. Several fatalities resulted from apparent excessive use of force by security forces and so-called "civil patrols" – civilian militias in which Guatemala's largely indigenous peasants are forced to serve. At least 30 "disappearances" were reported, as were incidents of torture, including rape. Harassment

and intimidation, including death threats, were widespread.

The security forces continued to commit human rights violations with virtual impunity; little or no progress was made in bringing to justice those responsible either for new violations or for violations committed under previous administrations. Several clandestine cemetery sites were exhumed by independent forensic doctors, who unearthed remains believed to be those of primarily indigenous non-combatant victims of large-scale extrajudicial executions carried out by the army during its counter-insurgency campaign of the late 1970s and early 1980s. However, there were no convictions of those believed to be responsible. Similarly, little progress was made in investigating more recent extrajudicial executions.

In March 1994 the government and the armed opposition signed a UN-brokered human rights accord committing the government to respect human rights and to take firm action against impunity. The accord set the agenda for reaching agreement on refugees and the displaced, indigenous peoples, a cease-fire, constitutional reforms and a peace treaty, due to be signed in December. In June, in the context of the UN-brokered peace talks, the two parties agreed on a Clarification Commission to look into human rights and "acts of violence" that had "caused suffering to the Guatemalan people". However, the Commission was due to start work only when a final accord was signed by both sides and it would not be empowered to name perpetrators or initiate proceedings against them.

In August the armed opposition withdrew from the talks, saying that continuing violations were symptomatic of the government's failure to respect the accord; the government countered by saying that the opposition was still carrying out attacks in which civilians died. The peace talks restarted in October.

The March accord also mandated the establishment of the *Misión de Naciones Unidas para Guatemala* (MINUGUA), UN Mission for Guatemala, to monitor compliance with the accord. After many delays, the UN began deploying technical set-up staff in Guatemala in September.

There was some controversy as to whether the establishment of a Clarification Commission would mean that the

UN's Special Expert on Guatemala, mandated to examine the human rights situation in Guatemala and offer assistance to the government on human rights matters, would no longer be needed. In a January report, the Expert called for investigation of past abuses and dissolution of the civil patrols.

Only days after the signing of the March accord, President Ramiro de León Carpio reportedly considered suspending constitutional guarantees and increasing the internal security powers of the armed forces following a wave of violence sparked by the 1 April shooting of the President of the Constitutional Court, Eduardo Epaminondas González Dubón. President de León had been elected by Congress in June 1993 to finish the term of President Jorge Serrano, who was forced to leave office following a failed "self-imposed" coup (*auto-golpe*) (see *Amnesty International Report 1994*). Judge González Dubón had been viewed as instrumental in reversing the attempted coup. Although a number of common criminals were initially arrested, highly placed government officials publicly stated that there was no evidence to link them to the crime; by the end of the year, there had apparently been no convictions. In October Judge González' son, an employee of the Human Rights Procurator's Office, was dismissed, after describing its investigations into his father's death as "inefficient".

The number of extrajudicial executions escalated during the year. Those targeted included human rights workers, indigenous activists, suspected government opponents, returning refugees, students, academics, trade unionists and journalists. By mid-July 1994 the *Oficina de Derechos Humanos del Arzobispado de Guatemala* (ODHAG), the Archbishopric of Guatemala's Human Rights Office, had recorded more than 160 extrajudicial executions. Also in July, the country's Human Rights Procurator accused the government of being responsible for an increasing wave of violence in the country; by the end of the year his office had recorded 287 victims of extrajudicial executions.

Victims included Pascual Serech, a Cakchikel from Panabajal, Chimaltenango Department, who was shot and mortally wounded by three armed men in August. He had been a member of the Panabajal Human Rights Commission which actively

144

opposed forced recruitment into the army, forced service in the civil patrols, and the many abuses, including "disappearances" and extrajudicial executions, reportedly carried out by the military in Panabajal. Before he died, Pascual Serech reportedly named the local military commissioner, a civilian agent of the army, and his two sons, as his assailants. By the end of the year, no arrests had been reported.

Manuel López returned to Guatemala from a Mexican refugee camp in May 1994. He was found dead, his hands tied and his body showing signs of ill-treatment, near a temporary settlement for returnees in El Quiché Department in October. In 1992 refugee representatives and the Guatemalan Government had agreed a plan for the return of refugees living in UN High Commissioner for Refugees (UNHCR) camps in Mexico. The government, opposition and UN representatives signed a further accord guaranteeing the safety of all returned refugees and displaced communities in June 1994, in the context of the peace negotiations. Yet, since returns began in 1993, there have been numerous reports of threats, attacks and harassment against returnee communities, particularly in El Quiché, reportedly carried out by members of the army and their civilian adjuncts.

Several street children were extrajudicially executed by the police or government-licensed private security agents. They included 10-year-old Daniel Rosales and 13-year-old Rubén García González who were shot and killed by two private policemen in September 1994 as they slept on a street corner. Two policemen were reportedly detained in connection with the incident, but by the end of the year the case against them had not been concluded.

In August, two people died when riot police and private security agents apparently used excessive force in evicting peasants peacefully occupying the San Juan del Horizonte estate in Quetzaltenango Department to press the estate owners to pay the legal minimum wage. According to reports, police opened fire, killing Efraín Recinos Gómez, a trade unionist helping to bring food to the demonstrators, and Basilio Guzmán Juárez, an estate worker. Several others were wounded, two seriously, and over 40 taken into short-term detention. In Sep-

tember the Quetzaltenango departmental police chief was dismissed on the grounds that he had not complied with National Police guidelines for such evictions. The police said they were considering proceedings against him and that internal inquiries would continue to determine the degree of responsibility of the 300 police agents who participated in the operation. The badly mutilated body of Diego Orozco, a leader of the estate's rural workers' association, was found some 60 kilometres away shortly after those arrested during the eviction were released. Trade union sources alleged that private security police had first tortured him, and then thrown his body from a helicopter.

Over 30 people were reported to have "disappeared". In January Lorenzo Quiej Pu, a member of the *Consejo Nacional de Desplazados de Guatemala* (CONDEG), National Council for the Displaced of Guatemala, "disappeared" after leaving for work. The government informed the UN Working Group on Enforced or Involuntary Disappearances that the police were investigating, but CONDEG expressed fears that the investigations might be aimed at intimidating other CONDEG members, particularly Lorenzo Quiej's brother, a CONDEG leader, and might be related to plans to cause their "disappearance".

Alleged victims of torture during the year included Jorge Alberto and Gilberto Moral Caal, who were arrested by police with other Pokomhí Mayans in March in San Cristóbal Verapaz, Alta Verapaz Department, following the beating of a foreign tourist. Townspeople attacked the tourist, a US citizen, believing she was involved in the alleged kidnapping and "export" of Guatemalan children for adoption and the organ trade. The attack was one of several similar incidents around that time, which were reportedly instigated by people working closely with the army.

In January, two young indigenous girls from San Miguel Chicaj, Baja Verapaz Department, a Quiché-speaking region, said they had been raped by a group of men led by the local military commissioner, well-known in their area for previous abuses. The girls decided not to press charges after a representative of their village was threatened and insulted when he went to the local military base to file a complaint concerning the alleged rapes.

When victims of violations attempted

to pursue complaints through the courts, they, their relatives, witnesses, lawyers and judges involved in the cases were themselves victimized on a number of occasions. Judge María Eugenia Villaseñor was forced to flee Guatemala temporarily in September after she received a series of threats, apparently connected to her involvement in a number of high-profile human rights cases. In July an anonymous caller told Judge Villaseñor he would kill her if she did not drop the cases. Shortly afterwards, a policeman assigned to protect her was seized by men in plain clothes, beaten, and interrogated about her. Judge Villaseñor had been involved in two cases in 1993 in which members of the security forces had been convicted of human rights crimes (see *Amnesty International Reports 1993* and *1994*). She had also sentenced Noel de Beteta, a low-ranking member of the security section of the Estado Mayor Presidencial (EMP), presidential guard, to 30 years' imprisonment for the 1990 killing of anthropologist and writer Myrna Mack (see *Amnesty International Reports 1991* to *1994*.) Assertions first reportedly made by Noel de Beteta in 1993, that he carried out the killing under orders from a superior, were not pursued (see *Amnesty International Report 1993*). In 1994 Guatemalan radio reportedly broadcast a tape of Noel Beteta describing how he was given the order to carry out the murder by his superior officer.

Witnesses and relatives were threatened in the course of inquiries into the apparent extrajudicial execution of prominent politician and publisher Jorge Carpio Nicolle in July 1993. The wife of opposition commander Efraín Bámaca, a US citizen, missing since 1992, also reported intimidation by officials during her campaign to press the government for information. She believed that her husband was secretly detained by the military; they maintained that her husband was killed in combat (see *Amnesty International Report 1994*). Foreign forensic experts helping exhume victims who had been extrajudicially executed by the army in the late 1970s and early 1980s also reported threats, as did relatives of those believed to be buried in the clandestine cemeteries.

Amnesty International addressed the government repeatedly, calling for inquiries into reported violations. It also repeatedly reiterated to both the government

and the opposition that it was vital for the Clarification Commission and MINUGUA to ensure that those responsible for gross violations in Guatemala in recent years, including massive extrajudicial executions directed largely at Guatemala's indigenous peoples, did not benefit from any sort of pre-trial amnesty that would in effect grant them impunity for violations.

In July Amnesty International published details of a selection of unresolved extrajudicial executions in Guatemala since President de León took office, cases in which sufficient information already existed for a Clarification Commission to initiate immediate in-depth inquiries. The organization also pointed out at that time that since President de León had come to office, it had already called on him to initiate inquiries on over 50 separate occasions involving reported or feared violations against some 300 people.

In March, in a written statement, Amnesty International urged the UN Commission on Human Rights to continue to monitor the situation in Guatemala, pointing to the marked increase in death threats and other forms of intimidation. In June the organization drew the attention of the International Labour Conference's Committee on the Application of Standards to recent "disappearances" and extrajudicial executions of trade unionists and members of rural workers' associations in Guatemala.

GUINEA

At least 11 government opponents were imprisoned for up to one month and appeared to be prisoners of conscience. Several suspected government opponents arrested in previous years were held without charge or trial throughout the year. Reports of torture and ill-treatment were widespread. Liberian refugees were victims of serious human rights violations; at least 140 were detained without charge and several reportedly died in custody, and others were forcibly returned to Liberia. A Liberian armed political organization reportedly carried out deliberate and arbitrary killings of Liberian refugees with the support of some officials in Guinea.

The security forces continued to harass

146

opponents of the government of President Lansana Conté, who was returned to power in elections in December 1993. Legislative elections scheduled to take place during 1994 were postponed until 1995. Public meetings by opposition parties were banned for most of the year and several of those which did take place were broken up by the armed forces. For example, in August soldiers broke up a meeting of the opposition *Rassemblement du peuple de Guinée* (RPG), Guinean People's Rally, in Kérouane, 700 kilometres east of the capital, Conakry, killing two people and injuring many others.

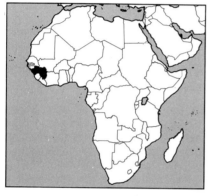

In December the government announced that the death penalty, which had not been enforced since President Conté took power in 1984, would be imposed by the courts and carried out. The measure was part of an official campaign against violent crime. No death sentences were known to have been carried out by the end of the year.

The civil war in neighbouring Liberia continued to effect Guinea, particularly in areas close to the Liberian border. According to eye-witnesses, in these areas a faction dominated by members of the Mandingo ethnic group of the Liberian armed political organization, the United Liberation Movement for Democracy in Liberia (ULIMO), was reportedly allowed to operate with the support of local government officials and members of the Guinean security forces of the same ethnic origin, known as Malinké in Guinea (see **Liberia** entry).

Eleven RPG members were detained in Kankan province in January and appeared to be prisoners of conscience. Tidjane Traoré, Mamady Magassouba and others were arrested after a political campaign tour.

They were initially detained at a military camp in Kankan, where they were ill-treated, until they were brought to court on charges of inciting resistance. They were sentenced to between 15 days' and one month's imprisonment.

In December, 13 Islamist activists, including Seidou Sidi Beye, a Malian national, were arrested in Mandiana, 550 kilometres east of Conakry. They were brought to court, apparently on charges of violence and making inflammatory speeches, although it was not clear whether they had in fact used or advocated violence. At least five were given prison sentences of up to two years' imprisonment; others were given suspended prison sentences.

Other suspected government opponents remained held without charge or trial. Amadou II Diallo, arrested in October 1992 in connection with an alleged assassination attempt against President Conté (see *Amnesty International Report 1994*), remained in detention without charge or trial throughout 1994. Bassy André Diakité, a Burkinabè national reportedly arrested in Siguiri in March 1993 on suspicion of undermining the security of the state, was held without trial at the Central Prison in Conakry throughout 1994.

There were widespread reports of torture and ill-treatment, particularly of people held in the region near the border with Liberia. For example, detainees were subjected to a torture method known locally as "*tabey*": the arms are tied tightly behind the back with elbows touching, causing extreme pain, rope burns and sometimes paralysis.

There were reports that Liberian refugees in Guinea and, in some cases, Guineans suspected of helping them, were subjected to various human rights violations by Guinean officials who sympathized, on ethnic grounds, with certain Liberian armed factions. For example, some Liberian refugees who were not from the Mandingo ethnic group were reportedly accused of supporting Liberian armed political movements opposed to the Mandingo faction of ULIMO and were detained without charge or trial or, in some cases, killed. In July reports indicated that more than 140 Liberians were detained for this reason in Macenta; four had reportedly died as a result of ill-treatment and torture. They were apparently suspected of supporting the Lofa Defense Force (LDF), a militia which emerged in northeast Liberia in late 1993 to counter attacks from the Mandingo faction of ULIMO. In mid-July, four Liberian refugees and two Guineans accused of helping them were arrested and detained without charge in Macenta. Also in July, a nurse from Gbarnga in Liberia who was a refugee in Guinea was arrested and accused of spying for the National Patriotic Front of Liberia (NPFL), an armed political group based in Gbarnga and fighting ULIMO since 1991. She was reportedly taken to Macenta Prison. It was not possible to confirm whether any of these detainees had been released by the end of the year.

There were reports that Guinean army and immigration officials participated in the forcible return of Liberian refugees fleeing ULIMO forces in Liberia. In February a Liberian nurse fleeing to Guinea was reportedly forced at gunpoint to cross back into Liberia and shot in the back and seriously injured by a Guinean soldier.

Abuses were reportedly committed in parts of Guinea by ULIMO and there were allegations that they had been carried out with the cooperation of some Guinean officials. For example, Guinean soldiers reportedly allowed ULIMO fighters to wear Guinean army uniforms and to kill young men among the Liberian refugees in Guinea whom they suspected were LDF members. Three Liberians – Kulubah Piwi, Alfred Zeze and Augustine Moniba – were reportedly shot in this manner by ULIMO fighters in June in the Guinean town of Yezu. In none of the cases involving abuses by ULIMO were the Guinean authorities known to have intervened to protect refugees or bring to justice those responsible for abuses.

ULIMO forces deliberately and arbitrarily killed Guinean civilians. In one case, at least 28 civilians were killed in early January when ULIMO fighters attacked two towns on the Guinean side of the border.

Amnesty International was concerned about the imprisonment of apparently peaceful government opponents, the long-term detention without charge or trial of other political detainees and reports of torture and ill-treatment of detainees. The organization was also concerned about the alleged killing, torture and arbitrary detention of Liberian refugees; it was particu-

larly concerned about the failure of the judicial authorities or central government to take any action to ensure the protection of refugees or end the pattern of abuses against them.

GUINEA-BISSAU

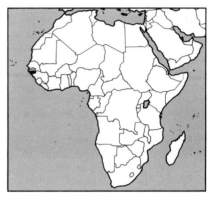

Members and supporters of opposition parties were arrested and beaten. Two prisoners of conscience were acquitted of complicity in an alleged coup attempt and released. Their trial, at which 14 other defendants were convicted and one acquitted, was unfair.

The ruling *Partido Africano da Independência da Guiné-Bissau e Cabo Verde* (PAIGC), African Party for the Independence of Guinea-Bissau and Cape Verde, won Guinea-Bissau's first multi-party elections in July. The head of state, President João Bernardo Vieira, narrowly won the presidential election after a run-off ballot in August. Members of opposition parties complained, both before and after the elections, of intimidation by government supporters and security personnel.

Two prisoners of conscience were briefly detained for exercising their right to freedom of expression. Luis Nancassa, president of the *Sindicato Nacional dos Professores*, National Teachers' Union, was arrested in February during a strike and demonstration against low pay and poor working conditions. He was accused of trying to prevent other teachers from working. He denied this but admitted using his legal right to call on teachers to join the strike. He was released uncharged after three days. António Nhaga, a journalist, was arrested in Cacheu, northeast of the capital, Bissau, in July. Police held

148

him for two hours and questioned him about a recording he had made of one of President Vieira's campaign speeches.

There were reports of suspected government opponents being arrested and sometimes assaulted. On the day of the teachers' strike, according to eye-witnesses and the local press, the Minister of Education stopped his car as he passed some teachers on their way to join the demonstration, fired his pistol into the air, grabbed one of the fleeing teachers and punched him. The minister reportedly apologized later. In the months following the elections several people were arrested and beaten, apparently because they had supported opposition political parties. They included Ussumane Embalo and a woman, Kodi Djata Djalo, who were briefly detained and assaulted by police in Gabú, in the east of Guinea-Bissau, in August. Opposition parties protested and the number of reported incidents declined.

Two prisoners of conscience, João da Costa and Tagmé Na Waié, both prominent members of opposition parties, were acquitted in January of complicity in an alleged coup attempt and released. They had been detained following a mutiny by soldiers in March 1993 in which a senior military officer was killed and which the authorities claimed was part of an attempt to overthrow the government (see *Amnesty International Report 1994*).

The trial of João da Costa, Tagmé Na Waié and 15 soldiers (not 14 as stated in *Amnesty International Report 1994*) was unfair. Many of the defendants said that senior military and security officials, whom they named, had forced them to sign statements implicating themselves and others in the alleged conspiracy. These statements constituted an important part of the evidence for the prosecution. The soldiers said that they had been demonstrating for better pay and conditions in the army. One soldier was acquitted and the others were sentenced to prison terms ranging from two to 15 years.

Details of torture and ill-treatment which took place in 1993 emerged at the trial. Amadú Mané, a soldier accused of the murder of the military officer in the mutiny, was reportedly stripped naked and held secretly for three days in a cell so small he was unable to lie down. Other defendants said they were threatened with death if they did not confess to complicity

in the alleged coup. In June 1994 a senior security official reportedly assaulted Amadú Mané during a visit to the prison where he and those convicted with him were held.

An Amnesty International representative observed part of the trial in January. The organization called on the government to establish a full and independent judicial inquiry into claims by the defendants that they had been forced to make incriminating statements. Amnesty International called for the officials responsible to be brought to justice. It also expressed concern about reports that law enforcement personnel had arbitrarily arrested and beaten suspected members of opposition parties.

GUYANA

There were reports of torture and ill-treatment of suspects by police. One person died in police custody under suspicious circumstances. Five prisoners were sentenced to death after retrials and some 15 people remained under sentence of death for murder. No executions took place.

There were reports of torture and ill-treatment of suspects by police. Four people alleged that they were kicked and beaten by police searching for weapons and marijuana in July in Cane Grove, Mahaica province. One of the four, Zabeeda Hussain, alleged that she suffered a miscarriage after police beat her with a belt and punched her in the stomach. She was held for six days in police custody before being taken to court to be charged and released on bail. A medical report on the day of her release recorded bruising below both eyes, bruises and multiple abrasions to her chest and back, and complaints of abdominal pain and uterine bleeding.

Shivnarine Dalchand died following his arrest on 19 August during a police raid in search of marijuana cultivators in Cane Grove. Relatives alleged that he and his brother were beaten before being taken away by police. During the next two days Shivnarine Dalchand was seen in custody, accompanying police during searches of other houses in the area. A witness alleged that Shivnarine Dalchand was again beaten by police and that he had told him he had been ill-treated while in custody. Four days after his arrest, police reported that Shivnarine Dalchand had drowned after jumping from a police boat into a canal. According to police statements, an autopsy conducted on 23 August showed no evidence that Shivnarine Dalchand had been beaten; however, other sources alleged that the autopsy report noted a number of external and internal injuries. No inquest had been held by the end of the year, nor had the autopsy report been made public.

Five people were sentenced to death after retrials, which were held after their first death sentences were overturned on appeal. There were no executions.

In September the Ministry of Home Affairs responded in a 17-page document to Amnesty International's past inquiries about eight cases involving alleged ill-treatment or disputed fatal shootings of suspects by police. The cases included the alleged ill-treatment of two teenagers at Vigilance police station in 1991, which the government said could not be substantiated after an investigation; the alleged torture of Hardatt Ramdass in 1992, where an investigation confirmed only some of the injuries claimed; allegations that the wife of a criminal suspect had been raped in 1992 which the government said inquiries had shown to be unfounded; the alleged beating of 10 youths in Mahaica in October 1993, which was still *sub judice*; and the cases of Rickey Samaroo and Joseph Persaud, whom the government said had been shot dead after they had attacked the police during a robbery in September 1993, and whose inquest was pending (see *Amnesty International Reports 1992* to *1994*). No reference was made, however, to the lawsuit against the police in the case of Michael Teekah who

had died in police custody in 1988 and in which Joseph Persaud had been due to give key testimony at the time he was shot. Amnesty International had called for an independent inquiry into the circumstances of the death (see *Amnesty International Report 1994*).

Amnesty International wrote to the Guyanese authorities in December calling for a full, independent inquiry to be held into the allegations of ill-treatment of Cane Grove residents in July and August and the death of Shivnarine Dalchand.

HAITI

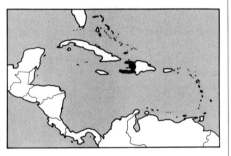

There was a marked upsurge in extrajudicial executions and "disappearances" during the first nine months of the year directed primarily against supporters of Haiti's exiled president, Jean-Bertrand Aristide, in an attempt to prevent his return. Hundreds of suspected Aristide supporters were detained without charge or trial; many were tortured. Reports of rape by the security forces and their civilian allies escalated. Some Haitian asylum-seekers attempting to reach the USA by sea who were forcibly returned by US forces were subjected to abuses after their return.

President Aristide, who had been ousted by a military coup in September 1991, had originally been due to return to power in October 1993 under the auspices of the Governor's Island Agreement of July 1993 brokered by the UN and the Organization of American States (OAS). However, his projected return had been repeatedly delayed by increasing abuses against his supporters by military and paramilitary forces under the command of Commander-in-Chief of the Haitian Armed Forces, General Raoul Cédras, and Port-au-Prince Police Chief, Michel François, who became

150 the country's effective rulers. Increasing violence was also cited by the UN as the reason for its withdrawal of the UN/OAS civilian human rights observer mission, MICIVIH, from October to December 1993 (see Amnesty International Reports 1992 to 1994).

Tens of thousands of Haitians fled the violence and the increasingly severe effects of a UN-sanctioned embargo, to live en marronage (in hiding), or to seek asylum abroad. Many were drowned as they tried to flee in unseaworthy craft; others were forcibly returned without even a cursory hearing of their asylum claim after interception at sea by US ships (see Amnesty International Reports 1993 and 1994). Some asylum-seekers who had been intercepted at sea were subjected to abuses once returned to Haiti, including arbitrary arrest, ill-treatment and torture. Others managed to reach other countries in the region only to be held in sub-standard conditions or to find that their applications for asylum were not dealt with according to international standards for the consideration of asylum claims.

In July the US Government altered its policy towards Haitian asylum-seekers, first agreeing to hear Haitian asylum claims on off-shore ships in the area or in neighbouring countries, then promoting a policy of "safe havens" for them throughout the region (see USA entry). These policy shifts provoked a renewed exodus of Haitians towards the USA. Also in July MICIVIH was expelled by the Haitian military authorities a second time. The US Government renewed its efforts to gain support for military intervention and by the end of July the UN Security Council had passed Resolution 940, authorizing a multinational force led by US troops to "facilitate the departure from Haiti of the military leadership ... the prompt return of the legitimately elected President ... [and a] secure and stable environment that will permit the implementation of the Governor's Island Agreement".

The Haitian military's response to the UN Resolution was to impose a state of siege and a number of other measures to prevent information about the country's human rights situation, already severely curtailed by the expulsion of MICIVIH, from emerging.

Outright confrontation with US-led forces was averted through a last-minute agreement between the US Government and the Haitian authorities, brokered by a US delegation led by former US president Jimmy Carter, under which the entry of US-led troops on 18 September was not actively opposed by the Haitian de facto authorities. The Haitian military also agreed to permit the return of President Aristide by 15 October, and to relinquish power by that date or after the Haitian parliament agreed an amnesty. By the end of October, the Haitian parliament had passed an amnesty (although the extent of its application was not clear), President Aristide had returned, and the principal leaders of the 1991 coup left the country to go into exile abroad. MICIVIH also returned to resume human rights monitoring in the country.

There were hundreds of extrajudicial executions and "disappearances" during the year. Those responsible were the country's military and police and their paramilitary adjuncts, including the so-called attachés (civilian auxiliaries to the police and military), the chefs de sections (rural section chiefs who are members of the military), zenglendos (armed individuals generally believed to operate under the control of the military) and members of a political party formed in 1993 as the Front révolutionaire pour l'avancement et le progrès d'Haïti (FRAPH), Revolutionary Front for the Advancement and Progress of Haiti, renamed in 1994 as the Front révolutionaire armé du peuple Haïtien, Haitian People's Revolutionary Armed Front. MICIVIH reported in March that there had been 75 apparent extrajudicial executions in the preceding six-week period alone and at least 62 "disappearances". For example, Oman Desanges' badly mutilated body was found near the international airport in Port-au-Prince in January, two days after he had been taken into custody by soldiers accompanied by attachés. A handkerchief tied to his body referred to his support for President Aristide. Oman Desanges had fled the country in 1992, after several attempts by soldiers to arrest him apparently because of his work as founder member of a neighbourhood committee which had supported President Aristide. He and his family were intercepted at sea by the US Coast Guard, but allowed to go to the USA to lodge an asylum claim. However, Oman Desanges and several of his family were returned to Haiti in 1992.

About 50 people were apparently extra-judicially executed when the army attacked the village of Raboteau, Artibonite Department, in April. Raboteau had already been attacked on several occasions in the past by army and police seeking a local leader, Amio Métayer.

Another notorious extrajudicial execution in 1994 was that of Father Jean Vincent, a close associate of President Aristide, who was shot dead in August by unidentified men in Port-au-Prince, apparently as a warning to those contributing to the growing pressure to return President Aristide to Haiti.

One of the scores of people who "disappeared" was Emile Georges, a member of the human rights commission of a popular organization in Cité Soleil. He "disappeared" during a wave of abuses carried out in July, immediately following the expulsion of MICIVIH. Residents of Cité Soleil, a poor district of Port-au-Prince, were repeatedly abused by the military because they were believed to support President Aristide.

In the months leading up to President Aristide's return in October, hundreds of his suspected supporters were held without charge for longer than permitted under Haitian law, and tortured while held in severely sub-standard prison conditions. Among them were nine returned asylum-seekers arrested as they disembarked at Port-au-Prince after being repatriated by the US Coast Guard in February. Neither US nor UN officials were allowed access to them while in detention. All were later released.

Torture by the security forces was widespread. Seventeen-year-old "Chatte", a brother of Amio Métayer (see above), was severely tortured during almost 10 months' detention without charge. He received no medical care for the serious wounds he sustained under torture. He was released in September.

An increasing incidence of the use of rape as a weapon of political terror was also recorded. MICIVIH statistics showed that at least 66 women, including 10 girls and one woman who was six months pregnant, had been raped by the security forces and their supporters between the end of January and May 1994. In just one raid carried out by the army on shanty-town areas of Port-au-Prince in March, some 40 women were reportedly raped, including an eight-year-old girl and a 55-year-old woman. Mathilde, whose husband, a supporter of President Aristide, had been killed, was raped by four uniformed men who burst into her home. As a result, she lost the baby she was carrying.

In response to the escalating human rights crisis in Haiti, Amnesty International appealed to the authorities on behalf of numerous individuals. It also urged national and international bodies, including the UN Special Rapporteur on Haiti and the Inter-American Commission on Human Rights, to take steps to resolve the human rights crisis in Haiti.

In August Amnesty International published a report, *Haiti: On the Horns of a Dilemma: Military Repression or Foreign Invasion*, which summarized the organization's human rights concerns in the country, pointed to a number of past violations in Haiti that required urgent investigation, and expressed fears that human rights might be further abused in the context of an invasion. The organization also called on the US authorities, other members of the UN Security Council and the UN "Friends of Haiti" (countries that had played a special role in seeking a resolution to the long-term human rights crisis in Haiti) to ensure respect for human rights and basic principles of humanitarian law in the course of any military intervention in Haiti.

In August and September an Amnesty International delegation visited the Bahamas, French Guiana, the USA and the Dominican Republic to investigate the situation of Haitian asylum-seekers in the region. At the end of September, a further delegation visited Guantánamo Bay, Cuba, to research the situation of Haitian and Cuban asylum-seekers taken there after their interception at sea. Amnesty International concluded that Haitians there were being encouraged to repatriate on the basis of inadequate information on the rapidly changing situation in their home country. It called on the US authorities to ensure that no Haitians were returned to Haiti without their informed consent.

Amnesty International regretted that UN Resolution 940 had contained no provisions for a human rights plan for Haiti and called on the international community to make a long-term commitment to building institutions to protect human rights in

152 Haiti. Amnesty International also asked that independent human rights observers be allowed to observe any foreign military intervention and its aftermath, and that there be no impunity for human rights violators, no matter where they might flee.

Amnesty International called for all paramilitary groups to be disbanded and urged the intervening foreign troops not to remain silent witnesses of any abuses by Haitian law enforcement personnel. Following the shooting by US forces of up to 10 Haitian police and paramilitaries at Cap Haïtien on 24 September, Amnesty International asked for a full independent inquiry to determine whether international standards on the use of lethal force had been violated. The organization also called on the commanders of the foreign military forces operating in the country to ensure that international human rights standards were respected by forces under their command, including the treatment of prisoners, and that steps be taken to ensure the safety of prisoners still held who had been detained by the previous *de facto* authorities.

HONDURAS

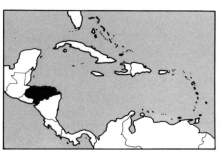

Several people were killed in the context of land disputes who appeared to be victims of extrajudicial execution. Two men allegedly abducted by the security forces were found dead. Human rights defenders seeking to clarify past human rights violations received death threats. Several minors were reportedly ill-treated.

In January President Carlos Roberto Reina took office, following the Liberal Party's victory in elections in November 1993. A former president of the Inter-American Court of Human Rights, President Reina identified human rights as a priority for his administration, pledging to under-

take a "moral revolution" and to put an end to impunity.

The ongoing process of human rights reform gained momentum. An Attorney General was appointed to head the Public Ministry, which was reformed in 1993 on the recommendation of the *Ad Hoc* Commission (see *Amnesty International Report 1994*). The Public Ministry became responsible for investigating all allegations of human rights violations. It was also responsible for the new *Departamento de Investigación Criminal* (DIC), Department of Criminal Investigations, which replaced the *Dirección Nacional de Investigaciones* (DNI), National Directorate of Investigations, which was controlled by the military. The DNI, implicated in numerous cases of killing, torture and "disappearance" in the past, was formally disbanded in June. But delays in creating the DIC left a vacuum, which fuelled popular anxiety about the state's capacity to respond to rising crime. The Attorney General's office was set up in June and contained special offices dealing with human rights, corruption, drug-trafficking, and the protection of children, the disabled, indigenous people and the environment.

A constitutional reform in May abolishing forced conscription reaffirmed civilian control over the military. Other human rights related reforms included measures to improve the administration of justice. A proposal was made to Congress to grant constitutional status to the office of the *Comisionado Nacional de Protección de los Derechos Humanos*, National Commissioner for the Protection of Human Rights, to allow it to play a supervisory role complementary to the investigative role of the Attorney General.

The new government pledged to follow up the recommendations made by the Commissioner, Dr Leo Valladares, in his preliminary report on "disappearances" under previous governments, published in December 1993 (see *Amnesty International Report 1994*). The Attorney General's office also said it would seek to ensure that those responsible for the human rights violations documented were brought to trial.

In December judicial investigations were opened into one of the 184 "disappearances" documented in the report. This followed the exhumation and identification of the remains of Nelson Mackay

Chavarría, a lawyer who "disappeared" in the custody of the DNI in February 1982. The exhumation was carried out in Los Amates, Valle department, by an international team of forensic anthropologists at the request of the Attorney General's office. Relatives, witnesses and members of the military were called to give evidence, including a colonel who in 1982 had publicly claimed to have information pertaining to the "disappearance" of Nelson Mackay and others. The investigation, hailed by the Human Rights Commissioner as "the beginning of the end to impunity", was ongoing at the end of the year.

Land conflicts, strikes and social unrest were reported in the context of deteriorating economic conditions. In May the government ratified the International Labour Organisation's Convention on Indigenous and Tribal Peoples, which specifies standards for the protection of indigenous rights.

Several indigenous people and peasant activists involved in land disputes appeared to be victims of extrajudicial execution. Rutilio Matute, a member of the Xicaque indigenous community in Olanchito, department of Yoro, was found dead on 31 May on waste land near his house. Circumstances suggested his killing may have been ordered by local landowners in conflict with the Federation of Xicaque Tribes of Yoro (FETRIXY), and carried out with the complicity of security force members. According to FETRIXY, Rutilio Matute was the 20th indigenous activist to have been killed since 1989 in the context of land disputes. In 1991 he had witnessed the killing of his uncle, former FETRIXY president Vicente Matute Cruz, who was shot dead after publicly accusing the government and military of unlawfully seizing land belonging to indigenous communities (see *Amnesty International Report 1992*). Another witness to the killing, indigenous activist Dionisio Martínez, was killed in February 1994 in suspicious circumstances. Other indigenous activists received anonymous death threats, including former FETRIXY president, Mauricia Castro Garmendia. Little progress had been made by the end of the year in ascertaining responsibility for the killings and death threats.

Evidence emerged about the apparent extrajudicial execution of a peasant activist in November 1993. Cleofes Colindres Canales, local leader of the *Central Nacional de Trabajadores del Campo* (CNTC), National Rural Workers' Union, in San Pedro Sula department, was found dead the day after he went to a meeting with members of the local military brigade. Members of the cooperative to which he belonged had been forcibly evicted four months earlier from land they occupied by the military brigade and Cleofes Colindres Canales had been actively involved in the continuing dispute. Witnesses and CNTC lawyers and activists cited clear indications of the military brigade's responsibility for the killing and claimed that official investigations had been suppressed by military pressure on the local judiciary.

A Nicaraguan citizen who was arrested in December 1993 by Honduran police was found dead in January (see *Amnesty International Report 1994*). Investigations by the non-governmental human rights organization *Comité para la Defensa de los Derechos Humanos en Honduras* (CODEH), Committee for the Defence of Human Rights in Honduras, indicated that Juan Pablo Laguna Cruz had been unlawfully killed by Honduran police. In June the dead man's sister, together with CODEH, brought formal charges against 18 security force officials, including the head of the *Fuerzas de Seguridad Pública* (FUSEP), Public Security Forces, for their role in carrying out or covering up the illegal detention and killing. However, proceedings against them had not advanced significantly by the end of the year.

Orlando Jiménez Antúnez, a bar manager from Elixir, department of Colón, was abducted from his home on 17 September by men in civilian clothing carrying weapons used only by the army. His whereabouts were not clarified until November, when his mutilated body was exhumed and identified in La Ceiba. After presenting a formal complaint in November against the army and civilian officials allegedly responsible, CODEH's regional president in La Ceiba, Andrés Pavón, was threatened by a gunman and his home placed under surveillance.

Human rights defenders seeking to clarify cases of "disappearance" in previous years also received death threats. On 2 March Berta Oliva de Nativí, coordinator of the *Comité de Familiares de Detenidos*

154 *Desaparecidos de Honduras* (COFADEH), Committee of Relatives of the Disappeared, was threatened with "disappearance" by a man identifying himself as a colonel. The previous day the Human Rights Commissioner had received an anonymous telephone death threat. Repeated incidents of threats and harassment were reported by other members of COFADEH, CODEH and the Commissioner's office, apparently linked to their campaigns against impunity for "disappearances" and other human rights violations.

Several minors were illegally arrested and ill-treated. On 9 April Martha María Saire, an 11-year-old street girl with behavioural problems, was raped by two uniformed members of a local military battalion guarding the Juvenile Guidance Centre in Támara, department of Francisco Morazán, where she lived. She was threatened with further violence if she complained about what had happened. Forensic examinations confirmed that she had been sexually assaulted. The case was presented to the courts in April, following a complaint by the children's organization *Casa Alianza*. Although one of the soldiers was reportedly in detention, proceedings had apparently stalled since May.

Sixteen-year-old Mario René Enamorado Lara was illegally detained by FUSEP in July near the *Casa Alianza* home in Tegucigalpa, the capital, where he lived. Accused of having stolen a watch, he was held for several hours in a cell with adults. A medical examination on his release supported his claims that he had been severely punched and kicked by police and beaten by male detainees in the cell. To Amnesty International's knowledge, the FUSEP members responsible had not been brought to justice by the end of the year.

This and similar cases highlighted broader deficiencies in the judicial treatment of juvenile offenders. Detained minors were often held with adults and were not always taken before minors' judges, who were frequently unavailable at weekends. In February a draft bill was presented to Congress to lower the age at which an individual can be held criminally responsible and admitted to the adult penitentiary system, from 18 to 16 years of age. There was concern that this would leave detained minors even more vulnerable to ill-treatment. At the end of the year the bill was still being studied by a special congressional commission.

Amnesty International appealed to the new government to ensure full investigations into the cases of possible extrajudicial execution, "disappearance" and ill-treatment, and to honour its commitment to end impunity for "disappearances" and other violations under past administrations.

An Amnesty International delegation visited Honduras in May and June and met the new authorities to discuss their human rights commitments. The delegates also assessed the progress of institutional reforms and of investigations into past "disappearances" and recent abuses. While encouraged by the government's manifest commitment to human rights reform, Amnesty International urged the administration to fulfil its obligations by making a historic break with impunity.

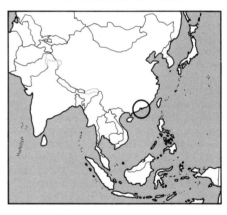

HONG KONG

Thousands of Vietnamese asylum-seekers remained in detention, some facing forcible return to Viet Nam. Hundreds of them were ill-treated by the security forces during transfer operations. The government took some steps to improve safeguards for human rights but failed to establish an independent human rights commission.

Uncertainty continued about the political and legislative structure of Hong Kong after it reverts to Chinese sovereignty in July 1997. In September China's National People's Congress adopted a resolution providing for the dissolution in July 1997 of Hong Kong's partly elected Legislative

Council (Legco) and of other elected agencies whose term of office would otherwise straddle the handover period. The resolution did not specify how the membership of the succeeding bodies would be chosen but Chinese officials indicated that the Preparatory Working Committee (PWC) for the Hong Kong Special Administrative Region, established by China in 1993 to oversee the transfer of sovereignty, would address this point before 1997. The PWC stated in April that it was reviewing the consistency of Hong Kong's laws with the Chinese Constitution. Laws found to be inconsistent may be abolished after 1997. By the end of 1994 the Committee had not yet completed its review of the Hong Kong Bill of Rights Ordinance, which enshrines many of the provisions of the International Covenant on Civil and Political Rights (ICCPR) in Hong Kong law.

In October Chinese officials reportedly indicated that they took the view that China was under no obligation to report to the UN Human Rights Committee on the implementation of the ICCPR in Hong Kong, although such reporting is mandatory under the provisions of the ICCPR. The 1984 Sino-British Joint Declaration on the Question of Hong Kong provides for the ICCPR and other international human rights treaties to remain in force after 1997. By the end of 1994 no arrangement to fulfil the reporting obligation after 1997 had been agreed.

In April members of Legco renewed calls on the government to establish an independent human rights commission (see *Amnesty International Report 1994*). In July the Hong Kong Government tabled before Legco a number of proposals aimed at improving existing safeguards for human rights, but falling short of establishing a commission. The proposals included a widening of the mandate of the Commissioner for Administrative Complaints, increased budgets for human rights education and changes in rules governing the provision of legal aid to citizens who complain that their rights have been violated and wish to bring a civil suit against the government. The proposals were approved by Legco in July.

By the end of the year, over 22,000 Vietnamese asylum-seekers remained in detention in camps in the territory, almost all of whom had been denied refugee status ("screened out") and were facing forcible return to Viet Nam if they did not opt for "voluntary repatriation". Another 380 had not completed the screening process. Many of those remaining in Hong Kong had spent several years in detention without effective access to judicial review of their detention.

In March members of the security forces raided barracks housing "screened-out" asylum-seekers in Whitehead Detention Centre, in order to transfer them to another camp pending their return to Viet Nam. Facing strong opposition from some asylum-seekers, the security forces used large amounts of tear-gas and physical force to complete the transfer. In the days that followed hundreds of asylum-seekers were reported to have sought medical assistance for bruises caused by batons and for burns and respiratory diseases allegedly resulting from the use of tear-gas fired at close range. An official inquiry into the incident, commissioned by Hong Kong Governor Chris Patten, concluded in September that excessive force had been used and criticized the lack of preparation by the security forces. In October two Correctional Services Department officers were given suspended prison sentences for beating asylum-seekers during the incident.

In March Amnesty International called on the Hong Kong Government to carry out an impartial and thorough investigation into the Whitehead incident. In April the organization published a report, *Hong Kong: Arbitrary detention of Vietnamese asylum-seekers*, calling on the government to end the arbitrary and indefinite detention of Vietnamese asylum-seekers. In another report, *Hong Kong and Human Rights: Flaws in the System – A Call for Institutional Reform to Protect Human Rights*, also published in April, Amnesty International urged the Hong Kong Government to establish an independent human rights commission, to ensure that those who complain of human rights violations have access to an effective and affordable procedure to seek remedy, and to develop training for officials on human rights law and human rights education programs. It also called on the British and Chinese Governments to agree with the relevant UN committees on methods to fulfil reporting obligations under international human rights treaties, such as the ICCPR, which are in force in Hong Kong but which China has not yet ratified.

156

HUNGARY

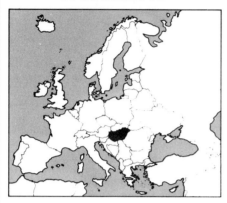

One possible prisoner of conscience was detained for 10 days. He and another person were allegedly ill-treated in detention.

In February Hungary acceded to the Second Optional Protocol to the International Covenant on Civil and Political Rights, aiming at the abolition of the death penalty. The European Convention for the Prevention of Torture and Inhuman or Degrading Treatment or Punishment was ratified in 1993 but its entry into force was delayed until March.

Throughout the year prosecutions were initiated against suspected perpetrators of gross human rights violations during the 1956 uprising.

On 19 January Hermán Péter was arrested in Szarvasgede and held for 10 days on charges which appeared to have been fabricated because of his non-violent political activity. He had campaigned against the decision of the local council to approve the construction of a medical waste incinerator. During his arrest, police officers reportedly sprayed him with tear-gas, manhandled him while putting on handcuffs and pushed him into a gutter. He was released on 28 January by order of a county court. Also on 19 January, his colleague Pálinkás József was taken to a police station in Szarvasgede for questioning about an apparently unrelated incident. During interrogation he was reportedly punched in the face by a police officer and forced to sign a statement.

In March Amnesty International urged the Minister of the Interior to initiate an independent and impartial inquiry into the alleged ill-treatment of Hermán Péter

and Pálinkás József and expressed concern that Hermán Péter had been held in detention apparently for exercising non-violently his right to freedom of expression. In September the Interior Ministry informed Amnesty International of the Public Prosecutor's decision not to charge officers involved in the alleged ill-treatment of the two men. No other inquiry appeared to have taken place.

In April Amnesty International expressed concern to President Göncz Árpád about the prosecution of Eörsi Mátyás and Lengyel László for defamation of public authority or officials, under the provisions of Article 232 of the Penal Code. The organization considered that this law could be applied in violation of the right to freedom of expression and urged the President to initiate a judicial review. In June the Constitutional Court abolished Article 232.

INDIA

Thousands of political prisoners were held without charge or trial. Torture and ill-treatment of detainees were routine, resulting in hundreds of deaths in police and military custody. Scores of political detainees "disappeared". Hundreds of people were reported to have been extrajudicially executed by the security forces. At least two people were judicially executed. Armed opposition or separatist groups committed numerous abuses, including deliberate killings of civilians and hostage-taking.

The government continued to face violent political opposition in several states, including Jammu and Kashmir, Punjab, Andhra Pradesh, Assam and other northeastern states. Jammu and Kashmir remained under direct rule by central government.

No legal reforms were implemented to safeguard detainees, although the government announced in May that it was considering a legal amendment that would require judicial inquiries into all deaths in custody. The amendment had not been passed by the end of the year.

Special legislation such as the Armed Forces (Special Powers) Act and the Terrorist and Disruptive Activities (Prevention) Act (TADA) remained in force. The TADA, which was in force in 22 of India's 25 states, grants the security forces wide powers of arrest and detention without trial under vague and imprecise provisions. Minimum legal safeguards for fair trial do not apply to those tried under TADA. The Supreme Court ruled in March that TADA was constitutional, but confirmed that police had frequently abused the Act in order to circumvent ordinary legal safeguards. The Minister for Internal Security admitted in August that TADA "had been misused extensively against Muslims".

The National Human Rights Commission (NHRC), established in 1993 (see *Amnesty International Report 1994*), pursued, apparently with determination, many complaints of human rights violations in various states. However, human rights groups complained that they were not informed about the outcome of investigations into specific complaints they submitted to the Commission. Its powers to investigate and act upon complaints of human rights violations from Jammu and Kashmir remained extremely limited. In August Andhra Pradesh police reportedly tried to prevent members of the Andhra Pradesh Civil Liberties Committee from testifying before the Commission.

Thousands of political prisoners, including prisoners of conscience, were held without charge or trial under various special laws. Many were held on suspicion of committing ordinary criminal offences but others were clearly held for political reasons.

Swaran Kaur and her sister were arrested by police in Punjab in April as they travelled to meet members of the NHRC. They were released only after the NHRC Chairman intervened on their behalf. Swaran Kaur told the Commission that she and members of her family had been tortured and harassed by police after her husband was killed in 1992 and that seven relatives, including her two-year-old child, were in police custody.

Among those arrested during the year under TADA was Ajit Kumar Bhuyan, a journalist who had been arrested on several previous occasions because of his human rights activities. He was arrested at his home in Assam on 5 July, and for three days police refused to disclose his whereabouts. He was released on bail on 27 September.

Hundreds of suspected political activists were detained without charge or trial under the National Security Act and, in Jammu and Kashmir, the Public Safety Act. In Jammu and Kashmir, two political leaders were rearrested under the Public Safety Act in May, immediately after the Supreme Court had ordered their release. Sayed Ali Shah Geelani and Abdul Gani Lone, both prisoners of conscience held without charge since October 1993, were released on 30 September. Shabir Shah, another prisoner of conscience, first held under the Public Safety Act and then under TADA, was released in October, having spent five years in detention without trial. A considerable number of children were held under the Public Safety Act, including 15-year-old Mushtaq Ahmad Wani, a student detained since June 1993.

Torture of detainees in police and military custody remained endemic. Criminal suspects and political detainees were routinely tortured to extract information and "confessions". Torture methods most often cited were beatings and, less frequently, suspension by the wrists or ankles, electric shocks and rape. In Jammu and Kashmir people were suspended upside-down, given electric shocks or burned, leaving some victims disabled for life.

Most torture victims came from underprivileged sections of society, particularly the scheduled castes and tribes. For example, four men, all members of the scheduled castes, were arrested in Ahmedabad district, Uttar Pradesh, on 14 August. All said they were beaten and one, Amrut Parmar, stated that he had been subjected to electric shocks. A medical report supported their allegations. No action was known to have been taken against the officers responsible.

In Jammu and Kashmir, deaths in custody as a result of torture or shooting reached extraordinary levels, sometimes being reported daily. During the year Amnesty International compiled a record of 706 such deaths reported between January 1990 and December 1994, 130 of them since January 1994. In other Indian states, at least 60 people died in custody in 1994, allegedly as a result of torture or shooting. Convictions of those responsible for these human rights violations were extremely rare. In Jammu and Kashmir none of the perpetrators was brought to justice.

In January a basket maker named Udayan from Palakkad district in Kerala was taken into custody, allegedly for carrying counterfeit money. He told his brothers he had been stripped and brutally tortured during the night. He died later that day. The police claimed that he hanged himself but an investigation by local human rights groups disputed this. After protests over his case, 32 people were arrested and 3,000 were charged with rioting and causing the death of a police officer who collapsed and died during a protest. The Chief Minister of Kerala agreed to set up an inquiry, but not an independent judicial inquiry.

In states other than Jammu and Kashmir, some courts convicted police responsible for custodial deaths reportedly committed several years ago and ordered compensation to be paid. On 16 April a sessions judge in Andhra Pradesh sentenced five policemen to prison sentences of between three and 10 years for beating T. Muralidharan to death in 1986. In May the Rajasthan High Court ordered that a commission be set up to establish the number of people who had died in custody in the state between 1990 and 1992 and that their families receive financial relief.

Senior police officials frequently participated in covering up torture and obstructing the rare cases where prosecutions of police were initiated. Archana Guha, a headmistress who was tortured in detention in 1974, was still pursuing her case in 1994, 16 years after court proceedings began. In February the Supreme Court expressed concern at the way police officers had escaped justice by repeatedly delaying proceedings.

In August a Criminal Investigation Department (CID) inquiry found evidence against 13 Provincial Armed Constabulary (PAC) personnel for killing 17 people in 1987 after taking them into custody during Hindu-Muslim riots in Meerut, Uttar Pradesh (see *Amnesty International Report 1988*). The PAC allegedly took them to a deserted spot, shot them and dumped their bodies in a canal. The state government was not known to have begun legal proceedings against the PAC personnel.

Scores of political detainees "disappeared" during the year. Most were young men suspected of having links with armed secessionist groups. Many were detained solely because they lived in areas where armed groups were active. Few "disappearances" were clarified. Sometimes officials eventually admitted that an arrest had been made, only to claim later that the "disappeared" person had "escaped" or was killed in an "encounter".

In Jammu and Kashmir the army and paramilitary forces were responsible for scores of "disappearances". For example, Mohammad Maqbool Dass was picked up by soldiers from his home on 9 April and has not been seen since. The army ignored requests by the district's Deputy Commissioner for relatives to have access to him.

In Punjab, most "disappearances" were carried out by the police. For example, Sukhwinder Singh Bhatti, a lawyer who had defended Sikh men held on political grounds, was abducted in May by armed men in plain clothes who were believed to be police. In mid-June the Punjab and Haryana High Court ordered a CID inquiry into his "disappearance" to report within three months, which it failed to do. The government denied that the police were responsible.

Hundreds of people were reported to have been extrajudicially executed by security forces. Five young men, members of the All Assam Students Union, were reportedly shot dead by the army at Dibru-Saikowa game sanctuary. Their bullet-ridden bodies were handed over to police on 23 February, reportedly bearing marks of torture including burns and bruises. The security forces claimed they had been killed in an "encounter", but two released detainees said all five had been tortured then shot. A magisterial inquiry was ordered but had not reported by the end of 1994.

Extrajudicial executions in Jammu and Kashmir continued throughout the year.

At least nine people travelling on a bus in Bandipore were killed by members of the Border Security Force (BSF) on 6 January. Witnesses said that the shootings were unprovoked. In August Abdul Rashid Dar was shot dead at point-blank range after being dragged out of his house in Batamaloo by members of the BSF. He was killed in front of his family. The police authorities apparently took no action in this case.

In Bombay, the judicial investigation continued into killings during intercommunal riots in December 1992 and January 1993, including several alleged extrajudicial executions (see *Amnesty International Report 1993*).

In Arunachal Pradesh members of the Chakma and Hajong communities, who are long-term settlers, apparently received little state protection from attacks by civilians calling for the expulsion of foreigners. Amnesty International appealed for their safety in September. The neighbouring state of Assam issued "shoot at sight" orders against any non-nationals entering the state.

At least two people were judicially executed in Rajasthan and Orissa.

Armed opposition groups committed grave human rights abuses, including hostage-taking, torture and deliberate and arbitrary killings. The victims included politicians and suspected informers. For example, in Jammu and Kashmir, 10 Congressmen were reportedly abducted in Srinagar in mid-June by the Islamic Front. Five were released, but the fate of the other five was not known. Pankaj Kumar Sinha, a former legislator of the Congress Party, was held captive by an armed group, *Al-Umar Mujahideen*, for a year before being released in June. In the northeast, civilians including Muslim immigrants were targeted for abuses by armed opposition groups. In Andhra Pradesh, members of the Naxalite People's War Group tortured and killed suspected police informers.

Amnesty International called on the government to release prisoners of conscience and to ensure that all other political prisoners were brought to trial promptly and fairly, or released; to investigate all allegations of torture and deaths in custody and to bring to justice those responsible; and to implement safeguards against torture. Amnesty International

welcomed the government's decision to consider requiring judicial inquiries into all deaths in custody and urged all political parties to support such a reform. Amnesty International appealed for the commutation of death sentences and the abolition of the death penalty.

In January Amnesty International made its first visit for 14 years to Maharashtra state to conduct research. The delegation visited the state capital, Bombay, and met senior government and police officials, as well as victims of human rights violations, lawyers and human rights groups. The delegation also met senior Indian Government officials, who said that Amnesty International's repeated request for permission to visit Jammu and Kashmir was still under consideration. In May Amnesty International submitted a memorandum to the government detailing widespread unacknowledged detentions, frequent beatings and other torture of suspects, and broad police powers to use lethal force. The memorandum contained 15 recommendations to remedy the situation. In August Amnesty International received a response from the government which dismissed nearly all the recommendations.

In March Amnesty International published a report, *India: Reports of rape in 1993*, and in June another entitled *India: Deaths in custody in 1993*. In August Amnesty International publicly challenged the government to respond seriously to more than 200 cases of "disappearance" in Jammu and Kashmir and Punjab, following a disappointing government response to a report issued by Amnesty International in 1993 (see *Amnesty International Report 1994*). In November Amnesty International published *India: The Terrorist and Disruptive Activities (Prevention) Act: The lack of "scrupulous care"*, which expressed concern that the act had been grossly abused and that several provisions contravened international human rights standards.

Amnesty International appealed to armed opposition groups to stop human rights abuses. In June it publicly urged them to release all hostages held in Jammu and Kashmir, and rejected a request by one of the groups, *Harkatul Ansar*, for a meeting in Pakistan. Amnesty International deplored the taking of hostages as a blatant violation of humanitarian law, and

160 said it would never play a part in negotiations for releases.

UN Special Rapporteurs on torture and extrajudicial, summary and arbitrary executions were not invited to visit Jammu and Kashmir as they requested.

INDONESIA AND EAST TIMOR

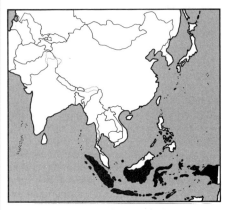

At least 350 political prisoners, many of them prisoners of conscience, were held, including some 40 sentenced during the year. Hundreds of people were arrested and held briefly without charge or trial. Torture of political detainees and criminal suspects was common, in some cases resulting in death. Several people were extrajudicially executed, and scores of criminal suspects were shot and killed by police in suspicious circumstances. The fate of possibly hundreds of Acehnese and East Timorese who "disappeared" in previous years remained unknown. Some 35 prisoners remained under sentence of death, at least three of whom were sentenced in 1994. No executions were reported.

Despite continuing claims of a commitment to "political openness", the government of President Suharto increased restrictions on civil liberties and intensified the harassment of alleged government critics and human rights activists. Dozens of peaceful seminars and meetings were broken up during the year. In April the government launched an anti-crime drive, "Operation Cleansing", deploying some 16,700 police and soldiers in Jakarta. Three of the country's leading news maga-

zines were banned in June. A draft presidential decree imposing severe restrictions on domestic non-governmental organizations was published. The human rights situation deteriorated in the run-up to the Asia Pacific Economic Cooperation (APEC) summit held in Jakarta in November, as security forces sought to rid the capital of "economic and political criminals".

The government faced continued armed and peaceful opposition from groups seeking independence for Aceh, East Timor and Irian Jaya.

The report by the UN Special Rapporteur on extrajudicial, arbitrary or summary executions of his visit to Indonesia and East Timor was published in December 1994. It concluded that members of the Indonesian security forces were responsible for the 1991 Santa Cruz massacre in Dili, East Timor, and that the government had failed to satisfactorily clarify the cases of those killed and "disappeared". By the end of the year the government had yet to implement most of the recommendations contained in the 1992 report of the UN Special Rapporteur on torture and the UN Commission on Human Rights Resolution 1993/97.

The government-backed National Human Rights Commission, whose members were appointed in December 1993, began to operate early in the year. The Commission surprised some critics by its occasional outspokenness but there were continuing concerns about its independence, mandate and methods of work. Access by international and domestic organizations to East Timor and parts of Indonesia continued to be restricted, preventing effective human rights monitoring. Individuals attempting to disseminate human rights information were often themselves detained and tortured. Hundreds of thousands of former members of the Indonesian Communist Party (PKI) remained subject to heavy restrictions on their freedom of movement and other civil rights.

Dozens of peaceful human rights and political activists were sentenced to prison terms after unfair trials during the year. In February Nuku Soleiman was sentenced to four years' imprisonment for "insulting the president". Access to his trial was restricted and the court agreed to hear only one of the 17 witnesses requested by the defence, in contrast to the 19 witnesses appearing for the prosecution. In May his sentence was increased to five years following an appeal to the High Court in Jakarta. Nuku Soleiman was a prisoner of conscience. Also in May, 21 university students were sentenced to six months in prison on the same charge for participating in a peaceful protest in December 1993. In mid-June the sentences against all 21 were increased by between two and eight months by the High Court. By December 1994, all but one of the students had been released.

Three student prisoners of conscience – Bonar Tigor Naipospos, Bambang Subono and Bambang Isti Nugroho – who had been sentenced in 1989 to between seven and eight and a half years in prison, were conditionally released in May and June.

Scores of trade unionists were jailed in connection with widespread labour unrest in Medan, North Sumatra, in mid-April. They included at least 11 labour activists charged with "inciting" workers to demonstrate and to strike. The 11 received prison sentences ranging from five months to three years. Among them was Dr Muchtar Pakpahan, the national chairman of the independent Indonesian Prosperous Workers' Union, who was sentenced to three years' imprisonment in November. From trial documents and observation of his trial, Amnesty International concluded that the charges against Dr Pakpahan and the 10 others tried with him were politically motivated, and that they might be prisoners of conscience.

Some 24 East Timorese prisoners of conscience were serving sentences of up to life imprisonment imposed after unfair trials. At least six were tried during the year for their peaceful pro-independence activities. They included José Antonio Neves, a theology student, whose trial had not been completed by the end of the year. He was accused of seeking to gain international support for East Timor's independence, a crime punishable by up to life imprisonment. Five other East Timorese – Isaac Soares, Miguel de Deus, Pantaleão Amaral, Rosalino dos Santos and Pedro Fatima Tilman – were tried and each sentenced to 20 months' imprisonment. They had taken part in a peaceful pro-independence demonstration during a visit to East Timor by foreign journalists in April. According to reports, they were not accompanied by lawyers during either their interrogation or trial. All were prisoners of conscience.

Hundreds of suspected supporters of independence for East Timor were subjected to short-term detention, ill-treatment and harassment. Up to 22 people were detained after police and military forces broke up a peaceful demonstration by students in Dili on 14 July. On 12 November, the anniversary of the 1991 Santa Cruz massacre, widespread and sometimes violent demonstrations broke out in Dili, East Timor. More than 125 people were detained but most were released after questioning. Some were known to have been badly beaten by their captors. Police officials said that 30 people would be tried for criminal offences; there was concern that some were peaceful pro-independence protesters.

Around 50 alleged supporters of the armed pro-independence group *Aceh Merdeka*, many of whom were believed to be prisoners of conscience, continued to serve sentences of up to life imprisonment imposed after unfair trials in previous years (see previous *Amnesty International Reports*). At least eight other alleged members were tried during the year, including three men convicted of subversion in March and sentenced to 19 years' imprisonment.

At least 50 political prisoners, over half of whom were prisoners of conscience, remained in prison for advocating independence for Irian Jaya. Most had been sentenced after unfair trials in 1989 and 1990 (see previous *Amnesty International Reports*).

Around 150 Islamic activists continued serving sentences of up to life imprisonment. At least 50 of them were prisoners of conscience. About 30 elderly prisoners, some of whom were ill, continued to serve prison sentences imposed in the 1960s after unfair trials for alleged involvement in a 1965 coup attempt or for membership of the PKI. Most were believed to be prisoners of conscience. Six were on death row.

Torture and ill-treatment of political detainees continued to be routine throughout Indonesia and East Timor. A farmer in Central Java was reportedly beaten and ill-treated by military officers in September after he initiated legal action over the forced appropriation of his land. The farmer was struck on the leg and his hair was repeatedly pulled. He was forced to sign a statement revoking the legal action.

On 3 January Salvador Sarmento, an East Timorese student suspected of pro-independence activities, was arrested and held for five days at the military intelligence headquarters in the Colmera district of Dili. He was repeatedly beaten, given electric shocks and threatened with death. He was released only after he had been forced to sign a confession.

Torture and ill-treatment of criminal suspects was also commonplace, sometimes resulting in death or serious injury. In April Jery Manafe, a university student, died after being beaten by up to 10 police officers and cadets in Kupang, West Timor. In November, five police officers went on trial before a military court charged with his murder. If convicted they faced jail sentences of between one and three and a half years.

Extrajudicial executions of political and criminal suspects continued to be reported both in Indonesia and East Timor. On 13 March the body of Rusli was found floating in the Deli River near Medan, North Sumatra. Two days earlier he had taken part in a strike which was violently broken up by the security forces. Police said Rusli had fallen into the river; relatives, co-workers and human rights organizations believed he was beaten by members of the security forces before either falling or being pushed into the river. An autopsy revealed a wound on his forehead, possibly caused by a blunt instrument.

An anti-crime drive known as "Operation Cleansing" led to an apparent increase in arbitrary police killings of alleged criminals. More than 60 criminal suspects were killed in suspicious circumstances during the year. Some were reported to have been shot dead while in handcuffs as they allegedly tried to attack police officers or grab their weapons. Others were shot directly in the head or the torso, rather than in the legs. One victim, Sulaiman, was reportedly shot while handcuffed by police on 28 April as he pointed out the hiding place of fellow gang members in East Jakarta. Concern was heightened by official statements that appeared to condone the killings.

No thorough investigations were conducted into reported extrajudicial executions, and the perpetrators were seldom brought to justice. By the end of the year, the authorities had clarified the fate of only a fraction of the estimated 270 people killed and 200 others thought to have "disappeared" during and after the Santa Cruz massacre. No official investigations had been initiated into the extrajudicial executions of at least 2,000 civilians in Aceh between 1989 and early 1993. The fate of possibly hundreds of Acehnese and East Timorese who "disappeared" in previous years remained unknown and those responsible had yet to be brought to justice. Nine civilians were sentenced to terms of up to 17 years in prison for the May 1993 abduction and murder of labour activist Marsinah, and a military officer received a nine-month sentence for failing to report the crime to his superiors. However, serious irregularities during the trials, including the acceptance of confessions extracted under torture as evidence, gave rise to doubts about the trials' fairness. No steps were taken against the military authorities believed to be responsible for the murder. Following the overturning of the guilty verdict against the main suspect, Judi Susanto, the National Commission on Human Rights called in December for the police to reopen the investigation.

At least 35 people remained under sentence of death, including at least three men convicted of drug-smuggling in September. No executions were reported during the year but several prisoners, convicted of both criminal and political offences, were in imminent danger of execution after their appeals for presidential clemency were turned down.

Amnesty International appealed throughout the year for the immediate and unconditional release of all prisoners of conscience, for the fair trial or release of other political prisoners, and for urgent steps to be taken to stop torture, extrajudicial executions and the use of the death penalty. It published 16 reports during the year including: in February, *Indonesia and East Timor: Fact and Fiction*; in July, *East Timor: Who is to Blame?*; and in November *Indonesia: "Operation Cleansing" – Human Rights and APEC*.

In September Amnesty International launched an international campaign to draw attention to the continuing human rights crisis in Indonesia and East Timor and published a major report, *Indonesia and East Timor: Power and Impunity,*

Human Rights under the New Order. The government said that the campaign was "politically motivated" and that the report did not reflect the human rights situation in the country.

In late July the government invited Amnesty International to visit Jakarta for official talks in the first week of August, but ruled out immediate access to East Timor. The organization welcomed the invitation but, because of the short notice, proposed alternative dates in September. In early September the government stated that the new dates were not convenient and that, following the publication of Amnesty International's most recent report, the situation was no longer conducive to a visit.

In oral statements to the UN Commission on Human Rights Amnesty International included reference to its concerns in both Indonesia and East Timor. In an oral statement to the UN Special Committee on Decolonization, Amnesty International described its concerns about extrajudicial executions, torture and other human rights violations in East Timor.

IRAN

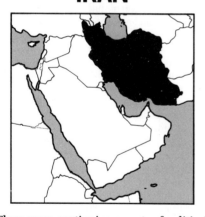

There were continuing reports of political arrests, torture, unfair trials and summary executions. Among the thousands of political prisoners held during the year were prisoners of conscience; some were detained without charge or trial, others were serving long prison sentences imposed after unfair trials. Judicial punishments of flogging and amputation of fingers continued to be implemented. Four religious leaders were killed in Iran and at least one prominent opponent of

the government was killed abroad in circumstances suggesting they may have been extrajudicially executed. At least 139 people were executed, including political prisoners.

The government headed by President 'Ali Akbar Hashemi Rafsanjani continued to face armed opposition from the Iraq-based People's Mojahedin Organization of Iran (PMOI), and organizations such as the Kurdistan Democratic Party of Iran (KDPI) in Kurdistan and Baluchi groups in Sistan-Baluchistan. The government blamed the PMOI for a bomb attack in June in a holy shrine in Mashhad in which over 20 people were killed, and accused the PMOI of trying to plant several other bombs during 1994. The PMOI denied responsibility for these acts.

In February police attacked demonstrators who had gathered outside a Sunni mosque in Zahedan to protest against the demolition of a Sunni mosque in Mashhad the previous month. Several people were killed and many injured, and scores were arrested. Among those detained was the Imam of the mosque, Moulavi 'Abdolhamid. There were further arrests of demonstrators in August in Qazvin and in Tabriz. At least 13 people were reportedly shot dead by Revolutionary Guards and 80 wounded in Qazvin; the circumstances in which these killings took place were not clear.

In February the UN Commission on Human Rights adopted a resolution whose recommendations included urging the Iranian Government to refrain from activities directed against Iranians living outside the country. The Commission again called on the government to investigate and rectify human rights issues identified by the Special Representative, particularly regarding the administration of justice and due process of law. It also encouraged Iran to offer the Special Representative its full cooperation, particularly by allowing him to pay another visit to the country. He had not been allowed access since 1991. The Commission extended the mandate of the Special Representative for a further year.

In August the UN Sub-Commission on Prevention of Discrimination and Protection of Minorities condemned human rights violations in Iran, including the use of excessive force in suppressing public demonstrations, and called on the government to cease involvement in "state

164

AMNESTY INTERNATIONAL REPORT 1995

sponsored terrorism against Iranians living abroad and the nationals of other states".

Retired General Azizollah Amir Rahimi, a former Commander of the Military Police, was arrested in November, allegedly for his open criticism of the government, and reportedly beaten by members of the secret police. His son, Mehrdad Amir Rahimi, was arrested a few days later after he had protested to the foreign media about his father's arrest. Both remained held as prisoners of conscience and their whereabouts were unknown.

A number of followers of Ayatollah Shirazi, a leading jurist, were arrested in Esfahan. Among them were Sheikh Makki Akhound, arrested in May and allegedly tortured, 'Abdolamir Akhound, aged 60, and 'Abdolrasoul Akhound, both reportedly arrested in October. At the end of the year they remained held as possible prisoners of conscience.

At least nine followers of Ayatollah Hossein 'Ali Montazeri were reportedly arrested in October, after he had publicly criticized the authorities in an open letter. Their fate and that of five of his followers arrested in 1993 (see *Amnesty International Report 1994*) remained unknown.

A well-known poet and satirical writer, 'Ali Akbar Sa'idi-Sirjani, was arrested in March together with another poet, Sa'id Niazi Kermani, ostensibly for possessing drugs. Officials publicly accused 'Ali Akbar Sa'idi-Sirjani of drug abuse, brewing alcohol, homosexual acts, links with espionage networks and receiving money from "counter-revolutionary" circles in the West. Some of these offences carry the death penalty. However, the real reason for his arrest appeared to be open letters he had written to the government objecting to censorship: most of his writings were effectively banned in Iran. 'Ali Akbar Sa'idi-Sirjani was held in incommunicado detention until 27 November when the Islamic Republic News Agency (IRNA) reported that he had died that day of a heart attack in an unspecified Tehran hospital. His family reportedly stated that he had no history of heart trouble. Sa'id Niazi Kermani was reported to have been released in September.

Some political prisoners and prisoners of conscience were still held after years in detention without trial. For example, Hossein Javadi-Gsor, a teacher and possible

prisoner of conscience, had reportedly been held without charge or trial since 1985 in his home town of Oromieh.

Other political prisoners were serving long prison terms following unfair trials: they included supporters of the PMOI; at least 24 followers of Dr 'Ali Shari'ati; members of left-wing organizations such as the *Tudeh* Party, *Peykar* and *Razmandegan*; supporters of Kurdish organizations such as the KDPI and *Komala*; and members of other groups representing ethnic minorities such as Baluchis and Arabs (see previous *Amnesty International Reports*).

Several amnesties were declared during 1994. For example, in February Ayatollah 'Ali Khamenei, Iran's spiritual leader, pardoned and commuted the sentences of 1,503 prisoners. No further details were made available. In November he pardoned 190 women convicted by ordinary and revolutionary courts.

Political trials continued to fall far short of international standards for fair trial. Trial hearings were almost always held *in camera*, often inside prisons. Proceedings were summary with hearings often lasting only a few minutes. Reports consistently indicated that political detainees were denied access to legal counsel at any stage of judicial proceedings, despite official assurances to the contrary. Mohammad Hussein Khotani, a businessman arrested in Tehran in April, was reportedly tried by an Islamic Revolutionary Court in November and sentenced to eight months' imprisonment. He was apparently denied access to a lawyer. Charges were reported to have included the distribution of anti-government leaflets among businessmen in Tehran. He was released in December.

There were continuing reports that prisoners were tortured or ill-treated to extract confessions or statements to be used as evidence at trials. The most frequently cited methods were beatings, particularly on the back and on the soles of the feet, and being suspended by the wrists or ankles. Former political prisoners testified that they had been beaten with sticks and cables, and had been held blindfolded for long periods while held in incommunicado detention. For example, Sheikh Makki Akhound (see above) was reportedly subjected to two months of torture, including beatings and lashing. He was ill and was believed to be suffering from high blood pressure. At the end of the year he had not been charged or tried.

Flogging and amputation as judicial punishments remained in force. Scores of women were reported to have been sentenced to flogging for violating the dress code. Flogging was frequently imposed for a wide range of other offences, often in conjunction with prison sentences. Mary Jones, a US national, was sentenced in April to 80 lashes, a fine and deportation to the USA reportedly for alcohol-related offences. The flogging was administered in public. In March Mohammad Hossein Honar-Bakhshi and Karim Gol-Mohammadi each had four fingers of their right hand amputated in Qom's Central Prison, in the presence of other prisoners, after being convicted of theft.

Religious minority figures were victims of possible extrajudicial executions. Reverend Haik Hovsepian Mehr, Superintendent of the Church of the Assemblies of God, was found dead in January. He had campaigned for the release of prisoner of conscience Reverend Mehdi Dibaj, a pastor in the same church who had been imprisoned since 1984 (see Amnesty International Report 1994). The body of Reverend Mehdi Dibaj was found in a forest in West Tehran on 5 July; he had been released from prison in January, still facing charges of apostasy, and was last seen alive on 24 June. The body of Reverend Tatavous Michaelian, Chairman of the Council of Protestant Ministers, was discovered on 2 July with gunshot wounds to the head.

Sunni leader Haji Mohammad Zia'ie was found dead on 20 July, five days after he was summoned for interrogation at the security headquarters in Laar, Fars province. His mutilated body was discovered beside his car some 200 kilometres from Laar. Security officials attributed the death to a car accident, but eye-witnesses reportedly disputed this. Haji Mohammad Zia'ie was a government critic and had been arrested, reportedly tortured and harassed in previous years.

A government opponent was killed in Turkey in January in circumstances suggesting the possible involvement of Iranian government agents. Taha Kermanj, a leading member of the KDPI (Revolutionary Command), was shot dead near his home in Çorum. He had fled to Turkey early in 1993 from northern Iraq, where he had reportedly received death threats from Iranian agents. He was a recognized refugee awaiting resettlement in a third country. This was the third killing of an Iranian political opposition figure in Turkey since mid-1993 (see Amnesty International Report 1994).

The threat of extrajudicial execution extended to many Iranian nationals abroad, as well as to non-Iranians such as the British writer Salman Rushdie whose killing had been called for in a fatwa (religious edict) in 1989.

At least 139 people were executed. Some were hanged in public. As in 1993, the number of executions reported in the Iranian media was far lower than in previous years. However, Amnesty International believed that the real number of executions for political and non-political offences, such as drug-trafficking and murder, was considerably higher than publicly reported.

Political prisoners continued to be sentenced to death by Islamic Revolutionary Courts using procedures that fell far short of international standards for fair trial. Among those reported to have been sentenced to death during 1994 was Seyed Nasrollah Mirsa'idi. He was arrested in March 1992, apparently in connection with his past activities with an underground left-wing organization.

Among political prisoners executed during 1994 were Hossein Sobhani, Bahman Khosravi and Raouf Mohammadi, who were reportedly executed in February. They had been imprisoned in Kermanshah since July 1992. A 77-year-old member of the Jewish community, Feyzollah Mechubad, was executed in February, allegedly because of his religious beliefs and activities. According to reports, his body bore the marks of severe torture, including the gouging out of his eyes. Bahram 'Abbas-Zadeh was publicly hanged in Zahedan in August, after being convicted of attempting to plant a bomb in Zahedan in June.

Salim Saberniah and Mustafa Ghaderi, two alleged members of Komala (see Amnesty International Report 1994), reportedly remained under sentence of death. It was not known whether Mitra Zahraie, who was sentenced to death for murder in 1993 when she was 15 years old, had been executed (see Amnesty International Report 1994).

Amnesty International repeatedly called for the immediate and unconditional release of all prisoners of conscience. It urged the government to introduce safeguards to ensure that political detainees would receive fair and prompt trials and to take steps to eradicate the use of torture. Throughout the year Amnesty International appealed for death sentences to be commuted, expressing particular concern about Mitra Zahraie.

Amnesty International appealed for immediate, thorough and independent investigations into the deaths of the four religious leaders killed in suspicious circumstances, as well as the death of 'Ali Akbar Sa'idi Sirjani. Officials claimed that the killings of Tatavous Michaelian and Mehdi Dibaj had been carried out by a young woman who had confessed to carrying out the crimes on behalf of the PMOI. The PMOI denied any involvement in the killings. Amnesty International also called for an investigation to establish the circumstances of the killings in February at the Sunni mosque in Zahedan.

The government replied to some of Amnesty International's inquiries, although it failed to answer most requests for information on particular cases. The government responded to Amnesty International's 1993 report, *Iran: Victims of human rights violations* (see *Amnesty International Report 1994*), accusing the organization of double standards and selectivity.

Amnesty International delegates continued to be denied access to the country.

IRAQ

Thousands of suspected government opponents and their relatives were detained during the year and tens of thousands arrested in previous years continued to be held. Among them were prisoners of conscience. Torture remained widespread and new punishments were introduced by law involving the mutilation of criminal offenders. The fate of many detainees arrested during the year remained unknown and the cases of thousands of detainees who "disappeared" in previous years remained unresolved. The scope of the death penalty was widened significantly and unknown numbers of judicial
and extrajudicial executions were carried out. Widespread human rights abuses were committed in areas of Iraqi Kurdistan under Kurdish control, including arbitrary arrests, torture and deliberate and arbitrary killings.**

Economic sanctions against Iraq imposed by a UN Security Council cease-fire resolution in April 1991 remained in force. Two "air exclusion zones" over northern and southern Iraq continued to be imposed. The distribution of humanitarian relief under the terms of a previous UN-sponsored Memorandum of Understanding continued on a reduced scale. In November Iraq announced its intention to recognize its border with Kuwait under the terms of UN Security Council Resolution No. 833.

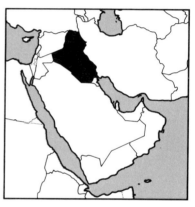

The Revolutionary Command Council (RCC), Iraq's highest executive body, introduced cruel, inhuman and degrading punishments for at least 12 criminal offences in decrees issued from April onwards. These punishments, carried out by medical personnel in public hospitals, involve the amputation of the right hand for a first offence, and of the left foot for a second offence, or the severance of one or both ears. People convicted under these laws are also branded on the forehead with an identifying symbol. Offences punishable in this way include, under certain circumstances: theft, monopolizing rationed goods, defaulting or deserting from military service, and performing plastic surgery on an amputated arm or leg, or removing the mark branded on the forehead.

The RCC also widened the scope of the death penalty to cover at least 18 new offences. These included embezzlement, forgery or bribery by military personnel;

possessing and trading in medicines or medical equipment obtained from non-official sources; and deserting or defaulting from military service on three occasions. People accused of the last two offences are tried before special courts set up at the ministries of the Interior and Defence respectively.

In June the RCC gave certain Arab Socialist Ba'th Party members and other civilian officials the power to detain people without trial for up to five years, outside the official penal system, for offences involving rationed goods and foreign currency.

Kurdish opposition forces retained control of parts of the northern provinces of Duhok, Arbil, Sulaimaniya and Kirkuk. These areas continued to be administered by the Council of Ministers for the Iraqi Kurdistan Region. The economic blockade imposed on the region by the Iraqi Government in October 1991 remained in force. In May widespread clashes broke out between forces of the Kurdistan Democratic Party (KDP), the Patriotic Union of Kurdistan (PUK) and the Islamic Movement in Iraqi Kurdistan (IMIK), which continued intermittently until August. Serious human rights abuses were perpetrated by all sides during and after these clashes (see below). In November an agreement was signed between the main political parties to end their differences and proposing a series of political reforms. However, clashes between KDP and PUK forces broke out again in December.

Widespread arrests of thousands of suspected government opponents were reported during the year but it was generally not possible to obtain further information on the detainees' fate or whereabouts. Most arrests were carried out by security and intelligence forces in Baghdad; there were also arrests in Mosul, Kirkuk, al-'Amara, al-Najaf and other places. In the south, hundreds of civilians were reportedly arrested following armed attacks in June on villages in Misan Province and in the region of al-Majar al-Kabir in al-'Amara Province. In July and August, widespread arrests were carried out in the Imam Qassem, Rahim Awa and Shorjah districts of Kirkuk by the security forces, reportedly on the pretext of searching for army deserters. Military personnel suspected of involvement in anti-government activity were also arrested during the year,

among them First Lieutenant Tayyar Ra'ad Isma'il al-Jibburi who was arrested in August. Several members of the medical profession were also said to have been arrested after refusing to perform operations involving the amputation of limbs, ears or branding. Among them were 'Abbas Qalandar and Nahrain Yusuf, both employed at the Baghdad Health Directorate.

At least three foreign nationals, two Bangladeshis and one Indian, were believed to be still held in Abu Ghraib Prison near Baghdad after being accused of illegal entry into Iraq. Eight Pakistani nationals and four Romanian nationals imprisoned in 1992 and 1993 for the same offence were released in February and April respectively.

Reports of the torture of detainees and sentenced prisoners continued to be received. Among those who died in custody were seven Ba'thist government opponents arrested in 1993 and under sentence of death. It was unclear whether they had died under torture or whether they were tortured and then executed. They included Muhammad 'Abd al-Ta'i from Diyala, Muhammad Ayyub al-Dulaimi from Mosul and Walid Shaker al-'Ubaidi from Baghdad. Their bodies were returned to their families in August and September, reportedly disfigured by torture. The eyes of six of the victims had allegedly been gouged out. Other detainees were said to have died under torture shortly after arrest; among them was Karim al-Jihari who was arrested in April in Misan Province during a wave of arbitrary arrests in the south. There were also numerous reports of the security forces beating relatives of army deserters to find out their whereabouts.

The new judicial punishments of amputation of the hand or foot, severance of the ear and branding were imposed widely, with hundreds of cases reported in Baghdad, Mosul, Basra and elsewhere. The majority of victims were people convicted of theft and army deserters. The first sentences of amputation of the hand were imposed by the Diyala criminal court in June on two people convicted of stealing carpets from a mosque. In some cases victims were later shown on television; one such case was that of 'Ali 'Ubaid 'Abed 'Ali, whose right hand was amputated and forehead branded in September following his conviction for theft. Some

168

army deserters had their ears severed in military hospitals, allegedly without the use of anaesthetic or in other appalling conditions. Hassan 'Ali Kadhim and Khaz'al 'Abed Mansur, whose ears were severed in al-Nasiriyya in September, reportedly died subsequently from infection. Others were reported to have died through haemorrhaging.

New information was received about some of the many detainees who had "disappeared" in previous years. Details emerged of 25 Feyli Kurds (Shi'a Muslims) who were arrested in 1980 and 1981, including 'Ala'uddin Molaei al-Haydari and his nephew Deler who had been arrested in Baghdad in June 1981. Thirty other relatives arrested with them were held for four months and then forcibly expelled to Iran. During the 1970s and 1980s several hundred thousand Shi'a Muslims, both Arabs and Kurds, were forcibly deported to Iran. Thousands of male members of such families were detained in Iraq, however, and many "disappeared". The cases of over 100,000 Kurds who "disappeared" during the 1988 and 1989 "Anfal Operations" remained unresolved (see previous *Amnesty International Reports*), as did the cases of an estimated 625 Kuwaiti and other nationals arrested by Iraqi forces during the occupation of Kuwait in 1990 and 1991, who were believed to be held in Iraq. The Iraqi Government reportedly said in September that 43 of the group of 625 were no longer alive but this could not be independently confirmed.

Numerous executions were reported during the year but it was not possible to determine the total number or whether they were judicial or extrajudicial executions. Death sentences continued to be imposed for a wide range of criminal offences, including murder, rape and drug- trafficking, as well as political offences. In February the Court of Cassation upheld the death sentences passed on five people convicted of drug-trafficking in December 1993, but it was not known whether the sentences were carried out. Eight people convicted of murder and theft were executed in March; several of them were members of the Iraqi Communist Party who had reportedly been arrested on account of their political affiliation. Five others were also executed in March in Abu Ghraib Prison following conviction for currency speculation; among them was

'Abbas al-'Aoun, a money-changer from Baghdad. Several military and intelligence officers were reportedly executed in October and November after being accused of involvement in alleged coup attempts.

An unknown number of unarmed civilians were extrajudicially executed in the southern marshes region, where military and special forces continued to launch deliberate and indiscriminate military attacks on civilian targets, including the settlements of al-Jibayesh, al-'Uwaili and al-Saigal. Armed government opponents were reportedly shot dead after capture; among them were Faleh al-Bazzuni and 'Adnan Khashan, who were arrested following an attack in the region of Umm al-Juwaish near al-Mdaina in March. Scores of families were displaced after their homes were destroyed or after fleeing to escape artillery shelling. Although over 4,000 refugees crossed the border into Iran during the year, the journey became increasingly hazardous as the widespread drainage of the marshes enabled Iraqi Government forces to cut off most escape routes.

Extrajudicial executions of suspected government opponents also continued to be reported. In April a prominent government opponent, Shaikh Talib al-Suhail al-Tamimi, was shot dead in Beirut. The Lebanese authorities arrested two Iraqi diplomats said to have been implicated in the killing; they apparently later confessed to working for Iraqi intelligence. Also in April a German journalist, Lissy Schmidt, and her Kurdish bodyguard, 'Aziz Qader, were shot dead near Sulaimaniya in Kurdish-held territory. Two people arrested by the Kurdish authorities reportedly confessed to working for Iraqi intelligence. In July Muhammad Taqi al-Kho'i, son of the late Grand Ayatollah Abul-Qasim al-Kho'i, died after a car accident on the al-Najaf-Karbala' road. There were fears that he might have been killed by Iraqi intelligence, who had caused the deaths of numerous government opponents in apparent "accidents" in the past. Muhammad Taqi al-Kho'i had been threatened and harassed since his release from prison in 1991, in particular for seeking to raise the cases of 106 Shi'a Muslim clerics, scholars and students who "disappeared" in custody following their arrest in 1991 (see *Amnesty International Report 1992*). Several cases were also reported in which government opponents were poisoned with thallium. Among the victims was Safa' al-Battat, a merchant who was allegedly poisoned by government agents in Shaqlawa in December.

Kurdish opposition groups were responsible for a wide range of human rights abuses during the May clashes and their aftermath. Several hundred fighters and party cadres were taken prisoner by the KDP, PUK and IMIK; although most were later released in prisoner exchanges, at least 59 were believed to have been killed after surrender or capture in Qala Diza, Rania, Koisanjaq, 'Aqra, Salahuddin, Khormal, Halabja and other places. The bodies of some of them were reported to have been subsequently mutilated. Scores of unarmed civilians were arbitrarily detained on the basis of their political affiliation, held in unacknowledged places of detention and tortured, including with beatings and electric shocks. Civilian demonstrators were also killed. In one incident in June, over 20 people taking part in a funeral procession in Sulaimaniya were killed by PUK forces who reportedly fired at random into the crowd. Information was also obtained about torture and killings of prisoners by PUK and IMIK forces during clashes in December 1993 (see *Amnesty International Report 1994*).

At least nine people were sentenced to death by the Sulaimaniya and Arbil criminal courts, all but one after being convicted of premeditated murder. Two of the sentences were upheld by the Court of Cassation, three others were reduced to life imprisonment and the rest were pending review at the end of the year. No death sentences were ratified and no executions carried out. At least 16 other prisoners sentenced to death in 1992 and 1993 for premeditated murder remained held.

In February and July Amnesty International delegations visited Iraqi Kurdistan to investigate reports of human rights abuses committed in December 1993 and in May. The organization interviewed scores of detainees and former detainees, torture victims and eye-witnesses to deliberate and arbitrary killings. It raised its concerns with leaders of the PUK, KDP and IMIK, urging that thorough and impartial investigations be conducted into the abuses. In June Amnesty International publicly urged the Kurdish leadership to put an end to deliberate and arbitrary killings and

the abduction, killing or torture of civilians based on their political ties. By the end of the year no investigations had been set up and none of the perpetrators had been brought to justice.

Amnesty International continued to appeal to the Iraqi Government to halt human rights violations, including the detention of prisoners of conscience, arbitrary arrests of political suspects, unfair trials and "disappearances". It expressed concern at the introduction of the punishments of amputation and branding, and urged that these penalties be abolished. The organization also appealed for the commutation of all death sentences. No substantive responses were received.

In an oral statement to the UN Commission on Human Rights in March, Amnesty International drew attention to its grave concerns in Iraq and urged that the UN Secretary-General make available without further delay the necessary resources to establish a human rights monitoring operation for Iraq. The Commission adopted a resolution condemning the "massive violations of human rights" perpetrated by the government, extended the mandate of the UN Special Rapporteur on Iraq for a further year and requested the UN Secretary-General to provide "appropriate additional resources" for human rights monitors for Iraq. A resolution adopted by the UN Sub-Commission on Prevention of Discrimination and Protection of Minorities in August also called on the UN Secretary-General to provide "all necessary assistance to the Special Rapporteur to undertake his mission". In December the UN General Assembly passed a resolution requesting the UN Secretary-General to "approve the allocation of sufficient human and material resources" for setting up a human rights monitoring operation for Iraq. By the end of the year the human rights monitoring operation had not been set up.

170

ISRAEL AND THE OCCUPIED TERRITORIES

(INCLUDING AREAS UNDER THE PALESTINIAN AUTHORITY'S JURISDICTION)

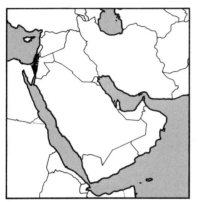

About 6,500 Palestinians were arrested on security grounds by the Israeli authorities; 6,245 were tried before Israeli military courts. More than 700 Palestinians and nine Israelis were held in administrative detention without charge or trial. At least 5,450 remained held at the end of the year, including almost 240 administrative detainees. Approximately 5,000 Palestinian prisoners and detainees were released, most in the context of agreements between Israel and the Palestine Liberation Organization (PLO). Prisoners of conscience included administrative detainees and conscientious objectors to military service. Torture or ill-treatment during interrogation remained systematic. At least 82 Palestinians were shot dead by Israeli forces, some in circumstances suggesting extrajudicial executions or other unlawful killings. One man was sentenced to death. The Palestinian Authority's security forces arrested, apparently arbitrarily, hundreds of Palestinians and there were reports of torture and ill-treatment: one Palestinian died in custody. At least 15 people died after being shot by Palestinian Authority forces in circumstances which suggested they were unlawfully killed. Palestinian armed groups committed human rights abuses including hostage-taking and deliberate and arbitrary killings.

In May the Israeli Government headed by Yitzhak Rabin and the PLO signed an Agreement on the Gaza Strip and Jericho Areas establishing the Palestinian Authority with jurisdiction over those areas. PLO Chairman Yasser Arafat returned to the Gaza Strip as head of the Palestinian Authority in July.

In the Occupied Territories, the Israeli authorities continued to make extensive use of firearms, arrests and restriction orders confining Palestinians to the Occupied Territories.

In February at least 29 people were killed in the Haram al-Ibrahimi mosque in Hebron by Baruch Goldstein, an Israeli settler, who was himself killed. More than 30 people were killed by Israeli forces in the two weeks following, mostly during demonstrations or riots. Two Jewish militant groups, *Kach* and *Kahane Hai,* were banned after the massacre. A judicial inquiry concluded that the settler had acted alone, but that there had been security failures. It recommended that open-fire regulations be clarified. An international monitoring force, the Temporary International Presence in Hebron (TIPH), was deployed between May and August in Hebron.

Attacks by armed Palestinians continued. About 75 Israeli civilians and 13 members of the Israeli security forces were killed in such attacks, as were over 70 Palestinian civilians. Many were carried out by Islamist groups such as *Hamas,* Islamic Resistance Movement.

More than 600 renewable administrative detention orders of up to six months were imposed on Palestinians. Appeals under a two-step process of judicial review usually took place several weeks after arrest. In most cases, detainees and their lawyers were not provided with crucial information about the reasons for detention. Prisoners of conscience held in administrative detention included Qasem al-Khaliliyya Tawfiq Qasem, who was released in February after three months' detention. At his appeal, which was rejected, the judge stated that he had not been involved in any violent activities. Other Palestinian administrative detainees included Fatmah 'Ataynah, allegedly a member of Islamic Jihad. She was held between February and August. Ahmad Qatamesh, allegedly a senior official of the Popular Front for the Liberation of Palestine (PFLP)

AMNESTY INTERNATIONAL REPORT 1995

and detained since September 1992, had his administrative detention order renewed twice (see *Amnesty International Reports 1993* and *1994*). Nine members of *Kach* and *Kahane Hai* were administratively detained for periods of between three and six months. Baruch Marzel, the leader of *Kach*, was released in September and placed under house arrest for six months.

Israeli prisoners of conscience included conscientious objectors to military service. For example, Peter Weiner was sentenced in March to 28 days' imprisonment for refusing to serve in the Occupied Territories.

Mordechai Vanunu remained held in solitary confinement for the eighth consecutive year (see *Amnesty International Reports 1988* to *1994*). Amnesty International believed his treatment to be cruel, inhuman and degrading and called for his immediate release as redress for the past and persistent violations of his human rights. Avraham Klingberg, a 76-year-old physician and university professor held since 1983 on spying charges (see *Amnesty International Report 1994*), had an appeal for his release on medical grounds refused.

In May Israeli forces abducted Mustafa al-Dirani, the leader of the Faithful Resistance, a Lebanese armed group, from his home in south Lebanon. The Israeli authorities said they interrogated him about the whereabouts of Ron Arad, an Israeli airman missing in Lebanon (see **Lebanon** entry), but gave no information on his whereabouts or legal status. He was still held at the end of the year. More than 30 Lebanese and other foreign nationals also remained held in Israeli administrative detention. They included Shaikh 'Abd al-Karim 'Ubayd, abducted from Lebanon with three others in 1989, and six Lebanese Shi'a Muslims transferred secretly to Israel in 1990 after having been detained by the Lebanese Forces militia in 1987 (see *Amnesty International Report 1994*).

Over 200 detainees were held incommunicado without charge or trial at any one time in the Khiam detention centre in an area of south Lebanon controlled by Israel and the South Lebanon Army (see **Lebanon** entry).

Some 6,245 Palestinians were tried by Israeli military courts on charges includ-

ing acts of violence. The maximum period adults could be held before being brought before a judge was reduced from 18 days to 11 days. Detainees were frequently denied access to lawyers and relatives for longer periods. Confessions obtained during incommunicado detention were often the main evidence against detainees. Over 5,000 Palestinians were released, most in the context of negotiations between Israel and the PLO.

Palestinian detainees continued to be systematically tortured or ill-treated during interrogation by the General Security Service (GSS), often while held incommunicado. Methods used included hooding with dirty sacks, shackling in painful positions for prolonged periods, beatings, sleep deprivation and confinement in dark, closet-sized cells. For example, Hani Muzher said that he had been deprived of sleep for at least a week and shackled in painful positions for prolonged periods during his interrogation in Ramallah Prison in July and August. Following an appeal to the High Court of Justice, the GSS agreed that he would no longer be deprived of sleep. His trial on charges of activities in the PFLP began in December. Members of a group of 12 Jewish militants, who were arrested in September and October, said that they were tortured. Oren Edri, an officer in the Israel Defence Force, alleged that he was hooded, insulted, roughly handled and confined in a dirty cell. He was later charged with passing weapons to Jewish militants.

In February new legislation provided for complaints against GSS interrogators to be investigated by the police or the Ministry of Justice. In November, following the taking as hostage of an Israeli soldier by *Hamas* in October, the authorities revealed that they had relaxed the secret interrogation guidelines laid down by the Landau Commission in 1987. The Landau Commission guidelines themselves permit the use of "moderate physical pressure".

In April the UN Committee against Torture considered Israel's initial report. The Committee found the authorization of the use of "moderate physical pressure" to be "completely unacceptable" and expressed concern at the "large number of heavily documented cases of ill-treatment in custody". The Committee recommended that the interrogation procedures be published and that all interrogation practices in

172 breach of the Convention be ended immediately.

At least 82 Palestinians were shot dead by Israeli forces. Some were shot during armed clashes; others were killed in circumstances suggesting that they may have been victims of extrajudicial executions. For example, in March, six members of *Fatah*, the main faction of the PLO, were shot dead apparently without warning by an undercover unit in Jabalia Refugee Camp in the Gaza Strip. One was reportedly shot in the head after being wounded and apprehended. The authorities later said that their killings had been a mistake, as none was sought for arrest, but said that the open-fire guidelines had been correctly applied.

In November Hani 'Abed, associated with *Islamic Jihad* and suspected of involvement in the killing of two Israeli soldiers in May, was killed in a car-bombing in the Gaza Strip. His death followed statements by Israeli officials suggesting that those responsible for armed attacks against Israelis might be targets for extrajudicial executions. Israel did not deny responsibility for his death, nor for an explosion in Lebanon which killed three people, including two members of *Hizbullah* (see **Lebanon** entry).

According to the authorities, 12 Israeli soldiers were tried for violating military orders. In July disciplinary measures were reportedly taken against six border police, including a chief officer for the West Bank, for incidents in Hebron, including the mosque massacre. Two border guards were dismissed in July after beating at least one prisoner in a detention centre in Bethlehem.

In November a military court in Jenin sentenced Sa'id Badarnah to death for plotting a suicide bomb attack in Hadera in April. An automatic appeal to the Military Court of Appeal in Ramallah had not concluded by the end of the year. The last execution was that of Adolf Eichmann in 1962.

The Israeli authorities used massive firepower against houses in which suspects were believed to be hiding. In other cases, houses were sealed or destroyed. In November the house of the family of the suicide-bomber Salah Nazzal, who killed 23 people in a bus-bombing in October, was destroyed after the Supreme Court rejected an appeal against a demolition order.

The Palestinian Authority's security forces arrested hundreds of Palestinians, many apparently arbitrarily. Most were suspected members of Islamist and other groups opposed to the peace agreement with Israel. They included prisoners of conscience. All were released without charge after spending between a few days and two months in detention, nearly all without access to lawyers or a judge. For example, two journalists, brothers Taher and 'Amer Shriteh, were arrested in October and held for nine days, apparently for faxing a *Hamas* leaflet. Scores of Palestinians said to have collaborated in the past with the Israeli authorities were also detained; none was brought before the courts but they reportedly had access to lawyers and judges.

Reports of torture in the Palestinian Authority's areas were received. Methods used included beatings. In July Farid Abu Jarbu' died in the interrogation centre of Gaza Prison where he had been held incommunicado for about two weeks on suspicion of having collaborated with the Israeli authorities. The Palestinian Authority acknowledged he died as a result of violence and set up an official investigation. Four officials were arrested in connection with his death. All were reportedly released and no trial had been held by the end of the year.

At least 15 people were killed by Palestinian Authority forces after May, some in circumstances suggesting unlawful killings. Salah al-Sha'er, aged 15, was shot in the abdomen in Rafah in August following a wedding, when the group he was with had an argument with policemen. He died shortly afterwards. Seven policemen were arrested and an investigation launched. The seven were later released pending the outcome of the investigation. In November, 13 Palestinians were killed by Palestinian Authority forces during a demonstration by *Hamas* supporters outside a mosque in Gaza City; the lives of the security forces had not been in danger. A judicial commission of inquiry was established.

Palestinian armed groups committed grave human rights abuses including deliberate and arbitrary killings and hostage-taking. In April and October, suicide bombers killed at least 35 people, most of them civilians, in Afula and other towns. *Hamas* claimed responsibility for these and other attacks as well as for the hostage-taking of Nachshon Waxman, an Israeli soldier, in October. He was killed, along with three of his captors and one Israeli officer, when Israeli forces attempted to free him. Over 70 Palestinians, mostly suspected of "collaborating" with the Israeli authorities, were also killed by Palestinian groups.

Amnesty International sought the immediate and unconditional release of prisoners of conscience and called for all administrative detainees to be tried promptly and fairly, or released. It sought clarification on the use of firearms and called for impartial investigations in cases of killings by Israeli forces. It urged the Israeli Government to dissociate itself from any policy of extrajudicial executions. It also called for a thorough review of policing methods used by Israeli forces in the Occupied Territories, and for the mandate of the TIPH to include effective human rights monitoring. In April Amnesty International published a report, *Israel and the Occupied Territories: Torture and ill-treatment of political detainees*. Its recommendations included prompt access to judges and lawyers, the prohibition of any "physical pressure" during interrogation, and the effective investigation of allegations of torture.

Amnesty International expressed concern about attacks on houses possibly containing suspects. The authorities denied that such attacks were a form of punishment, stating that all suspects were given the opportunity to surrender. However, the authorities did not clarify evidence presented by Amnesty International in 1993 that explosives were used after houses were stormed (see *Amnesty International Report 1994*).

The Israeli authorities provided information on a number of individual cases and commented on the *Amnesty International Report 1994*, arguing that the situation on the ground had been ignored.

In an oral statement to the UN Commission on Human Rights in February, Amnesty International referred to its concerns in the Israeli-Occupied Territories, including south Lebanon, calling for on-site human rights monitoring in the West Bank and Gaza Strip.

Amnesty International urged the Palestinian Authority to introduce clear procedures governing arrest, detention and interrogation and called for impartial investigations into abuses. The Palestinian Authority had not responded to cases raised with it by the end of the year.

Amnesty International condemned hostage-taking and deliberate and arbitrary killings by Palestinian armed groups. It called on them to respect fundamental principles of humanitarian law and to halt human rights abuses. *Hamas* informed Amnesty International that it was "anxious not to inflict any harm on civilians" but said this could only be guaranteed "if Jewish settlers were disarmed and forced out of the territories they illegally occupy". Amnesty International stressed that respect for basic principles of humanitarian law was unconditional.

ITALY

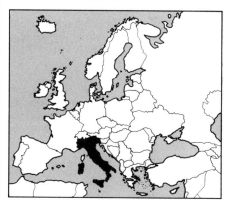

There were numerous allegations of ill-treatment by law enforcement and prison officers. The death penalty was abolished for all offences.

A bill reforming the existing system of conscientious objection to compulsory military service, approved by the Chamber of Deputies in 1993 after numerous delays (see *Amnesty International Reports 1989 to 1994*), was awaiting consideration by the Senate when parliament was dissolved in January to make way for general elections in March. These brought the new six-party coalition government of Prime Minister Silvio Berlusconi to power. A new bill, based largely on the 1993 text, was still under consideration by the Senate at the end of the year.

In October parliament gave its final approval to a bill eliminating the death

174

penalty from the Wartime Military Penal Code, thereby abolishing the death penalty for all offences.

Officers from all law enforcement agencies were accused of ill-treating detainees and a number of court proceedings were under way into such allegations.

In June, 13 officers of the Palermo Municipal Police were committed for trial in 1996 following an investigation into the alleged ill-treatment of Filippo Campanella in March. The officers were accused of forcing him out of his car and kicking and punching him until he lost consciousness, after he had asked if he could remain briefly double-parked on a Palermo street. He suffered a spinal injury resulting in neurological damage to his right leg. During the investigation the officers apparently claimed he had thrown himself to the ground, pretending to be hit. The officers were also accused of using threats and violence to take a roll of film from the camera of a bystander who had photographed their assault. Filippo Campanella was also committed for trial on a charge of refusing to give the officers details of his identity.

In May, two Turin police officers were charged with deliberately inflicting injuries which led to the death of Antonio Morabito following his street arrest for robbery in December 1993. Numerous eye-witnesses had stated that, after handcuffing him, police officers kicked and punched him, hit him with the butt of a gun and fired a shot close to his head. He was taken to a central police station but died a few hours later during transfer to hospital. Autopsy and forensic reports established that he had suffered numerous head injuries and damage to the peritoneum resulting in a fatal intestinal haemorrhage. The trial opened in October.

In October a *carabiniere* officer was charged with the manslaughter of Tarzan Sulic, an 11-year-old Rom shot through the head while detained in a *carabinieri* barracks near Padua in September 1993. His 13-year-old female cousin, wounded by the same shot, had alleged that both were ill-treated by *carabinieri* during their detention and that the accused officer had threatened the boy with a gun just before it fired. In December Padua's military authorities charged the officer with infringing regulations through illegal use of his firearm.

Allegations of ill-treatment by law enforcement officers often concerned immigrants. In June Naser Hasani, a Rom from former Yugoslavia, lodged a complaint after being stopped by three police officers while driving in a car with two companions in Florence. He said they checked his identity documents and accused him of using a hammer they found in his car to carry out robberies. They asked him to follow their police car to the central police station but instead led him to a park on the outskirts of the city, where he alleged they kicked him, struck him with the hammer and racially insulted him. After the police left the scene his companions took him to a local hospital which issued a medical certificate recording multiple cuts and bruises.

In August doctors attached to a Milan hospital drew the attention of police and judicial authorities to the allegations made by a drug addict who claimed that the injuries which had necessitated an emergency operation to remove his spleen had been inflicted by a *carabiniere* officer some hours earlier. Khaled Kablouti, a Moroccan immigrant, said that he had been on the point of injecting himself in a Milan underpass when the officer ordered him to throw away his needle. He said that he complied but that the officer then kicked him in the stomach, knocking him down, and kicked him again in the same place when he tried to stand. The officer then left the scene. A judicial investigation was apparently opened.

A mass demonstration held in Milan in September against the closure of a social centre led to violent clashes between demonstrators and law enforcement officers. In a subsequent complaint to the Milan Chief of Police and to the Minister of the Interior, journalists and press photographers claimed they were kicked and beaten by police while reporting on the demonstration and that officers assaulted some photographers while they were taking pictures of police armed with truncheons beating demonstrators. The Milan Chief of Police apologized to the journalists and photographers injured by the police, but apparently no disciplinary investigation was announced. Journalists claimed that they also saw bystanders, including passengers on a stationary bus, being beaten by the police. Some members of the public lodged formal complaints of ill-treatment. Enrica Personé alleged that she and her daughter were standing at a bus stop when they saw police officers beating a youth with their truncheons. She said that when they called on them to stop the police officers beat her daughter. A local hospital later issued a certificate recording that Enrica Personé was in a state of shock and that her daughter had extensive bruising on her legs.

There were further allegations of ill-treatment by prison officers. In January inmates of Sulmona prison claimed that officers had beaten them in reprisal for a protest they had carried out in December 1993, apparently over the alleged medical neglect of a fellow prisoner. By the end of the month inmates had reportedly lodged 13 complaints accusing prison officers of inflicting severe beatings, issuing death threats, abusing their authority and committing acts of deliberate humiliation and extortion.

In an open letter published by the press in early February inmates of Secondigliano prison expressed concern about the isolation of a fellow prisoner, Giacomo De Simone, since a court appearance on 12 January when he had complained of ill-treatment by prison officers. They claimed he had been repeatedly beaten by prison officers over a two-day period immediately preceding the court hearing and threatened with further ill-treatment if he reported the beatings to the judges. In February it was also reported that five prison officers and their commandant had been committed for trial on various charges, including abuse of authority, aggravated fraud, calumny, perjury and instigating others to commit offences, as a result of the judicial investigation opened in early 1993 into the alleged systematic ill-treatment of some 300 inmates of Secondigliano prison (see *Amnesty International Report 1994*). A further 108 officers were apparently under judicial investigation during the year in connection with the alleged ill-treatment.

In July the UN Human Rights Committee considered Italy's periodic report on its compliance with the International Covenant on Civil and Political Rights. Its principal concerns included cases of ill-treatment by law enforcement agencies and the "increasing number of cases of ill-treatment in prisons", noting that they were not always investigated "thor-

oughly". The Committee recommended that torture be made a criminal offence and that effective steps be taken to protect detainees from ill-treatment.

Some authorities responded to Amnesty International's inquiries about allegations of ill-treatment, giving information about the status of court proceedings.

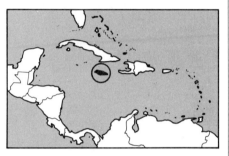

JAMAICA

Corporal punishment was imposed as a sentence for the first time for over 20 years. At least eight death sentences were imposed. There were no executions.

In August a High Court judge sentenced a man to six strokes with a tamarind rod and a prison term on conviction of wounding with intent. Corporal punishment had not been implemented since the early 1970s but had remained in the statute book despite a recommendation by a government-appointed committee in 1976 that flogging (with the cat-o'-nine-tails) and whipping (with a tamarind rod) be abolished as punishments. Corporal punishment may be imposed for offences such as rape, indecent assault and robbery with violence. In September, three other men were sentenced to three strokes and prison terms for robbery and illegal possession of firearms. The sentences had not been carried out by the end of the year.

The Judicial Committee of the Privy Council (JCPC) in London, Jamaica's final court of appeal, rejected the appeal of Albert Huntley in December. Albert Huntley had appealed against the Court of Appeal's dismissal in November 1993 of a constitutional motion in which he had claimed that the review of his case (provided in the Offences against the Person (Amendment) Act of 1992 for those already under sentence of death to classify their offences into capital or non-capital

176 murder) had violated his right to protection under the law and to a fair hearing (see *Amnesty International Reports 1993* and *1994*). He argued that he had not had the opportunity to be heard or to have legal representation of his choice during the classification review proceedings. The hearings of the cases of all other prisoners who had had their cases classified as capital murder were suspended in 1993 pending the resolution of Albert Huntley's appeal. No death sentences were commuted as a result of the November 1993 JCPC ruling that execution more than five years after sentencing would constitute "inhuman and degrading punishment or other treatment" (see *Amnesty International Report 1994*). The JCPC had further advised that in order to achieve justice swiftly, the Governor General should refer all relevant cases to the Jamaica Privy Council which should recommend commutation instead of waiting for all those prisoners who had been under sentence of death for five years or more to appeal individually. However, no action was taken in the cases of dozens of prisoners due to have benefited from the ruling.

At least eight people were sentenced to death for capital murder. There were no executions and at the end of the year there were over 150 prisoners on death row. The last hanging was carried out in February 1988.

The trial of five police officers charged with manslaughter in connection with the deaths of three men in the Constant Spring Police Station in October 1992 started in February. An inquest had found criminal negligence amounting to manslaughter as the cause of death. The men died from suffocation while being held in an overcrowded, unventilated cell (see *Amnesty International Report 1993*). At the end of the five-week trial the jury did not find the officers to be criminally liable for the three deaths and they were acquitted in late March. It was reported that the government intended to settle pending civil claims on the case.

Several policemen were tried on murder charges for killing people in previous years when they could have apprehended them instead. In one case, relating to the death of Rudolph Edwards in 1990, the jury could not reach a unanimous decision and a retrial was ordered.

In February the Minister of Justice and National Security replied to Amnesty International's 1993 report on the four death row prisoners who were shot dead by warders on 31 October 1993 after allegedly trying to take warders hostage (see *Amnesty International Report 1994*). The report also described concerns about previous deaths of inmates of the prison as well as allegations of ill-treatment and threats to prisoners. The Minister said that the police had been asked to carry out a thorough investigation into the deaths.

In June the Minister replied more fully to the concerns raised by Amnesty International in the above report about ill-treatment of prisoners between 1989 and 1993. He said that in the case of a disturbance at St Catherine's District Prison in May 1990 in which three prisoners died after allegedly being beaten by warders, a coroner's jury had decided in 1992 that there were people criminally responsible and the police had been asked to "carry out further investigations in order to obtain additional information about these persons" (see *Amnesty International Report 1991*). On the 31 October 1993 deaths he said that the report of an investigation by the Inspector of Prisons had been sent to the office of the Director of Public Prosecutions (DPP) for a ruling on the question of criminal responsibility, but that it had not been found necessary to appoint an independent Commission of Inquiry as recommended by Amnesty International.

In October Amnesty International replied, welcoming the inquiry conducted by the prison Inspectorate into the 31 October incident and the fact that the DPP would examine the report to see whether there was evidence of any criminal wrongdoing on the part of individuals. It regretted, however, that without the publication of a full report setting out the terms of reference, the sources examined and the findings, such an investigation could not be shown to have the impartiality and thoroughness that is required under international standards. Amnesty International reiterated its appeal for a full, independent inquiry and urged that, in the first instance, the report of the Inspectorate should be made public at the earliest date.

In March Amnesty International wrote to the Attorney General urging that all relevant death sentences be commuted under the 1993 JCPC five-year ruling. It also called for the commutation of all death sentences.

In September Amnesty International wrote to the Minister of National Security and Justice expressing its concern about the whipping sentence imposed in August. It pointed out that this sentence violated international standards to which Jamaica is a State Party and called on the government to introduce legislation to abolish corporal punishment and to ensure that the punishment was not carried out. In November the Minister replied stating that the sentence was legal under the current law. He added that when amendments to the Constitution, which were under discussion, came into force it would be "appropriate to consider whether this particular piece of legislation authorizing sentences of whipping and flogging can remain as part of our law in the light of current international conventions and practices".

JAPAN

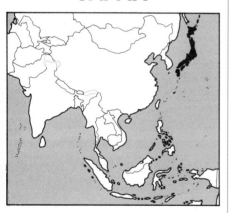

Two prisoners were executed in secret. Scores of others were still on death row after more than 20 years. There were continuing reports of ill-treatment of prisoners and of suspects in police custody. Asylum-seekers continued to be at risk because of the authorities' failure to fulfil their international obligations towards refugees and asylum-seekers.

The Liberal Democratic Party, which had ruled Japan for most of the post-war period until 1993, re-entered the government in August as part of a tripartite coalition led by Social Democratic Party chairman Murayama Tomiichi who became Prime Minister. In a package of political reform laws adopted by the Diet (parliament) in November, the electoral system was changed. In August the Prime Minister suggested that measures be considered to compensate women from several east and southeast Asian countries who had been forced into prostitution by the Japanese armed forces or their agents during World War II. Proposed legislation to set up a compensation fund was delayed in November; no action had been taken by the end of the year.

In November an all-party association of Diet members urged the government to call a five-year moratorium on the death penalty, encourage debate about its abolition and disseminate relevant information to the public. However, Prime Minister Murayama refused to take such an initiative. In December the Minister of Justice stated that his ministry was considering publishing more information on the death penalty.

In December Ajima Yukio and Sasaki Kazumitsu were executed. They had both been convicted of murder. Ajima Yukio had been held on death row for 16 years in Tokyo Detention Centre. In keeping with established practice, the executions were carried out in secret and were not announced to the relatives or the lawyers of the prisoners; the prisoners themselves were believed to have been given only a few hours' notice before their hanging.

About 90 prisoners were on death row at the end of the year, including 57 whose death sentences had been confirmed by the Supreme Court. At least four had been on death row for more than 20 years.

There were numerous reports of ill-treatment of detainees by police and prison guards. In May Kanazawa Hitoshi, a former prosecutor from the Sendai District Public Prosecutor's Office, was given a suspended sentence of two years' imprisonment for assaulting witnesses in October 1993 during an investigation into corruption. He had been dismissed in November 1993. In June and October two other prosecutors, Masuda Yasuo and Shinbo Hitoshi, both from the Tokyo District Public Prosecutor's Office, resigned after being suspended for three months for alleged ill-treatment of suspects during interrogation. These incidents led the Minister of Justice to formally discipline Public Prosecutor General Yoshinaga Yusuke for lack of adequate supervision. However, no changes were made to legislation and

178

practices which allow the lengthy detention of suspects in police custody and have led to frequent reports that interrogators had beaten, kicked and threatened suspects to extract confessions from them.

Mehrpooran Arjang, an Iranian national, died in June in Manamisenju Police Station in Tokyo, a day after being arrested on suspicion of illegal residence. His wife alleged that he had been beaten by police; an autopsy reportedly indicated that he had suffered several internal haemorrhages. A suit for compensation filed against the government by Mehrpooran Arjang's relatives was still pending at the end of the year.

In November Yahia Radwan Allam, an Egyptian national, filed a suit against the government alleging that he had been beaten in March while in solitary confinement at the Tokyo Detention House (TDH). He alleged that blows inflicted by guards left his hearing impaired and that he had contracted a skin disease following a previous period of solitary confinement in unsanitary conditions in October 1993. Another TDH detainee from Nigeria alleged in a suit also brought in November that he had been ill-treated on three occasions between February and August. On the last occasion he alleged he had been repeatedly thrown on the floor and against a wall by several guards, suffering as a result from prolonged bleeding and back pain.

In December Akiyama Takeshi, a former immigration officer, told the press that he had witnessed several cases of ill-treatment of foreigners while working at a detention centre in Tokyo in 1993. He alleged that foreign detainees who did not obey orders had been taken to isolation rooms and repeatedly beaten and threatened. Former detainees, their relatives and lawyers later confirmed these allegations. The Ministry of Justice said it had investigated Akiyama Takeshi's allegations and found them groundless. The investigation was reportedly carried out by Immigration Bureau officials over a weekend. It appeared to be neither independent nor impartial.

In November, 11 asylum-seekers from Myanmar had their applications denied on the basis of the "60-days rule", under which applications can normally be considered only when submitted within 60 days of an asylum-seeker's arrival in Japan, with no consideration of the substance of their claim by the authorities. Guidelines by the Executive Committee of the UN High Commissioner for Refugees prohibit governments from denying requests for asylum on the sole basis of the failure of asylum-seekers to meet administrative requirements.

In January Amnesty International published a report entitled *Japan: Asylum-Seekers Still at Risk*, outlining the organization's continuing concerns about Japan's laws and practices on the treatment of asylum-seekers. This followed a statement by the government dismissing as incorrect an earlier report on the same concerns published by Amnesty International in March 1993 (see *Amnesty International Report 1994*). In July Amnesty International published *Japan: An Agenda for Human Rights*, an open letter to the then newly appointed Prime Minister, urging that the death penalty be abolished, asylum-seekers be better protected and ill-treatment of suspects in police custody be ended. It also urged the government to ratify the Convention against Torture and Other Cruel, Inhuman or Degrading Treatment or Punishment and other relevant international human rights standards. By the end of the year the government had neither replied to Amnesty International, nor implemented any of these recommendations.

JORDAN

About 450 security detainees, including possible prisoners of conscience, were arrested during the year and many were held in prolonged incommunicado detention. Most were released without charge, but at least 40 were brought to trial before the State Security Court whose procedures do not satisfy international standards for fair trial. There were allegations of torture by the General Intelligence Department (GID). Fourteen people were executed.

The state of war between Jordan and Israel ended in July and a peace treaty was signed in October. Measures taken against opponents of the treaty included a ban on independent preachers giving sermons in mosques and on demonstrations.

Several journalists were prosecuted

under the Press and Publications Law during the year. For example, Nidal Mansur, editor of the newspaper *al-Bilad*, was detained twice, once for three hours and the second time for three days, in connection with articles published in the paper. Other journalists, including Ramadan al-Rawashidah, a journalist for the newspaper *al-Ahali*; its former editor, Jamil al-Nimri; and Sana 'Attiyah and Georges Hawatmah, both with the *Jordan Times*, were fined in connection with articles published in 1993 concerning allegations of torture raised during a trial before the State Security Court (see *Amnesty International Report 1994*).

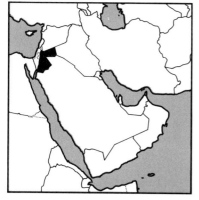

About 450 security detainees were arrested. Most were detained by the GID, frequently in prolonged incommunicado detention. The majority were released without charge. At least 10 members of an Islamist organization, the Liberation Party in Jordan (LPJ), including prisoners of conscience, were detained by the GID. Two were arrested in August after giving sermons in mosques opposing the ending of the state of war with Israel. One of them, Al-Shaikh Taher 'Abd al-Hamid, was released without charge after three weeks. The other, Salem al-Ja'fari, was held for over a month before his release on bail. He was tried before the State Security Court and acquitted of charges of slandering the King. Eight others were arrested during November. Four of them were held as prisoners of conscience after conviction of membership of an illegal organization and distribution of leaflets opposed to the King. They were sentenced by the State Security Court to three years' imprisonment. The other four had not been charged by the end of the year.

In February between 15 and 30 members of Fatah–Revolutionary Council (FRC), a Palestinian group led by Abu Nidal, were arrested in the wake of the assassination of a Jordanian diplomat in Lebanon (see **Lebanon** entry) for which FRC members were allegedly responsible. They were held for more than a month by the GID and were denied visits by lawyers or family members. They were then released without charge.

Up to 40 people were arrested after two cinemas were bombed in January and February, injuring several people. Twenty-five people were eventually charged, three *in absentia*, with forming an illegal organization; conspiracy to carry out terrorist activities; illegal possession of explosives with the intent to carry out subversive actions; and concealing crimes related to national security. The group was alleged to have been composed largely of "Arab Afghans" – men who had returned from fighting with Islamist groups in Afghanistan. Some were also alleged to have been members of the Palestine Liberation Army in Jordan. The trial of the 25 before the State Security Court began in August. Eleven of the accused were sentenced to death (three *in absentia*) in December.

The trial before the State Security Court of five military cadets and five others (including two who were tried *in absentia*) ended in January (see *Amnesty International Report 1994*). All 10 were convicted of plotting to kill King Hussein bin Talal, and four were convicted of membership of the LPJ. Isma'il Wahwah and the two tried *in absentia* were sentenced to death. Three others were sentenced to life imprisonment, and four to 15 years' imprisonment. An appeal against their sentences to the Court of Cassation had not been concluded by the end of the year.

There were allegations of torture by the GID. At least 16 of those on trial in the "Arab Afghans" case (see above) retracted their confessions during their trial, alleging that they had been extracted as a result of "physical pressure". They had been held incommunicado for up to six months before being transferred to prison. It was not clear whether the court had ordered an investigation into their allegations of torture.

At least 14 people were executed during the year. People on death row are informed of their execution only minutes

180

beforehand. Their families do not have the opportunity for a last visit and are informed only after the execution has taken place. At least two men, 'Uthman Subh and Muhammad Abu Zinah, have apparently been held under sentence of death since 1976.

Amnesty International received reports that some Iraqi asylum-seekers, deported to Jordan from third countries, had been forcibly returned to Iraq where they were at risk of human rights abuses. No information about their fate or whereabouts was known.

Amnesty International called for the commutation of all death sentences and expressed concern about the use of prolonged incommunicado detention which facilitates torture and ill-treatment. In March Amnesty International published a report, *Jordan: Human Rights Reforms: Achievements and Obstacles*, which discussed the human rights reforms introduced since November 1989 and Amnesty International's persisting concerns in the country. Recommendations included the review of legislation restricting freedoms and regulating interrogations; prompt access for detainees to judges, lawyers and families; and effective protection for asylum-seekers. The report was submitted to the UN Human Rights Committee which considered Jordan's third periodic report on the implementation of the International Covenant of Civil and Political Rights in July. The Committee welcomed the changes introduced in Jordan since 1989, but expressed concern about the death penalty and about reports of incommunicado detention, torture and ill-treatment. The Committee recommended that measures be taken towards abolition of the death penalty and of the State Security Court. It also recommended steps to prevent torture and ill-treatment, to restrict administrative and incommunicado detention and to place detainees under judicial supervision. In March Amnesty International issued a report, *Jordan: Executions on the Increase*.

The authorities provided information on specific cases raised by Amnesty International and stated that arrest and detention orders for detainees held by the GID, and orders denying access, are the responsibility of the Public Prosecutor of the State Security Court, and not of the GID itself. However, Amnesty International was

unaware that these functions had been carried out by anyone other than GID officials, some of whom can act as public prosecutors.

KAZAKHSTAN

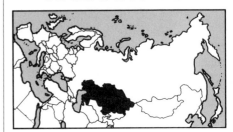

A conscientious objector to military service sentenced to one year's corrective labour but released on appeal was a prisoner of conscience. At least six death sentences were passed.

Multi-party elections in March to a new parliament returned a majority of deputies supporting President Nursultan Nazarbayev. The elections were criticized for procedural irregularities by monitors from the Conference on Security and Co-operation in Europe (CSCE).

Conscientious objector Roman Grechko, a Jehovah's Witness, was sentenced in March to one year's corrective labour for "evasion of active military service". He was a prisoner of conscience. In May a court upheld his appeal against the sentence and substituted a non-custodial punishment. The law in Kazakhstan does not offer an alternative service for all people who declare a conscientious objection to compulsory military service (see *Amnesty International Report 1994*).

At least six death sentences were known to have been passed for murder; the true number was probably much higher, but no statistics were available on the application of the death penalty. Amnesty International also learned during the year of five death sentences passed in 1993.

Amnesty International called for the immediate and unconditional release of Roman Grechko. It called for commutation of all death sentences and continued to urge the total abolition of the death penalty.

In January Amnesty International wrote to the Minister of Justice requesting him to provide clarification of the status of Article 170-3 of the criminal code ("infringement upon the honour and dignity of the President"), and Article 170-4 ("infringement upon the honour and dignity of a people's deputy"). Amnesty International had consistently lobbied for the repeal of these articles on the grounds that they placed unwarranted restrictions on freedom of expression (see *Amnesty International Report 1994*). In February the Minister replied that Article 170-3 had been repealed, but that Article 170-4 remained in force.

Amnesty International wrote in July to the chairman of a newly created parliamentary commission set up to reinvestigate demonstrations in 1986 in the capital, Almaty. The organization urged the commission to include in its activities a reinvestigation of the death in suspicious circumstances of Kairat Ryskulbekov, a participant in the 1986 demonstrations who was subsequently prosecuted and was found hanged in his prison cell in 1988.

KENYA

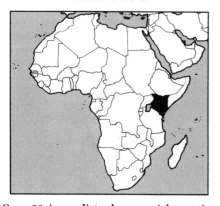

Over 80 journalists, human rights activists, opposition politicians and government critics were detained for short periods during the year, many of whom were prisoners of conscience. At least two were sentenced to several months' imprisonment. Four prisoners of conscience who faced mandatory death sentences if convicted were brought to trial. At least five other possible prisoners of conscience were held on non-bailable capital charges. There were widespread reports of torture and ill-treatment of prisoners.

Prison conditions were harsh. At least 30 people were killed in continuing political violence allegedly instigated by the government, many of them apparent victims of extrajudicial executions. A total of 568 people was under sentence of death by the end of the year, including at least 26 people convicted during 1994. No executions were reported.

Outbreaks of political violence continued sporadically during the year, although fewer lives were lost in inter-ethnic clashes than in previous years. The government of President Daniel arap Moi was accused of instigating the violence to undermine democratic reforms and the political opposition. By the end of 1994 over 1,500 people were estimated to have been killed since the violence began in late 1991 and over 300,000 – mainly women and children – displaced.

A former district commissioner, Jonah Anguka, charged with the murder in 1990 of Foreign Minister Robert Ouko was acquitted in July at the end of a lengthy trial. Following his release opposition members of parliament announced they would institute a private prosecution. However, the Attorney General refused to allow it and no further investigation into the murder had begun by the end of the year.

Human rights activists, critics of the government and journalists attempting to investigate or report political violence continued to be harassed. A book critical of the authorities by former prisoner of conscience Kenneth Matiba was banned in January and several editions of newspapers carrying articles critical of the government were impounded during the year. In December the Minister for Information and Broadcasting threatened to ban the *Daily Nation* newspaper if it continued to publish articles critical of the government.

Although opposition political parties continued to operate freely, they were prevented from functioning properly by, for example, the detention of members of parliament. There were over 56 arrests of opposition members of parliament during the year. Those arrested, many of whom were prisoners of conscience, were detained for several days or weeks and then released without charge or charged with political offences and released on bail. In many cases charges were then dropped or withdrawn after several months. Some cases were still pending before the courts

182

at the end of the year. Members of parliament were most often arrested after attempting to hold public meetings which did not have the required official authorization. Licences to hold political meetings were frequently denied or withdrawn at the last minute by the authorities. For example, in April Joseph Mulusya, Democratic Party member of parliament for Kangundo, was arrested and charged with holding an illegal meeting. He was acquitted in December.

Opposition groups, churches, women's groups and others were also prevented from holding educational seminars and workshops, even though these did not require a permit. For example, in June a seminar organized by the Kenya League of Women Voters in Kirinyaga was disrupted by heavily armed policemen who reportedly beat and detained a number of women present. Among those arrested was opposition member of parliament Martha Karua.

University lecturers and doctors, who were on strike for the right to form trade unions, were also arrested and harassed during 1994. For example, Korwa Ader, a leader of the striking university lecturers, was arrested several times.

Human rights activists were targeted for arrest. The executive director of the non-governmental Kenya Human Rights Commission (KHRC), Maina Kiai, was arrested with 10 others in September, following a protest march against the authorities' failure to issue identity cards to youths in Nakuru. He was later released without charge. Also in September, 14 members of the Released Political Prisoners (RPP), a non-violent group campaigning for the release of all political prisoners in Kenya, were arrested. All 14 were held incommunicado for up to six days.

Over 20 journalists were arrested during the year, many of whom were prisoners of conscience. For example, in April David Njau, a journalist from the *Daily Nation*, was arrested and charged with sedition for an article alleging that government helicopters had been used to transport "Kalenjin warriors", members of an ethnic group who appeared to be responsible for much of the violence. The charges against him and several other journalists were dropped following a review of a number of cases of sedition and subversion by the Attorney General in June. The

editor and a journalist on *The People* were sentenced to several months' imprisonment in June. They had been found guilty of contempt of court after an article by David Makali questioned the independence of a ruling by the Court of Appeal concerning the university lecturers' strike. The two were prisoners of conscience; they were released in September. In July one foreign journalist was deported after being held incommunicado for eight hours.

In April the trial of Koigi wa Wamwere, a human rights activist and former member of parliament, and three other men began. They had been arrested in November 1993 and charged with attempted robbery with violence, which is punishable by a mandatory death sentence (see *Amnesty International Report 1994*). They had been charged with 11 others who were released in January. All four were prisoners of conscience. The charges against them appeared to be fabricated and the police appeared to be using false capital charges to detain non-violent critics of the government: prisoners charged with capital offences cannot get bail. At the end of the year their trial was still continuing.

At least five other possible prisoners of conscience were detained on robbery with violence charges. They included Josephine Nyawira Ngengi, a member of the RPP, who was arrested in May and held illegally and incommunicado for 22 days when she was reportedly tortured. In June she was charged with a group of 18 others with robbery with violence. She and some of her co-defendants were prosecuted on two separate occasions during the year; both times the case was withdrawn by the prosecution and she was rearrested and charged with the same offence. She was still being detained at the end of the year. The same charge was brought against Geoffrey Kuria Kariuki, a former political prisoner (see *Amnesty International Report 1994*), who had earlier been charged with Koigi wa Wamwere, his cousin. The earlier charge against him was withdrawn and he was released on 29 January; he was rearrested in July and held incommunicado for 10 days before being charged with robbery with violence. He reportedly received serious head injuries as a result of torture but had not received any medical treatment by the end of the year.

The charge against the General Secretary of the Central Organization of Trade Unionists, Joseph Mugalla, was dropped in February. He had been arrested in May 1993 after calling for a general strike, and charged with inciting disobedience to the law (see *Amnesty International Report 1994*).

There were widespread reports of torture and ill-treatment of prisoners, including women prisoners who were reportedly subjected to beatings and sexual assaults. In June six men, charged with robbery with violence in November 1993, had the case against them dismissed when the magistrate refused to accept their confessions – which had evidently been obtained as result of torture. All six men had been whipped, forced to walk on sharp objects and had had their finger- and toenails removed.

In December one man had his arm amputated and three others received hospital treatment after they had reportedly been suspended from trees in Nakuru National Park and beaten by the police.

One possible "disappearance" was reported. Mohamed Wekessa, an Islamic Party of Kenya activist, was last seen when he was arrested on 19 August. The authorities denied that he had ever been arrested.

At least 30 people were killed, many of them apparent victims of extrajudicial executions, and thousands of people fled their homes following attacks by government supporters or armed pro-government groups during the year. Incidents occurred mainly in Rift Valley Province, but also in Coast Province, where eight people were killed and 26 seriously injured in May.

In January James Irungu, a hawker, was beaten to death by Nairobi City Council security personnel. By the end of the year no one had been charged in connection with his death. In August a street boy was killed by a police reservist. Following a national outcry the reservist was arrested and was charged with murder in September. The case had not gone to trial by the end of the year.

Prison conditions remained extremely harsh, with severe overcrowding and frequent shortages of food, clothing, clean water and basic medication.

At least 26 people were sentenced to death, mostly for actual or attempted robbery. No executions were reported. A total of 568 people were under sentence of death at the end of the year. In December an opposition member of parliament moved a motion to abolish the death penalty, which was defeated.

Amnesty International criticized the government for the continued harassment and arrest of human rights activists, journalists and others. It concluded that a number of people facing criminal charges were prisoners of conscience and that robbery with violence charges were being misused to detain government critics without any right to bail. The organization published two reports calling for the release of prisoners of conscience: in July, *Kenya: The Imprisonment of two prisoners of conscience – Bedan Mbugua and David Makali*; and in November, *Kenya: Abusive use of the law – Koigi wa Wamwere and three other prisoners of conscience on trial for their lives*. Amnesty International urged the government to introduce safeguards against torture and to abolish the death penalty.

KOREA
(DEMOCRATIC PEOPLE'S REPUBLIC OF)

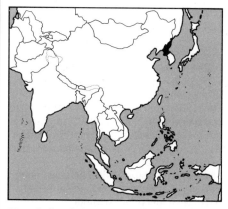

New information emerged about dozens of political prisoners, including possible prisoners of conscience, but it remained unconfirmed. However, the authorities provided information on several political prisoners, including a prisoner of conscience. The death penalty remained in force for many offences.

The death of President Kim Il Sung in July led to widespread public manifestations of mourning across the country, and

184

to the cancellation of a summit meeting with the President of the Republic of Korea (South Korea). The principle of that meeting had been agreed in June during negotiations between the Democratic People's Republic of Korea (DPRK) and the USA to resolve differences over the nuclear program of the DPRK. An agreement on that issue, involving modifications in the DPRK's nuclear program and the provision of international financing for some of its energy needs, was signed in October.

The positions held by President Kim Il Sung until his death, including those of President of the DPRK and General Secretary of the ruling Workers' Party of Korea (WPK), were still vacant at the end of the year. However, his son Kim Jong Il, Supreme Commander of the Korean People's Army and a member of the WPK Presidium, was frequently referred to in the official press as the main leader following the death of his father.

An unknown number, believed to be many hundreds, of political prisoners were held in unacknowledged detention. Information about their cases was extremely difficult to obtain and verify. New information emerged about some political prisoners and possible prisoners of conscience, but could not be confirmed. Kim Duk Hwan, an engineer, was detained in late 1961 or early 1962 in Sinyang District, about 100 kilometres north of Pyongyang, apparently because he had studied in the Soviet Union from 1953 to 1957, and had married a Soviet citizen. His detention was apparently related to the deterioration of Soviet-Korean relations in the early 1960s. His family in the Soviet Union had last heard from him in 1966. Amnesty International believed that, if still detained, Kim Duk Hwan was a prisoner of conscience.

New information also emerged about dozens of political prisoners reported to have been detained without trial, sometimes for decades, and to have been held in 1990 in Sungho village, east of Pyongyang. They included Li Ra Yong, an historian who had not been heard of since the 1960s, and over 20 Koreans who had formerly lived in Japan. There were unconfirmed reports that the detention centre in Sungho had been closed following the transfer of the prisoners.

In June the government acknowledged that Shibata Kozo, a Japanese national who had resettled in the DPRK in 1960, had been sentenced, under the Korean name of Kim Ho Nam, to 20 years' imprisonment in 1964 on espionage charges. Amnesty International believed him to be a prisoner of conscience (see *Amnesty International Report 1994*). The authorities stated that he was tried and given an additional six-year prison sentence for "instigating other prisoners to commit an anti-state plot" and that he died with his whole family in a train accident in March 1990, three months after his release. This official account was not consistent with Amnesty International's information. According to unofficial sources, Shibata Kozo was unaware of the reason for his supplementary six-year sentence and did not receive a formal trial.

The authorities also provided further information on other reported political prisoners. They stated that Shin Sook Ja and her daughters, who were reported to have been detained in 1987 after Shin Sook Ja's husband sought political asylum abroad, were not detained and were living in the capital, Pyongyang. Amnesty International was unable to confirm this during the year.

The death penalty remained mandatory under the Criminal Law for a number of political offences, and an optional punishment for certain violent crimes. No executions were officially reported, although unofficial reports received in earlier years suggested that several executions take place every year, some of them in public. An official source indicated to Amnesty International in August that in recent years two people had been sentenced to death and executed, including a man accused of murder in 1992 (see *Amnesty International Report 1994*). There was no information about the other reported case. Unofficial sources alleged that people accused of economic offences such as smuggling had been summarily executed during 1994 in areas close to the border with China, but there was no confirmation of these allegations.

In June Amnesty International published a report, *North Korea: New Information about Political Prisoners*, in which it detailed the cases of two reported political prisoners, and listed the names of 49 others. In another report in September, the organization detailed its continuing concerns about the case of Shibata Kozo. In meetings with representatives of the DPRK in August, and in letters to the authorities throughout the year, Amnesty International sought further information about these cases, including that of Kim Duk Hwan, but received no response. It did, however, receive some information from the DPRK authorities about reported prisoners it had named in a report in October 1993 (see *Amnesty International Report 1994* and above).

KOREA
(REPUBLIC OF)

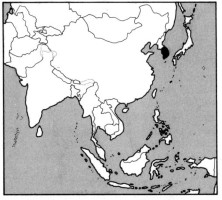

Hundreds of opponents of the government were detained throughout the year, the majority under the National Security Law which restricts the rights to freedom of expression and association. Some 200 other political prisoners arrested in previous years remained in prison, including dozens of long-term prisoners believed to have been convicted after unfair trials. Ill-treatment of political detainees continued to be reported. There were 15 executions and some 50 prisoners remained under sentence of death.

A proposed summit meeting between President Kim Young-sam and North Korean President Kim Il Sung was cancelled following the latter's death in July. Tension mounted between the two countries following his death and appeared to be a factor in the increased number of arrests made under the National Security Law during the second half of the year.

In October government officials told Amnesty International that the country would soon ratify the UN Convention against Torture. Officials also told Amnesty International that labour legislation would shortly be amended to remove the ban on third-party intervention in labour disputes.

A revision to the Code of Criminal Procedure was before the National Assembly but had not been passed by the end of the year. It incorporated some human rights safeguards but failed to bring procedures for arrest and interrogation fully into line with international human rights standards.

Hundreds of people were arrested under the National Security Law, especially between June and September. Eight members of a singing troupe, *Heemangsae*, Bird of Hope, who were arrested in March and April under the National Security Law, were prisoners of conscience. They were accused of trying to stage a musical based on a poem deemed by the authorities to "praise" and "encourage" North Korea and of sending parts of the poem via a computer communications network. They were released after trial with suspended prison sentences. Another prisoner of conscience was Kim Yon-in, owner of *Heem* Publishing Company, who was arrested in March and sentenced to one year's imprisonment for publishing allegedly pro-North Korean literature. He remained in prison at the end of the year.

In June, 23 people were arrested under the National Security Law for their alleged involvement with *Kukukchnui*, National Front for the Salvation of the Fatherland. The main defendant, 61-year-old Ahn Jae-ku, was accused of establishing this organization in order to spy for North Korea. There was, however, no convincing evidence that Ahn Jae-ku and other alleged members had been involved in espionage activities and he was considered to be a prisoner of conscience. In November Ahn Jae-ku was sentenced to life imprisonment, although the prosecution had asked for the death sentence.

Throughout the second half of the year dozens of students, dissidents, writers, publishers, academics and members of socialist organizations were arrested under the National Security Law for allegedly "praising" and "benefiting" North Korea. Many were adopted as prisoners of conscience. Charges against them included attempts to send messages of condolence to North Korea following the death of Kim Il Sung, the publication and distribution

186

of allegedly pro-North Korean material, membership of socialist groups deemed to be pro-North Korean, and participation in demonstrations against the government. Some were accused of being *Jusapa* (supporters of North Korea's *Juche* ideology).

Prisoners of conscience included four members of *Pomminnyon*, Pan-National Alliance for the Reunification of Korea, including the 74-year-old Reverend Kang Hui-nam. They were arrested in July at the border village of Panmunjom as they tried to visit North Korea. Others were dissident leaders Lee Chang-bok and Hwang In-sung who were arrested in August and charged with supporting North Korea's views about reunification and expressing sympathy on the death of Kim Il Sung. In December Lee Chang-bok was sentenced to 10 months' imprisonment.

Dozens of people belonging to socialist groups, arrested under the National Security Law for their alleged pro-North Korean views, were also considered to be prisoners of conscience. They included nine members of *Saminchong*, Union of Socialist Youth, arrested in August on charges of spreading leftist and allegedly pro-North Korean ideology among workers and students, and three members of *Sam* (Spring) youth group, charged in September with spreading *Juche* ideology among high-school students.

Over 100 workers were arrested in the course of industrial disputes, most accused of taking illegal strike action or resorting to violence during confrontations with riot police. In some cases the charges of violence appeared to have been unjustified and the prisoners were held in violation of their right to freedom of association. They included prisoner of conscience Suh Son-won, a trade union official of *Chongihyop*, an unauthorized trade union of national railroad workers, who was arrested in September during a peaceful sit-in protest at a temple in Seoul, the capital.

Prisoner of conscience Kim Sam-sok was given a seven-year prison sentence in February, reduced on appeal to four years. His sister Kim Un-ju was given a suspended sentence and released (see *Amnesty International Report 1994*). In October a former informer for the Agency for National Security Planning (ANSP) said that he had helped to frame the two prisoners. He also claimed that the ANSP had

asked him to make links between alleged pro-North Korean organizations in Japan and several political non-governmental organizations in South Korea, which could be used to incriminate the latter.

Members of *Sanomaeng*, Socialist Workers League, continued to face arrest and imprisonment under the National Security Law as prisoners of conscience. At least 40 members remained in prison at the end of the year, including prisoners of conscience Chon Kyong-hee and her husband Baik Tae-ung, arrested in April 1992 and sentenced to three years' and life imprisonment respectively.

Dozens of long-term political prisoners believed to have been convicted after unfair trials under previous governments remained in prison. Most had been arrested during the 1970s and 1980s, held incommunicado for long periods and tortured. They were convicted largely on the basis of their own coerced confessions. They included prisoner of conscience Yu Chong-sik, sentenced to life imprisonment in 1975. He was reportedly in poor health and receiving inadequate medical attention. Lawyers and activists worked to re-open the cases of some prisoners but found it impossible to obtain the evidence required to initiate a retrial.

The Republic of Korea continued to hold two of the world's longest-serving prisoners of conscience. Kim Sun-myung, aged 69, was arrested in 1951 and Ahn Hak-sop, aged 64, was arrested in 1953. Their continued imprisonment appeared to be a result of their refusal to sign a statement of "conversion" to anti-communism. In May a lawyer who wished to represent the two prisoners was denied access to them and had still been unable to visit them by the end of the year.

Most political suspects claimed to have been deprived of sleep during interrogation by the National Police Administration or the ANSP. There were also reports of detainees being subjected to threats, intimidation and beatings during questioning. At his trial in May, Kim Tae-il, a member of the singing troupe *Heemangsae*, said police investigators had threatened to arrest his fiancée unless he made a confession. At his trial in October Ahn Young-min said that after his arrest in June police officials had deprived him of sleep for 48 hours, beaten him and threatened to arrest other family members if he did not sign a confession. Jong Hwa-ryo, arrested in June, said he was beaten by ANSP officials during three days of interrogation and only permitted to sleep for two hours each day.

In October, 15 people convicted of murder were executed in Seoul, Pusan and Taegu prisons. These were the first executions since December 1992, and were carried out by order of the Minister of Justice. At the end of 1994 there were some 50 other people who had been convicted of murder under sentence of death, including Kim Chol-oo who claimed to have been beaten during interrogation by the police and forced to confess to some of the charges against him.

Throughout the year Amnesty International called for the release of prisoners of conscience and for a review of the cases of long-term political prisoners said to have been convicted after unfair trials. It called for amendments to the National Security Law and to labour legislation limiting the rights to freedom of expression and association. It sought an end to ill-treatment of detainees and called for impartial investigations into all allegations of ill-treatment. It urged the commutation of all death sentences and abolition of the death penalty. In March the organization published a report, *South Korea: Human rights violations continue under the new government*, describing human rights violations which had occurred since February 1993 when the administration took office and past violations which the government had failed to address.

In October Amnesty International delegates visiting the country met officials of the Ministry of Justice and the Ministry of Foreign Affairs. They were refused meetings with the National Police Administration and the ANSP.

KUWAIT

Over 160 people, among them possible prisoners of conscience, continued to serve prison terms imposed after unfair trials in 1991, 1992 and 1993. At least 150 other political prisoners, including possible prisoners of conscience, who were arrested in 1991 on charges of "collaboration" with Iraqi forces during the occupation of Kuwait, remained in

custody awaiting trial. The fate and whereabouts of at least 62 detainees who "disappeared" from custody in 1991 remained unknown. Six people were sentenced to death and one person was executed. Thirteen death sentences imposed in previous years were reduced to terms of imprisonment.

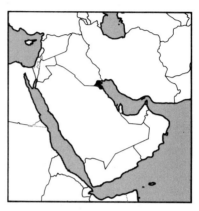

In February the parliamentary Committee for Legislative and Legal Affairs completed its examination of the Law on the Combat of Drugs (No. 74 of 1983). It proposed a number of amendments to the law, including the introduction of the death penalty for a wide range of offences. Under Article 31, the death penalty would be introduced as an optional punishment for importing drugs for commercial purposes, producing or manufacturing drugs for commercial purposes and for growing or importing drug-producing plants. The death penalty would become mandatory in certain circumstances for buying or possessing drugs and for receiving payment or other gain in return for facilitating the use of drugs. The National Assembly voted in favour of these amendments in March when the draft law had its first reading. However, the draft law failed to gain majority support at its second reading. No further information was available by the end of the year.

One of the country's leading human rights groups, *al-Jami'a al-Kuwaitiyya lil-difa' 'an Dahaya al-Harb*, the Kuwaiti Association to Defend War Victims, had to vacate its premises in October under government orders. Since a decree was issued in August 1993 ordering the dissolution of all unlicensed organizations, the group had been unable to obtain government registration to continue working on behalf of

188

Kuwaitis missing and believed to be held in Iraq since 1991 (see *Amnesty International Report 1994*).

Over 160 political prisoners, including 13 women, continued to serve prison terms in Kuwait Central Prison following their conviction on charges of "collaboration" with Iraqi forces during the occupation of Kuwait. At least 20 of them were prisoners of conscience. Fifty-nine had been sentenced by the Martial Law Court in 1991 and the others by the State Security Court in 1992 and 1993 after trials which did not satisfy international standards for fair trial (see *Amnesty International Reports 1992* to *1994*).

At least 150 other political prisoners, including possible prisoners of conscience, were believed to be held following their arrest in 1991 on suspicion of "collaboration". At the end of 1994 no information was available about the precise number of detainees awaiting trial or how many had been brought to trial.

'Abd al-Amir Sabati, an Iranian national who had lived in Kuwait since 1950, was reportedly arrested by State Security personnel on 21 February. According to information received by Amnesty International, he was not charged with any crime and was denied access to his family and lawyer.

A Kuwaiti police detective was reported to have been detained in August for the alleged torture of Ahmad al-Mubarak, a Sudanese national, during interrogation at a police station. It was also reported that the same detective had previously been sentenced to several years in prison on charges of torture but that he had not served his sentence. No information was available about progress in other cases of prosecution for alleged torture in previous years, including the case of seven policemen implicated in the torture of a Sri Lankan detainee who died in June 1992 (see *Amnesty International Reports 1993* and *1994*).

The fate and whereabouts of at least 62 Palestinians, Jordanians, Iraqis and other nationals who "disappeared" in custody between February and June 1991 remained unknown at the end of the year (see *Amnesty International Report 1993*). Among them was a Palestinian with Jordanian nationality, George Victor Salsa, who was arrested from his home by members of the State Security forces in May

1991 and subsequently "disappeared". In January the Minister of Information told Amnesty International that: "A thorough investigation was conducted, which unfortunately resulted in no information concerning the whereabouts of Mr Salsa". Fears also remained over the fate of Khalid Rashid Muhammad Agha-Mir, an Iraqi Kurd born in Kuwait, who worked as a cashier at al-Salam Gynaecological Hospital before his arrest in April 1991 at his home by soldiers and armed civilians. He was reportedly seen at al-Salmiyya police station and subsequently moved to an unknown destination.

In June the State Security Court sentenced to death five Iraqi nationals and a Kuwaiti for participating in an alleged assassination attempt on the former US President, George Bush, during his visit to Kuwait in April 1993 (see *Amnesty International Report 1994*). Among those sentenced were Bandar 'Ujail Jaber al-Shummari and 'Adel Isma'il 'Issa al-'Utaibi. Seven other defendants in the same case, all Iraqi nationals, were sentenced to prison terms ranging from six months to 10 years; one Kuwaiti national was acquitted. The trial proceedings fell short of international standards for fair trial: for example, the defendants were not allowed access to lawyers before the trial and were denied full right of appeal. The main prosecution witness in the trial was a senior officer in State Security Intelligence who led the operation to arrest the defendants. His evidence during the trial was reportedly based on "secret sources" and the information, which he claimed proved that the defendants were linked to Iraqi intelligence, was not made known to the court. The defence lawyers complained that they could not challenge the "secret information" as it was not available to them. The officer's evidence was also based on the confessions made by the defendants. Some of the defendants had initially confessed to the charges against them, but later retracted saying that they were innocent. Some stated that they had been beaten during interrogation. The six death sentences were to be reviewed by the Court of Cassation before ratification by the Amir, al-Shaikh Jaber al-Ahmad al-Sabah. The Court of Cassation had not given a verdict by the end of the year.

Muhammad 'Ali Qulaib al-Rashidi, sentenced to death by the Criminal Court in August 1993 following his conviction for rape, was executed in August after his sentence was upheld by the Court of Cassation (see *Amnesty International Report 1994*).

The Court of Cassation reduced to terms of imprisonment 13 death sentences imposed by the State Security Court in 1992 and 1993 following proceedings which failed to conform to international standards for fair trial. The defendants were 10 Jordanian men, two Iraqi men and one Kuwaiti woman who were convicted of "collaboration" with Iraqi forces during the occupation of Kuwait (see *Amnesty International Report 1994*).

In February Amnesty International published a report, *Kuwait: Three years of unfair trials*, which detailed the organization's concerns about the trials of alleged "collaborators" which took place before the Martial Law Court in May and June 1991 and the continuing trials before the State Security Court which began in April 1992. The report contained a series of recommendations to the government, including the release of all prisoners of conscience, the fair trial or release of all political prisoners and the abolition of special courts. The organization also urged the authorities to clarify all cases of "disappearance" and to investigate all torture allegations and deaths in custody. Amnesty International called for the commutation of all death sentences.

The Minister of Information responded in a television interview by denying the allegations of unfair trials, but added: "I am not here to deny the negative things that did take place after the liberation". He invited Amnesty International to visit Kuwait. The organization welcomed the invitation, but stated that for such a visit to be productive, it would be helpful if Amnesty International were to receive beforehand a substantial portion of the information requested over the past three years, including details of investigations into cases of "disappearance" and allegations of torture, and details of the evidence against defendants convicted by the Martial Law Court and State Security Court. In May Kuwait's Ambassador to Belgium described the report's contents as "hostile to Kuwait ... and a repetition of old allegations", but failed to address the substance of any of Amnesty International's concerns.

Early in the year the Ministry of Justice provided Amnesty International, at its request, with the names of 625 Kuwaitis arrested during the occupation in 1990 and 1991 and believed to be still in Iraq (see **Iraq** entry).

KYRGYZSTAN

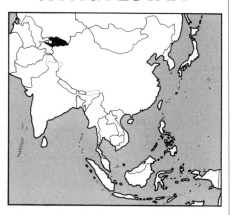

There were allegations that criminal suspects were tortured or ill-treated in police custody. At least four death sentences were passed; one was carried out and three were commuted.

President Askar Akayev dismissed parliament in September after members announced a boycott which would have rendered a forthcoming session inquorate. The government then resigned. A referendum in October endorsed constitutional amendments establishing a bicameral parliament and the principle of holding referendums on all future constitutional and major legislative changes. Elections to the new parliament were due in early 1995.

There were allegations that criminal suspects were tortured or ill-treated in police custody. In March, three teenage boys claimed that they were tortured until they confessed to assaulting a police officer. They were arrested in the capital, Bishkek. During interrogation they were allegedly beaten about the head, punched in the kidneys and thrown against walls, and one of them had a gas mask with its airway blocked put over his face to prevent him breathing. In a similar case, also in March, four teenage boys complained that they were beaten at a police station in Dzhalal-Abad. Two of them needed hospital treatment as a result. In June it was

190

reported that police abuses had been officially admitted in these cases, and that officers involved had been dismissed and were the subject of criminal investigation.

At least four death sentences were passed. The defendants in these cases alleged that police had beaten and intimidated them into making false confessions which formed the main evidence on which they were convicted of murder. One of these sentences was carried out and three were commuted – two of them to 20 years' and one to 15 years' imprisonment. Two women sentenced to death in 1992 and 1993 also had their sentences commuted to 15 years' imprisonment. During the year information was received about an execution carried out in 1993.

Amnesty International wrote in May to the government calling for investigations into allegations of torture and ill-treatment in police custody. It called for commutation of all death sentences and continued to urge total abolition of the death penalty.

LAOS

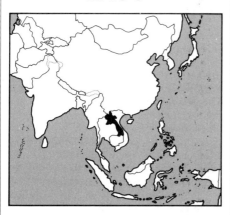

Three prisoners of conscience continued to be held throughout 1994. Three political prisoners continued to serve sentences of life imprisonment imposed after an unfair trial.

Information about political prisoners and the death penalty was limited as a result of restrictions on freedom of expression and a lack of official information.

Three prisoners of conscience continued to be held in the northern province of Houa Phanh. Thongsouk Saysangkhi, Latsami Khamphoui and Feng Sakchittaphong had been sentenced to 14 years'

imprisonment in November 1992 after a trial that failed to meet international standards for fairness. Although official charges against them included preparing for a rebellion, Amnesty International believed that they were detained for peacefully advocating a multi-party political system. They were believed to be still detained in "Re-education" Camp 7, where conditions were harsh and no medical facilities were available (see *Amnesty International Report 1994*).

One untried political prisoner, Ly Teng, was allowed to leave a village in Sop Hao, Houa Phanh province, to which he had been restricted, and move to Vientiane, the capital, with his family. Two other untried political prisoners – Tong Pao Song and Yong Ye Thao – were also reported as having been released from their restriction to Sop Hao, but they remained living in the area. All three had been detained or had their freedom of movement restricted for the purposes of "re-education" since 1975 (see *Amnesty International Report 1993*).

Three political prisoners – Pangtong Chokbengboun, Bounlu Nammathao and Sing Chanthakoummane – who had been detained without charge or trial for more than 17 years, continued to serve sentences of life imprisonment imposed after an unfair trial in 1992 (see *Amnesty International Report 1993*). They remained in detention at Sop Pan camp, Houa Phanh province. Bounlu Nammathao and Sing Chanthakoummane were reportedly in poor health.

Amnesty International continued to call for the immediate and unconditional release of prisoners of conscience, and the fair trial or release from detention or restriction of other long-term political prisoners. By the end of the year no response had been received from the Lao authorities.

LATVIA

At least two people were sentenced to death.

In September Maris Gailis replaced Valdis Birkavs as Prime Minister.

At least two people were sentenced to death. Michael Abramkin was convicted on three counts of murder by the Latvian

Supreme Court in February. The same court found Uldis Lujans guilty of aggravated murder in May. At the end of 1994 the two men were believed to be waiting to hear the outcome of petitions for clemency submitted to President Guntis Ulmanis. Reports indicated that two other death sentences may have been passed during the year.

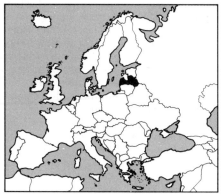

In January Amnesty International received confirmation from the Ministry of Justice that no death sentences had been passed the previous year (see *Amnesty International Report 1994*). In October the organization appealed to the authorities to commute the death sentences passed during 1994 and urged them to abolish the death penalty. In December Amnesty International asked the authorities for clarification of the number of people under sentence of death. No replies had been received by the end of the year.

LEBANON

Hundreds of people, including possible prisoners of conscience, were arrested on security grounds; some were released uncharged, while others were brought to trial. Allegations of torture or ill-treatment were received. Three people died in custody in suspicious circumstances. The fate of thousands of people abducted in previous years remained unknown. Four people were executed and at least two others were sentenced to death. Armed political groups committed human rights abuses.

The Lebanese army strengthened its control of most of the country. However, the South Lebanon Army (SLA) militia and

Israeli armed forces retained control of a "security zone" along the Lebanese/Israeli border extending northwards to the Jezzine region. Some parts of south Lebanon were controlled by *Hizbullah*, the main armed political group fighting the SLA and Israeli forces in Lebanon. With the agreement of the Lebanese Government, Syrian forces remained deployed throughout most of the country.

In March, following investigations into the bombing of a church in February in which at least 10 people died, the government dissolved the Lebanese Forces (LF) party, a former Christian militia, and banned news broadcasts by private radio and television stations until July. Also in March the death penalty was extended to a further category of murder as well as to politically motivated killings.

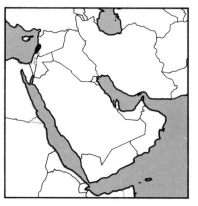

Hundreds of suspected political opponents, including possible prisoners of conscience, were arrested by government forces and Syrian personnel stationed in Lebanon. Fifteen people were arrested between December 1993 and February 1994 and charged with having supplied Israel and the USA with information on the Syrian army, *Fatah*-Revolutionary Council (FRC) and *Hizbullah*. All were allegedly tortured. For example, Georges Haddad's arm was broken, apparently as a result of beatings. Gabi Karam alleged that he was tortured in Syria where he was held for approximately six weeks before being returned to Lebanon. None was granted access to independent doctors. They were sentenced in July to between one month's and five years' imprisonment, apparently on the basis of statements made in incommunicado detention. In December seven of them had their sentences reduced on appeal to between nine months' and two years' imprisonment with hard labour.

In March and April, following the church bombing, hundreds of LF members were arrested. Most were released without charge after a few days; some were held for up to three months. There were reports that many had been tortured or ill-treated in detention. The LF leader, Samir Gea'gea', and his deputy, Fu'ad Malek, remained held. In June they were charged in connection with the church bombing together with Jirjis Khoury and five others *in absentia*. Also in June Samir Gea'gea', Camille Karam and Rafiq Sa'deh were charged with assassinating Dany Cham'oun, a former militia leader, and his family in October 1990. Ten others were charged *in absentia*. The trials of both cases began in November before the Court of Justice and were continuing at the end of the year. There is no right of appeal against sentences of this court. All those detained were held in the Ministry of Defence, which is not a recognized place of detention. In December the lawyers in the cases walked out after the court refused to consider a petition for the transfer of the detainees to a recognized detention facility.

In April, 12 members of the illegal pro-Iraqi wing of the Arab Socialist Ba'th Party, including Hasan Ghurayeb and Ne'meh Jamil, were reportedly detained by Lebanese security forces without arrest warrants after the assassination in Beirut of al-Shaikh Taleb al-Suhayl al-Tamimi, an exiled Iraqi opposition figure (see **Iraq** entry). Four Iraqi nationals, including three diplomats, and one Lebanese national were detained in connection with the killing, but had not been brought to trial by the end of the year. In September Rafiq Abi Yunes, a leader of the party, was also reported to have been arrested. The 13 men apparently did not undergo any judicial process in Lebanon, and some or all may have been taken to Syria.

About 20 people said to be supporters of General 'Aoun, a former military leader living in exile, were arrested in September in connection with the distribution of leaflets opposing the Syrian presence in Lebanon. Most were released without charge, but two men – Hikmat Dib and Aleftari Atanasio – and three women – Huda Yamin, Lina Ghurayeb and Muna Shkayban – were charged with state secur-ity offences before a military court. All five were allegedly tortured or ill-treated while held in the Ministry of Defence and may have been prisoners of conscience.

Samir Nasr, a possible prisoner of conscience, was sentenced in February by a military court to two years' hard labour, reduced to one year on appeal. He had been convicted of being an accessory to dealing with the enemy in connection with alleged links between the Guardians of the Cedar, a political party, and Israel (see *Amnesty International Report 1994*). No investigation appeared to have been conducted into his allegations of ill-treat-ment. He was released in November.

Other reports of torture or ill-treatment were received. Methods described in-cluded severe beatings on all parts of the body, *falaqa* (beatings on the soles of the feet), suspension by the arms from a pul-ley, and electric shocks. Joseph Faddul and his two sons, Tony and Fawzi, were arrested in March and held for about 36 hours in the Ministry of Defence, where they were reportedly kicked, beaten with rifle butts and verbally abused. Yusuf Sha'ban, Yusuf 'Abwani and Bassam 'At-tiyah, all members of the FRC on trial be-fore the Court of Justice for the murder of a Jordanian diplomat in January, alleged that they had been beaten in order to ex-tract confessions. The court refused to consider this evidence on the basis that such complaints could not be raised after charges had been brought. The court or-dered an investigation, but it was not known to have been carried out. Yusuf Sha'ban was sentenced to life imprison-ment and the two others to 10 years' im-prisonment.

Complaints about torture were ignored by officials or inadequately investigated. For instance, the Lebanese authorities did not respond to 'Ubad Zwayn's allegations of torture in 1993 by Syrian personnel sta-tioned in Lebanon (see *Amnesty Interna-tional Report 1994*). In April the Minister of Justice denied that Georges Haddad and others had been tortured, but gave no de-tails of any investigation.

At least three people died in custody in suspicious circumstances. In March Tareq al-Hassaniyah died in Beit al-Din Prison, reportedly from injuries sustained when his head was beaten against a wall. Up to seven members of the security forces were reportedly arrested in connection with his death. In April Fawzi al-Rasi, an LF member, died while under interrogation in the Ministry of Defence. Official sources said that an autopsy showed that he had suffered a heart attack. However, Fawzi al-Rasi's relatives were reportedly not allowed to see the body before burial. In July Mufid Sukkar died while held by the anti-drugs unit. A government investigation into his death was initiated.

No information was published on the investigation into the killing of nine people during an apparently peaceful demonstration in September 1993 (see *Amnesty International Report 1994*).

In April judicial executions resumed for the first time in 11 years. Bassam Saleh al-Muslah was hanged after conviction for rape and murder (see *Amnesty International Report 1994*). Two Syrian soldiers, 'Abd al-Karim Hujayj and Muhammad Za'tar, were hanged for murder a week later. In May Shaker al-Buraydi was executed by firing-squad for killing three policemen. At least three others were believed to be held on death row at the end of the year.

More than 200 prisoners continued to be held at any one time by the SLA in the Khiam detention centre in the "security zone". They were held outside any legal framework and without access to their families or the International Committee of the Red Cross. Some or all may have been hostages. Most were suspected members of armed groups opposed to the Israeli presence in Lebanon. Many were believed to have been tortured during interrogation. At least two people reportedly died shortly after release from Khiam. Poor conditions and medical care may have contributed to their deaths.

Armed political groups committed human rights abuses. *Hizbullah* was reported to have detained possible prisoners of conscience. For example, Ghassan Sheet, a lawyer from south Lebanon, was reportedly held for 65 days in a detention centre in Bir al-'Abed, apparently because he had tried to visit a client also detained by *Hizbullah*.

Dozens of people were killed, apparently for political reasons, although those responsible were often unknown. At least some may have been victims of deliberate and arbitrary killings by armed groups. In March SLA forces reportedly shot dead a member of the Democratic Front for the Liberation of Palestine after he had surrendered during a confrontation. In April, three men were killed by unknown assailants in separate incidents: Husayn Abu Zayd, a leading member of Fatah, the main faction of the Palestine Liberation Organization; Ne'meh Haydar, an official of the armed political group *Amal*; and Isma'il Julaylati, reportedly affiliated to the political group Islamic Tawhid. In December, three people, including two members of *Hizbullah*, were killed in an explosion in Beirut. Security forces later arrested three people in connection with the bombing, which the security forces claimed had been masterminded by Israeli intelligence forces (see **Israel and the Occupied Territories** entry).

In February Husayn 'Awadah, aged 16, was killed in Ba'albek, apparently by *Hizbullah* members with the acquiescence of local Lebanese security officials. He had apparently been "tried" at the request of his family by religious leaders under *Shari'a* (Islamic law) who found him to be responsible for the murder of a woman and her two sons. In response to a letter detailing Amnesty International's concerns about this killing, *Hizbullah* told Amnesty International that it had had no connection with the killing of Husayn 'Awadah.

The fate of thousands of people, including Lebanese, Syrian, Palestinian and other nationals taken prisoner by armed groups since 1975 remained unclear.

Amnesty International called on the Lebanese Government to release any prisoners of conscience and to investigate allegations of torture, deaths in custody and the killing of Husayn 'Awadah. The organization was concerned about possible arbitrary arrests and the fairness of trial proceedings. It expressed deep regret at the resumption of executions and the expansion of the death penalty and urged the commutation of all death sentences. In February officials said the section covering Lebanon in *Amnesty International Report 1993* was "largely inaccurate" and denied that 'Adel Hawila had been tortured. In April the Minister of Justice, replying to Amnesty International's concerns about Georges Haddad and others, said that Amnesty International "had been misled by an inexact and tendentious presentation of the facts". Amnesty International delegates sought access to the

194

country in May but had not been granted visas by the end of the year.

In an oral statement to the UN Commission on Human Rights in February, Amnesty International called for the release of Lebanese and other detainees held in Khiam and in Israel, as well as Israeli soldiers and SLA members missing in Lebanon, if they were being held as hostages.

LESOTHO

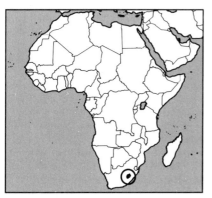

At least 10 people were shot dead by security personnel in circumstances suggesting unlawful killings. Prison warders ill-treated prisoners during a prison protest. Two prisoners remained under sentence of death.

In the first half of the year the government of Prime Minister Ntsu Mokhehle, which took office in April 1993 following Lesotho's first nationwide elections since 1970, faced repeated mutinies by the security forces. Disagreements over army pay and attempts by the government to promote one particular army unit were the ostensible causes of the conflict, but an underlying tension was the government's fear that most members of the security forces remained loyal to Lesotho's former military rulers. In April, in an attempt to force the government to address their grievances, disaffected soldiers took hostage four government ministers for several hours. They shot dead the Deputy Prime Minister, Selometsi Baholo, apparently while trying to capture him. Government ministers were again held hostage in May by officers of the Royal Lesotho Mounted Police who were on strike over pay demands.

On 17 August King Letsie III issued Order No. 1 of 1994, which dissolved the government and parliament, suspended certain provisions of the Constitution, and appointed a Council of Ministers to govern the country. Order No. 2 of 1994 granted immunity from prosecution to the security forces for a broad range of acts committed "in the public interest" on or after 17 August. A nationwide dusk-to-dawn curfew was imposed.

These actions provoked mass popular demonstrations of support for the ousted government. The High Court issued a preliminary ruling declaring the King's actions null and void, but the Chief Justice went ahead and swore in the Council of Ministers. After diplomatic pressure from neighbouring Botswana, South Africa and Zimbabwe, King Letsie restored the ousted government on 14 September and both parties agreed to participate in a broad national dialogue to resolve areas of conflict between the monarchy, the security forces and the government.

Soldiers and police officers shot dead at least 10 people in circumstances suggesting unlawful killings. In the worst single incident, on 17 August, soldiers on guard outside the King's palace in Maseru, the capital, fired on unarmed demonstrators gathered outside the palace to petition the King in support of the ousted government. Eye-witnesses said the demonstration had already begun to disperse when an army vehicle tried to force its way through the crowd. Soldiers on the vehicle hit people in the crowd with rifle butts, whereupon members of the crowd threw empty drinks cans at the vehicle. Soldiers at the palace gates then fired indiscriminately into the crowd. Four people were killed and at least 16 injured, one of whom died later in hospital. Other people were shot dead during August and September by police enforcing the curfew.

The 14 September agreement which ended the constitutional crisis provided immunity from prosecution for the King, his appointed council, public servants and security personnel for their actions between 17 August and 14 September. This was confirmed by the international guarantors of the agreement – Botswana, South Africa and Zimbabwe. Late in the year it was still unclear what the legal consequences would be, in particular for any investigation into the killings of demonstrators and curfew-breakers.

Prison warders on strike assaulted prisoners at Maseru Central Prison on 11 May and reportedly shot at some who had fled on to the prison roof. Prisoners were protesting against the suspension of court hearings and visiting rights as a result of the strike. A number of prisoners required hospital treatment for their injuries, including two former officials of the Lesotho Union of Bank Employees (LUBE) who were awaiting trial (see *Amnesty International Report 1992*) and who appear to have been singled out for ill-treatment. There were also further reports during the year of police ill-treatment of suspects in criminal investigations.

In a rare exception to the virtual impunity enjoyed by security personnel in Lesotho, a police officer was brought to trial in May for fatally shooting 17-year-old Bathobakae Mokhuthu in Maseru in 1990 (see *Amnesty International Report 1991*). The police officer was acquitted in October.

Two prisoners remained under sentence of death. One, a soldier, was convicted in 1991 of the 1986 murders of two government ministers and their wives (see *Amnesty International Report 1991*). The other was also convicted of murder. Both had their sentences confirmed on appeal in July and were awaiting the decision of the Pardons Committee on Prerogative of Mercy. There were no reports of new death sentences.

Amnesty International continued to call on the authorities to investigate human rights abuses and provide safeguards in law and practice against further abuses. The organization expressed concern in May about the safety of government ministers taken hostage by the police. At a September meeting of European Union and Southern African Development Community member states, it also raised its concerns about the shooting of unarmed demonstrators on 17 August and the granting of immunity from prosecution to the security forces.

LIBERIA

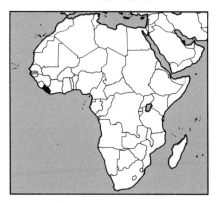

The killing of civilians increased as fighting intensified between the armed political groups contesting control of Liberia. In addition, these groups tortured and ill-treated civilians and non-combatants and took hostages.

On 7 March, under the terms of the 1993 Cotonou peace accord, the Interim Government of National Unity handed over power to the Liberian National Transitional Government. The Transitional Government was made up of representatives of the three parties to the accord – the Interim Government and the two armed groups which then controlled large areas of Liberia, the National Patriotic Front of Liberia (NPFL) and the United Liberation Movement for Democracy in Liberia (ULIMO). However, the peace accord was undermined by the subsequent proliferation of armed factions and increased fighting. The Transitional Government exercised authority only in areas controlled by the forces of the Economic Community of West African States (ECOWAS) Ceasefire Monitoring Group, known as ECOMOG, which held the capital, Monrovia, and the coastal strip to Buchanan, but was unable to enforce a cease-fire and demobilize the warring factions in the rest of Liberia. ECOMOG soldiers allegedly sold arms and ammunition to groups opposed to the NPFL. The national army, the Armed Forces of Liberia (AFL), increasingly acted as an armed group independent of the Transitional Government.

In April the UN Security Council renewed the mandate of the UN Observer Mission in Liberia (UNOMIL), established in September 1993 to help implement the

196

Cotonou peace accord, but in October the number of its military observers was reduced from 370 to 90.

In May a dissident faction within ULIMO, dominated by the Krahn ethnic group and led by ULIMO Chief of Staff General Roosevelt Johnson, seized control of ULIMO's headquarters in Tubmanburg, Bomi County, from ULIMO Chairman Alhaji G.V. Kromah and his faction, largely composed of members of the Muslim Mandingo community. Fighting and killings of civilians on ethnic grounds forced some 36,000 civilians to flee the area. In November the two factions agreed a cease-fire.

In August three NPFL ministers in the Transitional Government, who had previously been ministers in the NPFL's administration in Gbarnga, Bong County, broke with NPFL leader Charles Taylor and set up a rival NPFL faction. They subsequently joined in a coalition with other armed political groups: the AFL; the Liberian Peace Council (LPC), a Krahn offshoot of the AFL; the Krahn faction of ULIMO; and the Lofa Defense Force (LDF), a militia fighting the Mandingo faction of ULIMO in the northeast since late 1993.

In early September the Mandingo faction of ULIMO and coalition forces attacked the NPFL's base in Gbarnga. Large numbers of civilians were reportedly killed by fighters from all the forces involved. During continued fighting throughout September, ULIMO, coalition and NPFL forces all claimed control of Gbarnga or parts of it; in late December NPFL forces retook it. In September NPFL forces were driven out of Maryland County in the southeast by the LPC; there was heavy fighting in September and October and human rights abuses by both sides were reported. Tens of thousands of people fled, both to Monrovia and to neighbouring Guinea and Côte d'Ivoire, the largest exodus since 1992. International aid operations were halted in most areas outside the ECOMOG-controlled zone.

On 12 September an agreement brokered by ECOWAS, the Organization of African Unity and the UN was reached in Akosombo, Ghana, between Lieutenant-General Hezekiah Bowen, Chief of Staff of the AFL, Charles Taylor and Alhaji Kromah. It aimed to give their factions more control of a new Transitional Government and to facilitate disarmament. The agreement was opposed by civilian groups meeting in a National Conference in Monrovia. Further talks, which included civilians and other armed groups, led to a cease-fire in December.

On 15 September a coup attempt by members of the AFL led by former Lieutenant-General Charles Julue was thwarted by ECOMOG forces. Five civilians subsequently arrested were released by the courts but were rearrested in late September and charged with the capital offence of treason. In November General Julue and 37 other officers were charged with treason before a court-martial. None had been tried by the end of the year.

The civil war continued to be fought by armed young men and boys who lived by looting and extortion. Fighters from all the warring factions tortured and deliberately killed unarmed civilians suspected of opposing them, often because of their ethnic origin, as they seized control of territory or raided another group's territory. Ritual killings and cannibalism were also reported. It was usually not possible to confirm reports of killings, the identity of perpetrators or whether abuses were criminally or politically motivated.

Both AFL and LPC fighters – who sometimes operated together – were reported to have been responsible for human rights abuses. On 15 December more than 50 civilians, including 28 children under 10 years old, were massacred at Paynesville near Monrovia. Responsibility was unclear, but witnesses said the attackers were Krahn AFL soldiers. Nine AFL officers were reportedly arrested and the Transitional Government ordered an inquiry which had not reported by the end of the year.

LPC fighters were responsible for killing civilians in central and eastern Liberia, often because they were suspected of supporting the NPFL. On 11 September LPC fighters reportedly assembled the inhabitants of Kpolokpai, Kokoya District, Bong County, killed 30 alleged NPFL fighters and supporters with machetes, then shot dead 15 other civilian prisoners and fired into the crowd. Also in September LPC fighters in Greenville, Sinoe County, were reported to have killed Marie Tokpa, a girl from the Kpelle ethnic group, who resisted being raped. In early October LPC fighters apparently fired on assembled civilians in Zanzaye, Nimba County, killing scores of them. In November LPC fighters allegedly killed 12 residents of Sabo Wofiken, Glibo District, Grand Gedeh County, including Joshua Duweh, William Kuwor and David Hinneh.

The LPC reportedly tortured many civilians by burning them with heated machetes. In Barnabo Beach in July LPC fighters allegedly tied their victims' arms behind their backs, burned them severely with heated machetes, forced them to carry looted goods to another village and shot dead one man who had collapsed on the way. In September they allegedly cut off the fingers and ears of Albert Mende, a journalist taken prisoner in Kokoya District, Bong County. In November they reportedly took 10 girls captive in Sabo Wofiken, slashing their feet and forcing them to walk back to the fighters' base in Sinoe County.

The AFL and LPC also took hostage and detained civilians and non-combatants. In May the LPC reportedly detained 10 Ugandan ECOMOG soldiers, releasing them a few days later. In June AFL soldiers detained UNOMIL staff at Schieffelin barracks near Monrovia for three days. In July LPC fighters beat and detained for five days a civilian in Buchanan who resisted having his bicycle stolen.

Prisoners held under the authority of ECOMOG were released. In April 800 prisoners, held without charge or trial in Monrovia Central Prison in harsh conditions since the NPFL attack on Monrovia in October 1992, were released. They included people caught in possession of weapons as well as others suspected of supporting the NPFL. In May Peter Bonner Jallah, a civilian detained by ECOMOG since November 1992, was released without charge. In September the Supreme Court ruled that ECOMOG had no legal authority to arrest or detain.

All the armed opposition groups were responsible for deliberately and arbitrarily killing civilians and non-combatants. On 23 September armed men reportedly killed displaced civilians and medical staff at Phebe Hospital near Gbarnga; responsibility was not clear but the killings apparently occurred after NPFL forces overran the area.

In August the NPFL was reported to have executed as many as 80 of its own fighters, without any trial, and to have tortured and killed Lieutenant-General Nixon Gaye, an NPFL Commander, for leading a mutiny against Charles Taylor. In September NPFL fighters robbed and killed civilians as they fled the Gbarnga area. In one incident they tied up at least 20 men, women and children and threw them into the St John River at Bahla bridge. In another, they reportedly shot dead some 100 people in Palala, Bong County, on suspicion of being ULIMO supporters. From October NPFL fighters reportedly killed scores of civilians in Maryland County whom they suspected of supporting the LPC, among them Simon Gyekye, a Ghanaian school principal in Plebo.

Although human rights abuses by NPFL fighters went mostly unpunished, an NPFL commander and some fighters were reportedly detained by the NPFL in October in connection with the killing of civilians at the St John River. In December the NPFL executed six senior commanders held responsible for the fall of Gbarnga in September, apparently after a court-martial.

Fighters with the LDF were also reported to have killed civilians. In July LDF fighters reportedly killed more than 70 civilians in the village of Rusie, near Zorzor, Lofa County.

The two ULIMO factions also killed civilians. Mandingo ULIMO fighters reportedly killed at least four civilians and took women hostage for money when they burned and looted villages in the Tienne area, Cape Mount County, in mid-June, apparently accusing the villagers of supporting the Krahn ULIMO faction. In August Mandingo ULIMO fighters allegedly killed at least 20 civilians in Gbesseh, Cape Mount County. In August and September they also reportedly killed civilians in Lofa and Bong Counties. Some victims were apparently killed and eaten for ritual purposes, for example, Paul Tarwoi, a traditional healer who was reportedly captured in Zowolo, Lofa County, and killed in Gorlu. In Gbarnga, a ULIMO tribunal reportedly ordered the "execution" by firing-squad of civilians whom it found to be NPFL supporters.

At least two Tanzanian ECOMOG soldiers were killed in Kakata in September, 50 kilometres northeast of Monrovia, when Krahn ULIMO fighters reportedly attacked a convoy of civilians fleeing Gbarnga which included UNOMIL observers and aid workers.

All the armed opposition groups tortured and ill-treated captives and civilians.

198 They routinely subjected prisoners to "*tabey*", a form of torture where the victim's elbows are tied together behind the back, sometimes leading to long-term paralysis and nerve damage.

In late June Krahn ULIMO fighters took hostage six unarmed UNOMIL officers in Tubmanburg for two days, reportedly beating them and subjecting them to mock executions. In September large numbers of civilians and refugees were beaten and raped and their property looted by the armed groups involved in the fighting around Gbarnga. All the armed groups were reported to have forcibly recruited boys and young men to fight for them, and to have used civilians as slave labour to carry supplies, harvest crops, mine diamonds and carry looted goods to the border for sale.

Some of the armed opposition groups took hostage ECOMOG troops, UNOMIL observers and foreign aid workers. In July the NPFL was reported to be holding about 25 ECOMOG soldiers and 30 long-term political prisoners. In August it reportedly detained and ill-treated two chiefs in Bong County, Ruth Kollie and Willie Bestman, who tried to persuade the NPFL to attend the National Conference in Monrovia, and in September 30 civilians from the Bassa ethnic group in Butuo, Nimba County, accused of supporting the LPC. In September NPFL fighters reportedly detained 43 UNOMIL officers and six aid workers in various parts of the country for up to 10 days.

In separate incidents in May Mandingo ULIMO fighters held hostage 17 UN employees delivering food aid and 16 Nigerian ECOMOG soldiers, accusing them of supporting the rival Krahn ULIMO faction. They were released after a few days.

An Amnesty International delegation visited Liberia in July to investigate human rights abuses and to raise its concerns with officials of the Transitional Government, AFL, ECOMOG and UNOMIL. No response was received to requests to meet the NPFL in Gbarnga, and renewed fighting prevented the delegation from travelling outside areas under ECOMOG control.

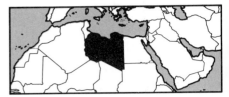

LIBYA

Scores of suspected government opponents arrested in connection with an alleged army revolt in 1993 remained held without charge or trial; some appeared to be facing imminent execution. Five prisoners of conscience held since 1973 continued to serve life sentences. At least 600 other political prisoners arrested in previous years, including prisoners of conscience, continued to be held without charge or trial. Torture and ill-treatment by the security forces were reported. New laws extended the use of the death penalty and allowed for the judicial punishments of flogging and amputation. At least 17 people were executed.

The UN sanctions against Libya (see previous *Amnesty International Reports*) were renewed in April for a further year. The sanctions were imposed in 1992 in response to the Libyan Government's refusal to hand over two Libyan nationals to British or US authorities who wished to bring them to trial. The two men were accused of the 1988 bombing of a civilian airliner which crashed on Lockerbie in Scotland, the United Kingdom, killing 270 people. In August the two men agreed to stand trial before the International Court of Justice in The Hague. The men's lawyer said the trial should be conducted according to Scottish law with an international panel of judges instead of a jury. No further steps had been taken in the case by the end of the year.

Early in the year the General People's Congress approved new laws – so-called "purification laws" – extending the use of the death penalty and allowing for the imposition of the judicial punishments of flogging and amputation, punishments that Amnesty International considers to be cruel, inhuman and degrading. According to the laws' provisions, which came into effect in February, murder, rape and some sexual offences are punishable by death, and theft is punishable by amputation of the limbs. It was not known whether any floggings or amputations were carried out during the year.

Five prisoners of conscience, all suspected members of the prohibited Islamic Liberation Party, continued serving life sentences in Abu-Salim Prison in Tripoli (see *Amnesty International Reports 1991 to 1994*). They included 'Omar Salih al-Qasbi and Muhammad al-Sadiq Tarhouni.

Scores of military personnel and civilians arrested following the alleged October 1993 army rebellion in Misrata and Bani Walid (see *Amnesty International Report 1994*) were still being held at the end of the year, apparently without charge or trial. The authorities continued to deny there had been a rebellion and said that all those arrested were "spies". In March it was reported that 16 of those detained were facing imminent execution. Among them were Miftah Qarrum al-Wirfali, who suffers from leukaemia, and Lt Col. Daw al-Salihin, who reportedly had had a leg amputated as a result of injuries sustained under torture. Earlier in March Libyan television had broadcast a film of three men, including Miftah Qarrum al-Wirfali, "confessing" to being US spies. They were believed to have been tortured to make them confess. It was feared that many others arrested after the alleged 1993 rebellion were at risk of execution.

In early 1994 members of the Urfala tribe were arrested by the security forces, reportedly in connection with the disturbances in the Bani Walid area in October 1993. They remained imprisoned without trial.

At least 600 political prisoners, including possible prisoners of conscience, were still detained without charge or trial: most had been held incommunicado since their arrest in previous years. Among them were scores of government opponents, including members or supporters of banned Islamist groups, who had been arrested in the 1980s. They included Dr 'Abd al-Mun'im Jbhiri al-'Awjali and Hassan al-Suwayheli Istayta, professor at the College of Agriculture in al-Bydha, who were arrested in May 1984 in connection with a clash at Bab al-'Aziziya between the security forces and members of the opposition National Front for the Salvation of Libya (see previous *Amnesty International Reports*). Also still held were suspected members of banned Islamist groups arrested between January 1989 and May 1991, such as Muftah 'Ali Salem al-Gawzi, a laboratory technician, and Muhammad Khayrallah al-Zawi, a university student (see previous *Amnesty International Reports*).

Seventeen government opponents sentenced to life imprisonment after unfair trials in previous years remained in Abu Salim Prison (see *Amnesty International Reports 1991 to 1994*). They included Mu'ammar Hassan 'Ali, who was arrested in May 1984 and summarily tried by a Revolutionary Court in Abu Salim Prison. His death sentence was commuted in June 1988.

Torture and ill-treatment of detainees continued to be reported. Among the victims were some of those arrested following the alleged October 1993 rebellion (see above). Dr Musa al-Keilani, a diplomat and former member of staff at the University of Gar Yunis, was reportedly tortured following his arrest in January to force him to confess to having participated in the October rebellion. His fate and whereabouts remained unknown at the end of the year.

There were grave concerns about Mansur Kikhiya who "disappeared" during a visit to Cairo in December 1993 (see *Amnesty International Report 1994*). A prominent member of the Libyan opposition and a human rights activist, he had been living in exile in France since 1980. He remained missing and there were fears that he had been abducted by Libyan agents and was being held in Libya.

At least 17 people were executed. Three executions were shown on television on 16 November, together with an announcement that the prisoners had been convicted of murder.

Throughout the year Amnesty International continued to appeal for the immediate and unconditional release of all prisoners of conscience and for the fair trial or release of the hundreds of other political prisoners.

Following the introduction of the "purification laws", Amnesty International urged the authorities to abolish the judicial punishments of amputation and flogging, and to replace them with punishments that are not cruel, inhuman or degrading. It also urged the authorities not to use the death penalty. Amnesty International sought assurances from the Libyan leader, Colonel Mu'ammar Gaddafi, that

200 Mansur Kikhiya had not been abducted and taken back to Libya. The organization received no response to its inquiries.

LITHUANIA

Two people were executed and at least three others were under sentence of death.

Two people were executed after President Algirdas Brazauskas rejected their petitions for clemency. Vidmantas Zibaitis had been sentenced to death by the Supreme Court of Lithuania in September 1993. Antanas Varnelis was sentenced to death by the same court at the beginning of the year. Both men had been found guilty of premeditated murder under aggravated circumstances. The executions by shooting took place in January and September respectively.

At the end of the year at least three other people were under sentence of death, including Boris Dekanidze who was convicted in November of ordering the assassination of a journalist the previous year. Both the other men under sentence of death were believed to have been denied the right to appeal against their convictions and sentences and were awaiting the outcome of petitions for clemency submitted to the President.

Throughout the year Amnesty International appealed to the authorities to commute all pending death sentences and to abolish the death penalty. The organization also asked the authorities in February to provide statistical information on the use of the death penalty. Amnesty International had received no reply to its request by the end of the year.

LUXEMBOURG

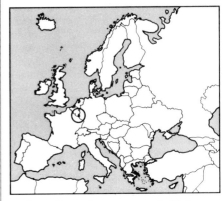

At least five prisoners were held in prolonged isolation.

The prisoners were kept in prolonged isolation in Schrassig prison for disciplinary reasons. In June Satko Adrovic completed a six-month period in solitary confinement as a punishment for attempting to escape. He had spent an even longer period in isolation the previous year for a similar offence (see *Amnesty International Report 1994*). Amnesty International believes that prolonged isolation may have serious effects on the physical and mental health of prisoners and may constitute cruel, inhuman or degrading treatment or punishment.

In April the government announced several changes to the practice of solitary confinement in response to criticisms made in 1993 by the Committee for the Prevention of Torture (CPT), a body of experts set up under the European Convention for the Prevention of Torture and Inhuman or Degrading Treatment or Punishment (see *Amnesty International Report 1994*). The changes included employing instructors in Schrassig prison in order to organize stimulating activities for prisoners in isolation, and improving exercise facilities. The CPT's recommendation that the authorities should reconsider using solitary confinement as a punishment was rejected for "reasons connected with order and security".

In March Amnesty International asked the government what measures the prison authorities had taken to alleviate the physical and psychological effects of prolonged isolation on Satko Adrovic. No reply was received.

MACAO

Three men faced extradition to the People's Republic of China, where they were at risk of being sentenced to death.

In October Chinese members of the Sino-Portuguese Joint Liaison Group, which deals with issues surrounding the transfer of Macao to Chinese administration in 1999, indicated that they would not object to a proposed revision of the Macao Penal Code formally excluding the death penalty, which was abolished in Macao in the 19th century. However, the revised Penal Code did not appear to effectively guarantee that the death penalty, widely used in China, would not be restored after 1999. The Basic Law of the Macao Special Administrative Region, adopted by China's National People's Congress in 1993 and due to come into force in 1999, lacks safeguards against the death penalty. It also lacks adequate safeguards against torture and ill-treatment, guarantees for fair trial, guarantees to protect the exercise of all fundamental human rights, and safeguards against the curtailment of basic rights under a state of emergency. It also fails to safeguard fully the independence of the judiciary in accordance with international standards.

In July journalists in Macao wrote to Portuguese President Mario Soares to express concern about complaints brought by Macao authorities against three Portuguese-language newspapers, which they alleged amounted to restrictions on their freedom of expression. In May the President of the Macao Supreme Court reportedly initiated proceedings against the newspaper *Futuro de Macau*, apparently for reproducing comments by Amnesty International on a Supreme Court decision relating to extradition cases (see below). The case against the newspaper was apparently dropped later in the year. Some of the other cases were still pending at the end of the year.

Three men were threatened with extradition to China, where they were at risk of being sentenced to death on criminal charges. Yeung Yuk Leung and Lei Chan Wa, detained in 1993, and Leong Chong Men, detained in April 1994, were wanted by the Chinese authorities in connection with criminal charges carrying the death

penalty. In April and September the Macao Supreme Court ruled that the three could be extradited, despite a Portuguese presidential decree prohibiting the extradition of alleged offenders to countries where they may face execution. The Chinese authorities had reportedly given assurances that the death penalty would not be sought by prosecutors in any of these cases, but the legal status of the assurances remained unclear. All three men appealed to the Constitutional Court in Portugal. In July the European Commission on Human Rights called on the Portuguese authorities to ensure that the extraditions remain suspended pending the Constitutional Court's decision. The cases were still pending at the end of the year.

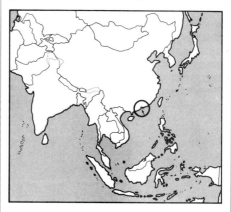

In March Amnesty International learned that a man facing a similar risk of execution had been detained in October 1993 by Macao police and handed over to the Chinese authorities without any judicial review whatsoever. James Peng, a Chinese-born Australian national, was reportedly arrested by police at his hotel in October 1993, taken a few hours later to the Chinese border and handed over to waiting Chinese officials. At the end of the year he was still in detention awaiting trial in China, and risked being sentenced to death on charges of embezzlement. No inquiry into the circumstances of his arrest in Macao and transfer to China was known to have taken place.

In February and again in April, Amnesty International expressed concern about the threatened extraditions. In April an Amnesty International representative visited Macao to inquire about these cases and about legislation concerning freedom of expression.

202

MACEDONIA
(THE FORMER YUGOSLAV REPUBLIC OF)

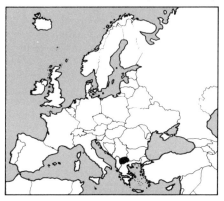

One ethnic Albanian was apparently a prisoner of conscience. Ten ethnic Albanians imprisoned on political charges were allegedly ill-treated while awaiting trial. People seeking protection were arbitrarily expelled.

In January the Former Yugoslav Republic of Macedonia succeeded to the International Covenant on Civil and Political Rights and the International Covenant on Economic, Social and Cultural Rights. In January it also acceded to the 1951 Convention relating to the Status of Refugees and its 1967 Protocol.

In August an ethnic Albanian, Sabit Bakiu, was sentenced to 45 days' imprisonment by the court for petty crimes in Tetovo. He was reportedly prosecuted for displaying an Albanian flag from his car while taking part in a wedding procession.

In July, 10 ethnic Albanians were sentenced in Skopje to between five and eight years' imprisonment on charges of "association for hostile activity". Some were allegedly ill-treated during their interrogation and detention.

There were reports of arbitrary deportations of people seeking protection in Macedonia. In May, two refugees from Bosnia-Herzegovina, sisters Ilda and Dženeta Pašić, aged 17 and 15 respectively, were arbitrarily deported to the Federal Republic of Yugoslavia (FRY) where they may have been at risk of subsequent return to Bosnia-Herzegovina. There was no judicial or administrative procedure which would have allowed them to put forward reasons why they should not be expelled. Out of fear of what might happen to them, the two girls jumped from the moving train as it crossed the border into the FRY. Ilda died as a result. In December, 18 ethnic Albanians who were members of the self-proclaimed Kosovo "parliament" were deported to the FRY, where they may have been at risk of torture and imprisonment, apparently without any examination of the risks which they might face.

In June Amnesty International wrote to the authorities calling upon them to ensure that asylum-seekers would not be deported to countries where they would be at risk of human rights violations or to any third country without ensuring that they would be given effective and durable protection against return to a country where they might be at risk.

MALAWI

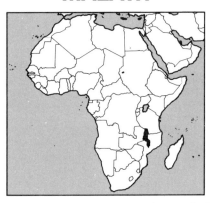

Over 100 prisoners on death row had their sentences commuted to life imprisonment in May after the election of a new government. Some remaining political prisoners held by the previous government were released and three prisons used to detain political prisoners in the past were closed. Ill-treatment of criminal suspects by the police continued to be reported. A commission of inquiry was set up to investigate the suspicious deaths of three government ministers and one member of parliament in 1983. There were no executions but at least two people were sentenced to death.

The first multi-party elections for over 30 years were held in May. They were won by the opposition United Democratic Front (UDF), whose chairman, Bakili

Muluzi, won the presidential election. He replaced Dr Hastings Kamuzu Banda, leader of the Malawi Congress Party (MCP), whose government had been responsible for widespread human rights abuses in the past.

In the early part of the election campaign in January and February, when the MCP was still in power, there were reports of intimidation and harassment of supporters of opposition parties in rural areas, particularly in the central region. Supporters of both the ruling MCP and of the opposition UDF were reported to have beaten opponents. The editor of *The Independent* newspaper received death threats in March for reporting allegations of corruption by supporters of the government. In Mangochi, southeastern Malawi, former members of the Malawi Young Pioneers (MYP), the paramilitary youth wing of the MCP, were said to be crossing the border from Mozambique and threatening people. Some 2,000 members of the MYP were reported to be encamped in neighbouring Mozambique, in camps controlled by the Resistência Nacional Moçambicana (RENAMO), Mozambique National Resistance, throughout the year. The MYP had been responsible in the past for many human rights abuses against government opponents. It was forcibly disarmed by the army in December 1993 and the law establishing the MYP was repealed in March.

In his inauguration speech on 21 May, President Bakili Muluzi announced the release of all remaining political prisoners, believed to be few in number, held by the former government. He also commuted all current death sentences – about 120 – to life imprisonment. He announced the closure of three prisons which he said had been used to detain and torture thousands of opponents of the former government.

A new provisional constitution was drawn up by the National Consultative Council, a body composed of government and opposition leaders, and was enacted the day before the election. It included a Bill of Rights and provisions for an Ombudsman and for a Human Rights Commission. These had not been established by the end of the year. The Constitution was to be provisional for one year, to allow for further discussion and changes. Hundreds of former political prisoners initiated cases in the courts seeking compensation for detention, torture and seizure of property by the former government.

In June a commission of inquiry was set up, chaired by a High Court judge, to investigate the deaths in May 1983 of three government ministers and a member of parliament, who had allegedly been extrajudicially executed (see *Amnesty International Report 1986*). It had not reported its conclusions by the end of the year.

In June two Malawians – Kelly Nkhoma and Sam Phiri – were extradited to Zambia, reportedly to stand trial for involvement in the deaths in Zambia of a journalist opposed to President Banda's government, Mkwapatira Mhango, and members of his family, who were killed by a bomb in 1989 (see *Amnesty International Report 1990*). However, they were instead charged with the murder of Tito Banda, a Malawian journalist, who turned out to be alive and living in Malawi. They were released in September by a magistrate's court in Zambia, for lack of evidence, and returned to Malawi.

Following the May elections there were reports of journalists being briefly detained. In July the editor of *The Enquirer* was held for four hours by the police. Also in July the then Attorney General and Minister of Justice banned an edition of *The Malawian* newspaper which had published a photograph of President Bakili Muluzi taken after he had been convicted of theft in the early 1960s. The editor, Chimwemwe Mputahelo, was charged under the Protected Flag, Emblem & Names Act, which had been used by the previous government to restrict freedom of expression. He was not detained and the charges were dropped in August on the instructions of the President. In September the editor of *The Independent* was reportedly beaten by the police and detained for several hours.

There were continuing reports that the police ill-treated criminal suspects. For example, a man detained in July claimed that he was whipped during interrogation by the police in an attempt to force him to confess to robbery.

Trials of death penalty cases, which until October 1993 had been heard in "Traditional Courts" which did not provide fair trials, were transferred to the High Court. Trials restarted in October. By the end of the year at least two people had been sentenced to death for murder. No executions were carried out.

204

In February Amnesty International published a report, *Malawi: A new future for human rights*, calling for human rights to be fully protected in the new constitution. Amnesty International representatives attended a symposium on the new draft constitution and met members of opposition parties, lawyers, journalists, religious leaders and new human rights groups. In May Amnesty International expressed concern that human rights abuses committed in the run-up to the election did not appear to be being adequately investigated or punished by the authorities.

After the election Amnesty International wrote to the new President welcoming the commutation of all death sentences and urging the government to abolish the death penalty. Amnesty International jointly sponsored a conference on human rights in Malawi with the Public Affairs Committee, a body of religious groups, in August. The conference brought together representatives from human rights groups, religious groups, lawyers, the police and the army to discuss the future of human rights in Malawi.

MALAYSIA

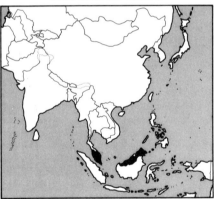

At least 11 leaders of a religious group, all possible prisoners of conscience, were detained for several weeks without charge under the Internal Security Act (ISA); four remained in detention. More than 150 members of the same group were arrested, charged and released on bail. At least six political prisoners remained in detention under the ISA. Restrictions imposed on seven released prisoners of conscience were lifted. Caning continued to be widely used as a punishment. **At least eight people were sentenced to death and another six people were executed.**

A separate Court of Appeal was established in September. Appeals against decisions by the high courts may now be submitted to the Court of Appeal. The Supreme Court remains the highest court in the country.

A national crack-down on members of *Al Arqam*, an Islamic sect, was launched after a ruling on 5 August by the National Fatwa Council that *Al Arqam*'s teachings and beliefs contravened Islamic practice and tenets. *Al Arqam*, which was founded in 1968, was declared unlawful under the Societies Act of 1966. To Amnesty International's knowledge, there is no evidence that *Al Arqam* has used or incited violence.

At least 11 leaders of *Al Arqam*, arrested between September and November, were accused of preaching "deviationist" Islamic teachings. One was held together with her six-month-old child. They were detained without charge or trial under the ISA, which allows preventive detention for up to two years. Seven of them were released in October and November after one of their leaders stated in a television program that he gave up his "deviationist" religious beliefs, possibly under duress. Four of those arrested, including Hasan Mokhtar, Supreme Council secretary of *Al Arqam*, remained in detention. Those released were prohibited by the Ministry of Home Affairs from making any religious or other statements and from joining any organization.

More than 150 other *Al Arqam* members were arrested throughout the country in August and September. All were released on bail after being charged with various offences under the Societies Act, including distributing leaflets and participating in *Al Arqam* activities.

At least six communists remained in detention. They had been held under the ISA after they voluntarily renounced armed opposition and surrendered to the authorities in December 1989. Their identities have not been disclosed (see *Amnesty International Reports 1993* and *1994*).

Restrictions on the freedom of movement imposed on Jeffrey Kitingan and six other former prisoners of conscience released in 1993 were lifted in January (see *Amnesty International Report 1994*).

Caning – which constitutes a cruel, inhuman or degrading punishment – continued to be widely inflicted as a supplementary punishment to imprisonment for some 40 crimes including drugs offences, rape, kidnapping, firearms offences, attempted murder, robbery and theft. Chong Chin Tak, an unemployed man, was sentenced in June to nine years' imprisonment and three strokes of the cane for credit card forgery. In September Amir Saad, an unemployed man, was sentenced to 13 years' imprisonment and 10 strokes of the cane for possession of heroin.

During the year, at least eight people were sentenced to death, five of whom were convicted of drugs offences and three of murder and firearms offences. The Supreme Court confirmed the death sentences on eight people, three of whom were Filipino nationals convicted of drug-trafficking. Nine other Filipinos, including one woman, had their death sentences reduced to life imprisonment. At least six people were executed.

Amnesty International appealed throughout the year for the release of members of *Al Arqam* and other political prisoners arbitrarily detained under the ISA, if they were not to be charged with recognizably criminal offences. It also called for the commutation of all death sentences and an end to the use of caning and the death penalty as punishments.

MALDIVES

At least 15 possible prisoners of conscience were arrested because of their political views or religious practices. Dozens of others were arrested in the run-up to parliamentary elections. Some detainees were reportedly ill-treated.

Parliamentary elections were held in December. Candidates stood as independents as no political parties are allowed in the country. A request to form a political party was submitted to the Ministry of Home Affairs in October but was turned down.

In July legislation was passed by the Citizens' Majlis (parliament) providing for between two and five years' imprisonment for people found guilty of involvement in "giving religious advice that contravenes independence and the government policy

... and the policy stated by the President".

Imam Mohamed Ibrahim, Adam Naseem and Abdul Gafoor were among at least 15 people arrested in March apparently because their political views or religious practices were different from those sanctioned by the government. Adam Naseem, a former presidential adviser, may have been arrested in connection with his poem, *Hayy 'ala Salah* (Call to Prayer), which was subsequently published in the newspaper *Aafathis*. The poem expressed concern about the deteriorating moral and political situation in the country. He was first held at Dhoonidhoo detention centre, and denied access to relatives; in July he was reportedly transferred to house arrest.

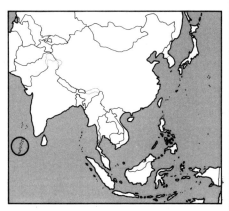

Ahamed Didi from Gan island was arrested on 17 May and kept in detention until 27 June; he was rearrested in early November and held without charge or trial until 5 December. His arrest may have been in connection with the parliamentary elections, in which he was standing. Mohamed Saeed Moosa Wajdee, a journalist, was taken into custody by the police in Male' on 19 October, possibly because of an article he had written in the newspaper *Haveeru*. The article warned that some candidates, including government officials, might abuse their position in order to gain votes in the parliamentary elections. Another journalist, Mohamed Nasheed, was arrested on 30 November and charged with spreading false information about the government. The charges reportedly referred to an article he had written about the parliamentary elections. The article had been published in a magazine in Manila, the Philippines. The trial had not concluded by the end of the year.

206 Mohamed Saleem, a member of parliament, who was among 22 people arrested in 1993 because of his apparent support for Ilyas Ibrahim, one of the presidential candidates (see Amnesty International Report 1994), continued to be held under house arrest pending trial. Charges of corruption were brought against him which may have been politically motivated. Sixteen of the others were reportedly sentenced to seven years' banishment. Nine of them had these sentences reduced to one year on appeal. There was no further information about the others.

There were reports of ill-treatment of detainees at a place of detention near the Air Maldives office in Male' and at Dhoonidhoo detention centre, where prisoners were held for months in solitary confinement.

Amnesty International expressed concern about the arrest of people because of their political views or religious practices and sought information about their cases. It urged the government to release all those held for the peaceful expression of their political or religious beliefs unless specific criminal charges were brought against them. It sought clarification about the law providing for terms of imprisonment for "giving religious advice". The government denied the allegations about arrests of candidates in the elections. It did not respond to requests for information about the 15 people arrested in March or about the arrest of Mohamed Saeed Moosa Wajdee.

MALI

Three prisoners of conscience were detained for short periods, two of them without charge or trial. Nine possible prisoners of conscience and about 10 other political detainees were held without trial until their releases in July and August. One person was sentenced to death. The former President and three former government ministers remained under sentence of death throughout the year. Government forces were reported to have extrajudicially executed at least 170 unarmed civilians in reprisal for attacks by armed political groups. Armed political groups, including a vigilante group,

were reported to have deliberately and arbitrarily killed at least 120 civilians.

Inter-ethnic violence in the north escalated during 1994, in which hundreds of people were reported to have been killed. Raids on northern towns and villages continued, despite the April 1992 peace accord between the government and the Mouvements et fronts unifiés de l'Azawad (MFUA), the Unified Movements and Fronts of Azawad, a coalition of Tuareg and Moorish opposition groups. It was unclear whether these armed robberies were politically motivated or the work of bandits, as claimed by the government and the MFUA, but from early 1994 there were increasing reports that dissident members or factions of the MFUA were involved. Government troops, who are predominantly from the majority black population, reportedly carried out reprisal killings of Tuareg and Moorish civilians from April onwards. A black vigilante group set up by former soldiers, the Mouvement patriotique malien Ghanda Koy (Ghanda Koy), Malian Patriotic Movement – Masters of the Land, was also responsible for killing Tuareg and Moorish civilians. Judicial investigations were ordered into two incidents of killings by soldiers but no one had been brought to justice in connection with any of the killings by the end of the year.

Under the terms of the 1992 peace accord, about 650 former Tuareg rebels (known as intégrés) were integrated into the armed forces. In May the MFUA signed a further agreement with the government, raising the number of former rebels to be integrated into the security forces and government services to over 2,000. In May and June the government increased the number of soldiers deployed in the north and civilian governors there were replaced by military personnel. However, the attacks and killings continued and many intégrés deserted and returned to former rebel bases. In August government troops in several cities went on strike over pay arrears and the government's failure to maintain security. By the end of the year, 25,000 more refugees had joined the 160,000 who had sought refuge in neighbouring countries since 1991.

Three prisoners of conscience were held for short periods. Two women – Diallo Fanta Dramé and Korotoumou Traoré – both members of local campaigning organizations, were arrested in Bamako, the capital, in May and held incommunicado for over two weeks before being released without charge. They were detained because of their involvement in a peaceful campaign for the release of about 40 students arrested following violent student demonstrations on 15 February; the students had all been released on bail or tried by July.

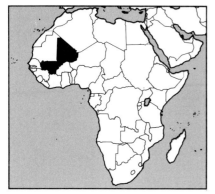

Sambi Touré, managing director of an independent newspaper, *Nouvel Horizon*, was detained for nine days in November after publishing an article about a meeting between President Alpha Oumar Konaré and armed forces officers in which the officers allegedly threatened to overthrow the government. He was a prisoner of conscience. He was released pending trial on charges of defamation and spreading false news.

Nine possible prisoners of conscience were released in July following an amnesty. Major Lamine Diabira, a former Minister of the Interior, and eight other army officers had been arrested in July 1991 and charged with conspiring to overthrow the transitional government (see *Amnesty International Reports 1992* to *1994*). They had been held without trial for three years, allegedly because Major Diabira had sought the prosecution in 1991 of officers he claimed were responsible for abuses committed under the government of former President Moussa Traoré.

In August the judicial authorities announced that they would not prosecute Lieutenant-Colonel Oumar Diallo, aide-de-camp to former President Traoré, and about 10 others, believed to be mostly soldiers, who had been detained in December 1993 after an alleged conspiracy to overthrow the government (see *Amnesty International Report 1994*). They were all released unconditionally except Lieutenant-Colonel Diallo, who remained in detention awaiting trial on embezzlement charges.

The wife, son and brother-in-law of former President Traoré remained in detention throughout the year, awaiting trial on charges of embezzlement and other "economic" offences (see *Amnesty International Reports 1992* to *1994*). All other officials of the former government and ruling party detained in 1991 had been released on bail by October.

One man, Kantara Traoré, was sentenced to death for attempted murder in August but no executions were carried out. Former President Traoré and three former government officials remained under sentence of death (see *Amnesty International Report 1994*), awaiting trial on further charges of embezzlement. President Konaré had not ruled on their plea for clemency by the end of the year.

Government forces were reported to have extrajudicially executed at least 170 civilians, and possibly many more. Most of the killings appeared to be in reprisal for earlier attacks by armed Tuareg and Moorish groups; soldiers targeted Tuareg and Moorish homes in towns and encampments and fired indiscriminately on civilians.

On 21 April, the day after two soldiers had been shot dead in a dispute with Tuareg *intégrés*, troops attacked Tuareg and Moorish homes in Ménaka, in the northwest, with machine-guns, rockets and grenades. Four civilians were shot dead, including an elderly woman, and seven women who were forced to flee from their homes and hide in the bush apparently later died from thirst and shock, one of them in an advanced stage of pregnancy. An internal inquiry investigated the incident and transferred the troops involved to different barracks, but no one was brought to justice.

In Timbuktu between 12 and 29 June at least 50 civilians, most of them Moors, were reportedly taken prisoner and extrajudicially executed by army commandos, apparently in reprisal for earlier attacks by *intégrés*. The victims included Baba Koutam, a 67-year-old businessman and community leader, who was arrested by soldiers on 22 June at the home of the *Kadhi* (Islamic judge) of Timbuktu; his body was found on the airport road, his limbs broken and throat cut. A member of the vigilante group *Ghanda Koy* had reportedly threatened him, then led the army commandos to him and taken part in the killing.

In October government troops and members of *Ghanda Koy* were reported to have killed about 40 Tuareg and Moorish civilians in and around Gao. These killings were in reprisal for an attack claimed by the *Front islamique arabe de l'Azawad* (FIAA), Arab Islamic Front of Azawad (see below). The government condemned the reprisal killings and ordered a judicial inquiry but no one had been brought to justice by the end of the year.

Some killings which the authorities said occurred during clashes between the armed forces and armed Tuareg and Moorish groups appeared in reality to be extrajudicial executions of Tuareg and Moorish civilians. In one instance, the army said that 22 *intégrés* had been killed while attacking an army convoy near Andéramboukane on 12 June. However, according to unofficial sources, the army killed 22 civilians in reprisal attacks on Tuareg and Moorish encampments; the bodies were buried in mass graves and were reported to include two elderly Moors. In October the government said that Jean-Claude Berberat, the Swiss consul in Mali, and Amoubareck Ag Alleyda, a Tuareg development worker, had been killed in Niafunké during an attack on a military patrol by armed bandits. In December a judicial inquiry found the military patrol responsible for the killings and apparently established that the killings had been unlawful. No legal action against the soldiers had been initiated by the end of the year.

Ghanda Koy was reportedly responsible for killing at least 20 and possibly more than 40 Tuareg and Moorish civilians during the year. Nine herdsmen travelling in a boat on the Niger river were reportedly shot dead by members of *Ghanda Koy* in late May. At around this time *Ghanda Koy* members were also reported to have killed four civilians in Fia near Bourem and 13 in the village of Tessit, southwest of Ansongo.

Tuareg and Moorish armed political groups were alleged to have killed more than 90 civilians because of their ethnic origin or in reprisal for killings by government forces. On 1 July an armed group reportedly killed nine people, seven of them civilians, in attacks on government buildings and a health centre in Tenenkou.

The FIAA also reportedly killed at least 70 civilians deliberately and arbitrarily. Between 18 and 25 market traders travelling in a lorry were ambushed and killed, allegedly by FIAA members, on 14 July on the Nampala-Niono road. At least 40 villagers were killed, reportedly by FIAA *intégrés*, on 25 July at the weekly market in Bamba near Gourma-Rharous; in December the MFUA said this was a reprisal attack by civilians. The FIAA acknowledged responsibility for an attack on Gao in October in which at least 13 civilians were killed.

Amnesty International appealed for the release of prisoners of conscience and for the trial or release of the army officers held without trial since 1991, who were released in July.

In September Amnesty International published a report, *Mali: Ethnic conflict and killings of civilians*, which documented the growing incidence of killings by government forces and armed political groups. Amnesty International appealed to the authorities to take measures to stop the extrajudicial executions of members of the Tuareg and Moorish communities. It called for an independent and public judicial inquiry into reports of unlawful killings by the armed forces, with a view to bringing to justice those found responsible. Amnesty International also appealed to the leaders of all armed political groups to condemn the deliberate and arbitrary killings of civilians and to put an immediate end to such killings by the forces under their command. In response the MFUA said in December that human rights abuses had not been carried out by MFUA groups but by dissident armed groups, armed bandits and civilians.

MAURITANIA

Two human rights activists held briefly were prisoners of conscience. At least 60 Islamists, some of whom may have been prisoners of conscience, were detained for about two weeks; some were reportedly tortured.

Many of the 60,000 black Mauritanians who were expelled or had fled from human rights violations in 1989 or 1990 (see *Amnesty International Reports 1990* and *1991*) remained in exile in neighbouring Mali or Senegal. Some who returned in 1994 were arrested or forcibly expelled when they tried to regain access to their land or property. Others were arrested on suspicion of having contact with those deported to Senegal or Mali. The level of human rights violations in southern Mauritania was lower than in 1989 and 1990: however, complaints about torture, extrajudicial executions and "disappearances" were not adequately investigated.

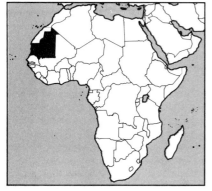

The government prevented judicial investigations into past human rights violations and the publication of information about such violations. A total amnesty had been enacted in 1993 for offences committed between 1989 and 1992, a period of intense and widespread human rights violations, and the pattern established in previous years of complete immunity from prosecution for human rights violations continued. Several newspapers and magazines were seized to prevent the circulation of human rights information and criticism of the government.

Two prisoners of conscience, both human rights activists, were detained briefly. Professor Cheikh Saad Bouh Kamara, President of the *Association mauritanienne des droits de l'homme* (AMDH), Mauritanian Human Rights Association, was held for five days in January shortly after he had met representatives of two visiting French human rights organizations. His house was searched and papers relating to his human rights activities were confiscated. The AMDH had not been given official legal status despite its application in 1992. In July Ly Haoussou Haïdara, a member of the support committee for the

victims of repression in Mauritania, was held briefly and questioned about her nationality. The real reason for her arrest may have been that she had recently met a delegation of deported Mauritanians who were on an official visit to Mauritania.

At least 60 Islamist activists, including foreign nationals, were detained for up to 16 days. It appeared that some had not used or advocated violence and were prisoners of conscience. Some of those arrested, including El Hacen Ould Moulaye Ely, were active members of the opposition *Union des forces démocratiques – Ere nouvelle* (UFD-EN), Union of Democratic Forces – New Era. Others, such as former minister Aboubekrine Ould Ahmed, were close to the government. All were arrested on or around 25 September in the capital, Nouakchott, and elsewhere. The same day the Minister of the Interior stated that secret organizations had been discovered which were operating under the guise of Islam, and which were training and arming people to destabilize Mauritania. Those arrested were held incommunicado and some were believed to have been beaten in custody. All were pardoned by President Maaouiya Ould Taya and released after 10 of them apparently confessed to belonging to secret Islamist organizations, such as the *Organisation du Jihad en Mauritanie*, Mauritanian Organization for Jihad, whose aim was to set up an Islamic state.

One criminal suspect died in custody. Ibrahima Diallo, a Senegalese national, was arrested and taken to a police commissariat in Nouakchott. He died on 13 June, apparently as a result of a fractured neck. No official investigation was reported to have been ordered to establish whether he died as a result of torture.

In July Seydi Boulo Bâ, a black Mauritanian who had returned from Senegal, was arrested in Kaédi when he tried to gain entry to his home which had been appropriated by someone else. It was not possible to establish if he had been released by the end of the year.

Amnesty International appealed for the unconditional release of Professor Kamara. Following the arrest of Islamist activists, Amnesty International urged the authorities to ensure that they were not tortured and that any held purely on account of non-violent religious or political activities were released immediately.

MEXICO

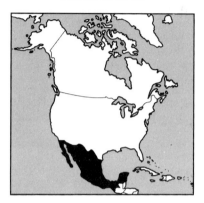

Scores of prisoners of conscience, mostly indigenous peasants, were detained. The widespread use of torture and ill-treatment by law enforcement agents continued to be reported. At least 20 people "disappeared" and the whereabouts of hundreds who "disappeared" in previous years remained unknown. Dozens of people were extrajudicially executed. Those responsible for human rights violations continued to benefit from impunity.

Zedillo Ponce de León, the candidate of the ruling *Partido Revolucionario Institucional* (PRI), Institutional Revolutionary Party, elected in August, took office as President in December.

On 1 January several towns in the southern state of Chiapas were seized by members of the *Ejército Zapatista de Liberación Nacional* (EZLN), Zapatista National Liberation Army, a previously unknown armed opposition group formed mostly by indigenous peasants. They demanded a series of rights, including land, healthcare, education and an end to abuses against indigenous people. Several violent clashes between the Mexican army and the EZLN were reported during the following days, during which the rebels retreated to the mountainous southern region of the state. At least 145 people died during the confrontations, and serious human rights violations by the army were reported during the conflict. The EZLN took hostages who were later released unharmed. Following a growing outcry against the human rights violations reported in Chiapas, President Salinas named a peace envoy and declared a cease-fire on 12 January. The cease-fire

lasted until the end of the year, despite the growing military presence in the region, which eventually amounted to more than 40,000 troops. Peace talks between the government and EZLN, mediated by the Roman Catholic Church, began in February, but were suspended in June. Tensions in the region increased following allegations of irregularities in the conduct of the August elections, in which the PRI won the state governorship. On 6 December the EZLN declared an end to the cease-fire although no further armed clashes had been reported by the end of the year.

Hundreds of people, including scores of prisoners of conscience, were arrested for short periods during the uprising in Chiapas. Most of those arrested were Indians and scores were tortured and ill-treated before being released without charge. About 70 were imprisoned for several weeks in Cerro Hueco, a prison in Tuxtla Gutiérrez, the state capital. Most faced false charges of participating in the uprising, based on confessions extracted under torture. Following public outcry, 38 of the prisoners were released in February and the rest in the following months.

Scores of prisoners of conscience were arrested in other regions of the country for their political or civil rights activities, and dozens of human rights monitors and journalists received death threats. These included Bishop Samuel Ruiz and members of a church-based human rights centre in Chiapas, the *Centro de Derechos Humanos Fray Bartolomé de las Casas*; Sergio Aguayo, president of the *Academia Mexicana de Derechos Humanos*, Mexican Academy of Human Rights; Juan Carlos Martínez Martínez; and Víctor Clark Alfaro.

In January several reporters and the deputy director general of *La Jornada*, a national newspaper, received anonymous death threats because of their coverage of the Chiapas uprising. The staff and directors of *El Tiempo*, a local newspaper in San Cristóbal de las Casas, Chiapas, were repeatedly threatened with death for the same reason. In April Edwin Bustillos, an Indian rights and environmental activist in the Sierra Madre region of Chihuahua, had a road accident after his car was tampered with by unidentified individuals; he was not injured. He had survived a near fatal beating by Guachochi municipal police in December 1993 and had received numerous death threats. Those responsible were not brought to justice and the anonymous death threats continued. Also in April Enrique Pérez López, chairperson of the *Asociación de Derechos Humanos Sur Este de Comitán*, a human rights organization, was attacked and abducted by armed civilians acting with local authorities in Chicomuselo, Chiapas, during a non-violent land dispute. He was severely beaten, threatened with death and transferred to a jail in Comitán, Chiapas, where he was held without charge until mid-May.

Manuel Manríquez San Agustín, an Otomí Indian and human rights activist convicted on the basis of confessions extracted under torture, had his appeal rejected by the high court in August. In October he presented another appeal. He remained in prison at the end of the year; he was a prisoner of conscience. Pablo Molinet, a poet imprisoned in Salamanca, Guanajuato, falsely accused of murder, was released in August after two years' imprisonment (see *Amnesty International Report 1994*).

Hundreds of people were tortured and ill-treated by the army and other security forces in Chiapas. In other parts of the country the frequent use of torture by law enforcement agents, particularly the state judicial police, continued to be reported. Torture methods included beatings; near-asphyxiation with plastic bags; forcing peppered water into the nose; electric shocks and burning. Some detainees died as a result. Confessions extracted under duress continued to be admitted as evidence in courts, and medical treatment for detainees who suffered torture was frequently not available. By the end of the year none of those responsible for any of the hundreds of cases of torture reported in Chiapas and throughout the country had been brought to justice.

Among the scores of Indian prisoners arrested after the Chiapas uprising and accused of links with the EZLN were Pedro and Benancio Hernández Jiménez who were arrested without charge by soldiers in Ocosingo on 9 January. They were held in secret detention for several days in a military installation where they were reportedly subjected to beatings, semi-asphyxiation with plastic bags and electric shocks in an effort to force them to confess to participating in the uprising. They were forced to sign a confession before a public prosecutor, before being transferred to Cerro Hueco, where they did not receive medical treatment for their injuries. They were not informed of the charges against them.

On 7 January three peasant leaders from Morelia – Sebastián Santis López, Severiano Santis Gómez and Hermelindo Santis Gómez – were reportedly severely tortured for several hours in their church when scores of soldiers raided their village. They then "disappeared"; their bodies were found near by in a shallow grave on 10 February. Forensic investigations concluded that the victims had been summarily executed. The army denied responsibility. Other men were forced at gunpoint to lie face down for several hours in front of the church, and dozens were detained and tortured by being beaten, semi-suffocated and burned. They were forced to confess to participating in the uprising, and transferred to Cerro Hueco.

Reports of torture in Chiapas continued throughout the year. On 4 June three young Tzeltal Indians – María Teresa Méndez Santis, Cristina Méndez Santis and María Méndez Santis – were raped and beaten by several soldiers at an army road-block in Santa Rosita Siabaquil. They were accused of belonging to the EZLN, but were released that day without charge.

There were reports of torture from other regions. In Mexico City on 2 September, student activist David Lozano Tovar was seized by unidentified men believed to be members of the security forces. He was beaten and given electric shocks in a secret detention centre before being released the next day. Félix Armando Fernández Estrada and Demetrio Ernesto Hernández Rojas, a trade union activist, were abducted by unidentified armed men in Mexico City on 20 October and transferred blindfolded to a clandestine detention centre, where they were interrogated under torture about their political activities. This included suspension from the thumbs, slaps to the ears, semi-asphyxiation in water and with plastic bags and electric shocks to various parts of the body including gums and teeth. They were handed over to the police in Mexico City and charged with offences, including terrorism, based on their forced confessions, and remained in prison at the end

212

of the year. They received no medical treatment for their injuries.

At least 20 people "disappeared", many in the context of the armed conflict in Chiapas. For example, at least 14 Tzeltal Indian peasants from the communities of San Miguel, La Garrucha, Patihuitz, La Galena and Prado Ocosingo "disappeared" after being detained by the army during the first week of the uprising. Their whereabouts remained unknown at the end of the year. No one was brought to justice for these "disappearances". Similarly, little progress was reported in the investigations into hundreds of past "disappearances" of political activists – most of which occurred during the 1970s and early 1980s.

Scores of people were extrajudicially executed by members of the security forces after the uprising in Chiapas, and dozens of other cases of extrajudicial executions were reported during the year throughout the country. At least 11 people, including patients, were reportedly killed on 3 January when members of the army entered a hospital in Ocosingo, in search of EZLN rebels. Their bodies, which were buried in a common grave, were exhumed later in January. The governmental National Human Rights Commission stated they belonged to members of the EZLN who had died in combat. Further investigations contradicted these claims, and at least three of the bodies were identified as belonging to non-combatant civilians, one of them a hospital patient. The bodies of at least five unidentified young men, their hands tied behind their backs, were discovered in Ocosingo marketplace on 4 January. The victims wore bandannas used by members of the EZLN, and all had been shot through the head at point-blank range. The army initially claimed that they had died in combat, but subsequent independent forensic investigations suggested they had been murdered in detention. The bodies of at least 14 men, many shot through the head, were discovered beside a civilian bus near the Rancho Nuevo army base in Chiapas. The army's claim that they had all died in combat was not consistent with the victims' injuries. Those responsible for the killings reported during the conflict in Chiapas were not brought to justice.

On 9 March Mariano Pérez Díaz and his son Jorge Pérez Núñez, both peasant activists in Simojovel, Chiapas, were shot by unidentified gunmen. The father died instantly, while the son survived his injuries. They had both received death threats from local paramilitary groups for their participation on behalf of Indian peasants in negotiations between the government and the EZLN. On 6 September Roberto Hernández Paniagua, a schoolteacher and municipal leader of the *Partido Revolucionario Democrático*, Revolutionary Democratic Party, in Jaltenango, Chiapas, was murdered by unidentified gunmen when cycling to work. He had been repeatedly threatened with death. Those responsible for his death remained at large at the end of the year.

On 8 September Rolando Hernández Hernández and Atanacio Hernández Hernández, prominent members of the Nahua and Otomí Indian community of Plan del Encinal, Veracruz, were abducted by members of the state police and hired gunmen, who raided their community. Their mutilated bodies were discovered near by on 17 September. In November and December local officials prevented the participation of independent forensic observers in the exhumation and autopsy of both men.

On 1 November four Zoque Indians from La Blanca community, Oaxaca – Efraín Cortés Coronel, Cristóbal Sánchez García, Finar Jiménez Sánchez and Hilder Jiménez Sánchez – were arrested by the municipal police and never seen alive again. Their bodies, shot at point-blank range, were discovered near their communities in mid-November. Investigations into their killings continued at the end of the year, and those responsible remained at large.

Those responsible for the 1993 killings of Luis Manuel Salinas Germán, Israel García Hernández and 13-year-old Omar Ricardo Mendoza Palacios, had not been brought to justice by the end of the year (see *Amnesty International Report 1994*).

Amnesty International repeatedly urged the authorities to end the impunity enjoyed by perpetrators of gross human rights violations. In January an Amnesty International delegation interviewed and medically examined 70 prisoners in Cerro Hueco, who were mostly Tzeltal, Tzotzil and Ch'ol Indians. An Amnesty International delegation also visited the country in December to investigate reports of human rights violations. In October the organization sent a memorandum to the President-elect, Ernesto Zedillo Ponce de León, which included more than 70 recommendations for strengthening human rights protection in Mexico.

MOLDOVA

At least 15 people were on death row at the end of the year. In the self-proclaimed Dnestr Moldavian Republic (DMR), at least three political activists were reported to have been detained repeatedly for short periods; they were possible prisoners of conscience. Reports of ill-treatment in custody in the DMR continued. One death sentence was commuted in the DMR.

Political parties favouring reunification with Romania fared poorly in parliamentary elections in February. A March plebiscite called by President Mircea Snegur confirmed overwhelming popular support for Moldova's status as an independent country. The DMR, which continued to regard itself as a separate entity (see *Amnesty International Report 1994*), introduced a state of emergency in January in the territory it controlled.

A new constitution adopted in July retained the death penalty as "an exceptional measure of punishment".

Comprehensive statistics were released on the application of the death penalty from 1980 to 1993, during which time 67 people were sentenced to death and 43 executed. One woman was among those sentenced. Eight death sentences were commuted to life imprisonment. In 1993 two men were sentenced to death for premeditated, aggravated murder, but the last

executions recorded took place in 1989. At least 15 people were believed still to be on death row at the end of the year (see *Amnesty International Report 1994*).

In the DMR at least three men were said to have been detained repeatedly for short periods solely because of their peaceful political opposition to the authorities. For example, Alexei Mocreac, leader of a movement advocating the territorial integrity of Moldova, was placed under administrative arrest in Grigoropol for three days in March. In August he was arrested again and held for the full 30 days allowed under state of emergency legislation. The charge, denied by him, was petty hooliganism.

Allegations of ill-treatment by law enforcement officers in the DMR continued. Alexei Mocreac reported that he was beaten on the first day of his detention by police officers who also threatened him with execution. Journalist Anatoly Holodyuk was said to have been beaten by a major in the DMR Security Ministry on 10 October. He had been threatened by uniformed security agents two days earlier for reporting on protests against the DMR's ban on using the Latin alphabet when writing in the Moldovan language.

One death sentence was commuted in the DMR in September. Ilie Ilaşcu had been convicted in 1993 of violent political acts after a trial that appeared to fall short of international standards (see *Amnesty International Report 1994*). One of the five other defendants, Petru Godiac, was released in June after serving his sentence. In October Vladimir Garbuz, the only defendant to plead guilty and whose testimony implicated the others, alleged publicly that his confession had been extracted under duress. He had been pardoned and released from his six-year prison sentence in July.

Amnesty International continued to urge that all pending death sentences be commuted.

The organization called on the DMR authorities to ensure that no one was imprisoned for the non-violent exercise of basic human rights. Amnesty International also urged a full and impartial investigation into all allegations of ill-treatment in detention. Amnesty International called for a review of the case of Ilie Ilaşcu and his co-defendants.

213

214

MONGOLIA

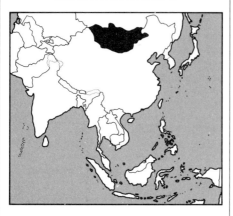

Prisoners in corrective labour institutions died of starvation. At least 26 people were sentenced to death.

Two weeks of anti-government protests in April in the capital, Ulaanbaatar, ended when parliament agreed to debate anti-corruption legislation and President Puntsalmaagiyn Ochirbat announced the preparation of a draft law to free the mass media from government control. In July the government banned demonstrations in Ulaanbaatar's central square.

Reports were received that inmates in corrective labour institutions had died from starvation because the administration did not have the money to provide sufficient rations. Out of an official figure of 90 deaths of prisoners in such institutions between late 1993 and late 1994, around 30 were directly attributed to starvation and an unknown number of the remainder to illnesses which may have been caused or exacerbated by starvation.

The death penalty remained in force for five offences (see Amnesty International Report 1994). At least 26 death sentences were passed. It was not known whether any executions took place.

At talks with officials in December, an Amnesty International delegation to Mongolia raised the issue of the gross neglect of prisoners' welfare which had resulted in deaths by starvation and called on the authorities to take immediate steps to alleviate this situation. Amnesty International continued to call for the abolition of the death penalty.

MOROCCO AND WESTERN SAHARA

Over 50 political prisoners and prisoners of conscience continued to serve long sentences imposed after unfair trials in previous years, although more than 350 political prisoners, including over 130 prisoners of conscience, were released under a royal amnesty. Dozens of prisoners of conscience were arrested and held briefly. Dozens of people were arrested on charges of arms smuggling and armed attacks on behalf of militant Islamist groups. Eight received long prison sentences after unfair trials. Torture and ill-treatment of detainees in *garde à vue* (incommunicado) detention continued to be reported, particularly in Western Sahara. At least four people died in police custody. Hundreds of Sahrawis and Moroccans who had "disappeared" in previous years remained unaccounted for. Over 300 former Sahrawi "disappeared" continued to remain under restrictions in Western Sahara. No executions were carried out and 196 death sentences were commuted.

The UN-sponsored referendum on the future of Western Sahara, originally scheduled for 1992, had still not taken place by the end of the year (see *Amnesty International Reports 1992* to *1994*) and it was postponed until late 1995. Observers from the UN Mission for the Referendum in Western Sahara (MINURSO) remained in place, but freedom of expression, association and movement in Western Sahara remained restricted.

In July the government repealed a 1935 *dahir* (decree) which had been frequently used to sentence prisoners of conscience to up to two years' imprisonment on vague charges such as "disturbing public order".

Among the prisoners of conscience convicted in previous years who were still held at the end of 1994 were 'Abdelkader Sfiri and Ahmed Haou. They were among a group of supporters of the illegal Islamist organization *al-Shabiba al-Islamiya* (Islamic Youth) arrested in 1983 after putting up anti-monarchist posters, distributing leaflets and taking part in demonstrations. In July 1984 they were sentenced to death for plotting to overthrow the monarchy.

Their convictions were based on confessions signed under torture during months of incommunicado detention. Their sentences were commuted to life imprisonment in March 1994. Another prisoner of conscience, 'Abdessalem Yassine, the spiritual leader of the banned Islamist association al-'Adl wa'l-Ihsan (Justice and Charity), remained under house arrest in Salé. He had been held without charge or trial since 1990.

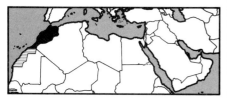

Over 350 political prisoners, including over 130 prisoners of conscience, were released under a royal amnesty in July. Most had been imprisoned after unfair trials in previous years on charges which included offences against state security, membership of illegal organizations, distributing leaflets and disturbing public order. The majority had been convicted on the basis of confessions extracted under torture. They included six people arrested after demonstrations in Bouznika in 1993; people arrested after demonstrations and riots in 1984 and 1990; and supporters of banned Marxist and Islamist organizations (see previous Amnesty International Reports).

Over 30 prisoners of conscience were arrested during 1994, including government critics and peaceful demonstrators. They were sentenced to up to two years' imprisonment, although most sentences were suspended or reduced on appeal to time already served.

Seven Berber activists from the association for Berber culture, Tilili (Freedom), who were also members of the Moroccan Association for Human Rights (AMDH) and the Confédération démocratique du travail (CDT), Democratic Trade Union, were arrested in Errachidia after peaceful demonstrations on 1 May. They had chanted slogans calling for the recognition of Berber as an official language in Morocco. Three were sentenced in May to up to two years' imprisonment on charges of chanting slogans attacking the Constitution, and the other four were acquitted. At the appeal in June the sentences were reduced to

two months' imprisonment.

Political trials continued to fall short of international fair trial standards. For example, 14 members of the Association of Unemployed Graduates arrested in June in Guercif after protesting peacefully about unemployment were sentenced to two years' imprisonment for holding an unauthorized meeting. All of them told the judicial authorities that they had been beaten by police during incommunicado detention, and some reportedly still bore marks and bruises several days later. A medical examination ordered by the Public Prosecutor was never carried out. In July their sentences were reduced to three months' suspended imprisonment.

In Western Sahara detainees were frequently held for up to several months in secret detention. Six Sahrawi women arrested in Laayoune after demonstrations in September 1992 were held incommunicado in secret detention until their release in April 1994. Beatings and torture or ill-treatment of detainees in police custody continued to be widely reported, especially in Western Sahara. Methods of torture which had been routinely used in the past – such as suspension in contorted positions for prolonged periods, electric shocks and suffocation with cloths soaked in chemicals – were again reported.

Torture was also alleged by several Moroccans, Algerians, and French citizens of Moroccan and Algerian origin who were accused of arms smuggling and armed attacks on behalf of Islamist militant groups, including an attack on a hotel in Marrakech during which two people died. According to reports they were visibly bruised when they appeared in court and they alleged that they had been tortured by being suspended from a metal bar in contorted positions and beaten during illegally prolonged garde à vue detention. No investigation was ordered by the courts into their allegations. Eight of them were sentenced in June by the military court in Rabat, the capital, to prison terms varying between five and 20 years' imprisonment; others remained detained awaiting trial; and others were released without charge.

At least four people died in police custody in Khouribga, Ouled Si Bouhia, Sidi Bennour and Salé, allegedly as a result of beatings and ill-treatment. Younes Zerzouri died of head injuries on 17 August

216

in Rabat, a few days after having reportedly been beaten by four policemen in front of his home. No independent investigation was ordered by the authorities into these and other deaths in custody which occurred over the past years, including three deaths in custody in 1993 (see *Amnesty International Report 1994*).

There was no new information on hundreds of Sahrawis and Moroccans who had "disappeared" after arrest since 1975. They included Faraji Mohamed-Salem Bueh-Barca, who "disappeared" in Laayoune in 1976 at the time of a Polisario Front attack, and Abdelhaq Rouissi, a trade union activist who "disappeared" in 1964. More than 300 former Sahrawi "disappeared" who were released in 1991 after up to 16 years in secret detention continued to have their freedom of movement and assembly severely restricted. Former Moroccan "disappeared" who were released from the secret detention centre at Tazmamert in 1991 began receiving monthly payments from the authorities, but hundreds of other former Sahrawi and Moroccan "disappeared" did not benefit from this measure. The families of some of the 34 people who died in Tazmamert between 1973 and 1991 received death certificates, but no inquiry was held into these and other cases of long-term secret detention and deaths in custody.

In March, 196 death sentences were commuted to life imprisonment. Up to 10 other people sentenced to death reportedly awaited a review of their cases by the Supreme Court. No new death sentences were imposed and no executions were carried out.

Amnesty International welcomed the commutation of the death sentences and the amnesty for more than 350 political prisoners. It called on the government to release immediately all remaining prisoners of conscience and all political prisoners convicted after unfair trials unless they were to be promptly retried in full accordance with international fair trial standards, and to shed light on the fate of hundreds of remaining "disappeared". The organization also welcomed the repeal of the 1935 decree, and urged the authorities to bring the Moroccan legal code into line with international standards, in particular to abolish the provisions that allow the imprisonment of prisoners of conscience.

In May Amnesty International published a report, *Morocco: The Pattern of Political Imprisonment Must End*. In August the Minister of Human Rights wrote to Amnesty International commenting on the content and presentation of the report and on Amnesty International's interpretation of the application of specific Moroccan laws. In November the UN Human Rights Committee recommended that Morocco take steps to ensure that past cases of "disappearance", deaths in custody and torture are investigated and that such abuses are prevented from recurring. The Committee also recommended that Morocco take steps to limit the use of the death penalty with a view to abolishing this punishment. Also in November the UN Committee against Torture recommended that Morocco set up a system of systematic monitoring of interrogation procedures in all police stations so as to ensure the protection of detainees.

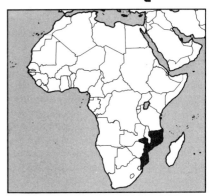

MOZAMBIQUE

Some people were detained without charge for political reasons. There were reports of beatings and floggings by police and soldiers. Two soldiers were convicted of human rights violations carried out in 1993. The opposition *Resistência Nacional Moçambicana* (RENAMO), Mozambique National Resistance, assaulted prisoners.

A second year of peace following the October 1992 General Peace Agreement between the government and RENAMO brought further advances but also some set-backs in the observance of human rights. Mozambique held its first multiparty elections in October. The governing

Frelimo Party and President Joaquim Chissano were returned to power but RENAMO gained 112 seats in the 250-seat parliament.

Under the terms of the 1992 peace agreement, ONUMOZ, the UN Operation in Mozambique, was to oversee the demobilization of soldiers and the collection of weapons. A 30,000-strong army was to be formed of volunteers from the former government and RENAMO armies. However, progress was slow. Soldiers confined to assembly camps grew impatient and between January and October there were mutinies up and down the country to back demands for food, pay and demobilization. Mutinous soldiers took hostages and committed acts of violence resulting in some deaths. Almost 80,000 soldiers, about a quarter of whom were RENAMO soldiers, were demobilized. A unified army of just over 11,500 was formed by December; fewer soldiers than expected enrolled. The UN collected nearly 200,000 weapons, including tens of thousands it found in 67 sites which the government had not declared to the UN and 79 undeclared RENAMO sites. ONUMOZ was unable to investigate reports of other arms caches before its mandate expired in December.

In January the UN decided to increase protection of human rights by raising the number of UN civilian police monitors (CIVPOLS) (see *Amnesty International Report 1994*) from 128 to over 1,100. Their task was to monitor the neutrality of the Mozambican police and also to monitor respect for civil and political rights and liberties in general, including during the election campaign. The monitoring activities of the CIVPOLS were severely restricted in areas formerly under RENAMO control as the Mozambican police were unable to re-establish police posts in these areas. CIVPOLS reported that they investigated 61 complaints of human rights violations. The commissions set up in December 1993 to monitor the police and security services (see *Amnesty International Report 1994*) also investigated allegations of human rights violations by police. The UN expressed regret that the impact of the CIVPOLS was reduced because, although human rights violations were reported to the commissions, this did not result in any corrective or preventive action.

In the second year of peace thousands more refugees returned. A peace movement grew and community leaders appealed for reconciliation and for weapons to be handed in. There was greater freedom of movement but RENAMO continued to restrict access to many areas. Acts of violence including beatings and stone-throwing by supporters of both Frelimo and RENAMO against members of the opposing party increased as the election campaign gained momentum. Almost 90 per cent of registered voters went to the polls despite RENAMO's last-minute announcement that it would boycott the elections. RENAMO then decided to participate in the elections which were extended for a third day. ONUMOZ pronounced the elections free and fair.

There were some reports of people being detained for political reasons. A journalist was illegally detained for five days in May after making a radio program which criticized transport police for forcing people to hand over possessions and for pushing passengers clinging to moving goods trains off the trains in Nampula. The journalist was released uncharged. Eight RENAMO members were arrested in Montepuez, Cabo Delgado province, in September and accused of attempting, apparently for political motives, to commit a murder. They had not been tried by the end of the year.

The commission set up under the peace agreement to monitor the security services reported that Alexandre Niquisse Macassa, a RENAMO soldier captured by government troops in 1989, had been held in Inhambane until August 1994 instead of being released under the terms of the October 1992 amnesty for all political prisoners (see *Amnesty International Report 1993*). The government denied this and said that the prisoner had been released in 1992 and that a release document had been issued by the Inhambane District Prison in August 1994 to enable him to receive the subsidies given to demobilized soldiers. There were reports that at least 10 other captured RENAMO soldiers continued to be held after their prison records were changed to class them as ordinary criminal offenders.

There were numerous reports of police subjecting detainees to beatings and other ill-treatment. In some police cells, conditions amounted to cruel, inhuman or degrading treatment. In one case, detainees were said to have been packed so tightly into a small, filthy police cell that they could not all lie down to sleep. Military and paramilitary personnel were also reported to have beaten and flogged prisoners. Military police in Nampula reportedly arrested a civilian in January, beat him severely and held him in a cell intended for detained soldiers until he paid a bribe to secure his release. Soldiers in Cabo Delgado province reportedly severely beat Santos Mulota Rosa because they suspected him of being a RENAMO member. In September members of the paramilitary Rapid Intervention Police claimed that some fellow police officers had been flogged on the orders of their commander.

Some police and soldiers accused of assaulting prisoners were prosecuted. Two soldiers tried by the Nampula Provincial Military Court in April each received 18-month prison sentences for assaults committed in June and September 1993 respectively. The first, a military counter-intelligence officer, was convicted of illegally arresting and torturing a soldier. The second had ordered a subordinate to administer 15 blows with a piece of wood to an imprisoned soldier, Maurício Mendes Ramucha, who sustained wounds which required surgical treatment.

Reports that a member of the Presidential Guard had "disappeared" or been killed when soldiers suppressed a disturbance at the Magoanine barracks in March 1993 (see *Amnesty International Report 1994*) were found to be incorrect. Agostinho Pedro Riquixa rejoined his family in Nampula in June 1994 after travelling from Maputo on foot and stopping frequently on the way. He said he had fled from the barracks when he saw his colleagues being shot and wounded by the troops sent to put down the disturbance. Agostinho Pedro Riquixa's father, who had made inquiries about his son's whereabouts, had reportedly received an official letter saying that his son had been demobilized before the shooting incident.

The commission set up under the peace agreement to monitor the behaviour of the police said that they had sent a delegation to Mozambique Island in Nampula province to investigate the alleged killing by police of Ossufo Buanamassari in June 1993 (see *Amnesty International Report 1994*) but that as so much time had passed, it had been impossible to gather reliable evidence.

The discovery of 150 skeletons in Gaza province in September was a reminder of the killings of civilians which both sides had carried out during the war. Villagers in the area believed that the victims had been abducted by RENAMO in Chokwe district in 1991. The provincial governor ordered a memorandum to be written but no further action was reported.

Abuses carried out by RENAMO included the arrest and beating of two local government officials whom they suspected of trying to disrupt a conference which RENAMO and other opposition parties held in the coastal town of Xai-Xai in May. The two were taken to a football ground where RENAMO officials beat them and threatened to throw them into the Limpopo river. One sustained a broken rib. The two men were later rescued by police. Non-governmental organizations continued to try to unite families who had been separated by war. They tried to find people such as Sandra Galego, who had been captured by RENAMO in 1986 (see *Amnesty International Report 1994*), and whose whereabouts remained unknown at the end of 1994.

An Amnesty International delegation visited Mozambique in January to make inquiries about the protection of human rights during the peace-keeping operation. In June it published a report, *Mozambique: Monitoring human rights – the task of UN police observers*. It also provided human rights education materials for CIVPOLs and Mozambican police including pocket-sized cards containing 10 basic rules of law enforcement. These materials were included in a human rights training course provided for CIVPOLs in Mozambique by the UN Centre for Human Rights.

MYANMAR

Hundreds of government opponents remained imprisoned, including dozens of prisoners of conscience. Some were detained without trial, but most had been sentenced after unfair trials. At least 17 people were arrested for political reasons, including five prisoners of conscience. Prisoners of conscience and other political prisoners were held in conditions amounting to cruel, inhuman or degrading treatment. Persistent human rights violations continued to be reported

from many parts of the country, with members of ethnic minorities particularly targeted. The violations included: arbitrary seizure of civilians to serve as military porters and labourers; demolition of homes; ill-treatment; and possible extrajudicial executions. Five people were sentenced to death.

The ruling military government, the State Law and Order Restoration Council (SLORC), chaired by General Than Shwe, continued to refuse to convene the People's Assembly elected in 1990. It also continued to suppress political opposition as well as freedom of expression and association.

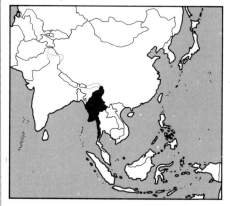

The National Convention, initially convened to draw up a new constitution in early 1993 (see *Amnesty International Report 1994*), reconvened in January and agreed basic principles for administering the state. The principles establish a leading role for the military in politics. They also stipulate that the country's president and vice-presidents must not be married to a foreigner, must not receive support from abroad and must have lived in the country for at least 20 years. It was widely believed that these conditions were designed to exclude Aung San Suu Kyi, the leader of the opposition National League for Democracy (NLD), from the office of president. The National Convention reconvened in September to discuss self-administered areas for ethnic minorities, the legislature, the executive branch and the judiciary.

Four armed opposition groups representing different ethnic minorities – the Karenni National People's Liberation Front, the Kachin Independence Organization, the Kayan New Land Party and the Shan State Nationalities Liberation Organization – signed cease-fire agreements with the SLORC during the year. In May the Burmese armed forces launched an offensive in the Shan State against the Muang Tai army led by Khun Sa. Cease-fire negotiations between the New Mon State Party (NMSP), representing the Mon ethnic minority, and the SLORC were stalled at the end of the year. Human rights violations against members of ethnic minorities continued throughout the year, both in areas where cease-fires were holding and in the context of counter-insurgency operations.

In February the UN Special Rapporteur on Myanmar submitted an extensive report to the UN Commission on Human Rights. In March the Commission adopted without a vote a resolution which extended the mandate of the Special Rapporteur for another year, and called on the Myanmar Government to release Aung San Suu Kyi and other detained political leaders and prisoners immediately and unconditionally. In December the UN General Assembly adopted without a vote a resolution expressing grave concern at the continued human rights violations in Myanmar and requested the Secretary-General to continue his discussions with the SLORC.

Hundreds of political prisoners, including dozens of prisoners of conscience, remained in detention; most had been convicted under laws which criminalized peaceful political activity and allowed unfair trials. Dozens of political prisoners sentenced to long prison terms after unfair trials before military tribunals (which were abolished in 1992) remained in jail.

Prisoner of conscience and co-founder of the NLD, Aung San Suu Kyi, remained under house arrest throughout the year. In February she was allowed to meet a US Congressman, her first visit from someone outside her family for almost five years. Aung San Suu Kyi told him that she had been informed her detention would continue until 1995. Later in the year she was allowed visits from an exiled Burmese Buddhist monk and was taken to meet leading members of the SLORC.

At least 17 people were arrested for political reasons, including five prisoners of conscience. In July Khin Zaw Win, a dentist and graduate student, was arrested at Yangon airport as he tried to board a plane for Singapore, where he was studying. He is a well-known NLD activist and was carrying documents relating to the political opposition movement in Myanmar when arrested. Six other NLD activists were arrested in August. One was later released but the others remained held. Four of them – Daw San San Nwe, a well-known writer and former NLD member, her daughter Ma Myat Mo Mo Tun, and NLD MPs-elect Khin Maung Swe and Sein Hla Oo – were tried with Khin Zaw Win before a civilian tribunal in Insein prison, Yangon, in October. Charges included spreading false information and contacting illegal organizations. All five were sentenced to between seven and 15 years' imprisonment.

More than 70 political prisoners were released during the year. The SLORC did not provide further details, but it was learned that among those freed were two prisoners of conscience: Zargana, a popular satirist imprisoned in 1990, was released in March; and Nai Tun Thein, an MP-elect for the Mon National Democratic Front, was released in August.

Political prisoners were held in poor conditions, sometimes amounting to cruel, inhuman or degrading treatment. A US Congressman visited four prisoners held in Insein prison, Yangon, in February. Their poor health, as described by the Congressman, reflects the lack of adequate medical treatment available to prisoners. Prisoner of conscience Dr Ma Thida, who was sentenced to 20 years' imprisonment in 1993 (see *Amnesty International Report 1994*), said she had a gastric ulcer and endometriosis. Min Ko Naing, former chairperson of the All Burma Federation of Students imprisoned since 1989, had a nervous tremor and appeared to have suffered emotionally from torture and ill-treatment inflicted during the early stages of his detention. Win Tin, a senior member of the NLD arrested in 1989, appeared to have been denied adequate medical care. Win Htein, a prominent NLD member arrested in 1989, was suffering from hypertension and headaches. All four prisoners were being held in solitary confinement in cells with little light. Family visits were restricted to 15 minutes fortnightly.

Human rights violations against members of ethnic minority groups, particularly the Mon, Karen and Shan, continued throughout the year. Soldiers routinely entered villages in ethnic minority areas, burned houses, stole livestock and crops and evicted villagers from their homes. Villagers who refused to move were beaten. Many were seized in their fields or homes, accused of supporting armed insurgents, and tortured. Some were reported to have been extrajudicially executed.

In March, for example, soldiers of the 99th Division approached a Karen village. Most of the villagers fled, but three men who carried on working were taken away and accused of being insurgents with the Karen National Union (KNU). Three young girls, who were also taken but later escaped, reported that the soldiers tortured the three men, beating them and submerging their heads in water. The girls said the soldiers then stabbed the men to death, and slit the throat of the youngest, a 14-year-old boy. The families of the victims found the bodies buried near the village.

Also in March a porter was killed by soldiers from the 339th regiment. His brother described how seven soldiers seized them both for porter duty while they worked in their fields. The soldiers accused the two men of being KNU members. The brother could not respond as he did not understand Burmese, so the soldiers slit his throat and shot him.

Thousands of members of ethnic minorities were arbitrarily seized by the military and forced to serve as porters carrying army supplies, or as unpaid labourers working on construction projects. Porters were held in army custody for periods ranging from a few days to a few months, and some were forced to work for the army for much of the year. They usually received little or no food, and frequently suffered from malnutrition and malaria. Most were not given medical attention and were forced to continue to work, sometimes until they collapsed and were left behind or killed by troops. Old people, pregnant women and children were among those conscripted. One man from Hlaingbwe township, Kayin State, for instance, was forced to be a porter 10 times in a year. When he lagged behind he was beaten on the back with a stick. During a military offensive against the Muang Tai army in May, hundreds of Shan and other civilians were seized by the military to serve as porters.

Thousands of people were forced to work on large construction projects, particularly a railway line between the towns of Ye and Dawei. Villagers were forced to leave their homes and live by the railway until they had completed a quota set by the army. Hundreds of refugees from the Mon State who had been forced to work on the railway fled to Thailand. The Thai authorities forced them to move to Halockhanie camp, which straddles the border with Myanmar (see **Thailand** entry). On 21 July soldiers from the 62nd Infantry Battalion of the Burmese army attacked the camp, burned down 60 houses and took 16 men to act as porters. At the end of the year, one was still missing; he was believed to have been sentenced to two years' imprisonment.

Five people were sentenced to death in January. One man was convicted of murder and possession of heroin. Four men were sentenced to death for murder two days after the crime was committed: their rapid trial may have been unfair. There were no reports of any executions.

The return of Muslim refugees from Bangladesh, under a Memorandum of Understanding signed with the UN High Commissioner for Refugees (see *Amnesty International Report 1994*), resumed during the year, and more than 115,000 had returned by the end of the year.

Amnesty International received no new information about abuses committed by armed opposition groups during the year. The organization remained concerned about the health and whereabouts of two prisoners held by a faction of the All Burma Students Democratic Front, an armed opposition group (see *Amnesty International Report 1994*).

In January Amnesty International published a report, *Myanmar: Human rights developments July to December 1993*. It called on the government to provide adequate medical care for prisoners, and to cease holding political prisoners in solitary confinement. On the fifth anniversary of the detention of Aung San Suu Kyi, Amnesty International called for the immediate and unconditional release of her and all prisoners of conscience. The organization later appealed for the release of the NLD activists arrested in July and August. In November Amnesty International published a major report, *Myanmar: Human rights still denied*, and called on the government to comply with international human rights standards.

In an oral statement to the UN Commis-

sion on Human Rights in March, Amnesty International included reference to its concerns in Myanmar.

NEPAL

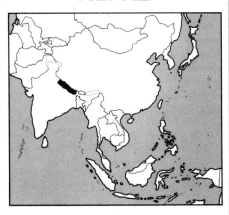

Eleven prisoners of conscience were reportedly detained. Several hundred people, including possible prisoners of conscience, were detained for short periods during a series of nationwide strikes and demonstrations. There were reports of torture and ill-treatment in police custody.

Prime Minister Girija Prasad Koirala resigned in July after losing a key parliamentary vote. King Birendra Bir Bikram Shah Dev dissolved parliament and ordered fresh elections, appointing Girija Prasad Koirala as leader of the interim government. A coalition of left-wing opposition parties, led by the Communist Party of Nepal-United Marxist Leninist (CPN-UML), demanded the dismissal of Girija Prasad Koirala and the reinstatement of parliament under an all-party government. The CPN-UML won parliamentary elections in November by a narrow margin but failed to secure an overall working majority. CPN-UML Chairman Man Mohan Adhikari was appointed Prime Minister.

Eleven Christians, one a Nepali national and the others ethnic Nepali refugees from Bhutan, were arrested in Ilam District in August on suspicion of proselytizing, an offence under Nepali law. They were prisoners of conscience. They were brought to trial at the district court in December but the outcome was not known by the end of the year.

Several hundred people were arrested

in July and August during nationwide strikes and demonstrations called by the alliance of left-wing opposition parties in support of their demands for the reinstatement of parliament. Some of the demonstrators threw stones and attacked public transport facilities. Most of those arrested, some of whom were possible prisoners of conscience, were detained for short periods and then released. According to a Home Ministry spokesperson, about 300 people were arrested during strikes called between 20 and 24 July, of whom 42 were charged under the Public Offences and Penalties Act, 1970, and 13 under the Anti-State Crimes and Penalties Act, 1989. Human rights groups maintained that, between 14 and 19 August, over 2,000 people were detained nationwide, although police reports put the figure at about 600. All those arrested and detained in July and August were reportedly released.

There were several reports of torture and ill-treatment in police custody, although ill-treatment of detained demonstrators was not reported on the scale it had been in previous years.

Laxman Rai, a farmer who was tried in June on charges of cutting down trees belonging to the Forestry Department, was reportedly tortured by forest guards at the Forest Ranger's offices in Kerakha. He had been arrested at Bidhakhola, Jhapa District, in early October 1993. He was beaten with a bamboo stick, including on the palms of his hands and the soles of his feet, and pins were stuck under his fingernails. Laxman Rai was reportedly found not guilty and released unconditionally.

Seventeen people who were detained in Khalanga, Pyuthan District, in May during a student demonstration were allegedly tortured in police custody and denied medical treatment. All were charged under the Public Offences and Penalties Act, but were reportedly not brought before the Chief District Officer within 24 hours of their arrest, as required by law. Seven of those arrested were reportedly released within days, but the fate of the remaining 10 was not known by the end of the year.

Bamdev Devkota, a student, was arrested during demonstrations on 20 July in Kathmandu, the capital, on suspicion of causing damage to a vehicle. He was taken to the Mahendra Police Club where he was reportedly beaten severely by police

officers, given electric shocks to his right hand and denied food for two days. During his six days' detention, he was reportedly not brought before a magistrate or informed of the charges against him.

Police officers remained immune from prosecution. There was not one case reported in 1993 or 1994 in which a police officer suspected of being responsible for torture or ill-treatment was prosecuted.

The Supreme Court heard a *habeas corpus* petition filed on behalf of Pravakar Subedi, a student who "disappeared" in Kathmandu in June 1993 (see *Amnesty International Report 1994*). The court ordered the police to identify a man alleged to be Pravakar Subedi shown in a photograph being arrested by four policemen. The Inspector General of Police responded by denying that the person in the photograph was Pravakar Subedi. The Supreme Court ordered all four policemen to be produced in court. The outcome of the case was unknown at the end of the year.

Amnesty International wrote to the government to express concern about reports of torture in police custody at Pyuthan, Kathmandu and Jhapa but had received no response by the end of the year. It urged the government to ensure that all reports of torture by police were promptly, thoroughly and independently investigated.

Amnesty International submitted information about its concerns regarding torture and ill-treatment in police custody to the UN Committee against Torture in April when Nepal submitted its first report under Article 19 of the UN Convention against Torture and Other Cruel, Inhuman or Degrading Treatment or Punishment. In October Amnesty International drew the attention of the UN Human Rights Committee to its concerns about unlawful killings in 1993 (see *Amnesty International Report 1994*) and about torture.

NETHERLANDS
(KINGDOM OF THE)

There were further reports of ill-treatment by prison guards and police officers in 1993 in the Netherlands Antilles, a Caribbean country forming part of the Kingdom of the Netherlands.

It emerged during 1994 that former

prisoners from Pointe Blanche prison in St Maarten had alleged that they had been beaten by prison guards in 1993. The former inmates claimed that they had been beaten with clubs and fists by at least three prison guards and kicked with steel-capped shoes. One alleged that following beatings he had severe scarring on his right arm and another claimed that he had a scar on his neck where a prison officer had shot him. Following these reports of ill-treatment, the Attorney General of the Netherlands Antilles visited the prison. He stated in a press interview that the prison director was conducting an investigation and claimed that over the past year police officers and prison guards had been convicted of ill-treating people in their custody.

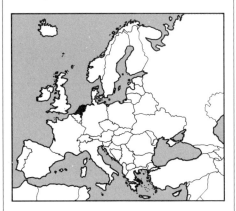

In December 1993 Cuthbert Athanaze, a bus driver, stated that he had been threatened and physically ill-treated by police officers following a dispute over a parking offence. He claimed that he was arrested on the bus, handcuffed and assaulted in front of witnesses and assaulted again at the police station. A judicial inquiry was opened. One officer admitted punching the handcuffed man in the left eye, which later required three stitches. The Public Prosecutor concluded that the officers had, for the most part, acted correctly, but the officer who admitted punching the bus driver was severely reprimanded.

Amnesty International sought information from the government about the progress of inquiries into these allegations of ill-treatment. In May the Public Prosecutor replied with details of his investigation and conclusions in the case of Cuthbert Athanaze. No reply had been received by the end of 1994 regarding the

investigation into the alleged beatings at Pointe Blanche prison.

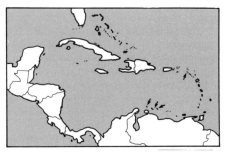

Amnesty International also asked the Attorney General to supply details of the prosecution of police officers and prison guards mentioned in his press interview. No reply had been received by the end of the year.

NEW ZEALAND

Prison officers dismissed in 1993 for alleged ill-treatment of prisoners were not prosecuted.

In February New Zealand passed the Human Rights Act, 1993, which replaced the Race Relations Act, 1971, and the Human Rights Commission Act. The new act widened the grounds of unlawful discrimination. For example, the act protects those who have AIDS or HIV infection from discrimination. It also prohibits discrimination based on disability or a person's sexual orientation.

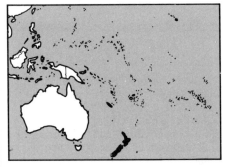

Six of the 12 prison officers from Mangaroa Prison who had been dismissed after an official investigation by the Department of Justice in 1993 in connection with ill-treatment of prisoners (see *Amnesty International Report 1994*) were reinstated to

224

serve at other prisons. The other six officers reportedly opted not to accept new jobs. All of them were reportedly paid lump sums of between $12,000 and $35,000 each. The reinstatements and the money were reported to be part of a secret agreement between the prison officers and the Department of Justice to stop personal grievance actions by officers against their dismissal. However, the Department was reported to have referred the findings of the internal inquiry into ill-treatment in Mangaroa Prison to the police for possible further investigation.

In October Amnesty International wrote to the government of Prime Minister James Bolger seeking further information about the reinstatement of the dismissed prison officers from Mangaroa Prison. The organization also asked about the implementation of prison reforms on which the government had embarked. It asked in particular about the recommendations of the Ministerial Inquiry into Management Practices at Mangaroa Prison relating to inmate complaints procedures and training and recruitment of new prison officers.

In a reply to Amnesty International in December the Minister of Justice confirmed that six of the 12 former officers from Mangaroa Prison had been reinstated at other prisons and that the remaining six had reached settlements which did not involve their re-employment as prison staff. He also gave details of various reforms which had already been implemented or were planned for 1995 concerning prison inmates' rights and complaints procedures, staff training and recruitment, and management training practices.

NICARAGUA

Numerous cases of ill-treatment by police were reported. There was an attempt on the life of a trade unionist in circumstances suggesting official involvement. A military court dismissed charges against nine members of the military accused in connection with the killing of a youth in 1990.

Amid growing political divisions between and within the government and the opposition *Frente Sandinista de Liberación Nacional* (FSLN), Sandinista National Liberation Front, military and constitutional reforms were passed by the National Assembly. In August the National Assembly approved the new Military Code aimed at strengthening civilian control over the armed forces. The new Military Code would, among other things, allow civilian courts to try military personnel charged with common criminal offences. A draft bill which would partially reform the 1987 Constitution drafted under the previous FSLN government was presented in October. The draft bill would modify 149 of the Constitution's 195 articles.

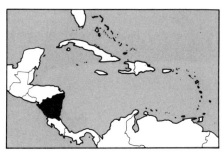

In March the Supreme Court rejected an appeal challenging the constitutionality of Article 204 of the Penal Code, concluding that it did not violate any of the rights guaranteed in the Constitution. The ruling upheld changes to the Penal Code introduced in 1992 to penalize homosexuality. Article 204 states: "anyone who induces, promotes, propagandizes or practices in scandalous form sexual intercourse between persons of the same sex commits the crime of sodomy" (see *Amnesty International Reports 1993* and *1994*). The law could result in the prosecution and imprisonment of prisoners of conscience. Its broad terms could permit the prosecution of individuals solely for their homosexuality, for activities such as advocating lesbian and gay rights, imparting health information concerning sexuality or having homosexual relations in circumstances which are not criminal if they involve heterosexuals.

Killings and abductions by groups of former rebels and former army combatants continued to be reported, linked partly to the government's failure to comply with demobilization provisions agreed at the end of the civil war. There was continued violence by a group of former rebel combatants in the north, who claimed that the government had breached agreements for the group's demobilization signed in April. A report by the *Ejército Popular Sandinista* (EPS), Sandinista Popular Army, covering the first five months of the year, indicated that military operations to combat rebel groups in the north had left nearly 200 people dead and over 100 injured: the victims included civilians as well as irregular troops and members of the army.

There were numerous complaints of ill-treatment of detainees by the police. The non-governmental human rights organization *Centro Nicaragüense de Derechos Humanos* (CENIDH), Nicaraguan Centre for Human Rights, recorded 20 complaints of human rights violations, including ill-treatment, in the first half of 1994. Although all the cases were submitted to the *Inspectoría General de la Policía Nacional*, the monitoring body of the National Police, no investigations were apparently initiated. Police reportedly ill-treated people during strikes protesting against government economic measures. In January scores of strikers were beaten by police during a transport strike in the capital, Managua. Many people were briefly detained, among them 26 juveniles and several people not participating in the strike.

In June, 12 members of the *Federación de Trabajadores de Comunicaciones Enrique Smidth*, Telecommunications and Postal Workers' Federation, were arrested and ill-treated by members of the *Brigada Especial de la Policía Nacional*, National Police Special Brigade. The trade unionists were demonstrating in Managua against the privatization of the telecommunications and postal services. They were allegedly beaten and kicked during their arrest and one, Adonis Montiel, required hospital treatment for internal injuries. All 12 were released a few hours later.

A trade union leader actively involved in opposition to the government's economic measures was attacked by unknown assailants in circumstances suggesting official involvement. In April trade union leader Roberto González Gaitán, a member of the National Board of the *Confederación Síndical Central Sandinista*, Sandinista Central Union Confederation, was shot at by unidentified armed assailants who fired at the car in which he was travelling. He lost control of the vehicle and crashed against a tree, suffering concussion and bruises. The attack was allegedly related to a public declaration made a few hours earlier by the head of the National Police, who described Roberto González Gaitán as a "dangerous individual and a destabilizing influence". A police investigation was initiated.

In June the military court of first instance dismissed charges against the head of the armed forces and eight of his military escorts. They were accused of carrying out or covering up the killing of Jean Paul Genie Lacayo, a 17-year-old shot dead on the Managua-Masaya highway (see *Amnesty International Reports 1993* and *1994*). The military court ruled that there was insufficient admissible evidence against the accused. The military court also ruled that the case should remain open until responsibility for the crime was established. In August an appeal to the Military Appeals Court against the ruling was passed on to the Supreme Court, whose decision was still pending at the end of the year. At the end of the year the case was being considered by the Inter-American Court on Human Rights.

In May Amnesty International wrote to President Violeta Chamorro expressing concern that the case of Jean Paul Genie Lacayo was under military jurisdiction, because military jurisdiction does not offer guarantees of due process and impartiality, and permits undue influence by the army high command at the appeals stage. In July the authorities sent Amnesty International the ruling of the military court of first instance. In November Amnesty International made public its concerns in the light of the ruling.

In October Amnesty International published a report, *Nicaragua: Article 204: Legalizing the repression of homosexuality*, which called on the government to guarantee that Article 204 would never be used to prosecute people solely for their homosexuality. It also urged the authorities to give serious consideration to amending or repealing Article 204, to ensure that the Penal Code did not interfere with fundamental rights.

226

NIGER

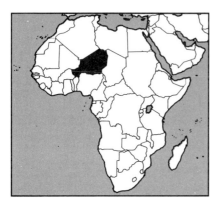

Dozens of members of the Tuareg minority ethnic group were detained without charge or trial, one for six months. Many were prisoners of conscience. Most were beaten and some were tortured; two reportedly died in custody as a result. There were reports of possible extrajudicial executions.

Throughout the year the authorities faced strikes by civil servants and students seeking financial compensation for the devaluation of the currency in January. In March a student was killed in violent clashes between students and the security forces on the university campus in the capital, Niamey.

There was conflict in the north of the country involving armed Tuareg political groups. From the beginning of the year onwards, tension increased in the north following the decision in December 1993 by one of the Tuareg armed organizations, the *Front de libération de Tamoust* (FLT), Liberation Front of Tamoust, not to renew the truce signed in June 1993 with the government of President Mahmane Ousmane. The rebels resumed attacks and at least two civilians were killed in January near Agadès, the main town in the north, when armed Tuaregs attacked a convoy of vehicles under military escort.

In October the government and the *Coordination de la résistance armée* (CRA), Coordination of the Armed Resistance, the coordinating body of all armed Tuareg groups, signed a peace agreement in Ouagadougou in neighbouring Burkina Faso. Both parties agreed to the creation of an international commission of inquiry into human rights abuses committed by the army and rebel Tuareg groups, but it was not clear who was to be asked to carry out the investigations.

Five people detained briefly in Niamey appeared to be prisoners of conscience. In January four students were arrested during a meeting. They were subsequently tried and each received a six-month suspended sentence for assault and battery against members of the security forces. There was apparently no evidence that they had been involved in acts of violence. Also in January the secretary general of the *Union des scolaires du Niger* (USN), Niger's Union of School Pupils, Boubacar Siddo, was arrested when he tried to visit the four detained students. He was accused of inciting violence but was released a week later after a court found no grounds for the charge against him.

Dozens of Tuareg detained during the year were prisoners of conscience, arrested solely on account of their ethnic origin. Although Tuareg armed groups resorted to violence, these prisoners were not known to have used or advocated violence and appeared to be detained as part of a policy of reprisals. For example, in August, two days after a violent attack by rebels in Tchirozerine, the army arrested some 60 civilians of Tuareg origin in Timia, most of whom were women and children. After three days of detention, all the detainees were released except three (see below). Dozens of others, briefly detained by the army solely because of their Tuareg origin, fled their villages and camps to take refuge in towns.

Although most Tuareg detainees were held for only short periods, one, Assalek Ag Ibrahim, arrested in Agadès in May, was held for six months and released uncharged in November. No reasons were given for his detention, but it appeared he was suspected of contact with the rebels.

Five nationals from neighbouring Nigeria were detained without trial throughout the year. All were members of the Movement for the Advancement of Democracy (MAD), which organized the hijacking of an airplane in October 1993 at Niamey airport in pursuit of demands for greater democracy in Nigeria. Four were arrested on the airplane and charged with hijacking. One other, Jerry Youssouf, suspected of complicity, was arrested in Nigeria in November 1993 and secretly transferred to custody in Niger where he was held uncharged for over a year. In June 1994 a court in Niamey ruled that there was no reason for his continued detention but he remained in prison and was finally charged in December with complicity in hijacking.

Many Tuareg detained by the army or gendarmerie were beaten and some were tortured. In May, five Tuaregs arrested in Agadès were severely beaten and two of them died in custody, apparently as a result. There was no official investigation into the cause of these deaths. The three others were apparently still held without charge or trial at the end of the year. In August, after a rebel attack near Tchirozerine, the army arrested dozens of Tuareg civilians. They were severely beaten and one of them, according to a medical certificate, had his ribs broken. The Tuareg detained in Timia in August were reportedly severely beaten and two pregnant women among them suffered miscarriages.

There were reports of possible extrajudicial executions. Three Tuareg men arrested in Timia in August – Ilias Ahwal, Ilias Algabit and Adam Hamane – were killed by soldiers apparently in retaliation for the killing of three soldiers by rebels some days previously.

At the beginning of 1994, details were received of two possible extrajudicial executions which had occurred near Agadès in December 1993: Warghiss Founta and Karbey Moussa, both market gardeners, were shot dead by soldiers at the oasis of Tchin-Tibizguit, six kilometres from Agadès, when they were transporting vegetables to the market. The killings appeared to be in reprisal for the theft of a vehicle some hours before in Agadès, allegedly by armed rebels. The Mayor of Agadès lodged a complaint about these killings but no judicial investigation was known to have been initiated.

Amnesty International publicly expressed its concern that some prisoners were detained by the security forces simply on account of their Tuareg ethnic origin and in the absence of any evidence that they were connected with armed groups. Amnesty International was also concerned at reports of beatings and torture and the failure of the authorities to account for their actions. It urged the government to investigate all allegations of torture, deaths in custody and extrajudicial executions and to bring those responsible to justice.

NIGERIA

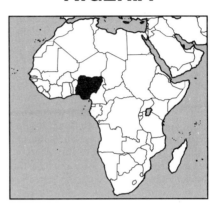

Hundreds of pro-democracy activists were arrested; many of them were prisoners of conscience, some of whom were still in custody at the end of the year. An estimated 600 people from the Ogoni ethnic group, many of whom were also prisoners of conscience, were arbitrarily detained without charge or trial. Many detainees were badly beaten and held in life-threatening prison conditions. At least 11 soldiers arrested in 1990 continued to be held in administrative detention. At least 50 people were reportedly extrajudicially executed by the security forces in Ogoniland. There was a dramatic increase in the use of the death penalty, with at least 100 people publicly executed.

The military government headed by General Sani Abacha continued to prohibit all political activity. In May the newly formed National Democratic Coalition (NADECO), comprising former civilian and military political leaders, demanded that the military government hand over power to the winner of the annulled presidential elections in 1993, Chief Moshood K.O. Abiola. NADECO leaders and Moshood Abiola were arrested and charged with treason. Pro-democracy protests in major southern cities led to widespread arrests and clashes with police in which dozens of people were killed. Trade unionists took prolonged strike action which paralysed parts of the country and threatened oil exports, Nigeria's main foreign currency earner.

Following the murder in May of four leading members of the Ogoni community in Rivers State in the southeast, there were reports of extrajudicial executions by the security forces and mass arrests among supporters of an Ogoni organization which campaigned against environmental damage by oil companies. Journalists, human rights and environmental observers who attempted to monitor events in Ogoniland were obstructed by the authorities; some were detained.

In September the government promulgated decrees which extended already draconian powers of detention, formally proscribed 15 newspapers and journals, dissolved the executives of the oil unions and the Nigerian Labour Congress, and removed the jurisdiction of the courts to challenge government authority and actions. The Attorney General was dismissed for criticizing the decrees. In October a further decree specifically removed the power of the courts to issue writs of *habeas corpus* or any other orders to the authorities to produce detainees before them.

Hundreds of people were detained for political reasons during the year. Most were prisoners of conscience and were released without charge.

In April three journalists on *Newswatch* magazine were detained after publication of an article critical of the government. A week later they and three others were charged with sedition and criminal intent to cause fear, alarm and disaffection, but the next day the charges were withdrawn and they were released.

Hundreds of members of the Ogoni community, many of whom were prisoners of conscience, were reportedly detained without charge or trial. In the weeks after the murder of four leading members of the Ogoni community on 21 May, soldiers arrested Ogoni indiscriminately and detained them at Bori military camp in Port Harcourt or at Kpor in Ogoniland. Most were subsequently released without charge but about 30 remained in incommunicado detention without charge or trial at the end of the year. They included prisoners of conscience Ken Saro-Wiwa, a writer, and Ledum Mitee, a lawyer, both leaders of the Movement for the Survival of the Ogoni People and for-

mer prisoners of conscience, who had been briefly detained in January apparently to stop their political campaigning. In a press conference, the authorities accused them of inciting youths to murder the Ogoni leaders. Initially reported to be held in leg irons, Ken Saro-Wiwa was denied hospital treatment prescribed by a military doctor for a heart complaint.

In June NADECO leaders who called for the military government to stand down were arrested. Six former members of the disbanded Senate, including Ameh Ebute, former President of the Senate, were arrested and charged with "treasonable felony", which carries life imprisonment. They were granted bail in July but five were rearrested in September and briefly redetained. Four others arrested and charged with treasonable felony were also released on bail. Among them was Dr Beko Ransome-Kuti, President of the Campaign for Democracy and the Committee for the Defence of Human Rights, who was detained in June and again in September. None of their trials had taken place by the end of the year. An earlier case of treasonable felony against Dr Ransome-Kuti and several other human rights activists, including the lawyer Chief Gani Fawehinmi, was struck out by the courts in January for lack of evidence.

Chief Moshood Abiola was arrested on 23 June at his home in Lagos by hundreds of armed police after he had declared himself head of state. He was detained incommunicado in harsh conditions and moved to several different places of detention. The government ignored two orders in June by the High Court in Lagos to produce him before the court and justify his detention. On 6 July Moshood Abiola was brought before a Federal High Court in Abuja, the capital. This court was appointed by the military government especially to try his case and could not be considered independent of government influence. He was charged with treason and refused bail despite his ill-health. On several occasions the authorities ignored court orders that he should be given regular access to his family and lawyers and continued to deny him hospital treatment. In November the Federal Court of Appeal in Kaduna granted his release on bail; the authorities did not release him and in December the court allowed a stay of execution of the order on security grounds pending an appeal to the Supreme Court. His trial had not started by the end of the year.

In August at least 40 people, mostly students, were detained following violent protests in and around Benin City. Some were reportedly beaten. In October, 12 were charged with criminal offences, including armed robbery and arson, and released on bail. Some appeared to have been prisoners of conscience.

Further NADECO leaders, including Chief Anthony Enahoro, a 71-year-old former government minister, were among 20 pro-democracy activists detained in Lagos and Kaduna in August and September. Some were released without charge but the government said that he and others were being held for "economic sabotage" and acts prejudicial to state security. In December Chief Enahoro was released unconditionally. Chief Frank Ovie Kokori, Secretary General of the National Union of Petroleum and Natural Gas Workers, and three other oil workers' leaders were reportedly still detained incommunicado and without charge at the end of the year.

At least 11 soldiers arrested after a coup attempt in April 1990 continued to be held in incommunicado detention, apparently under a decree allowing indefinitely renewable administrative detention.

Six prisoners who had been sentenced to death after an unfair trial by a special court were unconditionally released in March. Major-General Zamani Lekwot and five other members of the Kataf ethnic group had been convicted of murder in February 1993, in connection with religious riots in Kaduna State in 1992, by a Civil Disturbances Special Tribunal (see *Amnesty International Reports 1993* and *1994*). In August 1993 their death sentences had been commuted.

Many of those arrested during the year were reportedly beaten and held incommunicado in harsh conditions – with inadequate food, over-crowded and insanitary cells and no washing facilities, exercise or fresh air. In late June at least 60 Ogoni boys and youths were being held in two small, bare cells with no toilet facilities in Bori military camp. They had been arrested in early June and reportedly beaten.

At least 50 Ogoni were believed to have been killed and many wounded by the security forces in late May and June when soldiers reportedly attacked towns and villages in Ogoniland. Troops apparently fired at random, killed, assaulted and raped civilians, and destroyed homes. The twin villages of Uegwere and Bo-ue were reportedly attacked at night several times between 4 and 8 June: Nbari Vopnu, Lebari Eete and eight other people, including a 10-year-old boy, were reportedly killed. In the village of Buan, a pregnant woman, Leyira Piri, was apparently shot dead and six other people critically wounded. Other villages where people were shot dead by soldiers included Yeghe and Okwali. The military commander reportedly acknowledged that his men had killed six youths, but there was no judicial inquiry into these deaths nor into the many others alleged to have occurred in Ogoniland in 1993 and 1994 as a result of ethnic conflict and security operations.

Dozens of people were reportedly killed by police during pro-democracy demonstrations in the cities, for example, during riots in Lagos and Ibadan on 18 July. Some were reported to have been unlawfully killed – they were not involved in violent activities or posing a threat to the police. Following violent protests in Benin City and Ekpoma in Edo State in August, in which the homes and properties of government supporters were destroyed, at least four and possibly more people were allegedly killed by the security forces.

There was a dramatic increase in the use of the death penalty. The authorities were apparently reinstating a policy of mass executions: hundreds of prisoners had been executed under military governments in the mid-1980s, but none in the two years leading up to the 1993 presidential elections, when civilian state governors had been in office.

During the year, at least 100 people were executed. Executions took place in Akwa Ibom, Borno Enugu, Imo, Kano and Lagos states. Execution was by firing-squad, and executions were frequently held in public before large crowds. Most of those executed had been convicted by Robbery and Firearms Tribunals, special courts which do not guarantee a fair trial and from which there is no right of appeal.

Between February and June, 30 prisoners convicted of armed robbery were publicly executed in Akwa Ibom State, some

230

within days of being sentenced. On 24 May, four prisoners, including a woman, Elizabeth Oleru, were executed before large crowds at a race course in Kano. On 2 August, 38 prisoners were executed before a crowd of 20,000 people in Enugu, in the southeast. One of them, Simeon Agbo, survived and stood up an hour later, bleeding profusely, to protest his innocence and plead for water. Police reportedly threw him onto a lorryload of corpses and his subsequent fate was unknown.

Amnesty International urged the government to release pro-democracy activists and members of the Ogoni ethnic group who were prisoners of conscience. It also urged the government to end the practice of indiscriminate arrests and detention without charge or trial. Amnesty International called for immediate measures to be taken to protect the Ogoni people from attacks, and urged a thorough investigation into reports of extrajudicial executions in Rivers State. Amnesty International expressed its concern about the use of mass, public executions, and urged the commutation of all death sentences.

In November Amnesty International published a report, *Nigeria: Military government clampdown on opposition,* detailing one of the most serious human rights crises Nigeria had faced for decades. In December Amnesty International delegates visited Nigeria, but were denied access to detained prisoners of conscience and were not allowed to carry out independent investigations in Ogoniland. Amnesty International called on other governments to use their influence with the Nigerian authorities to bring an end to the human rights violations taking place in Nigeria.

OMAN

Hundreds of suspected members of an Islamist organization were arrested. Most were released but around 160, including possible prisoners of conscience, were sentenced to terms of imprisonment after an unfair trial.

In June the Ministry of the Interior announced that representation at its *Majlis al-Shura,* Consultative Council, was to be increased from 59 to 80 members. The Council has no legislative powers and is not a decision-making body. Its members are appointed by the Head of State, Sultan Qaboos Bin Sa'id.

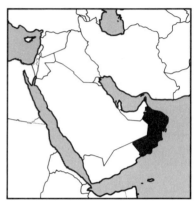

In May and June hundreds of people were arrested reportedly for setting up an illegal Islamist organization and distributing leaflets criticizing the authorities for hosting a conference attended by Israeli delegates. Those arrested included Omani, Jordanian and Egyptian nationals. Most of them were reported to be businessmen, university lecturers and civil servants. Many were released by the end of August, but around 160 remained held incommunicado in al-Ramis prison in Muscat, including four employees of Petroleum Development Oman, two Under-Secretaries in the Ministries of Agriculture and Commerce, a former ambassador to the USA, and a well-known Omani religious scholar, Salim al-Ghazali. His two brothers, Mohammad and Hamed, were reportedly held for several weeks before their release.

Those still detained were tried before the State Security Court and in November the court pronounced judgment. All the defendants were found guilty: the sentences ranged from the death sentence to varying terms of imprisonment with a minimum of three years. The death sentences were reported to have been commuted to prison terms by the Head of State. The trial was apparently conducted in secret and there were fears that defendants may not have had access to lawyers of their own choosing. No further information was available as to the exact charges of which they were convicted, their sentences, or whether they had the right to appeal before a higher court against their convictions and sentences. At the end of the year they were imprisoned in al-Ramis prison.

Sa'id Salim 'Ali, known as Abu Sakha, who had been arrested in 1993 following his return from studying in Kiev, Ukraine, reportedly remained in detention during the first half of the year. No further information was available.

In March Amnesty International wrote to the Minister of the Interior seeking clarification of the legal situation of Sa'id Salem 'Ali and urging his release if he was held as a prisoner of conscience.

In September Amnesty International wrote again to the Minister of the Interior requesting specific information about the hundreds of people arrested in May and June. In November the organization wrote to the Minister of Justice expressing concern about their trial. No response had been received by the end of the year.

PAKISTAN

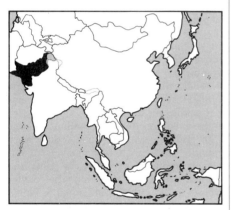

Several dozen prisoners of conscience charged with blasphemy were detained for weeks. Dozens of possible prisoners of conscience were among hundreds of political prisoners arrested by the army in Sindh and by police in other parts of the country. Torture continued to be widespread, reportedly resulting in at least 62 deaths. Dozens of sentences of flogging were carried out. Bar fetters continued to be used in jails. At least 35 extrajudicial executions were reported, some of them in staged "encounters" with the police. Thirty-two people were sentenced to death and one execution was reported.

Violent conflict between different ethnic and religious groups and political par-

ties persisted throughout the year. At least 700 people were deliberately and arbitrarily killed by such groups in Karachi alone. In November the government of Prime Minister Benazir Bhutto ended the army operation which had begun in mid-1992 in Sindh to combat criminal and political violence.

In February the Supreme Court cancelled special regulations governing the Provincially Administered Tribal Areas in North-West Frontier Province. Subsequently, a popular movement in Malakand in the province demanded the introduction of Islamic law. When the government conceded the demand but then failed to introduce it, activists in Malakand took dozens of people hostage to enforce their demands. Paramilitary troops were deployed in force in November to stop the uprising.

The governmental Human Rights Cell, established in December 1993 to monitor and investigate human rights violations and to recommend action against perpetrators, began its work.

The March 1994 deadline set by the Supreme Court for the completion of the separation of the judiciary from the executive was not met. Appeals by the governments of Sindh and Punjab provinces for an extension of the deadline were rejected. In June the Law Minister asked the provincial governments to complete the process within nine months.

A constitutional amendment which had in 1991 empowered the government to establish Special Courts for Speedy Trial for a period of three years (see *Amnesty International Report 1992*) lapsed in July and the related act was formally repealed by presidential ordinance in November. The Qisas and Diyat Ordinance which permits forms of cruel, inhuman or degrading punishment, including judicial amputation, was periodically re-promulgated with minor changes.

The government announced procedural changes intended to curb the abuse of the law against blasphemy which carries a mandatory death penalty. However, no concrete legislative measures were taken.

More than a dozen Christians and Ahmadis were in detention at the end of 1994 charged with blasphemy solely for exercising their religious beliefs peacefully. They were prisoners of conscience. During the year over 100 Ahmadis were

232

charged with various religious offences and detained for weeks. Over 130 Ahmadis faced charges of blasphemy under Section 295C of the Penal Code, which carries a mandatory death penalty for "defiling" the name of the prophet Mohammad. One of them, Dr Muhammad Akhtar Majoka, was arrested on 22 February for allegedly inviting others to watch a television program featuring the exiled head of the Ahmadiyya community. Police later added charges under Section 295C although there appeared to be no evidence to support the charges. He was released on bail on 12 March. His trial began in September.

Five Ahmadi journalists, all prisoners of conscience, were detained on 7 February for a month for publishing articles in which they allegedly "posed as Muslims" and "thereby injured the religious feelings of Muslims". They were subsequently charged with blasphemy under Section 295C. Their trial had not begun by the end of 1994.

Hundreds of people, mostly members of the *Mohajir Qaumi Mahaz* (MQM), Mohajir Qaumi Movement, were arrested during the army operation in Sindh. Dozens of them may have been prisoners of conscience. When MQM activists could not be found, their friends or relatives were arrested.

Several members of Sindhi political parties continued to be detained. Among them was prisoner of conscience G. M. Syed, the 92-year-old Sindhi nationalist leader, who remained under house arrest on charges of sedition throughout the year (see *Amnesty International Reports 1993* and *1994*).

On several occasions when opposition parties, particularly the Pakistan Muslim League (*Nawaz*), announced plans for mass demonstrations, the government imposed a ban on public assembly and arrested hundreds of participants defying the ban. Most were released within days, often without charge, but dozens were detained for weeks under the Maintenance of Public Order Ordinance. Some may have been prisoners of conscience.

Four Ahmadis, who had been arrested in 1984, falsely accused of murder and sentenced to 25 years' imprisonment by a military court (see *Amnesty International Report 1994*), were released in March following their acquittal by the Lahore High Court which found that their conviction had been unlawful.

In November Gul Masih, a Christian prisoner of conscience arrested in December 1991 and sentenced to death for blasphemy in November 1992 solely on the evidence of the complainant, was acquitted on appeal (see *Amnesty International Reports 1993* and *1994*).

Torture, including rape in police, military and judicial custody, continued to be widespread and resulted in at least 62 deaths. For example, Murad was arrested near Turbat, Balochistan province, on 24 July by the paramilitary Mekran Scouts and the Anti-Narcotics Task Force, apparently in place of a suspected drugtrafficker. The following day, the Mekran Scouts delivered his body to the Turbat hospital. A district administrator told the investigating Human Rights Commission of Pakistan, a non-governmental organization, that Murad had been tortured to death by the Mekran Scouts. A judicial inquiry was set up but the law enforcement agencies refused to cooperate. Murad's nephew lodged a complaint against the alleged perpetrators but then had two criminal complaints registered against himself, apparently to prevent him pursuing the complaint.

The police rarely investigated charges brought against law enforcement personnel, although some police officers were prosecuted for illegal detentions or torture. However, very few convictions were reported and the punishments were not always properly executed. In 1993 the Supreme Court had confirmed the conviction of a Deputy Superintendent of Police for torturing a prisoner and increased his sentence from a fine to six months' imprisonment. However, the policeman was not arrested until June 1994 after the case was raised in the Punjab assembly. A judicial team which paid a surprise visit to the District Jail, Faisalabad, Punjab province, in July found that the policeman was allowed to go home every night and still occupied government quarters.

In September the Sindh High Court noted with concern that a judicial inquiry held to establish whether police from Kharadar police station were responsible for a death in custody appeared to have been deliberately misleading. The inquiry had established that Nazir Ahmed had probably died as a result of torture but had failed to invoke relevant sections of the Penal Code. The High Court ordered the trial court to amend the charges accordingly.

Dozens of sentences of flogging continued to be imposed and carried out in jails. In September, two men were sentenced to 10 lashes each by a tribal *jirga* (council of elders) in the Khyber Agency for alcohol consumption which is punishable under tribal Islamic law. The punishment was carried out in public.

A sentence of judicial amputation of right hands and left feet of three men convicted of robbery in 1992, confirmed by the Supreme Court in December 1993, was not carried out during the year.

Prisoners and detainees awaiting trial continued to be kept for weeks in their cells in bar fetters and cross-bar fetters. This was despite the 1993 ruling by the Sindh High Court that the use of bar fetters was inconsistent with Article 14 of the Constitution and with the injunctions of Islam. International standards as well as Pakistani law only permit the use of instruments of restraint in strictly limited circumstances and for limited periods. The prohibition of the use of fetters was stayed in April pending the Supreme Court's ruling on an appeal against the High Court's decision, which was lodged by the Sindh government.

Several people, including political activists, were extrajudicially executed. On 3 May, five young MQM activists were reportedly arrested by police, the paramilitary Rangers and army personnel, blindfolded and taken to a police clerk's house where they were shot dead. Official sources said that five "dangerous criminals" had been killed in an "encounter" with law enforcement personnel, but human rights groups investigating the incident stated that all the evidence supported the local residents' view that they had been deliberately killed.

Dozens of people were alleged to have been deliberately and arbitrarily killed by militant groups because of their ethnic or religious identity; the government failed to investigate the incidents or prosecute the perpetrators. On 5 April Manzoor Masih, a Christian charged with blasphemy, was shot dead by religious militants in Lahore. Police arrested the three assailants identified by eye-witnesses, but in an unusually lenient decision they were released on bail and had not been tried by the end of 1994. On 21 April a Muslim doctor, Sajjad Farooq, was stoned to death by a group of people in Gujranwala who believed he was a Christian who had burned the Koran. They set his body on fire while he was probably still alive and dragged him through the streets. A complaint was lodged against five people but no arrests appeared to have been made. At least six Ahmadis, including prominent members of the community, were killed by religious extremists during the year. Police failed to arrest any suspects.

Several people who had reportedly "disappeared" remained untraced, although other "disappearances" were resolved. The whereabouts of police officer Mohammad Afaque, who was abducted by police and handed to the Qasim Rangers in Hyderabad in February 1993, remained unknown. Two villagers from Miranigoti near Hyderabad, Ramazan Otho and Mohammad Otho, who had reportedly "disappeared" in late 1992, were released in April. Four other men arrested at the same time for allegedly crossing the border illegally remained missing. Police authorities denied holding them.

At least 32 people were sentenced to death, mostly for murder. In October Rehan was hanged in Peshawar Central Jail, following his conviction in 1991 for murder. He had to wait for over 30 minutes with the noose around his neck while his family and the heirs of the victim sought a compromise. Under Islamic law a death sentence may be commuted if the heirs of the murder victim forgive the offender and accept monetary compensation.

In February the government banned public hangings which had been temporarily stayed in 1992 pending a Supreme Court decision as to their compatibility with human dignity. In July parliament passed a law extending the death penalty to drug-trafficking.

In January Amnesty International urged the government to reconsider its decision to refuse entry to Afghan refugees as this contravenes the internationally accepted principle of *non-refoulement*, which forbids the return of refugees into areas where their lives and safety would be at risk.

During the year Amnesty International called on the government to release all

234

prisoners of conscience and drop charges against Ahmadis accused of blasphemy. Amnesty International expressed concern that the police had failed to investigate attacks on and to protect members of the Ahmadiyya and Christian communities. The organization also expressed concern about mass arrests of MQM members and their relatives in Sindh province. It called again for the release of G. M. Syed.

In July Amnesty International issued a report, *Pakistan: Use and abuse of the blasphemy laws*, which highlighted cases of individuals who were falsely charged with blasphemy, ill-treated in custody, denied a fair trial and in two instances sentenced to death. In September Amnesty International urged the government to establish the whereabouts of Shaukat Ali Kashmiri, Secretary General of the Jammu and Kashmir People's National Party, who had reportedly "disappeared" in the custody of the military intelligence in August. He was released from an army detention centre one month later.

Amnesty International asked the government to clarify a response it received from the Human Rights Cell in October about the probable extrajudicial execution of Niaz Hussain Pathan in September 1992. The government said that a judicial inquiry had found that Niaz Hussain Pathan had been "killed in a genuine encounter" but that police officers in Kotdiji, Sindh province, had been charged with murder.

PANAMA

Over 200 former officials and military supporters of a previous government were pardoned. A former military leader and four soldiers were sentenced to prison terms for murder in two trials.

Elections in May returned the *Partido Revolucionario Democrático* (PRD), Democratic Revolutionary Party, to power. The PRD had supported the *de facto* military government of former Panamanian Defense Forces chief, Brigadier General Manuel Noriega.

In September the new President, Ernesto Pérez Balladares, announced a pardon for 222 former officials and military supporters of General Noriega. Some of them had been imprisoned without trial

since the USA invaded Panama and overthrew General Noriega in 1989. President Pérez said those pardoned had been prosecuted for political reasons, but opponents of the measure feared it granted impunity to people who had committed common crimes including murder and misappropriation of state funds. Amongst those benefiting were Jaime Simons, former director of the state savings bank, and former President Manuel Solís Palma, in exile in Venezuela (see *Amnesty International Reports 1993* and *1994*).

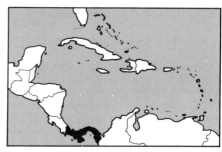

In March Manuel Noriega and a soldier were found guilty of murdering a major who had led an attempted coup in 1989. Both were sentenced *in absentia* to the maximum 20 years in prison by the Panamanian Supreme Court. However, Manuel Noriega was absolved of the murder of another rebel officer, Nicasio Lorenzo Tuñón, who died in prison after the failed coup, allegedly by committing suicide, a suggestion which his family disputed (see *Amnesty International Reports 1990* and *1994*).

In April, three former soldiers were sentenced to 15 years' imprisonment for the 1971 kidnapping and murder of Colombian priest Héctor Gallegos, who was apparently targeted because of his efforts to organize cooperatives among the rural poor (see *Amnesty International Report 1994*).

PAPUA NEW GUINEA

There were reports of torture and ill-treatment by police; one person died as a result. On Bougainville several supporters of an armed secessionist group were reportedly extrajudicially executed and ill-treatment of civilians continued,

although reports of human rights violations on the island declined. At least one "disappearance" remained unresolved and the government failed to investigate reports of human rights violations in 1993. An armed secessionist group also reportedly committed human rights abuses, including deliberate and arbitrary killings.

In August Sir Julius Chan became Prime Minister after a parliamentary election. The new government expressed support for human rights investigations and the establishment of a national human rights commission. The new government initiated peace negotiations with the secessionist Bougainville Revolutionary Army (BRA) to end the six-year conflict on the island of Bougainville. In October the government signed an agreement with 15 BRA commanders, but by the end of 1994 a settlement with key leaders of the secessionist movement had not been reached and fighting continued. The government announced that it would lift its blockade of Bougainville in October.

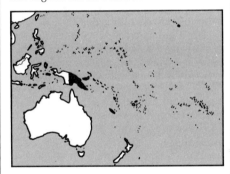

In March the UN Commission on Human Rights adopted a resolution noting the failure of the government to provide information about steps taken to address human rights violations by security forces on Bougainville or to prosecute the perpetrators. The resolution called on the government to invite the UN Special Rapporteur on extrajudicial, summary or arbitrary executions and the Special Rapporteur on torture to visit Bougainville to conduct independent investigations. To Amnesty International's knowledge, the government had failed to issue the invitations by the end of the year.

A Supreme Court challenge to the 1993 Internal Security Act, which could be used to detain peaceful political opponents of the government, declared sections

of the Act invalid. However, broadly worded sections of the Act remained intact, granting the head of state powers to ban organizations deemed to be "promoting or encouraging, or ... likely to or about to promote or encourage terrorism". Sections allowing for the imprisonment of alleged supporters of banned organizations also remained in force.

There were continued reports of torture and ill-treatment by police. On 1 November Babi Stevens, who was assisting a foreign film crew researching released young offenders, was stopped by police in Chimbu Province, arrested without charge and detained for two days. While in custody he was reportedly beaten with a gun barrel and kicked. Friends visiting him the day after his arrest said that as a result of the beatings he could not talk properly. The day after his release, he was again questioned by police and reportedly kicked. On 5 November Sande Alpane, a shopkeeper, was beaten to death by police in the streets of Port Moresby. Witnesses said that two car-loads of police hit Sande Alpane with their rifles and then left him lying in the street. He was pronounced dead on arrival at hospital.

There were continued reports of possible extrajudicial executions and ill-treatment of suspected BRA supporters by the Papua New Guinea Defence Force (PNGDF) on Bougainville. However, these reports were difficult to verify because of the continued blockade of the island. In August, four suspected BRA supporters were reportedly killed by the PNGDF in Central Bougainville. The four, along with 10 others, escorted a woman needing medical treatment to the Arawa care centre, a government-run camp for civilians. Two of the four were reportedly taken from the camp around midnight on 23 August and killed by the PNGDF. The other two were taken the following day to Loloho where they were shot by the PNGDF. The remaining 10 were reportedly taken to Loloho army base where they were subjected to mock executions.

The government-backed paramilitary Resistance Forces were also reportedly responsible for killings of suspected BRA members on Bougainville. Thomas Patoe, the brother of a BRA commander but himself a member of the Resistance Forces, disappeared for several hours after being given a gun and hand grenades, possibly

236

prompting speculation that he was liaising with the BRA. On his return he was taken to a Catholic mission compound by Resistance Force members and reportedly beaten, cut with knives and then shot.

By the end of the year, the government was not known to have investigated these and other reported human rights violations. There was no information about whether the government had investigated the reported extrajudicial execution of six men by the PNGDF in January 1993, when their boat was intercepted in waters off Bougainville (see *Amnesty International Report 1994*). The "disappearance" of Ken Savia, seized by government troops in Arawa in February 1993, also remained unresolved (see *Amnesty International Report 1994*).

Mechanisms for redressing human rights violations by the security forces remained inadequate. Victims of violations were often hampered in their use of them by inefficiency and obstruction, particularly by local police. However, the courts granted compensation to some complainants. In October a national court judge ordered compensation to be paid to Darius Ken, because he had been held illegally in police custody for four days without being charged. Also in October, a judge ordered compensation be paid to another individual alleging ill-treatment in prison.

No one was sentenced to death and no executions were carried out during the year. In June, two men were found guilty of wilful murder, an offence carrying the death penalty which was reintroduced in August 1991. In handing down the verdict, the judge asked the defence to argue why the defendants should not be sentenced to death. In this case the defence was successful.

The BRA continued to commit human rights abuses on Bougainville. There were reports of deliberate and arbitrary killings by the BRA of unarmed individuals and Resistance Force members.

In a report published in October, *Papua New Guinea: Human Rights Commission Mooted*, Amnesty International urged the government to demonstrate its commitment to human rights by establishing effective mechanisms for investigating violations. An Amnesty International request to visit Bougainville, sent to the government in November 1993, remained unanswered.

PARAGUAY

One person was killed in circumstances suggesting an extrajudicial execution. A peasant union organizer was shot dead and several others were injured when police apparently used excessive force to break up a demonstration. Peasant leaders were arrested and intimidated in the context of land disputes. Prosecutions for human rights violations under the past administration continued.

An unprecedented wave of unrest and disturbances swept the country in the first three months of the year. Numerous peasant protests and demonstrations took place, some of which were violently repressed by the state security forces. In February police violently broke up a blockade of Highway No. III near the town of Guayaiby, San Pedro department, by peasants, some of whom were armed with farming implements. At least 20 protesters were injured by the Police Special Operations unit when rubber bullets, tear-gas and buckshot were fired indiscriminately into the crowd. The demonstration had been called to protest at the violent eviction days before of a group of 400 landless peasant families from a farm belonging to a Senator of the ruling Colorado Party. At least 40 protesters were arrested. Digno Brítez Pérez, a lawyer working for the Interchurch Committee, a human rights organization, received repeated anonymous death threats reportedly because of his work representing the interests of the evicted peasant families. In March he presented a formal criminal complaint against the police alleging malicious wounding, death threats and torture in connection with incidents in Guayaiby.

The case had not been concluded by the end of the year.

In April peasant leader and former candidate for the governorship of Itapúa, Esteban Balbuena Quiñónez, was killed in circumstances giving rise to suspicions that ruling party officials might have been involved. Esteban Balbuena, who was a regional leader of the Itapúa Regional Farmers' Committee and a member of the Workers' Party, was shot dead as he approached his home in the community of Colonia 7 de Agosto, district of Carlos Antonio López, Itapúa department. The previous month Esteban Balbuena had requested the Commission for Investigation of Unlawful Acts of the National Congress to investigate alleged "political persecution" against him by a member of the governing committee of the ruling Colorado Party. Police authorities denied the murder was politically motivated and arrested a number of people from the community. Most were released without charge. The investigation was continuing at the end of the year.

Sebastian Larrosa, student and secretary of the peasant union Organization of Peasant Farmers for Integrated Development, was shot dead in May by a police sergeant when police apparently used excessive force to break up a demonstration in the town of Tacuara, department of San Pedro, during a general strike. Mariano Godoy, a journalist from the national newspaper *ABC Color*, was also shot and seriously wounded by the security forces when he went to Sebastian Larrosa's assistance. The commander of the National Police opened internal disciplinary investigations against the sergeant and 18 police agents who participated in the operation to disperse the demonstration. The sergeant was arrested and detained. The Minister of the Interior, who on the eve of the strike had reportedly said that any demonstrations would be repressed, denied that he had given orders to open fire on the demonstrators.

Leaders of peasant organizations reported constant intimidation and anonymous death threats as a result of their activities. Many reports were received of the participation of civilian gunmen, believed to be acting for landowners, in land conflicts. On several occasions civilian gunmen cooperated with the regular security forces in illegal evictions and detentions of squatters. In August, 11 landless peasants were seized by armed civilians from land they had been occupying in Santa Rosa de Monday, Alto Paraná department. The captured men were later handed over by the civilian gunmen to prison authorities in Ciudad del Este, where they were then charged with illegal land occupation.

Judicial investigations continued into torture and deaths in custody of political prisoners committed under the former administration of General Stroessner (see previous *Amnesty International Reports*). New evidence emerged from police records confiscated by judicial officials in December 1992 and from the records of other branches of the security forces uncovered in early 1993. However, sentences were passed in only one further case. In November Pastor Coronel, the former head of the Police Investigations Department (DIP-C), Sabino Montonaro, former Minister of the Interior, and Lucilo Benítez and Agustín Belotto, former DIP-C officials, were charged in connection with the torture and death of Amílcar María Oviedo Duarte, who was killed in detention in 1976. Pastor Coronel, already serving a prison sentence, was sentenced to a further 25 years in prison and the others to five years in prison.

PERU

Twenty-five prisoners of conscience and 255 possible prisoners of conscience remained in prison. At least 4,000 political prisoners awaited trial or were tried under judicial procedures which continued to fall far short of international standards. Torture of political prisoners continued to be widely reported. Some 65

238

new cases of "disappearance" were reported, of which 55 were from 1993. The security forces were reported to have extrajudicially executed 37 people. The armed opposition continued to commit numerous human rights abuses.

Significant areas of the country continued to be declared emergency zones, although there were fewer armed attacks by the clandestine *Partido Comunista del Perú (Sendero Luminoso)* (PCP), Communist Party of Peru (Shining Path), and the *Movimiento Revolucionario Túpac Amaru* (MRTA), Túpac Amaru Revolutionary Movement, during the year. However, the PCP remained militarily active in parts of the rainforest and around Lima, the capital. The government of President Alberto Fujimori did not accede to a renewed appeal by the leadership of the PCP to reach a "peace accord". A splinter group of the PCP, known as *Sendero Rojo*, Red Path, reiterated that it would continue the armed conflict.

In February President Fujimori approved a congressional law which led to the Supreme Court of Justice deciding that the La Cantuta human rights case (see *Amnesty International Report 1993*) should be resolved under the jurisdiction of a military, rather than a civilian, court. Jurists and the independent *Coordinadora Nacional de Derechos Humanos* (CNDDHH), Human Rights National Coordinating Committee, argued that this law violated constitutional principles, including that of the independence of the judiciary. In protest, the CNDDHH broke off talks with the government designed to improve the protection of human rights.

An international commission of jurists, established by agreement between the Peruvian Ministry of Justice and the Department of State of the USA, made recommendations to bring Peru's anti-terrorism legislation into line with international human rights standards. These were rejected by the Minister of Justice as "interference in the internal affairs of Peru".

In February the computerized *Registro Nacional de Detenidos*, National Register of Detainees, a measure designed to help prevent "disappearances", came into operation. However, by the end of 1994 the register covered only areas in and around the urban centres of Lima, Ayacucho and Tarapoto.

In April the government excluded the International Committee of the Red Cross (ICRC) from a battle zone in the Alto Huallaga region of the department of Huánuco. The exclusion order was justified as a measure to protect the safety of ICRC delegates. However, this meant that the ICRC could not promptly and effectively investigate allegations emanating from the area of gross human rights violations by the army. Also in April, the government used its majority in Congress to approve a motion criticizing the "irresponsible way" in which the CNDDHH made these allegations public.

In August the government established the National Human Rights Council, "a multisectoral body responsible for promotion, coordination, dissemination and advisory services for the protection and exercise of the fundamental rights of the individual". In November the *Ley de Arrepentimiento*, Repentance Law, was abolished. This exempted suspects of terrorism-related offences from prosecution and commuted the sentence of those convicted, in exchange for information leading to the arrest of other suspects. The Repentance Law had been widely criticized by independent human rights organizations for allowing uncorroborated evidence to be used by the courts to secure the conviction of political prisoners.

No investigation into the alleged existence of a "death squad" within the National Intelligence Service was known to have been initiated by the end of year (see *Amnesty International Report 1994*).

In November the UN Committee against Torture criticized the Government of Peru for not implementing legislative, administrative and judicial measures which conform to standards enshrined in the Convention against Torture and Other Cruel, Inhuman or Degrading Treatment or Punishment, ratified by Peru in 1988.

By the end of the year 25 prisoners of conscience, and at least 255 possible prisoners of conscience, continued to be held on terrorism-related charges. For example, in September María Elena Foronda and Oscar Díaz Barboza, both environmental activists, were detained and charged with "terrorism". They were prisoners of conscience. The charges were based on uncorroborated accusations against them by a prisoner who made use of the Repentance Law.

Prisoners of conscience Pelagia Salcedo Pizarro and her husband Juan Carlos Chuchón Zea were detained in December 1992 by the police and allegedly forced under torture to admit to storing explosives. In 1993 a military court sentenced them to 30 years' imprisonment for treason. Their sentence was subsequently upheld by the Supreme Council of Military Justice.

In August the Supreme Court of Justice annulled the 20-year sentences passed on prisoners of conscience Rómulo Mori Zavaleta and Wagner Cruz Mori (see *Amnesty International Report 1994*). Following this decision, the prisoners were released in November after being absolved by the Lambayeque High Court.

Eighteen prisoners of conscience were released during the year. Among them were Juan José Cholán Ramírez (see *Amnesty International Report 1994*) and his cousin, César Ramírez Yalta.

Thousands of political prisoners charged with terrorism-related offences were held pending trial or were brought before secret civilian and military courts, using procedures which fell far short of international standards. Defence lawyers were prohibited from calling as witnesses members of the security forces involved in the detention and interrogation of the accused and all trials, whether under civilian or military jurisdiction, continued to be held *in camera*.

According to their defence lawyer, twin brothers Rodolfo Gerbert and Rodolfo Dynnik Asencios, charged in April 1992 with terrorism-related offences under articles 319 and 320 of the Peruvian Criminal Code, were absolved of the charges by an examining judge. However, they were each subsequently sentenced to 10 years' imprisonment by a high court for offences defined in articles 321 and 322. These new charges were not, as required by law, examined by a lower court. In September 1993, following an appeal, the Supreme Court of Justice upheld the charges and sentences.

Thousands of political prisoners were forced to wait for unduly long periods before their trials began. For example, in October 1994 Sybila Arredondo Guevara was sentenced to 12 years' imprisonment for terrorism-related offences, after waiting over four years in jail for her trial to open.

Torture and ill-treatment were reported to have been inflicted by the security forces on most prisoners suspected of terrorism-related offences. The government acknowledged in February that "agents of the State resort to [torture]".

In March Francisco Alejos Murillo and three other leaders of an independent civil defence patrol in Sihuas, department of Ancash, were detained and reportedly tortured by members of the army and the police. After 10 days in incommunicado military detention, the four were transferred into the custody of the police. One of the leaders was immediately released. According to Francisco Alejos' statement, he was tortured, first by army personnel and then by the police, to force him to admit to being a member of the MRTA. Three months later a court unconditionally released him and the two other detainees. In April Ulises Espinoza Sánchez, governor for the district of Chavín de Pariarca, Huamalies province, Huánuco department, was detained by members of the army and reportedly "brutally beaten". The governor had been processing complaints by local people of thieving and looting by army patrols. In both these cases, complaints of torture were filed with the authorities, but by the end of the year those responsible had not been brought to justice.

No further progress was reported in judicial investigations into the deaths in military custody in 1993 of Alberto Calipuy Valverde and Rosenda Yauri Ramos. Prisoner of conscience Juan Abelardo Mallea Tomailla was released in April, but allegations that he had been tortured while in police custody remained unresolved (see *Amnesty International Report 1994*).

At least 10 "disappearances" were reported. On 19 March Jorge Pérez Rodríguez and Eloy Escudero Domínguez reportedly "disappeared" following their detention by members of the marines in Puerto Inca, province of Atayala, Ucayalli department. In late January a list of 55 people who "disappeared" in the custody of the security forces in the department of Huánuco between January and November 1993 was issued by a senior prosecutor to the Attorney General. In the light of this new information, claims made by the government that "disappearances" had significantly diminished in 1993 were called into question.

Extrajudicial executions by the security forces continued to be reported. For example, in January Víctor Ramírez Arias was reported to have been extrajudicially executed by an army officer near Lima. Separate investigations into this incident were initiated by military and civil courts. By the end of the year the Supreme Court of Justice had yet to rule which of these courts should have jurisdiction over the case.

In April the army was alleged to have extrajudicially executed 31 peasants in three separate incidents during a major offensive launched against PCP strongholds located on the left bank of the Alto Huallaga, in Huánuco department. In the wake of the allegations, representatives of the military and of the Congressional Human Rights and Pacification Commission claimed that human rights violations during the operation could not be ruled out. The results of separate investigations initiated by the military, Congress and an *ad hoc* prosecutor had not been made public by the end of the year.

In February the Supreme Court of Justice, in a decision which was widely regarded as having been politically dictated by the executive and the military, voted in favour of the La Cantuta case being resolved under the jurisdiction of a military court. In the wake of this decision, nine members of the army linked to the case were convicted and sentenced by the Supreme Council of Military Justice to terms of imprisonment ranging between one and 20 years for the illegal killing of a professor and nine students in 1992. However, one civilian and at least 10 high-ranking officers accused by dissident military officers and human rights defenders of being implicated in the case were never investigated by an independent judicial body.

In September the Supreme Court of Justice upheld the convictions of five police officers sentenced in November 1993 for the unlawful killings of brothers Rafael and Emilio Gómez Paquiyauri and student Freddy Rodríguez Pighi (see *Amnesty International Reports 1992* and *1994*).

The PCP continued to carry out a policy of deliberate and arbitrary killings against civilians. According to a report by an indigenous organization, on 27 March one boy and seven men from the community of Alto Chichineri, Satipo province, department of Junín, were detained, tortured and then killed by members of the PCP. On 20 June David Alberto Chacaliaza, an activist in the shanty town of Huaycán, on the outskirts of Lima, was shot dead in full view of witnesses. The killing was widely attributed to the PCP.

Amnesty International appealed to the authorities on numerous occasions to release all prisoners of conscience immediately and unconditionally and to bring anti-terrorism legislation into line with international human rights standards. The organization also called on the authorities to investigate thoroughly all human rights violations, and to ensure that those responsible were brought to justice before civilian courts.

In March Amnesty International noted the conviction of nine members of the army in the La Cantuta case. However, the organization expressed concern that other high-ranking officers and one civilian implicated in the killing had not been investigated by an independent judicial authority.

In April the Minister of Justice rejected Amnesty International's request for talks with President Fujimori and other high-level authorities, on the grounds that "we are not prepared to discuss matters which are internal to the country". In the event, talks were held in May with the presidents of Congress and of the Congressional Human Rights and Pacification Commission. The President of Congress told the delegation that the government would be setting up a "commission of notable jurists" to review alleged miscarriages of justice in terrorism-related cases. However, by the end of year no such commission appeared to be in operation.

Amnesty International wrote in May to President Fujimori expressing grave concern about extrajudicial executions reported to have taken place in the Alto Huallaga during April. The organization recommended that the Public Ministry name an *ad hoc* prosecutor to investigate the allegations, and that a presidential commission of notables be appointed to ensure the impartiality and independence of the investigations.

In November the organization published a report, *Peru: Amnesty International's concerns about torture and ill-treatment*. The report urged the government to take all measures necessary for the prevention and eradication of torture.

In an oral statement to the UN Commission on Human Rights in February Amnesty International included reference to its concerns in Peru.

PHILIPPINES

At least 43 people were victims of apparent extrajudicial executions and several "disappearances" were reported. Some political prisoners were released, but almost 300 remained in detention, among them possible prisoners of conscience. There were reports of torture and ill-treatment of suspected government opponents. Twenty-two people were sentenced to death but no executions were carried out. Armed opposition groups committed human rights abuses.

The government continued to face armed opposition from the New People's Army (NPA), the armed wing of the Communist Party of the Philippines (CCP); and from groups seeking independence for predominantly Muslim areas of Mindanao. Armed opposition groups committed abuses, including deliberate and arbitrary killings.

Peace negotiations between the government and opposition groups continued. Talks with the National Democratic Front, representing the NPA, took place in October, but broke down after two days over security guarantees. Talks with the Moro National Liberation Front (MNLF) in Jakarta led to limited agreement, and were to be resumed in 1995.

Two amnesty proclamations were issued by President Fidel Ramos in March. Those eligible were prisoners detained for criminal acts committed in pursuit of political objectives, and soldiers or police involved in coup attempts or who had committed crimes during counter-insurgency operations. After widespread protest, President Ramos amended the second proclamation in May to exclude perpetrators of "serious" human rights violations.

The government announced that the transfer of counter-insurgency functions from the Armed Forces of the Philippines (AFP) to the Philippine National Police (PNP), expected in 1993, would not be implemented in areas of Mindanao, Sulu, Tawi-Tawi, the Cordillera, Southern Tagalog, Bicol, Panay and Samar in 1994 or 1995. In March a report by the official Commission on Human Rights (CHR) named the PNP in 43 per cent of complaints filed in 1993. Senior PNP officials said they would investigate the allegations. The official militia, the Citizens' Armed Forces Geographical Units (CAFGU), were also accused of human rights violations during counter-insurgency operations. Some CAFGU companies were reportedly deactivated during the year.

Effective investigation of alleged human rights violations and related prosecutions continued to be obstructed by security forces. Methods used included threats and intimidation of witnesses, complainants, lawyers and judges; and refusal of access to information or military premises. Court proceedings were characterized by cumbersome, lengthy procedures, as were investigations by the CHR.

At least 43 people were victims of apparent extrajudicial executions by government and government-backed forces. Among those killed were former political prisoners and criminal suspects. Rural dwellers in militarized zones were also attacked and those killed included the very young and the elderly. For example, Antonio Pacis, a former political prisoner, and his wife were riding to their farm in Isabela province in February when they were shot dead, reportedly by CAFGU members.

Two CAFGU members were arrested and charged with murder in connection with the 1993 killing of Chris Batan, a human rights worker (see *Amnesty International Report 1994*). One reportedly "escaped", however, and despite numerous court hearings the case apparently had not been resolved by the end of the year.

"Disappearances" continued to be reported. In several cases detentions were acknowledged by the authorities after some weeks or months. However, the whereabouts of a man known as "Jun", who "disappeared" after being abducted by the security forces in May, remained unclear at the end of the year. The whereabouts of the majority who have gone missing remained unknown. The bodies of three people who "disappeared" in 1990 were recovered in May. Ernesto Biasong, Ladislao Pillones and Wilfredo Villaruz had reportedly been abducted by members of a military-backed vigilante group in Negros Occidental.

Some political prisoners were released but an estimated 291 others, including possible prisoners of conscience, remained in detention at the end of 1994. Most were accused of supporting armed opposition groups and charged with criminal offences. Among those held were Juanito Itaas and Donato Continente, sentenced to life imprisonment in 1991 for the killing of an army colonel from the USA. Both signed "confessions" said to have been extracted under duress.

There were reports of torture or ill-treatment of political suspects. Eddie Doños, arrested in June and accused of taking part in an ambush of a company of soldiers, was reportedly beaten and threatened with a gun during interrogation.

The death penalty, restored in 1993 for a wide range of crimes, was imposed on 22 people, the majority after conviction for rape or murder. No executions were reported during the year.

Deliberate and arbitrary killings were reportedly carried out by armed opposition groups. In January the NPA released a list of 345 individuals targeted for "execution". Leopoldo Mabilangan, a former NPA commander, was shot dead in April for supposed "heinous crimes". In Mindanao the Abu Sayyaf group abducted 74 people in June. The majority were quickly released, but 15 were killed and a Roman Catholic priest was held for two months before being released unharmed.

Throughout the year Amnesty International appealed to the government to conduct independent and impartial investigations into all apparent extrajudicial executions and "disappearances" and called for those responsible to be brought to justice. It called for the release of all prisoners of conscience and for political prisoners to be given fair trials or released. It urged the government to commute all death sentences. It appealed to opposition groups not to commit human rights abuses.

POLAND

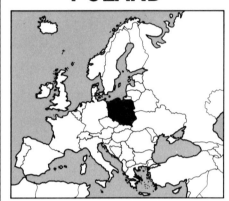

At least five conscientious objectors were imprisoned for refusing to perform military service and were prisoners of conscience. Two people were sentenced to death.

In September the National Assembly began debating seven draft constitutions submitted for consideration by various political parties, the President, the Senate and the trade union Solidarity.

During the year suspected perpetrators of human rights violations committed after the imposition of martial law in 1981 were brought to trial. In April a trial resumed in Wrocław of three former police officers accused of killing three Solidarity supporters in Lublin in August 1982 (see *Amnesty International Report 1983*). In June six former security service agents went on trial for the kidnapping and torture of Janusz Krupski in 1983. In September Czesław Kiszczak, former Interior Minister, went on trial for allowing riot police squads to use firearms, causing the death of nine miners at Wujek colliery, near Katowice, in December 1981 (see *Amnesty International Report 1982*).

Five conscientious objectors to military service were conditionally released after serving more than half their sentences, which were imposed in 1993 (see *Amnesty International Report 1994*). Dariusz Matczak was released in March, Tomasz

Jarosik in May and Robert Cygan was released in June.

One person was sentenced to death for murder in June and another in November.

Amnesty International called for the release of prisoners of conscience. The organization also called on the authorities to commute the death sentences and to abolish the death penalty.

PORTUGAL

There were further allegations of torture and ill-treatment by law enforcement officers. Judicial inquiries into such allegations were very slow but a few trials of law enforcement officers accused of ill-treatment were held during the year.

In July the European Committee for the Prevention of Torture (ECPT), established under the European Convention for the Prevention of Torture and Inhuman or Degrading Treatment or Punishment to examine the treatment of people deprived of their liberty, published its report on its visit to Portugal in January 1992 and the government's response.

The Committee reported that its delegation had heard "numerous detailed allegations of ill-treatment" inflicted by officers of all three law enforcement agencies: *Polícia Judiciária* (PJ), Judicial Police; *Polícia de Segurança Publica* (PSP), Public Security Police; and *Guarda Nacional Republicana* (GNR), Republican National Guard. The most common form of ill-treatment alleged was physical assault, including kicks, punches and blows with pistol butts. The delegation's medical expert examined several people who had complained of ill-treatment and recorded that some of them displayed physical injuries consistent with their allegations. On the basis of all the information received, the ECPT concluded that the ill-treatment of detainees was a "relatively common phenomenon".

In the government's response, dated October 1993, the Minister of the Interior, responsible for the PSP and GNR, commented that the ECPT's conclusions on ill-treatment appeared "manifestly excessive". He maintained that when officers who ill-treated people were identified they were "invariably severely punished". The Minister of Justice, responsible for the

PJ, said that he had no knowledge of complaints about acts of aggression or torture brought against his officers in the past two years. However, at the end of the year the Ombudsman was still conducting the investigation, which he had announced in December 1992, into 32 complaints against the PJ. Many of them were complaints of the use of violence by the PJ received by the Ombudsman in the preceding 23 months (see *Amnesty International Report 1994*).

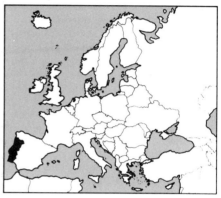

There were further allegations of ill-treatment, some of them relating to previous years. Long delays were reported in inquiries into such allegations. In March Carlos Rebelo complained to the Ombudsman that the judicial authorities had failed to investigate his allegation of ill-treatment by the PJ. He had been arrested in March 1993 in connection with investigations into bank robberies. He claimed that PJ officers had beaten him severely in a Lisbon police station. When he appeared in court, the judge remanded him in custody and ordered that he be taken to hospital and a report made on his injuries. Instead the officers took him to a police station where a doctor recorded minor injuries. After repeated requests by his family and a delay he was X-rayed and found to have five fractured ribs. Because of the delay, his other injuries, such as cuts and bruises, had healed. He alleged that although he had complained of ill-treatment immediately after his arrest, it was not until June 1993 that the prosecutor requested documents relating to his treatment. These were then supposedly sent for investigation by the police. Carlos Rebelo said that he was subsequently informed that the documentation could not be found by the police. A new inquiry into

244

his allegations was opened during the year.

In April the Faro prosecutor charged four PSP officers with insulting and physically injuring a PJ officer. In June 1993 the PSP officers had reportedly stopped the PJ officer from entering a party because he was wearing a motor-cycle helmet. When he persisted, claiming official status, it was reported that the PSP officers on duty kicked and punched him in front of witnesses. The PJ officer and a witness, who was apparently also attacked, were taken in handcuffs to the police station. They alleged they were further ill-treated on the way to and inside the station. The PJ officer was charged with verbally insulting the PSP officers.

In November, three trials of 12 GNR officers accused of assaulting civilians opened in the Second Military Tribunal in Lisbon. Seven officers were charged with seriously assaulting Francisco Carretas and a friend in February 1992 (see *Amnesty International Report 1994*). The court suspended the hearing until March 1995 because one of the accused officers did not appear. The court also tried five officers in two other, separate, cases of assault. Two defendants were sentenced to seven and nine months' imprisonment respectively. However, the sentences were not enforced as both officers had already been pardoned by an amnesty in 1991. The three other officers were acquitted.

Amnesty International urged the authorities to ensure that all allegations of torture and ill-treatment were promptly and thoroughly investigated and that those responsible were brought to justice.

QATAR

The judicial punishment of flogging continued to be applied. One case was reported during the year.

A British national, Gavin Sherrard-Smith, was sentenced to 50 lashes and six months' imprisonment by an Islamic Court in February on charges of selling alcohol. He was reportedly denied access to a lawyer and his sentence was upheld by the Court of Appeal in March. The 50 lashes were carried out in secret in May.

No information was received about two prisoners of conscience, M.V. Babu and Samuel Philip, who were arrested in January 1993 for allegedly holding an unauthorized Christian prayer meeting (see *Amnesty International Report 1994*). In March 1993 the authorities stated that a decision to deport the two men, both Indian nationals, "was taken in view of the breach of Qatari Visa Law No. 3 of 1963". At the end of 1994 it was still not clear whether or not they had been deported.

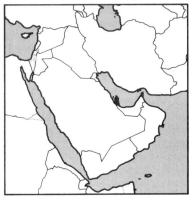

Amnesty International appealed in April to the Amir of Qatar, al-Shaikh Khalifa Ibn Hamad Al Thani, to exercise clemency by commuting the punishment of lashes, which the organization considers to be cruel, inhuman and degrading. It urged the authorities to replace this punishment in law by other more humane punishments. No response was received.

ROMANIA

At least three prisoners of conscience were held. Three Roma were arbitrarily detained, apparently because of their ethnic origin. There were reports of torture and ill-treatment by the police.

In February the Senate adopted a draft law for the revision of the Penal Code. The debate on this law in the Chamber of Deputies lasted throughout the year. Some of the adopted amendments imposed even greater restrictions on the right to freedom of expression than before. These concerned: dissemination of false news, offences against insignia, defamation of the state or nation, offences against the authorities and "outrage". An adopted amendment to Article 200, paragraph 1, was ambiguous and could lead to the imprisonment of homosexuals solely for engaging in private consensual sexual relations between adults. In December, however, the Chamber of Deputies rejected the draft law as a whole and returned it for a second debate to the Senate.

In March Council of Europe rapporteurs visited Romania to evaluate the human rights situation as well as the implementation of recommendations made on Romania's admission to the organization. They concluded that not all the obligations Romania had accepted had been honoured and recommended continued monitoring.

In July the Constitutional Court ruled that Article 200, paragraph 1, of the Penal Code was unconstitutional "to the extent to which it applies to sexual relations between adults of the same sex, freely consummated, not committed in public or not causing public scandal". The decision, however, had not come into force by the end of the year.

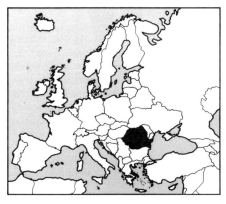

Some of those suspected of perpetrating human rights violations in the past were brought to trial. In May a former security service investigator was arrested and charged with illegally detaining four minors in 1989 for handing out leaflets opposing the then President Nicolae Ceauşescu. In June three army officers charged with the killing of 50 cadets and civilians at Otopeni airport on 23 December 1989 were brought to trial. Relatives and airport staff who were called as witnesses said they had received death threats and that they feared reprisals if the accused were convicted. The defendants remained free.

In November the intelligence service, *Serviciul Român de Informaţii*, in its annual report on national security referred to the human rights monitoring work of certain independent Roma organizations as destabilizing and unconstitutional.

In June Romania ratified the European Convention for the Protection of Human Rights and Fundamental Freedoms. In October it ratified the European Convention for the Prevention of Torture and Inhuman or Degrading Treatment or Punishment.

People continued to be imprisoned solely because of their homosexuality; they were prisoners of conscience. Cosmin Hutanu, who was convicted under Article 200, paragraph 1, of the Penal Code and had begun serving a 14-month prison sentence in July 1993 (see *Amnesty International Report 1994*), was conditionally released in March. Three other men convicted under the same law were serving concurrent sentences for other crimes. More information came to light during the year about imprisonments in 1993 under Article 200, paragraph 1. Traian Pasca was imprisoned solely under this charge for nine months in 1993. This contradicted information compiled by the Ministry of Justice in November 1993.

Prosecutions for defaming state authority, under Article 238, paragraph 1, of the Penal Code, led to people being imprisoned for peacefully exercising their right to freedom of expression. In September Ionel Buzoianu was released after 18 months in detention in Bucharest, the capital, pending trial. He had been charged in March 1993 for writing a slogan on his car accusing the police of corruption. At the end of the year his trial was continuing. In February Nicolae Andrei, a journalist in Craiova, was detained for five days for publishing an article which was considered defamatory of the President, Ion Iliescu. The case was still under investigation at the end of the year. Both men were considered prisoners of conscience.

The enforcement of the law on misdemeanours (Law 61/91) also led to apparently arbitrary political detentions. There was concern that this law was used to intimidate some people who complained about ill-treatment by law enforcement officers. Police harassment of Emil Macău, a Rom, reportedly began in August 1993 and was apparently motivated by his ethnic origin. On 17 April after returning from Bucharest, where he had complained on several occasions to the Parliamentary Commission for Human Rights, Emil

246

Macău and his brother Virgil were arrested by four officers in a shop in Victoria, Braşov County. Emil. Macău was reportedly beaten while two officers held his brother with a gun to his chin. They were then taken to Făgăraş and charged under Law 61/91 with disturbing the public peace because "their arrest caused indignation to around 200 people who had gathered in front of the shop". Emil Macău was sentenced to two months' imprisonment and Virgil Macău to 40 days. Their motion for a new trial was rejected by two judges of the same court which had tried them earlier.

In November 1993 Maria Moldovan, also a Rom, was ordered to pay a fine under Law 61/91 for "shouting that her son had been beaten". She appealed to the Tîrgu Mureş Court and a hearing had been set for 26 August. However, the same court issued an arrest warrant for Maria Moldovan, converting the fine into 33 days' imprisonment. She was arrested on 15 June and released two days later, apparently after the authorities recognized that a judicial error had been committed. In October the court rejected her appeal.

There were other reports of ill-treatment of Roma by police officers. In April Valentin Lacă went to the police station in Valea Largă to complain about a fine that he had been given. He was reportedly beaten and kicked by an official and two police officers.

Government investigations into ill-treatment of Roma by law enforcement officers and acts of racist violence were slow and appeared not to have been thorough or impartial. No one was prosecuted for a violent attack by soldiers on Roma in Bucharest in 1992 (see *Amnesty International Report 1993*). In November the General Prosecutor stated that the soldiers had been provoked and had "spontaneously beat Roma with rubber truncheons". He considered the decision of the Military Prosecutor not to charge anyone to be legally justified. There was also no prosecution of anyone involved in racist violence in Hădăreni in September 1993, when two Roma had been killed and one burned to death (see *Amnesty International Report 1994*). Three police officers from the village were "reprimanded and reassigned". One of them was transferred to Valea Largă, a village in the same county, where he was allegedly involved in the ill-treatment of Valentin Lacă.

There were many other reports of torture and ill-treatment by the police. In July Gabriela-Ioana Gavrilă was arrested by two police officers in front of her apartment in Bucharest. They reportedly twisted her hands and kicked her in the abdomen causing her to fall to the ground. She was then punched in the back and on the head and pulled into the lift. At the prosecutor's office she was questioned about the business affairs of a private firm where she was employed. A medical examination later that day confirmed that she had been beaten.

In November, in Galaţi, two journalists and a female city councillor who were investigating the operation of a firm which removed illegally parked vehicles were beaten by the firm's manager and four employees in the presence of two police officers who reportedly did not intervene to protect them.

A number of investigations into police abuses were completed. Two police officers were charged with illegal detention and abusive conduct towards Viorel Baciu in 1988 (see *Amnesty International Reports 1992* and *1994*). Viorel Baciu was released from Botoşani penitentiary in September following a presidential pardon. However, most of the other police officers considered responsible for abusive conduct were subjected only to disciplinary measures or fines; as in the case of two officers involved in the torture of Andrei Zanopol (see *Amnesty International Report 1994*).

Amnesty International urged members of parliament throughout the year to ensure that the revised Penal Code was consistent with Romania's legal obligations under international human rights treaties. In March Amnesty International published a report, *Romania: Criminal law reform on the wrong track*. The organization also expressed concern about the detention and prosecution of journalist Nicolae Andrei. In May it called for an impartial review of the case against Emil and Virgil Macău. In June Amnesty International expressed concern about the detention of Maria Moldovan. Amnesty International also repeatedly called for reports of torture and ill-treatment to be investigated and those responsible brought to justice.

The Romanian authorities responded giving information about investigations into reports of torture and ill-treatment and about the prosecution of suspected perpetrators of human rights abuses. In April Amnesty International was informed that the investigation into the deaths of Andrei Frumuşanu and Aurica Crăiniceanu (see *Amnesty International Reports 1993* and *1994*) had still not been completed. In July the government informed Amnesty International that Viorel Horia (see *Amnesty International Reports 1992* to *1994*) had been found, that he had left home of his own volition and had never been detained.

RUSSIA

There were numerous allegations of ill-treatment in detention. Conditions in some pre-trial prisons amounted to cruel, inhuman or degrading treatment. At least 125 people were sentenced to death, and three people were executed. The death penalty was abolished for four offences. There were reports of inadequate legal protection for asylum-seekers.

Inaugural sessions for both houses in the new bicameral legislature were held in January. That month the lower house, the State Duma, appointed Sergey Kovalyov, a former prisoner of conscience, to the new post of parliamentary Ombudsman for Human Rights. However, legislation establishing this post had not been adopted by the end of the year and Sergey Kovalyov exercised his functions through his existing position as chairman of the presidential Commission on Human Rights. In April the State Duma created a committee to investigate human rights violations in pre-trial detention.

In December Russian troops entered the self-proclaimed Chechen Republic-Ichkeriya, an area in the south of the country which had declared itself independent in 1991. Hundreds were killed in subsequent fighting.

The leaders of parliamentary opposition to President Boris Yeltsin who were detained after violent events in Moscow in October 1993 (see *Amnesty International Report 1994*) were freed under an amnesty declared by the State Duma in February. The amnesty also covered leaders of an attempted coup in 1991.

In July the death penalty was abolished for four offences: terrorist acts, terrorist acts against a representative of a foreign state, sabotage and counterfeiting.

Although the right of conscientious objectors to a civilian alternative to compulsory military service had been enshrined in the Constitution since April 1992, parliament again failed to introduce the necessary enabling legislation or to amend the criminal code to reflect the constitutional provision. Young men continued to risk imprisonment for refusing their call-up papers on grounds of conscience, and often had to initiate legal action themselves to avoid prosecution for evading conscription. Religious pacifist Pavel Zverev, for example, brought a civil action against the conscription board which had refused his request for alternative service. On 14 April a Moscow court ruled in his favour, in what was believed to be the first successful such action. Other conscientious objectors were prosecuted, although none was known to have been imprisoned. Jehovah's Witness Oleg Khmelnitsky, for example, was acquitted by a Moscow court on 19 May after the judge gave precedence to the Constitution over the criminal code.

Reports of ill-treatment in detention continued. In a July report on human rights observance, the chairman of the presidential Human Rights Commission condemned the penitentiary system for allowing regular and gross violations, and said beatings were widespread. Lack of effective supervision, he reported, meant that many violations were not investigated and that the guilty were not brought to justice.

In one instance that came to light, prisoner Sergey Osintsev alleged that he and other prisoners in solitary confinement cells at corrective labour colony YaP 17/1 in Stavropol Territory were assaulted on 12 April by special troops brought in to search the premises. He reported that the prisoners were forced to take off their clothes and then were severely beaten and

248

kicked by the troops, who were said to have wound elastic bandages round their hands in order not to leave visible marks. Sergey Osintsev further alleged that the troops threatened to return and kill him if he lodged an official complaint (as he had done following a similar incident in September 1993).

Conditions for those detained in many of the country's pre-trial prisons remained appalling. Gross overcrowding (the presidential Human Rights Commission reported that 76 per cent of the country's 177 such institutions were overcrowded) meant thousands of prisoners on remand were held in filthy, malodorous, pest-ridden cells with inadequate light and ventilation. Tens of thousands had no individual beds, having to sleep in two or three shifts, often without bedding. Insanitary conditions facilitated the spread of parasitic and infectious illnesses. Prisoners' health was further undermined by frequently inadequate food and medical supplies and by oppressively hot and humid conditions in summer which, according to the presidential Human Rights Commission, presented a "real threat to life and health from oxygen starvation". Some prisoners had waited years in such conditions for their cases to come to court. Speaking of two such prisons in Moscow, the UN Special Rapporteur on torture, who visited in July, said: "The senses of smell, touch, taste and sight are repulsively assailed. The conditions are cruel, inhuman and degrading; they are torturous".

Statistics became available on the application of the death penalty in 1993 and the first half of 1994. Two hundred and twenty-five people were sentenced to death in 1993, 123 death sentences were commuted to life imprisonment by President Yeltsin, and three people were executed. From January to June 1994, 125 people were sentenced to death, the President commuted 143 death sentences, and three people were executed. All executions were for premeditated, aggravated murder.

It was unlikely that these figures included eight men under sentence of death in the Chechen Republic-Ichkeriya. In August it was reported that five of the men faced execution after exhausting the territory's appeals process. However, armed conflict in the area made information gathering difficult and the men's situation remained uncertain at the end of the year.

On 17 December, six men and four women were said to have been shot dead by Russian troops while trying to flee fighting in the Chechen Republic. According to one account, after seven vehicles from a convoy of 10 had passed through a checkpoint near the village of Nesterovskoye, troops opened fire on the last three cars. Survivors alleged that troops fired without warning and continued firing on those seeking to escape. Official Russian sources confirmed that a number of deaths took place but said that the troops had opened fire in self-defence. An investigation was announced.

Reports were received that some asylum-seekers were not granted effective protection against forcible return to countries where they risked falling victim to human rights violations. For example, 20 Afghans who were said to have links with the former communist government of Afghanistan, and were therefore afraid of returning, were arrested on 8 August in the Krasnodar Territory and forcibly expelled via Uzbekistan to Afghanistan. Other asylum-seekers reported being subjected by the police to harassment, threats of deportation, extortion and confiscation of identity documents issued to them by the UN High Commissioner for Refugees.

Amnesty International submitted information about its concerns regarding ill-treatment in detention and conditions in pre-trial prisons to the UN Special Rapporteur on torture, who visited Russia in July. Throughout the year Amnesty International urged the authorities to investigate swiftly and impartially all allegations of ill-treatment, with the results made public and any perpetrators brought to justice. The organization also called for immediate improvements to conditions in pre-trial prisons.

Amnesty International welcomed the reduction in the scope of the death penalty, and President Yeltsin's wide exercise of his right to pardon, but throughout the year continued to urge the authorities to commute all death sentences and to take further steps towards total abolition.

Amnesty International called on the authorities to ensure that no asylum-seekers were returned to countries where they could face human rights violations, and to ensure the effective protection of asylum-seekers by establishing fair and satisfactory asylum procedures which meet international standards. In October the Foreign Ministry replied that the establishment of procedures on determining refugee status had begun, although they were progressing slowly. The Ministry also reported that President Yeltsin had ordered a review of instructions to officials governing the return of asylum-seekers.

Amnesty International called on all parties to the conflict in the Chechen Republic-Ichkeriya to protect all non-combatants in accordance with international humanitarian and human rights law. The organization urged the authorities to ensure that the investigation into the deaths reported near the village of Nesterovskoye was comprehensive and impartial, with the results made public and anyone found responsible for human rights violations brought to justice.

RWANDA

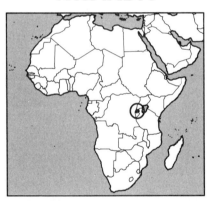

In a genocidal attack on the minority Tutsi ethnic group, over half a million people were massacred by soldiers and militias loyal to President Juvénal Habyarimana after he was killed in April. More than one million Rwandese fled the country, either to escape the slaughter or fearing reprisal killings by the Tutsi-dominated Rwandese Patriotic Front (RPF), which took over the country and formed a new government in July. RPF soldiers also carried out unlawful killings and other abuses.

In the first three months of 1994, the government of President Habyarimana delayed implementing the peace accord it had signed with the rebel RPF in 1993 (see *Amnesty International Report 1994*). Sup-

porters of the former ruling party, the *Mouvement républicain national pour la démocratie et le développement* (MRND), Republican National Movement for Democracy and Development, and its ally, the *Coalition pour la défense de la République* (CDR), Coalition for the Defence of the Republic, continued to carry out violent attacks on supporters of opposition parties which supported the peace accord. The MRND and the security forces were dominated by the majority Hutu ethnic group. The CDR was an exclusively Hutu political party.

On 6 April President Habyarimana was killed (together with President Cyprien Ntaryamira of Burundi) when his plane was hit by a rocket. An interim government led by the former speaker of the National Assembly, Théodore Sindikubwabo, was established. The interim government blamed the killing of President Habyarimana on the RPF and on Belgian troops serving with the UN Assistance Mission for Rwanda (UNAMIR) peace-keeping force, although government soldiers were widely believed to be responsible.

Within hours of the President's death, members of the security forces and MRND and CDR supporters began an orchestrated campaign of killings. Most of the victims were Tutsi, but Hutu who opposed the killings or supported sharing power with the RPF were also targeted. There were massacres in all parts of the country: only areas effectively controlled by the RPF were spared the worst of the carnage.

The massacres were systematic, planned and condoned at the highest level. Virtually all the killers belonged to the majority Hutu ethnic group, particularly the MRND militia known locally as *Interahamwe* ("They who attack together"). Others belonged to the CDR and its militia known locally as *Impuzamugambi* ("They who have the same goal"). In the preceding months, the militia, who from April were collectively known as *Interahamwe*, had been armed and prepared to kill virtually all Tutsi and Hutu government opponents. Hundreds of known or suspected RPF supporters, most of them Tutsi, and some suspected Hutu RPF sympathizers, including non-violent opposition leaders, had been killed during the first quarter of the year. Radio broadcasts, particularly by the *Radio-télévision libre des mille collines* owned by Hutu close to President

Habyarimana, incited Hutu to genocide, accusing all Tutsi of being enemies of the Hutu and supporters of the RPF.

As a result of the massacres, more than one million Rwandese fled to neighbouring countries and the RPF resumed an offensive against government forces.

UNAMIR troops largely failed to respond to the massacres, although 10 Belgian UNAMIR soldiers were killed in an unsuccessful attempt to defend Prime Minister Agathe Uwilingiyimana when Rwandese soldiers came to kill her. On 21 April the UN Security Council decided to withdraw about 2,000 members of its peace-keeping force, leaving less than 500 in Rwanda. On 16 May the UN Security Council authorized the deployment of a force of 5,500 troops with an enlarged mandate to protect civilians at risk and to use force if necessary. However, only a few hundred had been deployed by the time the RPF had achieved a military victory and an RPF-led government was formed in mid-July. On 25 May a Special Session of the UN Commission on Human Rights was held to consider Rwanda. It appointed a Special Rapporteur to investigate human rights violations in Rwanda. On 22 June the UN authorized France to send a 2,000-strong force to southwestern Rwanda to protect civilians from attacks by government forces and militia as well as the RPF. French troops were replaced by UNAMIR in late August. In August the UN also authorized the deployment of civilian human rights investigators, but only around 80 out of about 150 promised had been deployed by the end of the year.

By 19 July the RPF had taken control of most of Rwanda and declared a new government of national unity. The new government was made up of representatives of the RPF and of four other political parties. Both the President, Pasteur Bizimungu, and the Prime Minister, Faustin Twagiramungu, were Hutu. The new government announced its intention of bringing to justice all those who had ordered or taken part in the massacres and in July officials said that they hoped to try up to 30,000 people, if necessary by creating special courts. On 8 August the government stated that it would agree to trials before an international tribunal which was set up in November by the UN Security Council.

When mass killings started in April,

some 300,000 refugees fled to neighbouring countries, particularly Tanzania. As the RPF took control of Rwanda, at least a million more Hutu refugees fled abroad. Conditions in the refugee camps were atrocious: in Goma camp in Zaire up to 80,000 people died within weeks in a cholera epidemic. There were numerous killings of Tutsi refugees and Hutu by exiled former government and security officials and by Hutu gangs in Tanzania and Zaire.

In mid-September the UN High Commissioner for Refugees (UNHCR) stated that the Rwandese Patriotic Army (RPA), the armed wing of the RPF which became Rwanda's national army in July, had carried out numerous killings in the southeast. UNHCR suspended repatriation of refugees from neighbouring countries. UNAMIR sent soldiers to monitor the situation. The government, which denied that its troops had been involved in any massacres, said it would cooperate with a UN investigation team. The results of the investigation had not been published by the end of the year.

The massacres started in the capital, Kigali, and within days spread to the whole country. The victims were surrounded in their homes and villages. Many were trapped and slaughtered in public buildings such as churches and hospitals where they had sought sanctuary. Most killings were carried out with traditional weapons, such as clubs and machetes; the killers also used grenades and firearms.

The initial targets in Kigali were Hutu and Tutsi opposition leaders, human rights activists and other prominent Tutsi. The first reported victims were Prime Minister Uwilingiyimana, several other government ministers and the President of the Cassation Court, Joseph Kavaruganda, who were killed on 7 April by the Presidential Guard. Human rights activists including Fidèle Kanyabugoyi, a Tutsi, and Ignace Ruhatana, a Hutu, were rounded up and killed. Several dozen journalists, including Vincent Rwabukwisi, were also killed.

Soldiers then attacked a Roman Catholic centre in Kigali and killed about 17 Tutsi, mostly priests and nuns. Those killed included 67-year-old Father Chrysologue Mahame and Father Patrick Gahizi.

The militia set up road-blocks in Kigali

and its suburbs: anyone believed to be a Tutsi was summarily executed. The killers made no attempt to conceal what they were doing or to hide the bodies. Generally, government and security officials ordered or condoned the killings. The few who opposed them became victims themselves.

On 17 April more than 100 Tutsi were killed by soldiers and militia a few kilometres south of Kigali. They had been part of a group of some 2,000 Tutsi who were reportedly intercepted by soldiers and militia as they walked towards Amahoro stadium in Kigali, hoping for protection by UNAMIR troops camped there.

Most of the massacres in eastern Rwanda apparently took place in churches. For example, more than 800 people were reportedly killed on 11 April by government supporters and soldiers at Kiziguro Roman Catholic church, Murambi district of Byumba prefecture. Hundreds more were killed by *Interahamwe* and gendarmes at Rukara Roman Catholic mission in Kibungo prefecture's Rukara district. The attackers hurled grenades through the windows of the church and killed survivors with guns and machetes. Hundreds of similar killings were reported at Gahini Protestant church in Rukara district.

Massacres in Cyangugu prefecture in the southwest were among the most extensive. Many Tutsi took refuge in churches and in a stadium in Cyangugu town. Some were killed there, others were herded into administrative centres where they were killed. Hundreds of Tutsi fled to Mabirizi Roman Catholic parish in Cyimbogo district. Militia attacked them there, apparently led by a businessman and the recently elected administrator (*Bourgmestre*) of Cyimbogo. The victims resisted and on 18 April they were attacked with grenades, machine-guns and other automatic weapons. When most of the Tutsi men had been killed or injured, the attackers reportedly entered the church compound and killed all the males they found, including babies. Thousands were also reportedly massacred by militia at Mushaka, Nyamasheke and Nkaka Roman Catholic parishes.

More than 3,000 people, most of them Tutsi but including Hutu members of opposition political parties, were killed at Mukarange Roman Catholic parish in Kibungo prefecture's Rwamagana district in the east of the country. The victims were first herded into the parish main hall and grenades were hurled through windows. An estimated 2,500 people were killed there. Some 500 or more tried to run but were mown down by machine-gun fire in the church compound.

On 23 April government troops and militia killed about 170 patients and some staff at Butare hospital. From the hospital the killers went to a nearby camp for the displaced where they also reportedly killed people. On 1 May, 21 orphans and 13 local Red Cross workers were killed in Butare. The orphans had just been evacuated from Kigali to Butare where it was thought they would be safe.

There were also reports of human rights abuses by the RPF and RPA. Hundreds – possibly thousands – of unarmed civilians and captured opponents were reported to have been summarily executed by the RPA and by Tutsi supporters of the RPF. Many of the killings were arbitrary reprisals against groups of Hutu civilians.

In April and May scores of unarmed civilians were reportedly killed by units of the RPA in northeastern Rwanda. Witnesses reported that such killings took place at Nyabwishongwezi and Kagitumba in Byumba prefecture's Ngarama district. In both cases local people were summoned to public meetings by RPA soldiers, who then attacked them with guns, grenades, bayonets and hoes. Among those reported killed at Nyabwishongwezi were Jovans Nakabonye, who was shot, and her daughter, 12-year-old Felicita Busingye, who was bayoneted to death.

In late May and early June RPA soldiers were reported to have carried out numerous arrests of Hutu at "screening" centres in southern Rwanda used to identify those suspected of involvement in massacres and to have killed a number of them.

Prominent Hutu and others suspected of supporting former President Habyarimana and the interim government set up after his death were held by the RPA in camps, including one near Kabgayi. Some were subsequently killed or "disappeared". For example, Rwanda's Roman Catholic Archbishop, Vincent Nsengiyumva, a former MRND central committee member, and 12 other priests were killed by four of the RPA soldiers supposed to be guarding them at Byimana, south of

252

Kabgayi, near Gitarama. Other RPA soldiers shot dead one of the killers and the other three escaped.

More than 10,000 people, virtually all of them Hutu, accused of involvement in the genocide earlier in the year were being held in various Rwandese detention centres at the end of the year. Most of them had not been formally charged with any offence. Some were reportedly held in private houses and military installations without any supervision by judicial officials, amidst reports that some were tortured or severely ill-treated in custody, and that others had "disappeared". There were also numerous reports of abductions and "disappearances" carried out by the RPA after April.

Many prisoners held by the RPA were subjected to a torture method known as *kandoya* or "three-piece tying". The victim's arms are tied above the elbows behind the back, which sometimes results in permanent injury. From October there were reports of seven detainees or more dying daily in Butare, Gitarama and Kigali prisons and other detention centres from disease as a result of lack of medical care and unhygienic prison conditions exacerbated by overcrowding.

Amnesty International repeatedly appealed to former government and military authorities and to political leaders in Rwanda to condemn the massacres and to stop them. Amnesty International also called on the international community to bear its share of the responsibility for the slaughter, naming countries which had supplied weapons and trained the army and militias, and criticizing the UN for withdrawing most of its troops once the massacres began.

Amnesty International welcomed the special session in May of the UN Commission on Human Rights, at which it made an oral statement, and the Commission's decision to investigate the killings. However, Amnesty International called for stronger measures to protect human rights.

In May Amnesty International published a report, *Rwanda: Mass murder by government supporters and troops in April and May 1994*, which documented the killings and provided clear evidence that they were organized at the highest level and were an attempt at genocide. In June Amnesty International publicly condemned the killings of priests by the RPF.

In August an Amnesty International delegation visited Rwanda. The delegates met senior officials of the new government including the President, Vice-President and Minister of Justice, as well as local human rights groups, UN personnel and survivors of massacres. In the light of the continuing climate of fear, Amnesty International called on the international community to act urgently in four ways: by expanding international human rights monitoring; by sending UN civilian police monitors; by rebuilding Rwanda's judicial system; and by extending the jurisdiction of the international criminal tribunal established to deal with crimes against humanity in former Yugoslavia to Rwanda.

In October Amnesty International published *Rwanda: Reports of killings and abductions by the Rwandese Patriotic Army, April to August 1994*. It called for an independent and impartial investigation into reports of numerous human rights abuses committed by the RPA and for those responsible to be brought to justice. The organization appealed to the new government and the international community to take appropriate action to prevent such abuses from recurring.

SAUDI ARABIA

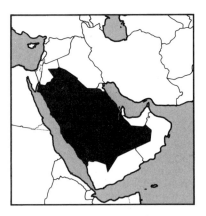

Hundreds of people, among them prisoners of conscience, were arrested during the year for their political or religious activities. The vast majority were suspected Sunni Islamist opponents of the government although several Christian worshippers were also detained. At least 30 Iraqi refugees from Rafha camp continued to

be detained without trial. New information came to light regarding the torture and ill-treatment of detainees in previous years. The judicial punishment of amputation continued to be imposed. At least 53 people were executed.

In January King Fahd bin 'Abdul-'Aziz opened the inaugural session of the *Majlis al-Shura*, Consultative Council, whose 60 members are appointed by the King and have an advisory role (see *Amnesty International Reports 1993* and *1994*). In April the banned Committee for the Defence of Legitimate Rights (CDLR) transferred its headquarters to the United Kingdom (UK) following the release of about 20 of its members and supporters at the end of 1993 (see *Amnesty International Report 1994*). Among them was Professor Muhammad al-Mas'ari, the CDLR's spokesperson, who fled Saudi Arabia and sought political asylum in the UK. During the year two Saudi Arabian diplomats based in the USA sought political asylum, allegedly because they feared reprisals for opposing the government's policies.

Hundreds of suspected Sunni Islamist opponents of the government were arrested during the year. A wave of arrests began in April following the transfer of the CDLR headquarters to the UK and the establishment there of offices of another opposition group, *Hay'at al-Nasiha wal-Islah*, the Advice and Reformation Committee. Among those detained was Anmar al-Mas'ari, son of the CDLR's spokesperson, who was arrested in April and held in al-Ha'ir prison with other detainees suspected of supporting the CDLR. He was released in late December without charge. There were further arrests in September; two leading CDLR members were arrested by *al-Mabahith al-'Amma*, General Intelligence, and held at an unknown location. 'Abdullah al-Hamid, a writer and lecturer at Imam Muhammad bin Sa'ud University in Riyadh, and Muhsin al-'Awaji had been detained in 1993 (see *Amnesty International Report 1994*) and released after giving a written undertaking to forgo any political activities deemed to be hostile to the Kingdom. All those detained were believed to be prisoners of conscience. Some remained held without charge or trial at the end of the year and there were fears that they were being tortured while in incommunicado detention.

In mid-September, two prominent religious figures and critics of the ruling royal family were arrested: Sheikh Salman bin Fahd al-'Awda, a religious scholar, and Sheikh Safr 'Abdul-Rahman al-Hawali, former Head of the Islamic Jurisprudence Department at Um al-Qura University. Hundreds of other suspected Sunni Islamist opponents were arrested in the same period, among them possible prisoners of conscience. They included religious scholars, businessmen, students and academics. The arrests were carried out by *al-Mabahith al-'Amma* and other security forces, principally in the towns of al-Buraida, al-'Unaiza and al-Bukayriya in al-Qaseem Province. All the detainees were held incommunicado without charge or trial in al-Ha'ir prison, *al-Mabahith al-'Amma* headquarters in al-'Ulaisha and in police stations in al-Qaseem Province and Riyadh. In late September the government acknowledged the detention of 110 people, whom it accused of sedition and conspiracy to threaten state security in co-operation with foreign forces. It stated that investigations launched into their cases might lead to the release of some of the detainees. Most of them were released, but some were still held at the end of the year.

The fate and whereabouts of suspected government opponents arrested in 1993, all said to be followers of *Salafiyya*, a Sunni Muslim doctrine, also remained unknown (see *Amnesty International Report 1994*).

At least nine Christians were arrested in August and held as prisoners of conscience. Sherif Fahmy Ishak, a Coptic Christian and an Egyptian national, was arrested at his home in Riyadh by *al-Mabahith al-'Amma*, who reportedly confiscated religious cassettes, a Bible and other possessions. Eight Filipino Christian worshippers were arrested during a religious service in Riyadh by members of the Committee for the Propagation of Virtue and Prevention of Vice (CPVPV), an official body which supervises the observance of the *Shari'a* (Islamic law). All were released by the end of the year. Nine other Filipino Christians arrested in 1993 were released at the beginning of the year (see *Amnesty International Report 1994*).

At least 30 Iraqi refugees arrested following a protest in Rafha refugee camp in March 1993 remained held without trial (see *Amnesty International Report 1994*). They were among an estimated 23,000 refugees still held in the desert camp in northern Saudi Arabia; all had fled from Iraq during and after the Gulf War or had been captured and held as prisoners of war. While the government continued to regard them as refugees, the International Committee of the Red Cross (ICRC) was understood to consider them as civilian internees to whom the provisions of the Fourth Geneva Convention of 1949 still applied. Disagreement over this issue led to the closure of the ICRC offices in Riyadh in January.

New information was received about the torture and ill-treatment of Iraqi refugees in Rafha and Artawiyya camps since 1991. Among the victims was 'Ali Muhsin Abu Zahra, a former drama teacher arrested in Artawiyya camp in March 1992 on suspicion of writing a play criticizing the camp's authorities. According to his testimony, he was stripped and threatened with rape, and subjected to *falaqa* (beatings on the soles of the feet), beatings all over his body and electric shocks. He eventually signed a "confession" to the effect that he had incited other refugees against the camp's authorities, and was released in April 1992 after one month in incommunicado detention. 'Ali L'aibj Abu Khanjar, son of a prominent tribal leader from southern Iraq, was beaten with cables after refusing to identify any of the refugees who had participated in a protest in Rafha camp in March 1993. He was subsequently taken to an unknown destination and his fate and whereabouts remained unknown.

No known investigation or inquiry was carried out into the death in custody in 1992 of Hussein al-Shuwaykhat (see *Amnesty International Report 1993*), whose body was returned to the family allegedly bearing the marks of torture. He had been held without charge or trial since March 1991 on suspicion of theft.

The judicial punishment of amputation continued to be imposed. Five Sudanese nationals convicted of theft had their right hands amputated in August in Jeddah. Mashooq Banj, a Pakistani national convicted of theft, had his right hand amputated in Jeddah in August.

At least 53 people were executed, all by public beheading. The victims included Indian, Nigerian, Pakistani, Saudi Arabian and Syrian nationals who had been convicted of murder, rape, or drug-trafficking.

The executions were carried out in several cities including Mecca, Medina, Jeddah, Khobar and Riyadh.

Amnesty International expressed concern during the year about the arrest of people for the peaceful expression of their political or religious beliefs, calling for the immediate, unconditional release of all prisoners of conscience. The organization also called for hundreds of suspected Islamist opponents of the government to be released unless charged with a recognizably criminal offence and tried in accordance with international standards. It sought assurances that all were being humanely treated and urged that they be allowed access to family members, defence counsel and doctors. The organization reiterated its opposition to the continued imposition of the cruel, inhuman or degrading punishment of amputation and of the death penalty, appealing for the commutation of all such sentences. No response was received.

In May Amnesty International published a report, *Saudi Arabia: Unwelcome "guests": the plight of Iraqi refugees*. It expressed concern about the pattern of torture and other cruel, inhuman or degrading treatment and punishment to which the refugees had been subjected; the detention of some refugees without trial and without access to legal counsel and family members; the excessive use of lethal force in the camps by the Saudi Arabian army and possible extrajudicial executions; and cases of forcible return of refugees to Iraq where they may face grave human rights violations. Amnesty International called on the government to initiate prompt, thorough and impartial investigations into all such cases and to take immediate steps to put an end to these practices and bring to justice those found responsible. The Saudi Arabian Ambassador to the UK promptly issued a statement denying that Iraqi refugees had been tortured or ill-treated. In mid-May Prince Sultan bin Abdul-'Aziz, the King's brother and Second Deputy Prime Minister, also rejected Amnesty International's findings.

In April Amnesty International submitted information about its concerns in Saudi Arabia for UN review under a procedure established by Economic and Social Council Resolutions 728F/1503, for confidential consideration of communications about human rights violations.

SENEGAL

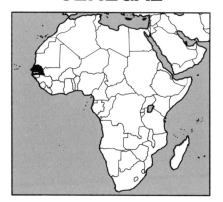

Eleven prisoners of conscience were held for a week. About 150 political prisoners were detained for five months after a violent demonstration, most of whom appeared to be prisoners of conscience; one died in custody, reportedly as a result of torture. The authorities failed to investigate reports of torture. Reports of torture and "disappearances" in previous years had still not been investigated.

Opposition to the government's economic policies intensified in February, after a currency devaluation, and there was controversy about whether opposition political leaders were responsible for the political violence which occurred. Following public protests, some of them violent, large numbers of people associated with opposition parties were arrested, especially members of the Islamist youth movement *Moustarchidina wal Moustarchidati*, Men and Women of Truth (known as the *Moustarchadines*). The *Moustarchadines* were allied to the *Coordination des forces démocratiques* (CFD), Coordination of Democratic Forces, an association of five opposition parties.

The murder in May 1993 of Maître Babacar Sèye, Vice-President of the Constitutional Council (see *Amnesty International Report 1994*), continued to have wide repercussions. Four men were tried in September and convicted of this apparently politically motivated murder, but speculation continued about who had ordered the killing; the authorities exploited the uncertainty in an attempt to discredit the opposition.

In May charges arising from Maître Sèye's murder were dropped against Maître Abdoulaye Wade, leader of the main opposition party, *Parti démocratique sénégalais* (PDS), Senegalese Democratic Party, and six other political figures. The prosecution appealed against the decision. Two of those against whom charges were dropped had spent more than a year in custody and were released only after going on hunger-strike, shortly before the decision was confirmed on appeal in September. One of the two was a PDS member of parliament, Mody Sy, who had reportedly been tortured in custody in May 1993.

The murder investigation itself was marred by a series of shortcomings, notably the apparent failure to hold a full autopsy, and the failure to investigate impartially different allegations. Members of the PDS, who were first implicated in the murder, were charged and detained, but subsequent allegations implicating the Prime Minister were apparently not pursued. Efforts by defence lawyers to persuade relevant witnesses to testify were discouraged by the presiding trial judge.

During the Africa Regional Preparatory Meeting in November for the 1995 UN World Conference on Women, Mauritanian human rights activists were prevented from displaying pictures of torture victims in Mauritania and were later deported from Senegal.

There were reports that Casamance separatist groups kidnapped and ill-treated some local government officials before releasing them. However, there was no repetition of the violence experienced in the first half of 1993. Four men from Casamance were extradited from Guinea-Bissau in June 1994 and remained held without trial in Dakar, the capital, at the end of the year. In November, they were questioned for the first time about allegations of buying arms and offences against the security of the state.

One prisoner was convicted in January and sentenced to one year's imprisonment; he appeared to be a prisoner of conscience. Moustapha Sy, spiritual leader of the *Moustarchadines*, was arrested in October 1993 after criticizing government policy at a PDS meeting. He was found guilty of activities aimed at discrediting the state. He was released in September following a presidential pardon.

Eleven prisoners of conscience were held for a week in February. They were all members of two opposition parties, the

PDS and the *Parti africain pour la démocratie et le socialisme* (PADS), African Party for Democracy and Socialism. They were arrested on 14 February for publicizing an authorized public meeting organized for 16 February by the CFD to protest against the currency devaluation. They were tried on 21 February and each given a one-month suspended sentence on the grounds that they had not obtained prior approval from government officials for their information sessions.

About 150 people, most of whom appeared to be prisoners of conscience, were held for five months. The majority were *Moustarchadines*, but also arrested were Maître Wade, leader of the PDS, and Landing Savané, leader of the PADS. They were arrested and charged with various offences, including undermining the security of the state, in connection with a demonstration which took place after the authorized CFD meeting on 16 February. Eight people were killed, six of them police officers, in violent disturbances after the meeting broke up. In the days following, about 150 people were arrested, but most appeared to have been detained because of their political activities rather than because of any evidence that they had organized or participated in acts of violence on 16 February. The authorities violated the parliamentary immunity of Maître Wade, Landing Savané and a PDS member of parliament, Pape Oumar Kane. Most of the detainees were released on 19 July and the charges against them were dropped.

After the July releases, 24 *Moustarchadines* remained in custody. In September they were tried and all but one were sentenced to between six months' and two years' imprisonment. Another member was sentenced *in absentia* to five years' imprisonment. They were found guilty of participating in an illegal march and violence leading to bloodshed. However, in some cases individual responsibility for acts of violence was not clearly established and allegations that testimonies used to convict people had been obtained under torture were not investigated by the court.

One suspect arrested after the February demonstrations, Lamine Samb, a leading member of the *Moustarchadines*, died in detention, probably as a result of torture. He was arrested on 17 February and died

two days later. He was reported to have been in good health at the time of his arrest and to have been tortured in custody. However, replying to these allegations, the Minister of Justice cited an autopsy report, which was never made public, in which five medical experts concluded that Lamine Samb had died as a result of a heart attack and extensive bruising; they made no attempt to account for the bruising. The Minister claimed that Lamine Samb had been seriously injured during the demonstration before his arrest. However, police did not arrange medical treatment for him until one hour before he died.

In June Amnesty International published a report, *Senegal: Mass arrests and torture*, about the large-scale arrests and reports of torture following the February demonstration. A submission to the authorities in November 1993 expressing Amnesty International's concern about cases of torture and "disappearances" in 1992 and 1993 (see *Amnesty International Report 1994*) was also published after receiving no response from the authorities.

In July the Minister of Justice replied to Amnesty International and stated that investigations into "disappearances" in the Casamance region requested in November 1993 were still under way but that there was no progress. He disputed the reports that Lamine Samb had died in custody as a result of torture. Responding to reports that Mody Sy and Ramata Guèye had been tortured in 1993 (see *Amnesty International Report 1994*), he stated that an official complaint lodged by lawyers in July 1993 had been passed to the gendarmerie and had been rejected for lack of evidence. Amnesty International considered the inquiries into these two cases to be completely inadequate. Despite calls from Amnesty International and a local human rights organization, the *Rencontre africaine pour la défense des droits de l'homme*, African Conference for the Defence of Human Rights, the authorities did not make public the full medical report on Lamine Samb.

SIERRA LEONE

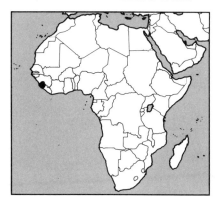

Hundreds of unarmed civilians were killed by insurgent forces, disaffected soldiers and government troops. Government troops tortured, ill-treated and extrajudicially executed captured or suspected insurgents. More than 200 political prisoners were detained without charge or trial during the year, including former government ministers, some of whom may have been prisoners of conscience. A trial of journalists charged with sedition and libel continued. Twelve soldiers were executed after being sentenced to death by court-martial. Armed opponents of the government committed gross human rights abuses, including deliberate and arbitrary killings.

Political violence increased in many parts of the country and it was frequently impossible to establish whether government troops, soldiers who had deserted or insurgents were responsible for killings and other abuses.

The National Provisional Ruling Council (NPRC), headed by Captain Valentine Strasser, which came to power following a military coup in 1992, reaffirmed its commitment to hand over power to an elected government in early 1996. An electoral commission was established and a new constitution drafted. A referendum on the constitution, and legislative and presidential elections were scheduled for 1995. However, return to civilian rule was jeopardized by the deteriorating security situation: local elections did not take place as planned and voter registration was delayed.

Although by the end of 1993 government troops had regained control of areas in the south and east previously held by rebel forces of the Revolutionary United Front (RUF), which had launched an attack from neighbouring Liberia in 1991, fighting intensified during 1994. Attacks by the RUF or other insurgents spread to the centre and north of the country, previously unaffected by the conflict, and were aimed largely at the civilian population, resulting in hundreds of dead and injured. Rape and mutilations were common. Thousands of people fled their homes, seeking refuge in displaced people's camps or neighbouring countries.

During 1994 the identity and motives of those carrying out attacks became increasingly difficult to establish. Although the government invariably claimed rebel forces were responsible, there was evidence that many attacks were in fact carried out by disaffected soldiers, some of them deserters but others still serving soldiers. Many attacks appeared to be carried out for material gain, but it also appeared that some were carried out by factions within the army opposed to the NPRC. Some disaffected soldiers appeared to have joined RUF forces, whereas others formed separate armed groups. Individuals claiming to represent the RUF publicly claimed responsibility for an attack in the far north in November during which civilians, including two foreign nationals, were abducted. Following this attack the NPRC called for dialogue with the RUF; a meeting between representatives of the NPRC and the RUF was officially reported to have taken place in early December but there was a subsequent escalation in violence.

The NPRC admitted that there were serious problems of indiscipline within the army: a number of soldiers were tried before courts-martial and some sentenced to death (see below). In July and August members of a Liberian armed group, the United Liberation Movement for Democracy in Liberia (ULIMO), which had been involved in operations alongside Sierra Leonean troops against the RUF, were disarmed and returned to Liberia, after complaints by traditional rulers in the southeast that they had attacked villages and looted property.

Government troops extrajudicially executed captured rebels and people accused of collaborating with rebel forces. Victims were mutilated: severed heads were sometimes displayed on army vehicles. Rebels who surrendered in February in Buedu, Kailahun District, in Eastern Province, were reported to have been summarily executed by soldiers. In April some 30 people, including children, from the village of Dodo Kotuma, also in Kailahun District, who had been hiding in the bush were reportedly taken back to their village by soldiers and then to Buedu where 25, apparently suspected of collaboration with rebels, were shot dead by soldiers.

As many as 80 Sierra Leoneans, an Irish priest, a Dutch doctor and his family were killed in an attack on Panguma, Kenema District, Eastern Province, in March. Although the attack was officially attributed to rebel forces, witnesses claimed that soldiers had been responsible for some of the deaths and property belonging to the murdered foreigners was later found in a soldier's home. An official inquiry concluded that two soldiers had contributed to the deaths through negligence but had not been directly involved; although arrested, they had not been prosecuted by the end of the year.

There was uncertainty about the identity of those responsible for other incidents. Major roads were a particular target for attacks; the routes between Bo and Kenema in the south and Makeni and Koidu in the north became impassable without military escort. On 5 August a convoy was attacked by men in army uniforms near Matotoka; at least three, but possibly more, civilians were reportedly shot, women were reported to have been stripped and raped and others were abducted. On 25 August another convoy was attacked, again by men in army uniforms, between Matotoka and Makali, resulting in many deaths of both civilians and soldiers; Captain Nasiru Barrie was reported to have been beheaded. The timing and precision of these attacks suggested collusion by some soldiers with the attackers.

Several journalists, in particular those covering the conflict, received anonymous death threats.

Suspected rebels were tortured and ill-treated by soldiers, often in public. Prisoners were bound tightly, sometimes with both arms and legs tied behind them, beaten and mutilated. For example, four suspected rebels were reportedly taken to a military barracks in March following an attack on Koribundu, Bo District. Their hands and feet were reportedly bound with wire and rope and they were thrown to the ground and kicked. They were then suspended head down from iron bars and kicked.

There were also reports of soldiers ill-treating civilians in areas not affected by armed attacks, for example, in Freetown, the capital. They appeared to act with impunity.

At the beginning of the year some 170 political detainees were held without charge or trial in the Central Prison, Pademba Road, in Freetown. Some had been held for more than two years. By June the number had increased to over 200. They were held under legislation introduced by the NPRC which allows indefinite administrative detention without charge or trial with no recourse to the courts. Most were held on suspicion that they were rebels but others were accused of involvement in alleged conspiracies to overthrow the government in November and December 1992 (see *Amnesty International Report 1993*). More than 10 of those arrested in November 1992 remained held. Two soldiers arrested in December 1992 also remained detained, although a student arrested at the same time, Sahid Mohamed Sesay, was released in late December 1993 (see *Amnesty International Report 1994*). During the year, the authorities reviewed the cases of uncharged political detainees. Some, including Sorie Daffey, a 73-year-old trader held since October 1992, were released during the first half of the year; some 220 others were freed on 23 December when the government announced that there was insufficient evidence to keep them in prison. It was not clear how many detainees remained held at the end of the year.

More than 20 former government ministers and others associated with the ousted government of former President Joseph Saidu Momoh were arrested in early May and detained in Pademba Road Prison where they were initially denied access to families and lawyers; one was reported to have been beaten by soldiers while in prison. Most had been arrested previously at the time of the coup in 1992 and detained without charge for periods of up to a year. Judicial commissions of inquiry, established in 1992 to investigate accusations of corruption by former government ministers, civil servants and state corporations, submitted reports directly to the NPRC. These reports were not made public but the NPRC subsequently published its decisions on the commissions' findings; it confiscated the property of some former ministers and ordered compensation to the state of sums alleged to have been misappropriated. Although the official reason for the arrests was non-payment of compensation, no criminal charges were brought and it appeared that some of those detained may have been held only because of their association with the former government and their suspected opposition to the NPRC. Most were released in August and September, others later in the year, but some were restricted under house arrest. At least two – Dr Bu-Buakei Jabbie and Ahmad Edward Sisay – were still in detention at the end of the year.

The trial of four journalists on an independent newspaper, *The New Breed*, and a printing company manager continued. They had been arrested in October 1993 and charged with seditious publication and libel after reporting allegations of government corruption (see *Amnesty International Report 1994*). They were released on bail but their trial before the High Court in Freetown was repeatedly adjourned. Lawyers representing the five, who included Dr Julius Spencer, the newspaper's director, and editor Donald John, challenged the High Court's proceedings on the grounds that a fair trial had been jeopardized by pre-trial publicity, but the Supreme Court ruled in July that the trial could resume. However, defence lawyers subsequently withdrew, questioning the trial's fairness, and the defendants were redetained on 12 December after appearing in court without legal representation. After several subsequent hearings, the trial was adjourned until January 1995.

Four foreign nationals arrested in October 1993 were detained until November. They had been arrested in Freetown on suspicion of involvement in a plot against the government and subsequently charged with treason (see *Amnesty International Report 1994*). A magistrate ruled in May that there was sufficient evidence to proceed to trial, although key evidence was not presented in court. In November the Attorney General announced that the government had decided not to proceed with the prosecution, giving no explanation.

Twelve soldiers, including a 77-year-old warrant officer, were executed on 11 and 12 November after being convicted by courts-martial in Freetown of charges which included collaborating with rebels, armed robbery and murder. Other trials before courts-martial of soldiers accused of similar offences also took place. It emerged that courts-martial had passed 25 death sentences since the NPRC came to power in 1992. Defendants before courts-martial had no right of appeal to a higher court against conviction or sentence. The then Attorney General, Franklyn Bai Kargbo, resigned in September in protest against the use of the death penalty and subsequently left the country. There were no executions of prisoners sentenced to death by ordinary courts.

Armed opponents of the government, including both RUF forces and disaffected government soldiers, were responsible for the abduction, torture and killing of hundreds of unarmed civilians. On 30 June some 60 villagers were killed at Telu Jaiama, Bo District, Southern Province; more than 20 others were seriously injured. Another 70 villagers were killed two months later at Telu Bongor, also in Bo District.

Some of those captured during attacks were forced to join rebel forces; others were held as hostages. For example, on 7 November rebels attacked Kabala, Koinadugu District, in Northern Province, an area until then considered safe; at least 10 civilians were killed and others, including two British aid workers, were abducted. Radio messages by alleged members of the RUF claimed they were holding the two men and demanded arms and ammunition. The two were still held at the end of the year.

Attacks intensified in late December. Dozens of people were reported killed in attacks around Bo and Kenema. For example, on 24 December many civilians were killed when rebel forces overran a displaced people's camp at Gondama, south of Bo, where an estimated 80,000 people had sought refuge; others drowned in the Sewa river attempting to escape. Five people, including prominent lawyer Patrick P. B. Kebbie, were killed in an attack on Kenema on 25 December.

Amnesty International expressed concern that, although the government continued to blame rebel forces for attacks on

260

unarmed civilians, there was evidence that some attacks had been carried out by serving government soldiers. Amnesty International also condemned the killings of civilians by rebel forces of the RUF and disaffected soldiers. In May Amnesty International called for the release of detained former government ministers unless they were to be charged and given a fair trial. It also called for the repeal of legislation allowing administrative detention without charge or trial and repeatedly called for a review of the cases of all other uncharged political detainees. The organization condemned the executions of 12 soldiers in November and urged that no further executions take place.

SINGAPORE

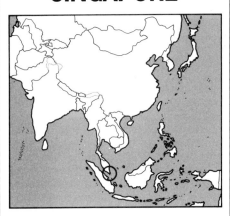

Two former prisoners of conscience continued to be subject to government orders restricting their freedom of expression and association. Criminal offenders were subjected to cruel, inhuman or degrading punishment. At least 10 people were sentenced to death and 32 were executed.

Restriction orders limiting freedom of association and expression continued to be imposed on Chia Thye Poh and Vincent Cheng, two former prisoners of conscience (see *Amnesty International Reports 1991* to *1994*).

Caning, which constitutes a cruel, inhuman and degrading form of punishment, remained a mandatory punishment for some 30 crimes, including armed robbery, attempted murder, drug-trafficking, illegal immigration and rape. In May Michael Fay, a teenager from the USA who was convicted of several charges of van-

dalism, was given four strokes of the cane in addition to a four-month prison sentence and a fine. In September Ramanathan Yogendran, a lawyer, was sentenced to 12 strokes of the cane and five years' imprisonment after he was convicted of five criminal offences including fabricating evidence and criminal intimidation.

At least 10 people were sentenced to death, of whom eight were convicted of drug-trafficking and two of murder. They included Sagar Suppiah Retnam, a labourer, who was sentenced to death in May for murder. Navarat Maykha, a Thai woman, was sentenced to death in July for drug-trafficking.

At least 32 people were executed. Yeo Choon Chau, Lai Kim Loy, Tee Seh Ping, Hanafiah Bedullah and Mat Repin Mamat, all Malaysian nationals, were executed by hanging on 13 May at Changi prison. All had been sentenced to death for drug-trafficking. Yeo Poh Choon was also executed on 13 May: he had been sentenced to death in September 1993 by the Court of Criminal Appeal despite having been acquitted in July 1993 by the High Court.

Amnesty International urged the authorities to lift the restrictions on the two former prisoners of conscience. It also urged the authorities to end the punishment of caning and to commute all death sentences.

SOMALIA

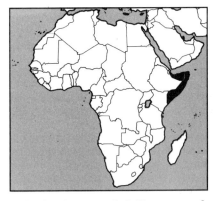

Hundreds of unarmed civilians were deliberately killed by members of armed political groups on account of their membership of a particular clan. Many women were raped by militias. A woman and 12 men had limbs amputated as punishments ordered by an unofficial Islamic court in Mogadishu, which also decreed and carried out a death sentence by stoning and over 160 floggings. There were at least two other executions in Mogadishu after unofficial courts condemned prisoners to death.

The UN peace-making operation, UNOSOM II, established in May 1993 with a two-year mandate to end fighting between the two main clan alliances and launch a national reconstruction program (see *Amnesty International Report 1994*), had failed to achieve many of its objectives by the end of the year. In March the UN Security Council authorized the withdrawal of the 20,000 western troops in its military operation, and in November it decided to pull out the remaining 15,000 African, Arab and Asian troops by March 1995, the planned end of the UNOSOM II operation. Yet fighting between General Mohamed Farah Aideed's Somali National Alliance (SNA) and Ali Mahdi's Somali Salvation Alliance (SSA) broke out frequently during 1994. Little progress had been made by the end of the year towards implementing a Peace and Reconciliation Declaration which both parties signed in Nairobi in March, or towards establishing a Transitional National Council as an interim government to administer the collapsed Somali state with UN assistance.

Somali civilians, including women who were raped, were the main victims of the continuing high level of inter-clan violence. The insecurity also seriously affected humanitarian operations run by international non-governmental organizations (NGOs). Several aid workers and journalists reporting on their relief work were killed or taken hostage for some weeks by armed groups, and most international NGOs, after losing relief supplies and property to looters, pulled out of the country. UN troops provided a measure of security in escorting food convoys but they were progressively pulled back to bases in Mogadishu towards the end of the year in the run-up to the planned withdrawal. Dozens of UN troops were killed in clashes, as well as Somali militia members and possibly hundreds of unarmed civilians.

In January the UN freed eight senior SNA officials it had detained the previous October. They were held in poor conditions without charge or trial, and denied access to their relatives or lawyers. UN Secretary-General Boutros Boutros-Ghali ordered their release on the recommendation of an independent jurist appointed by the UN to visit Somalia to review their detentions. Somalis detained by the UN during 1994 on suspicion of involvement in armed attacks on the UN or criminal offences were apparently transferred quickly to the custody of the new Somali police, prisons and judicial services established by the UN. No details were disclosed by the UN on people detained, charged, tried or released.

An Independent Expert appointed by the UN in August 1993 on the recommendation of the UN Commission on Human Rights visited Somalia in January but the Ombudsman function he proposed to undertake to examine complaints of human rights violations by Somali groups or militias or UN troops had not started by the end of the year. In late 1994 the UN released the report of an international commission of inquiry which it set up in 1993 to review the attacks on UN troops that year (see *Amnesty International Report 1994*). It criticized military aspects of the UN operation and proposed compensation should be paid for abuses by UN troops. The UN did not disclose what specific measures it was taking to meet these recommendations but during 1994 UN policy on the use of force changed and UN troops performed a predominantly defensive role.

In November and December there was fighting in Hargeisa, the capital of the breakaway Republic of Somaliland in the northwest, which had been under President Mohamed Ibrahim Egal's interim administration since May 1993. Tens of thousands of people fled to neighbouring Ethiopia. President Egal declared a state of emergency in December.

Despite the failure by the UN command force and the US Rapid Reaction Force to investigate alleged human rights abuses by their own troops, cases of alleged abuses involving soldiers of three national contingents continued to be under investigation by their own governments – in Canada, Belgium and Germany (see *Amnesty International Report 1994*). In Canada, seven soldiers were brought to court, mostly in connection with the death of a Somali prisoner in 1993; one was convicted of

262

manslaughter and imprisoned for five years, two were convicted of lesser offences, three were acquitted, and a seventh case was pending. A public inquiry was announced after the publication in November 1994 of photographs depicting ill-treatment of a Somali intruder into the Canadian army compound in Mogadishu in March 1993. In Belgium, 13 cases continued to be under judicial investigation since 1993 and a court martial of eight alleged offenders began in December, for offences including manslaughter. In Germany in September, a military inquiry investigated reports of ill-treatment of detained Somali criminal suspects in 1993.

Hundreds of unarmed civilians, including women and children, were deliberately killed by members of armed political groups on account of their membership of a particular clan during fighting between opposing clan factions. Many women were raped by members of clan-based militias. Information was difficult to obtain, and details of individual incidents hard to verify. Hundreds of civilians and many more fighters were killed in flare-ups of fighting in Mogadishu in October and December between General Aideed's SNA and Ali Mahdi's SSA. There was also fighting at times, although on a less serious scale, between clan-based groups in Belet Huen, Baidoa and Kismayu. Scores of unarmed civilians as well as fighters were killed in clashes between troops loyal to President Egal and his Somali National Movement (SNM) party and armed men of a clan group supporting former Somaliland President Abdirahman Ali Ahmed in November and December in Hargeisa.

In a part of northern Mogadishu controlled by the SSA, an unofficial Islamic court was established in August which imposed cruel, inhuman and degrading punishments. A woman and 12 men were convicted of violent robbery and sentenced to amputations of a hand or a hand and a leg, which were carried out immediately in public. The court also ordered and publicly carried out over 160 floggings of between 20 and 100 lashes each.

On 8 December the same court condemned a man to death by stoning for rape and he was immediately stoned to death by a crowd. At least two other people were executed on the orders of unofficial courts in 1994.

Amnesty International appealed to the UN and Somali political groups to work together for justice and human rights. In a letter to the UN in March, Amnesty International criticized the lack of emphasis placed on human rights in the UNOSOM operation, and particularly the inadequacy of investigations into killings by UN and US troops in 1993, arbitrary detentions without charge or trial, and the absence of any real program of human rights. Amnesty International called for the UNOSOM Human Rights Office to be fully activated and supported, and for the Ombudsman to be established. It recommended human rights training for all UN troops and for officers in the new Somali police and prison services, and urged the UN to report regularly and publicly on its work to re-establish the judiciary and develop protection of human rights. The organization welcomed steps being taken by the Canadian, Belgian and German authorities to bring to justice any soldiers found to be responsible for human rights abuses.

Amnesty International urged General Aideed and Ali Mahdi to assert control of their armed militias and supporters and to end the summary executions and ill-treatment of members of other political or clan groups. It condemned the stoning execution, amputations and floggings in northern Mogadishu, and called on Somali political leaders not to allow these cruel, inhuman and degrading punishments and to intervene to prevent any executions.

SOUTH AFRICA

After months of political uncertainty and violence, the country's first non-racial national elections were held successfully in April. At least 2,683 people were killed in political violence during the year – some of whom were extrajudicially executed. At least two thirds of the deaths occurred before the elections. Further evidence emerged of collusion by the security forces in past political killings. Torture of detainees by the police and army was reported; at least 32 died in police custody in suspicious circumstances. Twenty-five people were sentenced to death and 450 remained on death row. There were no executions.

AMNESTY INTERNATIONAL REPORT 1995

The African National Congress (ANC) won the April elections, with over 62 per cent of the vote. The National Party (NP) and Inkatha Freedom Party (IFP) secured sufficient votes to be allocated cabinet posts in the government. On 10 May Nelson Mandela was inaugurated as President. The new National Assembly and Senate opened in late May, and in the following months nine new provincial governments began operating.

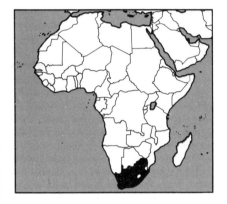

On 24 May the National Assembly and the Senate, sitting jointly as a Constitutional Assembly, began reviewing the interim constitution, which must be adopted in final form by May 1996. The interim constitution guarantees certain "fundamental human rights", including the right to life and the right not to be tortured. It also provides for institutions to protect these rights, including a Constitutional Court.

The new parliament approved the establishment of a Human Rights Commission to promote and protect "fundamental rights", monitor legislative and executive measures which may affect these rights, and investigate alleged violations.

In July the Ministry of Safety and Security published a bill intended to reform the Police Act. Its proposals included the establishment of an independent "mechanism" to investigate complaints against the police. The bill had not gone to parliament by the end of the year. In November the Ministry of Justice published the draft Promotion of National Unity and Reconciliation Bill, providing for the establishment of a commission to investigate past human rights violations, to consider requests for amnesty for politically motivated acts, and to recommend compensation for victims of human rights violations.

In October South Africa signed a number of human rights treaties, including the International Covenant on Civil and Political Rights.

Further evidence emerged through court proceedings and commissions of inquiry that members of the security forces had colluded with paramilitary groups to foment political violence, resulting in thousands of deaths since the late 1980s, and to commit serious human rights violations. In March the judicial commission of inquiry chaired by Judge Richard Goldstone released an interim report confirming that three senior police generals had authorized the illegal supply of weapons to and the training of IFP members by a unit of the South African Police (SAP), which had also organized violence through IFP-dominated hostels against township communities and commuters on trains. The report implicated, among others, Colonel Eugene de Kock, the former commander of a security police counter-insurgency unit based at Vlakplaas. In early May the Transvaal Attorney General confirmed that there was *prima facie* evidence linking certain members of the police to "crimes [including] murder, bombings, and the unlawful possession and supply of arms and ammunition". Later that month, Colonel Eugene de Kock was arrested and was subsequently denied bail. He was due to stand trial in 1995 on 121 charges, including one for the 1991 murder of human rights lawyer Bheki Mlangeni (see *Amnesty International Report 1993*). A number of other former Vlakplaas operatives were also facing charges in the same trial.

Between 1 January and the elections, at least 1,600 people were killed in political violence, the majority in Natal Province, the East Rand near Johannesburg and in the Bophuthatswana "homeland".

In Natal province the death toll rose dramatically from mid-March with at least 429 people killed in the following four weeks. Paramilitaries trained in a camp set up by KwaZulu "homeland" government officials, the IFP and members of the security forces attacked ANC-aligned communities and individuals involved in preparing for the April elections, which at that stage the IFP was boycotting. Hundreds of residents fled the Ndwedwe area

264

near Durban, for instance, following repeated attacks by heavily armed men supported by KwaZulu police officers. In one incident, 11 employees of a private company who were distributing voting procedure pamphlets in Ndwedwe were abducted on 12 April by the local IFP-aligned chief and others. They were tortured for several hours, including with hot wires, and then shot. Eight died and three escaped. The level of killings in Natal decreased substantially from late April as a result of the increased presence of the South African Defence Force (SADF) and the IFP's 19 April decision to contest the elections.

On the East Rand, the withdrawal of the SAP's Internal Stability Unit (ISU), which had been implicated in torture and extrajudicial executions, and the presence of SADF patrols also led to a marked decrease in the number of political killings. However, some SADF members committed human rights violations, including the extrajudicial execution of Jeffrey Sibiya, an IFP member and National Peace Accord worker.

At least 53 people were killed and several hundred wounded when shooting erupted in central Johannesburg during an IFP anti-election campaign rally on 28 March. Investigations by the police and the Goldstone Commission failed to clarify who was responsible for the majority of the deaths, which occurred when snipers fired on the marchers as they reached Library Gardens. Eleven people were killed when ANC security guards fired on a group of the marchers outside the ANC's Shell House headquarters. Police investigations into the latter incident continued throughout the year. Members of the new parliament criticized the ANC for failing to cooperate promptly with the investigation.

In the Bophuthatswana "homeland", repression intensified as the government of Lucas Mangope resisted participating in the national elections. On 12 February, for instance, 19-year-old Mary Keitumetse Gaolaolwe died when she was shot in the face by a police officer who was dispersing ANC supporters in the village of Mareetsane, southwest of Mafikeng.

Dozens of black civilians were killed and a number of journalists were assaulted by white right-wing paramilitaries who entered the "homeland" at the behest

of its government on 10 March. The following day two paramilitaries were extra-judicially executed by the police after sections of the "homeland" security forces joined the popular rebellion against the "homeland" government.

After the national elections, the level of political violence subsided in most parts of the country, except in Natal. Towards the end of 1994 the death toll in this province rose sharply, with at least 75 people killed in December. In many incidents the police failed to protect ANC-supporting communities, trade unionists and IFP leaders involved in peace initiatives. In some cases the police appeared to have supplied arms and ammunition to the killers. In one incident, 15 people were killed when approximately 100 men armed with traditional weapons and guns attacked the village of Gcilima, south of Durban, on 27 October. The ISU based in the area failed to intervene despite having been warned days before that an attack on Gcilima was imminent. In November the Minister of Safety and Security summoned senior provincial police officers to Pretoria to account for their failure to arrest the perpetrators of political killings.

There were also some political killings in other areas after the elections. On 29 April, in Driefontein in the Eastern Transvaal Province, the body of Lazarus Yende, the ANC Youth League Chairperson, was found floating in a reservoir. He had been abducted from the local ANC office several days earlier. The police had been warned that named people were planning to kill Lazarus Yende and other prominent ANC members, but they took no steps to protect them. On 31 July Hendrietta Nkabinde, an executive member of the South African Rural Women's Movement, was shot dead outside her home in Driefontein. Other prominent members of the community received death threats. By the end of the year no one had been brought to justice for these crimes.

Several cases involving past political killings were resolved. In May Judge Neville Zeitsman ruled that four Eastern Cape political activists had been murdered by the security forces in June 1985 (see *Amnesty International Report 1986*). In November a Cape Town magistrate ruled that six police officers from Nyanga police station had unlawfully killed a former member of the ANC's military wing,

Khaya Simani, in April 1993 (see *Amnesty International Report 1994*). Both cases were referred to the Attorney General.

In December the Circuit Court in Mtunzini convicted three people, including two members of the KwaZulu Police, of extrajudicial executions committed in the Esikhawini area of northern Natal in 1993. Reports by the pre-election multi-party Transitional Executive Council's (TEC's) Task Force on the KwaZulu Police concluded that senior members of the KwaZulu Police, including the acting commissioner, had aided assassins within the police force and obstructed investigations into alleged political killings by IFP members. The Task Force called for the suspension of several senior police officers, but those named were still on duty at the end of the year. However, the new Minister of Safety and Security ordered further investigations into the allegations.

Torture of political detainees and criminal suspects was frequently reported. The allegations implicated in particular members of police murder and robbery squads and other special investigation units, and the ISU.

For example, in January teenagers Petrus Nyamande and Michael Mathe were arrested by ISU members in the East Rand township of Katlehong. Both were assaulted during arrest and tortured during interrogation. They were kicked and beaten, attacked by a police dog, and repeatedly subjected to partial suffocation with rubber tubing pulled over their faces. All charges against both were later dropped.

On 19 February Thebiso Lephoto and seven others, including two 14-year-olds, were arrested in Thokoza township by soldiers and taken to Steenpunt army base. There, they were stripped, beaten and tortured with electric shocks while being interrogated about the activities of self-defence units in the township. One of the detainees was threatened with being buried alive and had a gun forced into his mouth.

In August the national Minister of Safety and Security ordered an independent investigation into persistent reports of torture by members of police special investigation units based in the Vaal Triangle area south of Johannesburg. The victims were predominantly criminal suspects. The investigation was precipitated

by the discovery by visiting Dutch police officers in May of torture equipment in a police station. By the end of the year more than 100 investigated complaints of torture had been referred to the Attorney General for possible prosecution. On 16 September one complainant, Don Molebatsi, was shot dead by the police officer whom he had alleged had tortured him.

In a number of cases, criminal suspects died in circumstances suggesting extrajudicial execution. For instance, on 7 November Nazeem Jacobs was shot dead in the custody of the Bellville murder and robbery squad. The police said that they had shot him when he attacked a police officer with his handcuffs. The previous day Nazeem Jacobs had told his family that he had been tortured and feared he would be killed.

In a few cases perpetrators of past violations were brought to justice. In August the Graaff-Reinet Regional Court convicted Detective Sergeant Willem van Heerden of intent to do grievous bodily harm, common assault and defeating the ends of justice, for the torture in 1993 of six farmworkers. During interrogation the farmworkers had been handcuffed, blindfolded, suspended from a pole under their knees and subjected to electric shocks or partial suffocation with rubber tubing.

In October a prison warder was sentenced to nine years' imprisonment on conviction of murdering an ANC security official, Msizi Mchunu, by shooting him in the back at Ulundi police station on 23 April. At the end of the year the trial was continuing of seven men, including an ANC security guard, who were charged with the abduction and assault of six people, including a 14-year-old boy, in the ANC's regional headquarters in Johannesburg in April.

Twenty-five people were sentenced to death. President Mandela's government maintained the moratorium on executions.

Prior to the elections, Amnesty International campaigned to expose continuing human rights violations, particularly those affecting the prospects for free and fair elections. The organization lobbied bodies responsible for conducting and monitoring the election process, including the government, TEC, Independent Electoral Commission, and the UN and other intergovernmental organizations' observer missions.

266

In an oral statement to the UN Commission on Human Rights in February, Amnesty International highlighted the positive post-election prospects inherent in the new constitution, but stressed that these could be jeopardized unless firm steps were taken before the election to curb political killings and other human rights violations and to restore public confidence in the police and criminal justice system.

Amnesty International issued two reports in March addressing the human rights crisis in Bophuthatswana and issues of justice and accountability left outstanding after the "homeland" government collapsed.

Amnesty International delegates visited South Africa during the election period to gather information about long-standing human rights concerns.

After the elections, Amnesty International called on the government to ratify international human rights instruments, abolish the death penalty and to bring to justice perpetrators of human rights violations. It appealed to the new national and provincial authorities to investigate new reports of extrajudicial executions and torture and to provide safeguards in law and practice against further abuses.

In July Amnesty International submitted comments to the government on the proposed complaints investigation mechanism in the draft Police Bill. In November Amnesty International delegates met the Minister of Justice in London to discuss the proposed Commission for Truth and Reconciliation. On request, Amnesty International also provided documentation on the abolition of the death penalty.

SPAIN

There were further allegations of torture and ill-treatment by law enforcement and prison officers. There were numerous trials of officers accused of torture and ill-treatment.

Attacks by the armed Basque group, *Euskadi Ta Askatasuna* (ETA), Basque Homeland and Liberty, on the security forces and civilians continued throughout the year. Thirteen people, including four civilians, were killed and more than 20 people were injured.

Special legislation regarding armed groups remained in force. People suspected of belonging to or collaborating with an armed group can be held incommunicado for up to five days by judicial order, 48 hours longer than the normal limit, and are denied the right to designate lawyers of their choice.

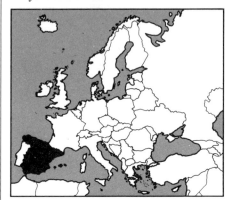

A major national human rights organization, the Association against Torture (ACT), recorded 267 complaints of torture by law enforcement and prison officers in its report for 1993 published in October. This was a significant increase over the previous year. ACT stated that its examination of judicial action on torture allegations revealed "the continuation of the policy of reward and pardon" which effectively provided impunity for officers convicted of torture.

In March a judicial investigation opened into the alleged suicide of José Luis Iglesias Amaro, who had been found on 28 February hanging by his shoe laces in an isolation cell in Picassent II prison, near Valencia. He had a history of self-injury and a few days before his death had attempted to escape from a hospital where he was receiving treatment for self-inflicted injuries. Fellow prisoners alleged that he was taken on a stretcher to the cell where he later died. According to their statements, he was repeatedly beaten by prison guards armed with truncheons in the days leading to his death. Photographs of the deceased and the autopsy revealed numerous injuries, two to four days old, including large blood clots in the head and severe bruising to the face and body. The injuries were consistent with blows from truncheons. The investigating magistrate failed to interview fellow prisoners, stating that he considered it unnecessary.

The inquiry was still open at the end of the year.

Numerous trials of officers charged with torture and ill-treatment took place.

In January the Provincial Court in Valencia sentenced a police officer to four months and one day in prison for assaulting and seriously injuring Hamid Raaji, a Moroccan national (see *Amnesty International Report 1994*). In September the Supreme Court rejected the officer's appeal against this sentence. The officer was not imprisoned, as custodial sentences of less than one year and one day are customarily not served.

The trial of 16 prison officers accused of ill-treating 17 prisoners in the Modelo prison in Barcelona in 1990 (see *Amnesty International Reports 1991* and *1993*) opened in October. In November, 12 officers were found guilty of injuring the prisoners and using "unnecessary severity". Two officers were suspended for four years and 10 for three years; four others were acquitted.

In October a police officer in La Coruña was committed for trial in December on charges of ill-treating and injuring Carlos Viña Pena, a Civil Guard reservist (see *Amnesty International Report 1994*). However, the court hearing was postponed on procedural grounds at the plaintiff's request.

Two Civil Guards and three policemen were charged in October with beating, ill-treating and threatening Mohamed Hegazy and Raed Shibli in Ibiza in 1991 (see *Amnesty International Reports 1992* and *1994*).

In November the Provincial Court in San Sebastian retried five Civil Guard officers charged with torturing Juan Carlos Garmendia Irazusta in 1982. In July the Supreme Court had ordered the retrial after overturning the 1993 acquittal of these officers by the Provincial Court in San Sebastian (see *Amnesty International Report 1994*). Three officers were found guilty and the court passed minimum sentences of two months' imprisonment. The other two officers were acquitted.

In June the government granted the petition for pardon of a lieutenant colonel in the Civil Guard. He was the senior officer among nine defendants sentenced in 1990 to terms of imprisonment, fines and disqualification from duty for torturing Tomás Linaza Euba in 1981 (see *Amnesty International Reports 1982* and *1991*). The officers did not serve their sentences, claiming that proceedings relevant to their convictions were pending. In February the Provincial Court of Vizcaya ordered the lieutenant colonel to prison to serve his six-year prison sentence. Two other officers were not imprisoned as they had been sentenced to less than the customary custodial term of one year and one day. The court also opposed the granting of the lieutenant colonel's petition for pardon. Four months later the government pardoned and released him.

At the end of the year the government was considering the appeal for pardons of five Civil Guard officers found guilty in October 1992 of torturing Joaquín Olano in 1983 (see *Amnesty International Reports 1984* and *1993*).

Amnesty International urged the authorities to ensure that all allegations of torture and ill-treatment were thoroughly and impartially investigated and to bring those responsible to justice.

SRI LANKA

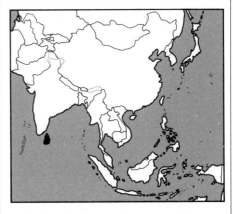

Hundreds of Tamil people, including prisoners of conscience, were detained, particularly in the early part of the year. Torture and ill-treatment of detainees in police and military custody were widespread; at least one person died allegedly as a result of torture. Legal safeguards for detainees were flouted. At least 10 people were reported to have "disappeared". Several people may have been extrajudicially executed. Further evidence came to light of gross human rights violations in

the south between 1987 and 1990, but impunity for those responsible remained a serious concern. The Liberation Tigers of Tamil Eelam (LTTE) were responsible for numerous human rights abuses, including "executions" of prisoners.

In August the People's Alliance (PA), a coalition of parties headed by the Sri Lanka Freedom Party, won parliamentary elections and formed a government together with the Sri Lanka Muslim Congress party, bringing an end to 17 years of government by the United National Party (UNP). The leader of the PA, Chandrika Bandaranaike Kumaratunga, was sworn in as President after winning presidential elections in November. The UNP presidential candidate, Gamini Dissanayake, was among more than 50 people killed at an election rally on 24 October by a suicide bomber suspected of belonging to the LTTE.

The new government established three commissions to investigate "disappearances" and extrajudicial executions that had occurred since 1 January 1988. However, the commissions were not mandated to investigate the approximately 700 unresolved "disappearances" which took place between 1984 and 1987. The new government introduced legislation to give effect to the UN Convention against Torture and Other, Cruel, Inhuman or Degrading Treatment or Punishment, to which the former government had acceded in January. The cases of all prisoners held under the Prevention of Terrorism Act and the Emergency Regulations were reviewed. The new government also announced a review of Sri Lanka's status under international human rights instruments and said it would bring to justice the perpetrators of human rights violations, grant compensation to the victims, strengthen the constitutional protection of human rights and establish a national human rights commission. However, by the end of the year most of these measures had not been implemented.

Armed conflict between the security forces and the LTTE continued in the northeast. A number of goodwill measures were taken, including the release of prisoners by both sides. The government partially lifted the embargo imposed in June 1990 on the LTTE-controlled areas in the north of the country. Representatives of the new government and the LTTE met in mid-October. However, further meetings were suspended following the killing of Gamini Dissanayake and more than 50 others in October.

The state of emergency lapsed in July after the dissolution of parliament. It was briefly reimposed throughout the country after the parliamentary elections in August and following the killing of the UNP presidential candidate in October. At the end of the year, it remained in force in the northeast of the country, parts of Puttalam, Anuradhapura and Polonnaruwa Districts, and in the capital, Colombo, and surrounding areas. Under the ERs in force at the end of the year the security forces were no longer required to report arrests to the Human Rights Task Force (HRTF), a body set up by the government in 1991 to establish and maintain a central register of detainees and to monitor their welfare (see *Amnesty International Report 1994*).

Hundreds of Tamil people, including dozens of prisoners of conscience held solely on account of their ethnic origin, were detained in the northeast and in Colombo, particularly in the early part of the year. Most were released within a week. Some of those arrested were held in unacknowledged detention for several days. In February Sivasekaram Panchalingam was abducted in Colombo on his way to work by a group of armed men in plain clothes. He was reportedly kept blindfold and beaten daily for 16 days at an unofficial place of detention used by officers of the Special Task Force (STF). Throughout this period relatives were not given any information about his whereabouts. He was later handed over to the Criminal Investigation Department (CID) and was still held without charge or trial at the end of the year.

According to figures published by the HRTF in August, 3,850 people were held under the Emergency Regulations or the Prevention of Terrorism Act: 646 in detention camps, 204 in rehabilitation camps, about 2,000 in police stations and about 1,000 in army camps. At the end of the year an estimated 700 detainees remained held.

There were persistent reports of torture and ill-treatment from all parts of the country. In April a young farmer collecting his identity card from an STF camp in Batticaloa District was taken into custody on suspicion of supporting the LTTE. He was beaten and lost consciousness when

STF officers attempted to strangle him with a nylon rope. In May police at Gokarella, Kurunegala District, arrested W.A. Ranjan Weerasuriya in connection with a robbery. He alleged that he was hung upside-down and beaten on the chest and shoulders for about two hours; that he was made to inhale burning charcoal and chilli powder; that a piece of wood was inserted into his anal passage and that his testicles were hit with a club.

In the south, an army deserter who had been arrested died at Panagoda army camp in early April, allegedly as a result of torture. A post-mortem revealed multiple injuries to his body, limbs and head, all caused by blunt instruments.

At least 10 "disappearances" were reported from the east. On 13 January, Pannichan Kumarakulasingham and his brother-in-law, Krishnapillai Thanabalasingham, were taken from their homes at Thalankuda, Batticaloa District, in the middle of the night by STF personnel. Despite eye-witness accounts of the arrest, STF officials at various camps in the area denied that the two men were in their custody. Their fate and whereabouts remained unknown at the end of the year.

A lawyer, several opposition politicians and journalists involved in the excavation of mass graves at Suriyakande in January received death threats.

Several possible extrajudicial executions were reported from the northeast. In the Jaffna peninsula, at least 10 civilians were reportedly killed during shelling and bombing carried out by the security forces in apparent retaliation for attacks by LTTE cadres on military targets. At Valaichenai, Batticaloa District, a 13-year-old boy was killed and three other people were injured when police fired indiscriminately inside a mosque. Seven police officers were arrested in connection with this killing; others were transferred out of the area.

Further evidence came to light of gross human rights violations perpetrated in southern Sri Lanka between 1987 and 1990, but impunity for those responsible remained a serious concern. No action was known to have been taken on the findings of the Presidential Commission of Inquiry into the Involuntary Removal of Persons (PCIIRP) – established in January 1991 to investigate "disappearances" – and none of the PCIIRP's reports on the 130 or so cases it had examined since its estab-

lishment was made public. Following the change of government in August, exhumations took place of about a dozen clandestine graves. They were thought to contain the remains of people abducted by the security forces who subsequently "disappeared" between 1988 and 1990. Eight army personnel and a school principal were committed to stand trial in September 1995. All were charged with abduction with intent to murder and wrongful confinement of a group of young people at Embilipitiya between late 1989 and early 1990. Five prison officers were charged in connection with the killing of five remand prisoners at Mahara prison in 1993 (see *Amnesty International Report 1994*).

The LTTE "executed" several people, including a suspected robber at Navakuddy in August, and an LTTE member suspected of embezzlement at Sittankerni in September. LTTE cadres abducted and killed several Sinhala and Muslim fishermen, particularly in the Kalpitiya area, Puttalam District, north of Colombo. In early January, K. Jeevaratnam, the UNP candidate in the local elections in Kaluwankerny, Batticaloa, was killed. A note was reportedly left by his body stating that all who tried to contest the elections would suffer the same fate. The exact number of political opponents held in unacknowledged detention and people held for ransom by the LTTE was unknown. Relatives were denied access to detainees held by the LTTE.

An Amnesty International delegate visited Colombo in January to investigate reports of the widespread arbitrary arrest and detention of Tamil people in the city. The organization published a report, *Sri Lanka: Balancing human rights and security; abuse of arrest and detention powers in Colombo*, containing 14 recommendations for the prevention of human rights violations during security operations in Colombo. The government did not respond to the substance of the report. In July Amnesty International sent an open letter to all political parties participating in the parliamentary elections calling on them to make a public commitment to human rights protection. No responses were received. The organization called upon successive governments, first in January and later in September, to ensure that exhumations at mass graves thought to contain the bodies of victims of human rights violations were carried out under the supervision of a multi-disciplinary team of forensic experts so that evidence about the identity of the bodies and about the cause and time of death would not be lost. In September Amnesty International welcomed the news that independent commissions to investigate past "disappearances" and extrajudicial executions would be established but expressed concern that the new commissions would not investigate the hundreds of cases that took place before 1 January 1988.

Amnesty International appealed to the LTTE to respect human rights and humanitarian standards and to halt deliberate killings of non-combatant civilians. It also called for the release of people held hostage and urged that the whereabouts of those detained by LTTE forces be made known.

SUDAN

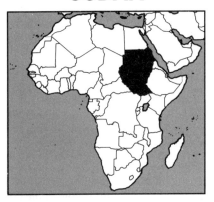

Hundreds of suspected government opponents, many of whom were prisoners of conscience, were arrested. Most were detained, often in secret, without charge or trial for periods ranging from 24 hours to a few months. The few political prisoners who were taken to court did not receive a fair trial. Torture was widespread, and numerous floggings were carried out as punishments. The fate of hundreds of prisoners who had "disappeared" in previous years remained unknown. Hundreds of people were extrajudicially executed in war-affected areas. Both factions of the armed opposition committed serious human rights abuses, including torture and deliberate and arbitrary killings.

Members of virtually every sector of

Sudanese society in both northern Sudan and the war-torn south suffered human rights violations. The government of President Omar Hassan Ahmad al-Bashir continued to suppress all independent political activity and a state of emergency remained in force. In the south and Nuba mountains, serious abuses were committed by all sides as the armed conflict, which has cost over one million lives since 1983, continued between the government and both factions of the Sudan People's Liberation Army (SPLA) – SPLA-Mainstream, led by John Garang de Mabior, and SPLA-United, led by Riek Machar Teny-Dhurgon. In September SPLA-United changed its name to the South Sudan Independence Army (SSIA).

At the start of the year the government's armed forces launched a major military offensive in the south, recapturing several towns they had not held for many years and burning down numerous villages. The military activity added to the millions of people already displaced. The UN estimated that over two million people required food aid during the year. In September peace talks between the government and both factions of the SPLA, mediated by the foreign ministers of Eritrea, Ethiopia, Kenya and Uganda, broke down.

In February the government said that it would no longer cooperate with the UN Special Rapporteur on Sudan following his submission of a critical report to the UN Commission on Human Rights. In August the government ignored his request for a visa to enable him to visit Sudan. In November the Special Rapporteur issued a further interim report to the UN General Assembly in which he concluded that "potentially all categories and strata of the population are affected by violations of human rights committed by agents of the Government".

Hundreds of people, many of them prisoners of conscience, were arrested for political reasons. They included members of banned political parties, trade unionists, army officers and aid workers. Most were detained without charge or trial for periods ranging from 24 hours to a few months. Detainees were often held in secret detention centres known as "ghost houses". Many suspected government opponents were made to report daily to security offices and wait there all day, effectively a form of day-time detention.

Prisoners of conscience arrested in previous years remained in jail throughout the year. Among them were at least two members of the banned Sudan Communist Party (SCP) who had been arrested in December 1992, including Farouq Ali Zacharia, an economist.

At least 50 members of banned political parties and trade unions were arrested in 1994. Former prime minister Sadiq al-Mahdi, the leader of the opposition Umma Party and of the *Ansar* religious order, was held for 24 hours in April and for 13 days in June and July. Other members of the Umma Party were arrested in February and May. In April Sarah Nugdallah, a leading member of the Umma Party, was detained. She was held for 10 weeks in Omdurman Women's Prison.

Members of other opposition political parties were also arrested. Osman Omar al-Sharif, a former minister of justice and prominent member of the Democratic Unionist Party (DUP), was held from February to April. He had previously been imprisoned from 1989 to 1991 and had been detained in 1993. Mahjoub Mohamed Sharif, a member of the SCP popularly known as "the people's poet", was arrested in May and held for over three months.

Trade unionists continued to be arrested, questioned, held uncharged, released and then rearrested. Magdi Mohamedani, a doctor active in the banned Sudan Doctors Union, was arrested in December 1993 and detained until April. He had been detained at least twice before. Ali al-Mahi al-Sakhi, president of the Central Mint Workers Union, was among six trade union activists arrested near Khartoum in June. This was at least the third time he had been taken into detention. He was known to remain in detention in mid-October but had been released by the end of the year.

Journalists and lawyers also faced abuses. In February Moatisim Mahmud, the news editor of *al-Sudani al-Dawliyya* (Sudanese International), the first Sudan-based independent newspaper reporting political events to be allowed to publish since the current government took power, was arrested. However, *al-Sudani al-Dawliyya* continued to publish articles critical of government policy and in early April its owner and editor-in-chief,

Mahjoub Mohamed al-Hassan Erwa, and two other journalists were detained and the newspaper banned. All four journalists were freed by June but the newspaper remained banned.

Lawyers arrested in 1994 included Ali Mahmud Hassanein, who took a leading role in the defence of 12 men charged with sabotage (see below). He was detained for two weeks in June. In September Mirghani Abdelrahman al-Kadro, a lawyer in the small eastern town of Rufa'a, was arrested with two women colleagues. The women were released within a week, but Mirghani Abdelrahman al-Kadro was taken into detention in Khartoum where he was known to remain in late October.

In the war zones, the security services continued to detain suspected government opponents. There were also persistent reports that troops from the Popular Defence Force (PDF), a government-created militia, on military operations captured women and children for use as domestic slaves.

Few political prisoners were taken to court and those who were failed to receive a fair trial. In January the trial of 29 men, including 17 in exile abroad and tried *in absentia*, opened in a specially convened court in Khartoum. The defendants faced charges relating to sabotage and had a defence team of several prominent lawyers, including Ali Mahmud Hassanein (see above). Detailed evidence emerged that at least five of the accused had been tortured. The judge acknowledged that they had been tortured but he allowed their confessions, which formed the bulk of the prosecution case, to be used in evidence. In April, five of the defendants were sentenced to prison terms ranging from two to seven years. The others present were freed.

There was widespread torture by the army, other security agencies and the PDF. The victims included children. Routine beatings, harsh physical exercise and prolonged exposure to the sun were apparently regarded as normal methods of dealing with prisoners. At the January sabotage trial, defendants testified that security officers had whipped and beaten them with sticks and lengths of plastic piping, inserted pins in their ears, pressed hot metal on their skin and threatened them with death. One man, al-Hassan Ahmad Saleh, lost an eye after being beaten during interrogation. Court-ordered medical

272

reports confirmed bruising and scarring consistent with their accounts.

In April Nadir Abdel Hamid Khairy, a political activist who had been in incommunicado detention since December 1993, died in Omdurman Military Hospital, apparently after prolonged beatings. The authorities refused to release the body to his family.

Suspected government opponents arrested in the war zones were at risk of torture in military detention centres and there were persistent reports that captured SPLA combatants were routinely tortured before being extrajudicially executed.

Cruel, inhuman or degrading punishments, including flogging, were imposed by court order. Many of the victims were poor women convicted of brewing alcohol. In mid-1994 the Khartoum authorities announced a campaign to eradicate the brewing and drinking of alcohol: in the first 16 days of June, 657 people were charged with alcohol-related offences and many were flogged.

The fate of hundreds of people who "disappeared" in previous years remained unknown. The vast majority were civilians from the war zones. The "disappeared" include 230 men arrested between June and August 1992 following an attack by the SPLA on Juba. Among them were Kennedy Khamis, a customs official arrested after he went to Juba military headquarters in search of his missing son; and Joseph W.D. Wai, a geologist who returned to Sudan in late 1991 after studying abroad.

The report of a commission of inquiry established by the government in late 1992 to investigate "the incidents witnessed by Juba town" (see Amnesty International Reports 1993 and 1994) had not been made public by the end of the year. In February the government commented that the commission blamed the delay on a "continuous flow of lists" of missing prisoners submitted by the UN Centre for Human Rights.

Hundreds of civilians and prisoners were reported to have been extrajudicially executed during the year. In the south, the army and PDF attacked villages and killed civilians. In one incident in April, soldiers on patrol from the town of Aweil in Bahr al-Ghazal came across three men fishing who were from the village of Awulic. Villagers who heard shooting subsequently found their bodies lined up on the river bank.

In January and June military trains which passed along the only railway line linking north and south Sudan carried troops who captured and then killed civilians along the route. Unescorted trains carrying aid used the same line, attracting people to the area. Eye-witnesses said that soldiers on the June train killed people at each station in territory not under government control. They reported that about 30 people were extrajudicially executed at Gana and at Kanji. Survivors reported that at Mondit 50 people were killed, that uniformed soldiers raped women and that both men and women were beaten with sticks and axes. A number of adolescent girls were reportedly taken captive into domestic slavery outside the war zones. There were further reports of killings along the railway line in December.

There were renewed reports of killings in the Nuba mountains at the start of the year. In January PDF members were said to have killed Mahmud Issa as he tried to defend his wife from being raped. The PDF also reportedly ambushed and killed over 60 civilians travelling from Lagowa to Dilling. Also in January, a group of Nuba was detained by PDF members at Kurgal. Seventeen were shot dead, among them Salah Ibrahim and Hussein Abdalla. A number of survivors were severely beaten by security officials during interrogation.

Each faction of the SPLA was responsible for gross human rights abuses. Troops loyal to two different SPLA-United commanders in Upper Nile deliberately killed an unknown number of civilians in early 1994 during internal fighting within SPLA-United. Tens of thousands of people were forced to flee their homes and the delivery of humanitarian assistance by the UN again became an imperative for survival.

Dissident SPLA prisoners held by SPLA-Mainstream since early 1993 were released in January, but at least two – Major Robert Akuak Kudum and Captain Gabriel Majok Nyieth – had died in SPLA detention the previous year. In August Carlo Madut Deng, a doctor, was abducted in Uganda and detained and reportedly tortured by SPLA-Mainstream troops in Nimule in southern Sudan. By December it had become clear that he had died in detention.

In June SPLA-Mainstream announced that Martin Majier Gai, a judge and an

273

influential Dinka politician, first arrested in 1984 and held until late 1992 before being rearrested in January 1993, had been "shot while trying to escape" in early 1993. The announcement followed the declaration of an amnesty by SPLA-Mainstream for political prisoners following which they would have had to produce Martin Majier Gai. It was believed he was deliberately killed in detention.

Amnesty International repeatedly appealed to the government to release prisoners of conscience and to ensure that all political detainees were promptly and fairly tried, or released. It called for action to end torture, floggings, "disappearances" and extrajudicial executions.

The organization made two attempts to send a high-level delegation to Sudan to meet senior government officials. The government requested Amnesty International to postpone its visit on each occasion.

In June Amnesty International representatives visited parts of Sudan under SPLA control and held meetings with SPLA-Mainstream and SPLA-United commanders. The organization urged both factions to observe basic humanitarian standards and to end deliberate and arbitrary killings and other abuses.

In July Amnesty International wrote to the Sudanese Government, both factions of the SPLA and the governments of Eritrea, Ethiopia, Kenya and Uganda, calling for human rights issues to be placed on the agenda of the peace talks.

In September Amnesty International published a report, *Sudan: Outside the war zones: secret detention and torture in northern Sudan*, urging the government to end the use of detention without charge or trial in secret detention centres and to stop the use of torture.

SWAZILAND

Dozens of prisoners of conscience were briefly detained. There were numerous allegations of torture in police custody. Police used excessive force against striking trade unionists. Five people remained under sentence of death.

All party political activity continued to be banned. In the face of increasing unrest, the government, led by Prime Minister Prince Mbilini, further restricted the rights to peaceful assembly and expression.

Several legislative changes restricted basic rights. In June an amendment to the 1993 Non-Bailable Offences Act (NBOA) (see *Amnesty International Report 1994*) obliged courts to deny bail to any person charged with offences listed in the Act, without police having to present evidence of the accused's involvement. One of these listed offences is "breach of the public order", which could result in the detention of government opponents for holding meetings. The Act was used during 1994 to deny bail to suspects charged with political offences.

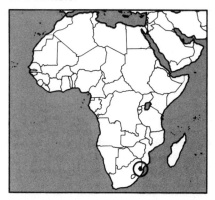

A proposed amendment to the Sedition and Subversive Activities Act, which included penalties of up to 10 years' imprisonment for publishing "seditious" material, was withdrawn after widespread opposition. The amendment would have effectively prevented newspapers from reporting critically on any branch of government.

The government-appointed Judicial Services Commission (JSC) formed in 1993 (see *Amnesty International Report 1994*) continued to compromise the impartiality of the judiciary. Four magistrates faced charges instigated by the JSC. For example, magistrate Sipho Dlamini was arrested and charged with defeating the ends of justice after he cautioned a suspect who alleged that he had agreed to confess to a crime because of torture by police officers. The magistrate told the suspect that confessions must be freely given and would be used against him, and the suspect withdrew the confession. Sipho Dlamini was subsequently acquitted by the High Court but immediately dismissed from his post by the JSC.

Dozens of opposition supporters were

274

briefly detained during 1994. For example, in April seven supporters of the People's United Democratic Movement (PUDEMO) were arrested at a peaceful demonstration marking the 1973 suspension of Swaziland's Constitution. They were charged under the King's Proclamation No. 12 of 1973, which bans political activity. They were held incommunicado in harsh conditions for two days before being released on bail. The charges were dropped in June.

In October, seven PUDEMO supporters were arrested at a demonstration calling for democratic reform. They were charged under the Sedition Act because they carried placards calling on the government to resign. They were also charged with a breach of the public order and were initially denied bail under the NBOA. In November they were acquitted of the sedition charge, but found guilty of participating in a demonstration without police permission. All seven were sentenced to seven days' imprisonment and released because of their time in pre-trial detention. However, two – Mphandlana Shongwe and Andreas Lukhele – were rearrested because they already had suspended sentences. At the end of 1994 they were free on bail pending the Appeal Court's decision on their appeal against their convictions.

There were numerous allegations of torture in police custody. In May a defendant told a court that he confessed to murder after being beaten and suffocated by police officers. Also in May a magistrate stated in court that police routinely treated suspects "so brutally" that he could not allow them to be remanded in police custody overnight. In August a defendant alleged that when he was arrested he was handcuffed and put in a car boot, and then assaulted at a police station for three days before being charged.

In July police officers used tear-gas and batons to disperse striking workers and reportedly assaulted Paul Dlamini, Secretary General of the Swaziland Manufacturing and Allied Workers' Union. Days later police officers shot and seriously wounded a striking worker, then briefly detained Jan Sithole, Secretary General of the Swaziland Federation of Trade Unions.

No new death sentences were imposed by the courts and two death sentences were overturned on appeal. Five people remained under sentence of death awaiting the outcome of appeals.

Amnesty International expressed concern about the imprisonment of PUDEMO supporters and others for exercising their rights to freedom of assembly and expression and about their prison and bail conditions. Amnesty International wrote to the government about the continuing existence of laws which provide for the imprisonment of peaceful demonstrators and those expressing their peaceful political views. Amnesty International was also concerned about the numerous allegations of torture in police custody.

SWEDEN

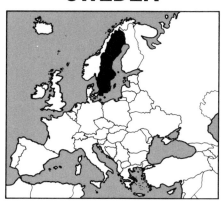

There were a few reports of ill-treatment in custody, some relating to previous years.

Sergio Nigretti, an Italian national, alleged that he had been ill-treated while held in isolation at Kumla prison in 1993. The regional public prosecution authority, which conducted an investigation into the allegations, concluded that there were no grounds for further proceedings.

In June the Appeals Court confirmed the suspended sentences and fines levied against three prison guards found guilty of breach of duty regarding the death in custody in July 1993 of Tony Mutka (see *Amnesty International Report 1994*). Tony Mutka had died in custody while being transported from prison to hospital wearing only underpants, lying face-down on the floor between the front and back seats of a van, handcuffed behind the back and with his feet chained. Guards sitting in the back seat above him had placed their feet on Tony Mutka and shortly before he died a guard had stood on him. The Appeals

Court did not consider the guards' conduct to be a gross breach of duty. In November the Supreme Court denied the family's and the prison guards' requests for further review. Revised procedures for transporting prisoners in need of treatment came into force in January.

Amnesty International wrote to the government in March and April calling for Sergio Nigretti to be medically examined and treated, urging that his allegations be independently investigated, and requesting to be informed about the findings of the investigation. In September Amnesty International received from the authorities the findings of the investigation.

SWITZERLAND

Scores of conscientious objectors to military service were sentenced to terms of imprisonment or compulsory work by military tribunals. There were allegations of ill-treatment by law enforcement officers.

In April the UN Committee against Torture considered the government's periodic report on its compliance with the UN Convention against Torture. The committee expressed concern about police ill-treatment and recommended reforms in legislation and procedures relating to police custody and preventive detention.

There was still no alternative civilian service available to conscientious objectors to compulsory military service. However, in June the government approved the text of a bill introducing such a service. Conscripts demonstrating their inability to reconcile military service with their consciences would qualify for the right to perform civilian service one and a half times

the length of ordinary military service. In November a parliamentary committee examining the bill proposed restricting access to civilian service to those objecting to military service on "ethical" grounds. Further parliamentary examination of the bill was scheduled for 1995.

Meanwhile, under the Military Penal Code, refusal to perform military service remained a criminal offence. However, where a tribunal concluded that a conscript was unable to reconcile military service with his conscience because of "fundamental ethical values", he was sentenced to a period of work in the public interest and did not acquire a criminal record. Conscientious objectors who failed to qualify because, for example, the tribunals considered that they had opposed military service on political grounds, continued to be sentenced to terms of imprisonment. However, few conscientious objectors reportedly served prison sentences during 1994 as many cantons had moratoriums on such sentences, pending the introduction of a civilian service. Those who were imprisoned were considered prisoners of conscience.

There were allegations of ill-treatment by law enforcement officers; many concerned foreign nationals. Emmanuel John and George James both claimed Sudanese nationality on applying for political asylum in Switzerland, but their nationality was disputed by the refugee authorities. They lodged a complaint claiming that two police officers had subjected them to an unprovoked physical assault and racial abuse following an identity check outside Sissach railway station, in the Canton of Basel-Land, in July. They alleged that one officer punched George James in the stomach, knocking him to the ground, and that a police dog was set on them. George James was apparently bitten by the dog on his thigh and Emmanuel John was bitten so severely on his buttocks and stomach that he lost consciousness. The officers then left the scene, but returned after George James sought assistance at a local police post. They called an ambulance which transferred both injured men to hospital where they were kept overnight for treatment. The officers accused them of obstructing the police by refusing to identify themselves. A judicial investigation was opened into the alleged incidents, but Emmanuel John and George

James were not questioned about their allegations for over three months. As their asylum applications had by then been rejected definitively they were obliged to leave the country shortly after being questioned.

Several allegations of ill-treatment came from the Canton of Geneva. In a complaint lodged in September, Denise Moreira, a Brazilian citizen, alleged that she had been ill-treated by two Geneva police officers following an identity check in August. She claimed that they subjected her to racist insults and used a disproportionate degree of force to remove her from her apartment after she refused to accompany them to the police station. She alleged that they siezed her, threw her down a flight of stairs and kicked and punched her repeatedly. She stated that in an attempt to escape the blows she tried unsuccessfully to bite the hand of one of the officers, upon which they attacked her more violently, leaving her prostrate on the floor. Neighbours stated that they had heard sounds of someone being hit, insulted by the police and crying for help. She was taken to the police station where she was seen by a doctor who supplied medication. She was formally accused of illegal residence and of using violence against the police and transferred to prison where she received a medical examination the next day. The examination found cuts and bruises on her right hand, elbow and side, on both knees and the stomach. A medical certificate issued by a local hospital after her release from prison two days later recorded bruises "compatible" with the blows she claimed to have received. The Prosecutor General filed Denise Moreira's complaint in December stating, apparently incorrectly, that she was an illegal resident and concluding that her injuries were "perfectly compatible with the legitimate use of force".

Amnesty International appealed for the release of prisoners of conscience and expressed concern that people continued to be punished for refusing military service on grounds of conscience. It welcomed the progress made towards the introduction of a civilian alternative to military service.

In April Amnesty International published a report, *Switzerland: Allegations of ill-treatment in police custody*. It concluded that the number of such allegations received by the organization, taken together with the findings of other international governmental and non-governmental organizations, indicated "a substantial cause for concern".

Amnesty International sought information from the authorities on the steps taken to investigate cases of alleged ill-treatment and the outcome of inquiries opened into such allegations. The authorities responded to the majority of cases raised by the organization. Some gave information about the status of investigations or court proceedings. Others stated that the allegations were unfounded or that injuries incurred by detainees were the result of police officers using the degree of force necessary to subdue a person violently resisting arrest.

SYRIA

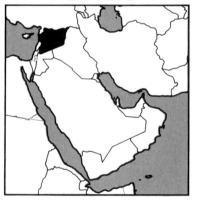

Hundreds of long-term political detainees, including prisoners of conscience, appeared before the Supreme State Security Court whose procedures fall far short of international fair trial standards. Many of the defendants were convicted and sentenced to up to 15 years' imprisonment. The outcome of most of the trials had not been made public by the end of the year. Few political arrests were reported to have taken place during the year. Several thousand political prisoners, including prisoners of conscience, remained in prison: some were serving sentences imposed after unfair trials; most were held without charge or trial under state of emergency legislation. Several political prisoners continued to be held after their sentences had expired. Torture of detainees was widespread. At least two people were executed.

Hundreds of suspected government opponents, including prisoners of conscience, appeared before the Supreme State Security Court (SSSC) whose procedures fall far short of international fair trial standards. The court, which was established in 1968 to deal solely with political and state security cases, is not bound by the Code of Criminal Procedure and denies defendants many of the rights guaranteed under this code, including the right of appeal. The defendants had been arrested between 1980 and 1993 and held without charge or trial. They were brought before the SSSC on charges of membership of, or activities relating to, various unauthorized political organizations. Many were sentenced to prison terms and dozens were acquitted or had the charges against them dropped. The outcome of most of the cases had not been made public by the end of 1994.

When the trials began in July 1992, most of the defendants were represented by lawyers chosen by their relatives, although some reportedly refused legal representation in protest against the SSSC's procedures (see Amnesty International Report 1994). However, by the beginning of 1994, most of these lawyers had withdrawn in protest at the conduct of the trials. They were replaced by other lawyers appointed by the Bar Association at the SSSC's request. All the defendants had been denied access to legal assistance in prolonged pre-trial detention, including during interrogation by the SSSC prosecutor before the court hearings. Defence lawyers rarely had prior access to their clients' files and were unaware of the specific charges against them. In some cases lawyers were denied the right to meet their clients in private or to call defence witnesses.

Over 300 prisoners charged in connection with Hizb al-'Amal al-Shuyu'i, the Party for Communist Action (PCA), were on trial before the SSSC. Most of them, including many prisoners of conscience, had been held without charge or trial for years, in some cases for over 12 years. They included Silya 'Abbas, a student of mathematics at Damascus University, who was reportedly held incommunicado. Her father, 'Abbas 'Abbas, detained for alleged links with the PCA since January 1982, was also on trial. During the year, many of these defendants were sentenced. Among

them was Anwar Badr, a radio and television journalist, who received a 12-year prison term. Dozens of defendants were released; the results of the trials of the remainder were not known.

About 30 people charged with membership of or links with al-Hizb al-Shuyu'i al-Maktab al-Siyassi, the Communist Party Political Bureau (CPPB), appeared before the SSSC. Most of them were sentenced to between eight and 15 years' imprisonment. Among them was Ahmad Faiz al-Fawwaz, a 62-year-old doctor, who received a 15-year prison sentence. Riad al-Turk, a leading member of the CPPB who was arrested in 1980, remained held in incommunicado detention without charge or trial. Throughout his detention he had been allowed only one visit by his wife and daughter, in 1993.

At least 18 people were tried for alleged links with two unauthorized Nasserist political movements, Hizb al-Ittihad al-'Arabi al-Ishtiraki fi-Suriya, the Arab Socialist Union Party in Syria, and al-Tanzim al-Sha'bi al-Dimuqrati al-Naseri, the Nasserist Democratic Popular Organization. Sixteen were released; no information was available regarding the remaining two defendants.

Dozens of political detainees suspected of links with unauthorized Kurdish organizations were tried during the year. Some of them were sentenced to up to two years' imprisonment and were released as they had been detained since 1992. They included Ahmad Hassu, who was arrested in 1992 and sentenced to two years' imprisonment in connection with the Kurdish Democratic Party (KDP). He was released in May. It was not known whether the court had reached a verdict in the remaining cases.

About 50 political detainees held in connection with Hizb al-Ba'th al-Dimuqrati al-Ishtiraki al-'Arabi, the Arab Socialist Democratic Ba'th Party, remained held. Most were believed to be facing trial before the SSSC, but the outcome of their trial was not known.

Few political arrests were reported to have taken place during the year, but no details were made public by the authorities.

Several thousand political prisoners, including prisoners of conscience, remained held. Some were serving prison sentences imposed after unfair trials; most were held without charge or trial.

Scores of prisoners of conscience continued serving lengthy prison sentences imposed by the SSSC in 1992 and 1993 (see *Amnesty International Reports 1993* and *1994*). Ten had been sentenced in March 1992 to between five and 10 years' imprisonment on charges connected with the Committees for the Defence of Democratic Freedoms and Human Rights in Syria, an unauthorized organization. They included Aktham Nu'aysa, a lawyer who was reported to be in poor health, and Nizar Nayyuf, a sociologist. The others had been sentenced in 1993 to between three and 15 years in prison for alleged links with the PCA. One of them, Khalil Husain Husain, a chemist, who had been sentenced to eight years' imprisonment in October 1993, was released in May. He had already spent more than eight years in pre-trial detention.

The majority of political detainees still held without charge or trial were alleged supporters of *al-Ikhwan al-Muslimun*, the Muslim Brotherhood (see previous *Amnesty International Reports*). Most remained in incommunicado detention and their whereabouts were unknown. A few were said to have been tried, but no details were available.

Three long-term prisoners of conscience, all former government and Ba'th Party officials, remained in al-Mezze Military Prison in Damascus, the capital; all had been detained without charge or trial since 1970 and were reportedly in poor health. They were: Muhammad 'Id 'Ashawi, aged 64; Fawzi Rida, in his sixties; and 'Abd al-Hamid Miqdad. Five former leading members of the Ba'th Party, all prisoners of conscience, were released in February and October. They had all been detained without charge or trial since their arrest between 1969 and 1972. They were: Ahmad Suwaidani, Mustafa Rustum, Hadithe Murad, 'Adel Na'issa, and Dafi Jam'ani, a Jordanian national.

At least 130 doctors, lawyers and engineers who had been arrested following a one-day general strike in 1980 remained held without charge or trial. They included Tawfiq Draq al-Siba'i, a doctor, who was reported to be in al-Mezze Military Prison in 1987. Since then there has been no news of his whereabouts. The government stated that two people arrested following the strike had been tried and

sentenced: 'Abd al-Majid 'Abd al-Qadir, a veterinary surgeon, was reportedly serving a life sentence; 'Abd al-Rahman Kittanji, a physician, was reportedly sentenced to 15 years' imprisonment in 1980.

Hundreds of Lebanese nationals and Palestinians arrested in previous years in Lebanon or Syria as suspected political activists remained detained (see previous *Amnesty International Reports*). Most were held incommunicado and their whereabouts were unknown. They included Khadija Yahya Bukhari, a singer, who had been held incommunicado since her arrest at Lebanon International Airport in April 1992. She was reported to have been tried in secret before a military court.

Several other political prisoners remained held despite having completed their prison sentences. They included Mustafa Tawfiq Fallah and Jalal al-Din Mirhij, former military staff whose sentences expired in 1985. No additional charges had been brought against them.

Eleven men who had been held incommunicado without charge or trial since August 1993 were released on 3 July. They had been detained shortly after attending the funeral of Salah Jadid, a former prisoner of conscience who died in custody in August 1993 after almost 23 years in detention without charge or trial (see *Amnesty International Report 1994*).

Torture of political detainees remained widespread. Commonly cited torture methods included *falaqa* (beatings on the soles of the feet) and *dullab* (the "tyre", whereby the victim is suspended from a tyre and beaten with sticks or cables). Many defendants who appeared before the SSSC alleged that they had been tortured and that their "confessions" had been extracted under duress. The court did not order investigations into their allegations. Government ministers told Amnesty International delegates who visited Damascus in October that torture was illegal in Syria and provided them with a list of some 40 officers whom they said had been referred for trial in connection with torture allegations. However, they provided no information about the cases of torture submitted by Amnesty International.

There were reports that Dani Mansurati, a Lebanese national, died in custody in April. He was reportedly arrested in May 1992 and held incommunicado at the Air Force Intelligence headquarters in

Damascus. No investigation into his death was known to have been carried out.

Scores of political prisoners arrested in previous years remained unaccounted for and it was feared they had "disappeared". They included Ghassan Abazid, a lawyer and member of the Syrian Bar Association, who was arrested in 1982 in Damascus.

Scores of asylum-seekers of various nationalities were held in contravention of international human rights standards or were at risk of being sent back to countries where they faced human rights violations. They included 'Abd al-Basit 'Azuz, a Libyan national. He was reportedly living in hiding in Syria after escaping from custody in October 1993 while he was being taken to the port of Lataqiyya in preparation for his forcible return to Libya. Another Libyan national was forcibly sent back to Libya at the same time: no information was available about his fate or whereabouts following his return. In response to Amnesty International's queries, the Syrian authorities claimed that the two had not informed them of any request for asylum. Other asylum-seekers were detained incommunicado for long periods and some were allegedly tortured or ill-treated. All were said to have been denied access to any asylum procedure or to the judiciary.

At least two people were executed. Both were convicted of murder.

Amnesty International continued to appeal for the immediate and unconditional release of all prisoners of conscience and for all other political prisoners to receive fair and prompt trials or be released. It urged the authorities to initiate impartial investigations into all torture allegations and to end the use of the death penalty. The organization also urged the authorities to ensure that all asylum-seekers were given access to fair refugee procedures and the judiciary.

In July Amnesty International sent a comprehensive memorandum to the government entitled *Amnesty International's Continuing Human Rights Concerns in Syria*. A delegation from the organization visited Damascus in October and discussed the memorandum with ministers, senior judges and officials. The authorities gave an undertaking to study the memorandum and respond to the issues and cases raised by the organization, but no response was received by the end of the year.

In April Amnesty International submitted information about its concerns in Syria for UN review under a procedure established by Economic and Social Council Resolutions 728F/1503 for confidential consideration of communications about human rights violations.

TADZHIKISTAN

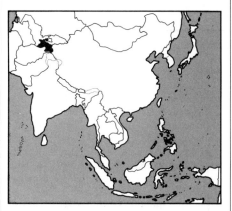

Two probable prisoners of conscience were among political prisoners released by the government in exchange for hostages held by opposition forces. Two journalists who were detained briefly for possessing an opposition newspaper were prisoners of conscience. A man who "disappeared" in 1992 was found dead. One political prisoner was executed, and at least six death sentences were passed. Armed opposition forces reportedly killed captured government soldiers.

Talks aimed at settling the armed conflict between government forces and armed groups supporting the outlawed opposition convened in Russia in April. They continued during the rest of the year in two further rounds held in Iran and Pakistan. The third round in September led to an agreement on a temporary cease-fire which took effect in October and was still holding at the end of the year. In September the outlawed opposition split when the Democratic Party repudiated its former alliance with the Islamic Renaissance Party.

While pursuing the peace negotiations, the government held a national referendum in November which approved a new

280

constitution. It also held an election to the reinstated office of President. The presidential election was won by the head of state, Supreme Council Chairman Imamali Rakhmonov. His opponent, former Prime Minister Abdumalik Abdullodzhanov, and independent observers alleged that there had been irregularities, including vote rigging and intimidation of voters by Imamali Rakhmonov's supporters. The Democratic Party sought to participate in the election, but the Islamic Renaissance Party called on its supporters to boycott it.

Two probable prisoners of conscience were released in November in an exchange of prisoners between the government and the armed opposition. Dzhumaboy Niyazov and Nuriddin Sadridinnov had been convicted in 1993 of illegal firearms possession (see *Amnesty International Report 1994*, where Sadridinnov's name is given incorrectly as Sadiriddinov). Also released by the government in the exchange were political prisoners Mirbobo Mirrakhimov, Akhmadsho Kamilov, Khayriddin Kasymov and Khurshed Nazarov (see *Amnesty International Report 1994*). The prisoners released by the opposition were captured government soldiers. In total, 27 prisoners were released by each side.

Journalists Maksud Khusaynov and Mukhammadrakhim Saydar were detained in August after state security agents searched their homes and discovered copies of an opposition newspaper published outside Tadzhikistan. They were prisoners of conscience. They were released from custody within days of being detained.

The body of Mirzonazar Imomnazarov, a Pamiri man who "disappeared" in December 1992, was found in a Dushanbe suburb in January. According to reports he had been killed recently, suggesting that he had been held in unacknowledged detention for over 13 months. The authorities began an investigation into his death.

Political prisoner Adzhik Aliyev was executed in September. He had been sentenced to death in 1993 after a trial which may have been unfair (see *Amnesty International Report 1994*). Six men were known to have been sentenced to death in 1994. At the end of the year the fate of these men and of five others sentenced to death in 1993 could not be confirmed.

Opposition forces reportedly killed some of a group of more than 50 government soldiers they captured in July near Tavildara, close to the Afghanistan border. It was not clear in what circumstances these killings occurred.

Amnesty International welcomed the news of the release of Dzhumaboy Niyazov and Nuriddin Sadridinnov, having previously called for a judicial review of their criminal convictions. It called for the immediate and unconditional release of Maksud Khusaynov and Mukhammadrakhim Saydar. It continued to call on the government to investigate reports of extrajudicial executions and "disappearances" dating from 1992 and 1993, and asked to be kept informed of the findings of investigations announced by the government. It called for a review of the case of Adzhik Aliyev on the grounds that he may not have received a fair trial. It urged commutation of all pending death sentences.

In July Amnesty International expressed concern about the fate of government soldiers captured near Tavildara, following reports that some of the soldiers had been killed. It called on the self-proclaimed "government-in-exile" to ensure that its armed forces, or those acting with its approval, fully respected human rights and the basic humanitarian standards set out in the Geneva Conventions and other relevant international standards.

In April Amnesty International sought official permission to visit Tadzhikistan. No response was received to its request.

TAIWAN

There were continued reports of ill-treatment of suspects in police custody. Military conscripts received disciplinary punishments reportedly amounting to torture or ill-treatment. At least 13 prisoners were executed.

Attempts by the Republic of China (ROC), Taiwan, to break out of its international diplomatic isolation continued and were marked by unofficial visits by President Lee Teng-hui to some countries in Asia. Taiwan's attempts to join the UN continued to face obstacles, partly because the governments of the ROC and of the People's Republic of China refused to recognize each other. Taiwan was unable to accede to any of the multilateral treaties relating to the protection of human rights, and the authorities made no public commitment to accede to them in future.

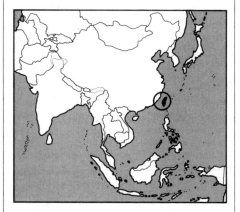

The Constitution was amended in July to allow the direct election of the president in 1996, when Li Teng-hui's term ends, and to provide more safeguards for the rights of indigenous people. In May, when the National Assembly convened to discuss the constitutional amendments, 572 judges called for reforms aimed at improving judicial independence. No judicial reform had been proposed by the government by the end of the year.

There were continuing allegations of ill-treatment of people in police custody and detention centres. In August Pan Chang died while serving a 30-day prison term in the southern city of Tainan for alleged violations of public order. According to an unofficial medical report, injuries seen on his body may have been caused by beatings. In the same month, Chou Hung-yu, a deaf and mute university student, was detained and reportedly beaten by police during a murder investigation. An opposition member of the Legislative Yuan stated that police had broken into Chou Hung-yu's room without a warrant. No inquiry into these incidents was known to have been concluded by the end of the year.

In January three army officers were sentenced to prison terms for beating to death an army conscript in July 1993 (see *Amnesty International Report 1994*). The court sentenced Kung Teh-huai to 12 years' imprisonment for beating and kicking conscript Chen Shih-wei. Two other junior officers, Ku Jung-feng and Chen Chia-hsiung, were sentenced to three and five years' imprisonment respectively.

In September the Control Yuan, an independent state agency empowered to investigate official misconduct, made public a detailed report of its investigations into complaints that police and prosecutors had ill-treated suspects in two related 1988 murder cases. The report concluded that several suspects were tortured into making false confessions during interrogation, by being suspended from a horizontal wooden pole, choked and gagged. In one incident, a female suspect was undressed and an investigator inserted an object into her vagina. The report recommended that the officials involved should be prosecuted, but no action was known to have been taken by the end of the year.

At least 13 prisoners were executed. Prisoners under sentence of death whose sentences had not been finally confirmed by the Supreme Court continued to be held permanently shackled. This practice amounts to an arbitrary additional punishment and constitutes cruel, inhuman or degrading treatment. A government statement in October denied that permanent shackling amounted to inhuman treatment but officials said that the treatment of prisoners under sentence of death was being reviewed.

The government made public the results of a public opinion survey on the death penalty carried out in 1993. It concluded that a majority of the respondents, while supporting the death penalty, did not believe that its increased use in previous years had improved public order. Most of those interviewed supported a temporary suspension of all executions, pending further studies.

In October an Amnesty International delegate visited Taiwan to gather information about reports of ill-treatment of criminal suspects and military conscripts. In meetings with government officials, the delegate stressed that Taiwan should implement relevant provisions of all international human rights instruments despite its inability to ratify treaties formally.

282

TANZANIA

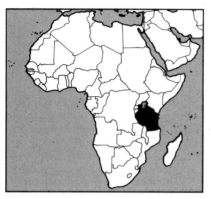

At least two supporters of an opposition party in Zanzibar imprisoned for sedition and others briefly detained were prisoners of conscience. Two journalists were charged with sedition. Courts continued to impose caning sentences. At least three people were sentenced to death and at least eight people were executed.

In August the ruling *Chama Cha Mapinduzi* (CCM), Party of the Revolution, announced its opposition to the creation of a Tanganyika government on the mainland equivalent in status to the government of Zanzibar. The Union government, led by President Ali Hassan Mwinyi, dropped plans to amend the Constitution in order to create a Tanganyika government.

There continued to be allegations of harassment by the authorities of members and supporters of opposition parties, notably in Zanzibar. The opposition Civic United Front (CUF) was repeatedly denied permits by the authorities to hold public meetings in the north of Zanzibar.

CUF members and supporters in Zanzibar were arrested for short periods and at least two people were imprisoned on charges of possessing seditious material in the form of recordings of CUF public meetings. Bosa Haji and another man were sentenced by Mkokotoni primary court to three months' imprisonment for possession of an audio-cassette of a CUF public meeting at which government officials were accused of corruption.

In March, two mainland journalists, Paschal Shija, editor of *The Express*, and Riaz Gulamani, its publisher, were arrested after an editorial accused the Union government of incompetence. They were released after 10 hours but were rearrested soon after and charged with sedition before being granted bail. If found guilty, they could face up to five years' imprisonment. Their lawyers challenged the constitutionality of the charges in the High Court. They had not been tried by the end of the year.

Outstanding charges from September 1993 against 10 opponents of the Zanzibar Government, including Huwena Hamad, the wife of the Vice-Chairman of the CUF, were dropped in 1994 (see *Amnesty International Report 1994*). They had been charged with organizing an illegal assembly and insulting Dr Salmin Amour, the President of Zanzibar.

Courts continued to impose sentences of caning – a cruel, inhuman or degrading punishment. In August a resident magistrate in Kisutu sentenced Emmanuel Charles and Joachim Chacha to 10 strokes each of the cane and 30 years' imprisonment for robbery with violence. It was not known if the sentences had been carried out by the end of the year.

At least three people were sentenced to death for murder. At least seven men and one woman were executed in secret in Dodoma in October. In June a judge ruled that the death penalty violated the Tanzanian Constitution and was accordingly null and void, when he sentenced two men found guilty of murder to life imprisonment. In October the Attorney-General appealed against his ruling to the Court of Appeal. The Court of Appeal had not ruled by the end of the year.

Amnesty International expressed its concern about the detention or imprisonment of prisoners of conscience and about the use of caning. It called on the Union government to abolish the death penalty.

THAILAND

At least five death sentences were imposed during the year, although there were no reports of any executions. Prisoners were reportedly held in conditions amounting to cruel, inhuman or degrading treatment. Refugees and asylum-seekers from Myanmar and other countries were also held in such conditions, and hundreds were returned to their countries

of origin, where they were at risk of human rights violations.

The five-party coalition government led by Prime Minister Chuan Leekpai, which came to power following elections in September 1992, continued to govern the country. Discussion continued in both houses of Parliament over redrafting the 1991 Constitution promulgated by the National Security and Peacekeeping Council (the military government of the time), but no progress was made on substantive reform. Despite the commitment made by the Thai Government to the UN World Conference on Human Rights in Vienna in June 1993 that Thailand would accede to the International Covenant on Civil and Political Rights, by the end of the year it had not done so.

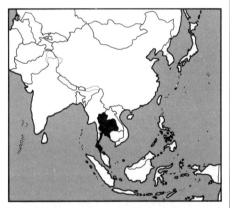

In July a group of non-governmental organizations arranged a conference to discuss human rights in southeast Asia to coincide with a meeting of the Association of South East Asian Nations (ASEAN). Three overseas delegates who arrived to take part in the conference were deported, on the grounds that they had not requested work permits 30 days in advance. Such a requirement had not been imposed before, and official condemnation of the conference by the Thai authorities suggested that the freedom of human rights groups to organize international meetings in Thailand might in future be subjected to similar arbitrary restrictions.

The whereabouts of 39 people who vanished during the security forces' violent crack-down on pro-democracy demonstrations in May 1992 (see *Amnesty International Reports 1993* and *1994*) had still not been established by the end of 1994; they may have been victims of extra-judicial executions. The government did not reveal the full results of a Defence Ministry investigation into the military's role in May 1992, although the report had been submitted to the government in July 1992. In May 1994 the Interior Ministry instructed provincial governors to work with the Office of the Supreme Attorney-General and the courts to make official declarations on those still missing in order to allow compensation to be paid to relatives. The families of the missing are entitled to compensation payments of 200,000 Thai baht, approximately US$8,000, each. Under the law, an official declaration can be made after a person has been missing for two years, but a court order is required and these are made on a case by case basis. The first of these cases was raised by the Office of the Supreme Attorney-General in June. According to the government, 30 families of the missing had received compensation as of July. A lawsuit demanding compensation from the leaders of the military government of 1992, filed by relatives of victims of the May 1992 crack-down, was dismissed by the Civil Court in June. The court based its decision on the amnesty granted by the government to those involved in the crack-down.

The trial on charges of lese-majesty of prominent social critic and Buddhist scholar Sulak Sivaraksa continued intermittently during 1994 (see *Amnesty International Report 1994*). If convicted and sent to prison, he would be considered a prisoner of conscience.

At least five death sentences were imposed during 1994, four for heroin-related offences and one for murder. Over 100 prisoners were believed to be under sentence of death at the end of the year. There were no reports of any executions. The King of Thailand granted amnesties in April to more than 10 prisoners facing the death penalty. In July the Interior Ministry called for more information from the Police Department on a draft bill which would impose mandatory execution for major crimes committed with war weapons. No further information on the status of this bill was available at the end of the year.

There were continuing reports of criminal prisoners being held in conditions amounting to cruel, inhuman or degrading treatment. These included the use of heavy leg chains for extended periods,

284

poor medical care and ill-treatment. In February the Police Director-General rejected news reports that foreigners had been summarily executed in Thailand, but admitted that some detainees had died in police custody. He said that most of them had committed suicide. The Police Director-General admitted that it was possible that some suspects had been physically abused, but said that this was an investigation method that police all over the world had used.

Immigration officials and police continued to detain asylum-seekers and refugees from Myanmar and other countries in harsh conditions, sometimes amounting to cruel, inhuman or degrading treatment. After the authorities announced a crackdown on illegal immigration in 1993, thousands of asylum-seekers and refugees were arrested and charged with illegal immigration. Even asylum-seekers who were registered with the UN High Commissioner for Refugees (UNHCR) were arrested, detained and, in some cases, forcibly returned to their country of origin. Asylum-seekers convicted of illegal immigration have to pay a fine or serve a prison term at the Immigration Detention Centre (IDC) in Bangkok. Former detainees complained of chronic overcrowding, lack of food and ill-treatment, including beatings by officials, at the IDC. Refugees and asylum-seekers were detained even after they had served their sentences, because they did not have the money to pay for their own deportation.

Throughout the year, refugees and asylum-seekers were sent back to countries where they were at risk of human rights violations. Hundreds of refugees from Cambodia were deported to an area of Cambodia controlled by the armed opposition group, the *Partie* of Democratic Kampuchea (Khmer Rouge). The UNHCR strongly condemned the forcible return of the Cambodian refugees. Hundreds of refugees from the Shan State in Myanmar, fleeing from forced portering and other human rights violations committed by the Burmese army, were forced back across the border to Myanmar by the Thai authorities.

Refugees and asylum-seekers from Myanmar who were convicted of illegal immigration were sent to Halockhanie (Halakhanee) refugee camp. The camp, to which thousands of refugees were moved

by the Thai authorities in April, straddles the border with Myanmar. In July Burmese armed forces attacked the camp, burned 60 houses and took 16 people prisoner (see **Myanmar** entry). Refugees fled back across the border to Thailand, but were forced to return to Myanmar in September by the Thai authorities. Deportations continued to Halockhanie throughout 1994, where refugees were at risk from further attack by the Burmese military forces.

Four Malaysian nationals, including a six-month-old baby, all members of the Islamic sect *Al Arqam*, were arrested in September and handed over to the Malaysian authorities. The four were taken to Malaysia, where they were held in incommunicado detention until their release at the end of October. Malaysia outlawed the *Al Arqam* sect in August, and its followers risk up to five years' imprisonment (see **Malaysia** entry). The Thai authorities said that the Malaysian authorities had declared the passports of the four invalid, and that the four were therefore living in Thailand without valid documents.

In May Amnesty International called upon the Thai authorities to stop immediately the forcible return of Burmese refugees to Shan State, Myanmar. In September Amnesty International published a report, *Thailand: Burmese and other asylum-seekers at risk*, detailing the organization's concerns about the treatment of refugees and asylum-seekers. Amnesty International urged Thailand to accede to the 1951 Convention relating to the Status of Refugees, and to its 1967 Protocol, and to ensure better protection for refugees in the country. An Amnesty International delegation met the Thai Prime Minister in September and discussed Thailand's treatment of refugees and asylum-seekers. A military spokesman later stated that the forcible return of refugees to Myanmar complied with the government's policy of expelling those who had entered the country illegally.

TOGO

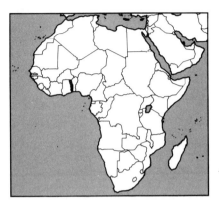

At least 60 people were extrajudicially executed by the armed forces in January. At least five prisoners of conscience were sentenced to prison terms. Several other political prisoners appeared to be prisoners of conscience. There were reports of torture and ill-treatment. At least eight people "disappeared".

Togo's first multi-party legislative elections were held in February, ending a transition period which began in 1991 with a National Conference and led to presidential elections in 1993 in which President Gnassingbé Eyadéma was returned to power (see *Amnesty International Report 1994*). The February elections were marked by violence by members of President Eyadéma's *Rassemblement du peuple togolais* (RPT), Assembly of the Togolese People, as well as by members of opposition parties. The Togolese Armed Forces, supposedly confined to barracks during the election period, continued to harass opposition supporters, particularly members of the *Comité d'action pour le renouveau* (CAR), Action Committee for Renewal. A special security force, the *Forces de sécurité publique*, Public Security Force, set up to keep order during the elections, was also implicated in human rights violations.

The CAR and the *Union togolaise pour la démocratie* (UTD), Togolese Union for Democracy, won a majority of seats in the National Assembly. In mid-April President Eyadéma appointed the UTD leader, Edem Kodjo, as Prime Minister, provoking a rift between the two opposition parties: the CAR subsequently refused to participate in the new government.

The new Prime Minister promised to re-establish the rule of law and improve respect for human rights, and in September the army chief of staff declared that the police would resume full responsibility for law and order. Despite this, none of the human rights violations committed by the security forces during the transition period or subsequently was known to have been fully or independently investigated, nor were those responsible brought to justice. Moreover, in mid-December the National Assembly passed a general amnesty law covering all crimes of a political nature committed prior to 15 December 1994, which appeared to grant impunity for all human rights violations committed by the security forces prior to that date.

In October it was publicly announced that the head of the Presidential Guard had been arrested in connection with the murder of a lawyer in Lomé in June. However, it appeared that the real reason for his arrest was his suspected opposition to President Eyadéma and he and at least four other officers remained in detention at the end of 1994.

After the elections, the security forces reportedly continued to harass and intimidate opposition supporters and those involved in the political transition process. According to unofficial sources, armed militias operating in collusion with the security forces were also responsible for killings and "disappearances". Between May and September at least six people with opposition connections – mainly prominent businessmen or their relatives – were killed in a series of assassination attempts by armed individuals, some of whom wore military uniform.

Armed opposition supporters allegedly carried out attacks in January (see below) and October, when three members of the security forces and a civilian were killed in an attack on a police station in Vogan, 40 kilometres northeast of the capital, Lomé. Five suspects were arrested in connection with the attack, but had not been brought to court by the end of the year.

In August the UN Sub-Commission on Prevention of Discrimination and Protection of Minorities passed a resolution on Togo which condemned human rights violations, called for an end to impunity and urged the UN Commission on Human Rights to appoint a Special Rapporteur on Togo.

286

At least 48 prisoners were extrajudicially executed by soldiers following a shooting incident in Lomé on 5 January which the government alleged was an attack from Ghana on the headquarters of the *Régiment interarmes togolais* (RIT), Togolese Combined Regiment. After the shooting, at least 36 civilians were reportedly seized on the streets, taken into military custody at the RIT headquarters and executed on or around 6 January. Up to 12 others, who had been held for 10 months in military custody at the RIT headquarters on suspicion of involvement in an alleged attack there in March 1993 (see *Amnesty International Report 1994*), were also killed on 6 January because of their suspected sympathy with the attack the previous day. Among the victims were two soldiers, Private Amégadji and Private Djagri N'Teki Baba. At least 11 other people were extrajudicially executed or "disappeared" in Lomé in the days following the 5 January incident.

In February, three CAR activists were killed after being abducted by men in military uniform during the elections. Gaston Aziaduvo Edeh, a newly elected member of parliament, and three other CAR supporters were reportedly taken in their car by their abductors to a military building known as *la résidence du Bénin*, the Benin residence. The following day, the burned-out wreck of the car and the dead bodies of three of the men – Gaston Aziaduvo Edeh, Prosper Ayité Hillah and Martin Agbenou – were found. The fourth captive escaped and went into hiding. The army chief of staff denied that soldiers had been involved and claimed that the killings were the work of civilians wearing military uniform. President Eyadéma asked the government to set up a commission of inquiry, but those responsible were not identified or brought to justice.

Several prisoners of conscience were held during the year. Martin Dossou Gbenouga, publishing director of an independent newspaper, *La Tribune des démocrates*, was sentenced in May to five years' imprisonment in connection with an article which criticized President Eyadéma and the French Government's support for him. His arrest and conviction were part of a pattern of arrests and harassment of independent journalists, newspaper publishers and vendors.

In early February, six members of the opposition *Union des forces du changement* (UFC), Union of Forces for Change, were arrested and charged with electoral fraud for distributing pamphlets calling for a boycott of the legislative elections. They were prisoners of conscience. At least four of them were sentenced to prison terms in May. Two were reportedly beaten and deprived of food in pre-trial custody. All six were released before the end of the year.

Several other political prisoners appeared to be prisoners of conscience. Trade union leader Komi Dackey was arrested in January and held without trial until late December when he was released under the terms of the general amnesty. The authorities claimed that he was held, with a number of other detainees, on suspicion of involvement in the alleged attack on the RIT headquarters in January. However, the real reason for his arrest appeared to be his trade union activities. In November he was secretly transferred to a military camp in Kara, in the north, together with a number of other political detainees, including five soldiers held since March 1993 (see below).

Several political prisoners arrested in 1992 and 1993 were reportedly released prior to the general amnesty, including Louis Amédome, Kanlou Odanou, Kokou Okessou Mbooura, Ali Akondo and Tampoudi Dermane (see *Amnesty International Reports 1993* and *1994*). Others were released at the end of the year as a result of the general amnesty. Among those freed were at least five soldiers detained without charge or trial since the alleged March 1993 attack on the RIT headquarters; Attiogbé Stéphane Koudossou and Gérard Akoumey (see *Amnesty International Report 1994*); at least 10 people arrested after the events of 5 January (see above); and four relatives of Corporal Nikabou Bikagni, held without charge or trial since October 1992 (see *Amnesty International Reports 1993* and *1994*). Corporal Bikagni, who was arrested in October 1992 apparently because of his allegiance to former Prime Minister Joseph Kokou Koffigoh, was convicted in January of importing and carrying arms and ammunition and was sentenced to three years' imprisonment; he reportedly remained held at the end of the year. The court refused to investigate allegations that he had been tortured in custody.

Torture and ill-treatment of detainees were reported to be routine. In February Akuete Kodjo, a CAR member and brother of a soldier extrajudicially executed in March 1993 (see *Amnesty International Report 1994*), was detained for four months at the *Gendarmerie nationale*, the paramilitary police headquarters, in Lomé, where he was tortured. In June one man was reportedly arrested by soldiers and detained for 19 days in a secret detention centre where he was beaten, tortured with alternating jets of cold and scalding water, and interrogated about his views on democracy and freedom.

At least eight people "disappeared". Gavi Komi, a salesman and CAR member, "disappeared" after he was abducted from his home in Lomé by five soldiers on 6 January. Six people, including Kowouvi Kobono and two women, "disappeared" in mid-February after being stopped by soldiers at a check-point in Adétikopé. David Bruce, a civil servant, "disappeared" after he was abducted in Lomé on 6 September from his car by three armed men, one of whom had a machine-gun. The assailants were travelling in a mini-bus followed by two military vehicles. Between 1991 and 1993 David Bruce was a senior adviser to the President of the High Council of the Republic.

Amnesty International repeatedly expressed concern to the authorities about human rights violations including extrajudicial executions, torture and "disappearances".

In September Amnesty International published a report, *Togo: A new era for human rights?*, which detailed human rights violations in the period between President Eyadéma's re-election in 1993 and the 1994 legislative elections. It called on the new government to investigate past violations, bring those responsible to justice, and implement urgently needed human rights reforms, including measures to eradicate torture, the release of prisoners of conscience and a review of the cases of political prisoners. The government did not respond in detail, but indicated a willingness to hold talks with the organization and informed Amnesty International about the general amnesty.

TRINIDAD AND TOBAGO

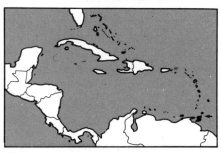

The first execution since 1979 was carried out and two prisoners came close to being executed. At least one death sentence was imposed.

The first execution in nearly 15 years was carried out. Glen Ashby, convicted of murder and sentenced to death in 1989, was executed on 14 July. This was the first hanging to be carried out in three years in the English-speaking Caribbean. The execution caused international consternation not only for marking a resumption of executions but also because it was carried out in contravention of national and international law. The death warrant was read to Glen Ashby less than 48 hours before the execution was due to take place; the practice has been to read a death warrant on Thursday for execution on Tuesday, providing time for the prisoner to seek legal advice on any proceedings still available and to make any final personal arrangements. On 13 July the Attorney General gave an undertaking to the Judicial Committee of the Privy Council (JCPC) in London, Trinidad and Tobago's final court of appeal, that "there would be no execution until all possibility of obtaining a stay of execution, including an appeal to the Board [JCPC], has been exhausted". In view of this statement the Court of Appeal, sitting at the time the execution was carried out, did not grant a stay of execution requested by lawyers in order to file a constitutional motion on grounds of, among other things, the very short notice given of intended execution. This issue was pending a decision of the Court of Appeal in the case of Lincoln Guerra and Brian Wallen (see below) and therefore Glen Ashby's execution should have been stayed pending a decision.

Glen Ashby was ·just six days away from completing five years under sentence of death and thus becoming eligible to have his sentence commuted under the JCPC's November 1993 ruling that execution after five years constitutes "inhuman or degrading punishment" (see *Amnesty International Report 1994*, **Jamaica** entry). At the time of Glen Ashby's execution, the JCPC was communicating by fax to the Attorney General its decision to grant a stay of execution.

On 6 July Glen Ashby asked the Human Rights Committee (HRC) to consider his case, which takes several months. No time was allowed by the government for the HRC to consider Glen Ashby's case. International standards provide that no execution may "be carried out pending any appeal or other recourse procedure"; these obligations were ignored by the government. In a statement issued in late July, the HRC expressed its "indignation" at the failure of the government to allow time to review Glen Ashby's communication and said that there was "no precedent in the Committee's practice in capital cases" of such an attitude. The HRC decided to continue considering Glen Ashby's complaint.

On 24 March a warrant was issued for the execution of Lincoln Guerra and Brian Wallen the next day, only three days after the JCPC dismissed their petition for leave to appeal against conviction. Both men had been convicted of murder and sentenced to death in May 1989. The prisoners filed constitutional motions arguing that executing them would be a violation of their constitutional rights and requested a stay of execution. The High Court refused to grant the stay. An appeal was filed immediately but was dismissed; however, they were granted a 48-hour stay and leave to appeal to the JCPC. The JCPC subsequently adjourned the hearing of the prisoners' application until 25 April and granted a stay until after determination of the application.

On 18 April the Court of Appeal dismissed their constitutional motion and refused a stay of execution pending an appeal. However, the Attorney General made a commitment that the two men would not be executed until determination of an appeal to the Court of Appeal; he refused, however, to give a similar undertaking to cover the appeal to the JCPC.

On 9 June the Court of Appeal heard the appeal on the constitutional motion and reserved judgment.

In view of the circumstances surrounding the execution of Glen Ashby (see above), Lincoln Guerra and Brian Wallen sought an undertaking from the Attorney General on 19 July that they would not be executed pending the determination of any further appeals available to them; however, this was not forthcoming. The two men petitioned the JCPC on 25 July to grant them a stay of execution should the Court of Appeal rule against them, so that they could pursue further appeals. The JCPC stated that "their Lordships were much concerned that ... the petitioners might be executed before they had an opportunity to exercise their right of appeal to the Judicial Committee". The JCPC, after giving careful consideration to the matter of jurisdiction, directed that "the sentence of death be not carried out ... until after determination of such appeal by the JCPC". On 27 July the Court of Appeal issued its decision (pending since June) rejecting the men's appeal. It strongly criticized the JCPC decision and the lawyers for taking action "to pre-empt the jurisdiction of this court" but granted the men leave to appeal to the JCPC. A full hearing was pending at the end of the year.

At least one death sentence was imposed during the year for murder; at the end of the year there were about 60 prisoners under sentence of death.

The court hearing in the case of an 11-year-old boy sentenced to 20 strokes in April 1993 and flogged with a leather belt was held on 14 November (see *Amnesty International Report 1994*). He was seeking redress and compensation from the government.

In April Amnesty International wrote to the Prime Minister, Patrick Manning, expressing its concern at the attempt to execute Lincoln Guerra and Brian Wallen. The organization pointed out that there had been a departure from normal practice on the issuing of death warrants; that the two men were only two months away from completing five years under sentence of death and therefore becoming eligible to have their sentences commuted to life imprisonment; and that no time had been allowed for them to submit their case to the HRC or the Inter-American Commission on Human Rights. Amnesty International urged the Attorney General to ensure that this situation did not arise again. It further urged the authorities to commute all death sentences and to take steps to abolish the death penalty.

In July Amnesty International called on the government not to execute Glen Ashby and expressed its "deep regret and strongest condemnation" after his execution, noting that the hanging had been carried out in violation of national and international law.

There had been no reply from the government by the end of the year.

TUNISIA

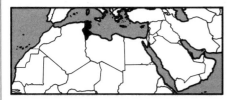

Hundreds of suspected supporters of the unauthorized Islamist organization *al-Nahda* and of the unauthorized *Parti communiste des ouvriers tunisiens* (PCOT), Tunisian Communist Workers' Party, and other government critics were arrested. Most of them were prisoners of conscience. Many were released without trial, but scores were given prison sentences. Over 2,000 political prisoners, most of them prisoners of conscience sentenced after unfair trials since 1991, remained held. Prolonged *garde à vue* (incommunicado) detention continued to facilitate torture and ill-treatment of detainees held in the Ministry of the Interior and in police stations across the country. Cruel, inhuman or degrading treatment of political prisoners was reported to be widespread. At least four political detainees died in custody.

A new wave of repression of government opponents and critics further restricted freedom of expression and association. At least six foreign newspapers were banned, foreign journalists and observers were expelled or denied access to Tunisia, and government critics were prevented from leaving the country. A former socialist leader was arrested for questioning in April and was refused permission to register a "*forum démocra-*

tique" (democratic forum). In May a group of women who signed a petition calling for respect for public liberties were summoned by police for questioning. The *Ligue tunisienne des droits de l'homme* (LTDH), Tunisian Human Rights League, resumed its activities in February, but its communiques could not be published in the government-controlled press.

Presidential elections were held in March and according to official sources President Zine el Abidine Ben 'Ali was re-elected with over 99 per cent of the votes. He was the only candidate. The two people who had announced their intention to stand as candidates were arrested. Moncef Marzouki, the former president of the LTDH, was arrested in March and detained for four months on charges of having insulted the Tunisian judiciary in an interview with a foreign newspaper. He was released on bail and was still awaiting trial at the end of the year. 'Abderrahmane Hani, a lawyer, was arrested in February and held for over two months on charges of setting up an unauthorized association and spreading false information. He was later sentenced to eight months' imprisonment, suspended.

Several people were imprisoned as prisoners of conscience as a result of legislation introduced in 1993 which allows prosecution of people for offences committed in other countries even when the offences are not recognized as crimes in those countries (see *Amnesty International Report 1994*). 'Adel Selmi, a Tunisian academic resident in France, was arrested in June on arrival at Tunis airport. He was held in illegally prolonged *garde à vue* detention but the arrest date was falsified to conceal this. Showing his wrists and ankles which still bore marks, he stated in court that he had been suspended in contorted positions and had his head plunged in buckets of water to force him to sign a confession without knowing its content. He was sentenced to four years and two months' imprisonment for belonging to an unauthorized organization (*al-Nahda*), participating in an unauthorized demonstration and collecting funds without authorization. The charges related either to *al-Nahda* meetings outside Tunisia, which he denied participating in, or to events which were beyond the statute of limitation.

Wives and other relatives of Islamist

290

political activists who were in prison or abroad were often detained for questioning. Many were reportedly ordered to stop wearing the headscarf and subjected to ill-treatment and harassment, including sexual harassment and threats of rape. Those known or suspected of having given financial assistance to families of Islamist detainees, or of having themselves received financial assistance, were imprisoned on charges of unauthorized collection of funds. Monia Mannai, whose husband continued to serve a long prison sentence for alleged political activities on behalf of *al-Nahda* and whose brother was being sought by police for the same reason, was sentenced in July with four other women to one year's imprisonment for membership of an unauthorized association, participating in unauthorized meetings and unauthorized collection of funds.

Hundreds of prisoners of conscience and possible prisoners of conscience sentenced in previous years remained in prison. Most of those released were ordered to report to a police station daily, weekly or in some cases twice a day, and were denied passports.

Torture and ill-treatment of both male and female detainees during *garde à vue* detention continued to be reported. The 10-day statutory *garde à vue* limit, which itself contravenes international human rights standards, was often illegally prolonged. No independent and impartial investigations were carried out into any of the allegations of torture and illegally prolonged *garde à vue* detention. Hamma Hammami, a leading PCOT figure arrested in February, stated in court that he was tortured and ill-treated in the police station and in the Ministry of the Interior. He stated that he was severely beaten, sexually humiliated and threatened with rape and death. Days after his arrest he still bore bruises and marks on his face and neck. He had been sentenced *in absentia* in December 1992 to four years and nine months' imprisonment for maintaining an unauthorized organization, holding unauthorized meetings and distributing leaflets, and was in hiding at the time of arrest. After his arrest he was also accused of assaulting two police officers and carrying a false identity card. He was sentenced in April to nine years and seven months' imprisonment, reduced by one year on appeal in June. In April an Amnesty Interna-

tional delegate who planned to observe his trial was refused access to Tunisia.

Ill-treatment in prisons continued to be widely reported. Prisoners of conscience who went on hunger-strike were put in isolation cells and kept chained by the foot. Inmates were reportedly beaten by prison guards inside the prisons and sometimes taken back to the Ministry of the Interior and beaten and ill-treated. Political prisoners were also often denied medical treatment and family visits.

Courts ignored complaints by defendants who retracted their confessions stating that these had been extracted under torture, even when the marks of torture or ill-treatment were still visible at the time of the trial. These confessions were accepted as evidence, as were confessions of other detainees who were never brought to court for cross-examination as requested by defence lawyers.

At least four people died in custody during the year. Isma'il Khemira and 'Ezzeddine Ben 'Aicha died in prison in February and August respectively, and Lotfi Gla'a and 'Amar el Beji died during *garde à vue* detention in police custody in February and November respectively. The authorities did not reply to requests for clarification of the causes and circumstances of these deaths. The government took no further action to investigate the death in custody of Faisal Barakat, Rachid Chammakhi and at least six others in 1991 and 1992, despite compelling evidence of torture prior to the deaths. No further information was made available about Kamal Matmati, who "disappeared" after arrest in 1991 (see *Amnesty International Report 1994*).

In November the UN Human Rights Committee expressed concern at the deterioration in the human rights situation in Tunisia since 1990, about continuing reports of abuse, ill-treatment and torture of detainees, deaths in custody under suspicious circumstances, and about the lack of independence of the judiciary.

Amnesty International renewed its call for the release of all prisoners of conscience and for the fair trial or release of other political prisoners. It called for full and independent investigations into allegations of torture and ill-treatment and into all cases of death in custody in recent years. It also expressed concern at the continuing denial of access to Tunisia of an

Amnesty International delegate, and at the continuing harassment of its Section in Tunisia. In January Amnesty International issued a report, *Tunisia: Rhetoric versus reality, the failure of a human rights bureaucracy.*

TURKEY

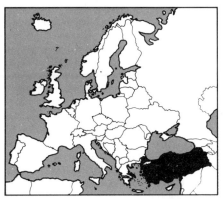

Hundreds of people were detained as prisoners of conscience. Some were soon released, but dozens were sentenced to prison terms. Torture of political and criminal detainees in police stations was routine and systematic, and there were at least 29 reported deaths in custody as a result of torture. At least 55 people reportedly "disappeared" in security force custody. There were hundreds of political killings in the mainly Kurdish southeastern provinces, many in circumstances that suggested that the victims had been extrajudicially executed by the security forces. There were no executions, but death sentences were passed during the year. Armed opposition groups were responsible for at least 170 deliberate and arbitrary killings of prisoners and other non-combatants.

State of emergency legislation was in force throughout the year in 10 southeastern provinces, where the 10-year-long conflict between government forces and the secessionist *Partiya Karkeren Kurdistan* (PKK), Kurdish Workers' Party, claimed 3,500 lives, including civilians, during the year.

Hundreds of people suspected of supporting Kurdish separatism were arrested, many of them at public meetings and demonstrations, and held for hours or days in police custody as prisoners of con-

science. Article 8 of the Anti-Terror Law, which outlaws any advocacy of separatism, was increasingly used to prosecute and imprison people for the peaceful expression of their opinions. In May Mehdi Zana, the former mayor of Diyarbakır, began serving a four-year prison sentence under Article 8 of the Anti-Terror Law for testifying before the Human Rights Sub-Committee of the European Parliament in Brussels in December 1992. Günay Aslan, author and television journalist, who had been arrested in October 1993, continued to serve an 18-month sentence because of a historical book he had written.

In January Ahmet Zeki Okçuoğlu, a lawyer, began serving a 20-month sentence for "spreading separatist propaganda" because of an article in a political journal. In October Mahmut Akkurt, another lawyer, began a 14-month prison sentence for a speech he made in 1992 as president of the Balıkesir branch of the Turkish Human Rights Association (HRA). Four members of the board of the Diyarbakır branch of the HRA, Melike Alp and the lawyers Mahmut Şakar, Nimetullah Gündüz and Abdullah Çağer, were arrested in December and remanded in custody on charges of "separatist propaganda" and membership of the PKK. The indictment against them contained no evidence to support the charges of membership of the PKK. All were prisoners of conscience.

Torture by police or gendarmes (soldiers carrying out police duties in rural areas) continued to be reported from all parts of Turkey, particularly the major cities and the southeast. Detainees suspected of links with illegal armed organizations were held for up to 30 days in incommunicado detention, unprotected by even the most basic safeguards against torture. A 13-year-old boy, Abdullah Salman, wrongly accused of theft, reported that he had been blindfolded, beaten, choked and given electric shocks while being interrogated at Şişli Police Headquarters in Istanbul. Bruising on his shoulders, arms and neck was confirmed by a medical report.

There were at least 29 deaths in custody apparently as a result of torture. Those who died included criminal suspects and people detained on suspicion of involvement with armed political organizations. Garip Ölmez of the village of

292

Yoğurtyemez in the Ahlat district of Bitlis province was arrested in April and interrogated at Bitlis Gendarmerie Headquarters. Ten days later Garip Ölmez's family were asked to collect his body from the mortuary of Bitlis State Hospital. They found that the body had severe injuries to the head and stomach. The ankles bore marks of bindings and the feet had apparently been burned with melted plastic. The family submitted a petition of complaint to the Ahlat Prosecutor's office, but it was reportedly rejected.

Abdullah Baskın was detained with 14 other Kurdish villagers from Gümüşgörgü in the Kozluk district of Batman province in July. They were interrogated at Batman Gendarmerie Headquarters because they had refused to participate in the system of village guards (villagers armed and paid by the government to fight the PKK). After 13 days in custody Abdullah Baskın, who was in good health before being detained, was taken to hospital where he died. The other villagers said that they were tortured and that Abdullah Baskın had been tortured particularly severely – that he was subjected to hanging by the wrists tied behind the back, continually beaten and subjected to electric shocks. No judicial investigation appears to have been carried out into Abdullah Baskın's death.

There were reports of ill-treatment of inmates in prisons, particularly when police or gendarmes entered prisons during hunger-strikes and other protests by prisoners, or when prisoners were travelling to or from court in the custody of gendarmes. In September the female inmates of Konya E-type prison were returned to their dormitory by force when they protested that their exercise period was being curtailed. Later that evening approximately 80 prison warders and an equal number of soldiers entered the women's dormitory and beat the women with sticks, truncheons and pipes. Many women were injured, including Çınar Yaşar whose ribs were broken.

In October scores of prisoners at Diyarbakır E-type Prison were injured when soldiers and plainclothes police attacked a barricaded prison ward with firearms and explosives. Two prisoners, Ramazan Özüak and Süleyman Ongün later died of their injuries.

Hayriye Gündüz and 11 other prisoners on trial for membership of the illegal armed organization *Devrimci Sol* (Revolutionary Left) were severely beaten by gendarmes who were guarding them at Istanbul State Security Court No. 3 in October. The attack was witnessed by three lawyers, who reported that the gendarmes shouted, "Get the lawyers out, we are going to kill this lot." Police hustled the lawyers away. The prisoners were beaten in the court corridor before being dragged into a yard where they were kicked and punched by plainclothes police and members of the Mobile Force (an anti-riot squad).

At least 55 people were reported to have "disappeared" in the custody of police or soldiers. Mehmet Gürkan, head of the village of Akçayurt in Diyarbakır province, and the inhabitants of his village were forcibly evacuated by security forces in July. At a press conference in Ankara, the capital, Mehmet Gürkan publicized the plight of his village, where security forces had burned both houses and crops, and asked the government for help. He returned in August to the village to collect his belongings and was seen being detained by members of the security forces and taken away in a helicopter. He has not been seen since.

Kenan Bilgin "disappeared" in unacknowledged detention in Ankara following his arrest in the Dikmen district of the city in September. Nine people, including a lawyer, who were detained at Ankara Police Headquarters in September claim to have seen a person answering Kenan Bilgin's description, apparently being interrogated under torture. Another detainee who knew Kenan Bilgin spoke to him. The police denied holding Kenan Bilgin.

Hundreds of people were victims of political killings, many of which may have been extrajudicial executions. Those targeted included journalists, members of the *Halkın Demokrasi Partisi* (HADEP), People's Democracy Party, which campaigned for political rights for the Kurdish minority, and people who had been imprisoned for or interrogated about separatist offences, or whose relatives had joined the PKK.

Necati Aydin and Mehmet Ay were detained in March. In April they appeared in Diyarbakır State Security Court on charges of supporting the PKK. The court ruled that they should be released. The prosecutor lodged an objection, demanding that they should remain in custody. The objection was overruled, but the two men were never released or seen alive again: seven days later their bodies were found in a field.

Muhsin Melik, a founder of the Şanlıurfa branch of HADEP, was attacked in June. Before he died of his wounds he said that he recognized the faces of three of his attackers and that they were members of the police team following him.

In March several villages in Şırnak were bombed, reportedly by jet aircraft. Thirty-six people were killed, including 17 children. Official statements claimed that the bombing was accidental, but local inhabitants said that just days before the bombing they had been threatened with death by the security forces for refusing to join the village guards.

There were also allegations of extrajudicial executions in Istanbul and Ankara during police operations against *Devrimci Sol*. Fuat Erdoğan, who was wanted by police, Elmas Yalçin and İsmet Erdoğan were shot dead by police in a café in the Beşiktaş district of Istanbul in September. Istanbul police claimed that the three opened fire when approached for an identity check. However, the café owner said that police evacuated the café before the shootings took place, and a lawyer who visited the scene of the killing on behalf of the HRA found no evidence of shots fired from inside the café outwards. The three victims had bullet wounds to their heads.

After 10 years in which no judicial executions had been carried out, Turkey became *de facto* an abolitionist country. However, the death penalty remained in force and a number of death sentences were passed during 1994.

PKK guerrillas were responsible for over 170 deliberate and arbitrary killings. Most of their victims were Kurdish villagers who participated in the system of government-armed village guards. Village guards captured by the PKK during the course of attacks were frequently "executed", as were their extended families. Sixteen women and children were killed by grenades thrown by PKK members into a building during an attack on village guards in Ormancık, Mardin province, in January. The PKK also claimed responsibility for bomb attacks which were clearly directed at civilian targets. In January Ali Ertuğrul Tokaç and Ruhi Can Tul were killed by bombs placed on buses in

Ankara. Also in January a six-year-old boy was killed by a bomb planted in the Diyarbakır governor's office. In June, 12 foreign tourists were injured by a bomb in Marmaris, southwest Turkey, for which the PKK claimed responsibility. One later died. In September PKK forces raiding the village of Kazanköyü, Ağrı, entered the house of a primary school teacher, Sait Korkmaz, dragged him out, bound his hands and legs, and shot him dead. Guerrillas of the PKK reportedly shot dead four primary school teachers in Mardin province in November.

Amnesty International condemned these grave abuses and in June publicly called on the leadership of the PKK to ensure that all PKK forces were instructed to respect human rights and basic international humanitarian standards.

Amnesty International published a number of reports including *Turkey: Time for Action* in February, *Turkey: More people "disappear" following detention* in March, and *Turkey: Dissident voices jailed again* in June. Throughout the year the organization appealed for the release of prisoners of conscience and urged the government to initiate full and impartial investigations into allegations of torture, extrajudicial executions and "disappearances". In January an Amnesty International delegate observed a hearing in the trial of 16 lawyers at Diyarbakır State Security Court. The lawyers faced charges of assisting the PKK, but Amnesty International believed that the real reason for their prosecution was their work for human rights. At the end of the year, the trial was continuing. In May an Amnesty International delegate observed a hearing in the trial of Soner Önder at Istanbul State Security Court. In October he was sentenced to life imprisonment on charges of participating in an arson attack on a department store, in which 12 people were killed. Amnesty International believed that Soner Önder's trial was unfair. In August an Amnesty International delegate observed a hearing in Ankara in the trial of eight Kurdish members of parliament being tried for treason. In December the parliamentarians were convicted of assisting the PKK and sentenced to long terms of imprisonment.

In September the Turkish Government refused to admit an Amnesty International researcher into Turkey on the grounds that he had links with the PKK. Amnesty International denied this and asked the authorities for specific information. This was not provided.

In an oral statement to the UN Commission on Human Rights in February Amnesty International included reference to its concerns about extrajudicial executions and "disappearances" in Turkey. In October in Budapest at the Conference on Security and Co-operation in Europe (CSCE) Review Conference, Amnesty International raised concerns about human rights violations against human rights defenders in Turkey. Amnesty International also continued to urge that a CSCE expert mission be sent to the country (see **Working with International Organizations**).

TURKMENISTAN

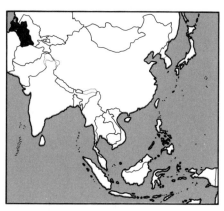

Two probable prisoners of conscience were detained. A third person detained briefly in connection with the same case was reportedly tortured. A probable prisoner of conscience was confined to a psychiatric hospital. At least one person was executed.

In January a referendum confirmed the extension of President Saparmurad Niyazov's term in office for a further five years and presidential elections scheduled for 1997 were cancelled.

Yusup Kuliyev was detained for around 15 days in October and November by agents of the State Security Committee (KGB) and questioned about an alleged plot to assassinate the President. He was reportedly tortured in detention. Shortly after he had been detained Khoshali Garayev and Mukhammad Aymuradov,

both Russian citizens of Turkmen origin, were arrested in Uzbekistan by Turkmenistan KGB agents. Both were reportedly also charged with plotting to assassinate President Niyazov. However, sources alleged that the charge had been fabricated to punish them for their opposition sympathies. They were still in detention at the end of the year and there were fears that they too had been tortured.

Valentin Kopusev, a probable prisoner of conscience, was reportedly confined against his will in a psychiatric hospital not for medical reasons but to punish him for his opposition to the authorities. Reportedly, his detention came after he wrote a letter to the President complaining about the lack of democracy, human rights and fundamental freedoms in Turkmenistan.

The death penalty remained in force for 13 offences in peacetime (not 18 as reported in *Amnesty International Report 1993*). Information was received that the death penalty had been repealed for one offence in 1991 and for two others in 1993. At least one person convicted of murder was executed in 1994.

In February the Minister of Foreign Affairs sent a detailed reply to the Amnesty International report, *Turkmenistan: A summary of concerns about prisoners of conscience, ill-treatment and the death penalty*, published in November 1993, in which he rejected the report's conclusions and recommendations on the grounds that they were based on "free interpretations and emotions". He also denied that people described in the report as prisoners of conscience had ever been arrested or detained for political reasons.

Amnesty International sought further information about the criminal charge against Khoshali Garayev and Mukhammad Aymuradov, and called on the authorities to ensure that they were not tortured. Replying in December, the Ambassador of Turkmenistan to the USA declined to provide further information about the charge, but asserted that "the Government of Turkmenistan does not condone the maltreatment of detainees or prisoners".

Amnesty International sought further information about the detention of Valentin Kopusev in a psychiatric hospital. It continued to call for the abolition of the death penalty.

UGANDA

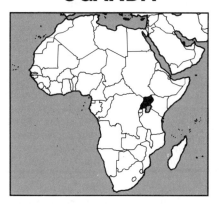

More than 160 people, many of whom appeared to be prisoners of conscience, were unlawfully detained without charge or trial in areas affected by insurgency. Two members of an opposition party and a journalist were detained briefly in the capital; they were prisoners of conscience. There were reports of torture and ill-treatment of prisoners. Courts continued to impose sentences of caning. At least seven civilians may have been victims of extrajudicial execution by the security forces. At least 22 death sentences were passed and there was one execution. An armed opposition group was responsible for serious human rights abuses.

Armed opposition to the government of President Yoweri Museveni continued to decline. In January the armed opposition Uganda People's Army announced that it had abandoned its insurgency. However, negotiations between the Lord's Resistance Army (LRA), the largest armed opposition group active in the north, and the government failed to produce a settlement. The government armed thousands of members of local militias and there were numerous reports of forced conscription into these militias.

In March elections were held for a Constituent Assembly. The Assembly had the task of promulgating a new constitution, but it had not done so by the end of 1994.

A commission of inquiry into the administration of justice, established in 1993, and the Uganda Human Rights Commission, established in 1986 to investigate human rights abuses before President Museveni's government came to power, were reported to have handed in final reports to the government during the year. Neither had been published by the end of 1994.

Between September and November at least 168 people were unlawfully detained without charge or trial in Gulu military barracks in northern Uganda. They were taken into military custody for "screening" after being identified as "rebel coordinators" by former members of the LRA now working as informers for the army. Many of those detained appeared to be prisoners of conscience, imprisoned for the political views they held, or were assumed to hold by virtue of their ethnic origin. All the detainees were members of the Acholi ethnic group. Tobias Ali, who had been studying in Jinja, was arrested by army officers in Gulu town while visiting his family. He was arrested because an army informer arbitrarily pointed him out on the street as a "rebel coordinator". He was released without charge after four days in detention after relatives and local officials interceded on his behalf. Patrick Okot, a teacher at Pece primary school, was detained for five weeks before being released without charge on condition that he report to the authorities every two weeks. By the end of the year at least 100 of those detained had been released without charge and none of those who remained in detention appeared to have been charged.

Two members of an opposition party and a journalist were detained briefly in the capital, Kampala. They were prisoners of conscience. In March the National Chairman of the Uganda People's Congress (UPC), Haji Badru Kendo Wegulo, and one of his colleagues, Patrick Rubaihayo, were charged with publishing and printing seditious material. The charges related to the UPC's manifesto for the Constituent Assembly elections in March, which alleged that Uganda was being ruled by Tutsi of Rwandese origin. A court threatened to dismiss the charges in September after repeated prosecution requests for adjournments, but had not done so by the end of the year. Also in October, the editor-in-chief of *The Monitor* newspaper, Wafula Oguttu, was arrested and detained for 18 hours on charges of defamation and publishing false statements. The charges were quickly dropped.

No further official action appeared to have been taken in relation to a sedition charge lodged in October 1993 against two journalists on *The Shariat* newspaper.

296

Teddy Sseze Cheeye, editor of the *Uganda Confidential* newsletter, was also charged with sedition in October 1993 and again in December 1993 (see *Amnesty International Report 1994*). The first charge was dropped but trial proceedings began in relation to the second.

In contrast to 1993, there were no reported releases from custody of political prisoners who had been detained without trial for prolonged periods on the capital charge of treason. There continued to be long delays in bringing political prisoners to trial. Sergeant Kabanda, charged with treason in June 1993 after having been held for three years in military custody without charge or trial, had still not been brought to trial by the end of the year.

There were continued reports of torture and ill-treatment of criminal suspects by soldiers, members of paramilitary groups and police. For example, in June police officers in Mukono District were accused of having tortured Fred Mukisa during more than a year's detention without trial. It was not known whether he was charged with an offence or what official action had been taken by the end of the year regarding the allegations of torture against the police.

Courts, particularly Resistance Committee courts, continued to impose sentences of caning – a cruel, inhuman or degrading punishment. For example, in July a Resistance Committee court in Bweyogerere, composed of local councillors with no legal training, imposed sentences of eight strokes of the cane upon a man and a 12-year-old girl after they were found guilty of having had sexual intercourse.

There were reports of extrajudicial executions by army personnel in March in Gulu District in the context of military operations against the LRA. Soldiers based in a detachment in Binya village were reported to have killed at least seven civilians. For example, Lino Okot and Janani Oywello of neighbouring Layoko village were reported to have hidden in the bush during fighting between soldiers and LRA combatants. According to witnesses, the two men encountered soldiers after the fighting had died down and were asked to show identification. Although they did so, they were shot and killed on the spot. The soldiers were also reported to have tortured and ill-treated other inhabitants

of Binya village and neighbouring villages. There were unconfirmed reports that the officer in charge of the army unit concerned was subsequently detained, but no information was made available about official investigations by the end of the year.

The Army General Court Martial began the task of hearing appeals from over 100 individuals under sentence of death whose trials by army tribunals in previous years had been declared "illegal and incompetent" in September 1993 by the Minister of State for Defence (see *Amnesty International Report 1994*). At least 15 people had their death sentences quashed. In September the Court Martial found that a unit disciplinary committee had wrongly sentenced to death three army corporals on charges of aggravated robbery. The Court Martial found that they should have been charged with a lesser, non-capital offence.

Professor Isaac Newton Ojok, who was arrested in 1988 for alleged links to the armed opposition Holy Spirit Movement of Alice Lakwena, was acquitted by the High Court after a retrial in January on the grounds of insufficient evidence. He had been charged with treason in 1990 and sentenced to death in 1991 (see *Amnesty International Report 1992*). In November, two men charged with treason in 1990, Brigadier Smith Opon Acak and Ahmed Ogeny, were acquitted by the High Court and released.

There was one execution. In December a soldier was executed by firing-squad after being found guilty by an Army Field Court Martial in Gulu District of killing three people at a night club. The High Court sentenced at least 14 people to death, including two soldiers, for a variety of offences. The Army General Court Martial sentenced to death at least eight soldiers on charges of robbery and murder. In May it was reported that there were over 200 prisoners on death row in Luzira Maximum Security Prison.

The LRA was responsible for serious human rights abuses, including rape and deliberate and arbitrary killings. Joyce Maku was captured in February in Moyo District along with five other women. She escaped in April after having been sexually abused by three LRA combatants. She was pregnant on her escape. Civilians were deliberately killed in raids by the LRA on buses and villages in the north. Sixteen people were reported to have died after a bus was attacked on the Gulu-Kitgum road in April. It was reported in March that at least 20 people had been killed after the LRA attacked and burned homes in Abulu village in Apac District. Amnesty International condemned the abuses of human rights by the LRA and urged it to abide by basic humanitarian standards.

During the year Amnesty International continued to urge the government to investigate past and recent killings by the security forces which might have been extrajudicial executions. In August Amnesty International published a report, *Uganda: Recommendations for safeguarding human rights in the new constitution*, expressing concern that the draft constitution failed to meet the requirements of international standards in the safeguarding of human rights. In December it published a report, *Uganda: Detentions of suspected government opponents without charge or trial in the north*, in which it called for the immediate release of prisoners of conscience being detained in Gulu military barracks and for all uncharged political detainees in custody to be released if they were not promptly to be charged and brought to trial.

UKRAINE

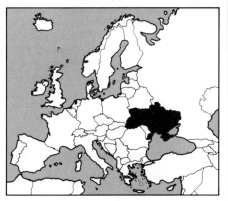

At least 200 people were sentenced to death. At least one execution came to light during the year, but the true figure was believed to be much higher; information was received of 181 executions in 1992 and 1993. There were reports of inadequate protection for asylum-seekers.

Parliamentary elections took place in March. Following presidential elections in July Leonid Kuchma succeeded Leonid Kravchuk as President. Discussions continued throughout the year on the draft of a new constitution (see *Amnesty International Report 1994*).

At least 200 people were sentenced to death by October 1994. Detailed statistics on the application of the death penalty were released for 1992 and 1993. In 1992, 79 people were sentenced to death and 103 executed. In 1993, 117 death sentences were passed, all for premeditated, aggravated murder, and 78 people were executed. The same year, 11 death sentences were quashed on appeal and one was commuted.

Sessions of the presidential clemency commission were delayed in the second half of 1994 following the July elections. Among those awaiting the outcome of a petition for clemency was Vasily Krivonos, who was sentenced to death for murder in November 1993. He had just turned 18 at the time of the crime and he was said to have learning difficulties and psychiatric problems. His appeal had been rejected by the Supreme Court in February. Vasily Krivonos was reportedly beaten and taunted by prison guards.

Among those known to have been executed in 1994 was Anatoly Lyubarsky, who had been sentenced to death for murder in October 1993. His appeal was turned down in January and he was executed after President Kravchuk rejected his petition for clemency in July.

In July reports were received of inadequate protection of at least eight Iraqi asylum-seekers who, if forcibly returned to their country of origin, could have risked falling victim to human rights violations. The authorities were said to have intended expelling them without examining their reasons for seeking protection or the risks they faced in Iraq. They were believed still to be in Ukraine at the end of the year.

Throughout the year Amnesty International urged the President to commute all pending death sentences. The organization also called for a full investigation into allegations that Vasily Krivonos had been beaten while on death row. Amnesty International urged that no asylum-seeker, including the eight Iraqis, be expelled without a thorough examination of his or her case, and that asylum-seekers at risk of

298

human rights violations in their own countries be granted effective and durable protection against forcible return. No replies had been received by the end of the year.

UNITED ARAB EMIRATES

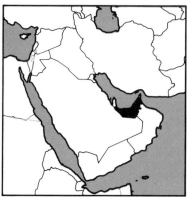

Four prisoners of conscience, all Indian nationals, were held until December. One person was sentenced to death and at least five people were executed.

In February the President, al-Shaikh Zayed bin Sultan Al Nahayan, issued a special decree referring certain criminal cases, including adultery, drug-trafficking and murder, to the Islamic courts, which apply *Shari'a* (Islamic law). Most of these offences are punishable by death.

Four prisoners of conscience, all Indian nationals resident in the United Arab Emirates (UAE), continued to serve prison sentences imposed for allegedly insulting Islam because of their involvement in a play staged at the Indian Association in Sharjah in May 1992 (see *Amnesty International Reports 1993* and *1994*). They were released in December.

The fate of three foreign nationals who were arrested in 1993 for alleged anti-Islamic activities and appeared to be prisoners of conscience (see *Amnesty International Report 1994*) remained unknown at the end of the year.

In February the President pardoned 112 prisoners. Those released had reportedly served half their prison sentences. It was not clear whether there were any political prisoners among them.

A pregnant foreign national was con-

victed of adultery and reportedly sentenced to death by stoning. The Court of Appeal overturned this sentence, imposing instead a prison sentence of nine months and 100 lashes to be administered 45 days after the birth. It was not known whether the sentence was carried out.

A Pakistani national was reportedly sentenced to death on charges of drug-trafficking and had his sentence confirmed by the Court of Appeal in the emirate of Sharjah in January. This was apparently the first case in which the death sentence had been imposed for drug-trafficking offences in the UAE. It was not known whether the execution was carried out.

Mashal Badr al-Hamati remained on death row (see *Amnesty International Report 1994*). The prisoner, who was 17 years old at the time of the offence, had not been executed by the end of the year.

At least five people were executed. In September Qismatullah Haji Fadl Manan, a Pakistani national, was executed after having been convicted of murder. In the same month a UAE national and three members of the *"Bidun"* community (stateless Arab) were executed: Anwar al-Ma'mari was convicted of rape, while Ishaq Jumu'a, Muhammad Tahar and Ibrahim 'Abbas were convicted of murder.

Amnesty International wrote to the Minister of Justice calling for the immediate and unconditional release of all prisoners of conscience. Amnesty International welcomed the decision to commute the death sentence in the case of the foreign national convicted of adultery. However, the organization expressed concern at the use of flogging, which it considers to be a cruel, inhuman or degrading form of punishment, as a judicial punishment. Amnesty International urged the President to commute all outstanding death sentences.

UNITED KINGDOM

Police officers charged with misconduct in connection with miscarriages of justice were acquitted. Reports on interrogation centres in Northern Ireland urged the introduction of further safeguards. Allegations of ill-treatment of deportees were investigated; three police officers were charged in connection with the death of

Joy Gardner in 1993. **The inadequacy of inquests was highlighted in some cases of disputed killings. Armed political groups carried out deliberate and arbitrary killings until cease-fires were declared.**

On 1 September the Irish Republican Army (IRA), a predominantly Catholic Republican armed group, declared a cessation of its "military operations". Republican armed groups seek unification of Northern Ireland with the Republic of Ireland. On 14 October the Combined Loyalist Military Command declared a cessation of "all operation hostilities" by the Ulster Defence Association (UDA) and the Ulster Volunteer Force (UVF). Loyalist armed groups, predominantly Protestant, seek to maintain Northern Ireland as part of the United Kingdom. Armed groups claimed responsibility for killing 60 people in Northern Ireland in 1994.

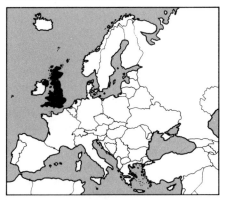

The Criminal Justice and Public Order Act became law in November. Under it, courts can draw adverse inferences against defendants remaining silent during interrogation and at trial in England and Wales; similar legislation already operates in Northern Ireland. The law also gives police new powers to stop and search and creates criminal sanctions against protesters, travellers and others.

In February the government amended legislation on the age of consent for homosexual acts in private, lowering the age from 21 to 18. The age of consent for heterosexual acts remains 16.

In June, in the *Murray v. UK* case, the European Commission of Human Rights concluded that the applicant's rights to a fair trial and to legal assistance had been violated by restrictions on his access to a lawyer. It rejected the argument that adverse inferences drawn against the accused for remaining silent during interrogation and at trial violated his right to a fair trial. The Commission referred the case to the European Court of Human Rights.

The trial of seven people charged with a bomb attack in the Ballymurphy area of Belfast (see *Amnesty International Report 1994*) finished in November. Four of the defendants were acquitted during the proceedings after the judge ruled that their confessions were inadmissible. The judgment on three defendants had not been delivered by the end of the year. An Amnesty International delegate attended part of the proceedings.

Four police officers, charged with attempting to pervert the course of justice in connection with the conviction in 1986 of four UDR soldiers for murder, were acquitted in September. The judge ruled that although interview notes had been rewritten, this did not necessarily mean any crime had been committed.

In April the Northern Ireland Court of Appeal quashed the conviction of Paul Hill for the murder of a police officer in 1974. A lawyer attended the proceedings on behalf of Amnesty International. Paul Hill had also had his conviction for the 1975 IRA pub bombings in Guildford and Woolwich, as one of the "Guildford Four", quashed in 1989. In a report published in June Sir John May concluded that the wrongful convictions of the "Guildford Four" were due to individual failings by police officers, prosecutors and lawyers and "not due to any specific weakness or inherent fault in the criminal justice system" (see *Amnesty International Reports 1990* to *1994*).

Two senior police officers, charged in connection with the prosecutions of the "Tottenham Three", were acquitted in July. They were charged with conspiracy to pervert the course of justice after scientific analysis showed that interview notes had been altered (see *Amnesty International Report 1992*).

The report of an *ad hoc* visit to Northern Ireland in July 1993 of the European Committee for the Prevention of Torture was published in November. It concluded that detainees held under emergency legislation ran a significant risk of psychological ill-treatment and, on occasion, of physical ill-treatment. It emphasized the need for further safeguards, including immediate access to a solicitor, legal assistance during interrogation, and the possible electronic recording of interrogations.

In January the Independent Commissioner for the Holding Centres, Sir Louis Blom-Cooper, published his first annual report on police interrogation centres in Northern Ireland. The report was critical of some conditions at Castlereagh. It concluded that "public confidence can be secured only if there is in place ... a method of accountability" for the conduct of detectives carrying out interrogations. The report also proposed the creation of a legal advice unit at Castlereagh; this proposal was criticized by the Law Society and human rights organizations as undermining the detainees' right of access to a lawyer of their own choice.

In May the Independent Assessor of Military Complaints, David Hewitt, published his first annual report. He reviews the procedures for non-criminal complaints by members of the public in Northern Ireland. The report stressed the need to address the "widespread perception that the Army is failing to provide reasonable satisfaction to genuine complainants". A total of 210 formal non-criminal complaints, including harassment and abuse, had been made during 1993; 16 of these were substantiated, in eight of which disciplinary action was taken.

Charges of manslaughter were brought in April against three police officers from the deportation squad of the London Metropolitan Police in connection with the death of Joy Gardner in August 1993; they had not been tried by the end of 1994. Joy Gardner died after being gagged and strapped into a body-belt (see *Amnesty International Report 1994*). After her death a joint review was carried out by the Home Office and the police into deportation procedures involving the police. The results, which were released in January, included the decision to ban mouth gags as a form of restraint. Internal Home Office investigations into allegations of ill-treatment by private security guards of other deportees found no evidence of excessive use of force.

Allegations were made that police officers and private security guards physically ill-treated people protesting against the building of roads; however, very few charges for the ill-treatment were brought.

Two reports by Chief Constable John Stevens into alleged collusion between the security forces and Loyalist paramilitaries (see previous *Amnesty International Reports*) were forwarded to the Northern Ireland Director of Public Prosecutions in March and October, but had not been made public by the end of the year.

Allegations about the lack of equal protection by the Royal Ulster Constabulary (RUC) of the Catholic community were highlighted by the killing of Paul Thompson in April. He was shot dead by UDA gunmen who had climbed through the "peaceline fence" in West Belfast. Eight hours earlier a resident had informed both police and government authorities that the fence had been broken.

In January the RUC officer charged with the murder of 19-year-old student Kevin McGovern in 1991 was acquitted (see *Amnesty International Report 1992*). The acquittal highlighted the need for a review of legislation governing the use of lethal force by the security forces.

The trial of two soldiers charged with the murder of Peter McBride in 1992 took place in June; no verdict had been given by the end of the year.

The inquests into the killings of six people, shot dead in 1982 by a special anti-terrorist squad of the RUC, were closed in September by the coroner who stated that his aim in holding the inquests was "no longer achievable". The RUC and the government, through the issuing of Public Interest Immunity Certificates, blocked disclosure to the inquest of the report of the Stalker/Sampson inquiry (see previous *Amnesty International Reports*).

The inquest in October into the deaths of John McNeill, Edward Hale and Peter Thompson was unable to examine the full circumstances of the killings by undercover soldiers in 1990 (see *Amnesty International Report 1991*) because of restrictions placed on inquest procedures. An Amnesty International delegate observed the proceedings.

The European Commission of Human Rights issued its decision in March in the case of *McCann, Farrell, and Savage v. UK* (the three people killed by undercover soldiers in Gibraltar in 1988 – see *Amnesty International Report 1989*). The Commission concluded that the use of force had been no more than "absolutely necessary". The Commission referred the case to the

European Court of Human Rights.

Karamjit Singh Chahal's petition to seek leave to appeal against his deportation order was rejected by the Appeal Committee of the House of Lords in March (see *Amnesty International Report 1992*). His petition to the European Commission of Human Rights was declared admissible in September.

Armed political groups carried out deliberate and arbitrary killings until ceasefires were declared. Loyalist armed groups claimed responsibility for killing 36 people, of whom 20 were killed by the UVF and 11 by the UDA. In June, six people were killed and five others injured when a UVF gunman sprayed a bar, frequented by Catholics, with gunfire. Kathleen O'Hagan, a Catholic and mother of five, was killed by UVF gunmen in her home in August; she was pregnant. Sixty-eight men were shot in the limbs and 38 were reported to have been beaten by Loyalist groups as "punishment".

The IRA claimed responsibility for killing 18 people, of whom seven were members of the security forces and 11 were civilians. The Irish National Liberation Army (INLA) claimed responsibility for killing six people. A police station cleaner, Fred Anthony, was killed when an IRA bomb exploded under his car in May. His wife and two children were injured. Two leading Loyalists, Colin Craig and Ray Smallwoods, were shot dead by the INLA and IRA respectively in June and July. Members of the IRA killed post office worker Frank Kerr during a robbery in November; the IRA leadership stated it had not sanctioned the operation. Republican groups also carried out 32 beatings and shot 54 men in the limbs as "punishment".

Amnesty International urged the government not to adopt new legislation curtailing the right of silence and to repeal similar legislation already operating in Northern Ireland. The organization was also concerned about provisions in the Criminal Justice and Public Order Act.

Amnesty International expressed concern about the government's failure to refer the life imprisonment of three men charged with the murder of two army corporals (see *Amnesty International Report 1994*) to a judicial authority for review.

In February Amnesty International published a report called *United Kingdom: Political Killings in Northern Ireland*, which examined patterns of killings falling within the organization's mandate. These included killings by members of the security forces, killings by paramilitary forces carried out with the acquiescence, collusion or complicity of the security forces, and deliberate and arbitrary killings by armed political groups.

Amnesty International reiterated its long-standing concerns about the ineffectiveness of inquests dealing with disputed killings by the security forces, as well as the government's intervention in particular cases to block the disclosure of crucial evidence. The organization urged the government and the RUC to release the Stalker/Sampson report to the *McKerr, Toman and Burns* inquest. The government replied that Public Interest Immunity Certificates were issued because it was "sometimes necessary to safeguard information which would otherwise be useful to terrorists".

Amnesty International submitted written comments to the European Court of Human Rights in the case of *McCann, Farrell and Savage v. UK*. The organization urged the Court to declare that the intentionally lethal use of firearms could only be compatible with the European Convention on Human Rights when its use was strictly unavoidable in order to protect life.

In July Amnesty International published a report, *United Kingdom: Cruel, inhuman or degrading treatment during forcible deportation*, which detailed allegations by four deportees of ill-treatment by police officers and private security guards. Unauthorized equipment was used to restrain deportees, including mouth gags, adhesive tape and plastic straps. The organization urged the government to open impartial investigations into the allegations. It also urged the government to set up an independent inquiry into the accountability of all agencies involved in the deportation process and to create a statutory authority to regulate the Immigration Service and private security firms. The report was submitted to the Home Affairs Select Committee inquiry into the private security industry. The Prime Minister, John Major, wrote to Amnesty International in August rejecting the need for an independent statutory authority, or an independent inquiry.

302

Amnesty International urged that the protection of human rights be placed centrally on the agenda in the search for a political settlement in the context of the cease-fires in Northern Ireland.

UNITED STATES OF AMERICA

Thirty-one prisoners were executed in 13 states. Three states carried out their first executions in more than 30 years. More than 2,870 prisoners were under sentence of death in 35 states. Political activists in San Francisco were repeatedly arrested. There were reports of deaths in police custody in disputed circumstances and allegations of torture and ill-treatment by police and prison officers. Thousands of Cuban and Haitian asylum-seekers were held at a US naval base in Guantánamo Bay, Cuba.

The use of the death penalty under federal civilian law was extended to cover some 60 new crimes. These included the murder of federal officials and certain non-homicidal offences such as treason, espionage and major drug-trafficking. President Bill Clinton supported the passage of the Crime Bill and signed the legislation on 13 September. This move clearly conflicted with Article 4(2) of the American Convention on Human Rights, which the USA has signed but not ratified.

Kansas reinstated the death penalty in April, becoming the 37th state to authorize its use. The governor of Kansas, who personally opposed the death penalty, allowed the reinstatement bill to become law without her signature.

In October the USA ratified the UN Convention against Torture and Other Cruel, Inhuman or Degrading Treatment or Punishment. The same month the Senate gave its consent to ratification of the International Convention on the Elimination of All Forms of Racial Discrimination.

The death penalty continued to be used extensively. Thirty-one prisoners were executed, bringing the total number of executions since 1977 to 257. Three states – Idaho, Maryland and Nebraska – each carried out an execution for the first time in more than 30 years. Texas carried out 14 executions. Executions were also carried out in Arkansas (five), in Virginia (two) and in Delaware, Florida, Georgia, Illinois, Indiana, North Carolina and Washington (one each).

William Hance, a black man who was borderline mentally retarded, was executed in Georgia on 31 March. He had been tried in Columbus, Georgia (Chattahoochee Judicial Circuit), where there is strong evidence of racial discrimination in the application of the death penalty (see *Amnesty International Report 1991*). The jury contained only one black member; all other black prospective jurors were excluded by the prosecutor (Columbus' population is 34 per cent black). Shortly before the execution, two jurors stated in affidavits that deliberations at William Hance's 1984 resentencing trial had been marked by misinformation, misconduct and racial bias. The one black juror on the panel swore that she had not voted for the death penalty on account of William Hance's mental condition, but that she had been ignored and a unanimous verdict announced. Another juror corroborated this account and described racially derogatory remarks made during the jury deliberations. The Georgia Board of Pardons refused to grant clemency despite appeals for mercy from the family of the murder victim.

Harold Lamont "Wili" Otey was executed in Nebraska on 2 September; this was the first execution in the state for 35 years. Wili Otey, a black man, was convicted of the 1977 rape and murder of a white woman. In June 1991 the Nebraska Board of Pardons denied clemency by two votes to one. His attorneys argued that the clemency hearing had been unfair because the Attorney General, who prosecuted the case and sought to expedite the execution, was a member of the Pardons Board.

Grounds for clemency included the fact that Wili Otey had no prior criminal record; his rehabilitation in prison; and other mitigating factors.

Members of Food Not Bombs (FNB), a group distributing free food and information to homeless people in San Francisco, were repeatedly arrested. One member was convicted in February 1994 of violating a court injunction forbidding FNB from distributing food in public places without a permit. The group had been unable to obtain such a permit since 1990 when the authorities stopped issuing them. The group's leader, arrested more than 90 times since 1988, faced prosecution at the end of the year on various charges including assault. The alleged victims and witnesses were employees of City Hall, several of whom had openly opposed the activities of FNB. Some of those arrested reported that they were ill-treated by police.

There were reports of deaths in police custody in disputed circumstances and allegations of torture and ill-treatment by police and prison officers. Ernest Sayon, a black man, died during his arrest on Staten Island on 29 April. His death was classified as a homicide caused by asphyxia by compression of chest and neck while his wrists were handcuffed behind his back. Witnesses alleged that Ernest Sayon was beaten by the arresting officers and placed in a choke-hold. A grand jury investigating the case voted in December not to file criminal charges against the three officers involved.

A grand jury investigating the May 1993 death in police custody of Johnny Cromartie, a black man, voted in March not to indict any of the officers involved, on the ground that the use of force to subdue him during an escape attempt had been justified. Johnny Cromartie's death from heart failure was found to have been caused by several factors including stress caused by blows by the police officers and the difficulty he had breathing while lying face down with his wrists manacled behind him (see *Amnesty International Report 1994*).

Felipe Soltero, aged 17, of Latin American origin, was shown on a video tape being beaten by a black police officer in Los Angeles County, California, on 29 July. The police officer struck the teenager four times on the head and face with a metal baton, and continued to beat him as he lay on the ground. Felipe Soltero reportedly sustained severe bruising. The officer was suspended and a grand jury began hearing evidence in the case in August.

On 30 September Timothy Prince Pride was fatally shot in the back by a prison guard in San Quentin prison, California, reportedly after being involved in a minor altercation with another prisoner. According to a statement by the prison authorities, rubber bullets were fired as a warning to break up a fight between Timothy Pride and the other prisoner. However, a guard using live ammunition reportedly opened fire at the same time in what appeared to be an excessive use of lethal force.

A Los Angeles jury failed to reach a verdict in the trial in September of a police officer charged with second-degree murder for the killing of John Daniels Jr (see *Amnesty International Reports 1993* and *1994*). A new trial was ordered.

The Knox County Sheriff's Department, Tennessee, and the Federal Bureau of Investigation (FBI) initiated inquiries after a newspaper report published in July alleged that during 1993 inmates in Knox County jail had been handcuffed spread-eagled to bars for periods of an hour or more. The newspaper also claimed other inmates were punished by being placed in a special restraining chair and forced to wear a helmet with the visor blacked out, which was then struck by prison guards using fists, flashlights and other objects.

Prisoners in Oklahoma State Penitentiary's H-Unit, a super-maximum security unit which opened in November 1991, were kept for between 23 and 24 hours per day in underground, concrete, windowless cells with virtually no natural light or fresh air. H-Unit houses nearly 400 inmates, including all male prisoners under sentence of death in the state. The American Correctional Association, a private agency that administers national accreditation for US and Canadian prisons, delayed reaccrediting the penitentiary after receiving a highly critical report on H-Unit by Amnesty International which concluded that conditions constituted "cruel, inhuman or degrading treatment" (see below).

Judgment was still pending at the end of the year in a civil suit brought in 1993 on behalf of inmates of Pelican Bay Prison, a maximum security prison in

304

California (see *Amnesty International Reports 1993* and *1994*).

Haitian boat people held by the US Government in camps at the US naval base at Guantánamo Bay, Cuba, were encouraged to return to Haiti, often without being given adequate information about the unstable situation prevailing there. A substantial number of the approximately 32,000 Cuban asylum-seekers held by the US authorities in camps at Guantánamo Bay and in Panama during the year were believed to have fled the risk of human rights violations in Cuba.

Amnesty International made numerous appeals on behalf of prisoners sentenced to death, urging clemency in all cases.

In an open letter to President Clinton in January, Amnesty International called on the federal government to set up a Presidential Commission into the use of the death penalty, and to introduce a moratorium on all executions until the Commission reports its findings. The letter showed that death sentences in the USA are imposed disproportionately on the poor, on members of ethnic minorities, on the mentally ill or retarded, and on those without adequate legal counsel. This, the organization said, was a matter for the US federal authorities to investigate and remedy with the utmost urgency. Eleven areas of particular concern were cited, including the execution of juvenile offenders and the mentally impaired. No substantive response had been received from the US Government by the end of the year.

Amnesty International remained concerned that Gary Tyler, in prison in Louisiana for murder, was denied a fair trial in 1975 and that racial prejudice played a major part in his prosecution. It wrote to the Board of Pardons and Louisiana's governor in December, urging that he be pardoned (see *Amnesty International Reports 1990* to *1992*).

Amnesty International wrote to the authorities in San Francisco in October to request further information on the charges against the FNB leader and some 20 others. It expressed concern that the group had reportedly been subjected to a pattern of harassment, arrest and ill-treatment by police over a six-year period and that members may have been targeted on account of peaceful beliefs and political activities.

In May Amnesty International wrote to the New York City Police Commissioner

regarding deaths and ill-treatment of suspects in custody. The organization was disturbed at the deaths of several suspects, including Ernest Sayon, in recent years after they were placed face-down in restraints, which can inhibit respiratory movement. Amnesty International also remained concerned at the use of lethal force in the case of Johnny Cromartie, who was unarmed, epileptic and in need of medical attention.

Amnesty International wrote to the authorities in Tennessee in October regarding allegations of ill-treatment of inmates in the Knox County jail. It wrote to the authorities in Arizona, California, Florida, Maryland and Ohio about other allegations of deaths and ill-treatment in custody. Cases included Felipe Soltero in Los Angeles, California; Timothy Pride in San Quentin prison, California; three people who were shot dead by the Los Angeles Police in 1992 and 1993; and Michael Bryant who died in March 1993 in Los Angeles, California, after being "hog-tied" by police (see *Amnesty International Report 1994*). The Los Angeles Police Department told Amnesty International in September that Michael Bryant's death had been thoroughly investigated and that "no fault" was found in the officers' actions, but that new procedures had since been introduced to restrain suspects. In November the California Department of Corrections told Amnesty International that an investigation was being conducted into the shooting of Timothy Pride.

In March an Amnesty International delegation visited H-Unit at Oklahoma State Penitentiary. Amnesty International's report, published in June, concluded that the conditions constituted "cruel, inhuman or degrading" treatment in violation of international standards. It urged the Oklahoma prison authorities to act on the organization's findings and recommendations. Some conditions, including lack of access to natural light and fresh air, violated the UN Standard Minimum Rules for the Treatment of Prisoners. Amnesty International also raised concerns regarding H-Unit's failure to meet American Correctional Association standards for prisons including adequate cell furnishings and unencumbered cell space for two occupants.

In September an Amnesty International delegation visited the US naval base at

Guantánamo Bay, Cuba, to investigate the situation of Cuban and Haitian asylum-seekers held there after being intercepted at sea by the US authorities. Amnesty International questioned the repatriation process to which Haitian asylum-seekers were subjected and expressed concern that some were volunteering to return to Haiti without being given adequate information about the unstable situation in the country. The organization believed that a substantial number of Cubans held in camps at Guantánamo Bay and Panama, who were not permitted to request asylum in the USA, could be at risk of human rights violations if required to return to Cuba. It urged that they be given the opportunity to present asylum applications in accordance with internationally accepted procedures.

URUGUAY

There were reports of excessive use of lethal force by members of the police during a demonstration, resulting in one dead and dozens wounded. There were reports of ill-treatment in police custody. Human rights violations committed during the period of military rule remained uninvestigated.

In November Julio María Sanguinetti of the Colorado Party was elected to succeed Luís Alberto Lacalle as President. The President-elect had served one term as President from 1985 to 1990, after 12 years of military rule. In November a military anti-guerrilla unit, *Organismo Coordinador de Operaciones Antisubversivas* (OCOA), known to have committed human rights abuses during previous military

governments, was disbanded. This was one of a series of military reforms set in motion nine years after the transfer of power to an elected government.

One person was killed when anti-riot police and mounted police of the *Guardia Republicana*, Republican Guard, charged and fired into a demonstration held in August in the capital, Montevideo, in what may have been excessive use of force. One demonstrator, Alvaro Fernando Morroni, was fatally shot and at least 75 people, including police, were injured. Esteban Massa, a male nurse of the emergency medical service, was shot in the back while attending to an injured demonstrator. At least two juveniles were seriously injured and many other demonstrators, among them children, were beaten and trampled by police horses. An investigation initiated into the incident had not concluded by the end of the year.

The demonstration was to protest at the imminent extradition to Spain of three suspected members of the Basque group *Euskadi Ta Askatasuna* (ETA), Basque Homeland and Liberty. The three men, who faced serious criminal charges, were in hospital following a 14-day hunger-strike. The three Spaniards were extradited to Spain in August by orders of the Uruguayan courts.

Reports of ill-treatment of detainees by the police continued. Criminal suspects were reportedly beaten in provincial police stations. In October Claudino Ferraz, a farm worker, was allegedly severely beaten by police attached to the Sixth District police station in Young, Department of Rio Negro, where he was taken for interrogation. As a result of the beating Claudino Ferraz had a ruptured spleen and several broken ribs. An investigation was apparently initiated but by the end of the year its outcome had not been made public.

The government again failed to take measures to bring to justice those responsible for human rights violations during the period of military rule. In August the presidential candidate Julio María Sanguinetti testified at the continuing civil court case brought by Sara Méndez in 1991 challenging the adoption of a boy she believes to be her "disappeared" son, Simón (see *Amnesty International Reports 1990* to *1994*). Julio María Sanguinetti was called to testify because as President he had been

306

responsible for closing an investigation into this case by a criminal court in 1989, on the grounds that the case was covered by the Expiry Law (see *Amnesty International Reports 1987* to *1994*). He said in his testimony to the Family Court that he had passed the case on to the Defence Ministry and the National Institute of Minors, which were responsible for clarifying "disappearances". The 1986 Expiry Law has effectively stopped all judicial processes against police and military personnel accused of human rights violations during the military government.

There was no progress in the complaint presented by a Uruguayan member of parliament before a Paraguayan court, requesting clarification of the fate of two Uruguayan citizens who had "disappeared" in Paraguay in the hands of Uruguayan, Argentine and Paraguayan personnel in 1977 (see **Paraguay** entry).

In August Amnesty International asked the authorities to investigate the violence during the demonstration against the extradition of three Spanish citizens and expressed its concern at the alarming number of civilian casualties. There was no reply. Amnesty International asked the Uruguayan Government to obtain guarantees from the Spanish Government that the three Spaniards would not be tortured or ill-treated in Spain if detained incommunicado under anti-terrorist legislation. The Uruguayan Minister of Foreign Affairs informed Amnesty International that he had raised concerns with his Spanish counterpart about the possible ill-treatment of the three men in Spain and had obtained "the utmost guarantees a state governed by the rule of law can offer".

UZBEKISTAN

Two prisoners of conscience and three probable prisoners of conscience were granted clemency and released early, but other probable prisoners of conscience were detained on allegedly fabricated criminal charges. Three people held briefly under "administrative arrest" for attempting to travel abroad to a human rights conference were prisoners of conscience. Reports were received of ill-treatment of detainees in police custody. At least five people were executed.

Elections were held in December to a restyled parliament, the 250-seat *Oliy Majlis*. The elections were contested by President Islam Karimov's People's Democratic Party and another party supporting the President's policies, and by candidates nominated by regional governments. Opposition parties remained banned and were not permitted to stand in the elections.

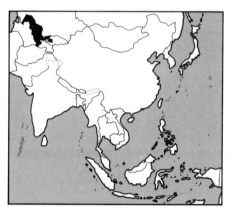

Otanazar Aripov and Salavat Umurzakov, former prisoners of conscience, were rearrested in March. At separate court hearings they were ordered to begin serving previously suspended prison sentences of, respectively, five and three years passed on them at the 1993 *Milli Mejlis* trial (see *Amnesty International Report 1994*). They were ruled to have violated a condition under which their sentences had been suspended by continuing their active involvement in the outlawed opposition party *Erk* (Freedom). However, in November they were released by a special presidential clemency decree.

Also freed by the November amnesty were probable prisoners of conscience Pulat Akhunov and Nosyr Zokhir (see *Amnesty International Report 1994*) and Inamzhon Tursunov. Nosyr Zokhir had been sentenced in August to two and a half years' imprisonment for illegal possession of a firearm and narcotics; sources suggested that the case against him had been fabricated. Probable prisoner of conscience Akhmatkhan Turakhanov did not benefit from the November amnesty. He had been arrested on the same day and in similar circumstances to Nosyr Zokhir (see *Amnesty International Report 1994*, where the name is given as Akhmadkhon Turakhonboy-ugly), and was sentenced in

September to 18 months in prison for illegal possession of a weapon.

Mikhail Ardzinov, Vasiliya Inayatova and Talib Yakubov were placed under "administrative arrest" for up to 10 days in May to prevent them travelling to Almaty in Kazakhstan to attend a human rights conference. They were prisoners of conscience. Vasiliya Inayatova's arrest by Uzbek police took place after she had already crossed by car into Kazakhstan.

There were further arrests and prosecutions of people on criminal charges which may have been fabricated. These people were probable prisoners of conscience. In May Sherali Ruzimuradov, a student, was arrested in Karshi and reportedly charged with illegal possession of a weapon. Sources claimed that he was being detained on a fabricated criminal charge to force disclosure of the whereabouts of his brother, Yusuf Ruzimuradov, an *Erk* activist who had escaped from police custody in April. In June Gaipnazar Koshchanov, an *Erk* organizer in Urgench, was sentenced to two years' imprisonment for illegal firearms and narcotics possession. Sources alleged that the charge had been fabricated to punish him for possessing copies of the *Erk* party newspaper.

There was no news of Abdullo Utayev, leader of the unregistered Islamic Renaissance Party, who apparently "disappeared" in 1992 (see *Amnesty International Report 1994*). Sources continued to allege that he was in the custody of one of the state law enforcement agencies.

Two Israeli citizens, Grigory Zalkind and Anna Korol, alleged that they suffered torture and ill-treatment while in police custody in Tashkent, the capital, in February. Both reported that they had been severely beaten by police officers and Anna Korol reported that she had been repeatedly raped by two officers. They received no response to their complaints to the authorities about their treatment.

The death penalty remained in force. At least six death sentences were passed, three of which were reported to have been carried out. One man convicted in 1991 and one man convicted in 1992 were also reported to have been executed during the year. The fate of three others convicted in 1992 and known to be under sentence of death at the beginning of 1994 could not be confirmed. It was reported that in some cases procedures for informing the family

of a prisoner facing the death penalty about decisions made at clemency hearings were no longer being strictly followed, leaving the family uncertain of the fate of the prisoner and in some cases unaware for long periods that execution had taken place.

Amnesty International called for the release of Otanazar Aripov and Salavat Umurzakov. It protested against the continuing use of "administrative arrest" to prevent people from exercising fundamental human rights. In cases of probable prisoners of conscience Amnesty International called for judicial review of criminal convictions where people had already been sentenced to terms of imprisonment, and for clarification of the charges against people in pre-trial detention. The organization asked to be informed about investigations into complaints by Grigory Zalkind and Anna Korol of torture and ill-treatment. Amnesty International continued to press the authorities to abolish the death penalty. In November it wrote to the clemency commission calling for stricter adherence to procedures for informing families of people under sentence of death about the outcome of clemency petitions.

In June Amnesty International published a report, *Uzbekistan: Further prosecutions in the "Milli Mejlis" case: prisoners of conscience Otanazar Aripov and Salavat Umurzakov.*

VENEZUELA

At least one prisoner of conscience was jailed during 1994 and at least eight others remained in prison. The widespread use of torture by the security forces continued to be reported. Prison conditions remained extremely harsh, and scores of prisoners died during violent incidents in jails. At least 10 people were extrajudicially executed by the security forces, and scores more were reported to have been unlawfully killed during police and army operations to combat crime. Most investigations into reported human rights violations made little progress.

President Rafael Caldera took office in February. On 27 June, in the context of a deepening economic crisis, President Caldera announced the suspension of certain constitutional guarantees, including the right not to be detained without warrant except when caught committing a crime. The suspension of guarantees was rejected by Congress on 22 July but the next day the executive overturned Congress' decision and suspended the guarantees until the end of the year.

Venezuela signed the Inter-American Convention on the Forced Disappearance of Persons in June but had not ratified it by the end of the year.

Community activists and their relatives continued to face threats, persecution and imprisonment. Several were prisoners of conscience. Gabriel Rivas Granadillo, leader of *La Chívera* peasants' union, was arrested without warrant on 2 July by the state police in Valencia under the *Ley de Vagos y Maleantes*, Law on Vagrants and Crooks. This permits administrative detention for periods of up to five years, without judicial appeal or review. He remained in detention as a prisoner of conscience in extremely harsh conditions for days before being released without charge. Other prisoners of conscience arrested in previous years remained in jail, including Henry Landino Contreras, a musician, the son of Bari Indian and peasant activist Mario Landino who was released without charge in March (see *Amnesty International Report 1994*). Henry Landino was arrested and tortured in the state of Zulia in March 1993, together with Guzmán Villalba Torres, a Colombian peasant. Both men were prisoners of conscience and remained imprisoned throughout 1994. Pedro Luis Peña Arévalo and José Luis Zapata were arrested in Maracaibo and Caracas in 1992 because of their homosexuality. They were detained under the Law on Vagrants and Crooks.

Jaime Rafael Lugo Acabán, a student activist, was arrested and tortured in Puerto La Cruz by members of the military intelligence agency *Dirección de Inteligencia Militar* (DIM), in May 1992. He was tried on charges of "military rebellion" and acquitted by a military court in July 1992. However, he remained in detention as a result of the court's failure to order his release owing to an unresolved conflict between military and civilian jurisdictions.

Human rights activist Fernando Arias Figueroa, who was arrested and tortured by members of DIM in February 1993 (see *Amnesty International Report 1994*), was released on bail in July.

Dozens of other prisoners of conscience, including community and student activists, were detained without warrant after the suspension of guarantees on 27 June. They were held for short periods and interrogated by members of DIM and the police intelligence agency, *Dirección de los Servicios de Inteligencia y Prevención* (DISIP). The human rights subcommission of Congress criticized such arbitrary arrests.

Scores of people continued to be imprisoned under the Law on Vagrants and Crooks despite government promises to repeal the law, which government and judicial authorities have acknowledged infringes the Constitution and international human rights treaties ratified by the country, including the International Covenant on Civil and Political Rights.

Most of those imprisoned in connection with the coup attempts in February and November 1992 were released during the year (see *Amnesty International Report 1993*).

Torture and ill-treatment by the security forces continued to be widely reported throughout the country and those responsible continued to benefit from impunity. Victims included men, women and children, many of whom belonged to underprivileged sectors of society. The most frequently cited methods were beatings; suspension from wrists or ankles for prolonged periods; near-asphyxiation with plastic bags; electric shocks; and mock executions. Torture was used extensively by the police and army to extract confessions from criminal suspects and such confessions continued to be accepted as evidence by the courts. State attorneys frequently failed to act effectively on complaints of torture and official forensic doctors regularly avoided documenting cases of torture. Torture and ill-treatment were also widely reported from prisons. Medical treatment for detainees who suffered torture was generally unavailable or grossly inadequate.

Among the scores of cases of torture reported were those of María García and her husband Luis Gelves, who were arrested without warrant together with eight other peasants by soldiers between 18 and 20 April in the community of Sector Socuavó, Zulia state. Although María García was seriously ill and awaiting an operation, they were transferred to a local army garrison. María García was held with four other women, one of whom was pregnant. They were repeatedly threatened with death, and on 22 April were brutally beaten by members of DIM to force them to confess to collaborating with Colombian guerrillas. Luis Gelves was tortured together with 27 other men while held in secret detention at a local army post. The men were beaten, nearly drowned and threatened with death. On 6 May María García, Luis Gelves and 11 other peasants were released, but the charges against them were not dropped.

Franklin Pérez was arrested by members of the *Policía Técnica Judicial* (PTJ), Criminal Investigations Police, in July in Tucupita, Delta Amacuro. He was allegedly beaten and semi-asphyxiated with a plastic bag while suspended from the wrists during interrogation. He was released without charge three days later.

In August community activists José Manuel Flores, José Gregorio Guedez, Rubén Sánchez and José Luis Sánchez were arrested by the state police in Valencia, Carabobo, on charges of participating in the November 1992 coup attempt and belonging to an armed opposition group, *Bandera Roja*. They were held in incommunicado detention by DISIP and were allegedly beaten, suspended by the wrists for prolonged periods, and given electric shocks. They were then transferred to a military prison run by the DIM in Caracas, the capital, where they remained awaiting trial before military courts.

There were no prosecutions of those responsible for past cases of torture. The perpetrators continued to benefit from impunity. In August two members of a non-governmental human rights organization, *Red de Apoyo por la Justicia y la Paz*, re-

ceived several anonymous death threats after publicly complaining about torture and extrajudicial executions by the police in Caracas.

Prison conditions were extremely harsh, often amounting to cruel, inhuman or degrading treatment. Government authorities publicly acknowledged the lack of security for prison inmates, the serious overcrowding and the extremely poor sanitary conditions, but failed to reform the prison system.

At least 108 prisoners were killed and dozens remained unaccounted for in Sabaneta prison, Maracaibo. In the worst recorded incident in Venezuela's prisons, on 3 January a group of inmates attacked and set fire to overcrowded cells. The guards failed to prevent and stop the attack, which according to reports was planned with the knowledge of some prison authorities. Few of those responsible had been brought to justice by the end of the year.

At least 10 people were extrajudicially executed by the security forces and scores were reported to have been unlawfully killed. Six prisoners who escaped from the *Centro Penitenciario de Aragua*, a prison in Aragua, on 4 January, were shot in the back by a member of the *Guardia Nacional* (GN), National Guard. The unarmed prisoners were recaptured at a nearby bus stop on the day of their escape, and forced to lie face down on the ground by the GN. Witnesses saw one of them shoot the prisoners in the back at close range. Rómer de la Cruz Morón Carrillo, a bystander, was shot in the leg when he protested. Those responsible were not brought to justice.

On 2 February around 30 soldiers raided the Yukpa Indian community of Kasmera in Zulia. They confiscated a shipment of wood, without a court order as required by law. Community members who protested were threatened and shot at by the soldiers. Three Yukpa Indians – Felipe Romero, José Vicente Romero and Carmen Romero – were killed and 17-year-old Francisco Romero was wounded in the attack. Those responsible had not been brought to justice by the end of the year.

Alibeth Blanco Nieves was killed by members of the *Policía Metropolitana* (PM), Metropolitan Police, in May as she stood with her relatives at a bus stop in Caracas. The police reportedly shot

310

indiscriminately at bystanders. Alibeth's 15-month-old son Anderson was slightly injured in the incident. The PM was accused of dozens of other arbitrary killings in Caracas during 1994, which were not investigated. The officers responsible for killings during 1993 (see *Amnesty International Report 1994*) were not brought to justice. The victims included three-year-old César García Villarroel and Sergio Rodríguez Yance, a human rights activist. Most killings by the security forces in previous years remained unpunished, including the 1992 massacre of at least 63 inmates in the *Retén de Catia* prison in Caracas (see *Amnesty International Report 1993*).

An Amnesty International delegation visited Venezuela in May and June and met President Rafael Caldera and other senior government officials, including the Interior Minister, the Justice Minister and the Defence Minister, as well as officials of the Ministry of Foreign Affairs, members of the Supreme Court, members of Congress and the Attorney General. The delegates urged the government to implement more than 70 recommendations contained in Amnesty International's 1993 report, *Venezuela: The eclipse of human rights*, including the abolition of the Law on Vagrants and Crooks. The President and other government officials acknowledged the organization's concerns, and expressed the government's willingness to end human rights violations.

VIET NAM

At least 60 prisoners of conscience and possible prisoners of conscience remained imprisoned in 1994, and there were more than 10 new arrests. Several political prisoners, including prisoners of conscience, were released. A trial of a political prisoner appeared to fall short of international fair trial standards. Eight death sentences were imposed but no executions were reported.

The government continued its policy of economic liberalization throughout the year, and the lifting of the trade embargo by the USA in February was welcomed by the authorities. The press and broadcast media remained under state control, and freedom of worship was limited to those groups approved by the government. Members of a Buddhist religious group were subjected to surveillance and arrest by the authorities in the latter half of the year.

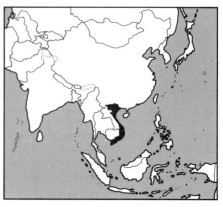

At least 60 prisoners of conscience and possible prisoners of conscience remained in prison throughout 1994, including Thich Han Duc, a Buddhist monk; Tran Thang Thuc, a former military doctor; Doan Viet Hoat, an academic; and Nguyen Dan Que, a doctor (see *Amnesty International Report 1994*). Prisoners of conscience Pham Hong Tho, Vo Van Pham and Nguyen Xuan De, who were sentenced to long terms of imprisonment in May 1993 for alleged "activities aiming to overthrow the people's government", remained in detention in 1994. Seven Roman Catholic priests also remained imprisoned. Paul Nguyen Chau Dat was arrested in 1987 along with 22 other members of the Congregation of the Mother Co-Redemptrix and charged with "undermining the policy of unity and disruption of public security". He was detained in a "re-education" camp in Xuan Loc district, Dong Nai province.

During the second half of the year, the authorities arrested at least nine members of the banned Unified Buddhist Church of Viet Nam (UBCV). The UBCV has refused to join the official Viet Nam Buddhist Church established with government approval in 1981. Surveillance of followers of the UBCV increased after the suicide by self-immolation in May of UBCV monk Thich Hue Thau in southern Vinh Long province, allegedly in protest against government restrictions on religious freedom and against high taxes imposed on the peasants in the Mekong Delta. In August

Thich Giac Nguyen was briefly detained after holding a three-day demonstration in front of the Ho Chi Minh City town hall. The authorities denied reports that 100 people were detained with him. Later the same month he was arrested at his temple in Ho Chi Minh City, allegedly for "dissident acts". He was apparently returned to his home province by the authorities, and it was unclear whether he had been released by the end of the year. In November, six members of the UBCV involved in a UBCV flood relief mission were arrested, allegedly because the mission did not have authorization from the authorities. Those detained included Thich Long Tri, a monk. They appeared to be prisoners of conscience. There were at least two further arrests in Hue in November during disturbances following the opening of a new Buddhist school of the official Viet Nam Buddhist Church. The UBCV Supreme Patriarch, Thich Huyen Quang, a prisoner of conscience under house arrest in his pagoda in Quang Ngai province since 1982, went on hunger-strike in December to protest against the arrests of members of his church. He was taken into custody on 29 December, then moved to another pagoda where he remained at the end of the year.

At least one other man was arrested for his peaceful political activities. Nguyen Ho, a former prisoner of conscience, aged 77, was rearrested in March. He was reported to have written an article critical of the Communist Party of Viet Nam. From 1990 to May 1993 he had been under house arrest for allegedly giving "unauthorized" interviews to foreign journalists.

In October the UN Working Group on Arbitrary Detention visited Viet Nam to examine the legality of arrests, sentencing and detention. Unconfirmed reports stated that political prisoners at one prison camp visited by the delegation were prevented from meeting the UN group by the camp officials.

At least eight political prisoners were released during the year, including three prisoners of conscience. Among them were Tran Vong Quoc, a former instructor in a military academy for the former Republic of (South) Viet Nam (RVN) during the Vietnam war; Quach Vinh Nien, a former lieutenant in the army of the RVN; and Nguyen Ngoc Anh, a Protestant pastor. Four other ethnic minority lay Protestants were reported to have been released during the year.

A political prisoner was convicted after what appeared to be an unfair trial. In February the Ho Chi Minh City People's Court sentenced Pham Van Quang to 15 years' imprisonment on the charge of "rebellion". According to reports, he was alleged to have waved the flag of the former RVN and fired gunshots in the air to attract attention when Ho Chi Minh City was hosting an international marathon in December 1992. There were no international observers at Pham Van Quang's trial, and he would not have been allowed access to a defence lawyer of his choice.

Eight people were reportedly sentenced to death after being convicted of offences including robbery, murder, destruction of national security projects, fraud and drug-trafficking. The death penalty may be applied for around 30 criminal offences. In August a Vietnamese court sentenced Le Thi Thu Ha, a police captain, to death for fraud. She reportedly confessed to lying to 41 people and two state companies in order to misappropriate gold and cash worth thousands of dollars in 1993. Nguyen Si Tuan was sentenced by the People's Court of Hanoi to death for heroin trafficking. However, no executions were reported in 1994.

Throughout the year, Amnesty International called for the release of prisoners of conscience and expressed concern about unfair political trials. Amnesty International also wrote to the authorities in May asking for Doan Viet Hoat to be allowed regular access to his family (see *Amnesty International Report 1994*). In May Amnesty International published a report, *Socialist Republic of Vietnam: Buddhist monks in detention*, which expressed concern about the continued detention of members of the UBCV. Amnesty International also wrote to the government in November, requesting further information on the arrest of Buddhist monks and lay people from the UBCV. The authorities did not respond.

In February Amnesty International sent a memorandum to the government outlining Amnesty International's human rights concerns in Viet Nam and asking permission for a delegation to visit the country. The memorandum focused on national security legislation and other legal concerns, the imprisonment of prisoners of

312 conscience and possible prisoners of conscience, concerns about the fairness of trials of political prisoners and the death penalty. It also included specific recommendations to strengthen the protection of human rights in the country. The government did not respond by the end of the year but an Amnesty International delegate visited Viet Nam in September and met a government official to discuss the organization's request to send a delegation to the country in 1995.

YEMEN

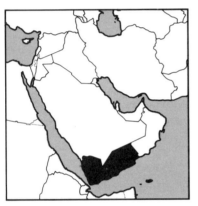

Thousands of civilians, among them prisoners of conscience, were detained without charge or trial following the outbreak of full-scale war in Yemen. Thousands were released after an amnesty was announced in May, but arrests of critics of the government continued. Political detainees and prisoners arrested in the northern provinces in previous years and held in unlawful detention or following unfair trials remained in prison. Torture and ill-treatment of both civilian and military detainees arrested after May were widespread, and scores of people may have been extrajudicially executed. The fate of hundreds of people who "disappeared" in previous years in the north and south remained unknown. At least 25 people were executed.

President 'Ali 'Abdullah Saleh, leader of the General People's Congress (GPC), and Vice-President 'Ali Salem al-Bidh, leader of the Yemeni Socialist Party (YSP), signed a "Document of Accord and Commitment" in February in 'Amman, Jordan. The agreement was aimed at resolving

differences between the north and south (which had united in 1991 to form a single state); it laid down the principles governing their future relations. However, none of its 18 clauses was ever implemented and military clashes erupted shortly afterwards between units of the northern and southern armies. In early May full-scale war broke out between the two sides. In the third week of May the authorities in the south led by 'Ali Salem al-Bidh announced the creation of the "Democratic Republic of Yemen" and designated 'Aden as its capital. The UN Security Council adopted a resolution at the end of May calling for an immediate cease-fire, but the war continued until early July when southern forces were defeated. In August President 'Ali 'Abdullah Saleh announced that 16 former YSP leaders who had fled the country would not be pardoned and would be sought to stand trial for high treason. In September the Council of Representatives (parliament) amended the country's Constitution, abolishing the Presidential Council, previously the highest executive body in the country, and re-confirming President 'Ali 'Abdullah Saleh in his post.

Following the outbreak of fighting in May, there were widespread arrests and detentions of suspected opponents, including prisoners of conscience, by both sides. In the north, thousands of civilians were arrested during the first week of fighting in Sana'a, Ta'iz, al-Hudaida, 'Ibb and other cities. The vast majority were suspected members of the YSP, who were reportedly held in incommunicado detention at undisclosed locations. Others were independent political activists considered critical of President 'Ali 'Abdullah Saleh. In the south, scores of suspected members or supporters of Islamic Jihad, the GPC and 'Islah, the Yemeni Grouping for Reform, were arrested in 'Aden, Hadhramaut, Dhali' and other cities.

An amnesty announced in the third week of May by President 'Ali 'Abdullah Saleh resulted in the release of thousands of political detainees held in the north. However, hundreds of others arrested during and after the fighting continued to be held without charge or trial. Most were initially held at al-'Anad military base in Lahj Province and at al-Hoban military garrison on the outskirts of Ta'iz. They were subsequently transferred to Political

Security detention centres and other locations throughout the country. With few exceptions, they were denied access to defence counsel, relatives and independent medical attention. Among them were prisoners of conscience, arrested solely on the basis of their region of origin or because of their suspected association with the YSP and its leaders. They included three university students – 'Ali 'Abd al-Wahid Yahya, Sadiq Nasir Salim and Muti' 'Abdullah Salim Hawash – who were arrested in May while visiting relatives at the home of Yassin Sa'id Nu'man, former Speaker of Parliament and a leading YSP figure. They were held at the Political Security detention centre in Sana'a. Others included 'Ali Ahmad Muhammad al-Daudahi and Fadhl Hashim Abu Bakr, both farmers from Lahj Province arrested in June and held at the Political Security detention centre in Ta'iz. All five were among 65 named detainees whom the government stated in September had been released.

As President 'Ali 'Abdullah Saleh strove to consolidate his authority throughout the country following the war, censorship measures were tightened and anyone openly critical of the government was liable to arrest. Among those arrested were scores of YSP activists or sympathizers, trade unionists and Islamists. Civilian and military personnel who fled after the conflict and returned following an amnesty announced in July were also arrested. In August, in Sa'ada in north Yemen, members of the security forces reportedly attacked the house of Badr al-Din al-Huthi, a member of parliament and leading member of Hizb al-Haq, a Shi'a Islamist opposition party. He escaped arrest but 56 members of his party were arrested instead. Twenty-nine members of this group remained in Sa'ada Political Security detention centre at the end of the year. On 3 December Amin Ahmad Qasim, a businessman from Ta'iz, was arrested, reportedly because of his business connections with the YSP. At the end of 1994 he had not been charged nor had access to his family, lawyer or doctor.

Most political detainees were held for short periods. Some were apparently held in unacknowledged places of detention. The exact number of detainees held at the end of the year was not made public by the authorities.

The vast majority of political detainees were arrested by army personnel and Political Security officers. However, other arrests were carried out by the 'Islah progovernment armed militia, particularly in the southern and eastern provinces. Members of this militia were present at government check-points and police stations, and apparently operated openly with the consent of senior government and military officials. Those arrested by members of 'Islah were reportedly held in secret detention, where they were believed to be at risk of being tortured or killed.

Political detainees and prisoners arrested in the northern provinces in previous years and held in unlawful detention or following unfair trials continued to be held. Mansur Rajih, a prisoner of conscience under sentence of death, remained held after more than 11 years' imprisonment (see Amnesty International Report 1993). At least 20 government opponents, among them possible prisoners of conscience, also remained in prison. All were suspected members of the former National Democratic Front (NDF), the main opposition group in the former Yemen Arab Republic (YAR) (see previous Amnesty International Reports).

A number of political detainees who had been held in prisons in the southern provinces escaped after the outbreak of fighting in May. Among them were nine suspected members or supporters of Islamic Jihad arrested in 1993 and held without trial and without access to legal counsel (see Amnesty International Report 1994).

Torture and ill-treatment of detainees were reported throughout the year, particularly of civilian and military detainees arrested by government forces during the conflict. The methods of torture used included beatings with cables, electric shocks, rape and "Kentucky Farruj" (suspension from a metal bar inserted between the hands and knees which are tied together). Detained military personnel were said to have been routinely tortured to force them to divulge information. One such victim was Colonel Muhammad Saleh al-Najjar, a member of the southern armed forces who was arrested in June. He was reportedly tortured while held at the Political Security detention centre in Ta'iz, as a result of which he frequently vomited blood and suffered acute kidney

314

pains. In mid-July he was transferred to an unknown destination and his fate and whereabouts remained unknown.

Another case was that of Yahya Ahmad Ahmad al-Jahari, a labourer and YSP member arrested in Sana'a in June. He was held in an underground solitary cell at the Political Security detention centre in the city and shackled for 18 days. During interrogation he was said to have been beaten with cables on his wrists and legs, resulting in severe injuries.

There were several killings in circumstances suggesting the involvement or complicity of the authorities, before the outbreak of hostilities. Among the victims was 'Abd al-Karim Saleh, a leading YSP member who was shot dead outside his home in Sana'a in January.

There were also killings of government supporters, who were apparently targeted for political reasons, but it was not known which group was responsible. Among the victims were Ahmad Mas'ud al-Serafi and Mahdi Muhammad al-Shubeih, both prominent GPC members who were shot dead in February in Sana'a.

Following the outbreak of fighting in May, scores of civilians and military personnel were killed in circumstances which suggested that they may have been extrajudicially executed. In two such incidents the killers were said to have been army personnel and members of the 'Islah militia. In May an army unit surrounded the offices of the Central Committee of the YSP in al-Safia district of Sana'a. According to eye-witnesses, tanks and heavy weaponry were used to overpower a small number of lightly armed security guards stationed outside the offices. The guards were reportedly given no opportunity to give themselves up. An unknown number of people, including bystanders, were killed in the attack. In another incident in 'Aden in July, an inebriated man was reportedly shot dead at point-blank range after an altercation at a check-point in the district of Ma'alla. The check-point was manned by army personnel and members of the 'Islah militia. According to an eye-witness account, the victim was killed after making derogatory remarks about President 'Ali 'Abdullah Saleh.

The fate of hundreds of detainees who had "disappeared" in previous years in the former People's Democratic Republic of Yemen (PDRY) and in the former YAR

remained unknown (see previous *Amnesty International Reports*).

At least 25 people were publicly executed during the year. All had been convicted of premeditated murder and sentenced to death at different times in the mid- and late 1980s in the former YAR, following trials which were believed to have fallen short of international standards for fair trial. Five prisoners were executed in late July and the others in September. Hundreds of people convicted of capital offences in previous years remained under sentence of death.

In January Amnesty International submitted a memorandum to the government detailing its concerns about human rights violations committed both before and after the unification of the YAR and PDRY. Amnesty International's recommendations included the release of all prisoners of conscience; judicial review of the cases of political prisoners convicted after unfair trials; the investigation of all outstanding "disappearances"; the prompt and fair trial or release of all political suspects held in untried detention; the investigation of incidents involving torture or ill-treatment of detainees and cases of alleged extrajudicial executions; judicial review of the cases of all prisoners on death row and the commutation of all pending death sentences. The government's responses did not adequately address the issues raised in the memorandum.

In May Amnesty International publicly urged both sides in the conflict to respect human rights and to observe international humanitarian standards. Amnesty International appealed for an end to the arbitrary arrest of civilians and for all detainees to be treated humanely. It also urged that detainees be given immediate and regular access to representatives of the International Committee of the Red Cross.

In July an Amnesty International delegation visited Yemen to investigate reports of widespread human rights violations committed during and in the aftermath of the fighting. The organization interviewed over 60 prisoners of conscience and other political detainees and held discussions with the Ministers of Justice, the Interior and Foreign Affairs as well as Political Security officials. In August a memorandum was sent to the government raising the organization's concerns and urging that measures be taken to put an end to human rights violations. Details of Amnesty International's concerns were published in September in a report, *Yemen: Human rights concerns following recent armed conflict.* The government responded by stating that 65 of the 75 political detainees whose cases were highlighted in the report had been released. However, this could not be independently verified by the end of the year. Amnesty International remained concerned that the government did not address fully all of the recommendations in its report.

YUGOSLAVIA

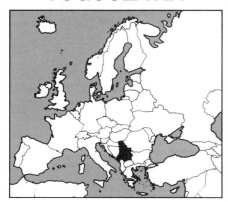

Some 300 people were detained for political reasons on charges of having sought to jeopardize Yugoslavia's territorial integrity by force of arms. Over 130 people – more than 90 ethnic Albanians and 45 Slav Muslims – were convicted in trials which violated international standards for fair trial. Some were prisoners of conscience. Other prisoners of conscience included conscientious objectors to military service. The first trial of a defendant accused of war crimes committed in Bosnia-Herzegovina began in November. Over 2,500 people were ill-treated or tortured by police primarily because of their ethnic identity. The majority of victims were ethnic Albanians in Kosovo province, but there were also many cases involving Muslims from the Sandžak region. There were also cases of police ill-treating or torturing Serbs and Montenegrins. Five men, four of them ethnic Albanians, died after ill-treatment in police custody and 10 others were shot dead by police, some in disputed circumstances. At least four men were sentenced to death for murder.

In August the Yugoslav Government publicly withdrew support from Radovan Karadžić and other Bosnian Serb representatives after they refused to accept a UN-sponsored peace settlement. In response the UN partially suspended sanctions imposed in 1992 on Serbia and Montenegro because of their involvement in the wars in Croatia and Bosnia-Herzegovina.

Around 450,000 refugees from Bosnia-Herzegovina and Croatia remained in Serbia and Montenegro. The majority were Serbs who had arrived since 1991.

Some 300 people were arrested and charged under Articles 116 and 136 of the Yugoslav Criminal Code with having sought to undermine Yugoslavia's territorial integrity by force of arms. They included over 250 ethnic Albanians in Kosovo province and some 45 Slav Muslims from the Sandžak area of Serbia and Montenegro which borders on Bosnia-Herzegovina. Over 160 were ethnic Albanian former police employees detained in November and December. Lawyers claimed that many of them had been severely tortured following arrest; one of them, Ramadan Ndrecaj, was admitted to hospital as a result of injuries inflicted by police.

Political trials took place which violated international standards for fair trial. Over 90 ethnic Albanians, many of them activists of the *Lidhja Demokratike e Kosovës* (LDK), the Democratic League of Kosovo, the main ethnic Albanian political party in Kosovo province, were convicted during 1994. Also convicted during the year were 45 Slav Muslims, including leading members of the *Stranka Demokratske Akcije* (SDA), the Democratic Action Party, which rallies Muslims in the Sandžak area.

In February, 17 ethnic Albanians, who had been detained since their arrest in 1993, were sentenced by a court in Priština to between one and 10 years' imprisonment. They were accused of founding an organization aimed at seeking by force of arms the secession of Kosovo province and areas of Montenegro inhabited by ethnic Albanians. Several were accused of having smuggled weapons into Kosovo. Almost all the accused stated in court that police had extorted statements from them by beatings and – in several cases – by electric shocks. Some were severely injured: among them Raif Qela,

316

whose injuries were confirmed by a medical certificate.

In October a court in Novi Pazar sentenced 24 Muslims, SDA members, to between one and six years' imprisonment, also on charges under Articles 116 and 136. They were accused of aiming to establish the Sandžak region as an independent state. They were charged with creating military and police units and with obtaining arms and organizing the training of terrorist groups. Most of the accused admitted distributing arms, which they said they had done to ensure the self-defence of the local Muslim population. They denied all other charges. They stated in court that they had made false confessions after police had beaten or threatened them. Six of the accused remained in detention; the others had been released earlier or were freed pending appeal. In December a further 21 Muslims, including leaders and members of the SDA in Montenegro, were sentenced to between two and seven years' imprisonment on similar charges by a court in Bijelo Polje. The accused alleged that following arrest they had been beaten with truncheons and subjected to electric shocks.

Characteristic of these and many other similar trials of ethnic Albanians was that most of the accused had been denied contact with their lawyers following arrest and during much or all of the investigation proceedings. Many alleged that as a result of torture or ill-treatment by police they had made false self-incriminating statements which they had repeated to investigation judges out of fear of reprisals. In some cases there was medical evidence to support allegations of ill-treatment, although in others medical examinations, if they took place at all, were too delayed to confirm or refute allegations. The limited information available about these trials suggested that some of the defendants were prisoners of conscience, among them Ismail Kastrati, Sylejman Ahmeti and Mustafë Ibrahimi, who were arrested in May. In October they were convicted of founding a Chamber of Commerce, one of the many institutions created by ethnic Albanians outside the structure of Serbian state institutions. They were sentenced to between two and two and a half years' imprisonment, but were released pending appeal.

Prisoners of conscience also included conscientious objectors to military service. Among them was Vilmos Almasi, an ethnic Hungarian from the Vojvodina, who was imprisoned from May to September for having refused, on grounds of conscience, to report for reserve duty in the (former) Yugoslav National Army in 1992. A number of ethnic Albanian men were imprisoned for failing to report for military service or for deserting from the (former) Yugoslav National Army in 1991. In most cases their draft evasion or desertion was probably politically motivated. They included Blerim Sejdiu, who was sentenced to five months' imprisonment by a military court in Niš in March for failing to report for military service, and Fatmir Osmani and Hajdar Jashari who were sentenced to eight months' imprisonment in December for deserting from the Army of Yugoslavia in 1993 while performing military service. In May the right to perform civilian service for those refusing military service on conscientious grounds was introduced, but the length of service was 24 months, twice the length of military service. This right did not apply retroactively.

In June the authorities extradited a suspected war criminal to the *de facto* Serbian authorities in Bosnia-Herzegovina. He was suspected of having led a Serbian paramilitary group which abducted two groups of Muslim civilians from Serbia and Montenegro in 1992 and 1993. In both cases they were travelling by public transport and were abducted as their route briefly took them into Bosnian territory. Their fate remained unknown (see *Amnesty International Reports 1993* and *1994*). It was not known whether any proceedings were started against him. The first trial in Yugoslavia of a defendant accused of war crimes in Bosnia-Herzegovina began in November. Dušan Vučković went on trial in Šabac on charges of having committed war crimes while operating with Serbian paramilitary units in Bosnia-Herzegovina. He was accused of killing 16 Muslim civilians and wounding 12 others while they were unarmed and under guard in a village near Zvornik in Bosnia-Herzegovina in 1992. He was also charged with rape and looting on Serbian territory just over the border.

There were daily reports of the ill-treatment or torture of ethnic Albanians in Kosovo province, most frequently in the context of systematic arms searches which were carried out throughout the year by the largely Serbian police force. Over 3,000 families underwent searches of this kind. In other instances police ill-treated ethnic Albanians held in police custody for questioning or when checking identities in the street. Up to 2,000 people were ill-treated, among them some children. Many of the victims were political activists, or teachers who rejected the curricula and education in the Serbian language laid down by the Serbian authorities. In February police beat Ali Murati, aged 90, until he lost consciousness, while carrying out an arms search at his home near Podujevo. In April a high-school student, Arian Curri, was arrested and beaten by police officers in Peć. One of them carved a Serbian symbol on his chest with a knife. In June Nebih Zogaj, a primary school headmaster and LDK activist, was arrested on 10 occasions by police in Suva Reka and repeatedly beaten. As a result he was admitted to hospital for treatment at least twice.

Police also systematically used violence and threats in the course of similar arms searches in the Sandžak. For example, in January and February police carried out mass house searches of Muslims in Prijepolje, arresting over 400 people, although in most cases no arms were found. Many of those arrested were severely beaten, sometimes with metal clubs; some were reportedly subjected to electric shocks or sexual abuse. Other forms of ill-treatment included deprivation of food, water and sleep and threats of death or imprisonment.

There were also reports of police violence against Serbs and Montenegrins. For example, in June police in Cetinje beat and injured Siniša Andjelić and Goran Vušurović, witnesses to a brawl, after they refused to sign statements which they regarded as untrue, compiled by police officers.

Four ethnic Albanians and a Rom in Kosovo province apparently died as a result of ill-treatment in police custody. They included Hajdin Bislimi, who was arrested in May in Kosovska Mitrovica and beaten over three days by police who reportedly suspected his young sons of having bought stolen goods. He was admitted to hospital with a perforated stomach ulcer and died in early July. In December Hasan Cubolli, aged 80, died the day after being detained and allegedly beaten by police in Podujevo. Two other ethnic Albanians apparently committed suicide as a result of police ill-treatment. It appears that no investigation of these deaths was undertaken.

Ten ethnic Albanians died and 11 others were wounded after being shot by police or soldiers. In several of these cases the authorities claimed that officers had acted in self-defence. However, in others it was clear that no officer was under attack. In July Fidan Brestovci, aged six, died after being shot by a police officer while his family were driving along a road near Uroševac; his mother and father were wounded. A police statement later said that the officer, Boban Krstić, had mistaken the family car for that of a criminal. Boban Krstić was detained for investigation but was reportedly released a month later, pending trial. He had not been brought to trial by the end of the year.

At least four men were sentenced to death during the year for murder. There were no executions.

Between January and March scores of Serb men who had sought refuge in the Federal Republic of Yugoslavia from conscription were forcibly returned by the Yugoslav authorities to Serb-controlled areas of Bosnia-Herzegovina and Croatia to be mobilized into Serbian armed forces there.

Amnesty International called for the immediate and unconditional release of prisoners of conscience and for other political prisoners to receive fair trials. It urged the authorities to institute independent and impartial investigations of all allegations of torture and ill-treatment and called for the perpetrators to be brought to justice. In February, April and September the organization issued three reports, including *Yugoslavia: Ethnic Albanians – Trial by truncheon*, documenting its concerns about unfair trials and torture and ill-treatment of ethnic Albanians in Kosovo province.

318

ZAIRE

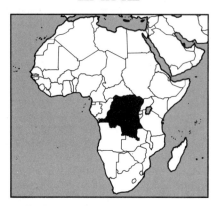

Hundreds of opponents of President Mobutu Sese Seko were detained without trial; most were prisoners of conscience. Torture and ill-treatment of detainees were widespread. "Disappearances" continued and the fate of scores of people who "disappeared" in previous years remained unknown. Dozens of unarmed civilians were extrajudicially executed by the security forces. Zairian soldiers attacked Rwandese refugees in eastern Zaire, killing at least five. Two soldiers were sentenced to death. No executions were reported.

In January President Mobutu dismissed the prime minister he had appointed in 1993 (see *Amnesty International Report 1994*) and announced the formation of a transitional parliament, the High Council of the Republic – Transitional Parliament. In June the transitional parliament elected Léon Kengo wa Dondo as Prime Minister, a post he had held twice in the 1980s. His election was vehemently opposed by supporters of Etienne Tshisekedi, leader of the *Union pour la démocratie et le progrès social* (UDPS), Union for Democracy and Social Progress, who had been appointed Prime Minister by the National Conference in 1992 but dismissed by President Mobutu in January 1993 (see *Amnesty International Reports 1992* to *1994*).

In July Prime Minister Kengo wa Dondo embarked on a program to end the crisis affecting most aspects of life in Zaire, in particular widespread violence and insecurity, ineffectiveness of the judicial system, lack of discipline in the army and the widespread and uncontrolled use of weapons by soldiers and some civil-

ians. One of several initiatives aimed at reducing violence and human rights abuses was new legislation limiting the circumstances in which members of the security forces can use firearms. It was unclear, however, whether the new government had the authority to enforce these measures, as the security forces effectively remained under the control of President Mobutu and his allies. There were fewer reports of military units rampaging through towns and cities than in previous years, but the security forces continued to arrest and detain people arbitrarily with virtual impunity.

In June the UN Commission on Human Rights appointed a Special Rapporteur on Zaire, and in November he visited the country. He was scheduled to submit a report to the 1995 session of the Commission.

Hundreds of people, including political activists, journalists and trade unionists, were arrested during the year. The majority were prisoners of conscience. In most cases they were detained by the security forces and held incommunicado and outside the framework of the law for weeks or even months. Few detainees were charged and even fewer were brought to trial. The courts were given no opportunity to rule on the legality of most cases of political imprisonment.

On 20 January, 440 members of the *Parti lumumbiste unifié* (PALU), United Lumumbist Party, were reportedly arrested by members of the Civil Guard during a peaceful demonstration to protest against what they called the President's interference in the democratic process. They were taken to the Civil Guard's headquarters in the capital, Kinshasa, where they were allegedly tortured. Some were seriously injured. More than 400 of them were released uncharged by the end of January; the fate of the rest was unknown.

A wave of political arrests began on 12 June when Etienne Tshisekedi was arrested by members of the *Division spéciale présidentielle* (DSP), Special Presidential Division, near its Kibomango barracks, 60 kilometres from Kinshasa, together with three bodyguards and his driver. He was freed after nine hours, but his bodyguards and driver remained in custody for two months. The driver and two bodyguards were released following a government decision in August to release all political

AMNESTY INTERNATIONAL REPORT 1995

prisoners (see below). It was not clear whether they had been charged. The authorities claimed that the third bodyguard, Christophe Ntumba, had escaped, but there were reports that he had "disappeared" in custody and might have been killed.

On 11 July DSP soldiers assaulted Etienne Tshisekedi's residence in Kinshasa, reportedly killing one UDPS member and wounding at least five others. The assault was in reprisal for a confrontation earlier that day between soldiers and UDPS activists who were said to have objected to the presence of soldiers around Etienne Tshisekedi's house. During the confrontation four soldiers were seriously injured. At least seven UDPS supporters were subsequently detained at Kinshasa's Makala Central Prison, some of them suffering from injuries inflicted by the soldiers. The seven, together with five others, were charged in July as a result of an investigation into the incident ordered by the authorities. A court ordered their provisional release shortly afterwards. One of the seven, Kabongo Kadila, died in September, reportedly from his injuries and lack of medical care while in custody. The authorities denied any responsibility for his death.

Journalists were subjected to death threats and other forms of intimidation, and several were detained for writing or publishing articles critical of the President and his allies, or for supporting the UDPS. Wilfried Owandjankoi, a columnist for the newspaper La Tempête des tropiques, was arrested on 22 June by members of the DSP and detained for several hours. He was arrested because of two articles he had written which criticized the President. Tshibanda Kabunda, a journalist for La Voix du Zaïre (Voice of Zaire), the national radio and television station, and a former prisoner of conscience, was arrested by members of the Civil Guard on 1 July. He was accused of showing UDPS supporters in Matadi a video he had recorded of a UDPS meeting. It was not clear for how long he was detained, but he was freed by mid-July, apparently without charge.

At least three trade union leaders – the three workers' representatives in the transitional parliament – were arrested on 16 August during a peaceful demonstration by civil servants in Kinshasa demanding payment of their salaries. They were arrested by members of the Civil Guard and the Gendarmerie's Brigade spéciale de recherche et de surveillance (BSRS), Special Investigation and Surveillance Brigade, which was trying to prevent the demonstration. Those arrested included Benjamin Mukulungu, president of the Syndicat des Enseignants, Teachers' Union, and Kibaswa Kwabene Naupess, secretary general of the Syndicat des agents de santé, Health Workers' Union. They were reportedly taken by jeep to a secret detention centre. At the end of the year it was unclear whether they had been charged or whether they were still in custody.

A possible prisoner of conscience, Jérôme Koy-Kashama, was sentenced to three years' imprisonment at Lodja in Kasaï-Oriental province for rebellion. He was apparently arrested after protesting against the use of torture by local security force members.

In July a judicial commission was set up by the Ministry of Justice to visit all detention centres. The following month the government announced that all political prisoners identified by the commission would be released, and in October it said that all had been freed. It was unclear, however, whether the commission had had the authority to check all places of detention controlled by the security forces and whether all prisoners had been released unconditionally.

Torture and ill-treatment of prisoners, particularly beatings of political detainees, were widespread. For example, Léon Kadima, a member of the UDPS and Etienne Tshisekedi's special envoy, was reportedly tortured after his arrest on 5 July. He was said to have been subjected to electric shocks while in custody at the Higher Institute of Building and Public Works, used by the Civil Guard as a secret detention centre. He was released in September without charge. No investigation into the alleged torture was initiated.

Conditions were so harsh in some prisons that they amounted to cruel, inhuman or degrading treatment. Scores of deaths as a result of starvation and lack of medical care were reported in Makala prison and other prisons around the country. In Bunia prison in Haut-Zaire, prisoners were immobilized with leg-irons which caused severe injuries. In August the Minister of Justice promised to release from

Makala prison all prisoners who were ill. It was not known how many were released.

"Disappearances" of suspected government opponents were reported. Most victims were arrested by the security forces and taken to a secret detention centre before "disappearing". Four members of the UDPS, including Théodore Kongo Mukwa, reportedly "disappeared" after their arrest by unidentified men following a UDPS meeting in Kinshasa on 5 June. The fate of dozens of people who "disappeared" in previous years remained unknown and it was feared that they had been extrajudicially executed. The government made no attempt to investigate the reported "disappearances". For instance, there was no investigation to discover the fate of Nelly Lengwa, a member of the *Forces novatrices de l'union sacrée*, Innovating Forces of the Sacred Union, who "disappeared" after her arrest on 13 July 1993 by three members of Civil Guard. She was reportedly taken away in a jeep without a number plate.

Dozens of deliberate and unlawful killings by members of the security forces were reported throughout the year, some of which were extrajudicial executions. In those cases where inquiries were ordered by the authorities, it was difficult to assess whether they took place and were independent. Pierre Kabeya, a journalist working for the newspaper *Kin-Matin*, was found dead on the night of 8 June in a street near Loano military camp in Kinshasa's Kintambo district. His death appeared to be linked to an article he wrote about the 1991 trial of those implicated in the 1990 attack on the Lubumbashi University campus (see *Amnesty International Report 1991*). Pierre Kabeya's body had been mutilated and a copy of *Kin-matin* placed conspicuously near the body. The government stated in October that the procurator in charge of the investigation had concluded that insufficient evidence was available to identify Pierre Kabeya's killers.

On 28 October Adolphe Kavula, director of the newspaper *Nsemo*, was kidnapped by armed men, believed to be members of the security forces. He was found dying by the roadside on 6 November. He was a founder of the UDPS and had recently published articles about the President's personal finances.

On 27 June, three people were reported to have been killed by members of the local police in Mbuji-Mayi, capital of East Kasai region, when an opposition meeting at the headquarters of the UDPS was violently broken up. Those killed included Kalenga Kasongo and Joseph Mulamba. At least 12 others were injured, two seriously. The government subsequently denied that anyone had died, claiming that no one had lodged complaints about relatives being killed.

Rwandese refugees fleeing to eastern Zaire's North and South Kivu regions from mid-July onwards were attacked by Zairian soldiers; at least five refugees were killed. Refugees attacked and killed several Zairian soldiers in reprisal.

Two soldiers were sentenced to death on 1 October by a Military Court in North Kivu; they were convicted of murder and attempted murder, apparently in connection with offences against refugees. No executions were reported.

On 27 November the Zairian authorities forcibly returned 37 Rwandese refugees to the Rwandese authorities, who detained them.

In February Amnesty International published a report, *Zaire: Collapsing Under Crisis*, and called on the international community to put pressure on President Mobutu to take action to end the cycle of human rights violations and to introduce effective human rights safeguards.

In September Amnesty International issued a public appeal to the new Prime Minister, welcoming the measures announced in July and calling on his government to implement them rigorously and to introduce the organization's recommendations to safeguard human rights and to establish the rule of law. A 13-page response was received from the government in October, commenting on some of the cases cited, reiterating the government's intention to end human rights violations, but urging comprehension at an international level for the difficult situation facing Zaire.

In December Amnesty International asked about the forcible return of Rwandese refugees and sought guarantees that no further such deportations would occur. No response had been received by the end of the year.

ZAMBIA

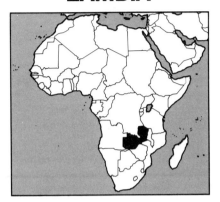

Nine journalists were briefly held as prisoners of conscience. Two refugees were detained without charge or trial for a prolonged period. There were reports of torture and ill-treatment of prisoners in police custody. At least 20 prisoners were sentenced to death, but there were no reports of executions.

The ruling Movement for Multi-Party Democracy (MMD), led by President Frederick Chiluba, faced allegations of corruption both from within its ranks and from its opponents. Three government ministers and the Vice-President, Levy Mwanawasa, resigned during the year. The former head of state, Kenneth Kaunda, who had retired from politics after his electoral defeat in 1991, announced that he was returning to politics.

Nine journalists from an independent newspaper, *The Post*, including Fred M'membe, its managing director, were briefly held as prisoners of conscience. They were each detained for a number of hours at different times during the year and charged with a range of offences, including defamation of the President, revealing classified documents and "publishing false information likely to cause public alarm". Fred M'membe faced charges on all these counts. The defamation charges were challenged in the High Court on the grounds that they were not constitutional; the court had not given a ruling by the end of the year. None of the nine journalists had been tried by the end of the year.

Two refugees from Burundi, Japhet Kabura and Leonard Bazirutwato, who had been detained without charge or trial since April 1993, were released in June. They were detained after publicly claiming that the Government of Burundi had sent a hit squad to Zambia to eliminate exiled political opponents.

There continued to be reports of torture and beatings in police custody. In February, two Lusaka police officers were charged with the murder of a taxi-driver, Oscar Chimbainga. They were reported to have beaten him with planks and fists at Chawama Police Post. It was not known whether their trial had taken place by the end of the year. In general, it appeared that the authorities failed to take effective action in relation to reports of torture and beatings of those in police custody.

The Commission on Human Rights, established by the government in 1993 to investigate allegations of human rights abuses under both previous and current governments, continued its investigation into allegations that at least two of those detained without charge or trial during the state of emergency in 1993, Cuthbert Nguni and Henry Kamima, had been ill-treated (see *Amnesty International Report 1994*). It had not reported its findings by the end of the year. Cuthbert Nguni died in September, his health reportedly permanently damaged by the ill-treatment which he had suffered.

At least 20 prisoners were sentenced to death during the year for murder or aggravated robbery. There were no reports of executions.

Amnesty International was concerned about the use of charges such as defamation and "publishing false information" to harass government critics. It was also concerned about continuing reports of torture and ill-treatment of those in police custody.

ZIMBABWE

A journalist was held briefly as a prisoner of conscience. There were reports of torture and ill-treatment of prisoners in police custody. At least five people were sentenced to death but there were no executions. Other death sentences were commuted.

In March the Supreme Court ruled that the section of the Law and Order (Maintenance) Act imposing restrictions

322

on certain demonstrations violated the constitutional guarantee of freedom of expression. The law prohibited any demonstration which had not been given prior police approval. The ruling followed a challenge brought by six members of the Zimbabwe Congress of Trade Unions (ZCTU) who had been charged with participating in an illegal demonstration in 1992. The law had not been repealed by the end of the year.

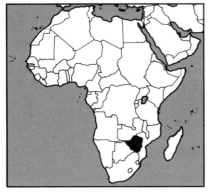

A journalist detained and charged with receiving and publishing classified documents was briefly a prisoner of conscience. Basildon Peta, a journalist on the *Daily Gazette*, was briefly detained three times in March in connection with a story he had written alleging official corruption. The police demanded that he reveal his sources. After refusing to comply with this demand, both he and the editor of the *Daily Gazette* were charged with receiving and publishing classified documents. However, they were never formally arraigned and the charges appeared to have been dropped by the end of the year.

There were reports of torture and ill-treatment of prisoners in police custody. Brian Nyamutsamba died in a cell at Harare Central Police Station in January, allegedly as a result of being denied access to the inhaler necessary to treat his asthmatic condition. An inquest was opened but had not concluded by the end of the year.

Four police officers were convicted and sentenced to two years' imprisonment in May for assaulting two civilians at a police post in Mutare in December 1993. Sarudzai Chimbudzi and Collins Sanyamaropa had been arrested after a row broke out in a nearby shop. They were handcuffed and assaulted with axe han-

dles and batons by the four police officers and forced to drink large quantities of water. They sustained various injuries, including a ruptured bladder and extensive injuries to the spine and chest.

The inquest into the death of 15-year-old Happy Dhlakama (see *Amnesty International Report 1994*), who was allegedly beaten to death in police custody in Mutare in July 1990, found that he had been assaulted in custody but was unable to determine whether the assault had actually caused his death.

There was widespread public criticism of the decision taken by President Robert Mugabe in January to pardon two members of the ruling Zimbabwe African National Union-Patriotic Front (ZANU-PF) convicted in 1993 of the attempted murder in 1990 of opposition parliamentary candidate, Patrick Kombayi (see *Amnesty International Report 1994*). The two men had lost an appeal against the conviction in the Supreme Court earlier in January.

At least five people were sentenced to death for murder, but there were no executions. In April it was reported that at least 56 prisoners remained on death row. In the same month the Minister of Home Affairs stated that since June 1993 over 50 prisoners who had been on death row for a prolonged period had had their death sentences commuted to life imprisonment (see *Amnesty International Report 1994*).

Amnesty International was concerned about the use of the charge of receiving and publishing classified documents to harass a government critic. It was also concerned about reports of torture and ill-treatment of prisoners in police custody.

APPENDICES

AMNESTY INTERNATIONAL VISITS 1994

DATE	COUNTRY	PURPOSE
January	Mozambique	Talks with government/Research
January	Guinea-Bissau	Trial observation
January	Botswana	Research
January	Sri Lanka	Research
January	India	Talks with government/Research
January	Mexico	Research/Talks with government
January/February	Moldova	Research/Talks with government
February	Russian Federation	Research
February	Northern Iraq (Kurdistan)	Research
February	Malawi	Research
February/March	United Kingdom	Trial observation
February/March	Colombia	Relief
February	Croatia	Research/Trial observation
February	Turkey	Trial observation
March	USA	Research
March	Colombia	Research/Talks with government
March	Tunisia	Trial observation
March/April	Indonesia	Research/Trial observation
April/May	Hong Kong	Talks with government
	Macao	Research
April	Egypt	Talks with government/Research
April	Thailand	Research
April	Croatia	Research
April	South Africa	Research
April	Brazil	Research
April	Kenya	Trial observation
May	Peru	Talks with government/Research
May	Ethiopia	Research/Talks with government
May	Romania	Research/Court hearing
May	Turkey	Trial observation
May/June	Venezuela	Talks with government/Research
May	Cambodia	Research
May	Denmark	Talks with government
May/June	Lebanon	Talks with government
May/June	Honduras	Research/Talks with government
May/June	El Salvador	Research
June	Sudan	Research
June	Israel/Occupied Territories	Research/Talks with government
June	Bulgaria	Research
June	France	Research
July	Equatorial Guinea	Research/Talks with government
July	France	Trial observation
July	Liberia	Research/Talks with government
July	Northern Iraq (Kurdistan)	Research

July	Tunisia	Talks with government
July	Yemen	Research/Talks with government
July	Colombia	Campaign
August	Algeria	Research
August	Rwanda	Research/Talks with government
July/August	Burundi	Research/Talks with government
August	Turkey	Trial observation
August	Germany	Research
August	Trinidad & Tobago	Research
August	Dominican Republic	Research
August	Barbados	Research
September	Viet Nam	Research
September/October	Brazil	Research/Talks with government
September	Albania	Research
September	USA/Dominican Republic/ French Guiana/Bahamas/ Guantanamo Bay, Cuba	Research
September	United Kingdom	Research
September/October	Uzbekistan	Research/CSCE Seminar
September/October	Bosnia-Herzegovina	Research
October	South Korea	Research/Talks with government
October	Taiwan	Research/Talks with government
October/November	USA	Research
October	United Kingdom	Observe inquest
October	Syria	Talks with government/Research/Observe trial
November	Pakistan	Research
November	Uganda	Research
November	Colombia	Talks with government
November	United Kingdom	Court hearing
November	Cambodia	Research
November/December	Israel/Occupied Territories/ Palestinian Authority areas	Research
November/December	Romania	Research
December	Cyprus	Research/Development
December	Nigeria	Research/Talks with government
December	Mongolia	Research/Talks with government
December	Azerbaijan	Research/Talks with government
December	Mexico	Research

STATUTE OF AMNESTY INTERNATIONAL
Articles 1 and 2

**As amended by the 21st International Council,
meeting in Boston, USA, 6 to 14 August 1993**

Object and Mandate

1. The object of AMNESTY INTERNATIONAL is to contribute to the observance throughout the world of human rights as set out in the Universal Declaration of Human Rights.
   In pursuance of this object, and recognizing the obligation on each person to extend to others rights and freedoms equal to his or her own, AMNESTY INTERNATIONAL adopts as its mandate:

   To promote awareness of and adherence to the Universal Declaration of Human Rights and other internationally recognized human rights instruments, the values enshrined in them, and the indivisibility and interdependence of all human rights and freedoms;

   To oppose grave violations of the rights of every person freely to hold and to express his or her convictions and to be free from discrimination by reason of ethnic origin, sex, colour or language, and of the right of every person to physical and mental integrity, and, in particular, to oppose by all appropriate means irrespective of political considerations:

   a) the imprisonment, detention or other physical restrictions imposed on any person by reason of his or her political, religious or other conscientiously held beliefs or by reason of his or her ethnic origin, sex, colour or language, provided that he or she has not used or advocated violence (hereinafter referred to as "prisoners of conscience"); AMNESTY INTERNATIONAL shall work towards the release of and shall provide assistance to prisoners of conscience;

   b) the detention of any political prisoner without fair trial within a reasonable time or any trial procedures relating to such prisoners that do not conform to internationally recognized norms;

   c) the death penalty, and the torture or other cruel, inhuman or degrading treatment or punishment of prisoners or other detained or restricted persons, whether or not the persons affected have used or advocated violence;

   d) the extrajudicial execution of persons whether or not imprisoned, detained or restricted, and "disappearances", whether or not the persons affected have used or advocated violence.

Methods

2. In order to achieve the aforesaid object and mandate, AMNESTY INTERNATIONAL shall:

   a) at all times make clear its impartiality as regards countries adhering to the different world political ideologies and groupings;

   b) promote as appears appropriate the adoption of constitutions, conventions, treaties and other measures which guarantee the rights contained in the provisions referred to in Article 1 hereof;

   c) support and publicize the activities of and cooperate with international organizations and agencies which work for the implementation of the aforesaid provisions;

   d) take all necessary steps to establish an effective organization of sections, affiliated groups and individual members;

   e) secure the adoption by groups of members or supporters of individual prisoners of conscience or entrust to such groups other tasks in support of the object and mandate set out in Article 1;

328

f) provide financial and other relief to prisoners of conscience and their dependants and to persons who have lately been prisoners of conscience or who might reasonably be expected to be prisoners of conscience or to become prisoners of conscience if convicted or if they were to return to their own countries, to the dependants of such persons and to victims of torture in need of medical care as a direct result thereof;

g) provide legal aid, where necessary and possible, to prisoners of conscience and to persons who might reasonably be expected to be prisoners of conscience or to become prisoners of conscience if convicted or if they were to return to their own countries, and, where desirable, send observers to attend the trials of such persons;

h) publicize the cases of prisoners of conscience or persons who have otherwise been subjected to disabilities in violation of the aforesaid provisions;

i) investigate and publicize the "disappearance" of persons where there is reason to believe that they may be victims of violations of the rights set out in Article 1 hereof;

j) oppose the sending of persons from one country to another where they can reasonably be expected to become prisoners of conscience or to face torture or the death penalty;

k) send investigators, where appropriate, to investigate allegations that the rights of individuals under the aforesaid provisions have been violated or threatened;

l) make representations to international organizations and to governments whenever it appears that an individual is a prisoner of conscience or has otherwise been subjected to disabilities in violation of the aforesaid provisions;

m) promote and support the granting of general amnesties of which the beneficiaries will include prisoners of conscience;

n) adopt any other appropriate methods for the securing of its object and mandate.

The full text of the Statute of Amnesty International is available free upon request from: Amnesty International, International Secretariat, 1 Easton Street, London WC1X 8DJ, United Kingdom.

AMNESTY INTERNATIONAL AROUND THE WORLD

There were 4,329 local Amnesty International groups registered with the International Secretariat at the start of 1995, plus several thousand school, university, professional and other groups, in over 89 countries around the world. In 55 countries these groups are coordinated by sections, whose addresses are given below. In addition, there are individual members, supporters and recipients of Amnesty International information (such as the monthly *Amnesty International Newsletter*) in over 150 countries and territories.

SECTION ADDRESSES

Algeria:
Amnesty International,
Section Algérienne,
BP 377
Alger RP 16004

Argentina:
Amnistía Internacional,
Sección Argentina,
25 de Mayo 67, 4º Piso,
1002 Capital Federal,
Buenos Aires

Australia:
Amnesty International,
Australian Section,
Private Bag 23, Broadway,
New South Wales 2007

Austria:
Amnesty International,
Austrian Section,
Apostelgasse 25-27, A-1030 Wien

Bangladesh:
Amnesty International,
Bangladesh Section,
100 Kalabagan,
1st Floor, 2nd Lane,
Dhaka-1205

Barbados:
Amnesty International,
Barbados Section,
PO Box 872, Bridgetown

Belgium:
Amnesty International,
Belgian Section (*Flemish branch*),
Kerkstraat 156, 2060 Antwerpen

Amnesty International,
Section belge francophone,
Rue Berckmans 9, 1060 Bruxelles

Benin:
Amnesty International,
BP 01 3536, Cotonou

Bermuda:
Amnesty International,
Bermuda Section,
PO Box HM 2136, Hamilton HM JX

Brazil:
Anistia Internacional,
Seção Brasileira,
Rua Vicente Leporaçe 833,
CEP 04619-032,
São Paulo, SP

Canada:
Amnesty International,
Canadian Section
(*English-speaking branch*),
214 Montreal Rd, 4th Floor, Vanier,
Ontario, K1L 8L8

Amnistie Internationale,
Section canadienne francophone,
6250 boulevard Monk,
Montréal, Québec H4E 3H7

Chile:
Amnistía Internacional,
Sección Chilena,
San Martin 575, Oficina 401,
Casilla 4062, Santiago

Colombia:
Señores,
Apartado Aéreo 76350,
Bogotá

Côte d'Ivoire:
Amnesty International,
Section Ivoirienne,
04 BP 895, Abidjan 04

330

Denmark:
Amnesty International,
Danish Section,
Dyrkoeb 3, 1166 Copenhagen K

Ecuador:
Amnistía Internacional,
Sección Ecuatoriana,
Casilla 17-15-240-C, Quito

Faroe Islands:
Amnesty International,
Faroe Islands Section,
PO Box 1075, FR-110, Tórshavn

Finland:
Amnesty International,
Finnish Section,
Ruoholahdenkatu 24 D,
00180 Helsinki

France:
Amnesty International,
Section française,
4 rue de la Pierre Levée,
75553 Paris, Cedex 11

Germany:
Amnesty International,
German Section,
Heerstrasse 178, D-53111 Bonn

Ghana:
Amnesty International,
Ghanaian Section,
PO Box 1173, Koforidua E.R.

Greece:
Amnesty International,
Greek Section,
30 Sina Street, 106 72 Athens

Guyana:
Amnesty International,
Guyana Section,
c/o PO Box 10720, Palm Court Building,
35 Main Street, Georgetown

Hong Kong:
Amnesty International,
Hong Kong Section,
Unit C 3/F, Best-O-Best,
32-36 Ferry Street, Kowloon

Iceland:
Amnesty International,
Icelandic Section,
PO Box 618, 121 Reykjavík

India:
Amnesty International,
Indian Section,
13 Indra Prastha Building,
E-109 Pandav Nagar,
N. Delhi-92

Ireland:
Amnesty International,
Irish Section,
Sean MacBride House,
8 Shaw St, Dublin 2

Israel:
Amnesty International,
Israel Section,
PO Box 14179, Tel Aviv 61141

Italy:
Amnesty International,
Italian Section,
Viale Mazzini, 146 – 00195 Rome

Japan:
Amnesty International,
Japanese Section,
Sky Esta 2fl,
2-18-23 Nishi-Waseda,
Shinjuku-ku, Tokyo 165

Korea (Republic of):
Amnesty International,
706-600 Kyeong Buk RCO Box 36,
Daegu

Luxembourg:
Amnesty International,
Luxembourg Section,
Boîte Postale 1914,
1019 Luxembourg

Mauritius:
Amnesty International,
Mauritius Section,
BP 69 Rose-Hill

Mexico:
Sección Mexicana
de Amnistía Internacional,
Apartado Postal No. 20217, San Angel,
CP 01000 México DF

Nepal:
Amnesty International,
Nepalese Section,
PO Box 135, Bagbazar,
Kathmandu

Netherlands:
Amnesty International,
Dutch Section,
Keizersgracht 620, 1017 ER Amsterdam

New Zealand:
Amnesty International,
New Zealand Section,
PO Box 793, Wellington 1

Nigeria:
Amnesty International,
Nigerian Section,
PMB 59 Agodi, Ibadan, Oyo State

Norway:
Amnesty International,
Norwegian Section,
Maridalsveien 87, 0461 Oslo 4

Peru:
Señores,
Casilla 659, Lima 18

Philippines:
Amnesty International,
Philippines Section,
95 Times Street,
West Triangle, Quezon City

Portugal:
Amnistia Internacional,
Secção Portuguesa,
Rua Fialho de Almeida,
Nº 13, 1º,
1070 Lisboa

Puerto Rico:
Amnistía Internacional,
Sección de Puerto Rico,
Calle Robles No 54-Altos,
Oficina 11, Río Piedras,
Puerto Rico 00925

Senegal:
Amnesty International,
Senegalese Section,
CEDHOSSAI, BP 10.494
Dakar Liberté

Sierra Leone:
Amnesty International,
Sierra Leone Section,
PMB 1021, Freetown

Slovenia:
Amnesty International,
Komenskega 7,
61000 Ljubljana

Spain:
Amnesty International,
Sección Española,
Apartado de Correos 50318,
28080 Madrid

Sweden:
Amnesty International,
Swedish Section,
PO Box 23400,
S-104 35 Stockholm

Switzerland:
Amnesty International,
Swiss Section,
Erlachstr. 16B, CH-3001 Bern

Tanzania:
Amnesty International,
Tanzanian Section,
PO Box 4331,
Dar es Salaam

Tunisia:
Amnesty International,
Section Tunisienne,
48 Avenue Farhat Hached,
3ème étage, 1001 Tunis

United Kingdom:
Amnesty International,
British Section,
99-119 Rosebery Avenue,
London EC1R 4RE

United States of America:
Amnesty International of the USA
 (AIUSA),
322 8th Ave, New York, NY 10001

Uruguay:
Amnistía Internacional,
Sección Uruguaya,
Yi 1333 Apto 305,
Montevideo, Casilla 6651, Correo Central

Venezuela:
Amnistía Internacional,
Sección Venezolana,
Apartado Postal 5110,
Carmelitas 1010-A, Caracas

COUNTRIES AND TERRITORIES WITHOUT SECTIONS
BUT WHERE LOCAL AMNESTY INTERNATIONAL GROUPS EXIST
OR ARE BEING FORMED

Albania	Gambia	Morocco
Aruba	Gaza Strip and West Bank	Pakistan
Bahamas	Georgia	Paraguay
Bolivia	Grenada	Poland
Botswana	Hungary	Romania
Bulgaria	Jamaica	Russia
Cameroon	Jordan	Slovakia
Central African Republic	Kenya	South Africa
Chad	Kuwait	Taiwan
Costa Rica	Lesotho	Thailand
Croatia	Lithuania	Togo
Curaçao	Macao	Uganda
Cyprus	Malaysia	Ukraine
Czech Republic	Mali	Yemen
Dominican Republic	Malta	Zambia
Egypt	Moldova	Zimbabwe
Estonia	Mongolia	

Amnesty International groups in Sudan have ceased activities following the banning of all political parties, trade unions and non-governmental organizations including the Sudanese Amnesty International Organization, under which the Sudanese groups were officially registered in Sudan.

INTERNATIONAL EXECUTIVE COMMITTEE

Ross Daniels/Australia
Celso Garbarz/Israel
Elizabeth Jenkins/United Kingdom
Menno Kamminga/Netherlands
Mardi Mapa-Suplido/Philippines
Gerry O'Connell/Italy
Marie Staunton/United Kingdom
Tracy Ulltveit-Moe/International Secretariat
Susan Waltz/United States of America

Update on Abolition of the Death Penalty

Amnesty International is unconditionally opposed to the death penalty and works for its abolition. The organization regularly monitors death sentences and executions around the world and appeals for clemency whenever it learns of an imminent execution.

During 1994, at least 2,331 prisoners were executed in 37 countries and 4,032 people were sentenced to death in 75 countries. These figures include only cases known to Amnesty International: the true figures are certainly higher. As in previous years, a small number of countries accounted for the great majority of executions.

In October Italy abolished the death penalty for all crimes. A bill eliminating the death penalty from the Military Penal Code in Time of War received its final approval from the Italian parliament on 5 October and was promulgated on 25 October.

By the end of 1994, 54 countries had abolished the death penalty for all offences and 15 for all but exceptional offences, such as war crimes. At least 27 countries and territories which retained the death penalty in law had not carried out executions for the past 10 years or more.

During the year, Denmark, Hungary, Malta, Namibia, Slovenia, the Seychelles and Switzerland became parties to the Second Optional Protocol to the International Covenant on Civil and Political Rights, aiming at the abolition of the death penalty, bringing the number of States Parties to 26. Ireland, Romania and Slovenia became parties to Protocol No. 6 to the European Convention for the Protection of Human Rights and Fundamental Freedoms ("European Convention on Human Rights") concerning the abolition of the death penalty, bringing the number of States Parties to 23. Uruguay became a party to the Protocol to the American Convention on Human Rights to Abolish the Death Penalty, bringing the number of States Parties to three; Brazil signed the Protocol, signifying its intention to become a party at a later date.

On 4 October the Parliamentary Assembly of the 32-member Council of Europe adopted a recommendation calling for the creation of a further protocol to the European Convention on Human Rights on the abolition of the death penalty. Unlike Protocol No. 6, which provides for the abolition of the death penalty but allows for its retention in time of war or imminent threat of war, the new protocol would constitute an agreement among States Parties to abolish the death penalty in all circumstances with no exceptions. Following the action by the Parliamentary Assembly, the Council of Europe's Steering Committee for Human Rights appointed a rapporteur to prepare an opinion on the proposal.

SELECTED INTERNATIONAL HUMAN RIGHTS TREATIES

States which have ratified or acceded to a convention are party to the treaty and are bound to observe its provisions. States which have signed but not yet ratified have expressed their intention to become a party at some future date; meanwhile they are obliged to refrain from acts which would defeat the object and purpose of the treaty.

(AS OF 31 DECEMBER 1994)

	International Covenant on Civil and Political Rights (ICCPR)	Optional Protocol to ICCPR	Second Optional Protocol to ICCPR, aiming at the abolition of the death penalty	International Covenant on Economic, Social and Cultural Rights (ICESCR)	Convention against Torture and Other Cruel, Inhuman or Degrading Treatment or Punishment	Convention relating to the Status of Refugees (1951)	Protocol relating to the Status of Refugees (1967)
Afghanistan	x			x	x(28)		
Albania	x			x	x*	x	x
Algeria	x	x		x	x(22)	x	x
Andorra							
Angola	x	x		x		x	x
Antigua and Barbuda					x		
Argentina	x	x		x	x(22)	x	x
Armenia	x	x		x	x	x	x
Australia	x	x	x	x	x(22)	x	x
Austria	x	x	x	x	x(22)	x	x
Azerbaijan	x			x		x	x
Bahamas						x	x
Bahrain							
Bangladesh							
Barbados	x	x		x			
Belarus	x	x		x	x(28)		

	International Covenant on Civil and Political Rights (ICCPR)	Optional Protocol to ICCPR	Second Optional Protocol to ICCPR, aiming at the abolition of the death penalty	International Covenant on Economic, Social and Cultural Rights (ICESCR)	Convention against Torture and Other Cruel, Inhuman or Degrading Treatment or Punishment	Convention relating to the Status of Refugees (1951)	Protocol relating to the Status of Refugees (1967)
Belgium	x	x*	s	x	s	x	x
Belize					x	x	x
Benin	x	x		x	x	x	x
Bhutan							
Bolivia	x	x		x	s	x	x
Bosnia-Herzegovina	x			x	x	x	x
Botswana						x	x
Brazil	x			x	x	x	x
Brunei Darussalam							
Bulgaria	x	x		x	x(22)(28)	x	x
Burkina Faso						x	x
Burundi	x			x	x	x	x
Cambodia	x			x	x	x	x
Cameroon	x	x		x	x	x	x
Canada	x	x		x	x(22)	x	x
Cape Verde	x			x	x	x	x
Central African Republic	x	x		x		x	x
Chad						x	x
Chile	x	x		x	x	x	x
China					x(28)	x	x
Colombia	x	x		x	x	x	x
Comoros							
Congo	x	x		x		x	x
Costa Rica	x	x	s	x	x	x	x

	International Covenant on Civil and Political Rights (ICCPR)	Optional Protocol to ICCPR	Second Optional Protocol to ICCPR, aiming at the abolition of the death penalty	International Covenant on Economic, Social and Cultural Rights (ICESCR)	Convention against Torture and Other Cruel, Inhuman or Degrading Treatment or Punishment	Convention relating to the Status of Refugees (1951)	Protocol relating to the Status of Refugees (1967)
Côte d'Ivoire	x			x		x	x
Croatia	x			x	x(22)	x	x
Cuba	x				s	x	x
Cyprus	x	x		x	x(22)	x	x
Czech Republic	x	x		x	x	x	x
Denmark	x	x	x*	x	x(22)	x	x
Djibouti	x						
Dominica	x			x		x*	x*
Dominican Republic	x	x		x	s	x	x
Ecuador	x	x	x	x	x(22)	x	x
Egypt	x	s		x	x	x	x
El Salvador	x			x		x	x
Equatorial Guinea	x	x		x		x	x
Eritrea							
Estonia	x	x		x	x		
Ethiopia	x			x	x*	x	x
Fiji						x	x
Finland	x	x	x	x	x(22)	x	x
France	x	x		x	x(22)	x	x
Gabon	x			x	s	x	x
Gambia	x	x		x	s	x	x
Georgia	x*	x*		x*	x*	x*	x*
Germany	x	x	x	x	x	x	x
Ghana				x		x	x

	International Covenant on Civil and Political Rights (ICCPR)	Optional Protocol to ICCPR	Second Optional Protocol to ICCPR, aiming at the abolition of the death penalty	International Covenant on Economic, Social and Cultural Rights (ICESCR)	Convention against Torture and Other Cruel, Inhuman or Degrading Treatment or Punishment	Convention relating to the Status of Refugees (1951)	Protocol relating to the Status of Refugees (1967)
Greece				x	x(22)	x	x
Grenada	x			x			x
Guatemala	x			x	x	x	x
Guinea	x	x		x	x	x	x
Guinea-Bissau	x			x		x	x
Guyana	x	x		x	x		
Haiti	x					x	x
Holy See						x	x
Honduras	s	s	s	x		x	x
Hungary	x	x	x*	x	x(22)	x	x
Iceland	x	x	x	x	s	x	x
India	x			x			
Indonesia					s		
Iran (Islamic Republic of)	x			x		x	x
Iraq	x			x			
Ireland	x	x	x	x	s	x	x
Israel	x			x	x(28)	x	x
Italy	x	x	s	x	x(22)	x	x
Jamaica	x	x		x		x	x
Japan	x			x		x	x
Jordan	x			x	x		
Kazakhstan							
Kenya	x			x		x	x
Korea (Democratic People's Republic)	x			x			

	International Covenant on Civil and Political Rights (ICCPR)	Optional Protocol to ICCPR	Second Optional Protocol to ICCPR, aiming at the abolition of the death penalty	International Covenant on Economic, Social and Cultural Rights (ICESCR)	Convention against Torture and Other Cruel, Inhuman or Degrading Treatment or Punishment	Convention relating to the Status of Refugees (1951)	Protocol relating to the Status of Refugees (1967)
Korea (Republic of)	x	x		x		x	x
Kuwait							
Kyrgyzstan	x*	x*		x*			
Lao People's Democratic Republic							
Latvia	x	x*		x	x		
Lebanon	x			x			
Lesotho	x			x		x	x
Liberia	s			s		x	x
Libyan Arab Jamahiriya	x	x		x			
Liechtenstein	x	x			x(22)	x	x
Lithuania	x	x		x		x	x
Luxembourg	x	x	x	x	x(22)	x	x
Macedonia (former Yug. Rep. of)	x*	x*		x*	x*	x*	x*
Madagascar	x	x		x		x	
Malawi	x			x		x	x
Malaysia							
Maldives							
Mali	x			x		x	x
Malta	x	x	x*	x	x(22)	x	x
Marshall Islands							
Mauritania						x	x
Mauritius	x	x		x	x		
Mexico	x			x	x		
Micronesia (Federated States of)							

	International Covenant on Civil and Political Rights (ICCPR)	Optional Protocol to ICCPR	Second Optional Protocol to ICCPR, aiming at the abolition of the death penalty	International Covenant on Economic, Social and Cultural Rights (ICESCR)	Convention against Torture and Other Cruel, Inhuman or Degrading Treatment or Punishment	Convention relating to the Status of Refugees (1951)	Protocol relating to the Status of Refugees (1967)
Moldova	x			x			
Monaco					x(22)	x	
Mongolia	x	x		x			
Morocco	x			x	x(28)	x	x
Mozambique	x*		x			x	x
Myanmar (Burma)							
Namibia	x*	x*	x*	x*	x*		
Nauru							
Nepal	x	x		x	x		
Netherlands	x	x	x	x	x(22)	x	x
New Zealand	x	x	x	x	x(22)	x	x
Nicaragua	x	x	s	x	s	x	x
Niger	x	x		x		x	x
Nigeria	x			x	s	x	x
Norway	x	x	x	x	x(22)	x	x
Oman							
Pakistan							
Panama	x	x	x	x	x	x	x
Papua New Guinea						x	x
Paraguay	x			x	x	x	x
Peru	x	x		x	x	x	x
Philippines	x	x		x	x	x	x
Poland	x	x		x	x(22)	x	x
Portugal	x	x	x	x	x(22)	x	x

AMNESTY INTERNATIONAL REPORT 1995

	International Covenant on Civil and Political Rights (ICCPR)	Optional Protocol to ICCPR	Second Optional Protocol to ICCPR, aiming at the abolition of the death penalty	International Covenant on Economic, Social and Cultural Rights (ICESCR)	Convention against Torture and Other Cruel, Inhuman or Degrading Treatment or Punishment	Convention relating to the Status of Refugees (1951)	Protocol relating to the Status of Refugees (1967)
Qatar							
Romania	x	x	x	x	x	x	x
Russian Federation	x	x		x	x(22)	x	x
Rwanda	x			x		x	x
St Christopher and Nevis							
St Lucia							
St Vincent and the Grenadines	x	x		x		x	x
Samoa						x	x*
San Marino	x	x		x		x	x
São Tomé and Príncipe						x	x
Saudi Arabia							
Senegal	x	x		x	x	x	x
Seychelles	x	x	x*	x	x	x	x
Sierra Leone					s	x	x
Singapore							
Slovakia	x	x		x	x	x	x
Slovenia	x	x	x*	x	x(22)	x	x
Solomon Islands				x			
Somalia	x	x		x	x	x	x
South Africa	s*			s*	s		
Spain	x	x	x	x	x(22)	x	x
Sri Lanka	x			x	x*		
Sudan	x			x	s	x	x
Suriname	x	x		x		x	x

	International Covenant on Civil and Political Rights (ICCPR)	Optional Protocol to ICCPR	Second Optional Protocol to ICCPR, aiming at the abolition of the death penalty	International Covenant on Economic, Social and Cultural Rights (ICESCR)	Convention against Torture and Other Cruel, Inhuman or Degrading Treatment or Punishment	Convention relating to the Status of Refugees (1951)	Protocol relating to the Status of Refugees (1967)
Swaziland							x
Sweden	x	x	x	x	x(22)	x	x
Switzerland	x	x	x*	x	x(22)	x	x
Syrian Arab Republic	x			x			
Tadzhikistan						x	x
Tanzania	x			x		x	x
Thailand							
Togo	x	x		x	x(22)	x	x
Tonga							
Trinidad and Tobago	x	x		x			
Tunisia	x			x	x(22)	x	x
Turkey					x(22)	x	x
Turkmenistan							
Tuvalu						x	x
Uganda	x			x	x	x	x
Ukraine	x	x		x	x(28)		
United Arab Emirates							
United Kingdom	x			x	x		x
United States of America	x			s	x*		x
Uruguay	x	x	x	x	x(22)	x	x
Uzbekistan							
Vanuatu							
Venezuela	x	x	x	x	x(22)		x
Viet Nam	x			x			

	International Covenant on Civil and Political Rights (ICCPR)	Optional Protocol to ICCPR	Second Optional Protocol to ICCPR, aiming at the abolition of the death penalty	International Covenant on Economic, Social and Cultural Rights (ICESCR)	Convention against Torture and Other Cruel, Inhuman or Degrading Treatment or Punishment	Convention relating to the Status of Refugees (1951)	Protocol relating to the Status of Refugees (1967)
Yemen	x			x	x	x	x
Yugoslavia (Federal Republic of)	x	s		x	x(22)	x	x
Zaire	x	x		x		x	x
Zambia	x	x		x		x	x
Zimbabwe	x			x		x	x

s – denotes that country has signed but not yet ratified

x – denotes that country is a party, either through ratification, accession or succession

* – denotes that country either signed or became a party in 1994

(22) denotes Declaration under Article 22 recognizing the competence of the Committee against Torture to consider individual complaints of violations of the Convention

(28) denotes that country has made a reservation under Article 28 that it does not recognize the competence of the Committee against Torture to examine reliable information which appears to indicate that torture is being systematically practised, and to undertake a confidential inquiry if warranted

SELECTED REGIONAL HUMAN RIGHTS TREATIES

(AS OF 31 DECEMBER 1994)

ORGANIZATION OF AFRICAN UNITY (OAU)
AFRICAN CHARTER ON HUMAN AND PEOPLES' RIGHTS (1981)

Algeria	x	Madagascar	x
Angola	x	Malawi	x
Benin	x	Mali	x
Botswana	x	Mauritania	x
Burkina Faso	x	Mauritius	x
Burundi	x	Mozambique	x
Cameroon	x	Namibia	x
Cape Verde	x	Niger	x
Central African Republic	x	Nigeria	x
Chad	x	Rwanda	x
Comoros	x	Saharawi Arab Democratic Republic	x
Congo	x	São Tomé and Príncipe	x
Côte d'Ivoire	x	Senegal	x
Djibouti	x	Seychelles	x
Egypt	x	Sierra Leone	x
Equatorial Guinea	x	Somalia	x
Eritrea		South Africa	
Ethiopia		Sudan	x
Gabon	x	Swaziland	
Gambia	x	Tanzania	x
Ghana	x	Togo	x
Guinea	x	Tunisia	x
Guinea-Bissau	x	Uganda	x
Kenya	x	Zaire	x
Lesotho	x	Zambia	x
Liberia	x	Zimbabwe	x
Libya	x		

x – denotes that country is a party, either through ratification or accession

This chart lists countries which were members of the OAU at the end of 1994.

ORGANIZATION OF AMERICAN STATES (OAS)

	American Convention on Human Rights (1969)	Inter-American Convention to Prevent and Punish Torture (1985)	Inter-American Convention on the Forced Disappearance of Persons (1994)*
Antigua and Barbuda			
Argentina	x(62)	x	s
Bahamas			
Barbados	x		
Belize			
Bolivia	x(62)	s	s
Brazil	x	x	s
Canada			
Chile	x(62)	x	s
Colombia	x(62)	s	s
Costa Rica	x(62)	s	s
Cuba			
Dominica	x		
Dominican Republic	x	x	
Ecuador	x(62)	s	
El Salvador	x	s	
Grenada	x		
Guatemala	x(62)	x	s
Guyana			
Haiti	x	s	
Honduras	x(62)	s	s
Jamaica	x		
Mexico	x	x	
Nicaragua	x(62)	s	s
Panama	x(62)	x	s
Paraguay	x(62)	x	
Peru	x(62)	x	
St Christopher and Nevis			
St Lucia			
St Vincent and the Grenadines			
Suriname	x(62)	x	
Trinidad and Tobago	x(62)		
United States of America	s		
Uruguay	x(62)	x	s
Venezuela	x(62)	x	s

s – denotes that country has signed but not yet ratified

x – denotes that country is a party, either through ratification or accession

(62) – denotes Declaration under Article 62 recognizing as binding the jurisdiction of the Inter-American Court of Human Rights (on all matters relating to the interpretation or application of the American Convention)

* By the end of the year, this Convention had not yet entered into force.

This chart lists countries which were members of the OAS at the end of 1994.

COUNCIL OF EUROPE

	European Convention for the Protection of Human Rights and Fundamental Freedoms (1950)	Article 25	Article 46	Protocol No. 6*	European Convention for the Prevention of Torture and Inhuman or Degrading Treatment or Punishment (1987)
Andorra	s				
Austria	x	x	x	x	x
Belgium	x	x	x	s	x
Bulgaria	x	x	x		x
Cyprus	x	x	x		x
Czech Republic	x	x	x	x	s
Denmark	x	x	x	x	x
Estonia	s			s	
Finland	x	x	x	x	x
France	x	x	x	x	x
Germany	x	x	x	x	x
Greece	x	x	x	s	x
Hungary	x	x	x	x	x
Iceland	x	x	x	x	x
Ireland	x	x	x	x	x
Italy	x	x	x	x	x
Liechtenstein	x	x	x	x	x
Lithuania	s				
Luxembourg	x	x	x	x	x
Malta	x	x	x	x	x
Netherlands	x	x	x	x	x
Norway	x	x	x	x	x
Poland	x	x	x		x
Portugal	x	x	x	x	x
Romania	x	x	x	x	x
San Marino	x	x	x	x	x
Slovakia	x	x	x	x	x
Slovenia	x	x	x	x	x
Spain	x	x	x	x	x
Sweden	x	x	x	x	x
Switzerland	x	x	x	x	x
Turkey	x	x	x		x
United Kingdom	x	x	x		x

s − denotes that country has signed but not yet ratified

x − denotes that country is a party, either through ratification or accession

Article 25: denotes Declaration under Article 25 of the European Convention for the Protection of Human Rights and Fundamental Freedoms, recognizing the competence of the European Commission of Human Rights to consider individual complaints of violations of the Convention

Article 46: denotes Declaration under Article 46 of the European Convention for the Protection of Human Rights and Fundamental Freedoms, recognizing as compulsory the jurisdiction of the European Court of Human Rights in all matters concerning interpretation and application of the European Convention

* Protocol No. 6 to the European Convention for the Protection of Human Rights and Fundamental Freedoms: concerning abolition of the death penalty (1983)

This chart lists countries which were members of the Council of Europe at the end of 1994.

Amnesty International's 15-Point Program for Implementing Human Rights in International Peace-keeping Operations

This set of recommendations is aimed at the incorporation into all peace-keeping and other relevant field operations of essential measures to ensure respect for human rights as well as monitoring, investigation and corrective action in respect of violations. The 15-Point Program is addressed to all those involved in the establishment of such operations – the parties to the conflict, observer governments involved in the process and other states as well as the UN Secretariat and other UN bodies and specialized agencies. They include structural suggestions as to how UN officials and governments involved at the political level should address human rights issues at all stages of peace-keeping or peace-building in a country. These recommendations are designed for use in all types of operations: cease-fire monitoring, implementation of peace agreements, peace enforcement or the delivery of humanitarian assistance. Member States and the UN are urged to pay greater attention to the importance of addressing human rights in a serious way in the planning and implementation of all peace-keeping operations. Amnesty International is convinced that human rights protection is essential to the success of any such operation and that, as long as the UN avoids tackling these issues effectively, it is seriously damaging its own credibility and thereby its capacity to undertake peace-keeping and peace-building operations in other contexts and countries in the future.

1. The political role of the international community

The UN and its Member States should give early, consistent and vigorous attention to human rights concerns when designing and implementing peace settlements and should plan for a continued human rights program in the post-peace-keeping phase. The international community must be prepared to publicly condemn human rights violations during and after the settlement process and to ensure that recommendations for institutional reform are fully and promptly implemented. Human rights protection measures should be kept under review, strengthened as necessary and properly evaluated at the end of the operation.

2. No international 'silent witnesses'

All international field personnel, including those engaged in military, civilian and humanitarian operations, should report through explicit and proper channels any human rights violations they may witness or serious allegations they receive. The UN should take appropriate steps, including preventive measures, to address any violations reported.

3. Human rights chapters in peace agreements

Peace agreements should include a detailed and comprehensive list of international human rights laws and standards to be guaranteed in the transitional and post-settlement phase, as well as providing for specific and effective oversight mechanisms. Peace settlements should require eventual ratification of any human rights treaties and adherence to any international systems of human rights protection to which the state concerned is not yet a party.

4. Effective and independent human rights verification

A specialized international civilian human rights monitoring component should be part of all peace-keeping operations. These components should have adequate resources and staff with human rights expertise. Their mandates should include human rights verification, institution-building, legislative reform, education and training. Monitors should be trained and should operate under consistent guidelines and in conformity with international standards. Human rights components should be explicitly and structurally independent from the political considerations of the operation and ongoing negotiations relating to the settlement, and their decision-making mechanisms must not be constructed so as to permit parties to the conflict to obstruct investigations. Effective human rights mechanisms, such as advisers or independent jurists, should also be established in less comprehensive peace settlements and should have an oversight role in matters such as the release of prisoners and the guarantee of rights to freedom of speech and assembly.

5. Ensuring peace with justice
Peace settlements should provide for impartial investigation of past abuses, processes aimed at establishing the truth and measures to ensure that any perpetrators of human rights violations are brought to justice. Individual responsibility for human rights violations, past and present, must be made explicit and sweeping pre-conviction amnesties should not be part of peace settlements.

6. On-site human rights monitoring
Human rights monitors should be mandated to carry out investigations and verify compliance with human rights obligations and to take corrective action in respect of violations. They should have broad access to all sectors of society and relevant institutions and the full protection of those who are in contact with them must be assured. Peace-building measures, such as institutional and legislative reform and education and training, must complement but never replace the verification role.

7. Frequent and public reporting
To guarantee the effectiveness, security and credibility of international human rights personnel there must be frequent comprehensive public reports of their activities and findings which should be broadly disseminated nationally as well as internationally.

8. International civilian police monitors
Civilian police monitors should monitor, supervise and train national police and security forces and verify their adherence to international human rights and criminal justice standards. Police monitors should cooperate fully with any human rights component or mechanisms and should themselves be trained in and fully respect international human rights and criminal justice standards at all times. There should be full public reporting of their activities.

9. Long-term measures for human rights protection
Human rights components in peace-keeping operations should assist in the establishment of permanent, independent and effective national institutions for the long-term protection of human rights and the reinstitution of the rule of law, including an independent judiciary and fair criminal justice system. Other mechanisms, such as ombudsmen or national commissions, may be encouraged to reinforce respect for human rights. Such mechanisms must be impartial, independent, and competent with the necessary powers and resources to be effective. They should conform to international guidelines and must never be a substitute for a fair and independent judicial system. While national institutions are being constituted, consideration should be given to establishing an interim relationship with relevant international tribunals.

10. Human rights education and advisory assistance programs
Public education and training on human rights standards and complaints procedures should be provided to all sectors, particularly the judiciary, lawyers and law enforcement officials. Other technical assistance programs should be provided, including drafting legislation in conformity with international standards and support for national human rights non-governmental organizations (NGOs). Such programs should not be a substitute for human rights verification by a specialized monitoring component.

11. The protection of refugees, internally displaced persons and returnees
Refugee repatriation programs should include an effective monitoring and protection aspect for as long as necessary. International refugee law and protection standards must be adhered to at all times, including the principles of *non-*

refoulement, the right to seek asylum and repatriation only on a voluntary basis with international supervision.

12. The gender dimension

Measures should be taken to guarantee consideration and respect for the particular needs of women in armed conflict situations. Peace-keeping personnel should receive information on local cultural traditions and should respect the inherent rights and dignity of women at all times. Human rights components should include experts in the area of violence against women, including rape and sexual abuse.

13. Adherence of international peace-keeping forces to human rights and humanitarian law standards

The UN should declare its formal adherence to international humanitarian law and human rights and criminal justice standards, including in relation to the detention of prisoners and the use of force. The UN should ensure all troops participating in international peace-keeping operations are fully trained in those standards and understand their obligation to adhere to them. There should be specific mechanisms at the international level for monitoring, investigating and reporting on any violations of international norms by peace-keeping personnel and to ensure that personnel responsible for serious violations are brought to justice in accordance with international standards.

14. Prosecution of war crimes and attacks on international peace-keeping personnel

The investigation and prosecution of violations of humanitarian and human rights law or attacks against international peace-keeping personnel should be undertaken by appropriate national authorities or under international jurisdiction. Any international mechanisms must conform to international fair trial standards and the creation of a permanent institution for the prosecution of international crimes should be encouraged.

15. Continued promotion and protection of human rights in the post-settlement phase

Effective international human rights monitoring and assistance should be continued for as long as necessary, until it is clear that the government concerned is implementing international human rights guarantees effectively. The UN's human rights bodies should develop a more effective and comprehensive role in the post-settlement phase.

INTER-AMERICAN CONVENTION ON THE FORCED DISAPPEARANCE OF PERSONS

The Inter-American Convention on the Forced Disappearance of Persons was unanimously adopted on 9 June 1994 in Belém do Pará, Brazil, at the 24th regular session of the General Assembly of the Organization of American States. The Americas became the first region to adopt a binding instrument aimed at the prevention, eradication and punishment of the crime of enforced disappearance.

Preamble

The member states of the Organization of American States signatory to the present Convention,

Disturbed by the persistence of the forced disappearance of persons;

Reaffirming that the true meaning of American solidarity and good neighborliness can be none other than that of consolidating in this Hemisphere, in the framework of democratic institutions, a system of individual freedom and social justice based on respect for essential human rights;

Considering that the forced disappearance of persons is an affront to the conscience of the Hemisphere and a grave and abominable offense against the inherent dignity of the human being, and one that contradicts the principles and purposes enshrined in the Charter of the Organization of American States;

Considering that the forced disappearance of persons violates numerous non-derogable and essential human rights enshrined in the American Convention on Human Rights, in the American Declaration of the Rights and Duties of Man, and in the Universal Declaration of Human Rights;

Recalling that the international protection of human rights is in the form of a convention reinforcing or complementing the protection provided by domestic law and is based upon the attributes of the human personality;

Reaffirming that the systematic practice of the forced disappearance of persons constitutes a crime against humanity;

Hoping that this Convention may help to prevent, punish, and eliminate the forced disappearance of persons in the Hemisphere and make a decisive contribution to the protection of human rights and the rule of law,

Resolve to adopt the following Inter-American Convention on the Forced Disappearance of Persons:

Article I

The States Parties to this Convention undertake:

a) Not to practice, permit, or tolerate the forced disappearance of persons, even in states of emergency or suspension of individual guarantees;

b) To punish within their jurisdictions those persons who commit or attempt to commit the crime of forced disappearance of persons and their accomplices and accessories;

c) To cooperate with one another in helping to prevent, punish and eliminate the forced disappearance of persons;

d) To take legislative, administrative, judicial, and any other measures necessary to comply with the commitments undertaken in this Convention.

Article II

For the purposes of this Convention, forced disappearance is considered to be the act of depriving a person or persons of his or their freedom, in whatever way, perpetrated by agents of the state or by persons or groups of persons acting with the authorization, support, or acquiescence of the state, followed by an absence of information or a refusal to acknowledge that deprivation of freedom or to give information on the whereabouts of that person, thereby impeding his or her recourse to the applicable legal remedies and procedural guarantees.

Article III

The States Parties undertake to adopt, in accordance with their constitutional procedures, the legislative measures that may be needed to define the forced disappearance of persons as an offense and to impose an appropriate punishment commensurate with its extreme gravity. This offense shall be deemed continuous or permanent as long as the fate or whereabouts of the victim has not been determined.

The States Parties may establish mitigating circumstances for persons who have participated in acts constituting forced disappearance when they help to cause the victim to reappear alive or provide information that sheds light on the forced disappearance of a person.

Article IV

The acts constituting the forced disappearance of persons shall be considered offenses in every State Party. Consequently, each State Party shall take measures to establish its jurisdiction over such cases in the following instances:

a) When the forced disappearance of persons or any act constituting such offense was committed within its jurisdiction;

b) When the accused is a national of that state;

c) When the victim is a national of that state and that state sees fit to do so.

Every State Party shall, moreover, take the necessary measures to establish its jurisdiction over the crime described in this Convention when the alleged criminal is within its territory and it does not proceed to extradite him.

This Convention does not authorize any State Party to undertake, in the territory of another State Party, the exercise of jurisdiction or the performance of functions that are placed within the exclusive purview of the authorities of that other Party by its domestic law.

Article V

The forced disappearance of persons shall not be considered a political offense for purposes of extradition.

The forced disappearance of persons shall be deemed to be included among the extraditable offenses in every extradition treaty entered into between States Parties.

The States Parties undertake to include the offense of forced disappearance as one which is extraditable in every extradition treaty to be concluded between them in the future.

Every State Party that makes extradition conditional on the existence of a treaty and receives a request for extradition from another State Party with which it has no extradition treaty may consider this Convention as the necessary legal basis for extradition with respect to the offense of forced disappearance.

States Parties which do not make extradition conditional on the existence of a treaty shall recognize such offense as extraditable, subject to the conditions imposed by the law of the requested state.

Extradition shall be subject to the provisions set forth in the constitution and other laws of the requested state.

Article VI

When a State Party does not grant the extradition, the case shall be submitted to its competent authorities as if the offense had been committed within its jurisdiction, for the purposes of investigation and when appropriate, for criminal action, in accordance with its national law. Any decision adopted by these authorities shall be communicated to the state that has requested the extradition.

Article VII

Criminal prosecution for the forced disappearance of persons and the penalty judicially imposed on its perpetrator shall not be subject to statutes of limitations.

However, if there should be a norm of a fundamental character preventing application of the stipulation contained in the previous paragraph, the period of limitation shall be equal to that which applies to the gravest crime in the domestic laws of the corresponding State Party.

Article VIII

The defense of due obedience to superior orders or instructions that stipulate, authorize, or encourage forced disappearance shall not be admitted. All persons who receive such orders have the right and duty not to obey them.

The States Parties shall ensure that the training of public law-enforcement personnel or officials includes the necessary education on the offense of forced disappearance of persons.

Article IX

Persons alleged to be responsible for the acts constituting the offense of forced disappearance of persons may be tried only in the competent jurisdictions of ordinary law in each state, to the exclusion of all other special jurisdictions, particularly military jurisdictions.

The acts constituting forced disappearance shall not be deemed to have been committed in the course of military duties.

Privileges, immunities, or special dispensations shall not be admitted in such trials, without prejudice to the provisions set forth in the Vienna Convention on Diplomatic Relations.

Article X

In no case may exceptional circumstances such as a state of war, the threat of war, internal political instability, or any other public emergency be invoked to justify the forced disappearance of persons. In such cases, the right to expeditious and effective judicial procedures and recourse shall be retained as a means of determining the whereabouts or state of health of a person who has been deprived of freedom, or of identifying the official who ordered or carried out such deprivation of freedom.

In pursuing such procedures or recourse, and in keeping with applicable domestic law, the competent judicial authorities shall have free and immediate access to all detention centers and to each of their units, and to all places where there is reason to believe the disappeared person might be found, including places that are subject to military jurisdiction.

Article XI

Every person deprived of liberty shall be held in an officially recognized place of detention and be brought before a competent judicial authority without delay, in accordance with applicable domestic law.

The States Parties shall establish and maintain official up-to-date registries of their detainees and, in accordance with their domestic law, shall make them available to relatives, judges, attorneys, any other person having a legitimate interest, and other authorities.

Article XII

The States Parties shall give each other mutual assistance in the search for, identification, location, and return of minors who have been removed to another state or detained therein as a consequence of the forced disappearance of their parents or guardians.

Article XIII

For the purposes of this Convention, the processing of petitions or communications presented to the Inter-American Commission on Human Rights alleging the forced disappearance of persons shall be subject to the procedures established in the American Convention on Human Rights and to the Statute and Regulations of the Inter-American Commission on Human Rights and to the Statute and Rules of Procedure of the Inter-American Court of Human Rights, including the provisions on precautionary measures.

Article XIV

Without prejudice to the provisions of the preceding article, when the Inter-American Commission on Human Rights receives a petition or communication regarding an alleged forced disappearance, its Executive Secretariat shall urgently and confidentially address the respective government and shall request that government to provide as soon as possible information as to the whereabouts of the allegedly disappeared person together with any other information it considers pertinent, and such request shall be without prejudice as to the admissibility of the petition.

Article XV

None of the provisions of this Convention shall be interpreted as limiting other bilateral or multilateral treaties or other agreements signed by the Parties.

This Convention shall not apply to the international armed conflicts governed by the 1949 Geneva Conventions and their Protocols concerning protection of wounded, sick, and shipwrecked members of the armed forces; and prisoners of war and civilians in time of war.

Article XVI

This Convention is open for signature by the member states of the Organization of American States.

Article XVII

This Convention is subject to ratification. The instruments of ratification shall be deposited with the General Secretariat of the Organization of American States.

Article XVIII

This Convention shall be open to accession by any other state. The instruments of accession shall be deposited with the General Secretariat of the Organization of American States.

Article XIX

The states may express reservations with respect to this Convention when adopting, signing, ratifying or acceding to it, unless such reservations are incompatible with the object and purpose of the Convention and as long as they refer to one or more specific provisions.

Article XX

This Convention shall enter into force for the ratifying states on the thirtieth day from the date of deposit of the second instrument of ratification.

For each state ratifying or acceding to the Convention after the second instrument of ratification has been deposited, the Convention shall enter into force on the thirtieth day from the date on which that state deposited its instrument of ratification or accession.

Article XXI

This Convention shall remain in force indefinitely, but may be denounced by any State Party. The instrument of denunciation shall be deposited with the General Secretariat of the Organization of American States. The Convention shall cease to be in effect for the denouncing state and shall remain in force for the other States Parties one year from the date of deposit of the instrument of denunciation.

Article XXII

The original instrument of this Convention, the Spanish, English, Portuguese and French texts of which are equally authentic, shall be deposited with the General Secretariat of the Organization of American States, which shall forward certified copies thereof to the United Nations Secretariat, for registration and publication, in accordance with Article 102 of the Charter of the United Nations. The General Secretariat of the Organization of American States shall notify member states of the Organization and states acceding to the Convention of the signatures and deposit of instruments of ratification, accession or denunciation, as well as of any reservations that may be expressed.

SELECTED STATISTICS

AMNESTY INTERNATIONAL MEMBERSHIP

At the beginning of 1995 there were more than 1,100,000 members, subscribers and regular donors in over 170 countries. There were 4,329 local Amnesty International groups registered with the International Secretariat, plus several thousand school, university, professional and other groups, in 89 countries.

PRISONER CASES AND RELEASES

At the end of 1994 Amnesty International groups were working on 4,002 long-term assignments, concerning over 8,000 individuals, including prisoners of conscience and other victims of human rights violations. During the year action began on 463 new Action Files, many of which concerned more than one individual. A total of 320 cases involving the release of prisoners of conscience and possible prisoners of conscience was recorded.

URGENT ACTION APPEALS

During 1994 Amnesty International initiated 532 actions which required urgent appeals from the Urgent Action Network. There were also 276 calls for further appeals on actions already issued. Members of the Urgent Action Network were therefore asked to send appeals on 808 occasions. These actions were on behalf of people in 91 countries.

The 532 new actions were issued on behalf of people who were either at risk or had been the victim of the following human rights violations: torture – 166 cases; political killing – 88 cases; "disappearance" – 80 cases; judicial execution – 100 cases; death threats and other threats to safety – 203 cases; and legal concerns – 79 cases. (These categories are not mutually exclusive; more than one concern may have been featured in an action.) Other concerns included ill-health, deaths in custody, *refoulement* (forcible repatriation) of asylum-seekers, amputation and forcible exile.

REGIONAL ACTION NETWORKS

Amnesty International's Regional Action Networks deal with human rights abuses in every country of the world. During the year, 2,444 Amnesty International local groups participated in the Regional Action Networks, which worked on the cases of thousands of victims of human rights violations.

AMNESTY INTERNATIONAL FUNDING

The budget adopted by Amnesty International for 1994 was £14,724,000. This sum represents approximately one quarter of the estimated income likely to be raised during the year by the movement's national sections. Amnesty International's national sections and local volunteer groups are primarily responsible for funding the movement. A central fund-raising program is being developed. No money is sought or accepted from governments. The donations that sustain Amnesty International's work come from its members and the public.

RELIEF

During 1994 the International Secretariat of Amnesty International distributed £212,789 in relief (financial assistance) to victims of human rights violations such as prisoners of conscience and recently released prisoners of conscience and their dependants, and to provide medical treatment for torture victims. In addition, the organization's sections and groups distributed a further substantial amount, much of it in the form of modest payments by local groups to their adopted prisoners of conscience and dependent families.

Amnesty International's ultimate goal is to end human rights violations, but so long as they continue it tries to provide practical help to the victims. Relief is an important aspect of this work. Sometimes Amnesty International provides financial assistance directly to individuals. At other times, it works through local bodies such as local and national human rights organizations so as to ensure that resources are used as effectively as possible for those in most need. When Amnesty International asks an intermediary to distribute relief payments on its behalf, it stipulates precisely the intended purpose and beneficiaries and requires the intermediary to report back on the expenditure of the funds.